WILLIAM MICHELSON is a member of the Department of Sociology and Director of The Child in the City Programme at the University of Toronto. He is author of *Man and his Urban Environment*, and *Environmental Choice, Human Behavior, and Residential Satisfaction.*

SAUL V. LEVINE is a member of the Department of Psychiatry and Associate Director of The Child in the City Programme at the University of Toronto.

ANNA-ROSE SPINA is Project Coordinator of The Child in the City Programme at the University of Toronto.

What do we know about the implications of the major changing forces in urban life for children? What should be our priorities for new policies and practices for children in cities? The traditional view of children as 'dependants' obscures the complexity of the urban experience children face. Their social environment is not limited strictly to institutions such as the family and the church. But neither do children have access to the full range of societal offerings.

This volume evaluates the basis of current issues of public concern and debate and constructs an agenda for future research, policy, and practice concerning children and families. The perspectives of many disciplines are brought together and integrated in the consideration of such factors as family structure and child care arrangements, urban dilemmas for adolescents, legal structures and practices, urban social organization and service delivery systems, housing and neighbourhood contexts, and ethnic diversity.

The book as a whole identifies the fundamentals of a broad issue of concern and offers guidelines for shaping a humane future.

THE CHILD IN THE CITY PROGRAMME

University of Toronto

The Child in the City: changes and challenges

WILLIAM MICHELSON

SAUL V. LEVINE

ANNA-ROSE SPINA

in collaboration with

Katherine Catton, Martha Friendly

Linda Hagarty, Susan Hodgson

Ellis Roberts, Suzanne Ziegler

UNIVERSITY OF TORONTO PRESS

Toronto Buffalo London

© University of Toronto Press 1979
Toronto Buffalo London
Printed in Canada

Canadian Cataloguing in Publication Data

Main entry under title:

The Child in the city

Vol. 1 originated from the proceedings of a lecture
series organized and presented by the Child in the
City Programme at the University of Toronto.
Vol. 2 edited by William Michelson, Saul V. Levine
and Anna-Rose Spina.
Contents: [1] Today and tomorrow. – [2] Changes
and challenges.
Includes indexes.

ISBN 0-8020-2314-2 (v. 1) bd. ISBN 0-8020-6337-3
(v. 1) pa. ISBN 0-8020-2315-0 (v. 2) bd.
ISBN 0-8020-6338-1 (v. 2) pa.
1. City children – Addresses, essays, lectures.
2. Child welfare – Addresses, essays, lectures.
I. Michelson, William, 1940–   II. Levine, Saul,
1938–   III. Michelson, Ellen, 1941–
IV. Child in the City Programme.

HT206.C45   301.43'14   C78-001509-6

The Child in the City Programme is a Canadian contribution
to the UNESCO Programme on Man and the Biosphere.

Dedicated to the Memory of John Law,

who worked to improve the condition of

the child in the city.

Contents

THE CHILD IN THE CITY: CHANGES AND CHALLENGES

1

Introduction

WILLIAM MICHELSON AND
SAUL V. LEVINE

Our interest is 'The Child in The City.' In this volume, we shall explore the physical and social context of health, welfare, and opportunities explicitly and systematically.

Concern about children in cities is not new. It goes back at least to the industrial revolution, when great numbers of persons of all ages flocked to cities for the first time in history. Although big cities had been known previously, increasingly large *proportions* of the population of nations began to reside in cities.

People continued to move to cities in recognition of indisputable benefits associated with urban life (particularly in comparison to the disadvantages of remaining where they were), but they discovered new kinds of problems as well, which caused them worry and eventually led to a variety of new legislative and administrative practices (particularly in the areas of work and welfare). Inasmuch as adults typically view children as physically and intellectually incomplete, dependent beings, considerably more susceptible to harmful forces at any time or place, it is no wonder that so many of the new practices focused on the perceived good of the child. Even as large cities became part of the established fabric of society, reformers like Jane Addams continued to refer to the 'abnormal fabric of city life for children.'[2]

While now a significant force in society, cities are no longer new. The great shifts from rural to urban societies have long since been carried out, and approximately 80 per cent of the residents of Western, industrialized nations now live in urban areas. Nonetheless, people are still uncertain about the situation of the child in the city: the nature and extent of the positive and negative aspects and the balance between the two.

We might regard such a continued concern with the child in the city, a concern which is continually fueled by media references to 'the concrete jungle' and other aspersions of 'inhumanity,' as anachronistic and even romantic were there not definite components of the child-city relationship to which one can point as the potential basis for uncertainty. Since these components serve as the conceptual basis for the work reported in this volume, let us turn to them now.

SOME CONCEPTUAL UNDERPINNINGS FOR LOOKING AT THE CHILD IN THE CITY

We do not regard the city as a rigid, physical entity. The focus is not only on the centre of established cities, often the locus of problems related to poverty and/or race. Nor do we place the city in a position of opposition to the characteristics of any other place (e.g. the small town or the countryside). Our concern is with the general implications for children of all the areas and aspects making up the modern metropolitan area, for reasons and with implications that are not irrelevant to other types of settlement. Specifically, aspects of (1) *social change*, (2) *scale*, and (3) *organization* convey implications for the situation of children. The impact of the foregoing aspects is magnified by (4) the particular *transition* children make from dependency to relative autonomy.

Social Change
Most changes and innovations now *first* appear in the city. Diffusion – whether referring to labour-saving devices, life-styles, alterations in social structure, or coiffures – occurs in a non-random geographic pattern. Redfield introduced a theory of an 'urban-rural continuum'[3] by showing that crucial differences among various sizes and forms of community were related to the way in which innovations are introduced and communicated. They appear first in the largest, most easily accessible urban centre and then, depending on ease of internal communication, wend their way to the smallest settlements.

In our view, cities are not unique entities, but they are the 'cutting edge' of society. Most of what is new is found there in its most highly developed form, though not necessarily absent elsewhere. All-reaching forms of communication surely do not restrict knowledge of innovations to urban areas for long, but it may take longer for changes to be as fully incorporated into the fabric of outlying areas. Figure 1 shows one view of cities and change.[4]

The meaning of social change is accentuated in the city by the second of our central aspects of the city – scale.

Scale
A critical mass is the minimum number of participants necessary for an activity to develop to its logical extent. Many new activities – innovative industrial work, ethnic food, a drug culture, modern music, specialized medical practices, Hare

Figure 1 Urban phenomena are not restricted to cities but take on special circumstances there due to timing, scale, and complexity. (Published by permission of King Features Syndicate, Inc.)

Krishna, etc. - appeal to only limited segments of the population, yet need a reasonable number of people participating to function smoothly. Hence, large numbers of people who are accessible to one another are required to produce enough participants for such activities to develop into something meaningful. Larger cities provide the 'personnel' to support an ever-changing variety of specialized interests and vices.[5]

In addition, where changes bring about unexpected negative consequences to certain segments of society (e.g. unemployed youth), the scale of the city implies that the affected parties are not as likely to be 'just' scattered individuals but accumulations of persons large enough to become social groups with a life and effects of their own (e.g. gangs, countercultures, etc.).

Thus, many of the opportunities and problems of the large city (not to speak of the nature of their solutions) require an understanding of how the scale of the city accommodates and extends the tangible manifestations of social change. Yet, the implications of urban scale and change for children do not become fully apparent without considering the next of our series of concerns - organization.

Organization

If the city is indeed a place where new phenomena materialize and take on significant dimensions (thus inviting significant responses) because of urban scale, we must still ask how this does or does not reach the individual child.

The city in North America is hardly a computer, within which all relevant entities are automatically connected or maintained apart, as desired, by the various persons involved. For example, if a social welfare or health agency institutes a service to deal with certain children placed in need of help because of some major phenomenon (e.g. teenage girls bearing children and then neglecting them), by what logic does the service effectively reach its clients - and vice versa - in a place as large and diversified as the modern city? Conversely, if parents do not wish their children to come in contact with something 'new' (e.g. earlier sexual initiation), by what logic can parents monopolize the channels of communication linking their children to the outside world?

To really understand the situation of the child in the city, we must therefore have some way of *linking* the child with what is happening or desired.

We often make convenient assumptions about the child, and we create services based upon these assumptions. For example, we frequently assume that the child is an integral unit in a family and that this family will find appropriate help for the child whenever required - whether it be medical, educational, or something similar. We make similar assumptions about reaching children in schools, in churches, and so on.

There are several reasons, however, why assumptions based on an overly optimistic view of the child's primary memberships are incomplete.

1 Important phenomena reach children either directly (e.g. pollution) or via non-institutionalized channels (e.g. peer groups). When negative, these phenomena create unexpected problems.
2 Parents are often unable to make the connections which their children require, while, conversely, service providers usually lack the mandate, funding, and/or skills to locate each and every family with a child in need.
3 Although children are clearly members of several primary groupings, these connections are not enough to explain what happens to them even in these contexts. Families and schools are themselves affected by social changes which have implications for children. The connections of the child *through* the family and other institutions to significant ongoing trends must be understood.
4 Nonetheless, even though the child is vitally connected to such institutions, this does not mean that they are primarily organized in support of the *child's* interests, as compared to those of the adult members of the institutions. Housing studies, for example, consistently show that the child is usually last in line when parents allocate space in a new residence.[6]
5 Even if adult intentions are optimal, this does not mean that the child is necessarily affected by conditions in the same ways as adults. We shall return shortly to this consideration.

Thus the place of the child in urban society is not, on the one hand, rigidly limited to a small number of institutions like family and church. Nor, on the other hand, is the child connected (with or without his or her family) to the full range of societal offerings. The child in the city is surely entirely subject to a wide range of influences and opportunities; some of these reach without intervening persons or groups, others are encountered insofar as the family or other institution succeeds in making the link, while others may be missed.

Convenient, traditional assumptions must therefore be replaced by empirically based knowledge of the place of the child in urban society. Where children stand vis à vis the rest of society and what it offers them is complex. We must always view the answers in terms of *which* children and *which* aspects of the city and urban society. But a failure to plan on the basis of the *de facto* organization of families and children in urban society results in services and facilities which lack appropriate clients and children who 'fall between the cracks' in all too great numbers.

Neither children nor institutions can be understood in a vacuum. The connections must be made, and the overall context must be charted.

The Particular Transition Children Make
from Dependency to Relative Autonomy
Our focus on children is not meant to imply that the foregoing considerations are irrelevant to the lives of *adults* in the city. With minor modifications, the

same points could have been made for adults. But there is certainly an additional perspective which plays a major role in our understanding of the child in the city. This is a developmental perspective.

Children enter the world in a state of total dependence. Children then enter a series of phases of development, within which they have capacity to learn and cope with some phenomena but not others. This means that, at any time short of adulthood, children differ from adults in their ability to react to external forces. Eventually, children assume adult autonomy, developing feelings of more or less competence and independence from those persons and groups with whom they have meaningful contact.

Because cities offer a physical and social context for child development which includes innovation and change, the world facing new adults in cities differs in many ways from that of older generations. The result is that children who would face crucial developmental challenges at different ages in the course of growing up even in the most stable settings find themselves 'cutting their teeth' and 'winning their spurs' in unprecedented contexts in cities.

Thus, the combination of developmental challenge and unfamiliar context, as magnified by urban scale and muddied by the ambiguities of urban organization, makes for an overall situation leading people to express uncertainties about the child in the city, even though urban life is hardly novel any more.

We therefore feel that any attempt to deal explicitly and systematically with the situation of the child in the city, our objectives, must take a perspective on the subject which is broad enough to include social change, urban scale, organization, and child development - not merely components of these viewed in a vacuum.

POINTS OF DEPARTURE FROM
TRADITIONAL RESEARCH ON CHILDREN

We do not argue that valuable research work has not already been done on urban children. But it has been addressed primarily to special situations facing only particular subgroups of children or to aspects of child-raising and development whose context was viewed as irrelevant.

It is our contention that the conceptual framework and results of 'The Child in the City'[7] differ from those of previous, voluminous research efforts that have looked at children from the perspective of each of the disciplines which comprise this programme and others. Traditional research approaches, which have made up this vast majority of studies on children, valuable as many of them have been, have often suffered from a restriction of perspective. Studies have certainly been done in all the areas we have described which look at children in particular social or physical environments. But very few studies have examined the *inter-action* between the environmental context and the children. Similarly most researchers have been interested in their subject from the relatively narrow perspectives of their own particular fields, usually without input from other disciplines.

Environmental Research
For example, in the area of environmental research, architects, planners and geographers, and the social scientists working with them, have primarily focused on the effects of housing type and the design of play space on children. Numerous writers have commented on the problems caused by high-rise apartments for families and young children. Younger children in these settings are not allowed outside to play as often as children in single family housing because of the barrier between home and play space, and there is an accompanying sense of frustration and isolation. As a result of these approaches, suggestions have been made that correct some of the physically caused problems: toilet facilities on the ground floor, better soundproofing in the walls between apartments, and similar improvements.

Other researchers, including a subgroup of the Environmental Design Research Association called 'Childhood City,' have concerned themselves with the optimal design of play space. Although this work has ranged in many directions (see Chapter 7), its most concentrated focus has been on the PLAYGROUND, with particular reference to quasi-philosophical issues like the degree of structure, the extent to which it might compensate for deficits in the child's residential community, etc.

Although both types of inquiry have produced results of value for improving children's environments, they cover only a small, home-centred part of the physical surroundings which affect the daily lives of most of the children in the city. Wider-based concerns include the variety of recreational and commercial services available within the spatial range of urban children of various ages. In addition, the availability and accessibility to children of an urban system of transportation are of particular concern, since the opportunities, or dangers, afforded by the city are usually contingent on mobility. The environment may itself provide clean air or poisonous contaminants differentially to children in different neighbourhoods. Moreover, the spatial and social organization of the environment implicitly conveys messages directly to children and through their parents about control and mastery as opposed to powerlessness and alienation.

Developmental Psychology
In the field of developmental psychology, there have been a number of major contributions[8] which define the sequential progression of children through stages

of growth along different dimensions such as cognitive or moral development, but the impact of the environment on the child's progress and on the end result has been, until fairly recently, largely ignored.

There is also a large experimental literature in psychology which examines particular dynamics, such as learned helplessness, or attachment, usually as dependent variables. While vitally important, the experimental approach also fails to deal adequately with the environment in which a child functions. We can and obviously do learn much from theories of development and research in experimental settings about the existence and working of various phenomena, but the translation to the natural setting often involves a quantum jump. The complexity of the setting increases significantly and many factors are no longer subject to rigid control or even measurement.

Even the work done in child-rearing environments, such as in daycare and to a lesser extent in compensatory preschool interventions, has concentrated largely on assessing the impact on outcome variables such as IQ without addressing the question of what aspects of the programme or environment, if any, explain the observed effect.[9]

Slowly, however, developmental psychologists are working in 'real' settings[10] and cross-culturally[11] in an attempt to document and analyse the effects of the social and physical environments in which the child functions. And increasingly, sophisticated analytic techniques are being brought to bear on the data, resulting in more precise and conclusive findings.[12]

However, the scope of these efforts remains too narrow in that, with few exceptions, the richness of the child's social life within the family and elsewhere is rarely considered.[13] The environments to which a child is exposed, such as home and daycare, are considered separately, precluding an assessment of the effects of the 'Gestalt' of the child-rearing system.[14] The environments themselves are not often examined as dependent variables reflecting the influence of the child[15] or the influence of the larger social context in which child-rearing occurs.[16] And there is a failure to make a connection between the research of developmental psychologists and the needs for information of those rearing children.[17] Perhaps by raising and beginning to address these issues with respect to contemporary childrearing a step can be made towards understanding a child's development in its complexity.

Urban Anthropology and Ethnicity
With some notable exceptions, anthropologists have studied neither children nor cities. Cultures as systems have largely been investigated through the adults of the society – their kinship patterns, rituals, beliefs, and customs. Sometimes ethnographic descriptions of a culture include a chapter on 'the life cycle,' but seldom are the processes of transmission of culture investigated.

There has been, however, a minority interest in cultural transmission – in enculturation, or what could be called cultural socialization. An early and important paper is Ruth Benedict's 'Continuities and discontinuities in cultural conditioning,' published in 1938 in the journal *Psychiatry*. Her student, Margaret Mead, both stimulated and executed more work in the field than any other anthropologist. Mead edited 'Childhood in contemporary culture' in 1955, a selection of readings in the anthropology of children; and in 1974 a volume called *Socialization as cultural communication* (T. Schwarz, editor) was dedicated to her as the ancestral figure of this tradition with the discipline. Most recently, the editors of *Culture and infancy* (Leiderman et al., 1977), a valuable collection of readings in child-rearing across cultures, acknowledge the debt to Mead of anthropologists, and especially of psychologists. Mead's own work often emphasized cultural transmission as it affects the lives of developing adults, as in *Coming of age in Samoa*, among many titles.

But very few North American anthropologists have followed her lead or have been fellow-travellers. The principal exceptions are John and Beatrice Whiting, whose work in the field spans the three decades between *Becoming a Kwoma* (J.W.M. Whiting, 1941) and *Children of six cultures* (B. Whiting and J.W.M. Whiting, 1975).

In British social anthropology as well, children and socialization have been neglected. This neglect and the reasons for it are discussed by Phillip Mayer in his introduction to *Socialization: The approach from social anthropology*, a volume he prepared from material presented at a conference in 1967 on socialization, sponsored by the Association of Social Anthropologists of the Commonwealth. Mayer states that 'socialization seemed a rather daring choice for the theme of the 1967 conference ... considering how little the subject has figured in British social anthropological discourse in the last twenty or thirty years' (p.xi).

The papers in the Mayer volume, based on field work in Africa and Southeast Asia, describe rural settings, in almost all cases. One exception is LaFontaine's paper, which discusses youth groups and youth culture in Kinshasa (Zaire). La Fontaine's emphasis on the urban setting within which the youths he studied were living and operating is a most unusual one, in anthropology.

If anthropologists can be accused of child-neglect, they are even more guilty of neglecting the urban context within which so very many children operate. This has been deliberate, of course. Anthropologists are only now looking at cities, and indeed at the western world. When they do so they find themselves ill-equipped, historically. Thus, when current scholars attempt to use a cross-cultural base to examine a current situation, they often find that the data available to them are of doubtful comparability, because of their rural, peasant bias. A recent example is the work of Weisner and Gallimore on child and sibling caretakers.[18] They use the Human Relations Area File, a voluminous if uneven collection of data on hundreds of cultures, the purpose of which is to make cross-cultural comparisons possible. From it, the authors are able to document the predominance of sibling caretaking worldwide, in peasant societies. But the HRAF can say little about the prevalence of the same practice in the Western world, or in urban settings.

In the important areas of ethnicity and heterogeneity of urban communities, and the immigrant experience, there have been numerous studies, but virtually none predominantly concerned with children. For example, studies of the process of cultural adaptation in the developed world have been largely focused on the poor, have considered racial but not ethnic differences, and have concentrated mainly on adults. The literature on social networks among urbanized Africans also deals entirely with adults, most often men who are unmarried or who have left their families behind, in the home village. Consequently, the network data, while a fascinating literature on urban adaptation, do not touch on children directly or indirectly (that is, on social modelling as a form of enculturation).

Acculturation studies of children are almost as rare as enculturation studies. Anthropological-like studies which include a focus on children, adolescents, and young people in cities, and as cultural groups, have been until recently undertaken by urban sociologists: viz Liebow,[19] Suttles,[20] and Whyte.[21] But there is increased interest in urban settings in anthropology. *Urban Anthropology*, which published its first issue in 1972, is flourishing, and anthropologists are publishing urban studies in interdisciplinary and sociological journals, as well as in their own. The reason is clear: the world is depleted of primitives; isolated societies do not exist; most people live in cities, and it is increasingly hard to study culture, society, or individuals without leaving the farm. But the world is not in danger of running out of adults, and there is little indication that more than a few anthropologists are becoming interested in children qua children.

Sociology
Sociologists have studied children primarily in families, schools, and gangs. Let us examine their treatment in the former context for illustration.

Up to 1945, sociological studies of the family focused on the importance of the family as an institution. Concern in family studies focused on the responsibility for socialization and social control and the preservation of social values. The studies were from what social scientists call a 'macro' perspective and implicit was the understanding that what happened in the family was a private matter and not properly a topic for research.

There was, however, in this institutional focus, a concern with the relationship between family and community, and the common feeling was that family-centred or 'private' matters served to undermine community structure. There was concern that there be a balancing of institutional inputs in society. As in a homeostatic model, a successful family was one that balanced its activities of socialization with community concerns. From this perspective, it was striking to see the development of formal institutions in relation to the family. As other institutions took on economic and educational functions formerly residing within the family, the development was (and is) often used as evidence that the family was declining in importance.

By 1950, what was happening in the family did become important, and from 1957 to 1967 there was the addition of small group studies to the field of family sociology and a new concern with family interpersonal dynamics and family roles. Demographic and ecological studies declined and the unit of study within families was the individual, before and after marriage, the married couple, and parents. The social context of interest moved from family-in-community to individual-in-family. The concern with children as developing individuals in the family, the importance of socialization experience to growth and development, that is, the intersection of sociology with psychology and social psychology, are late 1960s and 70s phenomena.[22]

But the study of the child in urban society, with reference to family and community, is still in its infancy.

Social Work

In the field of social work, research relevant to 'The Child in the City' has been done in the areas of family and child services, public welfare, corrections, and community development, as well as in the social aspects of health problems. Child welfare studies, which have occupied the bulk of concern about children, have classically focused on issues such as the effect of placement and adoption of children in care. Jaffee and Fanshel[23] investigated the long-term adjustment of 100 children adopted 20 to 30 years previously through four New York city adoption agencies in order to determine the factors related to successful and unsuccessful outcome. Similarly, the effect of long-term placement in foster care has been the subject of studies by social workers in the United States and Canada.

Also in the field of child welfare, Alfred Kahn and his colleagues' (1972) investigation of child advocacy projects throughout the United States using questionnaires, interviews, and case studies is a good example of social policy research relevant to children's services.[24] In relation to the family, Geismar, a social worker whose family functioning scale is widely used in social work research, has been involved in the Rutgers Family Life Improvement Project which has been following 555 young families over a period of three to four years subsequent to the birth of their first child.[25] Schorr's study of *Poor kids*, which marshalled evidence to demonstrate the effects of poverty on the family and argued for a family allowance policy, is representative of a social work study in the arena of public welfare.[26]

To the extent that studies such as these address urban phenomena, they are more likely to be conceptualized in terms of the organization of urban services concerned with issues such as accessibility or lack of co-ordination and the like, or the social problems of inner city residents, than as physical or spatial variables. This is consistent with the fact that although 'environment' is a core concept in virtually all social work theory, it is almost invariably defined in purely social terms. A few social workers have been involved in research into urban family housing[27] but, in general, Scott Briar's summary observation in 1966 that 'virtually no recent empirical studies of ecological influences in family life – such as housing patterns, neighbourhood characteristics, physical environment, and so on – have been conducted in social work'[28] still holds true with only a few exceptions.

Social workers are frequently engaged in interdisciplinary research, principally because most of the settings in which they work are shared with other professions and disciplines. A recent study by Chaiklin et al.[29] which looked at the physical health status of urban delinquents and found antisocial youth to be in poor health is a typical example. An Ontario study[30] which analysed hundreds of cases of juvenile offenders in Waterloo county over a decade, and a study of a juvenile services project in Hamilton, Ontario,[31] are representative of social work research in the juvenile corrections field.

Law
Our laws are meant to inform, regulate, and constrain official decision-making in our society. Yet little empirical research has been undertaken to understand how law is translated into action and the consequences thereof. Our laws affect children both indirectly and directly. Children, as members of families, feel the consequences of the laws governing the formation or dissolution of family ties. Their life-styles may be altered radically, both emotionally and financially, by their parents' divorce. Custody arrangements and property and support settlements all have direct and lasting effects on them.

Moreover, children are the focus of many of our laws as individuals in their own right. Our child welfare laws attempt to define and protect children who are 'at risk' in their home environment. Our education laws seek to ensure that all children receive at least a minimum of learning so that they may, as far as possible, prepare to become functioning members of society. Our health care laws have rules respecting minors' consent to treatment. Even more basic, it is the law which defines who has the status of minor in our society, the consequences that flow therefrom, and the circumstances in which exceptions to this status are created. Last, our laws establish categories of conduct which are considered criminal or socially unacceptable. The euphemism of delinquency has been applied to such behaviour. Special proscriptions apply to children and a special court, the juvenile court, has been established to handle violations of these behavioural norms.

While, overall, little social science research has been undertaken on the effects of law respecting children, the field of delinquency has been an exception. Yet although considerable empirical research has been conducted, there is scant evidence that we have progressed significantly in knowledge of aetiology, prevention, or understanding the effects of intervention. Both Pink and White's review of the American picture[32] and Byles's overview of the Canadian data[33] point to the same conclusion to which Schur came in 1975: that, in the long term, nonintervention seems to work as well if not better than attempts to rehabilitate antisocial children.[34] Most children grow out of their antisocial behaviour and become normal adults.

In the many other ways in which our children interact with the legal system, while there is considerable speculation and theorizing, there is a dearth of empirical research providing us with even basic descriptive information. For example, there is little documentation of individuals' understanding of or perceptions of law and legal institutions, or description of the actual functioning of our courts and other legal structures, or evaluation of the effects of the reforms we do implement, to learn if, in reality, they function as we want them to. Moreover, social science research could be usefully employed to inform policy and legislative decision-making by narrowing and focusing the range of alternative reforms to be considered. Hence, in many areas where children are affected by laws, including their perceptions of law and legal structures, judicial discretion, legal representation of children, the children's rights movement, child neglect and foster care, and the like, hard data are woefully lacking.

Recently, however, social scientists have shown an increased interest in studying law. Legal scholars, too, are coming to recognize the assistance which empirical research methodology and data can give them in understanding the effects of laws as they currently exist and in guiding and monitoring the law reform process. The need for such joint endeavours is well expressed by the legal scholar, Michael Wald, in his guest editorial in the *Journal of Child Development* in which he issues a plea for more data so that those drafting legal policy can know the consequences of adopting one policy or another.[35] Recently, too, there have been a few major efforts to bring legal scholars together with social scientists from a variety of relevant disciplines. The Berkeley Project on Law and Government is one example, as is the Boys Town Project at Stanford, as well as our own Child in the City Programme. Yet these major studies merely focus on the tip of the iceberg. Much remains to be done.

Health

Socioeconomic and technical advances have changed the pattern of disease and resulting disabilities. The infant mortality rate in Canada has dropped from 61 per 1000 live births in 1931 to 17 in 1971.[36] Also, in the last decade, with the advent of birth control and changes in the abortion law, crude birth rate and total fertility rate have dropped significantly. In the paediatric age group, infectious disease, malnutrition, and diarrhoeal disease have been controlled, and primary care physicians are now more often consulted for newer types of morbidity such as episodic illnesses, behaviour and learning disabilities, chronic illnesses, well-child care, and immunization.[37]

At the present time survival in childhood is taken for granted; family size is restricted, and parents are concerned about the quality of life for their children.[38] This has led to a strong desire for the prevention of chronic disabilities, educational failures, and behavioural problems, or, if this is not possible, for their early identification and amelioration. Any chronic disorder or disability in early life may lead to restriction of the child's development and/or to a lifetime of lower potential and expensive support. The early identification of these problems via screening programmes is probably more important in early childhood than at any other time in life.[39]

With the introduction of governmental health insurance, Canada has achieved its formal objectives in provision of health care to its population. Canadians spent approximately seven per cent of their Gross National Product on health care, amounting to approximately 13 billion dollars in 1976.[40] However, we have not yet achieved the state of health equivalent to some other developed nations as measured by a number of different health indices, for example, infant mortality, potential years lost, morbidity, etc. The message is clear: we must change our emphasis from curative to preventive health care and should put major emphasis on health promotion and maintenance.

Screening programmes leading to early detection of deviations from normal childhood development offer hope. Much has been written about child-health screening in recent years.[41] Some reviews provide good overall assessments; however, there are publications that are too uncritical and lack sound supporting data. Whitby's plea for clarity of terminology is especially pertinent with respect to child health.[42]

It has been frequently suggested that maximum yield from screening programmes will occur in preschool children. Most children under one year of age receive adequate health supervision by primary care physicians, and once they go to school they are supervised by school health services. However, between the ages of one and four years most children have very little contact with health care systems except for episodic illness.

It is evident from epidemiological studies[43] that screening programmes for preschool children can detect previously unnoted or new physical, auditory, developmental, and vision problems in 10–25 per cent of the children. However, many of the proponents of the preschool screening programmes are from the United States where there is no national health insurance.[44] The Scandinavians and British, who have national health insurance, are advocating similar proposals,[45] and thus far the best available data for the yield from screening programmes of four-year-olds are available from Scandinavia[46] and indicate need for such a programme. The need for and utility of preschool screening programmes in the Canadian health care system requires further research.

Adolescence has been seen as a time of particularly good health. Infectious (communicable) diseases are largely a thing of the past, and the diseases of aging and stress have not yet taken their toll. Yet Cohen has shown that incarcerated urban adolescents are in extremely poor health.[47] Further, it is known that adolescents in general are a population at risk for a number of health-related problems – venereal disease, alcohol and drug abuse, early pregnancy, accidents, suicide – all of which are relatively high, and increasingly prevalent in this age group, especially in the urban context.[48]

Other issues which merit the attention of researchers and clinicians, and yet have been neglected until relatively recently, are clinical accountability, patients' and parents' *own* responsibility for health maintenance and promotion, burgeoning health costs, and preventive medicine, especially as it relates to environmental or negative life-style influence on health.

Psychiatry and Clinical Psychology
Clinical psychology and psychiatry have only recently taken more than passing note of the social context in which the child resides.

Early research on children in these fields stressed individual case studies, and psychopathology. Both of these approaches have proven to have limited value, either as heuristic impetus or applicability to children in general. Even when taking cognizance of the family system, for example, conclusions have been based largely on a priori biases to the exclusion of other factors both in and outside the family. Certainly, Freud paid little attention to the social setting of his patients in analysing their personalities. In fact, most of his writing and theorizing about children came from the recollections of his adult patients.

Even esteemed epidemiological studies like the Stirling County Study[49] or the Midtown Manhattan Project[50] spent almost no time on children *per se*. Similarly, the important Hollingshead and Redlich study of the relationship between social class and mental illness in an urban community deletes any mention of children.[51]

In the past decade, in conjunction with the growth of Child Psychiatry as a legitimate specialty and Social Psychiatry as a central focus for research, there have been significant changes. More good research is now done with children as a central focus. Much of the work in contemporary psychotherapy also concentrates as much on the social context as it does on the child. There are many studies on infants, not only as manifesting significant individual differences,[52] but as part of an interactional social system, a far cry from the *tabula rasa* of Watson. Pasamanik pioneered the study of children as vulnerable products of their social environment, beginning even prenatally.[53] Rutter has compared children in urban and rural settings along a number of dimensions with important findings.[54] Robins did a thirty-year follow up of 3,000 urban children designated as antisocial or neurotic in their youth.[55] There have been recent studies which show that powerful contextual and social expectations actually shape behaviour in children.[56] Similarly, studies of competence and self-esteem in children no longer concentrate solely on the psyche of the child.[57] Just as there has been increasing emphasis on the potentially deleterious effect on children of deprivation, increasing vulnerability and incidence of handicapping conditions in health, education and behaviour, so too there has been increasing interest in invulnerability and achievement in spite of a destructive social context.

Erik Erikson broadened psychosexual development to incorporate social factors, culminating in adolescence in the achievement of identity resolution.[58] While this concept has been considerably modified in the past few years, it has served as a major contribution to the interface between psychological and social factors. Offer and Adelson, among others, have studied large populations of urban adolescents to assess their values, attitudes, and aspirations in many areas.[59]

The picture is positive. The number of children involved in research has increased. Clinicians are much more interested in normal populations, and yet, there is still a dearth of multi-disciplinary research on urban children, particularly research dealing with the context of urban life, including how change, scale, and organization intersect with child development.

We must also note that several excellent policy studies have recently emerged which emphasize the importance of income differentials and their implications for children.[60] That we do not deal with this approach is by no means a denegration of it. Our concentration is on aspects of urban life rather than of life in general. Let us, therefore, turn to the nature of the current effort.

THE CURRENT EFFORT

Despite the wide scope of our frame of reference, we realize that no single effort can provide total coverage over so complex a subject matter. Studying 'The Child in the City' requires some degree of judicious choice as to what can be comprehended short of the whole but which is yet worth attention and amenable to intervention in and of itself.

The process of refining coherent, digestible units of inquiry from an inchoate universe cannot be understood apart from the structural situation of our research programme. The Child in the City Programme is under the sponsorship of the Hospital for Sick Children Foundation, Toronto. This foundation's mother institution, the hospital, celebrated its centennial in 1975. During its first century, the hospital built up an international reputation for its medical services; but the centennial celebration became a time also for taking stock of needs for future activities. Among other things, the city serving as the primary sending area to the hospital had changed enormously, with particularly rapid changes during the decade immediately before 1975. The population of Toronto and its suburbs had grown to about two and one-half million in 1977, virtually doubling in 25 years. This contributed to pressures on the area's only general children's hospital, particularly in light of the relative scarcity of medical services in newly built areas. And the foreign origin of many newly arrived residents of Toronto was associated with attitudes towards and use of medical facilities which were not familiar to the local medical practitioners and administrators.

In addition, other recent changes, found most highly developed in the city, appeared potentially related to problems involving paediatric medicine, directly and indirectly. For example, changes in urban physical structure which occasion additional kinds of accidents among children are of concern to paediatric medical practice.[61] Other changes reflecting more purely social trends (e.g. increasing maternal employment and greater numbers of latchkey children) but which potentially affect psychological conditions are no less relevant.

Thus, our search for ways of dealing with this subject, within the conceptual framework described earlier, turned to one of judiciously selecting recent changes, either in the city structure itself or in the social structure found there, with potential implications for children's health in the widest sense – including welfare and well-being.

After much thinking and discussion, five substantive areas were selected for further pursuit. Each of these areas represents a set of concerns with strong potential implications for children, about which some degree of community concern has built up and where the literature on the subject, when existent, has been relatively diffuse – covering particular points in depth at times, but seldom coming to grips with the total situation, its meaning, or its consequences for children.

In the overall process leading to a selection of research and demonstration projects, we chose as a first step to examine thoroughly the current state of knowledge and practice concerning these topics. This examination is the subject of the greater part of this book. The five substantive areas are as follows:

1 *Community services and their ability to help families and children in the city.* There are many services, some private and some public, set up to ameliorate the condition of life for children – most of them oriented towards reaching children through their families, although some dealing with the children directly. Great national differences in the provision of services reflect differences in philosophy and financing (not always unrelated). Yet, in the cities, with their characteristic size and scale, certain problems always need be dealt with. The existence and location of appropriate facilities are not necessarily known to people whose daily paths of travel and residential location happen not to coincide with services they have had no previous need to use. Hence, the match between people and services is an inevitable matter to be dealt with. Who knows about and uses the different kinds of services (health, legal, welfare, supportive, etc.) which have already been made available? From the point of view of the individual, where do people turn for help, if needed, without having perfect knowledge of the total system in existence? Even when people know the 'right' places to go for services they need or want, are they willing or able to approach those offering the services; conversely, to what extent do those offering services feel able or willing to extend them to all who seek help?

In a unit with the scale of the city, to what extent are service-givers aware of each other, of the total system of services available, and of the real nature of need for service? To what extent are they co-operative or competitive – and with what consequences? When a child experiences one or another form of service, when the system of services is provided at such a scale, to what extent is there a rational and systematic procedure of referrals and follow-up, so that the individual child is not 'lost' in this part of the urban fabric?

2 *Child care, parenting, and social support for parenting.* Both the structure of families and the daily activities of individual family members have altered in recent years. The city has long been an escape from the social pressures towards conformity characteristic of small towns and rural areas. High incidence of divorce, remarriage, and single parenthood have been associated with city life, although, as with all else, these are surely not excluded elsewhere. Furthermore,

large cities provide greater opportunities for paid female employment, one of the notable ascendant trends of the last ten years.

What does all of this mean for child-raising, particularly in the 'tender' years (when adults now choose to have children at all)? What are some of the services and other types of parental support which have arisen in response to pressures typically placed upon parents in various situations of family structure and employment?

What must the effects of general ideological influences be towards people's attitudes about having and raising children?

On a more specific level, very little is known about the effects on children of various ways of providing for daycare, before- and after-school care, and other services (many of which, at their best, strongly emphasize aspects of child development thought desirable for the child, quite apart from pragmatic reasons working parents might have for choosing daycare).

3 *The transition from childhood to adulthood in the city.* There are a number of aspects of this area which arouse public concern, not least because they are more visible than the problems of very young children. There are, for example, special legal superstructures and statuses for adolescents, hypothesized to reflect, however crudely, the developmental capacity of the 'child becoming adult.' The law carefully specifies ages when children can participate in adult structures, when they require special legal protection, when they have the right to seek and consent to medical practices apart from the dictates of their parents, and when they can or cannot perform certain behaviour or consume certain substances. However, both the validity and the observance of these complicated structurings is an open question.

Furthermore, the particular path of transition from childhood to adulthood seems unclear in certain important respects. For example, how one prepares for and then enters the world of work is highly chaotic - or so it appears. To take another example, the social position of the adolescent is visibly unclear, with neither the certainties of childhood nor the family or social group memberships of adulthood welcoming the teenager. Indeed, the very word 'teenager' is at least partly a response to a world which has created a chasm largely unbridged between childhood and adulthood, leaving the need for young people to create a reality to fill the vacuum. One consequence is the selection of a variety of fads and belief-systems which are not always comprehensible to the adult, but which young people feel fulfil a need in their lives.

Despite all that has been and is now happening to adolescents in the city, what do we really know about these processes which operate upon young people during the increasing number of years following childhood and preceding formal adulthood? The urban setting is surely not irrelevant to this context, inasmuch as the city makes available so many choices from which critical masses of teenagers can choose - and must choose - in the process of sorting out their lives. We felt that popular worries such as delinquency, adolescent sexuality, use of alcohol and drugs, relationships to authority (including their rights and responsibilities), and youthful unemployment all fitted more coherently under a perspective framing the kinds of questions just posed. And both legal and social-psychological approaches to such questions are needed.

4 *Increasing population diversity and its implications for children.* Toronto is an extreme example of the trend towards ethnic diversity, long since found in many North American cities and now extending to many in Europe. While there is a voluminous literature having to do with racial contrasts and contacts, and their effects on children, much less work has been pursued on what it means to grow up in a setting where many worlds and sets of values co-exist, compared to homogeneous settings in which particular definitions of right and wrong are promulgated without competition. Although it is highly conceivable for children to live in the equivalent of an 'urban village,'[62] a nearly self-contained homogeneous group within the confines of the city, total insularity is not the rule, and all sorts of variations occur in the degrees of mixture of young people - minority/majority relationships, and minorities to one another.

One might in fact argue that in the City of Toronto there is no majority group, at best a 'plurality' group. In any case, what is the nature of contact and attitude linking various groups under different conditions of mixture and under the influence, if any, of various specific programmes designed to foster multicultural harmony? To what extent does the experience of children at school and in the city have a bearing on their relationships with their parents and other relatives - and vice-versa? What effects on the development of values, of self-concepts, and on feelings of social competence are fostered among children in different situations of cultural contact? What use of societal institutions is made by children coming from different backgrounds and in different situations of multicultural contact?

5 *Altered housing and physical environments, and their implications for children.* As in the preceding topics, a number of different aspects of this area are of interest. Similarly, it is not a foregone conclusion that the consequences of these aspects are positive or negative. In a system as complex as the city, in fact, we should expect both - in response to variations in the causal factors and in the nature of the particular group affected.

One aspect of the physical environment undergoing change as cities grow and develop has to do with the nature and distribution of purely physical environmental hazards and other influences relevant to children. For example, certain airborne pollutants, such as lead, are known to have a greater impact on the health of 'smaller people.'

The second aspect has to do with the type of housing in which families live, which is tending towards multiple dwelling units in larger complexes. In this situation, to what extent are both the form and content of contact between child and parent altered? One might also ask if the locational aspects of children's activities vary according to the types of housing and new neighbourhoods created. In this event, one would expect forms of contact with both peers and various non-peer authority figures to be changed, leading perhaps to different types of upbringings and childhood experiences.

What is the nature of the community in which children now live? Whether it be a newly constructed high-rise community, or a low-density, dispersed suburban community in which interesting places and activities, if any, are far removed from where the child lives, is this not a different experience from that found in the central city, where most things are usually found at close range and experienced on a personal basis?

What about the relationship of the child to the larger city? How well is public transportation provided, contributing to the ease or difficulty with which children can actually take advantage of the facilities of the metropolis?

The Process of Synthesis
Although the above questions surely delimit the universe of inquiry, they certainly are not small or pat questions. When dealing with slices of real world problematics, it is impossible to approach any of these matters through the eyes of a single discipline or approach. Answering questions of inherent complexity cannot be accomplished by taking purely sectoral viewpoints. It is perhaps for this reason that the investigation of issues having to do with social policy is becoming increasingly interdisciplinary.

As a starting point for the work to be done on 'The Child in the City,' we took the position that none of the questions posed could be understood adequately from the point of view of a single discipline, even at the same time that a person trained in one or another discipline might be more suitable for the development of a given topic.

Therefore, we assembled people from a variety of backgrounds into a research team, with the intention of merging an interdisciplinary process with individual substantive responsibilities. Among the disciplines represented in one or another position on the team are sociology, psychology, psychiatry (medicine), geography, law, anthropology, education, urban planning, and social work. External advisers represent additional disciplinary perspectives, as well as the realities of service delivery and policy formulation.

Even though the chapters are written by and credited to specific individuals, in recognition of the degrees of ultimate responsibility such authorship involved, both the whole and the parts of this volume represent an unusually high commitment to interdisciplinarity. This reflects collaboration in: (1) establishing the general frame of reference; (2) defining topics to be included; (3) spelling out the content of each topic; (4) making explicit relevant theories; (5) specifying linkages between topics; (6) sharing data relevant to more than one topic; (7) co-authoring of sections representing overlapping interest; (8) drawing conclusions; and (9) reviewing and integrating all written material.

The chapters which follow are intended to represent this commitment. Although chapters authored by different people obviously take on individual characteristics, they nonetheless attempt to follow a common pattern. They start by specifying the kind of problem concerning the child in the city with which they deal, indicating as well why such an area is considered problematic. Then the current state of knowledge and practice about this area is detailed, followed by some conclusions concerning the kind of research and demonstration efforts considered necessary for the near future.

In the last chapter, a more generally synthesizing look is taken at a number of the common theoretical and practical strands brought up in the individual chapters. Furthermore, some attempt is made, after having specified the criteria to be used, to assign priority across sectors, to identify work considered to deserve the most immediate attention in the future.

NOTES

1 With the support and assistance of Katherine Catton, Linda Hagarty, Susan Hodgson, Anna-Rose Spina, and Suzanne Ziegler.
2 See the larger quotation cited by Robert Bremner in Volume 1. *The child in the city: today and tomorrow*, p. 41. It serves as an excellent set of objectives even now for a programme like 'The Child in the City.'
3 Redfield, Robert *The folk culture of Yucatan*, Chicago: University of Chicago Press, 1941. See, more recently, Claude Fischer, Urban to Rural Diffusion of Opinions in Contemporary America, *American Journal of Sociology 84:* 151-159, 1978.
4 *Toronto Star*, 18 May 1977.
5 Fischer, Claude *The urban experience*. New York: Harcourt, Brace & Jovanovich, 1976.

6 Keller, Suzanne Oral presentation to annual meeting of American Sociological Association, Chicago, 5 September 1977.
7 A research programme at the University of Toronto, which is the institutional base for the present collective effort.
8 Kohlberg, L. The development of children's orientation toward a moral order: I. Sequence in the development of moral thought, *Vita Humana 6:* 11–33, 1963. Piaget has done extensive writing on the stages of cognitive development. For an excellent review, see Baldwin, A. The theory of Jean Piaget, in *Theories of child development.* New York: John Wiley and Sons, Inc., 1967, pp. 171–300.
9 Gump, P.V. Ecological psychology and children, in Hetherington, E.M., ed., *Review of child development research* V. Chicago: University of Chicago Press, 1975, pp. 75–126.
10 Yarrow, L., Rubenstein, J., and Pederson, F. *Infant and environment.* Washington, D.C.: Hemisphere Publishing Corp., 1975; Wachs, T., Uzgiris, I., and Hunt, J. McV. Cognitive development in infants of different age levels and from different environmental backgrounds: an exploratory investigation, *Merrill-Palmer Quarterly 17:* 283–317, 1971; Caldwell, B., Wright, C., Honig, A., and Tannenbaum, J. Infant day care and attachment, *American Journal of Orthopsychiatry 40:* 283–317, 1970. White, B. and Watts, J.C. *Experience and environment.* Englewood Cliffs, N.J.: Prentice Hall, 1973.
11 Hunt, J. McV. The utilization of ordinal scales inspired by Piaget's observations, *Merrill-Palmer Quarterly 22:* 31–45, 1976; Kagan, J. and Klein, R.E. Cross-cultural perspectives on early development, *American Psychologist 28:* 947–61, 1973; Ainsworth, M. *Infancy in Uganda: Infant care and the growth of love.* Baltimore: Johns Hopkins University Press, 1967.
12 Yarrow et al. *Infant and environment*; Kohn, M. and Rossman, B.L. Cognitive functioning in five-year old boys as related to socio-emotional and background demographic variables, *Developmental Psychology 8:* 277–94, 1973.
13 Weinraub, M., Brooks, J., and Lewis, M. The social network: A reconsideration of the concept of attachment, *Human Development 20:* 31–47, 1977.
14 Caldwell et al. *Infant day care.*
15 Bell, R.Q. and Harper, L.V. *Child effects on adults.* Hillsdale, N.J.: Lawrence Erlbaum Associates, 1977.
16 Bronfenbrenner, U. Toward an experimental ecology of human development, *American Psychologist 32:* 513–631, 1977.
17 Williams, T.M.B. Infant development and supplemental care: A comparative review of basic and applied research, *Human Development 20:* 1–30, 1977.

18 Weisner, T. and Gallimore, R. My brother's keeper: Child and sibling care-taking, *Current Anthropology 18:* 169–80, 1977.

19 Liebow, Elliott *Tally's corner*, Boston: Little, Brown Publishers, 1967.

20 Suttles, Gerald D. *The social order of the slum: ethnicity and territory in the inner city*. Chicago: University of Chicago Press, 1968.

21 Whyte, William F. *Street corner society: the social structure of an Italian slum*. Chicago: University of Chicago Press, 1943.

22 Ruano, Betty J., Bruce, James D., and McDermott, Margaret M. Pilgrim's progress II: Recent trends and prospects in family research, *Journal of Marriage and the Family 31:* 688–698, November 1969; Mogey, John M. Research on the family: the search for world trends, *Journal of Marriage and the Family 31:* 225–232, May 1969; Hill, Reuben Sociology of marriage and family behaviour, 1945–1956. A trend report and bibliography, *Current Sociology 7:* 1, 1958; Aldous, Joan and Hill, Reuben International bibliography of research in marriage and the family, 1900–1964. Minneapolis, Minn.: University of Minnesota Press, 1967.

23 Jaffee, B. and Fanshel, D. *How they fared in adoption: a follow up study in adoption: portrait of 100 families*. New York: Columbia University Press, 1970.

24 Kahn, A., Kamerman, S., and McGowan, B. *Child advocacy: report of national baseline study*. New York: Columbia School of Social Work, 1972.

25 Geismar, L. *555 families: a social psychological study of young families in transition*. New Brunswick: N.J.: Transaction Books, 1973.

26 Schorr, Alvin *Poor kids, A report of children in poverty*. New York: Basic Books, 1966.

27 Head, Wilson, et al. *Families in highrise apartments*. Toronto: Social Planning Council of Metropolitan Toronto, 1973. Hagarty, Linda M. *The family at home: a comparison of the time budgets of families in highrise and detached homes in suburban metropolitan Toronto,* Doctoral dissertation, University of Toronto, Faculty of Social Work, 1975.

28 Briar, Scott Family services, in Mass, H.P., ed., *Five fields of social service; reviews of research*, New York: National Association of Social Workers, 1966.

29 Chaiklin, H., Chesley, F. and Litsinger, W. Delinquency and health status, *Health and Social Work 3:* 25–37, 1977.

30 Yelaja, S. A profile of juvenile offenders, *The Social Worker 43:* 46–55, 1975.

31 Byles, John and Maurice, Andrea The juvenile services project, Report to Department of Health and Welfare, Ottawa, 1977.

32 Pink, William T. and White, Mervin Delinquency prevention: The state of the art in Malcolm Klein, ed., *The juvenile justice system*. Beverly Hills, Calif.: Sage Publications, 1976.

33 Byles, J. and Maurice, A. The juvenile services project, 1977.

34 Schur, Edwin M. *Radical non-intervention: rethinking the delinquency problem*. Englewood Cliffs, N.J.: Prentice Hall Inc., 1973.

35 Wald, Michael S. Legal policies affecting children: A lawyer's request for aid, *Child Development 49:* 1-5, 1976.

36 *Perspective Canada*. Information Canada, p. 7, 1974.

37 Aldrich, R.A. Introduction to pediatrics: The change from pediatrics to child health and human development, in Kelleg, V.C. et al., eds., *Practice of pediatrics*. Hagerstown: W.F. Prior, Chap. 1, p. 1, 1967; Bergman, A.B., Dassel, S.W., and Wedgwood, R.J. Time-motion study of a practicing pediatrician, *Pediatrics 38:* 254-63, 1966; Shah, C.P. and Robinson, G.C. A comparative study of pediatric practice in the Vancouver General Hospital Outpatient Department and in four family practices, *Canadian Medical Association Journal 100:* 465-70, 1969.

38 Holt, H.S. *The quality of survival*. London: Butterworth, 1972.

39 Department of Health and Social Security, *N.H.S. Reorganization Circular HRC 74:* no. 5, Operation and Development of Services: Child Health Services; Sheridan, M.P. Children's development progress. *National Foundation for Educational Research*, Windsor, 1973; Chard, T. The fetus at risk: screening for disease, *Lancet*, Oct. 5–Dec. 31, pp. 6-8, 1974.

40 Bennett, J.E., Krasny, J., The nation's health, *Financial Post*, Mar. 26–May 7, 1977.

41 Bailey, E.N. Kiehl, P.S. et al. Screening in pediatric practice: *Pediatric Clinic of North America 21: 1:* 123-65, 1974; Holt, K.S. Screening for disease: Infancy and childhood, *Lancet:* Oct. 5–Dec. 21, p. 1495, 1974; Kohler, L. Health control of four-year-old children: An epidemiological study of child health, *Acta Pediatrica Scandinavica Supplement 235.* 1973; Nilsson, C., Sundelin, C., and Vuille, J.C. General health screening of four-year-olds in a Swedish county: An analysis of the effectiveness of the psychological examination program, *Acta Pediatrica Scandinavica 65:* 663-68, 1976; Kohler, L. and Stigmar, G. Vision screening of four-year-old children, *Acta Pediatrica Scandinavica 62:* 17-27, 1973; Kohler, L. and Holst, H. Auditory screening of four-year-old children, *Acta Pediatrica Scandinavica 61:* 555-60, 1972, North, A.F. Screening in child care, *American Family Physician 13:* 2, 85-95. 1976; Arbus, G.S. and Williams, R.C. Preschool detection of asymptomatic bacteriuria: A public health program, *Canadian*

Medical Association Journal 14: 315-18, 1976; Ellestad-Sayed, J. et al. Nutrition survey of school children in greater Winnipeg, *CMA Journal 11:* 490-96, March 1977; Wynn, A. Health care systems for pre-school children, *Proc. Roy. Soc. Med 69:* 14-17, 1976; Henzell, J.M. The expanded role of the school health nurse in pediatric screening, *Australian Paediatric Journal 13:* 44-8, 1977; Eisner, V. and Oglesby, A. Health assessment of children. The unexpected health defect, *The Journal of School Health XLII: 6:* 348-50, June 1972; Jacobs, R. and Hall, C.J. Periodic developmental assessment of pre-school children in Newham. *Public Health,* London: 1976, pp. 179-86; Uyeda, F.F. The detection of learning disabilities in the early school age child, specifically the kindergarten child, *Journal of School Health XLII: 4:* 214-17, 1972; Cvejic, H. et al. The evolution of a team approach to a kindergarten screening program, *Canadian Journal of Public Health 68:* 165-68, March/April 1977; Rogers, M.G.H. The early recognition of handicapping disorders in childhood, *Develop. Med. Child Neurol. 13:* 88-101, 1971; Maier, J. *Screening and assessment of young children at developmental risk,* The President's Committee on Mental Retardation, Dept. of Health, Education and Welfare Publication (OS): 73-90, Washington, D.C., 1973; Frankenburg, W.K. Pediatric screening, *Advances in Pediatrics 20:* 149-75, 1973.

42 Whitby, L.G. Screening for disease: Definitions and criteria, *Lancet II.* pp. 819-22, 5 October 1974.

43 Kohler, L. Health control of children; Nilsson, C., Sundelin C., and Vuille, J.C. General health screening of four-year-olds, *Acta Pediatrica Scandinavica 65:* 663-68, 1976; Kohler and Stigmar Vision screening, *Acta Pediatrica Scandinavica 62:* 17-27, 1973; Kohler and Holst Auditory screening, *Acta Pediatrica Scandinavica 61:* 555-60, 1972.

44 Bailey, E.N., Kiehl, P.S. et al. Screening in pediatric practice, *Pediatric Clinics of North America 21*(1): 123-65, 1974. North, A.F. Screening in child care, *American Family Physician 13*(2): 85-95, 1976.

45 Holt, H.S. Screening for diseases, *Lancet,* p. 1495, 1974. Kohler, L. Health control of four-year-old children, *Acta Pediatrica Scandinavica Supplement 235:* 1973.

46 Kohler, L. Health control of four-year-old children, *Acta Pediatrica Scandinavica Supplement 235,* 1973. Nilsson, Sundelin, and Vuille, General health screening of four-year-olds in a Swedish County, *Acta Pediatrica Scandinavica 65:* 663-68, 1976; Kohler and Stigmar Vision screening, *Acta Pediatrica Scandinavica 62:* 17-27, 1973; Kohler and Holst Auditory screening, *Acta Pediatrica Scandinavica 61:* 555-60, 1972.

47 Litt, I.F. and Cohen, M.I. Prisons, adolescents and the right to quality medical care: The time is now, *American Journal of Public Health 64:* 894, 1974.

48 Keniston, K. and the Carnegie Council on Children *All our children*, New York: Harcourt, Brace & Jovanovich, 1977.

49 Leighton, D., Harding, J., Macklin, D., Macmillan, A., and Leighton, A. *The character of danger, vol. III: The Stirling County study of psychiatric disorder and socio-cultural environment*, New York: Basic Books, 1963.

50 Srole, L. *Mental health in the metropolis: the midtown Manhattan project*, New York: McGraw-Hill Book Company, 1963.

51 Hollingshead, A. and Redlich, F. *Social class and mental illness, A community study*, New York: John Wiley and Sons, Inc., 1958.

52 Thomas, A., Chess, S., and Birch, H.G. *Temperament and behavior disorders in children*, New York: University Press, 1968.

53 Pasamanik, B. The epidemiology of behavior disorders in childhood, *Rev. Publ. Assoc. Nerv. Ment. Dis.*, Baltimore: Williams & Wilkins Publishers, 1956.

54 Rutter, M., Tizard, J., and Whitmore, K. eds. *Education, health and behavior: medical study of child psychological development*, London: Longman Group Ltd., 1970; Rutter, M. and Madge, N. *Cycles of disadvantage: A review of research*, London: Heineman, 1976.

55 Robins, L.N. *Deviant children grown up; a sociological and psychiatric study of sociopathic personality*, Baltimore: The Williams & Wilkins Company, 1966.

56 Rosenthal, R. and Jacobson, L. *Pygmalion in the classroom; teacher expectation and pupils' intellectual development*, New York: Holt, Rinehart and Winston, Inc., 1968.

57 Coopersmith, S. *Antecedents of self-esteem*, San Francisco: W.H. Freeman, 1967.

58 Erikson, E. *Identity: youth and crisis*, New York: William W. Norton, Inc., 1968.

59 Offer, D. *The psychological world of the teenager*, New York: Basic Books, Inc., Publishers, 1969; Adelson, J., The development of ideology in adolescents in ch. 4 in Dragastin, S. and Elder, G. (eds.), *Adolescence in the life cycle*, New York: John Wiley & Sons Inc., 1976.

60 National Academy of Sciences *Toward a national policy for children and families*, Washington: The Academy, 1976, and Keniston, K. and the Carnegie Council on Children *All our children*.

61 Hospitals are vitally concerned with the incidence of *preventable* pathologies despite their competence with the technical and qualitative aspects of bodily

repair, just as insurance companies care about the number of auto accidents regardless of the proliferation and expertise of auto body shop personnel.

62 Gans, Herbert *The urban villagers: group and class in the life of Italian-Americans*, New York: Free Press of Glencoe, 1962.

2

Children, Families, and Community Services

ANNA-ROSE SPINA AND LINDA HAGARTY

I INTRODUCTION

The 1970s contrast with decades in the late nineteenth and early twentieth centuries when adults showed little awareness of children as individuals and little consideration for their feelings. An estimated one hundred thousand homeless children were shipped from England to Canada and elsewhere to live, but mostly to work. Children 'drilled into usefulness' by parents and foster families looked elsewhere for appreciation and emotional support. Help was considered charity.[1] Problems we now see looming were not perceived or not acknowledged.

Owing to technical advances since the early 1900s, traditional child health problems, such as infant mortality, infectious disease, dental caries, hygiene, housing, and nutrition are considered amenable to solution. The continuing improvement in child health care depends not only on the search for new knowledge in preventive medicine, care for acute and chronic illness, and quality of environment and social problems, such as child abuse, but on '... our ability to apply what we have learned, and to deliver it to the community in some effective way.'[2]

The public health movement from the 1880s to 1914 focused on problems of infant mortality, child health in schools, and sanitation, lending support to community-based or civic health improvement. In 1920, with the establishment of the Canadian Council on Child Welfare, child health and welfare shifted from

* We wish to thank Brenda Billingsley, and our colleagues for their help in putting together and critiquing this manuscript. Linda Hagarty is responsible for Section VI, Anna-Rose Spina is primarily responsible for II, III, and IV. Both authors collaborated on I and V.

volunteer to professional status. The public health service changed the relationship of citizens to their community resources and access to them, and established a precedent on which to build.

Based on their study of child health in Monroe County (Rochester), New York, Haggerty and his colleagues found, 'The current major health problems of children, as seen by the community, are those that would barely have been mentioned a generation ago. Learning difficulties and school problems, behavioral disturbances, allergies, speech difficulties, visual problems and the problems of adolescents in coping and adjusting are today the most common concerns about children.'[3]

The 'new morbidity,' as Haggerty calls these problems, requires innovative approaches to health, broadly defined. The solutions may indicate a new community role for the paediatrician, as Haggerty and Richmond and others believe. A new link more firmly forged with education may also be necessary. It could be a welcome innovation in an era of 'shrinking school population, unfilled school houses, and unemployed teachers.'[4]

Local (community) councils may be vital to the provision and co-ordination of children's services so that 'a system for finding children and families in need of services can be found but one designed not to transgress the privacy and integrity of each family.'[5] But 'actual understanding of consumer behavior is needed before we can develop a more effective and efficient services system.'[6] There is general agreement among clinicians, social workers, and social science researchers that differences in utilization of services cannot be ascribed solely to lack of availability or to lack of money to pay for them.

How do communities ensure that families have access to the health and social services they need? Should children's services be separate or a part of an integrated system for families or for individuals of all ages? Will children end up 'second' under any arrangement? What are the boundaries of health and social services? People want help for problems not always defined by professionals as their domain. Defining boundaries and evaluating costs, as Haggerty and others suggest, may be two of the most important issues facing community health and social services. Assessing community needs and resources is most certainly another.[7]

Broadly, services for children and families are all those provisions which societies make for the support, protection, and development of their members. Education, health, employment, housing, and income maintenance provisions are distinct areas of service along with a sixth field increasingly referred to as the general or personal social services, a term that describes an array of services both professional and voluntary which complement, supplement, or substitute for, services rendered by family or friends on an individual basis.[8]

For the most part, family and child welfare services fall within the domain of the personal social services. In addition, Hepworth has added correctional and penal services as a major social service, while the Robarts' Commission included both recreation and public libraries in its purview of social policies in Metropolitan Toronto.[9] Generally, however, personal social services include: traditional child welfare programmes, such as adoption, protection, foster home placement; child care provisions, such as day nurseries and daycare; family life education; marriage and family counselling; budgeting and credit counselling; family therapy; and family support services, such as homemakers and home care for the sick; adolescent counselling and placement services; group homes, institutions and day treatment centres for children and adolescents, and information and community centres.

A diverse array of services such as this defies any simple description of their pattern of organization. Currently, in both Canada and the United States, these services constitute an incoherent patchwork of auspices and funding arrangements, statutory and voluntary provisions, levels of staffing, and eligibility requirements.

As we move towards the end of the seventies, services to children and families stand at an important crossroad. Worldwide economic problems associated with inflation have curtailed the wholesale expansion of costly labour-intensive human services and proof of their effectiveness is being demanded. At the same time, a movement to 'empower' the family[10] 'restoring authority and resources' also has important implications for the form and function of services in the future.

As Marvin Sussman has observed:

The increasing inability of the bureaucracy to deliver services points up the significance of successful linkages and the role of family systems in achieving goals by their own efforts. Moreover, the growing demand for social, health, educational, and welfare services is beginning to exceed the capacities of professional and para-professional organizations. Thus, the family – as a social unit with caretaking, therapeutic, socializing, facilitating and handling activities – must be recognized as a vital partner of bureaucratic service organizations that have health, welfare and rehabilitative objectives.[11]

In light of these shifts in perception of the role of the family in relation to services, this chapter draws on literature from the disciplines of sociology, social psychology, and social work to examine four separate but related themes: changes in the family; help-seeking behaviour; the need for services; and helping resources in urban communities.

This chapter begins with a summary review of trends with respect to the family for two reasons. First, changes in the family have implications both for the family's need for external support and the nature of family linkages to both formal and informal sources of help. Secondly, there is increasing recognition that if children are to achieve their potential, the veil of privacy that has shielded family life may have to be lifted to some extent.

In the second section, we have reviewed the literature on help-seeking in order to obtain another perspective on the process by which individuals and families recognize the need for outside help and go about seeking it. This is essentially an adult literature, but to the extent that it considers family variables it sheds some light on what children learn in the family about seeking help outside it.

The third section of this chapter deals with services from the perspective of the service provider. It is organized around the pivotal concept of need: how needs are assessed and responded to by the formal service system.

In the final section, we follow the direction of current social policy to focus on the family in the community. What resources do families themselves have for dealing with problems? What is known about the relationships that serve families as informal sources of assistance? Concluding this section is an overview of the self-help movement as a phenomenon that stands midway between formal and informal sources of help.

II THE FAMILY

Changes in the Family?
Social scientists, practitioners, and policy-makers have converged on the family in the past two decades. They may have accelerated a 'demythologizing of the family' through the examination of family stability, family functioning, interpersonal dynamics, and varying interpretations of history. But their work has also begun to yield insights into family life, and has focused worldwide concern on population growth, issues of fertility and abortion, divorce and the position of women, and their relevance to family issues.[12]

Concern on the part of professionals and policymakers about 'what is happening in the family' is also shared by people generally, particularly with respect to divorce. This general concern is increasing in that more children are living with one parent, at least for some part of their growing up period; divorce signals a change in the nature of the relationship with at least one parent; and remarriage creates a complex of new relationships for everyone in the family. Central to the discussion of these family issues is knowledge about how children adapt to changes in the family unit; the crucial aspects of family life for children and their future; and whether help is therefore indicated for all families, or just for some of them.

The changes in the family that are heralded by many may actually be the lifting of a shield of privacy, making public the ties (or lack of them) binding members to one another and to the community. Historians and others disagree on whether the family unit prior to the nineteenth century was nuclear, as we know it, consisting of a husband, wife, and children, or extended, with generations sharing the work and family life as a unit. One view is that the family has in recent centuries been nuclear but that family 'boundaries' have been loosened and tightened as relations changed between family and community. Katz's research indicates that in the mid-nineteenth century families shared socialization. Often there was a single young person from another family living in the household in a semi-autonomous state until experience away from home and a job made independence possible. These relatively loose family boundaries tightened, according to Katz, when families took on a greater share of the task of socializing their own members.[13]

According to Edward Shorter, the family changed in the nineteenth century by the crucial factor of sentiment: romantic love unseated material considerations as partners were selected for personal happiness; 'maternal love' gave priority to the mother-child relationship; the exclusiveness and unique ties binding members of the family to one another created a boundary or a shield of privacy between family and the surrounding community. As Shorter words it, community involvement was no longer a given but a choice, and '... the couple terminated its association with these outside groups ...'[14]

Shorter sees the relationship between the couple as inherently unstable and fluctuating as they sever community ties. As the children grow to maturity, he sees the parent-child relationship becoming increasingly tenuous. To Shorter, post-modern family life is evolving in directions that have no historical precedent: the cutting of generational ties; intensification of the explosive nature of marital ties; and the withdrawing from the family circle of women and teenagers, replacing the nuclear family with a 'free-floating couple.'[15]

There is some general agreement that approximately 98 per cent of the children in North America in the future, as now, will be brought up in families. Kenneth Keniston and the Carnegie Council on Children and Mary Jo Bane counter the disintegration thesis of modern family life. They question the assumptions that others have used in assessing mature family life. 'The general agitation about the decline of the family and the demise of community seems to assume that these two institutions once provided protection against the twin dangers of individual vulnerability and political alienation.'[16]

Assumptions by experts that parents are solely responsible for what happens to their children, that families should be free-standing, independent and autonomous units, or they are not adequate, are questioned by Keniston. 'Recognizing that family self-sufficiency is a false myth ...,'[17] Keniston sees new roles for parents acting as family executives rather than performing direct functions such as education and job training. Rising expectations for what parents want for their children and ought to give them, and the need to consult and depend on institutions and new specialists to meet the expectations, creates a need for help for all families. 'The problem is not so much to re-educate parents but to make available the help they need and to give them enough power so that they can be effective advocates with and coordinators of the other forces that are bringing up their children.'[18]

Family Trends
Three recent family trends illustrate the importance of re-evaluating assumptions about the family, considering its role as an executive or co-ordinating one, and re-thinking the relationship between the family and the community.

A New Life-Cycle Stage
Freedom, independence, and the development of each person's full potential are the overriding values in North America mentioned to account for what demographers and other social scientists, and many social commentators, see as two population trends since 1970: an increase in the number of adults under 35 years living alone; and an increase in the number of households formed, which outstrips national population increase.[19] According to some experts, the two trends reflect the tendency for young adults to leave home early and to marry late, the interim being a period of singleness or a transitional phase which is being added to one's life cycle.[20]

Factors contributing to this singleness are independence of young people from their parents; the growing career ambitions of women, and the easing of salary and credit discrimination; the mounting divorce rate which creates a wariness about marriage, and a preference for postponing marriage for the 'right' person; a need to build a life or career for oneself, particularly in the case of women who have experienced early divorce and who desire a period of independence.[21] A generally increasing social tolerance for more flexible or unconventional living arrangements has also contributed to the new life-cycle stage, along with greater social acceptance of divorce by religious denominations, as a means of resolving marriage difficulties, and changes in divorce laws.

Parenthood and Singleness
Alfred Kahn has stated that now proportionately more children are living with their natural parents than ever before in history, because adults are living

longer.[22] We do have more single parent families, and more divorce, but we also have more marriage and remarriage. Kahn estimates that 94 per cent of our children are living with at least one natural parent. For some children, the life-cycle phase of singleness of their parents means being brought up, for a time at least, in a single-parent family. Glick estimates that 30 per cent of children under 18 years in the U.S. were not living with a mother and father in a continuous marriage in 1970.

From the point of view of one of the practice professions, the increasing interest in the one-parent family in the 1960s and 1970s has been based not on concern for the family but on the reasons why the family has only one parent.[23] Whereas, in decades past, death was the primary cause of single-parent families, now, for the most part, families separate voluntarily and the phenomenon is viewed as a 'social problem' for several reasons: the vulnerability of such families to economic dependence, especially when the one parent is a woman; potential deleterious effects on the psychosocial development of the children; and threat to the stability of a social and economic structure predicated on the two-parent family as the basic social unit. Together with changes in the status of women and increased sexual permissiveness, these factors are seen by many as sowing the seeds of the destruction of the family.

But, clearly, in North America, the husband-wife family is the primary focus of child-rearing (94 per cent, Canada; 86.5 per cent, U.S.), although single parents do have the responsibility, at least for a time (6 per cent of Canadian families are one-parent; 14 per cent, U.S.).[24]

Glick estimates that four of five divorcees probably remarry; no known comparable data are available in Canada, although a study by Schlesinger indicates that remarriage for divorcees generally occurs in their mid-thirties, the age at which they are most likely to have children growing up. Remarriage generally takes place about two years after divorce, for both men and women.[25]

Research literature since 1960 seems to indicate that while single parents have more problems performing domestic responsibilities than married parents, if single parents have adequate financial resources and adequate care for their children, their situations are little different, since the amount of time a father-husband spends with his children alone or on household chores is usually minimal.[26] Current research on child development does not tend to lend support to the idea that a single-parent family is generally a 'highly hazardous context for child rearing.' In fact, some adoption experts believe that for children who are in need of an exclusive relationship with a parent, the single parent is the 'happiest choice.'[27] But, while evidence is accumulating, much information is still needed since research that deals with one-parent families usually concerns the functioning of individuals, especially children, and not families.[28] And, usually information on family structure concerns only whether the family has one or two parents, and is not an analysis of their family life day by day.[29]

The social support available to parents raising children alone is always important in sustaining the family, and is often crucial. Formation of self-help groups, such as Parents Anonymous and Parents Without Partners, are indications of the importance of personal support, as are parent education programmes sponsored by boards of education, e.g., Score, Toronto Board of Education. Recognition of their value by social service agencies, as well as public health organizations, schools, and the courts, is indicated by their adoption of (and experimentation with) family and group programmes as well as individual counselling.

Multi-parents and Multiple Parent Families

Whether or not evidence will continue to support the contention that a period of independent singleness before and after marriage and remarriage is a new life-cycle phase, marriage and remarriage introduce parents to 'additional' parenthood, and children to an additional (rather than a replacement) parent, and, potentially, to adoptive or step-siblings.

In a situation in which one or both parents remarry and biological parents are available, '... there is the potential for a new kind of extended family unique to the multi-parent family situation.'[30] The biological parent is a linking person for a child to the new family; the child links his parent to the non-resident parent. The potential exists for a supportive kinship network during the reorganization involved in the inclusion of new members and when family reorganization has been achieved. One hypothesis might be that, having achieved a workable multi-parent family, the children in such a family may actually be more capable of building social ties outside the family than children from intact families. Adults with such childhood experience may be better able to forge links as necessary to other persons and community services, and participate in community life.

Families with more supporting social and kinship ties outside the family group can be said to have looser boundaries. Potentially multi-parent groups have more ties binding members to one another and to members of the community in which they live; more ties than a single-parent family, which may have tighter boundaries and a more private existence. Families with 'built-in' support may be more able to get help from community resources when they need it.

III HELP SEEKING AND SERVICES

John B. McKinlay, in his review in 1972 of two decades of research on the use of medical and welfare services, concluded that areas worthy of further research were: the decision to seek help and the influence of immediate family, other kin, friends and social networks; the help-seeking process; and the relationship between clients and the service organizations they utilize.[31]

It appears that much of what we do not know about these issues involves a fitting together of pieces from several academic disciplines, and help in interpretation from those in the practice professions; not the traditional way of doing social science research. Perhaps because there has usually been a separation between practice and research and, therefore, between practitioners and researchers, the necessary data have been unavailable to researchers, as outsiders, until recently. As a result, issues that have been of interest to practitioners have not been of interest to researchers. Perhaps until medical and social service issues gained prominence, research on such issues was not considered fundable or accorded sufficient prestige to attract researchers. In addition, family dynamics and how they relate to child rearing and family-community relations did not become an established part of research on community service issues until the 1960s and 70s.

In large part, it was health as a social issue that prompted research into medical and social services. The 1960s became the decade of the development of self. Along with it came the idea that everyone should have an equal opportunity to reach one's potential. Health became a factor in the ability to achieve one's goals and the good life; the provision of health care and facilities for everyone became the means to this ideal. Concern for the environment and conservation became linked to health, and the search for it. Of course, the social importance of health was also measured in terms of productivity in industry and the GNP, but consumer advocates, including the advocates of child and community health care standards and children's rights, came to share the concerns of practitioners, even as they were questioning the authority of those in the 'establishment' and asking them to be accountable. Some who were convinced that the family was crumbling in the 1960s were compelled by their convictions to seek support for the institution and help for family members.

The complexities of medical and social service issues are reflected in the inconclusive findings and the unanswered questions and anomalies that result from research on these issues. The research on help-seeking concerns health and adults, for the most part. Social service literature on help-seeking is at an early stage of development, although its development may become more rapid because the importance of such services is becoming as widely recognized as the costs of delivering them. The social services are a more diverse array than medical services and vary to a greater extent with the needs of the people who are to be served.

Primarily two anomalies prompted further research into medical help-seeking. They were the findings that: (1) people with the same condition may or may not seek help, and if they do, it may be at different points; (2) accessibility and cost may not determine whether or not people will seek help. Researchers noted the influence of informal associations on individual beliefs and feelings, i.e., family, friends, and social relationships, as well as sociocultural factors, and suggested that the decision to seek help, and the factors that prompt the decision, could be generalized as help-seeking behaviour.

Seeking Help
Until 1960, most studies of help-seeking concerned illness and whether a layman's conclusion that he was ill agreed with a doctor's diagnosis. As an example, Sweetser's[32] study concluded that people are more likely to see a doctor for ambiguous health problems than for unambiguous ones, particularly if the condition is of recent onset and interferes with usual activity.

Freidson uncovered what he called a 'lay referral structure' interposed between an individual's first perception of symptoms and the decision to see a professional.[33] 'Lay referral structure ... consists in a network of consultants, potential or actual, running from the intimate and most informal confines of the nuclear family through successively more select, distant, and authoritative persons until the "professional" is reached.'[34] According to Freidson, lay referral is independent of interconnections among professionals and institutions. 'Interaction with non-professional consultants ... is just as responsible for the patient's not following doctor's orders, or not returning for further treatment, as are the cessation of symptoms and the patient's personal opinions about proper treatment.'[35]

In his study on help-seeking and lay referral networks,[36] the two critical variables Freidson cites are: 'The degree of congruence between cultures of the prospective client and the profession, and the relative number and cohesiveness of lay consultants who are interposed between the first perception of symptoms and the decision to see a professional.'[37] Freidson found that a localized lay referral system tended to have a greater influence on the individual because it also tended to be the most cohesive, and the individual was more dependent on it. He found that some respondents were more prone to make decisions without the aid of lay consultants outside the household because they were more secure in their own assessment.[38]

Stoeckle, Zola, and Davidson[39] also concluded that, even in the face of serious debilitation, the decision to seek help is based on extra-physical grounds, i.e., interference with social and personal activity, sanction from others that it was all right to seek help, and experiencing one's situation as a crisis. Stoeckle and his associates noted that distrust, fear, and misconceptions about professions and practitioners, as well as the help of friends and others, increased reluctance to continue treatment and to seek professional advice in the future.

Models of Service Utilization

Alongside efforts to study the relationship between the family and social networks, and help-seeking, were efforts to develop 'models' of the use of health care services. These were efforts to establish an ordering of social, social psychological, and demographic factors as they affect the use of both treatment and prevention services. As health gained importance as a means to the good life, health behaviour as well as illness behaviour became important.

Edward Suchman's work[40] is an important and often cited attempt to relate individual help-seeking, social group membership, and the use of health care facilities. Suchman found that ethnic exclusivity,[41] friendship solidarity, strong family ties and familism, i.e., submission to authority of the family, were associated with low knowledge of disease, scepticism about medical care, and dependency in illness. The influence of respondents' social groups affected individual orientations to medical care (as measured by number of visits to a physician or clinic, a dentist, or other medical services), depending on health status and socio-economic status. Increases in socio-economic status increased the likelihood of use of health care services, especially if health status was felt to be poor.

Suchman's study was replicated by Geertsen[42] and his colleagues in Salt Lake City in 1969, after almost a decade of increasing health awareness and health insurance programmes. Their data indicate that possibly knowledge of disease and family authority have independent effects on service use. Geertsen and his group conclude that persons who belong to close and exclusive groups, especially tradition-oriented families, are likely to seek medical care for a medical problem, if this is consistent with their cultural beliefs and practices. One might also reason that, as Freidson's work showed, when one's beliefs are congruent with those of the medical profession, with respect to health care and health education, one would probably use preventive and detection services as well as diagnostic and treatment services. In 1970 another attempt was made to replicate the Suchman study in Los Angeles by Leo Reeder and Emil Berkanovic.[43] They failed to find any relationship between social group membership and medical orientations, and use of health services. They concluded that during the decade the consumer movement had caused a drastic shift in the expectations and behaviour of health consumers and that, in the ethnic enclaves in Los Angeles, there was considerable knowledge about medical matters and little scepticism about the medical care available.

When Rosenstock's article[44] on why people use health services was published in 1966, social psychological attributes or personal characteristics were thought to figure more importantly in the use of preventive services than they were in the use of treatment services. He found that in the absence of symptoms, belief in high susceptibility and the benefits of seeking medical help resulted in more preventive action for adults in all levels of socio-economic status. According to

Rosenstock, the type of help one seeks depends on whether beliefs are in the efficacy of medical help *or* in the assistance of lay persons in a referral system. The use of treatment services was found to be greater among females and in older age groups. Males and people who are older and have less education were found to be more apt to delay treatment. Rosenstock found, however, that personal characteristics were more important than demographic factors in accounting for the use of treatment services. Income level did not play an important role in the use of medical services, although it was important in the use of dental services.

Since Rosenstock's article, models of health service utilization have included health status and social psychological variables. Typical of this kind of model is Anderson's,[45] which integrates the work of Suchman and Rosenstock and has three components: predisposing factors (family compositions, social structure, health beliefs); enabling factors (family and community resources); need (illness and individual response).

Studies of factors in the use of services also brought findings that user satisfaction with preventive services was always lower than it was for treatment services. Generally, those with the need for medical care, access to it, and the ability to pay, personally or through insurance, were satisfied. Those who believed health care to be a right, and were high utilizers of medical care, were not particularly satisfied. Wolinsky[46] studied insurance subscribers in 1972 and found that benefits have a 'ceiling.' Increases in the utilization of preventive care above that ceiling bring decreasing benefits and a decrease in satisfaction.

Social network variables (social group, kin and non-kin affiliations) and social psychological variables were combined by Langlie in 1973 to determine the impact of social networks and health beliefs on preventive health behaviour. There are anomalies in her findings that may be due to the validity of the indicators for what she calls Direct behaviours particularly.[47] However, Langlie found that Indirect behaviours were related to (a) perceptions that one has some control over one's health status, in the high benefits of preventive action and positive attitudes toward providers and (b) belonging to a social network characterized by high socio-economic status (as measured by neighbourhood, family income, education, occupation and frequent interaction with non-kin).[48] Indirect behaviours were not associated with age or sex. Pratt's work[49] on learning about health care and resources during childhood takes on additional importance in light of these findings. Learning as a child that one has some control over one's life,[50] and growing up in a family with knowledge about and links to community resources, may make one more able to use services intelligently, and to best advantage.[51]

Pratt's work is an example of a developing literature relating childhood learning and aspects of family life to the use of health and social services. 'Since health is a resource that enables individuals to achieve their own goals, develop them-selves ...,'[52] socialization for personal health practices and the use of professional medical services is an important function of the family for its members. To Pratt, pursuing personal health practices and medical services are forms of task perfor-mance requiring competent and dedicated coping activity. Therefore, the aspects of family life that tend to facilitate such coping are crucial.[53]

According to Pratt's studies, two aspects of family life are important to health behaviour and to seeking health care outside the family: the nature of the inter-action or the relationship between family members, i.e., the extent to which families control members' efforts at self-direction, and the extent of family links to organizations, activities, and resources in the community. Her research reveals that while close-knit extended family groups may impede the use of medical ser-vices, close-knit nuclear family relationships apparently encourage their use.[54]

Pratt finds that interaction within the nuclear family generates a flow of ideas that fosters competence, and this interaction is positively related to pursuing contacts outside the family. Such interaction within a larger group of kin tends to have a 'caging effect,' impeding activity outside the family. Pratt found, how-ever, that caging was counteracted to some extent by a high rate of communica-tion among family members, for both extended and nuclear family groups. Ex-tent of communication was positively related to the use of community medical services, even in the absence of established family links to community resources.

Emphasis in this research is on the importance of support within the family and, at the same time, the freedom of those in the family, i.e., children, to exer-cise autonomy and initiative. Accordingly, child-rearing that features the use of reasons and information, rewards for good behaviour and autonomy, as well as family communication (developmental mode), teaches children to care for them-selves, i.e., to cope, and to learn to forge links outside the family successfully. Overall, children reared in this mode had better personal health habits due to better self-management skills. The habits most affected were care of the teeth and cleanliness, not exercise, nutrition, smoking, or sleep habits, regardless of the socio-economic status of the family.

Because mothers spent most time with the children, their health habits were more important than fathers', although the effect of autonomy, reward, and in-formation training prevailed whatever the health habits of the parents. In fact, Pratt's results show that for the children of parents with poor health practices, the autonomy training had a stronger positive effect on child health habits than when parent practices were good. The reason, according to Pratt, is that as a child matures, health training, information and resources available outside the home combine with self-management ability to allow the pursuit of one's own interests.

General recognition of the importance of the family experiences of a child has given rise not only to a growing research literature, but also to parent education and community resource programmes. They highlight a growing awareness of possibilities for families to engage in some type of family life education and to increase their knowledge of community resources. Resource programmes have as their purpose general education for all families, not only families in crisis or 'at risk,' for whom services are indispensable. An exclusively therapy-service approach may tend to emphasize problems; family life education tends to encourage a voluntary sharing of information on parenting by parents and others in the community.

Finding Help

Do people know where to find the help they need? Pemberton[55] and his colleagues are more sanguine about the ability of people to get to sources of help than many other researchers and practitioners.[56] They found that respondents who had substantial knowledge about sources of help knew where to find it for a variety of problems. Those whose friends and relatives had experience in finding help had more knowledge about help sources than respondents who needed professional help themselves. Pemberton also found that a lay referral or informal support system may reduce the need for knowledge on the part of individuals and the demand for formal or professional services.

The Freidson and Stoeckle studies emphasized the relation between lay referral and use of services, and the importance of the congruence of professional and client expectations to receiving satisfactory help. Pemberton concluded that adults with the most education were more likely to define their problems in mental health terms and were, therefore, more successful in receiving help from professionals. In a Toronto study of help seeking, Tannenbaum states, 'The more ambiguous the jurisdiction and authority of the helper and the more ambiguous the expectations of the help seeker, the less likely is the possibility of a satisfactory solution.'[57] It may be valuable to have friends to talk to and to clarify problems, and friends who are well informed about help sources and where they are. In fact, a lack of informal help may keep people outside the network of formal services.

Tannenbaum studied the role of a neighbourhood information centre (NIC), a quasi-professional community organization, in protecting individuals seeking help from rejection or continual referrals that result from making inappropriate demands on professionals. She states that this link in the community may be necessary even for people with informal helpers and resources available in the community, since experience with helping agents may hinder help-seeking and may discourage future help-seeking. Respondents reported consulting medical doctors about non-medical problems more often than any other formal agent, but referral from a doctor to other formal agents was negligible.

A study of clients of a family service agency reveals the process of referral to the agency and the role of mass media information.[58] From whom did clients get information before making contact with the agency? Seventy-four per cent (48 clients) discussed the information with family members, even though most of these family situations were characterized by a lack of communication. When the first source of information about the agency was a personal contact, about one-third of the clients came to the agency through self-referral. 'Among those for whom the mass media was the first source of information, every case of self-referral came from among those whose initial knowledge of the agency was supplemented by information from interpersonal contacts.'[59] When the first source of information was the mass media, 70 per cent contacted the agency after being referred by some professional source or a personal contact. There was no significant difference in the amount of time it took the client to contact the agency after receiving information about it when considering whether the source of the information was personal or professional.

Few studies that compare sources of help for a particular problem or need are available.[60] Lee discusses personal sources of information and assistance leading to the help source; Haese and Meile compare professional help sources.

Lee found the most important sources of information about where to get an abortion were those of equal age, equal status contacts, e.g., same sex friends, people who voluntarily associate and share leisure activities, and the sexual partner. Generally, barriers to information were within kinship, particularly across generational lines, across authority lines, i.e., employers, employees, teachers, pupils, and those with whom one has no intimate relationship, such as neighbours, or co-workers. However, family members and physicians tended to be the most successful starting points from which to seek an abortionist, if their views were compatible. Lee also found that to know someone who had had an abortion was not necessarily to know how and where to get one; less than 50 per cent with such knowledge could use it to contact an abortionist if needed.

Do people consider alternate sources of help for problems? A finding unanticipated by researchers studying preferred sources of help for psychiatric problems was that persons preferring a psychiatrist seldom consider alternative help sources.[61] While the psychiatrist ranked third as the preferred source of professional help, behind clergymen and non-psychiatrist doctors, alternatives were not considered by 81 per cent of those electing psychiatric help. The psychiatrist was selected because he was believed to be the appropriate professional, not because he was known personally, as were the clergyman and other doctors.

Finding a source of help likely involves a search and screening process when information is learned through the mass media, an information centre or a professional, as well as when family and friends are consulted first.

In the family service agency study by Bolton and Kammeyer discussed above, clients were unsure of what problems the agency was equipped to handle or how counselling would be conducted, even when referred by a professional (only 16 of the 64 clients had prior experience with professional counselling). Perhaps their contact with the agency was a screening process in a search for the most appropriate type of help or the source of help with which they were most comfortable. Perhaps after they had talked about their problems with a counsellor in the agency, they were able to seek solutions to their problems.

Evidence of the dynamics of help-seeking behaviour and the variation in help-seeking by type of problem is not only hard to find, but it probably does not now exist in sufficient detail to draw any but the most tentative conclusions. Greenley and Mechanic suggest that investigations of factors in help-seeking for particular populations of patients or clients should not be confused with general help-seeking, and recommend a study of the various sources of help (services) for similar problems, as well as an examination of the process of seeking help for different problems.[62]

For the university students who were respondents in their study of seeking help for psychological problems, Greenley and Mechanic found no evidence that attitudes, knowledge of services, or social group membership (social networks) provided links to services, when factors such as age, marital status, religion, and social status were considered. They found these factors were independent factors in help-seeking. This finding, which differs from findings in other studies, may be accounted for by the particular population they studied, or the respondents and the type of help they needed. The investigators concluded that help-seeking for psychological distress is a transient phenomenon that does not predict well to help-seeking over a period as long as two years, and that the process of help-seeking is tailored by a particular population to their problems at any given time.

The Influence of Kinship and Friendship on when Help is Sought
What is the influence of kinship and friendship on when help is sought and the outcome?

Social networks or links between people are assumed to have two qualities: cohesiveness or closeness, and openness. Closeness provides emotional and instrumental support to members, potentially delaying the use of professional help; openness provides the potential for connections to social institutions. The more persons in the network not connected to one another, the more accessible is professional help. One hypothesis is that the people in the network, i.e., a combination of friends, kin, co-workers, should indicate something about the type of help utilized, i.e., informal or professional. In a study of a community mental health centre, Horwitz found that patients with open friendship networks and weak kinship ties (as measured by number of visits per month) had maximum access to resources, were more likely to enter the mental health centre with mild conditions, and remain for the shortest period of time.[63] Those with strong kin and closed friendship networks delayed treatment and entered after dramatic incidents, but did not stay longer than others. It is not clear whether the patients with weak kin ties entered treatment earlier because they had minimal emotional support and little help available and, therefore, no alternative to admission, or because the patients themselves and those in their networks had information and expressed attitudes encouraging their admission, thus outweighing the importance of available personal resources.

In the Horwitz study, connections to professional psychiatric help per se did not aid or impede help-seeking, but network members' evaluation of experiences with psychiatry did. Whether the persons consulted had positive or negative experiences influenced their advice to the help-seeker and influenced when help was sought and from whom it was sought.

On Outcome
Horwitz studied the relationship between type of kin and friend networks and when professional help was sought, and the length of time help was needed. A study of women whose husbands survived a year after a severe heart attack relates differences in outcome to type of social network.[64] Those with the best outcomes had the greatest range of informal support and the highest proportion of help from family (children). The least desirable outcomes were deficient in family help and help from kin.

The role of children in favourable outcomes was explained by Finlayson as follows: The longer education and more diversified contacts of adult children may increase the congruence of their experience and that of professionals, encourage utilization of medical and other services, and facilitate change of expectations with respect to the sharing of responsibilities within the family. Absence of children limits the informal network to members of the family of origin of the husband and wife. They are older, they may have limited experience, and tend to reinforce resistance to new information. They may, thus, discourage or delay utilization of professional services, and retain rigid expectations about who should maintain certain responsibilities within the family. Such expectations may actually hinder recovery from illness and the ability to benefit from the help that is received.

Social support, on the part of those who are most meaningful, may serve to help maintain status in the family, and positively affect the marshalling of resources. The outcome of the utilization of professional help probably depends on the interaction of these three factors.

Discussion

The literature reviewed in this section emphasizes the contribution of kin, friends, and others to individual decisions to seek help and to the ability to find it. Seeking help involves the search for information and the search for aid. Except for the Greenley-Mechanic study, social influence has been found to intervene and to hinder or facilitate the help-seeking process. During the 1960s, research findings concerning the role of social groups changed. They became potential links to information and to sources of help as well as potential barriers interposed between the help-seeker and help sources.

Individual help-seeking is prompted by the experience of uncertainty and ambiguity and conditions that interfere with usual activities, or are experienced as a crisis. Family, friends, neighbours, and others are important in clarifying and defining problems as well as interpreting information received from the mass media and sources such as community information centres. Individuals often take general problems and questions to professionals for clarification and referral. For these individuals, failure of professionals to help them or to refer them to appropriate sources may preclude their receiving help, or at least discourage or delay the search.

Who relies on what Freidson and others call lay referral? Freidson and Greenley and Mechanic, particularly, indicate that some people, at least for some problems, make independent decisions to seek help. Findings indicate that being able to explain problems in professional terms may increase confidence and independent decision-making. Congruence between client and professional expectations may be a matter of speaking the same language, and may lead to the use of preventive services, in addition to services that are necessary in a crisis.

When is family cohesiveness not a barrier to seeking help, but a support in the search for it? The Suchman study and the replications by Geertsen, and Reeder and Berkanovic indicate agreement with Pratt's findings that, in addition to family cohesiveness, positive orientations to seeking help from available community resources, and links to these resources, are necessary.

One hypothesis is that the more links individuals have to others and to community resources, or the knowledge to forge them and to keep their knowledge up to date, the more likely it is that when they need help or information they will get it. The same may hold true for families. This way of viewing the family lends meaning to the idea that parents are family executives or co-ordinators. Children may learn to value potential sources of information and aid, and learn how to develop them as they learn other skills. If they do not, future help-seeking may consist of trials and errors and may not be successful. For them, 'trouble' may be an even worse experience.

Marriage, divorce and remarriage, and changes in family membership may increase the diversity of family links. Without such support potential, one-parent families may be more vulnerable because they have fewer members and less support and they may have fewer links to the community. Accordingly, a small nuclear family is more apt to be vulnerable than a larger family or an extended group of kin.

IV PLANNING AND PROVISION OF SERVICES TO MEET NEEDS

To this point in the chapter, we have focused on trends and changes in the family and on the circumstances in which people, usually adults, seek out formal helping services. In this section we examine what children and their families need from the opposite perspective – that of the service-provider or planner. Drawing on literature primarily from the social services and policy field, the focus here is on exploring what is meant by 'need,' how needs of families and children are assessed and determined, and the nature of the service response to these needs.

Services for Children and Families
Services to children have developed for the most part independently of services to families and have themselves taken a variety of forms depending upon their auspices, funding and perception of need. Child welfare, child care, children's mental health, juvenile corrections, services for distinct groups of children, such as the mentally retarded, the physically handicapped, and more recently the learning disabled, have developed into relatively distinct service delivery systems. Each has its own origin, auspices, sources of funding, physical location, volunteer support, and major identification with a particular discipline or professional group. For example, the social work profession is predominant in child welfare services, psychiatry in children's mental health, and medicine in most areas of physical handicap.

Psychology has played a central role in relation to mental retardation and learning disability, while in the area of juvenile corrections both social work and law have major, and frequently competing, roles (cf. Chapter 4). Childcare workers, a paraprofessional group who receive two or three years of post-secondary high school training, are increasingly used to staff the residential facilities in any one of these service systems.

To the extent that different professions and disciplines have predominated in these areas of children's services, practice theories, helping methods, and terminologies have differed. Moreover, in Ontario prior to the formation of the Children's Services Division within one ministry, the provision of services under seven pieces of legislation administered by six ministries and departments contributed to duplication of costly facilities and lack of co-ordination of services, as well as to extreme inequity in funding arrangements.[65]

Depending upon which door of the service system a child enters and therefore which system labels the child (neglected, disturbed, retarded, learning disabled, delinquent, etc.), the resources available to help the child, the type and level of care received, the involvement of the family, and presumably therefore the outcome, vary considerably. This is illustrated in an article by the director of a large Ontario residential treatment centre which outlines three probable scenarios of the same child as 'treated' by the child welfare system, the educational system, and the children's mental health system.[66] The same problem prompts different service responses, depending upon what that system is geared to provide. Implicit here is a question that will be explored subsequently in this chapter, namely, how service providers determine what a child or family needs.

Like services to children, those which focus on the family have also developed in a variety of forms. Within the social welfare field, the term 'family services' is most frequently identified with the Family Service Association, a voluntary (that is, privately funded) agency with origins in the Charity Organization Societies of the nineteenth century. Today, family service agencies, staffed predominantly by professional social workers and funded by the United Way or religious charities, are found in most major centres in North America. Services provided under their auspices, traditionally marriage and family counselling, are expanding to include marriage preparation, family life education, groups for single or divorced parents, and family advocacy to address those social conditions which threaten family functioning.

Family counselling may also be a component of a children's service such as a child welfare agency or children's mental health centre. Family therapy, a more intensive treatment method involving the family as a group, may be offered by social workers and/or psychiatrists in family or children's agencies or treatment centres.

The concept of 'family support services,' a phrase increasingly in use as a concomitant of deinstitutionalization policies, encompasses many of the programmes and services defined as personal social services at the outset of this chapter. Homemakers, home helps, child care, visiting nurses, and allowances for the costs entailed in caring for family members at home are among the family support services currently being developed. A major issue in their delivery to date is the haphazard pattern of funding and restrictive eligibility requirements which are characteristic of many such services. Again, this is a point to which we will return in discussing the service response to needs.

The Concept of Need

Definition and Typologies
Need is one of the most pervasive concepts in social welfare. Individual need, community need, client need, unmet need, need for custody, need for service, and literally hundreds of specified references to the concept of need constitute the basis for discussions of theory, descriptions of programmes, and particularly, argumentation in proposals for new programmes. The word 'need' itself is shaded with various meanings, derived from its use as both noun and verb, its subjective and objective connotations, and its pivotal place in the lexicon of the helping professions. Addressing all of these factors, Ivan Illich has contended that 'Professions could not become dominant unless people were ready to experience as a lack that which the expert imputes to them as a need.'[67]

The Oxford dictionary defines need, the noun, as a 'want; requirement; necessity; time of difficulty; destitution; poverty,' implying both the subjective and objective dimension of the concept. References are made in the literature to minimum needs or subsistence needs, although Runciman, in developing the theory of relative deprivation (the sense of deprivation a person experiences in comparing one's own situation with that of some other person or group), holds that apart from the basic survival demands of the organism there are no absolute needs 'either in the sense of not relative or in the sense of universally valid. The level of so-called absolute need can be just as well fixed at one level as another.'[68] Maslow's hierarchical theory posits five levels of needs: physiological or survival; security; belonging (affinity); self-esteem; and self-actualization.[69] Satisfaction of a higher need in this scheme is thought to be dependent upon fulfilment of those at previous levels. Applying this framework to the field of family housing, it has been observed that the expectations families place on their homes and the needs which they seek to satisfy there vary with their socio-economic station in life. Poor families are said to evaluate their home on the basis of its capacity to protect them from physical and social danger, while the middle class resident, having met this more basic need, seeks to satisfy a desire for self-expression.[70] In large public housing projects, such as Regent Park in downtown Toronto (9000 tenants), the introduction of the community guardians, a low-profile security force, exemplifies the use of a service to meet tenants' security needs. This is accomplished both directly through the guardians' presence and indirectly through their programmes for adolescents in the project which are designed to prevent problems that threaten security, such as vandalism.

In addition to Maslow's hierarchy, several taxonomies of needs have been developed. In the United States, for example, an effort 'to describe the field of social welfare and the range of client, family, and community needs that fall within its purview'[71] resulted in the elaboration of three interlocking concepts. Needs and problems are grouped into a number of 'domains of living' such as health, employment, education, leisure, and so on. A second construct identifies the 'status of functioning' along a continuum ranging from permanent disability to a high level of well-being. The third element is a classification of the obstacles to functioning, again arranged along a continuum from unexpected catastrophes to personal deficiencies. Displayed on three sides of a cube, this formulation has proven to be a useful tool in two major Canadian studies now underway on manpower utilization in social welfare.[72]

Bradshaw's taxonomy of needs, which stands farther back from the front lines of service delivery, distinguishes four types: *normative* needs, defined in accordance with some agreed upon standard; *felt* needs, which may be less or more than commonly perceived, and expanded by imagination; *expressed* needs, in the form of demands, frequently evidenced by waiting lists; and finally, *comparative* needs, imputed to a group whose characteristics are similar to those already receiving services. This approach has been employed in analyses of needs for the planning of social services in Britain.[73]

Typologies such as these are addressed essentially to the needs of the consumer or potential consumer of services. But these are not the only needs to be met within the social service system. A service organization is continually faced with the challenge of harmonizing the needs of its own many components: consumers, local community, professional staff, board members, and funding bodies. A community's need for security may be in conflict with an agency's need for group homes. A client's need for concrete help such as cash assistance may be in conflict with a social worker's need for job satisfaction through the provision of in-depth counselling, and the funding body's need for evaluation data may be in conflict with the service-provider's need to meet immediate demands for service. On the other hand, a programme designed to meet the needs of one component may, in fact, meet those of several. Such a possibility seems to be inherent in a pilot project being conducted by the Ontario Ministry of Community and Social Services in conjunction with the Federal Department of Employment and Immigration. The project is designed to encourage a group of mothers receiving the provincial welfare allowance to become self-supporting through entering or re-entering the labour force. To accomplish this, the women are carefully selected on the basis of their potential to succeed, engaged in a course designed to build self-confidence, given special attention by Manpower counsellors with upgrading and skill training as required, and assisted to make arrangements for daycare, transportation, and any other needs arising from this vocational change. Legislatively, an amendment to the Family Benefits Act permitted women to maintain their eligibility for the benefits of the public assistance programme such as Ontario Hospital Insurance coverage until securely established in their new jobs, thus removing one of the strongest disincentives to employment that had previously existed.

If successful, the project will meet the province's need to hold down the increasing costs of income maintenance, especially to mother-led families. But it can also meet the Family Benefits consumer's need to break the poverty cycle that is a by-product of public assistance. A project designed to provide special support to women to accomplish their desire to get off welfare can thus meet consumer needs as well as system needs. Again, another set of needs being met is that of the counsellors or field workers administering the project who experience the satisfaction of seeing people 'improve' as a result of their efforts. Interestingly, the needs of a fourth and key party to this kind of undertaking – the children of the welfare mother – are rarely mentioned except in relation to daycare arrangements. Evaluation criteria tend to focus on changes in the woman's self-image, the nature of the employment found, and particularly the pay scale she will receive. Except anecdotally, there are no measures of changes in children's self-image, school performance, sibling relationships, community participation, or parent-child relationships. Yet apparently children can be deeply affected by the experience both of being on welfare and of having their only parent make such a major transition in household living arrangements. This is clearly an area that recommends itself for research, particularly since it offers the use of both experimental and control groups.

Finally, on the subject of the definition of needs, it should be noted that seldom are needs carefully specified in legislation. The Child Welfare Act of Ontario sets out the conditions under which a child may be considered 'in need of protection,' but leaves considerable discretion in interpretation to the court (see Chapter 4 by Catton for an elaboration). In her book *Child care: Needs and numbers*, Jean Packman, commenting on this aspect of child welfare legislation, concludes that it is, in fact, preferable that definitions of need 'should change and develop as the community's standard of living rises and as understanding and skill develop.'[74]

Children's Needs

The conceptualization of children's needs as distinct from those of adults finds its fullest expression in the field of developmental psychology. Yet, in one way or another, the needs of children and youth are also the subject of every chapter in this volume. From a theoretical perspective, as summarized in the Report of the Commission on Children with Emotional and Learning Disorders (CELDIC Report),[75] 'successful or normal development is dependent upon a well-functioning biological organism operating within a sheltering yet stimulating environment.' The dual tasks of the adults associated with the child are seen as providing nurture and opportunities for learning both basic skills and the limits of socially acceptable behaviour (see Chapter 3 by Susan Hodgson). 'In our society,' note the authors, 'parents and teachers are the people; and home, school, youth organizations, church groups, are the institutions largely responsible for discharging these tasks.'[76]

Services, particularly in the child and family welfare field, are intended both to assist parents and teachers to perform these tasks and to respond to the problems that ensue when they fail. In the professional training of social workers and other mental health personnel, the objective of the study of human growth and development is the ability to identify developmental difficulties, abnormalities, and deviance as the basis of a treatment plan. Erikson's epigenetic theory of the eight stages of development of the healthy personality – trust, autonomy, initiative and industry in childhood, identity in adolescence, and intimacy, generativity and integrity in adulthood – is invoked more frequently for its elaboration of the pathological alternatives to healthy resolution of each successive stage.[77]

Efforts to assess and catalogue children's needs rarely employ a conceptual framework, and as a result invariably contain an admixture of basic developmental needs and what the service literature refers to as 'unmet needs.' For example, a monumental state-wide study in Idaho of the needs of children to six years produced a list which included planned pregnancy and education for parenthood along with foster homes for victims of child abuse.[78]

In part, the lack of clear distinctions in this area can be attributed to the semantic difficulties associated with the word 'need,' noted earlier. A statement from an address by Henry Maas is illustrative: 'In this day and age we know enough about the needs of children in need to anticipate the damage which we know will occur if their needs are not met.'[79] The children in need who are of primary concern to service providers are also referred to as 'at risk' or as having 'special needs' deriving for the most part from conditions such as mental retardation and physical handicap or from circumstances such as neglect or being in conflict with the law. As a result, their needs are seen primarily in terms of available services for each of these categorical problems.

Approaches to Needs Assessment
All questions of definition aside, the assessment and priorization of needs in the human social services is not a simple or straightforward matter. In theory, the logical starting point for undertaking effective planning for services is an assessment of the needs of the community and consequent planning of services or

measures to meet those needs. A flow model of service would proceed from an assessment of needs and identification of problems (unmet needs), through priorization of needs, assessment of resources, establishment of objectives, design and implementation of programmes or services to meet objectives, and finally evaluation of programmes in the light of their objectives and the original needs. In practice, few existing programmes have gone through this process of development.

An Historical Note

Historically, social service programmes have come into being to respond to one form of economic or social casualty after another. The predominantly rural society of the eighteenth and nineteenth centuries saw the birth of institutions for orphans, the elderly, and the insane, followed by the gradual emergence of private agencies: 'They sprang up, usually in the first place on a local basis, in response to specific needs recognized by socially responsible groups of citizens in particular communities. Many of them were extensions of similar services in Great Britain, or were created in emulation of similar services in the old country.'[80] A prominent example is the Children's Aid Society, established in 1891 through the efforts of a Toronto newspaperman, John J. Kelso, to arouse public consciousness to the plight of neglected and deprived children. Following the passage of the *Children's Protection Act of 1893*, which defined a number of states of neglect or dependency which would justify community action on behalf of the child, societies were created throughout Ontario and the Act became a prototype for legislation in other provinces across Canada.

The same period also saw the establishment of many of the social agencies providing family support services today such as the Family Services Association, Departments of Public Health, the Family Day Care Services, and the various settlement houses. Like the Children's Aid Society, these and other more recently developed agencies came into being in response to specific needs or social problems. Once established, the natural tendency is for agencies to remain in operation, changing and adding programmes to meet new and emerging needs.

Because social services have in retrospect developed in a haphazard fashion,[81] there is increasing interest in needs assessment research to determine the extent to which current needs are being met by existing resources. The rapidly growing literature on needs assessment refers to a wide variety of methodologies being developed and employed.

Tools and Applications

Essentially, the study of human and social needs can be approached from either of two directions – the individual case or the statistical aggregate. The respective merits of both the deductive and inductive approach to the analysis of a problem finds frequent illustration in social research and policy development. Carefully designed longitudinal research like that of the British Child Development Study, which is monitoring 16,000 children born during one week in 1958,[82] presents compelling arguments for change based on the weight of accumulated evidence. But equally powerful in other instances can be the facts of a single case which symbolize a reality experienced by many. For example, Fruin cites the impact on hospitalization of children in Britain caused by a single documentary film presentation of a two-year-old going to hospital.[83] Media coverage in Ontario of the case of a fifteen-year-old girl who committed suicide in an institution to which she was sent as a last resort drew public attention to some serious problems in the delivery of children's services and thereby played a part in their recent reorganization.

Most needs studies, however, employ the statistical method because, 'while it is the individual who has needs and while it is to individuals that services are given, policy and planning decisions must usually be taken about groups of individuals.'[84]

A number of data sources and methodologies are employed in statistical analysis. In order to highlight the general needs and problems of a given locale and identify target areas for services, secondary analysis of census and other aggregate statistical data is frequently used. Surveys of people living in particular areas (territorial groups) or having certain common characteristics such as age or disability (affinity groups) can provide more pointed information, while general population surveys are used to examine awareness of services and community attitudes towards needs. Surveys of service populations constitute both a form of evaluation of the effectiveness of existing services and a key to gaps in services. Analyses of community and political opinion have been described as 'effective in learning views of potential supporters or detractors of service systems activities.'[85]

At the aggregate level, social indicators research is attempting to isolate those factors that contribute to 'quality of life' and to measure them quantitatively in order to monitor the state of society in relation to existing social policy. Constructs such as the Gross National Welfare Index, similar to economists' Gross National Product, reflect the alternative emphasis on indicators of social progress.

A variation on the theme of social indicators research is the use of social pathology statistics. Typically, these plot such data as the number of illegitimate births, evictions, truancies, instances of child abuse, venereal disease, or other indicators selected for their ability to represent the extent of social problems in a given area.

The uses of both census data and other social pathology statistics are illustrated in two documents prepared as background reports in the development of an official plan for Metropolitan Toronto. An investigation of the social structure by Leon Kumove uses census data to identify changes and trends in areas such as population, housing, employment, and leisure.[86] In *Correlates of social structure*,[87] the social 'disease' indicators used include unemployment rates, juvenile delinquency charges, assaults, drug offences, suicides, and infant deaths. To this picture the authors had intended to add statistics on the incidence of major diseases, visits to outpatient departments, and several other factors which proved to be both inaccessible and of questionable reliability. The attention drawn to this lack of appropriate data echoes an observation made in an overview of needs analysis in Britain: 'Without exception, all investigators of social needs have bemoaned the insufficiency, the unreliability and the invalidity of much of the data from case records to national statistical returns.'[88]

Two needs analysis tools employed in the planning of British social services are Davies's *Social conditions index*,[89] which uses eight variables to assess the relative need for services to the elderly in different districts and the index constructed for the Plowden Report on education.[90] The latter index includes eight variables with a more educational focus, such as the proportion of retarded, disturbed, or handicapped students; children unable to speak English; and truancy rates It was further expanded by the Inner London Education Authority with the addition of other variables: teacher stress, as indicated by the number of short absences; pupil turnover; parental interest, assessed from attendance at the child's first medical; and so on.[91] Data from these kinds of analyses are used in Britain to plot the location of social service offices, and in the case of the education study, to determine priority schools.

In the United States, in compliance with the provisions of the 1974 Social Security Act, a number of states and cities have undertaken assessment of needs. Reports on these highlight the use of a variety of methodologies, singly and in combination. For example, the 'community audit' developed by the Brockton Multi-Service Centre in Massachusetts, delineated human needs reflecting these '... human states of concern: undesired feelings; undesired behavior, including personal behavior, psychosis, alcohol abuse, juvenile problems, and drug abuse; parenting difficulty; child vulnerability; morbidity/disability; early death; malnutrition; unemployment; misemployment; inadequate income; inadequate housing; and inadequate recreation.'[92] In addition to a survey of 400 households, the audit collected secondary data from schools, hospitals, and social agencies.

In South Dakota, a model 'capable of transfer to all rural-oriented areas of the nation' distinguished five major human needs: survival, socialization, social control, social participation, and mutual support. Subdivided into sixteen areas of inquiry, these became the basis for surveys at the individual, community, planning district, and state levels.[93]

The needs assessment literature contains frequent reference to the gap between needs and resources, classification schemes for analysis of need and resource information, the utility of needs and resource data as social indicators, and the development of community resource inventories as a basic tool for information and referral services. Research investigations geared to an examination of service needs and access, such as one conducted in New York state, seek information on the use of particular services, frequency of contact, access to service, and perceived need for the particular service in the community.[94]

In summary, a wide variety of traditional and innovative approaches is being employed and developed to assess need at the community level. Many are promising, although Jones has pointed to problems in application such as vague definitions of key terms, and lack of guidelines for sample selection,[95] which may hinder their utility as planning tools.

Canadian Studies
In Canada, where no federal incentives have been systematically provided to encourage large-scale needs assessment research, there is a critical lack of organized data. Within the last decade, studies have been done on the needs of affinity groups and/or the need for particular services. Examples of the former are studies of the blind,[96] the aging in particular locales,[97] welfare recipients,[98] and one-parent families.[99]

Assessments of service needs have examined such services as daycare[100] and housing for the elderly.[101] A few recent investigations have been addressed to the social needs of a particular community. But not since 1963 has there been a major study of needs and resources in Metropolitan Toronto, and that investigation considered needs for welfare, health, and recreation services rather than human needs per se.[102] Noting this critical gap in information as a basis for decision-making, the Priorities Development Committee of the United Community Fund has recently called for a 'geocoding survey of Metropolitan Toronto to assist in the determination of needs and resources.'[103]

For the most part, the existing Canadian research in this area is relatively limited in both scale and sophistication. There are few parallels to the work currently being done in Britain or the various American states. Among the provinces, only Manitoba has reported a large-scale needs study and it was in relation to the aged.[104]

In the absence of federal funds earmarked for the assessment of needs and resources, and technical assistance with methodology and research tools, many social service organizations in Canada struggle on limited resources to assess needs in their own local or service communities. Again, when needs assessment is undertaken at all, the typical examination concerns the need for services offered or planned by the particular agency or department. Even the social planning councils, which in urban centres in Ontario have research capability and a history of conducting needs and resources studies during the fruitful period of social investigation prior to the mid-sixties,[105] are constrained by inadequate or irregular funding.

The only national study conducted in Canada was completed in 1975 by the Canadian Council on Social Development with a grant from the Department of National Health and Welfare.[106] After reviewing the piecemeal fashion in which Canada's current social security system developed to respond to various individual, family, and collective needs, the study set out to examine whether these measures are meeting the original needs, responding to new needs, and being utilized equitably. Included in the purview of the study were the sectors of health, employment, education, income security, housing, and several specific personal social services such as daycare, homemakers, and legal aid. Methodologically, a random sample was drawn of 2000 Canadian households, stratified by region and geographical area. Interviews were conducted during 1974 with a response rate of 65.3 per cent for a total of 1213. In selecting this method, the study sampled both public opinion towards existing and proposed services, and the attitudes of service consumers. There was a generally high degree of satisfaction expressed by users of services. Nevertheless, other data suggested a failure to respond to consumers' needs, particularly in the area of health services. For example, time spent waiting for appointments and travelling to doctors' offices was disproportionate for those with the highest needs on the index constructed for the analysis. The high costs of some services, such as child care, dental care, drugs, to population groups with the lowest income were questioned as possibly preventing 'those persons whose needs are relatively greater from using the service when it happens to be required.'[107] The author also draws attention to the cumulative impact of needs which occurs when 'the inadequacy of income produces a multiplicity of privations at all levels.'[108] This point is amply illustrated in a report on children in poverty in Canada by the National Council of Welfare:

To be born poor is to face a greater likelihood of ill health – in infancy, in childhood and throughout your adult life. To be born poor is to face a lesser likelihood that you will finish high school; lesser still that you will attend university. To be born poor is to face a greater likelihood that you will be sent to a 'correctional institution.' To be born poor is to have the deck stacked against you at birth, to find life an uphill struggle ever after.[109]

The majority of poor families are caught in a spiral of inadequate housing, poor nutrition, health problems, and lack of ability to participate in programmes like recreation. The family support services designed to alleviate stress such as day-care, homemakers, counselling are available frequently only to those who can pay some part of the cost and who live in the higher-cost centres where the services tend to be located. Even totally 'free' services may entail some expense. For example, in health services, taking a sick child to a doctor may require both a taxi and a babysitter for the children at home.[110]

In reviewing available data to support their position, the Council has assembled a number of Canadian studies of individual aspects of the problem such as the emotional development of poor and non-poor children, delinquency, and early school leaving. But they have had to rely heavily on the findings of the British Child Development Study, cited earlier, to obtain an overall picture of the effects of poverty. For this deficiency they are critical of Canadian social scientists whom they say 'have consistently ignored family income in their search for causes of social phenomenon.'[111]

Assessing Children's Needs

With more specific reference to children's needs, the Office of Child Development of the Federal Department of Health, Education and Welfare in the United States has among its many functions the enhancement of the states' capacity to assess children's needs, plan programmes, co-ordinate and allocate resources, monitor and evaluate programmes, maintain standards, and provide technical assistance to those delivering children's services. This is done through the funding of demonstration projects and the provision to the states of 'a continuing flow of innovative program designs, needs assessment techniques, and delivery systems for utilization by public and private agencies serving children.'[112]

To cite one example of a state study, the Idaho Office of Child Development focused on the needs of children to six years of age.[113] Their study featured a number of components, one or more of which could usefully be replicated elsewhere. In addition to reviewing child development literature and existing data such as the census and vital health statistics, the study team undertook a 'vendor' survey of every agency, public and private, which provided services to children. Follow-up interviews were conducted to determine sources of funding, types of service, and cost per child. A consumer survey was directed to a 2 per cent random sample of Idaho families with children under six, to evaluate home conditions, attitudes towards child care, and agency use and satisfaction. Also tested were the children's health, social language development and nutrition, with health forms to be completed in three days and mailed in by parents. A medical records survey was undertaken which involved 50 per cent of obstetricians and paediatricians and 25 per cent of general practitioners, while individual maternal and child health records in 90 per cent of hospitals were examined by two medical students. Other elements of this large-scale study of the needs of young children included 'community speak-outs' designed to elicit input from the public, a comparison of the needs of minority group children with those of the general population, an assessment of public acceptance in liberal and conservative districts of programmes designed to meet the needs identified, and finally, a widespread distribution of the results of the investigation.

On a more limited scale, a survey of youth in Denver, Colorado, identified eight underlying needs through factor analysis of the data: need for more counselling; problems with parents and family; leisure problems and boredom; medical need; racial tension and discrimination; police and legal problems; and the need for community leisure facilities.[114]

In Canada, New Brunswick has conducted a study of services to children provided by its departments of health, justice, and social services which in effect examined the resources but not the needs of children in the general population.[115] Similarly, a thorough inventory of services to the children of Windsor, Ontario, completed with the assistance of a federal grant as a Local Initiatives Project (LIP) served to surface a variety of needs unmet by existing resources.[116]

In Ontario, an interministerial committee, under the direction of John Anderson, investigated residential services to children and youth as well as to two other target groups of adults, and adults in conflict with the law. While massive in scope and extensive in its inquiry, the report was nevertheless confined to one type of service, albeit provided under a variety of auspices. The needs of children and youth discussed in the report were, in fact, their service needs at the point of admission to a residential facility.[117]

A survey of children's needs studies conducted as a background to a policy statement of the Children's Services Division of the Ontario Ministry of Community and Social Services located a total of forty-six reports of varying quality, many of which dealt with the need for a particular service such as daycare, group homes, or residential treatment facilities.[118] Reported methodologies for needs assessment included surveys of service-providers, deliberations of service-providers in conferences and workshops, analysis of service statistics, and in a few instances, systematic surveys and analysis of census data. In the course of this survey, it became apparent that local communities need to be resourced with technical assistance and guidelines if the energy expended on needs assessment is to have good returns.

Demand as an Indicator of Need

Lacking systematic assessments of needs as a basis for programme planning, agencies frequently rely on indicators of demand for service such as waiting lists.

Philosophically, demand has been associated with freedom and autonomy on the part of the potential consumer, an assessment of one's own needs and consequent seeking of resources perceived to meet them. From this perspective, demand is favourably contrasted with the less libertarian process of ascribing need to persons unable or unwilling to experience or express them. '... a person virtually ceases to be a legal person when he ceases to have demands and has only needs.[119] Implicit in this argument is the acknowledgment that effective demand is closely related to income. When services are distributed according to demand, the rich obtain a disproportionate share. The dilemma is captured in the observation that 'those people least likely to be capable of making demands upon policy makers, decision-takers, and service providers are very often the same people who stand in greatest need.'[120]

Advocacy services, on both a case and class basis, were developed to address this gap between needs and demands by removing all the obstacles that prevent people from exercising their rights or receiving their benefits and using the resources they need.[121]

Also affecting the demand for social services is the stigma of being a recipient. Programmes with means testing to determine eligibility are particularly prone to stigmatizing recipients,[122] but other types of social services can also have this effect on those who use them. According to Miller,[123] the results of stigmatization include loss of pride and self-respect, guilt, and distrust of social services among users. Fear of being stigmatized may also deter many who are entitled to a given service and who therefore do not show up in statistics on demand for services.

Waiting lists, although frequently cited to substantiate need for service, tend to be somewhat unreliable. On the one hand they can overestimate need as a consequence of the practice of putting one's name on several waiting lists. On the other hand they can underestimate the extent of need since many persons, and particularly those experiencing a crisis, are deterred by the very fact of a waiting period for service.

In the social services, the problems of using demand as an indicator are further complicated by the fact that social agencies generally keep statistics on services they provide, but make no provision for collecting information on unmet needs.[124] Similarly, descriptions of programmes offered tend to focus on achievements rather than limitations, the numbers served rather than the large numbers of eligible children or adults not reached by a given programme.[125] Even requests received by community information centres are said to be an unreliable indicator of community need although they can document emerging needs on a case basis.[126]

In contrast to those approaches to needs assessments reviewed under the heading of Tools and Applications, demand indicators and opinion surveys of service-providers address the needs of only those who are known to the service system. Consequently, their utility as a planning tool is considerably more limited than their widespread use would suggest.

Setting Priorities
The pervasive lack of Canadian data on questions of needs and resources constitutes a major obstacle to the rational setting of priorities in social programmes. Yet the need for priority setting is both obvious and intensified in periods of economic constraint.

At present there are few objective criteria for the determination of priorities. Too little programme evaluation has been done to establish any reliable basis for comparison of outcomes expected from different allocations of the same resources. However, the accelerated trend towards co-ordinated and integrated service delivery models, if adequately supported by government, harbingers a somewhat more rational approach to planning and priority setting.

Historically, whenever social agencies have come together for the purpose of planning, allocation of funds based on some priorities becomes a primary concern. Yet attempts to make the process of allocation more systematic and rational have met with limited success.[127] The United Community Fund of greater Toronto, which is charged with raising and distributing funds to approved social agencies in the voluntary sector, has developed a number of priority guidelines to classify programmes as high, medium, or low priority.[128] Yet the application of most of the guidelines relies on subjective judgments rather than objective data.

This is not to imply that data alone are a sufficient condition for the determination of priorities. Most attempts to establish priorities reach the impasse of limited resources beyond which decisions are necessarily political and value-based. Particularly in times of economic constraint there is competition for resources, not only between social expenditures and non-social ones such as roads and sewers, but among social programmes themselves. Recently, for example, there has been increasing speculation about the social policy implications of the demographic tilt towards a larger population of senior citizens requiring a higher level of services. If the birth rate continues to decline, money previously allocated to child welfare programmes may be redirected to the older age group. The fact that senior citizens have a political voice may heighten this probability, along with the development of what many are perceiving to be an anti-child bias in the North American culture.[129]

Even within a budget area such as children's services, who can say whether the needs of autistic children are more or less compelling than the needs of victims of child abuse, or whether pre-schoolers should receive more attention than adolescents. The question of whether funds for social programmes are better spent on one group or another highlights the inherent value questions. And since in a pluralistic society there are many competing value orientations at any given time, priority setting poses difficult decisions, particularly when the process is unsupported by sound data.

Further complicating the question is the pattern of increasing funding of services by federal and provincial governments which reflects their own rather than local priorities. Programmes tend to follow available funds rather than the reverse.[130] While chairing the Commission on Metropolitan Government in Toronto, John Robarts referred to this when he reported that 'many of those who made submissions to the commission claimed this system of financing results is fiscal irresponsibility in that too many programs are being initiated to take advantage of 20 cent or 50 cent dollars rather than to meet local needs.'[131]

Related to these extraneous influences on the setting of priorities are the fads and fancies that come and go in the human services. Fired by the failures of many existing programmes to make a difference in people's lives, new programmes are frequently ushered in with considerable fanfare and raising of expectations. According to Etzioni, one of the more recent 'policy fashions' which has implications for children's services is de-institutionalization whereby many who have been resident in institutions are turned back to the community. It is a policy currently affecting services to the retarded, disabled, delinquent, elderly, and those with chronic or mental illness. Reviewing the results of reducing the population of patients in American mental hospitals from 430,000 in 1969 to 300,000 in 1975, Etzioni observed pointedly:

'Returning to the community' is romanticized as though the community in question were a warm loving tribe instead of the urban slum awaiting many. What in fact has happened when de-institutionalization has been translated into policy is that thousands of individuals, at least initially unable to cope, have been left to fend for themselves in the streets.[132]

Without a concomitant investment in community facilities and services, de-institutionalization represents little more than a temporary and illusory cost-reducing mechanism. In the area of children's residential services, those who are experienced in running group homes in the community have warned that de-institutionalizing youth from correctional settings, while long overdue and socially just, will not be the inexpensive panacea some people envision. This quotation from an article by Theodore Levine summarizes the issues clearly:

From the vantage point of youth service in Philadelphia, the children in question are often difficult to handle and relate to, and the possibility of success is uncertain, costs are high, referral systems are inadequate, drain on staff is enormous, and negative forces within the urban community generate many problems and pressures for the youngsters and for those serving them.[133]

Unless these realities are confronted, and transitional policies designed, the backlash of communities which have not been prepared, educated, or supported to receive their discharged[134] children and adults looms as an additional burden for those being released.

Hinging as it does on the adequate provision of family support services, de-institutionalization incorporates some of the most pressing problems in priority setting that services have yet had to face.

The Service Response to Needs

Intake Activities

As noted earlier in this chapter, children's use of services such as health and education is primarily mediated through their parents. In the social services, the process of connection between the child and the social agency is rather different. Child welfare services, for example, administered in Ontario under the authority of the Child Welfare Act to protect children from abuse and neglect, obtain new cases in a variety of ways.

Children are said to 'come to the attention of' child welfare authorities through referral from other community representatives – the school, the police, public health nurses, homemakers, and other front-line service personnel. Less frequently, parents may contact the agency directly, requesting placement of their child or children, or a situation may be reported by a neighbour or relative. Research on patterns of referral to child welfare services, although still rather scanty, suggests that referrals by professionals are more likely to result in acceptance than either referrals from non-professionals or self-referrals.[135] (The relevant legislation is outlined in more detail in the Appendix to Chapter 4.) In the complex network of social services, source of referral is one of the most salient pieces of data, routinely collected on all new clients or patients. Information provided by the referring person or agency usually indicates whatever labelling has occurred. Because agency-based social workers generally have no direct access to children or families who have not been referred to them, front-line workers are encouraged, but rarely adequately trained, to watch for problems requiring services and make referrals to the appropriate one. Particularly in the area of child abuse, where the importance of early detection is critical, there has been a major investment both in the United States and in Ontario in training programmes to promote interdisciplinary co-operation and skills in detection and reporting.[136]

Once a child or family comes to the attention of a particular agency, the need for service must be established. Two major considerations contribute to this process – eligibility requirements and the characteristics of the individual case, including the 'presenting problem.' Whereas in voluntary services, eligibility requirements (e.g. age, religion, residence, financial status, willingness to accept the terms of treatment, etc.) can be used to deny services[137] or conversely to 'cream' the best clients, that is, those who appear most likely to benefit,[138] in statutory services there are fewer bases for refusing to accept a given case. Determination of the service need involves a relatively complex process of 'assessment' or 'psychosocial diagnosis' which takes into account factors such as the child's or family's social history, previous use of service, family constellation, social class, current behaviour, strengths and weaknesses, and motivation to change. On the basis of this judgment, the person is either accepted or referred elsewhere; it is almost axiomatic that a person is never simply refused service. As Wellman has noted, 'gate-keepers who control admission in agencies are trained to look for symptoms of mental distress in those who present themselves as candidates for receiving help and selectively perceive symptoms of distress.'[139]

From the perspective of the individual agency, the need or problem presented by a prospective client may be redefined in terms of services available. According to Kahn, analyses of failures of service programmes reveal that one of the reasons for complaints about service delivery is the lack of relevance of the service model to the need posed. Using the child welfare field as an example, he pointed out that an agency providing placement, protection, and services to unmarried mothers 'has within its own organization too few of the options needed to support family living or enrich youth development, and we know that often agencies offer clients what they are organized to do even if not exactly what clients need.'[140] (Section 5e of Chapter 4 indicates this is also true of services associated with judicial processing.) One of the few studies to examine the process by which people are recognized as being in need highlighted the important role played by receptionists and other non-professional staff in implicitly formulating the organization's definition of need.[141]

Intervention Activities
In theory, there are four points of intervention in the helping process: activities to promote positive social functioning; activities to prevent problems from occur-

ring; activities to help individuals resolve their problems; and finally, activities to support or maintain those who are unable to resolve their problems.[142] All social welfare activity can in some sense be classified under one of these headings. Yet, in practice, the day-to-day demand for the last two categories of service response has far outweighed the former. Referring, for example, to the field of child welfare, Bettye Caldwell has observed that the more clamorous needs of children and families in crisis have deflected attention from preventive programmes. 'Whenever resources are in short supply (and when are they not?) crisis situations cannot be ignored, while preventive services can.'[143]

Because of this characteristic orientation to crisis situations, child welfare services over the years have come to be identified primarily with the placement of children in settings apart from their own homes. Adoption, foster homes, institutions, group homes, residential treatment, and related themes such as placement decisions, separation anxiety, and home-finding have dominated child welfare theory and research.

In most regions of the world today, child welfare focusses on the residual problems of the child. That is, service is provided after a family is disrupted and/or personal damage affects the child. The child welfare worker is continually pressed to attend to children in crisis situations; one emergency after another requires the placement or replacement of a child.[144]

Along with others, Maas has pleaded for a broader view of child welfare services as more than placement, more than remedial casework, more oriented to the social environment that gives rise to problems. Studies in various countries of the precipitating family and social environments of children who come into care reveal consistencies such as high mobility, high unemployment, pressures on housing, a high illegitimacy rate, and social isolation of families from primary support networks.[145]

Policies and programmes directed to the promotion of strength within the family and prevention of child placement would include homemaker services, daycare, family counselling, subsidized housing, and adequate welfare allowances. Despite the repeated conclusion in national studies and reviews of research in the social services that placement can be prevented or at least abbreviated by the provision of such alternative community services,[146] money has not been made available to seek this goal. Indeed, in times of constraint, the small amounts of funds earmarked for prevention programmes have been the first to be cut.

As a result of this lack of investment in prevention in favour of responding to immediate demands, professionals tend to view needs in direct service terms.

Kelly, evaluating the Human Service Council in the Regional Municipality of Halton, noted the lack of questioning of the premises upon which human services are based. 'Essentially it is believed that individual and family problems in social functioning can best be handled through provision of more and improved case services, better co-ordinated to assure accessibility and smoother referral procedures.'[147]

This raises again a point highlighted by the needs assessment studies reviewed earlier, that needs may be viewed along a continuum. At one end are the normal developmental needs experienced by all human beings, and ideally met in interaction with the natural, built, and social environment. At the other end are service needs, particularly the need for remedial treatment arising from earlier unmet needs. In between are those needs once met by informal arrangements, for example care of children and the elderly, which Kahn believes should be publicly underwritten as 'social utilities.'[148]

A recent critique of the effects of funding structures on services to adolescents in Ontario, which included a proposal for the reallocation of resources, introduced the notion of identifying the special or particular needs of young persons in consultation with them and their parents and then contracting with resources to meet those needs. A list of general needs applying to all young persons was tentatively set out as including 'an opportunity to be productive, a variety of outlets for appropriate recreation, a choice in the types of services with which they become involved, and a home life that is enriching and growth oriented.'[149] Such an orientation to the basic human needs of the adolescent at least raises the possibility of identifying alternative modes of meeting them rather than simply supplying more services in the sense of activities performed by or under the supervision of professionals.

It is axiomatic that service-providers tend to perceive all human needs in terms of their service implications. The kind of community needs assessment studies cited earlier usually generate a larger number of service needs identified by professionals than by the community at large.[150] In other words, whereas citizens may identify the need for employment or a problem such as vandalism, professionals will perceive a need for a crisis centre or psychiatric services. Alternative or competing modes of meeting needs or solving problems such as self-help groups, religious organizations, or even a change of scenery are less likely to be perceived by professionals as beneficial than by other groups in the community.

In addition to these related issues of emphasis on remedial treatment and lack of attention to alternative methods of meeting need, the service response to need has been hindered by lack of co-ordination of services. Analysing this issue within an historical framework, Rein has identified three types of problems in the organization and distribution of social services: (1) the dispersal of similar functions; (2) the discontinuity of related functions; and (3) incoherence when different functions are pursued without relationship to one another. Among the resulting problems are duplication of services, multiplicity of independent and unco-ordinated home visiting, overuse of services by a small percentage of clients, and poor access and generalized underuse of services.[151] Studies in both Canada and the United States confirm that there exists what one called an 'all-pervasive underutilization of existing resources' along with a need for agency coordination and communication.[152]

Reorganizations of human services to achieve co-ordination are currently underway throughout Canada, the United States, and Britain, with strong incentives from funding bodies. In Ontario, services to children, having largely been brought under one administration, stand on the threshold of a major reorganization along functional rather than structural lines. Conceptual models are being developed to distinguish the various functions performed in the service to children (e.g. reception, assessment, service delivery, etc.) as a step in the direction of tailoring a package of services to the needs of the individual child.

If the new system can be successfully co-ordinated with other sectors serving children and families, particularly education, public health, and income maintenance, the major corner can be turned towards more effective and efficient services.

On Evaluating Service Programmes
In theory, the final step in the process of identifying and responding to needs should be evaluation of the effectiveness of the programmes in meeting need. Yet until recently, there has been little demand for evaluation on the part of either funding bodies or consumers of services. As a result, while now gathering considerable momentum, the art and science of programme evaluation is considered to be 'still in its infancy.'[153]

Traditionally, funding agencies were content with testimonials, case examples, and service statistics, being somewhat reluctant to question the efforts of obviously dedicated, overworked professionals. But with the ever increasing demands on the service dollar and the introduction of costly, large-scale programmes, interest has grown in obtaining the best results for money expended. Cost benefit concerns, filtering down to the local level from higher tiers of government, have ushered in an era of demands for professional accountability of which evaluation research is one consequence.

A further impetus to the interest of funding bodies in evaluation research has been the generally negative findings of research that *has* been conducted. Large-scale interventions such as Head Start and Mobilization for Youth, introduced with considerable fanfare and optimistic promise, failed in most instances to achieve their stated programme goals. The area of correctional services has been studied more than most others, with the weight of evidence indicating virtually complete lack of effectiveness in reducing recidivism.[154] Reviews of evaluation research in other areas such as casework services[155] and psychotherapy[156] show similarly disappointing results – although some have questioned the formulation of the research designs. As Hyman and Berger have noted, the question 'Is psychotherapy effective?' leads to oversimplified confusion. It is analogous to asking 'Is higher education effective?' without specifying what kind of higher education, practiced by what kind of teachers on which students.[157]

The publication of negative findings has had several consequences in addition to raising questions on the part of funding agencies. Not surprisingly, it has threatened service professionals and deepened their resistance to evaluation research. Direct service personnel are frequently poorly informed about research activities, intuitively convinced of the worth of their work and the impossibility of subjecting it to 'measurement,' and prone to view time spent on data gathering as vying with the more compelling needs of immediate caseloads. On their part, researchers have contributed to the antipathy between themselves and practitioners through insensitivity to the realities of practice and failure to report back their findings. Other factors leading to friction are personality and role differences and conflicting goals and values.[158] Finally, even when findings are fed back, their lack of application to the specific child or family being served by the practitioner renders them of questionable utility in his eyes.[159]

References to reviews of research may also give the erroneous impression that the story has been told, when, in fact, relative to the vast number of programmes in operation at any given time in all the service sectors, little has yet been subjected to evaluation. Indeed, an anomalous outcome of the current demand for evaluation is the fact that at the federal level, for example, new programmes such as the Local Initiatives Projects representing relatively modest expenditures have stringent programme evaluation requirements, while existing programmes that consume the bulk of federal spending receive no similar scrutiny.[160] A parallel situation exists in the voluntary sector where agencies' co-ordination activities lead to the evaluation of innovative and peripheral programmes but not core services of participating agencies. To date, evaluation of the latter has been considered too threatening to the autonomy of the agencies involved in voluntary co-ordination efforts.[161] For the most part, the evaluations produced in accordance with these requirements tend to dwell on effort (service statistics) rather than efficiency or effectiveness. Frequently evaluations which do employ rigorous scientific designs are nevertheless premature and therefore also of questionable value.[162]

Currently the primary obstacles to wide-scale evaluation efforts are lack of expertise, lack of funds earmarked for evaluation research, lack of criteria for both formative and summative evaluation, and most important, lack of the data base required for any systematic evaluation research. In many sectors there has not yet occurred the prerequisite description of programmes, their goals or effects, and the rationale that links the two. In effect, many programmes are not yet 'evaluable.'[163]

Information systems, usually designed for purposes of case tracking and monitoring, are only now being put in place in many of the major public and private agencies in Canada. Until adequate information is collected and the problems of applying it to social planning confronted,[164] the cycle of needs assessment, priority setting, programme development and delivery, and programme evaluation will continue to be broken at crucial points, thus rendering services less responsive to human needs.

Concluding Commentary

In reviewing the state of the art on the planning and provision of services to meet needs, one is constantly confronted by the conundrum that services to children are predominantly delivered separately from services to families.

Because there has been no coherent national family policy, a position elaborated by Schorr in the United States[165] and the Vanier Institute of the Family in Canada,[166] no service system is responsible for enhancing family functioning or monitoring the effects of other social policies on the family unit. Yet service systems such as employment and education, which have been traditionally geared to the individual, may have profound impact on the family. As Giovannoni and Billingsley have observed:

Were all families ... seen as a dependent unit of society, measures would be designed to enable them to maintain their viability and to meet effectively the needs of their members, especially the youngest ones. The responses to those needs must emanate from the most important systems of society that have a bearing on family life, chiefly the economic, housing, health care, and educational systems.[167]

Social services have tended to be identified with the poor and people with problems, not because the affluent and the healthy have no need for help, but because they have more resources available either informally or formally through purchased services. Virtually every social welfare service has a middle or upper class equivalent which may be purchased on the open market, whether one is considering homemaker services (housekeepers, private nurses), child care

arrangements (babysitters, boarding schools, summer camps), income maintenance (insurance, pension schemes, investments), or family counselling (private
psychiatrist, psychologist, group therapist). In Ontario, prior to the introduction
of universal health insurance, a similar disparity existed in medical care for the
poor.

Recognition of the fact that all families may need services of some type has
led social policy advisors such as Alfred Kahn[168] and the Canadian Council on
Social Development[169] to recommend publicly provided social utilities on a universal basis similar to the provision of education and public libraries. (See Chapter 3 by Hodgson for discussion of supports for parenting.) Kahn and Kamerman's book, *Not for the poor alone*,[170] takes its title from a review of personal
social services in European countries typically organized on a more universal
basis than those in North America. An alternative approach favoured by Keniston and the Carnegie Council on Children,[171] because it reflects the market
economy of the United States, would provide sufficient income supports to poor
families to allow them to purchase services. Such an approach would necessitate
more equitable employment and income policies as the basic ingredients of family support.

Whenever services to people are transformed from exchanges of mutual aid on
a friendly, familial, or neighbourly basis, to formal help, they become prohibi-
tively expensive. The anomalies of informally versus formally provided service
are most apparent within the home whenever it is necessary to obtain formal
substitutes. Only the most affluent can afford to engage housekeepers, chauf-
feurs, governesses, and gardeners. Foster parents employed by child welfare
agencies to care for children whose parents are unable or unwilling to do so are
paid for the services they perform. Yet if natural parents are in receipt of welfare
allowances, even the more generous provincial one, they receive significantly less
than foster parents doing the same job.[172] Similarly, as has been demonstrated,
the costs of adoptive parents' time and services is never included as a variable
when calculating the cost of adoption versus foster care.[173]

If the families who have been receiving costly services are to be asked to
assume more responsibility for the care of their children (and elderly parents),
new ways must be found to support them in these tasks. The most important
directions for research, therefore, would seem to lie in two areas: the evaluation
of service effectiveness so that limited funds can be allocated where they are
most needed; and exploration of what helps and what hinders the family in
meeting the needs of its members. As noted in the introduction, many of the
support services which families require are by definition those which complement, supplement, or substitute for services rendered by family or friend on an
individual basis. Many can be performed by volunteers or members of self-help

groups. Therefore, the most important trends in current social policy are those that seek to strengthen the family's and community's natural helping networks.

V URBAN HELPING RESOURCES – A CONTINUUM

The preceding discussion has emphasized the importance of the social relationships of families and their children for seeking and finding assistance from health and social services and the importance of giving consideration to these relationships in developing social policy. What evidence is there that such networks or groups of relationships actually exist, particularly in cities?

It has become a commonplace that 'The changing scale of social organization associated with accelerated rates of communication, transportation, and educational and occupational mobility has reduced the significance of the local neighborhood as a source of social integration. The residents of (these) neighborhoods have become urbanites and their relationships extend ... to larger territories and to the larger society ...'[174]

This lack of significance of local neighbourhood ties, and the decreasing importance of shared physical space have been used often as indications that people lack social relationships, and are disorganized, isolated or even anomic. What it may actually mean is that neighbourhood residents come together or must be brought together for specific reasons and that ongoing activities cannot necessarily be considered part of an established, ongoing social organization, it, in fact, they ever could be. Neighbourhood organization may not bear a necessary relation to the social networks within which people live their lives day by day, although neighbourhood may continue to be more important than some assume.

In his work on help-seeking and mental health, Warren concluded 'that regardless of how strong or weak the actual resources of a neighbourhood are, it is a critical part of the individual's capacity to meet many of life's crises and a vehicle for achieving individual improvement in family, job and other spheres.'[175]

Warren characterized neighbourhoods by extent of internal organization and the capacity for collective activity, and whether internal activity meshed with other institutions in the surrounding community. He used the resulting typology[176] of what he called neighbourhood contexts to study the relation of the context to use of informal and formal sources of help by people in the neighbourhood.

In neighbourhoods in which collective action was almost impossible, i.e., anomic and transitory (mobile population) with no institutions and with people 'going their own ways,' there was actually more neighbouring but it was viewed as of little use. This finding may have reflected less the preference for neighbourhood help than barriers to using non-neighbour helpers; a case of necessity over choice. In the more integrated, homogeneous neighbourhoods, neighbour help (integral and parochial) was not used as often, but, when it was, it was viewed as being helpful. Warren states that the explanation lies in the function of neighbouring, not as sociability or as a self-contained problem-solving system, but as a means to link the individual to other resources in the neighbourhood, and outside. Referral (or instrumental) behaviour was associated with a positive evaluation of the helping role of the neighbour. 'Just listening' was not associated with perceived helpfulness.[177]

One of the Warrens' conclusions was that 'neighborhoods differ not so much in their ability to provide a few key helpers in a time of need'[178] but in the flow of information about resources between neighbours and links between neighbourhood and community resources. Strengthening actual helping resources in neighbourhoods may not mean simply providing facilities and attempting to change attitudes about them, but facilitating the flow of information and the perception that sources of help are available.

Granovetter employs the use of network analysis to relate the strength of interpersonal ties to large-scale patterns of interaction, such as social cohesion. He defines strength of interpersonal ties as a combination of length of time, emotional intensity, intimacy, and reciprocal services. 'Weak ties are more likely to link members of different small groups than are strong ones which tend to be concentrated within particular groups.'[179] But there may be interesting paradoxes. 'While weak ties are indispensable to individuals' opportunities and to their integration into communities, strong ties, breeding local cohesion, lead to over-all fragmentation.' For the individual, what is the balance that can be struck between strong and weak ties, to ensure the necessary support for well-being and additional help when it is needed, and to give help to others. For the family, what is it? And, in the event that help is needed beyond that available from personal or informal sources, how are formal help sources (health and social services) and informal networks linked within a neighbourhood or a community?

Claude Fischer[180] has questioned the decline of community thesis and its implications on historical and sociological grounds. '... the lowering of social and spatial barriers and the consequent increase in the freedom to choose social relations have not led to less communal ties. And, it may just have led to the opposite. The disintegration of the monolithic community has perhaps led to the proliferation of many personal communities, each more compatible and more supportive to the individual than ascribed corporate groups.'[181] Fischer points out that residential mobility has not increased since the nineteenth century, although spatial mobility has changed to a phenomenon of the middle class. Now that people can more readily construct and maintain social ties with persons outside their localities, according to Fischer, the influence of neighbours has declined and there is less social control of 'constraint,' although not less attachment. Michelson's study of residential mobility and housing[182] indicates that high-rise and single family dwellers in the city and suburbs experience no lack of social relationships. Neither housing type nor location plays a major part in interpersonal contact. Forty to 49 per cent of all respondents saw friends and neighbours during a given weekday; friends and relatives made up most of their 'frequent' contacts. Although more apartment families know none of their neighbours (25 per cent), children in high-rise apartments know a larger number of other children than those living in suburban houses. Ability to borrow from friends is related to home ownership, but those in high-rise apartments downtown are slightly more likely than others to *actually* do so.

Using the same data as Tannenbaum (see n.57), Wellman[183] found that 83 per cent of the respondents had informal support they could rely on every day, and at least one emergency help source; 92 per cent of those with children under three years of age reported such help available. Such attributes as sex, age, and socio-economic status of the respondents were not significantly related to the availability of needed help, but the quality of the respondent's relationship with the source of help was, i.e., residential proximity, frequency of contact, and relatedness or kinship.

Relationships depend on the flow of information between persons. Wellman found that people who know a number of others, i.e., have a network with a wide range, are likely to have sources of help available. If a network contains a number of persons one knows well, or intimates (persons outside the home that one feels close to), the probability is increased that help and support will be available when needed. If a network contains a number of intimates who know each other, the likelihood is even greater that help and support will be available.

'While assistance in emergencies is clearly available from within the great majority of intimate *networks*, it is not generally available from most intimate *relationships*.'[184] Stronger interpersonal ties tend to be a linked set of dyadic relations, rather than a densely connected solidary or communal group. The stronger the relationship, the more likely it is that helping becomes a salient part of the relationship. Whether or not intimates live in the same neighbourhood may have little effect on provision of assistance.

In another essay, Wellman[185] notes the persistence of communities and little substantiation of the 'myth of the lonely urbanites.' Communities have also been despatialized and specialized based on interests, not on common socialization. This potential for personal network diversity gives greater access to more information on many different resources. Multiple community memberships become a possibility. With diversity has also come differentiation in relationships. Clearly, kinship relations continue to be important. Adams[186] asserts that contemporary urban social relations are not characterized by less primary social interaction, but by more secondary relations.

Relationships tend to be differentiated by kinship and interest. According to Adams, one's obligations with respect to mutual aid centre around aging parents and siblings, although adult sibling relations tend to be based more on interest. Adams found residential mobility to be prompted by kinship affairs. For close kin, distance was a qualifier, not a deterrent to frequency of contact, exchange of aid, and emotional ties. This was especially true of middle class respondents. The networks of blue collar respondents were generally less dispersed and separation from kin often led to isolation from them, with the exception of parents.

In the past, sociologists, social psychologists, and others have tended to view mobile people as isolated, marginal, and self-sufficient, cutting ties to family in order to be free to move 'up.' Adams found 'mobiles' to have as strong interactional ties as 'stables' in the middle class. He reasoned that mobility requires social support from parents and other kin, although the quality and type of relationship is likely to change.

Shulman,[187] too, has noted the differentiation of relationships into kin obligation and shared interests. He notes the stability of relationships, even in the absence of face-to-face contact. His data show that in personal networks of primary relationships kin were 41 per cent of the persons named, friends, 45, and neighbours, 14 per cent. Most persons were long-term acquaintances, 67 per cent of more than six years, 57 per cent of 10 years or more. Shulman stated that people tend to require only a few sources for exchange of goods and services in their relationships, although two-thirds of the networks he studied involved some exchange. People find it difficult to see close relationships in an instrumental way, according to Shulman, and see neighbours as sources of exchanges of goods, and kin as providers of aid and service.

If there is differentiation within networks into kin and those with similarity of interests, one might also say that there are contacts that provide information and those that take on the tasks involved in giving help. Summarizing the research cited here, probably the best of circumstances is enjoyed by those who have extensive personal social networks, and supportive friends and kinship relationships. The former may yield the necessary information and the latter may help make the best use of it. How do the parts of one's network serve to get help when needed and to offer the personal and other aid necessary? Data gathered and analysed by urban sociologists begin to show some of the dynamics.

Bott's work[188] indicates that the network of relationships in which husband and wife are involved prior to marriage (particularly relationships with kin) has a significant influence on their marital relationship. Bott states that the involvement of husband and wife in their own close-knit network increases the likelihood of segregation of activities within the marriage which serves to decrease conflict and increase stability, but also to decrease the amount of joint involvement and probably the amount of personal support available from each partner.

Recent work by Richards[189] suggests that the relationship between social networks and the marital relationship may vary by activity and affect each other in unexpected ways. Generally, the women in Richards's study with the most extensive local social networks, of kin and others, tended to have highly role-segregated households. But, high household role segregation was associated with joint husband-wife social activities, if kin were available to be included in the women's networks. Involvement in family networks supported joint social activities for the women and their husbands, contrary to the Bott findings.

For those whose kin were not available by reason of death, the lessened kin contact was not necessarily associated with any increase in husband-wife joint functioning; those who lived far away from their parents, presumably by choice, showed a high degree of sharing. Richards concludes that the marital relationship, the extent of traditional or shared roles, may suggest the extent of external supporting relationships necessary to sustain and support one's life, and not the other way around.

Are sources of help or support interchangeable? Is it possible to make up in extension or range of network for lack of kinship or other intimates? Gore[190] reports that lack of a spouse only slightly changes the general level of reliance for support on relatives, neighbours, other friends, and ex-co-workers. This implies that lack of intimate support cannot be compensated for easily by other sources of help. Her data indicate the prominence of kinship relations in providing both socio-emotional and instrumental support.

Neighbourhoods as sources of aid are sustained by the flow of information just as personal relationships are. Flow of information also serves to connect people with formal sources of help outside family and friends. What appears to be important is that people have their own bridges for the gap that often exists between information about available help and the source of the help. Recent work by Warren[191] emphasizes the importance not only of a balance of social relationships, i.e., a balance between strong and weak ties, but of diversity, i.e., a combination of social ties from neighbourhood, work place, and voluntary organizations. The diversity may furnish the crucial bridges within personal relationships and within neighbourhoods and communities.

The Links Between Informal and Formal Help
A continuum of helping resources appears to exist that ranges from the informal help provided by families and friends to the statutory services representing

society's most formal arrangements. Standing about midpoint between informal sources of help and support and professionally delivered services are groups organized on the basis of a shared concern or condition. These are variously referred to in a growing literature as self-help, peer helping, mutual aid, or self-care groups or organizations, to distinguish them from those organized and operated by professionals.

Although the phenomenon of mutual support has been traced back to primitive times and described as playing a leading part in evolution,[192] prototypes for the contemporary self-help organization date back to the 1930s and the emergence of Alcoholics Anonymous and various associations of parents of handicapped children. Since the 1960s the self-help phenomenon has burgeoned into a movement that has been called 'one of the most important social phenomena of the last third of this century, not only in the United States and other Western countries, but on a scale worldwide.[193]

Newsletters in the United States and Britain, which are clearing houses for information, evidence the existence of groups for such diverse concerns as ostomies, terminal cancer, narcolepsy, concerned relatives of nursing home patients, parents of gays and lesbians, manic depressives, child abusers, post-mastectomy women, parents of children with cancer, low-income senior citizens, women awaiting caesarian birth, cardiac patients, stroke patients, welfare rights groups, public housing tenants, mothers of young mongoloids, single parents, and hundreds of others, including gamblers and overeaters.

To select one example from the field of family and child welfare, Parents Anonymous groups to help child-abusing parents have grown exponentially in the United States since federal funding was made available to them through the Office of Child Development. As of April 1976, there were 519 chapters of Parents Anonymous with a membership of 3944. A two-year evaluation to that point revealed a significant decrease in physical abuse immediately after joining a group, a significant positive relationship between self-esteem scores and months in the group, an increase in knowledge of child development, and a reduction in the social isolation of members. In Ontario, Parents Anonymous groups are also receiving funding, albeit on a much more limited scale through the provincial Child Abuse Program.

The conditions favouring the development of the self-care movement have been seen as: the rising costs of professional services in a period of economic restraint which makes less costly alternatives attractive; a consciousness on the part of minorities, women, the poor, and the handicapped who want to speak for themselves; and the anti-leviathan 'small is beautiful' idea that things be constructed on a small scale.[194] In the field of health, the significance of life-style factors in the precipitating conditions of costly illnesses and the failure of professional medicine with respect to prevention in these areas has increased support for patients to assume more responsibility for their own care and has increased interest in 'health activation.'

The relationship between self-help groups and professionals is increasingly being subjected to analysis and appears to vary widely. Professionals may form groups, as in the case of Recovery Incorporated designed to help former psychiatric patients, act as resource and technical consultants to the group, or join the group as peers when they share the same condition. Some groups such as AA eschew any connection with professionals except as members, while others rely on professional support and/or government funding. Current issues in the area of self-help revolve around the questions of whether the groups will themselves become bureaucracies as a function of their size and influence, and perhaps more importantly, whether the movement will be used as an excuse by government to cut back on needed services.

The relationship between self-help groups and neighbourhoods needs further consideration as well. Self-help groups as special interest groups organized on a community or neighbourhood basis may be able to provide the links between individuals and families and professional resources and services.

VI CONCLUSION

Potentially, current trends in the provision of health and social services bode well for children and families. The decentralization of service organizations promises the development of service centres in communities, based on the needs and concerns of the people who live there. In communities, the emphasis is on multiservice organizations and the collaboration of professionals across specialities and disciplines. The potential exists for new partnerships between service-providers and consumers, citizens and policy-makers.

As providers and potential consumers take a new look at what health and social services are needed and how they can be provided, two of the issues are: the feasibility of providing services for 'everyone' as social utilities, and the development of alternatives to the traditional, formal services. The current situation of service budget constraints and cutbacks may tend to spur the study of alternatives to some of the formal services and limit the examination of services as social utilities. Together, practitioners, policy-makers, citizens, and consumers will have to find ways to set services priorities, plan services, and evaluate performance based on those priorities.

The patchwork of social services is sending planners and policy-makers to the drawing boards to design a 'rational' system of services delivery. Services to children are separate from family services and the services in each group are distinct.

But they are not more separate than other types of services. In North America, it is hard to identify a social service system or a system of health and social services. However, indications are that we have moved from an era of big is beautiful to one of small is better. The emphasis is on community services, decentralization, and the importance of tailoring services to local needs. Through this we may be learning how to cope with the big city, and the sprawling metropolitan areas. We may find, without trying to bring back the good old days, that a community is a viable unit of the city.

It is difficult for a human needs or 'social utilities' emphasis to emerge from the current concerns about economic constraint, the demographic tilt to an older population and political expedience, irregular funding, and lack of objective criteria and data for determining service priorities. Perhaps neighbourhood or community service centres seem more manageable than larger units to those who allocate federal or provincial sources of funds than to those who have the responsibilities for the neighbourhood services. Our review indicates that this trend may promote the well-being of families and children, if not the well-being of those who will have to find ways to develop services tailored to needs, deliver them, and secure funding, since programmes tend to follow funds rather than the reverse.

The potential new partnerships between service-providers and consumers, and citizens and policy-makers, will have to find ways to break with precedents. Individual health and social service organizations must forge new professional and service linkages that are flexible enough to change with changing current and future needs, but organized for adequacy and efficiency to meet current guidelines imposed by economic constraint. Alternate modes of service provision may be less likely to occur to the professionals involved than to other groups in the community. Evaluation means professional accountability. Committed service-providers may need researchers and planners to help evaluate their efforts and to provide the information to policy-makers and others who assist in establishing service priorities.

Service boundaries are also being explored and redefined. Formal services, or help provided by service organizations, are being linked to groups of service consumers who are helping themselves and personal associations or networks of family, friends, and neighbours who furnish social support to supplement, complement, and sometimes provide continuity to professional help. For many, informal and self-help groups substitute for professional assistance. What could be developing is a recognizable continuum of health and social services in which family, friends, and neighbours furnish the links to groups of service consumers and to help provided by service organizations and the professionals in them.

Issues of service co-ordination and service boundaries include the delineation of family services from those for children. When should they be combined or separated? The current social climate, in which individual rights and entitlement to social minimums are important issues, embraces concern about what is happening to modern family life. Social services imply intervention. How can provision of services support the family and its members without interfering with family integrity or creating dependence? One could argue that services can be integrated into the local community to support family life. At the same time, a co-ordinated system of services signals leviathan to many.

Neighbourhoods do exist as a potentially vital aspect of living in a city, especially for families and their children. Although the community disintegration thesis has become widely known and rather widely accepted, the role of the neighbourhood may once again come to be appreciated, particularly by medical and social planners, practitioners, and policy-makers.

Families and their children learn to 'negotiate' the city through their personal associations where they live. Literature on urban communities indicates that, despite the size of cities, personal relationships in neighbourhoods continue to exist and remain important anchor points. In fact, personal associations may provide the only links to neighbourhood facilities and services for some families, and furnish children with opportunities to learn how to live in the city.

Families and children live within a set of social relationships, i.e., kin, friends, neighbours, and others involved in school, occupational, and other settings. Generally, crisis help is available from these relationships to all but a few. Help with less well-defined problems may also be available from kin, friends, and neighbours, but if it is not, it is vital that help be perceived to be available elsewhere and that referral to available help be possible from among these relationships. Relatives and friends and work associates (in that order) are the most frequent sources of help for matters of general concern. Neighbours are the next most frequently used source. This appears to be a general finding in studies of community help-seeking. But, whether one gets to other than informal help sources may depend on the perception that one can get help, knowledge of help sources, and/ or a neighbour who can provide a referral to that source. The latter may depend on the organizational links within and outside the neighbourhood.

The studies we have reviewed indicate that one can learn to seek help as a child and that learning takes place in the family subject to the influences of other kin and friends. The more clearly defined the problem or situation is with respect to seriousness (crisis, interference with normal life), the less is the influence of social relationships. Medical problems probably fall into this category more than do psychological or emotional problems, except for the most debilitating of these. Perhaps medical and dental problem prevention and most socio-emotional problems are the most subject to interpretation by family and friends or to what we have called social network influence. Responses to these less well-defined problems may be learned behaviours and more dependent on childhood experience to develop, since seeking such help does not vary by age and sex, but by education and socio-economic status.

The more links the family has to others, the broader a child's experience is likely to be and the greater probability the child has of obtaining information and knowledge that differs from that shared in the family. Since the interaction between parent and child lends support to both, and since the attitudes of both should be reasonably congruent to enhance the development of competency and a sense of worth in the child, the need exists for a social climate that supports the efforts of both parenting and growing up.

The trend among providers of some social services is to use the social relationships of service consumers to help work out problems. In a time of service budget cutbacks and restraint, the use of alternative sources of help is likely to increase. The support of one's family and friends is important in learning to cope with or solve problems, faster and for a longer time. Our literature review indicates that we know little, or have recorded little, about the interaction of problem, person, and social network and personal characteristics. Although adolescents may have an involvement with health and social services apart from their families, family relationships remain important in this interaction which becomes more complex, i.e., family – adolescent – peers – service. There is no indication that relationships with peers supplant the family or that family relationships can substitute for those with peers in the provision of community services any more than they can in education.

While most children grow up in two-parent families, for some period of their childhood, many children live in single-parent families, and with replacement parents. Family relationships are being extended and redefined. Children growing up in these situations have potentially more contacts within and outside the family; more opportunities for both associations and difficulties. There is no evidence here to suggest how services to families should change based on family changes. However, we also have no evidence to suggest that family relationships are becoming less important as a result of social change, and there is considerable evidence to the contrary.

NOTES

1 Dr Thomas John Barnardo from London, England, sent 25,000 orphans to Canada, maintained a Canadian headquarters in Toronto and a home on

Jarvis Street. His operation officially closed its doors in 1951. *Toronto Star Weekend Magazine*, 3 December 1977, p. 14a. Sutherland, Neil Late nineteenth-century attitudes to children, in *Children in English-Canadian society, 1880-1920, framing the twentieth-century consensus.* Toronto: University of Toronto Press, 1976, pp. 3-12.

2 Richmond, Julius B. The needs of children, in *Doing better and feeling worse: health in the United States, Daedalus 106:* 253. Dr Richmond is U.S. Surgeon General and Assistant Secretary for Health, U.S. Department of Health, Education and Welfare; Reva Gerstein *Shift in commitment, A study of pediatric needs in Metropolitan Toronto,* Metropolitan Toronto Hospital Planning Council, Toronto, November 1975; Shirley Post, *Feasibility study, Canadian Institute of Child Health,* Hospital for Sick Children Foundation, Toronto, February 1976.

3 Haggerty, Robert J., Roghman, Klaus J., Pless, Ivan B. *Child health in the community,* New York: John Wiley & Sons, Wiley Interscience Publication, 1975, p. 316, also *One million children, the Celdic report,* the Commission on emotional and learning disorders in children, Toronto: Leonard Crainford, 1970.

4 Richmond, Julius B. The needs of children, *Daedalus 106:* 255, Winter 1977.

5 Ibid., 257.

6 Haggerty, Robert J. et al. *Child health in the community,* New York: John Wiley & Sons, 1975, p. 318.

7 Additional reading on these issues in Newberger, E.H., Newberger, C.N., and Richmond, J.B. Child health in America: toward a national public policy, in Health and Society, *The Milbank Fund Quarterly 54:* 249-98, Summer 1976; *Toward a national policy for children and families,* Report of the Advisory Committee on Child Development, Assembly of Behavioral and Social Sciences, National Research Council, National Academy of Sciences, Washington, 1976.

8 Hepworth, H. Philip *Personal social services in Canada: A review 10:* 24 Ottawa: The Canadian Council on Social Development, 1975.

9 Robarts, John P. O.C., C.C., Q.C., Commissioner *Metropolitan Toronto, A framework for the future,* reports I and II of Royal Commission on Metropolitan Toronto, Toronto, June 1977.

10 Keniston, Kenneth and the Carnegie Council on Children *All our children,* New York: Harcourt Brace & Jovanovich, 1977.

11 Sussman, Marvin B. Family, *Encyclopedia of Social Work 1:* 365. Washington: National Association of Social Workers, 1977.

12 An example of current dialogue on the family is The family, *Daedalus 106:* Spring 1977, with a preface by Groubard, Stephen R., ed.

13   Katz, Michael *The people of Hamilton, Canada West*, Cambridge, Mass:
Harvard University Press, 1975, pp. 209–308.

14   Shorter, Edward *The making of the modern family*, New York: Basic Books,
Inc., 1975, p. 7.

15   Ibid., 280.

16   Bane, Mary Jo *Here to stay: American families in the twentieth century*,
New York: Basic Books, Inc., 1976, p. 66.

17   Keniston, K. *All our children*, New York: Harcourt Brace & Jovanovich,
1977, p. 23.

18   Ibid., 23.

19   A report of the U.S. Census Bureau in February 1977, commented on in an
article, Trend to living alone brings economic and social change, *Sunday New
York Times*, 20 March 1977, quoted demographer Norton, A. and social
scientists, Bronfenbrenner, Urie, Cornell University, Hudson, John, Arizona
State University, Furstenberg, F., University of Pennsylvania. See also Nett,
E.M. The changing forms and functions of the Canadian family: A demo-
graphic view, in Ishwaran, K., ed., *The Canadian family*, Toronto: Holt,
Rinehart and Winston of Canada, Ltd., 1976, pp. 46–76.

20   Hodgson, Susan discusses the implications of rising expectations for parents
and children as they relate to shared childrearing in Chap. 3.

21   Glick, Paul C. A demographer looks at the American Family, *Journal of
Marriage and the Family 37:* 1, 15–26, February 1975.

22   Kahn, Alfred The personal social services and the child, in Chap. 3 in William
Michelson, Saul V. Levine, & Ellen Michelson (eds.), *The child in the city:
Today and tomorrow*, Toronto: University of Toronto Press, 1979.

23   Giovannoni, Jeanne M. and Billingsley, Andrew Family, one-parent,
Encyclopedia of Social Work 1: 397–408, Washington: National Association
of Social Workers, 1977.

24   Larson, Lyle E. *The family in contemporary society*, The study of the
family in Canada, Toronto: Prentice Hall, 1976, pp. 20–40.

25   Glick, Paul C. A demographer looks at the American family, *Journal of
Marriage and the Family* and Schlesinger, Benjamin Remarriage as family
reorganization for divorced persons, in Ishwaram, K., ed., *The Canadian
family*, Toronto: Holt, Rinehart and Winston of Canada Ltd., 1976, pp.
460–78.

26   Giovannoni, Jeanne M. and Billingsley, Andrew Family, one-parent,
Encyclopedia of Social Work 1: 401–5, Washington: National Association of
Social Workers, 1977; Stone, Phillip J. Child care in twelve countries, in
Szalai, Alexander, ed., *The use of time*, The Hague: Mouton, 1972, pp.
249–56.

27 Giovannoni, Jeanne M. and Billingsley, Andrew Family, One-parent, *Encyclopedia of Social Work 1:* 405, 408, Washington: National Association of Social Workers, 1977.
28 Ibid., 404.
29 Messenger, Lillian, Schlesinger, Benjamin, and Macrae, A. Remarriage in Canada: Statistical trends, *Journal of Marriage and the Family 30:* 300–4, May 1970; Schlesinger, Benjamin *The one-parent family: perspectives and annotated bibliography*, Toronto: University of Toronto Press, 1969.
30 Wald, Esther Family, multiparent, *Encyclopedia of Social Work 1:* 392, Washington: National Association of Social Workers, 1977.
31 McKinlay, John B. Some approaches and problems in the study of the use of services – an overview, *Journal of Health and Social Behavior 13:* 115–52, June 1975.
32 Sweetser, Dorian Apple How laymen define illness, *Journal of Health and Human Behavior 1:* 219–25, 1960. Reprinted in Folta, Jeanette R. and Deck, Edith S., eds., *A sociological framework for patient care*, New York: John Wiley & Sons, Inc., 1966, pp. 200–27. A study of sixty men and women, 20 to 50 years in Boston. Related studies are: Mechanic, David The concept of illness behaviour, *Journal of Chronic Diseases 15:* 189–94, 1962; Jenkins, C. David Group differences in perception: a study of community beliefs and feelings about tuberculosis, *American Journal of Sociology 71:* 4, 417–29, January 1966.
33 Freidson, Eliot *Patients' views of medical practice, a study of subscribers to a prepaid medical plan in the Bronx*, New York: Russell Sage Foundation, 1961.
34 Ibid., 146.
35 Ibid., 147.
36 In this chapter we are using the non-technical meaning of 'social network,' i.e., links between people.
37 Freidson, Eliot *Patients' view of medical practice*, New York: Russell Sage Foundation, 1961.
38 Ibid., 151.
39 Stoeckle, John D., Zola, Irving K., and Davidson, Gerald E. On going to see the doctor, the contributions of the patient to the decision to seek medical aid, *Journal of Chronic Diseases 16:* 975–89, 1963.
40 Suchman, Edward Sociomedical variations among ethnic groups, *American Journal of Sociology 70:* 319–31, November 1964. Social patterns of illness and medical care, in Jaco, E. Gartly, ed., *Patients, physicians and illness*, New York: Free Press, 1972, pp. 262–79. A study in 1960 and 1961 of 5000 adults in 2000 families in New York City.

41 Ziegler, Suzanne Chap. 6, section III Ethnic boundaries and social networks, for a discussion of access to health and social services and information about them in ethnic communities.

42 Geertsen, Reed, Klauper, Melville R., Rindflesh, Mark, Kane, Robert L., Gray, Robert A re-examination of Suchman's views on social factors in health care utilization, *Journal of Health and Social Behavior 6:* 226–37, June 1975.

43 Reeder, Leo and Berkanovic, Emil Sociological concomitants of health orientations: A partial replication of Suchman, *Journal of Health and Social Behavior 14:* 134–43, June 1973.

44 Rosenstock, Irwin M. Why people use health services, *The Milbank Memorial Fund Quarterly 44:* 3, part 2, 94–127, July 1966.

45 Anderson, C. Ronald *A behavioral model of families' use of health services*, Chicago, Ill.: Center for Health Administration Studies, University of Chicago, 1968.

46 Wolinsky, Frederic D. Health service utilization and attitudes toward health maintenance organizations: a theoretical and methodological discussion, *Journal of Health and Social Behavior 17:* 221–36, September 1976. A study of insurance subscribers in 487 households in Iowa in 1972.

47 Langlie, Jean K. Social networks, health beliefs, and preventive health behavior, *Journal of Health and Social Behavior 18:* 3, 244–60, September 1977. A study of adults in Rockford Illinois. Indirect Risk Preventive Health Behavior (PHB) included seat belt use, exercise and nutrition behaviour, medical checkups, dental care, immunizations and miscellaneous screening exams; Direct PHB included driving behaviour, i.e., speeds, gets tickets, signals turns; pedestrian behaviour, i.e., jaywalks, crosses against light, personal hygiene, smokes.

48 Ibid., 258.

49 Pratt, Lois V. *Family structure and effective health behavior*, Boston: Houghton Mifflin Company, 1975, pp. 230, and Child rearing methods and children's health behavior, *Journal of Health and Social Behavior 14:* 61–69, March 1973.

50 Hodgson, Susan discusses the development of competence in Chap. 3.

51 An additional source for models of health and illness behaviour is Roghmann, Klaus J. Models of health and illness behavior, in Haggerty, Robert J. et al., *Child Health and the Community*, New York: John Wiley and Sons, 1975, pp. 119–41.

52 Pratt, Lois V. *Family structure and effective health behavior*, Boston: Houghton Mifflin Company, 1975, p. 8.

53 Ibid., 144.

54 Ibid., 121, 143.

55 Pemberton, Alec G., Whitlock, F.A., Wilson, P.R. Knowledge about where to find help: A preliminary analysis, *Social Science & Medicine 9:* 433–39, 1975. A study in two suburbs, 8500–9500 population, Australia in 1970 and 1971. The 1096 respondents were 20–70 years old.

56 Kadushin, Charles *Why people go to psychiatrists*, New York: Atherton Press, 1969, p. 315.

57 Tannenbaum, Deborah People with problems: seeking help in an urban community, Centre for Urban & Community Studies, University of Toronto, Toronto, *Research Paper No. 64*, June 1974, p. 66. A random sample of 845 respondents interviewed in 1968 provided data for the Tannenbaum paper.

58 Bolton, Charles D. and Kammeyer, Kenneth The decision to use a family service agency, *The family coordinator 17:* 47–53, January 1968. Study of 64 clients in a U.S. university town of 10,000 population in 1961 and 1962.

59 Ibid., 51.

60 Lee, Nancy Howell *The search for an abortionist*, Chicago, Ill.: University of Chicago Press, 1969. A study of 114 urban U.S. women seeking an abortion in 1965–67.

61 Haese, Philip N. and Meile, Richard L. Considerations of alternative help sources, Folta, Jeanette R., Deck, Edith S., eds., *A sociological framework for patient care*, New York: John Wiley and Sons, Inc., 1966, pp. 228–35. A study of a random sample of adults in a large Midwestern U.S. city.

62 Greenley, James R., Mechanic, David Social selection in seeking help for psychological problems, *Journal of Health and Social Behavior 17:* 249–62, September 1976.

63 Horwitz, Allan Social networks and pathways to psychiatric treatment, *Social Forces 56:* 86–105, September 1977.

64 Finlayson, Angela Social networks as coping resources, *Social Science and Medicine 10:* 97–103, 1976. A study of 76 wives whose husbands recovered from heart attacks, under 60 years old, 28 with non-manual, 48 with manual occupations.

65 *Priorities*, The effects of funding structures on services to adolescents in Ontario, A proposal for reallocation of resources, Central Toronto Youth Services, Toronto, December 1976.

66 Shaw, Robert C. The three worlds of Jimmy, *Canadian Welfare 52:* 2, 10–13, May-June 1976.

67 Illich, Ivan Society is caught in the needs makers' grip, The *Globe and Mail*, 18 October 1976, p. 7.

68 Runciman, W.G. *Relative deprivation and social justice*, London: Routledge and Kegan Paul, 1966.

69 Maslow, Abraham H. *Motivation and personality*, New York: Harper & Row, 1954.

70 Rainwater, Lee Fear and the house-as-haven in the lower class, *American Institute of Planners Journal 32:* 1, 23–31, January 1966.
71 Teare, Robert and McPheeters, Harold L. *Manpower utilization in social welfare*, Southern Regional Education Board, Atlanta, Georgia, June 1970.
72 Segal, Brian and Jackson, John *Social Services Task Bank*, Carleton-Algonquin Social Work Education and Manpower Project, Carleton University School of Social Work, Ottawa, July 1976. The Canadian Association of Social Workers is also conducting a study of manpower needs and uses under the direction of Peter McMahon.
73 Bradshaw, J. The concept of social need, *New Society*, 30 March 1972, p. 640.
74 Packman, Jean *Child care: needs and numbers*, London: Allen and Unwin, 1968.
75 *One million children, the Celdic Report*, Toronto: Leonard Crainford, 1970.
76 Ibid., 20.
77 Erikson, Erik H. Identity and the life cycle, *Psychological Issues 1:* 50–100, 1959.
78 *Growing up in Idaho: the needs of young children*, Idaho Office of Child Development, 1974.
79 Maas, Henry S. Children in need, in *The environment and the child: an assessment and a plan*, Montreal: The Children's Service Centre, 1970, pp. 7–11.
80 Morgan, John P. Social welfare services in Canada, in Oliver, Michael, ed., *Social purpose for Canada*, Toronto: University of Toronto Press, 1961, pp. 130–67.
81 Haphazard in hindsight. No doubt at the time the development of services was seen as enlightened and purposeful.
82 Wedge, Peter and Prosser, Hilary *Born to fail?* London: Arrow Books Ltd., 1973.
83 Fruin David Analyses of need, in Brown, Malcolm F., ed., *Social issues and the social services*, London: Charles Knight, 1974.
84 Ibid., 33.
85 Baumheier, Edward C. and Heller, Gretchen A. *Analysis and synthesis of needs, assessment research in the field of human services*, Center for Social Research and Development, Denver University, Denver, Colorado, 1974.
86 Kumove, Leon *The social structure of Metropolitan Toronto*, Municipality of Metropolitan Toronto Planning Dept. Toronto, April 1975.
87 Schiff, Myra and Pilette, Ron *Correlates of social structure in Metropolitan Toronto*, Metropolitan Toronto Planning Board, Toronto, June 1975.

88 Fruin, David Analyses of need, in Brown, Malcom F., ed., *Social issues and the social services*, London: Charles Knight, 1974, p. 33.
89 Davies, B.P. *Social needs and resources in local services*, London: Joseph, Michael 1968, and Davies, B.P. et al., *Variations in services for the aged*, Occasional Paper 40 on Social Administration, London: Bell and Sons, 1971.
90 *Children and their primary schools*, Central Advisory Council for Education, 1967.
91 *Inner London Education Authority, Index of Educational Priority Areas*, R.S. 501-71, London, 1971.
92 Baker, Michael and Joshi, Madhukar *Methods of building and maintaining accountable human services system: Brockton Multi-Service Center, A method for conducting a community audit*, Brockton, Mass.: Brockton Area Human Resources Group, 1975.
93 *Needs research and demonstration project, final report*, Institute for Social Science for Rural-Urban Research and Planning, South Dakota State University, Brockings, June 1974.
94 *Service needs/access study data book: The study of services needs/access in Chemung, Schuyler, Steuben, Tioga, and Scholarie Counties, New York State*, Ithaca, N.Y.: Cornell University, 1973.
95 Jones, Judith Denton *Who needs social services?* The impact of differential perceptions of need for social services on the development of service programs for welfare recipients in New York City from 1969 to 1974. Doctoral dissertation, City University of New York, 1976.
96 Greenland, Cyril *Vision Canada: The unmet needs of blind Canadians*, Toronto: Leonard Crainford, 1976.
97 *Differentiation of unmet needs using analysis by age/sex cohorts of an elderly population: Aging in Manitoba*, Manitoba Dept. of Health and Social Development, Winnipeg; *Study of aging in downtown Niagara Falls*, Social Planning Council of Niagara Falls, Niagara Falls, Ontario, 1973.
98 Heppner, Barbara *The recipient and the welfare system: Living on welfare in Montreal*, McGill School of Social Work, Montreal, 1974.
99 *The one-parent family*, Ottawa: Canadian Council on Social Development, 1971; *The one-parent family in Edmonton*: Report of a study looking at conditions and needs of one-parent families and services available, Edmonton Social Services, Edmonton, 1975.
100 Johnson, Laura C. *Patterns of child care in Metropolitan Toronto*, July 1977; *Who cares?* A report of the Project Child Care, Survey of parents and their child care arrangements, November 1977; and *Taking care*, April 1978, Social Planning Council of Metropolitan Toronto, Toronto.

101 *Beyond shelter*, Ottawa: Canadian Council on Social Development, 1973.

102 *Needs and resources in Metropolitan Toronto*, Toronto: Social Planning Council of Metropolitan Toronto, 1963.

103 *Priorities guidelines for 1977 allocations*, United Community Fund of Greater Toronto, Toronto, 29 November 1976, mimeo.

104 *Differentiation of unmet needs using analysis by age/sex cohorts of an elderly population: Aging in Manitoba*, and *Update: aging in Manitoba*, Manitoba Dept. of Health and Social Development, Winnipeg, 1977.

105 Rose, Albert Some reflections on the history of social planning in Ontario, in *Sourcebook to pathways to social planning*, Province of Ontario, Ministry of Community and Social Services, Toronto, October 1975.

106 Laframboise, Josette *A question of needs*, Ottawa: Canadian Council on Social Development, September 1975.

107 Ibid., 138.

108 Ibid., 139.

109 *Poor kids, A report on children in poverty in Canada*, Ottawa: National Council of Welfare, 1975, p. 1.

110 Ibid., 12.

111 Ibid., 34.

112 *Research, demonstration and evaluation studies, fiscal year 1976*, Research and Evaluation Division, Office of Child Development, U.S. Department of Health, Education and Welfare, Washington, 1976.

113 The study is published in three volumes: I, *The prenatal, perinatal, and postnatal status of children in Idaho*, 1973; II, *The status of young children in Idaho*, 1974; and III, *The status of minority children in Idaho*, State of Idaho, Office of Child Development, 1974.

114 Mayor's Commission on Youth: *Youth needs and services*, Bureau of Sociological Research, University of Colorado, Boulder, Colorado, January 1974.

115 *Report of a study on social services to children*, New Brunswick Department of Social Services, September 1975.

116 MacDonald, Linda et al. *The children of the community of Windsor*. Legal assistance of Windsor, a joint service of the Faculty of Law, University of Windsor, and the Ontario Legal Aid Plan, Windsor, 1976.

117 Anderson, John et al. *Report of the interministry committee on residential services*, to the Cabinet Committee on Social Development, Ministry of Community and Social Services, Province of Ontario, April 1975.

118 Hagarty, Stephen et al. *The rational perspective*, A background report for policy statement on program priorities, unpublished background paper for the Province of Ontario, Ministry of Community and Social Services, Children's Services Division, January 1978.

119 Boulding, Kenneth E. The concept of need for health services, *The Milbank Memorial Fund Quarterly 44:* 4, 202–23, part II, October 1966.
120 Fruin, David *Analyses of need*, in Brown, Malcolm F., ed., *Social issues and the social services*, London: Charles Knight, 1974, p. 33.
121 Teare, Robert and McPheeters, Harold L. *Manpower utilization in social welfare*, Atlanta, Georgia: Southern Regional Education Board, Atlanta, Georgia, June 1970.
122 Jones, Judith Denton *Who needs services*, City University of New York, Doctoral Dissertation, 1976, and *One in a world of two's*, Ottawa: National Council of Welfare, 1976.
123 Miller, Herman P. *Rich man, poor man*, New York: Thomas Y. Crowell, 1971, pp. 87–105.
124 Fruin, David *Analyses of need*, in Brown, Malcolm F., ed., *Social issues and the social services*, London: Charles Knight, 1974, and Wharf, Brian *Social planning functions and social planning organization*, in *Sourcebook to pathways to social planning*, Toronto: Ontario, Ministry of Community and Social Services, October 1975, pp. 93–121.
125 *One million children, the Celdic Report*, Toronto: Leonard Crainford, 1970.
126 Lambert, Camille, Jr. *Community information centres as an input for social planning*, in *Sourcebook to pathways to social planning*, Province of Ontario, Ministry of Community and Social Services, October 1975, pp. 28–30.
127 Chetkow, B. Harold *Some factors influencing the utilization and impact of priority recommendations in community planning*, *Social Service Review 41:* 3, 271–82, September 1967.
128 *Priorities guidelines for 1977 allocation*, United Community Fund of Greater Toronto, Toronto, 29 November 1976, mimeo.
129 Novak, Michael *The family out of favor*, *Harper's 252:* 1511, 37–46, April 1976. In defense of children, *Children today*, January-February 1977, 28–9.
130 *Priorities*, Central Toronto Youth Services, Toronto, December 1976.
131 Robarts, John *Afternoon Address to the Conference on Coordinating Human Services in Metropolitan Toronto*, Social Planning Council of Metropolitan Toronto, Toronto, October 1976.
132 Etzioni, Amitai *Deinstitutionalization, a public policy fashion*, *Evaluation 3:* 9–10, 1976.
133 Levine, Theodore *Community-based treatment for adolescents; myths and realities*, *Social Work 22:* 2, 144–7, March 1977.
134 The role of the community in deinstitutionalization and alternative resources was the theme of the 1978 Annual Conference of the Ontario Welfare Council.

135 Purvine, Margaret and Ryan, William Into and out of a child welfare network, *Child Welfare 48:* 3, 144–47, March 1969.

136 The American programme material entitled *We can help*, a curriculum on the identification, reporting, referral and case management of child abuse and neglect, has been adapted for use in the Province of Ontario by the Ministry of Community and Social Services. Children's Bureau, Office of Child Development, U.S. Dept. of Health, Education and Welfare, Washington, September 1976.

137 Perlman, Robert and Jones, David *Neighborhood service centres*, U.S. Dept. of Health, Education and Welfare, Washington, 1967.

138 Kadushin, Alfred Child Welfare, in Maas, Henry S., ed., *Research in the social services: a five-year review*, New York: National Association of Social Workers, 1971, p. 43.

139 Wellman, Barry Pathways to mental caseness, revision of a section of Coates, Donald and Wellman, Barry *Conceptual framework for a mental health study*, University of Toronto, Toronto, August 1968, p. 3.

140 Kahn, Alfred J. The future of child welfare, in *The environment and the child: an assessment and a plan*, Montreal: The Children's Service Centre, 1970, pp. 12–16.

141 Hall, A.S. Client reception in a social service agency, *Public administration 49:* 25, 1971.

142 Teare, Robert and McPheeters, Harold L. *Manpower utilization in social welfare*, Southern Regional Education Board, Atlanta, Georgia, June 1970.

143 Caldwell, Bettye M. The child, the family and the state, in *The environment and the child*, Montreal: The Children's Service Centre, 1970, pp. 3–6.

144 Maas, Henry S. Children in need, in *The environment and the child*, Montreal: The Children's Service Centre, 1970.

145 See Packman, Jean *Child care: needs and numbers*, London: Allen and Unwin, 1968; Maas, Henry S. Children in need, in *The environment and the child*, Montreal: The Children's Service Centre, 1970; Kadushin, Alfred Child welfare, in Maas, Henry S., ed., *Research in the Social Services*, New York: National Association of Social Workers, 1971.

146 *One million children, the Celdic report*, Toronto: Leonard Crainford, 1970, and Kadushin, Alfred Child welfare, in Maas, Henry S., ed., *Research in the social services*, New York: National Association of Social Workers, 1971.

147 Kelly, Maurice *Halton Region Human Services Council: An evaluation*, Waterloo, Ontario: Wilfrid Laurier University, April 1976.

148 Kahn, Alfred J. New directions in social services, *Public welfare 34:* 2, 26–32, Spring 1976; Kahn, Alfred J. and Kamerman, Sheila B. *Social services in the United States: policies and programs*, Philadelphia: Temple University Press, 1976.

149 *Priorities*, Toronto: Central Toronto Youth Services, Toronto, December 1976.

150 Weiss, Audrey Teren The consumer model of assessing community health needs, *Evaluation 2:* 2, 71-3, 1975.

151 Rein, Martin Coordination of social services, *Social Policy*, New York: Random House, 1970, Chap. 2.

152 *Experiment in the development of a coordinated system for the delivery of human services in New Bedford, Mass.*, in Gans, Sheldon P. and Horton, Gerald T. *Integration of human services. The state and municipal levels*, New York: Praeger Publishers, 1975.

153 Wharf, Brian Social planning functions and social planning organization, in *Sourcebook to pathways to social planning*, Toronto, Ontario, Ministry of Community and Social Services, October 1975.

154 Martinson, Robert What works?: Questions and answers about prison reform, the *Public Interest 35:* 22-54, Spring 1977; Lipton, Douglas, Martinson, Robert, and Wilks, Judith *The effectiveness of correctional treatment: A survey of treatment evaluation studies*, New York: Praeger Publishers, 1975.

155 Fischer, Joel Is casework effective: a review, *Social Work 181:* 5-12, 1973.

156 See, for example, Levitt, Eugene E. The results of psychotherapy with children: an evaluation, *Journal of Consulting Psychology 21:* 186-96, 1957; Truax, C.B. and Carkhuff, R.R. *Toward effective counselling and psycho therapy*, Chicago: Aldine Publishing Co., 1967.

157 Human, Ray and Berger, Louis Reply to Eysenck, Hans J. The effects of Psychotherapy, *International Journal of Psychiatry 1:* 99-142, January 1965, and *International Journal of Psychiatry 1:* 317-18, April 1965.

158 Weiss, Carol H. *Evaluation research: methods of assessing program effectiveness*, Englewood Cliffs, N.J.: Prentice-Hall, 1972.

159 Kadushin, Alfred Child welfare, in Maas, Henry S., ed., *Research in the social services*, New York: National Association of Social Workers, 1971.

160 Rutman, Leonard and de Jong, Dick *Federal level evaluation*, Ottawa: Carleton University, 1976.

161 Kelly, Maurice *Halton Region Human Services Council: An evaluation*, Waterloo, Ontario: Wilfrid Laurier University, April 1976; Hanson, H.R. et al. Task Force on Community and Social Services, *Report on selected issues and relationships*, Province of Ontario, Ministry of Community and Social Services, Toronto, January 1974.

162 This point is made both by Rutman, Leonard and de Jong, Dick *Federal level evaluation*, Ottawa: Carleton University, 1976; Kahn, Alfred J. Service delivery at the neighbourhood level: experience, theory and fads, *Social Service Review 50:* 1, 23-56, March 1976.

163 Wholey, Joseph S. *Planning useful evaluations*, Evaluation Research Training Institute, Ottawa: Carleton University, School of Social Work, 1976.

164 *Sourcebook to pathways to social planning*, Province of Ontario, Ministry of Community and Social Services, Toronto, October 1975.

165 Schorr, Alvin Family policy in the United States, in *Explorations in social policy*, New York: Basic Books, 1968, Chap. 9.

166 This is a recurring theme in *Transition*, the newsletter of the Vanier Institute of the Family, Ottawa, Ontario.

167 Giovannoni, Jeanne M. and Billingsley, Andrew Family, one-parent, *Encyclopedia of Social Work 1:* 397–408, Washington: National Association of Social Workers, 1977.

168 Kahn, Alfred J. Service delivery at the neighbourhood level, *Social Service Review 50:* 1, 23–56, March 1976.

169 *Social Policies for Canada*, Part I, Ottawa: Canadian Welfare Council, 1969.

170 Kahn, Alfred and Kamerman, Sheila B. *Not for the poor alone: European social services*, New York: Harper & Row, 1975.

171 Keniston, Kenneth *All our children*, New York: Harcourt Brace & Jovanovich, 1975.

172 *Poor kids*, Ottawa: National Council of Welfare, 1975.

173 Culley, James D., Van Name, Judith B. and Settles, Barbara H. Measuring the indirect costs of child care, *Public Welfare 34:* 4, 6–13, Fall 1976.

174 Taub, Richard, Surgeon, George O., Lindholm, Sara, Otti, Phyllis Betts, and Bridges, Amy Urban voluntary associations, locality based and externally induced, *American Journal of Sociology 83:* 2, 426, 1977.

175 Warren, Donald I. Neighbourhood and community contexts in help seeking, problem coping, and mental health: data analysis monograph, summary version, University of Michigan, Ann Arbor, *Program in Community Effectiveness*, 31 August 1976, p. 480.

176 The typology is integral, parochial, diffuse, stepping stone, transitory and anomic, in Warren, Rachelle B. and Donald I. *The neighborhood organizer's handbook*, Notre Dame, Ind.: University of Notre Dame Press, 1977.

177 Warren, Rachelle B. and Donald I. The helping roles of neighbors: some empirical patterns. Research conducted under project 5 ROI–MH–24982 of the National Institute of Mental Health under the title of Helping networks in the urban community, no date.

178 Warren, Donald I. Neighborhood and community contexts in help seeking, monograph, *Program in community effectiveness*, Ann Arbor: University of Michigan, 31 August 1876, p. 12.

179 Granovetter, Mark S. The strength of weak ties, *American Journal of Sociology 78:* 6, 1376, 1973.

180 Fischer, Claude S. et al. *Networks and places, social relations in urban setting*, New York: The Free Press, 1977.

181 Ibid., 202.

182 Michelson, William *Environmental choice, human behavior, and residential satisfaction*, New York: Oxford University Press, 1977, pp. 181–214. A five-year study in Toronto of 761 families.

183 Wellman, Barry et al. *The uses of community, community ties and support systems*, Research Paper No. 4, Centre for Urban and Community Studies, University of Toronto, August 1971. A study of 845 adults in the Borough of East York, Metropolitan Toronto, 1968.

184 Wellman, Barry *Urban connections*, Research Paper 84, Centre for Urban and Community Studies, University of Toronto, Toronto, March 1976.

185 Wellman, Barry *The network nature of future communities: a predictive synthesis*, Research Paper 58, Centre for Urban and Community Studies, University of Toronto, Toronto, March 1973.

186 Adams, Bert N. *Kinship in an urban setting*, Chicago: Markham Publishing Company, 1965, pp. 1–16; 163–78. A study in Greensboro, North Carolina in 1963 and 1964 of 799 married adults.

187 Shulman, Norman Role differentiation in urban networks, *Sociological Focus 9: 2*, 149–58, April 1976.

188 Bott, Elizabeth *Family and social network*, London: Tavistock Publications, 1957, pp. 52–96.

189 Richards, Ellen Fitzgerald Network ties, kin ties and marital roles: a re-examination of Bott's hypothesis. Paper presented at the 72nd Annual Meeting of the American Sociological Association, Chicago, Ill., September 5–9 1977. Based on data from 331 married women, West End, Boston, Mass., 1958.

190 Gore, Susan Social supports and unemployment stress. Paper presented at the 72nd Annual Meeting of the American Sociological Association Chicago, Ill., 5–9 September 1977. An analysis of data that are part of a larger longitudinal study of black and white blue collar workers in Detroit receiving or waiting for unemployment insurance benefits.

191 Warren, Donald I. Social bonds in the metropolitan community. Working paper, Oakland University, Rochester, Michigan, February 1977.

192 Kropotkin, Peter *Mutual aid: a factor in evolution*, Avrich, Paul, trans., New York: New York University Press, 1972.

193 Katz, Alfred H. Self-help groups, *Encyclopedia of Social Work 2:* 1255, Washington: National Association of Social Workers, 1977.

194 Gartner, Alan Opening address to the New Human Services Institute Conference on Self-help and Health, held on 8 June 1976, as reported in *Self-help and health: A report*, New Human Services Institute, Queens College, New York, September 1976, p. 3.

3

Childrearing Systems:
The Influence of Shared Childrearing
on the Development of Competence[1]

SUSAN HODGSON

I INTRODUCTION

Many people in our culture believe that a mother is, and should be, responsible for the rearing of her children throughout their infancy and early childhood and some even argue that an exclusive and intensive relationship with the mother is every child's birthright.[2] The fact is that many mothers share the rearing of their children throughout early childhood. Yet, and perhaps because of the cultural value that a mother should rear her children, little effort has been made to understand the significance of shared childrearing for the child's development. Since shared childrearing is likely to continue to be a widespread social practice, it is time to make an effort to explore its significance and to weigh its advantages and disadvantages. I shall attempt to assess the current state of our knowledge of the significance of shared childrearing for the developing competence of children and to suggest questions about shared childrearing which remain unanswered and which require our attention.

There are four major sections in this chapter. In the introduction, I define what I mean by shared childrearing and make the argument that it will continue as a popular method. Since it is necessary to confine the discussion somewhat, I shall also explain in the introduction why it is that the implications of shared child-rearing for the ongoing development of competence is the focus for the remainder of the paper.

In the second section, some of the qualities necessary to a child's environment, if that environment is to be conducive to the development of competence, are suggested.

In the third section, these qualities serve as criteria in evaluating various forms of shared childrearing. Three questions about ways in which shared childrearing might affect the likelihood that a child's rearing provides the qualities important in the development of competence are raised. The first question has to do with whether or not fathers, siblings and peers, and daycare-providers *can* provide the necessary rearing environment. If not, then shared childrearing is a problem. If so, then when a mother cannot provide the necessary qualities, sharing can be a supplement to her efforts. The second question has to do with whether or not mothers can provide all that is necessary in a child's rearing or if others like fathers, siblings and peers, or daycare-providers make unique contributions to the development of competence. If so, shared childrearing is a necessity. If not, one person under favourable circumstances can rear a competent child. The third question has to do with how childrearing changes in nature by the fact that it is shared. Issues are raised by sharing which never arise when one person cares for a child. For example, the consistency or inconsistency of those rearing the child becomes a central concern in shared childrearing, as does the effect of sharing on a child's capacity for attachment, and the effect of sharing on a person's perception of responsibility for the child.

In summary, in the third section, various forms of shared childrearing are evaluated in terms of whether they can or cannot *supplement* a mother's efforts to provide the qualities necessary to the development of competence, whether they *complement* and therefore are necessary to a mother's efforts to provide the qualities necessary to the development of competence, and how the *changes in the nature of childrearing*, because it is shared, affect the likelihood that the qualities necessary to the development of competence are provided.

In the fourth section, a preliminary analysis of situations which hinder a mother's efforts to rear competent children is offered and the implications for shared childrearing as a support to a mother's efforts are considered. The paper closes with a brief summary statement.[3]

Definition of Shared Childrearing
Childrearing refers to an individual's efforts (self-conscious or not) to teach or facilitate a child's learning what it is important to know in the reality in which s/he functions. It can be characterized on dimensions such as responsiveness, consistency, and inclusiveness as well as on the dimension of sharing. On the simplest level childrearing is *shared* when more than one person is rearing the child. On a more complex level, the extent of sharing varies with factors such as the number of persons involved and their proportionate involvement. Shared childrearing can be characterized on various dimensions such as degree of specialization and consistency in expectations. As defined, everyone who has contact with a child could share in his/her rearing, because s/he could teach or facilitate the child's development. However, the concept will be used here to refer to an individual with whom the child has ongoing contact, be that person a parent, a daycare-provider, a sibling, or a peer.[4]

Prevalence of Shared Childrearing
The reasons why childrearing is shared are numerous. Many women, for example, have paid outside employment. In Canada, *the participation rate in the labour force for women* with only preschool-age children increased from 19 per cent in 1967 to 29 per cent in 1973.[5] The figures are comparable, if not higher, in the United States.[6] Thirty-seven per cent of women with preschool children were in the work force in 1976. In actual numbers, this translates in Ontario alone into an estimated 206,000 preschool-age children with mothers in the labour force in 1973. The rearing of these children is shared, whether it be with the father, a relative or a non-relative, or with family daycare or centre daycare. Also, it has been suggested that the increasing labour force participation rate of young women (from less than 50 per cent in 1961 to more than 65 per cent in 1975 for the 20-24 year old group) is an indicator of changes which are likely to maintain their participation at higher rates, even when they have children. Among the reasons offered are that the education level of young women is increasing and education is associated with higher labour force participation. In addition, given the increasing likelihood of divorce and the likelihood that the mother will support the children after divorce, working, which provides skills, is a means of providing greater economic security should single parenthood become a reality.[7] A final factor is that current economic conditions are such that a supplementary income is often perceived as necessary for maintaining the present standard of living. Should the economic situation alter, there are labour shortages predicted for the 1980s which are likely to contribute to women's participation in the labour force.[8]

Single parenthood, even if only a temporary status, is increasing. The number of children involved in divorce in Canada went from approximately 20,000 in 1969 to approximately 42,500 in 1974.[9] The number of illegitimate births in Canada has been approximately 31,000 annually over the last few years.[10] It is projected that by 1985 one in eight children will live in a single-parent family, an increase from one in twelve in 1971.[11] Single parenthood results in shared childrearing and is likely to continue to do so, because society prefers work to welfare. That single parents be self-supporting is more important than that they be home to rear their children.[12]

Cultural values are changing as well. Presumably, some percentage of the increase in working mothers involves women who work out of desire rather than perceived economic necessity. It may also include others who have experienced the social changes of the last few years as devaluing childrearing, so they no longer stay at home. As work becomes increasingly valued and mothering less so, there are likely to be those staying at home who need support for a demanding task no longer so valued. In each case again shared childrearing is likely to result.

The practice of shared childrearing seems particularly likely to continue if, in a time of diminishing support from values, there are increasing pressures associated with the task. These pressures are not often considered and so are presented in some detail here.

Pressures of contemporary childrearing. Society has beliefs about who should care for or socialize children, about how it should be done, about the qualities a child will have if the process is successful, and about whose fault it is if it is not successful. It seems reasonable to assume that these beliefs can influence the stress associated with childrearing and in consequence can influence the quality of care. For example, a culture which attributes a child's undesirable behaviour to 'evil forces' is likely to produce less anxiety in those charged with socializing children than one which attributes undesirable behaviour to the inadequacy of the socializing agent.

It can be argued that the current beliefs about child care in our society are making childrearing increasingly stressful. Assuming that, as the sources of stress associated with childrearing increase, the forms of childrearing will change in response, not having children and sharing childrearing can be seen as two responses to this increase in stress.

Three concurrent factors will be considered. They are: (1) *Influence* - attributing a causal role in shaping the child's character to the socialization agent in the child's early years, (2) *Responsibility* - giving primary responsibility for early socialization to the mother, and (3) *Uncertainty* - arising from an open-ended socialization process and rapid change in the principles governing childrearing.

Influence. Theories assuming the malleability of the individual at birth have had a widespread influence for some time,[13] at least since Locke in the seventeenth century, whose writings about children as being *tabula rasa* coincided with self-conscious attempts to socialize children. Two major psychological theories of the twentieth century, Freudian theory and behaviourism, share the premise that primary responsibility for an individual's character can be attributed to the early environment in which s/he functions after birth. These theories are likely to have had a role in sustaining this view in contemporary North American societies.

Responsibility. Of all the individuals in a child's environment, it has in recent history been the mother to whom the responsibility for socialization of a very young child falls. Within the tradition of a nuclear family, it is she who spends extended periods of time with the child.[14] It is within this relationship that much of the child's early education occurs.

Uncertainty. Berger et al. discuss consequences of modernization. In their view, one consequence is that 'modern identity is *"peculiarly open."* While undoubtedly there are certain features of the individual that are more or less permanently stabilized at the conclusion of primary socialization, the modern individual is nonetheless peculiarly "unfinished" as he enters adult life.[15] From society's point of view the open-endedness is functional. Currently, change is so rapid that skills required by the society are not constant within the time it takes a generation to mature. Open-endedness in identity means that the people in a society have the flexibility to fulfil newly evolving roles.[16] The open-endedness is also positive for individuals in that they can continue to explore and develop their potentialities.[17]

However, a consequence for mothers is very likely to have been a change in the nature of childrearing. What was once a detailed, concrete task to produce farmers, miners, wives, and mothers has become an open-ended task.[18] The changes in society are so rapid that the general assumption is that tomorrow will be different from today. As Slater has said 'There is some ambiguity as to how to socialize the child. "Socialization for what?" is the fundamental question.'[19] Mothers given the responsibility of preparing very young children to enter society do not know what they are preparing them for.[20]

The uncertainty associated with childrearing is not restricted to the 'to what end' aspect of socialization. It also seems to characterize the methods preferred by the society. In an article reviewing the recent history of preferred childrearing methods it is the rapidity of change from one method to another that is striking.[21] According to this article, the methods geared towards obedience and regularity of habits in the 30s and 40s were replaced by a more permissive child-centred approach in the 50s and 60s which, in turn, was replaced by a 'no comment,' 'do what you feel comfortable with' approach in the present. In an era of mass-communication, not only are more people likely to witness and be influenced by the change in philosophy, but the changes are also likely to be effected more rapidly, because of the ease with which information is disseminated.[22] What is the impact of the rapid change? It seems reasonable to assume that a pattern of rapid change weakens the credibility of a new philosophy, independently of its accuracy. The result is an uncertainty about how to raise children. It is an uncertainty that does not have the traditional remedy of turning to one's parents for help in childrearing for, because of the change, parents' information is now fallible. The result is a reliance on 'how to' books and consultation with experts,[23] who are often telling parents to do what you feel comfortable with, a response not likely to reduce uncertainty.

Three beliefs characterizing childrearing in contemporary modern society have been identified. Mothers are responsible in early childhood and are assumed to have an influence early in life. They are provided with ambiguous guidelines as to what the outcome is supposed to be and on how to achieve whatever outcome is desired. It is this combination of responsibility and influence with uncer-

TABLE 1
Percentage of ever married women who are childless

Age	Year	
	1963(%)	1971(%)
15–19	42.3	49.7
20–24	26.3	42.0
25–29	13.6	20.7

NOTE: Another interpretation of these data is that the increase in the percentage of ever married women who are childless reflects more effective birth control and not that fewer women desire to have children.

tainty which is likely to make the childrearing task seem difficult, if not overwhelming, to some mothers.

Sharing childrearing with others may be a way to reduce the stress. Others are available to consult as well as to share the blame in the case of perceived failure. Involving other people makes the task less preoccupying and one's self-esteem is less dependent on the outcome to the extent that free time is spent on other valued activities.

If shared childrearing is in part a response to the stress associated with contemporary childrearing, there should be other trends which are also plausible responses to the stress. For example, data should indicate that more people are deciding not to have children. There are data which suggest that this is the case, but it should be noted that the data are open to alternative interpretations. A tendency for women to wait longer to have children has been noted in both Canada[24] and the U.S.[25] Recent data from Canada are included in Table 1. Among the women aged 25–29 there is an increase of 50 per cent between the years 1963 and 1971 in the percentage of those ever married who are childless. After World War II, a similar lag in births was noted. As the women got older the percentage of those having children did not catch up to the percentage of women in earlier generations.[26] Should this be true again, the result would be fewer women having children. If so, there are fewer women having children and more sharing their child's rearing, each of which may reflect the stresses associated with contemporary childrearing.

There is evidently some concern that data such as these may represent a long-term problem. At an Ontario provincial seminar on the family in May 1977 the possibility was raised that the state may need to intervene and provide 'incentives to the family to raise children.'[27] And it has been argued that, if social policy regarding children's well-being does not change, the result may well be a 'flight from motherhood' and a 'flight from parenthood.'[28]

It has been suggested that there are numerous reasons why shared childrearing is prevalent and is likely to continue to be so. Therefore, it is important to understand the significance of shared childrearing for a child's development. Both the direct effect on the child and the indirect effect on the child through the effect on the people rearing the child are important to consider. Also, because the effects of shared childrearing are unlikely to be constant in all situations or for all infants and children, it is important to understand not only the advantages and disadvantages of shared childrearing as a phenomenon in general, but also, how the specific contexts in which it occurs heighten or diminish the expected effects.

It is not possible to consider the impact of shared childrearing on a child's development in total in this chapter. The area of competence has been selected as a focus. The following discussion of competence and how it develops in children will set the stage for a consideration of how shared childrearing directly and indirectly affects this aspect of a child's development.

The Development of Competence as a Focal Point
The discussion to follow focuses on the impact of shared childrearing on the *ongoing development of competence* – competence broadly defined as interacting effectively with the environment.[29]

There are four components of the ongoing development of competence which are important to identify for this discussion. The first is conceptual development, and entails learning the rules of the environment. In order to be effective or to have the intended effect in an interaction with the environment, it is necessary to have an understanding of the particular physical and social reality. If you do X, Y is likely to happen. However, this conceptual understanding is not sufficient. Effective action also implies a level of proficiency in acting which is acquired over time through practice and this is the second component of the ongoing development of competence. It takes time and practice to learn to do X so that Y will follow, even after you know it is possible. Each of the first two components, conceptual understanding and skilled action, evolves over time and depends upon opportunities to explore the environment, acquiring knowledge and using opportunities to practice actions with the intention of becoming proficient. Level of competence reflects a stage in a process of development and it is this process of development which is the third component of the ongoing development of competence. The fourth component is an assumption that in our society it is advantageous for the development of competence to be an ongoing process. It facilitates adaptation. The ongoing development of competence is an 'ongoing' exploration of the environment, adding to a conceptual understanding of the physical and social reality and an ongoing practice of skills needed to be effective in interactions.

As presented, the ongoing development of competence is a general concept. In this chapter, research on a range of behaviours is presented as relevant to an understanding of the development of competence, based on the assumption that the principles governing the learning of different kinds of competence are the same. For example, the process of learning to be effective in interaction with the physical and the social worlds is assumed to be similar even though what is learned is very different. Therefore, data from research on either are presented as relevant to the general process.[30]

There are two reasons for focusing on the general concept of the ongoing development of competence. First, being competent or effective is valued in our society and it is important to know how it is affected by shared childrearing.[31] Second, given rapid change in the society and the open-ended nature of socialization discussed earlier, it is important to focus on the *ongoing* development of competence because, if the process is ongoing, it is likely to contribute to the individuals' ability to adapt to the changing requirements of the society. Therefore, knowing how shared childrearing affects the motivation to acquire knowledge and master new skills is important because this motivation underlies an ongoing process which is adaptive in this society.[32]

II COMPETENCE AND EXPLORATORY BEHAVIOUR

At birth, infants have a range of competence essentially limited to eliciting caretaking behaviour.[33] They are not competent in an adult sense. As a consequence, infants and young children spend a great deal of time learning the competencies necessary in their society. They are motivated to do so, but the outcome depends on the environment. The next few pages elaborate briefly on these ideas to establish that the environment has an influence on the development of competence.

Innate Motivation
Many theorists assume that the development of competence would be unlikely if there were not an *innate motivation to explore the environment* in the interests of becoming effective in interaction with it.[34] Piaget[35] and Freud[36] both have been impressed with the infant's persistent attempts to master new behaviours and to deal with the environment. Piaget's focus has been on the development of mental representations (schema) of the physical realities a child encounters, such as the permanence of objects and conservation of matter. His description of a 10-month old child follows:

He grasps in succession a celluloid swan, a box, and several other small objects, in each case stretching out his arm and letting them fall. Sometimes he stretches out his arm vertically, sometimes he holds it obliquely in front of or behind his eyes. When the object falls in a new position (for example on his pillow) he lets it fall two or three times more in the same place, as though to study the spatial relation; then he modifies the situation.[37]

The self-initiated physical repetition of an event with variations on a theme is strikingly described and forms the basis of acquiring mental constructs about physical realities.

Freud focused more on a child's use of mental repetition. To deal with a fear-arousing event, such as a mother leaving a child alone, Freud suggests that the child re-enacts the event in his/her imagination, introducing symbolic variations which help the child master the fear. For example, the child may pretend that it was the child who left and that the child returns, accomplishing symbolic control over the situation and reassurance of the mother's return. Whether it be mental or physical repetitions of an event, both writers capture the very active way in which children grapple with the unfamiliar complexities of their world.

Evidence collected in recent years, building on Piaget's notions, showing the pleasure various forms of mastery provide to the infant at even a very early age, reinforces the notion of an innate motivation to explore. For example, Watson reports that infants 5-8 weeks old, who had mobiles in their cribs which they could move by turning their heads (contingent mobiles), learned to turn the mobile and were observed to smile earlier and more frequently than infants who had either a stabile or a non-contingent mobile in the crib. He concludes that since the 'machines were not rewarding, smiling and cooing, it seems reasonable to assume that the contingency experience was releasing these responses.'[38] The 'contingency experience' is the experience of one's action having the expected effect. Other work has shown that not only do infants take pleasure in having an effect on their environments, but that they also take pleasure in forming concepts or familiarizing themselves with a multitude of novel objects in their environments.[39] The complement to these findings also seems to be true. Losing the ability to control a part of the environment once under control, in this case a person, is aversive.[40] All these findings are based on work with infants less than six months old. Already active interaction with the environment is a prevalent source of pleasure. Both skilled action and conceptual development are sources of pleasure and the result is likely to be the development of competence.

In summary, these data are representative of findings suggesting that even very young infants experience pleasure when their efforts to master their environments, by acting on them or by developing concepts about them, are successful. On the contrary, loss of mastery is aversive. In a very young infant there is a motivation to improve inborn and developing rudimentary skills in order to be effective in interaction with the social and physical environments.

Environment as an Influence on Motivation and Competence
Infants cannot engage in this pursuit of mastery without help. The environment provided by the people on whom the infant is dependent is of great importance to the development of competence. There is a large literature documenting the emotional, physical, and intellectual malfunction occurring frequently among children raised in institutions.[41] These environments are often characterized by extreme deprivation of both stimulation and interpersonal contact, because children are left alone in cribs except for routine childcare. A major work by Skeels provides a stark example of the effects of inadequate environments on children's development. Thirteen children, not yet three years of age, scoring in the retarded range on an IQ test, were transferred from an orphanage to an adult ward for the mentally retarded. Twelve others of the same age, not quite as retarded in mental development, remained in the orphanage. All the children were later retested for changes in mental capacity. After stays ranging from five to fifty-four months in the adult ward, the thirteen children showed gains in IQ ranging from 7 to 58 points, most gaining more than 20 points. Of the twelve children who remained in the orphanage, one gained 2 points in IQ and the others lost from 8 to 45 IQ points.[47] A follow-up study twenty years later revealed that all thirteen individuals in the experimental group were self-supporting and independent, with a median education of Grade 12. Of the other group, five remained institutionalized. All the others, with one exception, had menial jobs and a median education of Grade 3.[43]

In less dramatic circumstances, it has been shown that the environment influences the level of proficiency at a given time. For example, biological capacity,[44] social interaction skills,[45] and cognitive development[46] have all been shown to be associated with specifiable aspects of the individual's environment early in life.

There are also data which raise the possibility that the strength of the motivation to explore is affected by early environmental influences. Watson's work with infants and mobiles suggests that an infant's tendency to learn to control an object in the environment can be affected by experiences as early as eight weeks. Infants who were exposed to the non-contingent mobile (moving independently of their own behaviour) did not learn how to control it when its movement became contingent. This was true even six weeks later. The infants' motivation to learn to control the environment may have been affected.[47]

Other research done with older children and adults suggests that experiencing a non-contingent environment can result in 'learned helplessness.' While learning what one can control and what it is a waste of effort for one to try to control is important, this research suggests that non-contingent experiences can result in an inappropriate belief that things cannot be controlled or that one is helpless to affect them. A person who believes that s/he is helpless is less likely to explore and gather information in the interest of interacting more effectively in the environment than a person who believes that s/he is able to obtain desired outcomes.[48]

As one would expect from this discussion, research has shown that low levels of responsiveness to the environment (apathy, reservedness) in kindergarten children are associated with less active hypothesis testing and less mental alertness[49] and with poor achievement in grades one and two.[50] A child whose response to the environment is to withdraw is not very likely to gain needed information and experience to support efforts at coping and growth.

To summarize, human infants are motivated to explore their surroundings. Exploring provides knowledge and opportunities to practice developing skills, thereby aiding infants to be effective in their interactions. Being effective and knowing that one can learn to have the desired effect, in turn, make continued exploration likely. In other words, exploration and competence are part of an interdependent cycle. The cycle begins with exploration. How it will evolve is in part dependent on the environmental conditions present.

Once one accepts the proposition that the child's environment has an effect on his/her level of competence by affecting knowledge, level of proficiency, and possibly motivation to expand and improve these levels, all of which are important to the continuing adaptation necessary in life,[51] the question of *how* the environment influences development becomes critical. This question is raised next. What are the conditions necessary in the development of competence? Then discussion turns to consider how shared childrearing might affect development and motivation by assessing the extent to which various forms of shared childrearing provide the conditions necessary in the development of competence. The final question for discussion is whether some forms of shared childrearing can actually supplement environments which are not likely to help children develop their competence.

Principles of Learning
Five variables are considered in this section. Each is assumed to be important in learning to be effective in interaction with the environment, and each is likely to be affected by the sharing of childrearing. If the interdependent cycle described earlier is accurate, since each is important in learning to be effective, each also has implications for whether or not exploration and continuing efforts at mastery are likely. Whenever data are available as to the effects of the environment on motivation, which is rarely, they will be presented.

First, it is assumed that learning depends upon *opportunity*. Second, given opportunity, it is necessary for a situation to elicit *attention* to what is to be learned. Third, given opportunity and attention, learning that one is effective requires that outcomes be experienced as *contingent on self-initiated actions*, and fourth, that they be the *intended outcomes*. The fifth variable, the subject of considerable debate, is the *security of the mother-infant attachment relationship*. A secure relationship is assumed by some to be necessary for exploratory behaviour and learning, even given all the other conditions. At a minimum, a secure mother-infant attachment is likely to support exploratory behaviour and amplify learning when all other conditions are present.

Stating that these are conditions necessary to learning does not mean that they need *always* be present. What is more likely is that a range of conditions will be suited to a child's development, the range depending on the child's individual characteristics.[52]

What follows is not a thorough discussion of each variable, but it is hoped that enough information is provided that the effect of shared childrearing on these conditions is seen to be an important concern. There are likely to be other conditions important in learning and later work will need to address these too.

Opportunity
In order to learn there must be an opportunity to learn. It follows that childrearing environments providing greater opportunity for learning will result in greater learning. Even though this statement is just good common sense, some of the research will be reported briefly.

As suggested earlier, it is through repeated exposure to objects or events that an accurate mental representation (schema) of them develops. When an individual is exposed to a new object, an effort is made to integrate it into existing schema. When that is not possible, then either new schema evolve or existing schema are modified as required. Based on these ideas, variety in the environment would be expected to be related to measures of schema development.[53]

The number and variety of inanimate objects in a child's environment and the variety of daily stimulation are related to cognitive development as measured by IQ at six months,[54] at three years,[55] and at five years,[56] and as measured by ability to use language from two to six years of age.[57] Also of importance to the likelihood of continuing cognitive development is the finding that a greater variety of inanimate objects in the environment goes with a greater tendency to explore a novel object at six months.[58] It would seem that variety not only contributes to conceptual development, but also sustains exploratory behaviour.[59] In summary, the variety provided in the child's environment seems to be important in the development of intellectual and language skills in children from early infancy to six years at least and to exploratory behaviour.

There are data which confirm that specific skills require skill-related opportunities for development. For example, it has been found that qualities of
the objects in the environment are related to conceptual development and
exploratory behaviour, but not to language development or social responsiveness.[60] Vocalization is more responsive to vocal imitation than to food or tactile
stimulation.[61] Wachs found that, among 21-month-old infants, being able to scan
the environment and finding more manipulable objects during scanning are both
related to learning that a stick can be used to bring a ball towards you, or, in
more abstract terms, in learning to use an object as a means to an end.[62]

Other studies suggest that language development is related specifically to exposure to language and the opportunity for its use provided in the environment.
Lytton et al.'s work with twins shows that twins' poor performance on intelligence tests,[63] and in vocabulary and language tests in particular,[64] may well be
attributable to less language stimulation.[65] Comparing parents' behaviour to
three-year-old twins and singletons in two three-hour home observations, they
found, among other things, that parents spoke less to twins, gave fewer com-
mands, reasoned and suggested less. The twins spoke less and their speech was
less mature than that of singletons. The importance of opportunities to language
development is confirmed again at age 11.[66]

Appropriate and diverse skill-related opportunities are more likely to result with greater variety than with less variety in the childrearing environment.

The long-term implications of the absence of skill-specific opportunity are
not clear. Wachs suggests that there may be critical periods for the provision of
certain kinds of stimulation.[67] His finding that both being able to scan the environment and having manipulable objects available are important to developing
the ability to use objects as a means to a goal is an example of a possible critical
period. The relationship appeared only at 21 months in assessments made every
three months from 12 to 24 months. However, from his data it is not possible to
say what the consequence is of a failure to provide skill-specific opportunities
within an optimum range. Perhaps it is less adequate development of the particular skill in the long run or perhaps it is just slower development. It is important
for future work to clarify this finding and the implications.

In summary, evidence suggests that the variety of stimulation provided in a
child's early environment influences the level of competence developed and possibly the strength of exploratory motivation. The long term implications of failure to provide opportunity at what may be optimal moments are not clear and
need to be addressed. There will be further discussion of opportunity when the
extent to which forms of shared childrearing affect the number and variety of
opportunities available to a child is considered.

Attention

Not all analyses involving differences in opportunity reveal that greater opportunity is associated with competence. For example, Wachs et al. found that the greater number of individuals in and out of the home and the number of trips downtown, the slower conceptual development was, measured in terms of progress through Piaget's stages of conceptual development.[68]

Opportunity, while a necessary condition, is not a sufficient condition for learning to occur. In order to learn it is necessary to attend to what is to be learned. Because environments are too complex to attend to everything in them, selective attention is necessary. Factors which influence attention, and through attention learning, have been the focus of theorizing and experimental work for the last twenty years at least.[69]

Cognitive criterion for attention: moderate discrepancy. Before the infant has acquired any mental representations of the environment, a *change* in stimuli elicits attention as long as it does not elicit fear and defensive attack or withdrawal. Through repeated exposure the infant becomes familiar with the stimulus and develops a mental representation of it. As already discussed, it is assumed that once a mental representation develops, a stimulus discrepant from it elicits attention.[70] Several theorists go one step farther to suggest that there is an optimal level of discrepancy for eliciting attention. Novel stimuli, moderately discrepant from existing schema, are assumed to be preferred and to facilitate conceptual development at an optimal rate. As the infant's experiences accumulate and mental representations become more complex, greater and greater complexity becomes optimal.

The evidence does not clearly support or refute the notion of optimal discrepancy,[71] but if it should, it adds stage-specific requirements to the development of competence. In this situation, the advantage of variety may be that it allows an infant to maximize his/her rate of development.

Contextual criterion for attention: optimal level of arousal. What factors, other than stimulus discrepancy, affect attention and thereby learning? There is considerable evidence that one of the most important influences on attention is the level of arousal or the level of alertness, ranging from sleep to frantic activity, mediated by the environment.

Arousal can affect development in many ways. For example, a high level of arousal can interfere with exploratory behaviour by producing withdrawal or fear.[72] High arousal can also interfere with the ability to notice or remember information.[73] The effect of the level of arousal on attention to information in the environment is considered in some detail here to demonstrate its significance to learning.

It has been argued that as arousal increases, the amount of information noticed and used by a person decreases. At first, increasing arousal should lead to improved performance through a more appropriate focusing of concentration. Irrelevant information is less likely to be perceived and to interfere with learning. However, as arousal continues to increase and the information attended to continues to decrease, relevant information is likely to be missed. Therefore, as arousal continues to increase, it will lead to a decrement in performance and learning. Increasing arousal at first facilitates and then interferes with learning and performance. It also seems that the amount of information required to perform or learn increases as the difficulty of the task increases. Therefore, the level of arousal optimal for performance and learning decreases as task difficulty increases because, as task difficulty increases, the range of cues requiring attention is greater.[74]

These notions explain the results of a highly celebrated study by Yerkes and Dodson in 1908.[75] Rats learning a task were shocked following incorrect responses, different groups receiving different intensities of shock. Presumably, arousal increases with increasing intensity of shock. Yerkes and Dodson found that the speed with which rats learned the task was curvilinearly (inverted U shape) related to the intensity of shock. Increasing arousal first facilitated learning. Then it interfered.

The same pattern appears with human subjects. Individuals were ranked according to assumptions about their prevalent state of arousal. Given an easy task to learn, the moderately aroused group performed better than either the low or high arousal groups. Given a more difficult task, the low arousal groups performed the best and the differences in performance between the moderate and high arousal groups diminished.[76]

The studies assume differences in arousal. To be sure that differences in arousal have the expected effect it is necessary to manipulate them. It has been found that Atropine, a drug which decreases arousal, improved attention, while Emphademine, a drug which increases arousal, interfered with attention, suggesting that changes in arousal are involved as expected.[77]

In summary, there seems to be, at first, a facilitating and then a debilitating effect of increasing arousal on learning, due, for example, to changes in attention to information relevant to the learning task. By focusing on the effects of arousal on attention, only one aspect in an extremely complex process has been identified. However, the implication from even this one area is that childrearing environments differing in the level of arousal they mediate will influence what is learned in them.

There has been little work done on the extent to which environments differ in the arousal they mediate. There is one study which is suggestive – that done by Wachs et al. with infants in their homes.[78] A striking set of findings emerges in their data. The greater the noise level, the less able the child is to escape the noise and the greater the activity level in the home, the less the cognitive development of the child. For the first two measures, this relationship was found in each of six assessments made at three-month intervals from seven to twenty-four months.

Noisy home environments may affect the child's level of competence well beyond infancy. It has been found that the ability to make auditory discrimination is poorer in disadvantaged than in advantaged pre-school children, and it is assumed to be partly an effect of a noisier home environment.[79] Less adequate auditory discrimination may in turn contribute to later reading difficulties for these children.[80]

Other findings suggest that the implications of overstimulation in the environment depend upon the source of stimulation. Variety which exceeds a child's capacity to process it can be overstimulating, whether it be number of people or settings the child is exposed to or variety of physical stimulation in the immediate surroundings. However, these forms of overstimulation seem first to hinder cognitive development for a period of time and then to facilitate it.[81] It may be that massive stimulation relevant to conceptual development challenges the infants' capacities to their utmost, in the long run resulting in accelerated development and a positive experience in coping with a demanding task. These findings suggest that it is important to distinguish among types of overstimulation. Some, like variety of stimulation, may be only temporarily problematic and in the long run facilitative. Others, like noise, hunger, or fear, may make high arousal a more pervasive problem for the development of competence. Perhaps the relevant distinction is between arousal mediated by the task itself and background sources of arousal.

In addition to having a direct impact on the infant, variables like noise are likely to have an impact on the other individuals in the environment. Using noise as an example, if the infant cannot escape the noise, it is likely that others in the environment cannot. If the noise affects the arousal of others, then they too are less likely to be able to attend to what is going on. One consequence may be that they are less likely to notice the infant. Unnoticed, the infant is less likely to elicit satisfactory caretaking from his/her environment. And so, the infant is less likely to maintain a sense of mastery vis à vis the environment. It is important not to overlook the potential of an overstimulating environment to disrupt the responsiveness of that environment.

To summarize, this section of the paper has argued that, in order to learn, the infant must be attending to what is to be learned. Attention is not automatic. Some environments can elicit more attention than others. While the evidence is far from complete, two assumptions characterize current thinking in this area. The aspects of the environment which have been suggested as influential in their capacity to elicit attention are first, the match between the environment and the developmental level of the infant, and second, the level of arousal mediated by the environment. Environments which provide stimuli moderately discrepant from an infant's current schema, in a surround which does not interfere with attention, are assumed to be most likely to facilitate learning.

It will be important in the discussion of various forms of shared childrearing to consider how they effect the likelihood that optimal discrepancy and optimal arousal exist.

Contingency

The two conditions of opportunity and attention have been touched on as relevant to learning. One cannot learn about things with which one has no experience, and for learning to occur at an optimal rate both the objects in one's environment and one's own state may need to meet certain conditions. However, opportunity and attention are not sufficient for learning to occur. A third aspect involves the notion of contingency. A response to one's action is experienced as contingent when it follows the action soon enough and frequently enough that the cause of its occurrence is assumed to be one's action. There are three aspects of contingency, thus defined. They are response delay, response consistency, and self-initiation of the action.

Response delay. Response delay refers to the delay between one's action and the occurrence of the event of interest.

Two studies assess the effect of delay in the responses of those caring for infants. They suggest that when an infant acts, and there is little delay in the response, the infant learns that s/he is effective and the refinement of skills is accelerated. This seems to apply to different kinds of learning. The data suggest that prompt, and presumably effective, maternal responses to an infant's distress are associated at six months with more advanced mental and psychomotor development in general and with specific skills such as goal-directedness[82] and with less crying and more differentiated communication at one year.[83]

Watson, whose work was discussed earlier regarding the pleasure eight-week-old infants experience when they learn to control their environments, suggests that delay is particularly important in infants' learning, not just because delay hinders the perception of contingency, but because infants have a short memory span and the response must occur before the infant forgets his/her action for learning to occur.[84] While older children have longer memory spans, too long a delay still means that they are unlikely to see a response as a consequence of their action.

Consistency. There is a second part of contingency that is involved in learning that a response is contingent upon one's action. It is consistency. If a person's response to a child's action is always prompt, but also always different (once smiling, once frowning), then the child is less likely to develop an awareness that his/her action is causing the result than when a person's response to the child is prompt and similar. Consistency then describes the similarity of the responses to a particular action of a child over time. Responses to a child's actions can be described on various dimensions, such as delay, acceptance of the action, or effectiveness of the response. Consistency is a characteristic which can be applied to each of these dimensions. It is assumed that as inconsistency increases on any one of the dimensions of the response, the likelihood of perceiving that one is the cause of the response decreases. Some dimensions are likely to be more important than others in that inconsistency will be more disruptive of learning. Also, inconsistency can characterize the responses of one person or it can characterize the pattern of responding of two people or more. The impact of inconsistency may or may not be the same in these two situations. These are some of the issues raised by a consideration of the concept of consistency.[85]

Even though concern about inconsistency is frequently expressed,[86] there is little research to confirm or refute these assumptions or to answer the questions alluded to above. The studies provide more of a patchwork effect, a piece here and a piece there, rather than a systematic whole.

Watson's work suggests that inconsistency has a particularly important role in an infant's efforts to learn, because inconsistencies managed by an adult are beyond the discriminative capacities of the child.[87] In one study 8 week old infants were exposed to two mobiles. One's movement was contingent on the infant turning his/her head and the other was not. There was an increase in head turning in response to both mobiles and then a decrease back to the baseline level, again for both mobiles. Another group of infants was exposed to a mobile which was partially contingent on their head turning responses. Either 40 per cent or 60 per cent of the time when an infant moved his/her head the mobile turned. In this situation the infants' head turning never increases above a baseline level of responding. When two almost identical stimuli had different patterns of contingency or when one stimulus was inconsistently contingent, the discrimination was too hard for the infant to learn. The infant's efforts at control were not effective. Taking this study as an analogy, inconsistencies beyond a child's discriminative capacity are likely to result in learning that one is not effective.

Another study which is suggestive found that mothers who report that they tried to be consistent in disciplining their children are more likely to have children with high self-esteem than mothers who do not report efforts to be consistent. High self-esteem goes with good academic performance, social adjustment, and creativity in this study.[88] It may be that consistency helped these children to acquire various necessary competencies and to develop their creativity (ongoing exploration?) by providing them with an environment in which they could learn to be effective.

In summary, although there is considerable confidence, there is very little literature confirming the interference of inconsistency in responses to the child's actions with the child's developing an ability to interact effectively. Research in this area is needed.

Self-initiation. The third aspect of contingency, important in learning that one's action has caused a response, is self-initiation. A child experiencing hunger pains who is fed without having a chance to cry for food is less likely to learn that s/he can be effective in interaction with the environment than a child who has to cry. Assuming in both cases that the mother's behaviour is responsive, that there is little delay after the onset of hunger pains, that the mother is consistent in responding, and that the mother's response alleviates the hunger pains, in the first case the infant has no chance to act to alleviate the need and so the development of competence is unlikely.

There is some research relevant to this concept. Home environments with fewer physical barriers to exploration and in which mothers did not interfere in the infant's exploration produced children who were more advanced in development.[89] It has also been found that, within a context of a variety of objects, mothers who provide the objects for the infants to explore have infants who are less advanced at six months than infants whose mothers had a less active role.[90] This work suggests that the infant's active role in taking advantage of opportunities available in the environment is an important component of learning.

Similar relationships have been reported between fathers' behaviours and their school-age sons' intellectual development. Nurturent, as opposed to restrictive, fathers had sons scoring higher in IQ tests. Interestingly, father's nurturance during a task went with lower performance.[91] It seems again that it is the opportunity to engage in self-initiated learning within a context of opportunity that is important to the development of competence.[92]

It is suggested, therefore, that interference with a child's actions, through anticipation or substitution, can impede the development of competence. There is a cognitive process parallel to this behavioural one which becomes increasingly important as the child matures. A child's desire to explore and to expand his/her range of competence can be weakened by rewarding the child's behaviour.[93] Hunt would say that the child's behaviour has been brought under the control of task extrinsic motivation, a reward. The consequence is to weaken the task intrinsic motivation, i.e. the child performs for the reward and not for the pleasure intrinsic to the task or to self-initiated action.

Lepper et al. worked with nursery school children who were selected on the basis of their high interest in the drawing task involved in the study. One group was offered a 'good player' award for their participation. Another group received the 'good player' award unexpectedly after completing the task. A third group neither expected nor received such an award. The childrens' interest in the task was measured by observing how much they drew in a free-play session. The children in the anticipated reward condition drew less and exhibited much less interest in the task than either of the other two groups. Receiving a reward per se did not lessen interest, because the unexpected award group got the same award as the expected award group, but drew more than that group in the free-play session.[94]

Why are rewards problematic? Assuming that when an individual observes an effect, either of his/her own action or of another's action, she/he looks for an explanation of that effect, Kelly suggests that 'the role of a given cause in producing a given effect is discounted if other plausible causes are also present.'[95] When a person does something, that person observes why s/he might have done it. If there are reasons other than personal interest, the explanation of personal interest is discounted. A reward is such a reason.[96]

In summary, self-initiation of behaviour appears important both in developing competence and sustaining practice and exploration. Either physical intervention in the child's activity or intervention through structures such as rewards may turn out to be what Condry calls 'enemies of exploration.'[97]

Summary. In addition to opportunity and attention, contingency is important to learning. Responses to an infant's action which are prompt and consistent enough that the infant can perceive that s/he is the cause facilitate the development of skills for interacting effectively with the physical and social environments.

Environments are likely to vary in the extent of contingent experience they provide and therefore in the extent to which they enable an infant to develop competence. But how the *pattern* of contingent experience provided by a childrearing environment influences the child has not been examined.

Non-contingency is a fact of life and young children seem to learn to recognize this. Pre-school children believe they are less able to influence their peers than their parents or teachers.[98] Black children in the U.S. assume less control over their outcomes when interacting with a white experimenter than with a black experimenter.[99] Infants whose mothers are insensitive and rejecting have been found to reject their mother's efforts at contact, but to explore their environments. In terms of control, these infants approach the approachable parts of their environments (objects) and avoid the uncontrollable (mothers).[100]

However, it is also true that non-contingent experiences can be generalized inappropriately within a situation,[101] and possibly, more importantly, across situations to become a belief that one's outcomes are beyond one's control.[102] There is evidence that individuals who believe that outcomes are not within their control make less effort to learn about the world around them,[103] are more dependent on external instruction to focus their learning,[104] have less focused attention on tasks when skill is important to the outcome,[105] are less fluent verbally,[106] and are less likely to persist.[107] The reverse picture is also true. People who believe that their outcomes are within their control are more likely to gather relevant information, to determine for themselves what they attend to, to be more focused in their attention, to be more fluent verbally, and to persist. From this description it is apparent that the belief that one is helpless to gain the intended effect is likely to interfere with the development of competence and the use of existing capabilities. More information about what aspects of the experience of non-contingency lead to a cognitive predisposition that outcomes are beyond one's control is needed.

Contingency is likely to be an important aspect of childrearing environments, and how the extent of contingency provided is likely to be affected by various forms of childrearing is further pursued later in this chapter.

Correspondence between Intention and Outcome
What if a response has all the aspects thus far described, but is not the one intended? That a response be the one intended seems fundamental to learning and interacting effectively. There is little work in this area with very young children, probably because the effectiveness of a response from the infant's point of view is difficult to measure. Infants cannot verbalize their intentions. However, there are data which can be interpreted as consistent with the expectation that effectiveness facilitates development. Mothers, who in responding to their infants' cries change their mode of response less, have infants who exhibit more advanced communication skill at one year.[108] Assuming that less change indicates effectiveness, then effectiveness is related to more advanced development. Other work has indicated that holding a child, especially in an upright position, is more effective in comforting than, for example, talking softly.[109] This may explain why the single most important variable in the Yarrow et al. study of infant development at six months was variation in the extent of kinesthetic stimulation.[110] Changing position by picking up and holding is a primary example of this kind of stimulation. Mothers who are more likely to pick up their children may be stimulating them more as Yarrow et al. suggest, but they may also be using a more effective method of comforting when the infant cries. The infant may be learning that s/he is effective in eliciting the desired response from the environment and this may be important to the advanced development exhibited by these infants at six months.

In terms of meeting very basic needs, the importance of those in the environment learning to respond with the desired response, be it food, comforting, stimulation, etc., probably cannot be overestimated. It is very likely to be the beginning of the infant's sense of trust, not only that the environment will provide but, given the other conditions here, that s/he is effective in eliciting what is needed from the environment.

Summary
The data suggest, though the conclusion must be taken as tentative, that in order to develop competence or a sense of effectiveness in interaction with the environment infants and children need to have the opportunity to observe the effects of *their* actions on outcomes and to function in situations in which desired outcomes are *contingent* upon their actions. Under these circumstances they are likely to perceive the world as one in which they can be effective. This perception goes with acting, exploring the environment, and learning, all of which are assumed to increase the sense of competence in a circular reinforcing fashion.

Attachment
There is an additional aspect of a childrearing relationship which is important to the development of competence. It is attachment, defined as 'strong interdependence and intense affect.'[111] The conditions which foster its development have also been described.

... attachment is fostered by the availability of someone who has a distinctive relationship with the infant, who is *contingently responsive* to the baby's signals, and who *engages him in a stimulating interaction*. The latter two qualities may be viewed together as maternal behaviour which *maximizes the infant's attentiveness* to the external world. When the mother responds promptly to his distress states, the infant is made free to attend to a wide range of external stimuli. At the same time, *the mother herself is a source of varied stimulation which engages the infant's attention.*

How did these findings fit with the widely held notions concerning the importance of maternal warmth and nurturance in infant care? We believe that warmth, nurturance, stimulation and contingent responsiveness are not distinctively different aspects of the mother-infant relationship. They refer to similar qualities at different levels of abstraction. For example, the behavioural referents of emotional warmth are sensitivity to the baby's signals, effectiveness in alleviating his distress, and provision of stimulation in order to engage his attention and responsiveness capacities.[112]

According to this description, attachment is the emotional component of a relationship which is characterized from the infant's point of view as one that provides opportunities to learn in a way which elicits attention and provides contingent feedback. If this description were sufficient to describe the dynamics involved in attachment, then discussion could end, because they would be indistinguishable from the conditions which contribute to the development of competence as they have been presented here. However, there are ways in which one can expand the notion of attachment. One can add a third question to those above – what is attachment and how does it come about? It is, what are the consequences of attachment independent of its being synonymous with conditions which facilitate learning.[113]

There are two ways in which attachment may facilitate the development of competence. The first involves evidence, circumstantial though it may be, which suggests that attachment figures have an impact on the level of arousal mediated by the environment. In discussing the conditions that facilitate attention, it was suggested earlier that the arousal mediated by the context in which learning occurs is a factor. Overstimulating environments interfere with learning by increasing arousal beyond the point where attention focuses on a broad enough range of information to result in appropriate learning. If attachment figures can reduce arousal in such situations, they facilitate learning.

A mother's presence may decrease the arousal potential of a novel environment. The mother is frequently the person who responds to the infant's needs and alleviates the stress associated with them, be it by feeding the infant, or by changing or comforting it. As a consequence, the mother is repeatedly present when there is a reduction in anxiety. Over time, the presence of the mother may come to automatically decrease arousal even when such activities are not involved.[114] If this is the case (no data test this specifically through measures of stress), then the presence of the mother may well facilitate learning by reducing an infant's anxiety response to novelty and thereby encouraging exploratory behaviour.

Consistent with this, there is evidence that children engage in more exploratory behaviour in a novel situation when their mother is present than when she is not. The extent of talking, movement, and play exhibited by approximately fourteen month old children and two-and-a-half-year-old children decreased when their mothers left the experimental room for the middle four minutes of a twelve-minute session. Children began to return to exploratory behaviour when the mother returned.[115]

A naturalistic observation of mothers and their fifteen- to thirty-month olds in a park also suggests that mothers have a role as anxiety reducers. Infants' behaviour was comprised of cyclical movements away from and then back to the mother. The infants explored their environment, but did so by maintaining some kind of psychological contact with their mothers.[116] These data suggest that the attachment relationship with the mother provides a means for dealing with the stress of a novel situation, or what has been called a secure base from which to explore.[117]

Other evidence suggests that fathers and older siblings can also help a child deal with the anxiety of a novel situation,[118] quite possibly as a result of attachment relationships. Additional work is needed to confirm these later findings and the role of attachment figures in general.

Secure attachment may contribute to learning in another way. Thus far a slowed rate of development has been attributed to the failure of the infant-environment interaction to support the innate drive to explore and master. A child may have other needs in addition to the need to explore which interfere with learning when they are not fulfilled. In other words, the need to explore is one need in a context of others.

It has been suggested that attachment behaviours such as proximity seeking (being near an attachment figure) are incompatible with exploratory behaviours.[119] If there is a *need for attachment*, then this need, if unsatisfied, interferes with development by eliciting attachment behaviours in lieu of exploratory behaviour. To examine this notion Ainsworth and her colleagues observed mother-infant interactions.[120] The data did not support it. Children whose mothers' behaviours were not conducive to a secure attachment relationship did not explore less and approach their mothers more. However, it may be that, because the mother is not responsive, the need for attachment is expressed in other relationships. There are some data which suggest that this might be so. A study by Harter is particularly interesting. Institutionalized retarded children learned a task more slowly when an approving, warm experimenter was present than when she was not. Retarded children who were not institutionalized performed better when the experimenter was present. The institutionalized children sought more contact with the approving adult, indicated by the higher incidence of task irrelevant comments directed to the experimenter, and this behaviour interfered with learning the task. It may be that children deprived of an attachment relationship seek one out elsewhere.[121] Attachment seeking behaviour may become part of relationships where they are inappropriate, for example, in a teacher-student relationship. In this way childrearing environments failing to provide a secure attachment may have negative repercussions for social interactions in other settings.

Additional work clarifying the role of an attachment relationship as making an independent contribution to learning and exploratory behaviour and as fulfilling a need which then does not compete with exploratory behaviour is important. If these dynamics are part of what is going on, they have implications for children's abilities to take advantage of optimal learning conditions in other situations. A secure attachment may be a precondition to an optimal rate of development.

In summary, it is being suggested that an attachment relationship may reflect more than provision of the conditions suggested here as important to learning. Two ways in which an attachment contributes to learning in ways not implied in the discussion thus far have been suggested. First, attachment figures may mediate a reduction in arousal in stressful situations. Second, attachment itself may be a need which, if unfulfilled, interferes with learning and exploratory behaviour. If so, attachment is indicative of a more complex set of dynamics than were suggested earlier and further work is needed in these areas.

It has been argued that various qualities are necessary in a childrearing environment if that environment is to be conducive to the ongoing development of competence. These include providing opportunities for learning in a context that elicits attention. Further, to learn to be effective, it is necessary that some as yet undetermined proportion of the events which occur in this context is experienced as the intended consequences of self-initiated action. It has also been suggested that this whole process is facilitated by attachment relationships.

While all of this is plausible, the interpretation of the evidence has been oversimplified. An attempt to broaden the context in which these findings are interpreted follows. The conclusions are not altered, only qualified. Then various forms of shared childrearing will be evaluated in terms of whether or not they provide the conditions necessary to the development of competence.

Context for Interpretation and Application of Findings
Interpretations of research findings take place in a context of current assumptions about what affects human behaviour. To the extent that these assumptions are incomplete, alternative interpretations of findings are likely to be overlooked and there is a risk of premature confidence in explanations of a phenomenon. When a new perspective on findings is offered, additional research is needed to establish the value of each interpretation. Much of the research which has been presented is in that intermediate stage of being open to more than one interpretation because of a change in perspective about what affects human behaviour. Two examples are considered briefly here because they are relevant to the research presented and also because they illustrate the value of a cautious perspective vis-à-vis the application of reasearch findings.

Competence: Capacity and then Performance
Competence was defined earlier as interacting effectively with the environment. It is assumed to result from a motivation to explore and master in a context which provides what is necessary for a skill to emerge. A question which has been frequently asked is how competent is one group of children with a particular childrearing environment when compared with another group exposed to a

different childrearing environment. Using IQ test results as an example, how do we interpret a difference in score? While it seems clear that one group is not as competent as the other, because its members are not interacting as effectively with the environment, a further interpretation is usually made. The lower scores are attributed to less advanced conceptual development, be it the result of less inherited potential or a less adequate childrearing environment. However, the situation in which testing occurs is likely to affect performance. If it affects children differently, then differences in performance may reflect the testing situation and not the children's actual level of conceptual development. And if children are tested in different situations, then it is even more likely that the differences in performance reflect the different testing situations.

To pursue this it is necessary to refine the distinction between the two aspects of competence alluded to. One aspect is *capacity* and the other *performance capability*. Capacity refers to having the skills to bring about desired outcomes. Whether the outcomes are physical, conceptual, or social, a person who is able to accomplish X has that capacity. Having capacity is to have potential. Whether or not the potential is realized depends in part on the situation in which the individual is to perform. Therefore, to have a capacity and to use it are here separated as aspects of competence. When a person is capable of performing up to capacity s/he has the highest level of performance capability.

To perform well on an IQ test means that the person has both the capacity and performance capability aspects of competence. However, it is being argued that a poor performance, often interpreted as indicating lack of capacity, could actually reflect lack of performance capability in that situation. Shaffer and Emerson found that a group of institutionalized infants, who were stimulated for twelve minutes prior to testing, performed significantly better on a test of development than a group of institutionalized infants, who were in a bland environment for twelve minutes prior to testing.[122] Insufficient arousal impeded performance, as would be expected from the earlier discussion of arousal.

The effect of excessive arousal is evident in a study by Zigler and Butterfield.[123] When an IQ test was administered to disadvantaged pre-school children in the standard manner, the children's performance was lower than when the IQ test was administered in an anxiety-reducing manner. The anxiety of the standard administration setting interfered with the children's performance reflecting their capacity.

The importance to performance of differences in the stimulation provided by the environment is evident from these studies. In none of the studies reviewed earlier was this alternative interpretation eliminated. For example, noisy environments were found to hamper conceptual development.[124] But since the infants were tested at home, perhaps noise interfered with performance and the underlying capacity was the same. Or perhaps the association between variety and conceptual development[125] involves better performance because of the greater stimulation available in environments with variety and not a difference in development.

The issue here is not whether there is a difference in competence in the children. There is. The issue involves how to explain it. The explanation is important because interventions are based on the explanation chosen. To provide intensive developmental experiences to increase capacity in a situation when the issue is one of anxiety in the testing setting is an inefficient use of limited resources.[126] For example, in the Zigler and Butterfield study, exposure to a preschool programme brought performance in the standard administrative setting up to the level obtained in the anxiety-reducing setting months earlier. It may be that experience in the pre-school programme helped children deal with their anxiety in the testing situation and that this was sufficient for them to be able to demonstrate their capacity. However, the intensive developmental intervention may not have been necessary for the improvement. Further work separating these effects is needed.

Environment: Cause and Effect

As was suggested earlier, the environment can influence the extent of conceptual understanding an individual has, the level of proficiency an individual acquires, and the level of motivation to explore and to continue developing competencies. While this point is important because shared childrearing is essentially a variation in the environment provided for the child, it is also important to realize that some researchers offer an alternative interpretation for many of the findings.

There has been a great deal of research examining mother-infant interaction in the last few years. A major finding is that mothers who are responsive, accepting, and co-operative have infants who are 'securely' attached to them.[127] The assumption is that the mother influenced the child. She may have. But as has been pointed out, it is equally plausible that the differences are a result of differences in the infants.[128] Taking a look at a set of three findings gives an example of how differences in infants could explain some of the variation of maternal responsiveness and therefore differences in the infant's attachment.

One of the major tasks of infancy is learning to control the amount of stimulus input in order to maintain it at a desired level.[129] When there is insufficient stimulation, crying can bring someone to provide more. When there is excessive stimulation, which is likely to be often, falling asleep can screen it out. It has also been suggested that gaze-aversion is a method of stimulus control available to very young infants when interacting with another person.[130] That is the first finding. The second is that eye-to-eye gazing, and not gaze aversion, is an important precursor of a mother's attachment[131] and responsiveness to her young infant.[132] Adding the third finding, that infants differ in the amount of stimulation they find pleasurable,[133] enables us to raise an interesting question. Is it not plausible that an infant who is particularly sensitive to stimulation will resort to gaze-aversion frequently to attempt to keep stimulation within a tolerable range, with the unforeseen consequence that the mother is less responsive and does not develop as strong an attachment for her infant as she would if her infant engaged in more eye-to-eye contact? If so, then clearly it is important to consider the infant's role in the caretaking and childrearing which evolves.[134] To restate, findings attributed to an influence on the child originating in the environment are attributed by some to the child eliciting particular responses from the environment. This is a plausible interpretation of most of the findings reported earlier. Conceptually advanced infants may have elicited more variety. Difficult infants may have elicited inconsistent responsiveness and so on.

While this perspective is important it is necessary to go one step further, for the limitations of assuming that childrearing is primarily a function of the infant's characteristics have also been pointed out. Sameroff and Chandler suggest that, given an infant with a 'high risk' for developmental difficulty because of prematurity or some other factor, whether or not the difficulty materializes depends upon the environment to which the infant is exposed.[135] The implication is that, rather than assuming that the infant or the environment has an over-riding effect on the outcome of childrearing, it is more appropriate to assume that the effect of the infant depends upon the environment in which s/he is, and vice versa, the effect of the environment depends upon characteristics of the infant.

According to this view, the development of competence is the result of a complex interplay between characteristics of both the infant/child and the environment. Table 2 is presented to set out the possible explanations of a child's level of competence which result from this assumption. In cells A and D the result is similarly influenced, either positively or negatively, by the characteristics of the infant and the environment and the outcome seems relatively straight-forward. In cells B and C, however, the characteristics of the infant and the environment have opposite implications and the outcome is more ambiguous. Possibly, the outcome is dependent upon the capacity of the infant or the environment to adjust to the disadvantageous characteristics in the other. While either high levels of competence or low levels of competence can result, the brief discussion to follow focuses on the outcome of low competence.

There are at least three possible explanations of low competence according to Table 2. Characteristics of the infant, such as gaze aversion, can result in a pattern of interaction which hinders the development of competence, even if the environment was initially advantageous (cell C). Characteristics of the environment, such as unresponsiveness, can result in a pattern of interaction which hinders the development of competence, even if the infant's characteristics initially

TABLE 2
Level of competence

Characteristics of the childrearing environment			
		Advantageous	Disadvantageous
Characteristics of infant/child	Advantageous	Highly competent A	Competent to not competent B
	Disadvantageous	Competent to not competent C	Not competent D

NOTE: The cells in the table represent one moment in time. At a later point in time a different cell might be appropriate. It would depend on whether or not the characteristics involved are modifiable through interaction or maturation or become less significant due to maturation.

favoured the development of competence (cell B). Or characteristics of both infant and environment may result in an interaction pattern which hinders the development of competence (cell D).

Suppose that intervening with the environment when it was the infant's characteristics which were originally problematic or intervening with the infant when it was the environment which was originally problematic is like responding to the symptom rather than the cause. If so, the interventions are not likely to be effective because the cause remains to begin the cycle again. There are all kinds of assumptions being made in these statements which need to be specified and assessed, such as whether causes are equally likely at all ages to contribute to an interaction pattern which hinders the development of competence. However, leaving these tasks for another time, the point is that interventions intended to foster the development of competence need to take into account as much as possible the diversity of factors influencing the process of development. This requires that research explore the dynamics of the different situations suggested in Table 2.

In summary, research for the most part has interpreted findings as reflecting the effects of the environment on the infant and child's developing competence. As a consequence, insight into these more complex patterns of influence is at present quite limited. Expanding the perspective to take into account the interplay between the infant and the childrearing environment is likely to facilitate appropriate application of the findings.

Reversibility of Effects

There is another important issue regarding application of findings and it has to do with how permanent the effects of the early environment are. There is considerable controversy at present. Some view the early years as a critical period in the development of competence, setting the limits within which later development occurs, both in the cognitive[136] and in the social and emotional domains.[137] Others have come to view little, if any, of what occurs in early childhood as irreversible.[138]

What little longitudinal research there has been has not confirmed the assumption of continuity of capacity, continuity being assumed to reflect irreversibility.[139] The failure can be explained in a number of ways; some leave the assumption of continuity intact, others refute it.

Yarrow et al. suggest that the methodology has not been adequate to tap continuity. 'The failure to find direct relations between experience in infancy and later development does not negate the significance of early experience, but rather emphasizes the need for forming more differentiated questions and for defining variables much more precisely.'[140] Earlier, Yarrow pointed out the difficulty of such tasks. For example, to tap an underlying dimension such as dependency is difficult because the indicative behaviours are likely to vary with age. There may be continuity in the trait indicated by a lack of continuity in behaviour.[141] If these are the reasons why research has not found continuity, then continuity may well exist.

Others assume that it does not. A view adopted by a large number of developmental psychologists in recent years is called a transactional approach. It is reflected in the relationship between infant and environment described earlier (see Table 2). The infant and environment, each as shaper and responder, evolve an interaction pattern. There are various views as to whether or not the result is a stable or changeable interaction pattern. One is to assume that the interaction pattern is evolving continuously. The infant influences the environment. The changed environment responds to the infant. The changed infant responds to the environment and so on in cycles of continuous change.[142] Another view is to assume that the reciprocal influence stabilizes into an interaction pattern which requires a more dramatic event to alter its course.[143] These views agree that change occurs. Continuity is not assumed. The difference lies in how readily change comes about.

Kagan takes a slightly different view, suggesting that in the first five years little is crystallized that does not change with accumulating experience. At five or six the capacities to represent the self symbolically and to establish consistency in interaction and expectations have developed sufficiently to influence behaviour. Then, there is some predictability for the future, or continuity.[144]

This debate is important. If Kagan is correct, then the advantages and disadvantages of shared childrearing in early years are not of concern to policy-makers and recommendations around early childrearing can take factors other than the child's welfare more fully into account. However, if early experience is important, then Kagan's position, and others with similar implications, inappropriately alleviate the urgency of evaluating the implications of changes in early childrearing practices for the well-being of children.

There is another point to be made. The debate has focused primarily on reversibility. It may be important to stress another dimension – the ease of reversibility. To say that developmental deficits *can* be reversed does not necessarily mean that they can be reversed with equal ease at any point in an individual's life. Perhaps early intervention is advantageous because change is easier then. Continuing research in this area is important because of the role that assumptions regarding reversibility have as context for policy decisions and interventions.

In this paper, it is assumed that early experiences are important. It is assumed, in accordance with revised psychoanalytic theory that 'what is laid out early in life, are patterns for interpersonal relationships, basic attitudes about the self (especially the sense of trustworthiness and effectance) and a basic posture toward the environment – that is, expectations concerning the physical and social world and beliefs concerning one's own potency in that world. All of these are subject to change, but since the person is viewed as an active shaper of experience, there is a tendency toward continuity.'[145]

It is time to end this somewhat lengthy digression and to turn to the main task of this chapter, to ask how shared childrearing is likely to affect the development of competence. More specifically, the question to be raised is how does sharing a child's rearing affect whether or not the conditions necessary to the development of competence are created?

III ECOLOGY OF CHILDREARING:
SHARED CHILDREARING AND THE LIKELIHOOD OF COMPETENCE[146]

A growing child's efforts to explore and to acquire the skills for effective interaction are very likely to be influenced by various aspects of his/her environment. Childrearing which provides exposure to stimulation of a kind and in a context that elicits attention, frequently to the immediate and intended consequences of self-initiated actions, is to some degree related to the ongoing development of competence. The secure attachment assumed to result in such childrearing relationships may enhance the benefits of enabling exploratory behaviours in situations otherwise too arousing or dominated by other needs.

With this as a framework, discussion now turns to the influence of shared childrearing in its various forms. It is usually the mother who assumes primary responsibility for childrearing. She spends more time than the father caring for and interacting with a child regardless of whether she works. Therefore, in considering shared childrearing it is assumed that it is the mother who is sharing it with others.[147] How does a mother's sharing a child's rearing affect the likelihood of the environment providing the necessary conditions?

It is important to keep in mind in such a discussion that the evidence regarding these aspects of the environments considered 'necessary' is tentative and incomplete. As a consequence, considering the influence of various forms of shared childrearing on these aspects of childrearing may result in inappropriate caution or enthusiasm, should the earlier assumptions be in error. Nonetheless, it is important to get a sense of where the issue stands.

Shared Childrearing

Fathers
How does a father's involvement in childrearing affect its course? Unfortunately, there is very little research on how fathers interact with their children and with what effect. This may be the result of fathers having been viewed as substitute caretakers, at least in a child's early years, instead of as childrearers.[148] However, in the early 1970s developmental psychologists began looking at how fathers interact with their children and began asking what impact they have. This work is presented here.

Fathers' level of competence. The notion that mothers are unique in their biological programming of responsibility to new-born children[149] suggests by implication that fathers, given the opportunity, would not be competent to identify and respond to an infant's needs. Should this be the case, then one might ask whether, 'by definition,' involving fathers in child care does not interfere with the development of competence. Those who assume a mother's unique biological programming have not provided evidence regarding fathers. Those who disagree with the assumption are beginning to provide data. Parke and Sawin believe that four assumptions about fathers are myths. These beliefs are that (1) fathers are uninterested in new-borns, (2) fathers are less nurturant than mothers, (3) fathers prefer to leave caretaking to mothers, and (4) fathers are less competent than mothers. They argue that these myths follow from an error in interpretation of the meaning of fathers' lack of involvement in caretaking. 'Too often the fact of low father involvement throughout history in the caretaking of children has been extended to the conclusion that the low level of involvement was equivalent to a low level of competence.'[150] As discussed earlier, low performance levels do not necessarily mean low levels of competence.

Parke and Sawin have begun to collect data in order to evaluate these beliefs. In observing fathers and mothers with their new-borns between six and forty-eight hours after delivery, there were no differences in the looking, smiling, vocalizing, kissing, touching, imitating, and exploring behaviours of fathers and mothers. Fathers held and rocked the infant more than mothers and mothers smiled at the infants more than fathers.[151] Since these fathers were a potentially unusual group in that half were in Lemaze classes, 18 of 19 were in the delivery room during birth, and all were well-educated, white, and middle class, a lower class sample where one might be more likely to find differences between fathers and mothers was observed. There were no differences when the mother or father was alone with the infant and when all three were together the fathers held the infant and looked at the infant more than the mother.[152] These data do not go with the notion of an uninterested father. In fact, they may reflect the 'engrossment' of a father with his new-born child about which there has been some theorizing.[153] Unfortunately, data Parke and Sawin present to reflect father's nurturance, that is, stopping feeding as readily as mothers in response to infant behaviour such as coughing and spitting up, are of ambiguous value. Since it is difficult to feed an infant who is coughing or spitting up, it is questionable if stopping feeding reflects nurturance. Other work in situations where voluntary responsiveness is more easily assumed is needed.

Parke and Sawin's approach to the question of whether men are inherently less interested and competent than women is to observe levels of involvement of fathers and mothers with their children at birth. Equal involvement is interpreted as indicating equal interest and competence. What if mothers' and fathers' involvement and competence diverge as children get older? Does this confirm that fathers suffer from a biological disadvantage? Not necessarily, because it is possible that a great deal more 'mothering' is learned than is always acknowledged. It is possible that men and women both start from square one and cultures then provide women with experiences which train them for child care.

There are data which suggest that learning plays an important role in 'mothering.' After studying patterns of child care in six cultures, Whiting and Whiting concluded that it is unlikely that there is an innate drive towards nurturance among girls. The best predictor of feminine behaviour among girls was the nature of tasks assigned to them in childhood, such as helping and comforting infants, preparing food, being attentive to motivational states, and being tolerant of demands for succourance and of interruption.[154] It is equally plausible that the levels of nurturance demonstrated by boys and men are related to their early experience in child care. Since the prevailing expectation in Western industrial societies has not been for men to care for children, the societies have not provided men with extensive caretaking experiences.

The question of inherent competence at nurturing and caring for young children is still an open one. At this point, it is not reasonable to conclude that fathers' involvement in child care is problematic. However, the data are sparse.

Fathers as opportunity. Sharing childrearing with fathers can mean that fathers provide an *opportunity* to interact with another adult and very likely add to the overall stimulation in a child's environment. That the benefit of these opportunities depends on more than just the father's presence in the household is suggested by data showing that the amount of time fathers interact with their sons (no girls tested) is related to the son's academic performance and cognitive development at age eight. Fathers who spent an average of two hours a day with their sons had sons who performed better than boys whose fathers were absent because of separation or boys whose fathers spent less than two hours a week interacting with them.[155] Actual sharing is important.

Specifically how are these advantages realized? Fathers' interactions with their children may facilitate development by increasing the frequency of a child's exposure to certain kinds of experience. One such example involves separation protest. Many infants go through a period of showing considerable distress when someone to whom they are attached departs. The protest has been argued to reflect the infant's inability to interpret the meaning of the departure and feeling anxiety as a result.[156] Data suggest that the more a father interacts with his child the shorter and less intense the child's experience of separation protest. Having two adults to interact with means that the child has experienced separation more often. The greater opportunity to experience separation, test out hypotheses as to its meaning and have them confirmed or disconfirmed may be what speeds the process of interpretation.[157] It seems likely that similar developmental advantages occur whenever the father's involvement in childrearing increases the frequency of exposure to experiences.

Fathers sharing childrearing may also provide opportunities for distinctive kinds of interaction. There are data which suggest that the time fathers spend with their children differs qualitatively from the time that mothers spend with their children. Fathers spend much less time than mothers in routine child care. Fathers spend a higher proportion of their time playing with or educating their children than do mothers. When the mother works, it may actually represent equal or more time than the mother spends playing with the children.[158] It also seems that fathers may play differently with their children than mothers. Fathers' play is more rough and tumble and more idiosyncratic, while mothers' play is more conventional.[159]

These data suggest that fathers sharing childrearing provide children with experiences otherwise unavailable to them. However, it may be that on the average fathers are not sufficiently involved in early childrearing to have the distinctiveness of their interactions realized in a developmental advantage. Rebelsky and Hanks report that fathers spend on the average 37.7 seconds a day interacting verbally with their children aged 3 months or less.[160] Ban and Lewis and Peterson and Robson found that fathers play with their children, ranging in age from 9 months to 1 year, around one hour a day.[161] Further work is needed to assess the significance of these amounts of time for developing competencies.

In summary, in terms of shared childrearing, father's involvement may contribute to a child's developing competence by providing additional opportunities for learning. His involvement may result in increased exposure to situations such as separation, thereby facilitating the child's conceptual understanding of it and making its anxiety-arousing aspect of shorter duration. This may be advantageous to the child's developing sense of being able to integrate and cope with anxiety-arousing situations without having to endure prolonged anxiety. Also, if future data confirm the existing patterns, fathers may provide qualitatively different experiences in interaction with their children than mothers, thus enabling the children to learn to deal with a broader range of experiences.

While suggestive, these findings are also open to alternative interpretation. Developmentally advanced children may elicit more involvement from their fathers, and therefore, the father's involvement is a consequence and not a cause of developmentally advanced children. A greater involvement by fathers may coincide with greater involvement by mothers, and therefore developmental gains are not necessarily related to the father's involvement. (This interpretation points to a failure thus far of research to observe both mothers and fathers of children and to assess their joint and unique impact on development.) When childrearing is shared, work exploring the effect of different patterns of sharing on development is needed.

Consistency and role differentiation. Shared childrearing means by definition that more than one person is involved in a child's rearing. This immediately raises the issue of possible inconsistency and questions as to its effects on a child's development. Earlier, it was suggested that intrapersonal or interpersonal inconsistency in a child's early environment might impede a child's developing sense of mastery. Two people sharing child care functions may differ both in their responses to the child and in their expectations of the child. At a very young age the child is unlikely to be able to discriminate that these differences are associated with different people. The result could be a limited sense of mastery of the social environment, because the task of learning how to elicit the desired response is beyond the child's capacities. In the extreme, the child could learn that s/he is helpless to control the social environment.

One way to lessen the likelihood of a young child experiencing inconsistency is to have parents perform different functions. The data cited earlier showing that fathers educate and play more with children and that mothers perform more of the routine caretaking functions and that even within the play category fathers have a different pattern of play suggest that a role differentiation exists. Perhaps role differentiation has evolved as a way of lessening the likelihood that children will experience interpersonal inconsistency during the same childcare activity before they are at an age when they have the capacity to discriminate the different individuals involved. This is worth exploring.

The question of whether inconsistency of all kinds is problematic also merits examination. For example, once discrimination of the two individuals is possible, then differences may facilitate rather than hinder the development of competence. It has been suggested that the fact of two parents being involved in the same childcare functions will introduce a tension into the situation which facilitates a child's learning. 'Having to relate to two similar but slightly different persons may ... force the child at an early age to be sensitive to social cues, to discriminate subtle differences between individuals, and to tolerate frustration generated during the process of learning differential expectations about fathers' and mothers' behaviours.'[162] The father's presence may facilitate perception of, attention to, and learning about the mother's behaviours by being different, by setting up a contrast. It may be that learning how to evoke desired behaviours from one parent is helped by having the contrast of either the same behaviours evoking different responses or of a different set of behaviours evoking the same response in the other parent. At least this is what is suggested, if one generalizes somewhat incautiously from data reported by Brooks and Lewis.[163] They found that children in general learned the label 'daddy' before the label 'mommy.' Those who learned 'mommy' earlier than others had mothers who were employed. The contrast of absence with presence in each case seems to have accelerated learning. This is likely to be only one example of the general function of contrast.

A key phrase in the above quote is 'two similar but slightly different persons.' Differences create contrast. However, not all contrasts are likely to facilitate attention and learning. Extreme differences could be problematic for developing social competencies. For example, should two parents have very different expectations of the child and should the child comply, then the perception of self-initiation of behaviour is likely to be weakened as the origin of behaviour is more clearly in the external expectations of the parents. Or, if two parents expect incompatible behaviour and are both present, the result is a conflict for the child which is quite stressful. Role differentiation could be important here as before. It may decrease the frequency with which parents make different, possibly incompatible, demands of the child. As a consequence, the child may be better able to develop means for coping with such conflict effectively. Unfortunately, there do not seem to have been investigations along these lines.

In summary, the consequence of interpersonal inconsistency is one of the central issues raised by shared childrearing. It has been suggested first that having both parents involved may make learning easier by the fact that they provide a contrast for one another, and second the benefits occur only when the inconsistency or contrast they provide does not exceed the developing discriminative and coping capacities of the child. Role differentiation can, under these latter circumstances, be an important mechanism allowing the child time to develop the means to handle inconsistencies. More research is urgently needed in these areas.

Attachment issues. To date, much of the work involving attachment has resulted from the assumption that the mother-child relationship is primary. Therefore, few data are available as to whether, how, and with what result children form attachments to others. However, with what is available it is possible to venture forth with some ideas about the implications of shared childrearing for attachments.

Concepts like opportunity and responsiveness outlined earlier in the paper do not require or imply that it is the mother caring for the child. When it is the mother, the result is a bond of attachment. Assuming that a child is not predisposed to form an attachment only to his/her mother, it seems reasonable to hypothesize that anyone who responds to the child by providing an environment that enables the development of competence will be the focus of attachment. It further seems reasonable to take the next step and hypothesize that, if a secure attachment to the mother provides a base from which to explore, secure attachments to significant others in the child's environment would have a similar effect. In other words, rather than competing with the mother for '*the* attachment bond', as if the child's capacity to form an attachment is limited to one relationship, it seems quite possible that fathers and others, to the extent that they are responsive to the child, become added objects of attachment. As a consequence, they enlarge the base of security from which the child can explore his/her environment, which in turn facilitates the development of competence.

Several assumptions are being made, and relevant, if limited, data are available for some. The focus here is on data regarding fathers. The first assumption is that children are capable of multiple attachments. This capacity has been recognized for some time[164] and has been confirmed more recently in studies showing, for example, that an infant's play is disrupted as much by his/her father's departure as by his/her mother's departure.[165]

The second assumption is that a father-child attachment evolves according to the same principles as the mother-child attachment. There are no data assessing the dimensions of a father-child interaction which facilitate the attachment bond comparable to Ainsworth's data on the mother-child interaction. However, data cited earlier, showing that fathers who are not restrictive and who allow self-initiated problem-solving have sons who perform higher on IQ tests, do suggest that the father-child relationship develops according to the same principles as the mother-child relationship.[166] If so, though it must be tentatively stated, it seems reasonable to assume that the attachment aspects of a father-child relationship develop in a similar way and have similar consequences to the attachment aspects of a mother-child relationship.

The third assumption is that fathers can provide a secure base from which to explore. It is supported by data showing that infants explore as much in a novel situation when their father is present as when their mother is present.[167]

The fourth assumption is that, as the child's number of secure attachments increases, there is a corresponding increase in the base of security which supports its interactions. There is no study which assesses this directly. However, part of this assumption is that forming a second attachment does not functionally alter the first. This part of the assumption is supported by data. Even when the presence of either parent sustains exploratory behaviour in anxiety-arousing situations, the child turns to the mother significantly more often than to the father.[168] This is consistent with the assumption stated earlier that the mother's relieving the child's discomfort gives her presence the ability to mediate a reduction in anxiety. As long as fathers are less involved in child care functions, it seems consistent that they can function as a secure base from which to explore, but less so when compared to mothers as an option. Another study, cited earlier, can also be interpreted as supporting this assumption. It showed that the more a father interacts with a child the less the child's separation anxiety.[169] Children whose fathers interact with them may have a larger number of secure attachments and the less separation anxiety reflects a larger base of security. Unfortunately, there are no data on the security of the attachment to the mother or the father to confirm this interpretation.

These data suggest that a second attachment figure does not alter the functioning of the first as a source of security. However, there is no specific information on how new attachments affect old ones nor has any comparison been made among children differing in number of secure attachments to see if a greater number facilitates the ongoing development of competence to a greater extent than a smaller number. Future research needs to determine if it is correct to assume that a major advantage of shared childrearing is the development of attachments which support the child's development beyond what is possible in the absence of wider attachment relationships.

Summary and additional issues. In reviewing the literature on fathers it is a striking, and as we shall see a recurrent, fact that the implications of shared childrearing remain unexplored, both theoretically and experimentally. The emphasis on mother-child interactions is too narrow, for it does not adequately represent the child's social reality.[170] What are the implications of a father's involvement in childrearing for a child's development? Some ideas have been suggested, but they are in a preliminary form.

The extent of a father's involvement in a child's life varies, but to the extent that the father shares the child's care, he provides additional opportunities for learning and in some instances may provide a contrast which greatly facilitates the learning process. Depending on the quality of his interactions with his child, he may become an object of the child's attachment and provide an important source of security which supports the child in developing his/her competencies. The sharing of childrearing between two people very likely means that the similarity of their responses and expectations becomes an important aspect of the child's social environment. It has been suggested that role differentiation may function in some circumstances to keep the developmental tasks within the range of the child's capacities and therefore may be important to his/her developing sense of mastery.

In addition to explaining these ideas, other questions are raised by the earlier discussion of conditions important to a child's development. What are the implications of a father's involvement in childrearing for maintaining an optimal level of arousal? Perhaps the contrast of two adults facilitates learning or perhaps the result is overstimulation. What is the likely effect of a father's involvement for the availability of self-initiated learning? As the number of people involved increases, do the opportunities increase or decrease? These and other questions need attention as the concept of shared childrearing is researched.

Siblings

Since a childrearing relationship was defined as ongoing contact in which a child learns about the reality in which s/he is to function, it is important not to overlook the role of siblings in one another's development. It is not only likely that a mother shares her child's rearing with other of her children,[171] it is increasingly seen as essential that children have contact with other children if they are to acquire the necessary skills to initiate and sustain social interactions.[172]

Not until recently has an effort been made to identify the unique contribution children make to one another's development.[173] The significance of siblings has been overlooked by proponents of psychoanalytic theory, by family historians[174] and by developmental psychologists alike.[175] Therefore, once again, the evidence presented is sparse and unsystematic, but some interesting possibilities can be considered.

Siblings as opportunity. Two different kinds of opportunities provided by siblings, which may facilitate the development of competence, are considered. The first has to do with benefits of interacting with siblings close in age. The second is a benefit to an older sibling of having a younger sibling to teach.

Starting with the assumption that adult-child relationships are qualitatively different from child-child relationships, it is hypothesized that, if a child does not have an opportunity to interact with peers, then s/he cannot acquire skills necessary in same-age relationships. There is some very general evidence consistent with this hypothesis. Younger children have been found to be better accepted by their peers than middle or first children.[176] This is consistent with the hypothesis if it is assumed that younger children have had more opportunity to learn interaction skills in a wider variety of situations and with a wider variety of people, that they have developed greater competence, and that acceptance is a response to social competence. A second study reports that children who had interacted more with other children before going to daycare were more skilled in their response to peers once in pre-school.[177] These data suggest that exposure to children is necessary to developing skills for interacting with children, but in each case the data are open to alternative interpretation and need to be followed up.

Hartup has begun to identify specific ways in which adult-child and child-child interactions differ, to allow more rigorous testing of the hypothesis that child-child interactions make unique contributions to a child's developing social competence.[178] Adult-child relationships are characterized by dependency and developmental disparities, each of which makes certain kinds of interaction difficult. Dependency makes the learning of reciprocity among equals difficult. Data consistent with this are provided by the six cultures studied by Whiting and Whiting.[179] Pro-social behaviour among children is more common in child-child than in adult-child interactions. The disparity in physical development makes aggressiveness more problematic in adult-child than in child-child interactions and aggressiveness is more common in child-child interactions.[180] The disparity in conceptual development between adult and child makes sustained play at the child's level more difficult in adult-child interactions than in child-child interactions and, though sustained play has not been examined, child-child interactions are characterized more by play than adult-child interactions.[181] Hartup argues that child-child interactions are more suited for these reasons than adult-child interactions for learning to express aggression functionally and for learning the reciprocal give and take so important in social interaction. These ideas are important and need further exploration. Also, establishing the extent to which the complementary contributions to a child's development made by adult-child and child-child interactions depend upon one another is particularly important from the point of view of shared childrearing.

In summary, interaction with siblings, particularly those close in age, may provide opportunities to acquire aspects of social competence difficult to obtain in adult-child interactions. A word of caution is necessary because much of the research was done with peers and not siblings. However, assuming similarities in sibling and peer interactions does not seem unreasonable.

Turning now to older sibling relationships with younger children, it has been suggested that one of the important opportunities provided within a sibling relationship is the opportunity to teach. This opportunity is offered as an explanation of why only children and last born children do not perform as well on IQ tests as one would expect.[182] A child in either of these positions in the family structure is less likely to have opportunities to teach than other children. Evidence does support the notion that teaching improves the level of skill of the child who is doing the teaching,[183] a greater improvement occurring for those initially performing at lower levels.[184]

A child's level of social competence is also assumed to benefit from tutoring because of opportunities to practise role-taking and helping behaviour which are assumed to be part of nurturance and sympathetic behaviour.[185] Along these lines there is some intriguing preliminary research into the therapeutic value of interaction with a younger child. The original work done with monkeys by Harlow showed that monkeys reared in social isolation lacked appropriate social behaviours.[186] Neither interaction with older monkeys or age-mates altered the isolates' behaviour. However, interaction with younger monkeys resulted in a decrease in bizarre behaviour and the acquisition of appropriate social behaviours.[187] Similar results have been reported for the effects of interaction with younger children on the socially withdrawn behaviour of pre-school children.[188] The hypothesis that the rehabilitative effect is the result of the opportunity to practise giving direction, guidance and suggestions, and behaviours necessary in initiating and maintaining a social interaction is now being assessed.[189]

It is important to note that the advantages of such teaching experiences have traditionally been, and apparently still are, more often available to girls than to boys. Girls were more often expected to care for and perhaps teach younger siblings than were boys in early hunter-gatherer societies.[190] Recent research has shown girls to have more sophisticated tutoring skills than boys of the same age, presumably gained through greater experience,[191] and that first borns in families of two children do become teachers more often than one would expect by chance, a finding accounted for by the women in the sample.[192]

The implication of these preliminary data is that an older sibling can under some conditions benefit from the teaching of the younger sibling and that the society may provide these opportunities more frequently for girls than for boys. However, since our concern is the effects of shared childrearing in general, it is important to ask if the younger child benefits from being tutored. The data are mixed. Some suggest that tutees do not benefit as much as tutors,[193] unless an adult is involved.[194] Other work suggests that older children, particularly girls, can improve the quality of performance in younger children,[195] the greater the age difference the greater the improvement.[196] However, here again, the involvement of an adult may explain the benefit that a young child derives, because the young child who benefited more from an older sister is one who can also benefit from his/her mother. It is likely that mothers who can teach children have children who can teach and that the benefits derived from the older sibling originate in the mother's skills.[197] In general, it seems likely that the extent to which a young child benefits from an older sibling's tutoring is a function of the support in terms of help and trust provided by the adult environment to the older child. As before, the question of how childrearing can be shared most beneficially remains to be addressed, in that the question of what characteristics of adult-child relationships are necessary for the benefits of the child-child relationship to be realized has not been asked. What is the complementary and perhaps interdependent nature of adult-child and child-child relationships underlying these potential advantages of shared childrearing?

In summary, the involvement of siblings in one another's rearing may provide important opportunities, some necessary to and others facilitative of the ongoing development of competence. The data are preliminary. The importance of the issues raised argues for increased research effort to improve our understanding of the quantity, nature, and effects of sibling interactions and how these effects are influenced by the context of the adult-child relationships within which they occur.

Contingency of siblings. The contingency of child-child interactions is also an important issue. Interactions up to two years of age are low in contingency in that they are characterized by a long delay in response to one another's initiatives.[198] It has also been suggested that responses are 'too variable to allow a baby to develop firm predictable expectations of links between his behaviour and the actions of a peer.'[199] As would be expected if this is the case, it has been observed that young children do not interact extensively with each other.[200] It has also been observed that year-old infants who had an older sibling (size of age difference unspecified) were not as positive in their responses to stranger peers as infants who did not have an older sibling.[201] Children with older siblings may have had more non-contingent experiences and as a consequence may have learned not to try to master the behaviour of a 'peer.'

As a sibling is increasingly older, his/her behaviour is likely to be more predictable and possibly as a consequence s/he is likely to be more of a facilitator than an inhibitor of the development of social competence. Lewis et al.,[202] who report positive qualities of peer interaction, found that they were more typical when a young child interacted with an older, perhaps more contingent, child than when the interaction was with a peer of the same age. Bates notes that spending time with peers at an early age seems to slow the acquisition of language. She suggests that part of the reason is that young children's communication is more egocentric (less attuned to the perspectives of the listener) than adult communication and that a young child as a listener gives little feedback as to comprehension of a message. As a consequence, child-child communication is not as likely to facilitate children's language learning as adult-child communication. More to the point here is her discussion of recent data which suggests that, by the age of four, children are making adjustments in their communication with younger children which are parallel to the adjustment adults make. They shorten sentences and speak in simpler terms. Also, they are more frequently giving 'listener cues' (nodding the head) indicating understanding.[203] Bates's discussion does suggest that as the space between siblings increases, the interactions, at least in the area of language, are increasingly like an adult's in being contingent and sensitive to the level of understanding of the younger child.

The long-term implications of early exposure to the non-contingency of peers or siblings for developing competence are not clear. It may be that the early effects of non-contingency are easily reversed and therefore are not a long-term concern, or it may be that the timing of exposure to siblings is an issue for concern. There are some data which suggest that timing is important to the development of certain competencies. As the number of siblings preceding a child increases, IQ performance decreases. However, the larger the space between siblings the less the decrement in the cognitive development of the younger child.[204] It could be that the closer in age the next older sibling the more detrimental it is to cognitive development because of early child-child interactions. However, it could also be that when children are closely spaced the younger child interacts less with his/her mother than when there is a larger space and that the decrement in mother-child interaction explains the decrement in IQ. Further work exploring the influence of the timing and nature of child-child interactions will be an important contribution to our understanding of shared childrearing.

Additional issues. There are other questions raised by the earlier discussion of how children learn. For example, how does the nature and course of children's attachment for one another influence the extent of security children feel in their interactions with the known and unknown aspects of their environment?[205] What are the implications of the presence of older children and of interactions with older children for the appropriateness of stimulation, both in terms of optimal discrepancy and optimal arousal? What are the implications of the presence of siblings for opportunities for self-initiated actions? These kinds of issues have not been researched and do need to be considered in the future.

In summary, it has been suggested that siblings provide an important and in some cases necessary exposure to peers in terms of developing social competencies of various kinds, such as the control of aggression, a capacity for give and take with equals, and a capacity to be responsible for and guide the learning of younger children. Data also show that as the number of siblings increases cognitive performance decreases, although opportunities to teach seem to compensate to some extent. That the decrement is in some way related to exposure to noncontingent peers is possible but not clearly established.

Perhaps the most important comment to be made is that the extent, nature, and function of sibling and peer relationships, both by themselves and juxtaposed with adult-child relationships, are virtually unexplored. Research in this area represents an indispensable contribution to our understanding of the influence of shared childrearing on the development of competence.

Family and Centre Daycare

As discussed earlier, many mothers are working, including increasing numbers of mothers with pre-school children. These families usually make arrangements for their children to be taken care of by other adults. A substantial number of the arrangements involve family daycare, which is care in another's home by a nonrelative. Another popular arrangement is group daycare in a centre. These two additional childrearing settings do not include all the alternatives, but are the focus of what little research has been done on developmental consequences, and are therefore the focus of this section of the paper.

Daycare in each case means sharing childrearing with unrelated adults and children outside the home. Many of the issues raised in considering the influence of fathers' and siblings' involvement in childrearing are relevant in a consideration of daycare, but have been explored even less fully. An attempt is made below to note these similarities and also to suggest how daycare is different from sharing childrearing with fathers and siblings. One other comment is important before beginning. Even though the focus in this section of the paper is on issues which arise when childrearing is shared with people outside the home, issues common to both family and centre daycare, it should not be assumed that family and centre daycare are not distinctive experiences. Research is beginning to compare these two forms of daycare and early findings suggest, as one would expect, that family daycare is more like home care than centre daycare,[206] but not the same as home care.[207] As research accumulates, the distinctive nature of each type of arrangement is likely to come into focus, even on the issues about to be discussed.

Daycare as opportunity. There are few data on which to base a discussion of the kinds of opportunities daycare provides and the consequences of these opportunities for development. However, a few studies are suggestive. At a general level, research, which has been done almost exclusively in high quality sites, shows that infant and pre-school centre daycare and family daycare experiences are not detrimental to a child's cognitive development.[208]

There is some evidence on more specific aspects of daycare. Daycare involves ongoing exposure to adults and children outside the family. As was suggested earlier in the case of fathers, daycare also may increase the frequency of a child's exposure to certain kinds of events. For example, it offers contact with peers and adults who were initially strangers. As one would expect, if such contacts result in opportunities to test out the reality of what peers and adults are like through intensified contacts, thereby facilitating the schema building process regarding strangers, the onset of stranger anxiety occurs sooner and the intensity is less for daycare as compared with home-reared children.[209] Other data have indicated that in a novel situation daycare children move away from their mothers more and closer to strange children and to strange adults than home-reared children.[210] The implications of what appears to be daycare children's ease with strangers for the development of social skills have not been explored, but need to be.[211] Is their ease a long-term difference or is it an acceleration of development resulting from greater opportunities to hypothesis test and learn?

The earlier discussion regarding sibling and peer interactions raises other questions about the effect of daycare on developing competence. Daycare is on the average likely to provide more opportunities than a home for interaction with peers. Little is known about the effects of such opportunities. In the area of cognitive development, work cited earlier suggests that infant and pre-school daycare children are as advanced cognitively as home-reared children. If, as assumed, daycare children interact more with peers than home-reared, then this finding is important. It contradicts the earlier suggestion that the non-contingency of young children's interaction slows their (language) development. More information is needed about the daily experiences of children in the different settings in order to clarify this contradiction.

Turning to the area of social development, some research has found that day-care children are more 'aggressive' than home-reared children.[212] Perhaps this is the result of spending more time in peer interactions, suggested earlier to be characterized by more aggression than adult-child interactions. Bearing in mind that the interpretation of the children's behaviour as aggressive may be problematic,[213] these findings raise an interesting question. To what extent does the socializing children do of one another, for example involving aggressive behaviour, depend upon the context provided by adult-child interactions? To rephrase, how might parent-child and daycare provider-child interactions differ as a context for the socializing children do of one another?[214] Research into these kinds of questions seems important if the distinct opportunities offered by daycare are to be understood.

So far discussion has focused on the increase in opportunity provided to day-care children through a daycare experience. There is also an important decrease in opportunity which needs to be considered. It was suggested earlier that parents of twins spend less time interacting with their children.[215] Presumably this reflects the fact that demands for individualized attention when children are very young quickly exceed the adult's capacity. This is also true in daycare.[216] However, in daycare there is less flexibility in the number of children an adult is responsible for. One possibility then, depending on a child's home environment, is that daycare will provide less individualized attention from an adult, which may affect the level of competence that a child acquires.[217]

In summary, there is to date little evidence on how the opportunities of day-care affect a child's developing competence. Daycare may provide greater opportunities of some kinds, such as learning to cope with strangers, learning to adjust to a new setting, spending a great deal of time in a child centred setting,[218] exposure to a greater diversity of people; but, these opportunities have not for the most part been researched.

What is needed is more detailed knowledge of how home and daycare environments compare. Time-use studies have begun to tell us how mothers and fathers spend their time, but have not focused on children. How the day of a daycare child differs from that of a home-reared child in terms of opportunities for interaction with adults and children is not known. As a consequence it is not yet possible to specify with confidence how the opportunities provided by sharing childrearing with daycare affect the child's development.

Consistency: towards a gestalt of childrearing. One of the major drawbacks of daycare research to date is that it treats childrearing settings as if they exist as encapsulated entities. This results in a restriction of our understanding of many children's social reality. A child who goes from home to daycare and back again has a qualitatively different experience than one whose life centres around the home, not only because of the 'day care experience' as opportunity. Experiences in either setting occur in the context of the whole, the gestalt of the childrearing system. The idea implied by 'gestalt' is that the whole is greater than the sum of its parts. A child care system involving a home environment and a daycare environment is more than the sum of the two settings. The whole has qualities, deriving from the juxtaposition of the parts, which are likely to have an independent influence on a child's development.

How children's environments fit together is recognized as an issue between formal socialization structures like school and home,[219] particularly in terms of the continuity in expectations and skills required. For example, one of the earliest acquisitions during socialization at home is learning how to learn. A child then moves on to a school environment where s/he applies these skills to new subject areas. Home environments (i.e. middle-class homes) with greater 'continuity' prepare children more adequately for school, not because of effort or superiority but simply because of continuity. The language and values acquired in the home are suitable in the school.[220]

This raises for daycare children the question of the impact of consistency or inconsistency between home and daycare environments on the child's developing competence. What happens if the family expects a child to obey his/her parents promptly and the daycare staff expects the child to voice his/her opinions freely? In a situation where the child disagrees and there is a chance to voice dissent with an adult's wishes a child will have learned two incompatible responses, to obey and to dissent. 'Response competition' has been suggested as a term to describe this situation,[221] and response competition is stressful and a threat to effective action.[222]

According to some researchers, the significance of this issue is overestimated because differences in opinion do not occur. Two studies assessing the childrearing values of parents and daycare staff failed to find a sufficient number of divergent values to believe they were due to real as opposed to chance differences.[223] One study does report that perceived differences (as opposed to actual differences of opinion) occur. However, they occur only in areas where they do not result in conflict. One person values integrity, the other curiosity. Both can be fostered without conflict.[224] It is possible that there are no differences of opinion which result in incompatible expectations, but it is unlikely. Perhaps the adults involved intuit the importance of such differences and either suppress or deny them.

Other research findings can be interpreted as indicating that these conflicts do occur. The greater aggressiveness found in daycare children mentioned earlier could be due to greater tension and frustration, arising when conflicting expectations exceed a child's capacity to cope with them. The plausibility of this explanation is enhanced by Fowler's finding that increases in belligerence occurred in daycare girls and children from disadvantaged homes, but not in the other children.[225] It is these children who are most likely to experience inconsistency between their two childrearing environments, their home and a university-supervised daycare centre. It may be then that the conflicts exist and adults do not readily acknowledge them.

It seems important that the impact of incompatible expectations on a child's development be explored. Perhaps, as was suggested in the case of fathers' involvement in childrearing, inconsistency can provide a contrast that facilitates development up to a point, but when inconsistency exceeds the child's capacity to develop adaptive responses it interferes with development. Work looking into factors such as the frequency, centrality, and intensity of such experiences and the responses children develop to them is important.

Since there has been little research on childrearing as a gestalt, the significance of these ideas and interpretations remains an open question. But they are an alternative interpretation of data which have been used to caution us against the ill effects of daycare, such as greater 'belligerence' in daycare children. Should this new interpretation be supported in future work, the question it raises has to do with the 'match' between a child's rearing environments and not with the ill effects of daycare. Future work would need to explore how to match environments so that the gestalt of childrearing facilitates both a child's development and coping. It is also important that future work follow up on the notion of the gestalt of a childrearing system. What other aspects of shared childrearing between two environments influence the child's development independently of the influence of each setting alone? In other words, in what other ways besides the extent of consistency is fit between environments important?

Attachment issues. Two issues regarding the impact of daycare on attachment are considered here. The first issue involves a concern that daily separation from the mother weakens or precludes a secure attachment to her. The second issue is whether or not children form attachments in daycare which expand the base of security from which they explore.

Turning first to the concern about daily separation, it has been assumed that daily separation from the mother interferes with the child's secure attachment to her which will in turn adversely affect the child's cognitive motivational development and competence in other social relationships. Findings to date are not definitive, but do suggest that concern over separation is exaggerated.

The basic comparison in the research is between the attachment behaviours of daycare children and home-reared children towards their mother. Several studies provide data.[226] In one study, home-reared and daycare children were observed during an interview with their mothers at the daycare centre. During the interview the behaviour of the children was not different in terms of affiliation, nurturance, hostility, permissiveness, happiness, or emotionality in interaction with the mother. The authors conclude that the daycare experience, which for these children had already been from 5 to 24 months at the age of 30 months, did not adversely affect the child's attachment for his/her mother.[227] Two more recent studies report analogous results from comparisons made between daycare, family daycare, and home-reared children in environments equated for novelty, an improvement over the original study.[228]

While these studies are important, they are incomplete. It is important to determine if daycare weakens 'secure' attachments in the home environment, for it is secure attachments that seem most advantageous to development. Doyle did assess secure and insecure attachments and reports that the daycare children were different from the home-reared children, matched on age, sex, parents' education and occupation, and the number of siblings on only one of the 11 attachment variables. They looked at a stranger less when the stranger entered an experimental room, perhaps because the stranger was less novel. The other variables are not reported, but the measures in the study after which this was modelled include crying, proximity seeking, and proximity avoiding. Unfortunately, it is unclear whether the settings in which the observation took place differed in the familiarity to the two groups of infants.[229]

Blehar, who also assessed qualitative differences in attachment, reports different results. Her findings suggest that in a situation novel to both the daycare and home-reared children, the daycare children exhibited less secure attachment behaviours compared to the home-reared. Three and a half year-old daycare children cried more, explored less, exhibited more proximity seeking towards their mothers, and exhibited more avoiding of the stranger than home-reared children of a comparable age. The two and a half year-old daycare group sought less contact with the mother at reunion, exhibited more proximity avoiding behaviour towards the mother and seemed more avoiding of the stranger than their home-reared counterparts. Blehar suggests that older daycare children exhibited more ambivalent attachment and younger daycare children exhibited more detached attachment than the respective home-reared comparison groups. She suggests that these data call for serious concern regarding the impact of daycare on secure attachments.[230] However, a recent attempt to replicate Blehar's findings failed to do so, suggesting that the daily separation of daycare is not *per se* a threat to a secure attachment relationship and that further work is needed to establish if, when, and how daily separation affects attachment.[231]

Since the data on reaction to separation are equivocal, one can ask if any other data might help to clarify the effect of daycare on children's attachment for their mothers. There are two studies which suggest the primacy of the mother-child relationship, even after extensive experience in daycare. As suggested, when stressed, children turn to mothers rather than fathers. It appears that, when stressed, they turn to mothers rather than to other caretakers as well. The data from one study show that when a daycare child is in a room with his/her mother, a familiar caretaker, and a stranger whose presence is intended to produce anxiety, the children spend 70 per cent of the time closer to the mother than to the others and significantly more time interacting with the mother.[232] A particularly interesting finding is that all the children who sought help in a problem-solving situation presented by the experimenters sought it from their mothers and not from their 'teacher' (15 of 23). The daycare centre in this study was unusual in that no one adult had primary responsibility for a child in the daycare setting. Another study's data suggest that the primacy of the mother does not depend on this kind of daycare setting and adds a home-reared comparison group. Once again children were observed in a situation with their mother, a familiar adult, and a stranger. Daycare and home-reared children did not differ in their interactions with the adults. They were equally likely to prefer their mothers under conditions of stress, either boredom or surprising adult behaviour.[233] While these two studies do not show that the child's attachment for his/her mother has not been weakened, they do suggest that the mother remains a salient source of comfort, as much for daycare as for home-reared children.

Together, these two lines of research suggest that concern over the effects of daycare on a child's attachment for his/her mother may be exaggerated, but certainly more work is needed in this area. Since one argument being made is that a secure mother-child relationship is important to later relationships, it is hoped that research examining the quality of later social and emotional relationships among daycare and home-reared children is forthcoming.

Other research suggests potential advantages arising from daycare experience in terms of expanding the attachments which a child has. Infants may develop attachments for a supplemental caretaker[234] and, as one would expect, the supplemental caretaker can soothe the infant's distress at being left with a stranger. These findings supplement the findings reported earlier, suggesting that infants develop attachments for their fathers and siblings and that fathers and siblings can function as a secure base from which to explore. A child who is 'cared for' by more than one adult may have a larger reservoir of security to call upon when confronted with the inevitable challenges of development.

Summary. There are data for few of the issues raised regarding the impact of daycare on a child's developing competence. What there is suggests that concern over daily separation is exaggerated. Daycare children appear to be as attached to their mothers as home-reared children and the quality of development is comparable, although the implications of the adult/child ratio have yet to be clearly established. However, the implications of inconsistency between environments have not yet been explored. Similarly, most opportunities provided by daycare have not been identified or the consequences assessed. The picture is incomplete. But as a general conclusion it seems reasonable to assert that daycare is in principle not a problem for a child's developing necessary competencies. The problems that do exist are likely to have solutions within the daycare setting or in finding an appropriate fit between the parts of the child's rearing system. Abandoning the idea of daycare does not seem necessary (or feasible for that matter).

Having said all this, it is important to note that thus far the daycare research often has been conducted in university-sponsored daycare centres. The centres are likely to be of high quality. The result is that we can say daycare as a concept does not seem to be a problem. However, this does not tell us what daycare is like on the average any more than knowing home environments can provide excellent care tells us how often they do.

The Effect of Sharing on Those Sharing

In the previous section the focus was on the impact of shared childrearing on the child. Questions were raised such as how does sharing a child's rearing affect a child's attachment for his/her mother? How does the involvement of siblings or peers influence a child's development in terms of providing unique opportunities or extensive non-contingency? How does the extent and type of inconsistency between parents or across childcare settings influence the child's acquisition of competence? In each case the direct effect on the child was the focus of the discussion and the questions raised.

In this section the focus shifts to consider what the effects of shared childrearing are on those rearing the child. Presumably, the effects on those sharing the rearing of the child will in turn affect the child, and are therefore called indirect effects. If there were few answers as to how sharing affects the child directly, there are even fewer as to how sharing affects the child indirectly by affecting those parenting. The section is therefore brief and meant primarily to stimulate thought in this area.

Sharing Responsibility

Sharing childrearing means sharing responsibility for a child. There is little research on either the notion of responsibility or on what the consequences of sharing it are. This is an important aspect of childrearing and some preliminary issues are identified here.

Taking responsibility implies both an ongoing assessment of whether or not an action is required and then acting when it is required. What happens to either or both of these aspects of responsibility, assessing the need for action and acting, when the responsibility is shared with another person? Possibly sharing hinders responsive childrearing. Possibly it facilitates it.

Some research, though not done on childrearing, suggests that sharing responsibility may result in a 'diffusion of responsibility.'[235] The idea is that when a person perceives that others are available to define and respond to a need, the person is less likely to identify a need or to respond promptly if the need is identified. Should this happen when childrearing is shared, it means that there would be a delay in responding, if not a failure to respond, to a child's needs. Aside from the foremost significance of a child's needs not being met, there is the issue of the consequences of the failure to act or a delay in action for the child's learning that s/he is effective in interactions with the environment. Shared childrearing may under some circumstances be less conducive to the development of competence than childrearing by one person.

On the other hand, sharing responsibility may alleviate some of the demands of childrearing which, if excessive, would interfere with an adequate response. There are studies which suggest that continual responsibility for childrearing may interfere with a person's capacity to foster the development of competence. For example, in an infant daycare centre, staff given no opportunity to rest during the day were more negative in responding to infants in the afternoon than staff given an opportunity to rest.[236] Mothers with less play space for children report child care to be more fatiguing,[237] which may again reflect the impact of continual contact and responsibility. Anthropological studies of childrearing indicate that, when mothers have exclusive responsibility for childrearing, they are less consistently positive in their emotional reaction to their children and express more hostility unrelated to their children's behaviour.[238] It was suggested earlier that contemporary childrearing involves the strains associated with exclusive responsibility, in a context of influence, and uncertainty about how to rear children. When this is the case, sharing responsibility might be more conducive to the development of competence than childrearing by one person.

There is another possible advantage of sharing the responsibility for a child's rearing with others. With a larger number of people involved, with different areas of expertise and different sensitivities, quite possibly the result will be adequate responding to a greater range of the child's needs than is possible by one person.

The concepts of both responsibility and sharing need to be explored. Questions about what influences the perception of responsibility, the willingness to act when responsible, and so on are important. It has been suggested that sharing is one possible influence. In examining the influence of sharing on a person's taking responsibility, issues such as whether areas of responsibility overlap, whether there are variations in expertise, and whether sharing is sought or resorted to are important to explore. In general, sharing responsibility is an important aspect of shared childrearing and needs attention.

The Sharing Relationship

It seems likely that the relationship which develops through sharing will affect the extent to which those involved provide an environment which fosters the development of competence. However, there is no research known to this author which examines how the sharing relationship between or among those parenting develops and in turn affects their behaviour towards the child. This is true of childrearing shared between parents as well as childrearing shared by parents with non-family providers.

There are numerous questions which arise in the context of earlier discussion. A few are mentioned here as examples. How does the agreement or disagreement between a husband and wife about how to rear a child affect their responsiveness when they are with the child? How does a family daycare provider's liking or disliking a parent affect the amount and quality of individualized attention given the child? Should it arise, how does a feeling of competition for a child's affection affect people's interactions with the child? The answers to these questions are important and highlight the need for research on how sharing childrearing can affect the quality of care.[239] In summary, the effects of sharing childrearing on those who are doing the rearing have not been explored and need to be. It is important to determine what kinds of sharing relationships between or among those rearing a child produce behaviour conducive to the child developing competence. It is also important to be sensitive to possible unintended consequences of sharing, such as less adequate responding resulting from ambiguous or diffused responsibility.

Shared Childrearing as a Support for Parenting

Childrearing does not occur in isolation. It is process embedded in a larger context, a physical and social environment. Environments vary on many dimensions, some of which are likely to influence the childrearing process. Therefore, children reared in some environments are less likely to develop competence than children reared in others. The final issue to be considered is whether shared childrearing can benefit a child when an environment is not conducive to the development of competence. In other words, can shared childrearing support the parenting process in a context where existing supports are not sufficient? In answering this question it is important to remember that shared childrearing is only one of the responses which can be considered as a support for desired child care. There may be alternatives or there may be additional aspects of support required to complement shared childrearing. But for now the focus is on shared childrearing as a response.

Two ways in which a person's capacity to help a child in the ongoing development of competence can be hampered by the context will be considered.[240] They are, first, contexts which result in lack of knowledge or inappropriate beliefs about childrearing and, second, contexts in which the resources available to the person parenting are insufficient to meet the demands on him/her. By considering these topics the intention is not to be thorough, but rather to demonstrate another way of looking at shared childrearing.

Knowledge and Beliefs

Both the knowledge and beliefs of an individual are likely to be a reflection of where she/he is located in the society. Assuming that knowledge and beliefs affect childrearing, this is an important aspect of reality.[241] As an example of the influence of location in the society, Bernstein suggests that those who are more mobile (geographically, occupationally, etc.) need a more elaborated language in order to communicate with those of different backgrounds whom they encounter. More of their experience must be explicitly stated in order that both parties to an exchange share a starting point of conversation. Therefore, they have more complex language skills than those whose encounters are mainly with others similar to themselves. Talking with individuals similar to yourself, according to Bernstein, does not require elaboration. In fact, it results in a verbal shorthand, or a restricted language pattern.[242] The implication is that, depending on location within the society, a person's knowledge of language differs and as a consequence his/her ability to teach a child may be more or less adequate.

Another example comes from Coser's work.[243] She suggests that jobs vary in the kind of experiences they provide, some offering little opportunity for self-initiated decision-making. She argues that a different sense of self and set of skills result from taking responsibility for the outcome of decisions. Once again, the implication is that skills depend upon location in the society. Different jobs result in different skills. Some may limit people's ability to provide important experiences for their children, such as self-initiated decision-making opportunities.

The argument has been made that each of the above situations is disproportionately associated with being poor. In other words, knowledge important in rearing competent children is less available to the poor. Being poor is also more likely to result in a belief that one cannot influence one's outcomes,[244] a belief likely to affect childrearing.[245] There is no evidence to confirm it, but it does seem probable that a mother who does not believe that she can influence her own or her family's outcomes will be less likely to structure an environment full of contingent experiences or encourage self-initiated exploration in the interest of the ongoing development of competence in her infant than a mother who believes she can influence her outcomes.

These examples suggest undocumented, but plausible, consequences of the social context in which childrearing takes place. The social context is likely to influence the quality of childrearing by setting the experiential boundaries within which those who care for children operate.[246] Both knowledge and beliefs are likely to reflect personal boundaries in a society and in turn are likely to affect childrearing.

What are the implications of environments such as these for shared childrearing? One is to share the childrearing in order to expose the child to an environment that provides lacking elements, to compensate for the limits of the home environment. Previous discussion suggests that in doing this it is critical to be sensitive to how this sharing will affect the child and those parenting. The question is what kinds of sharing support the parenting system, because it is a system and not just a collection of environments. Different interventions might be appropriate, depending on the child and on those parenting. It is interesting to note that the concept of shared childrearing does not appear in the literature describing Headstart, Home Start, or Parent-Child Centers in the U.S., all compensatory interventions. Despite the fact that Headstart is a decade old, the analysis of the experiences as a shared childrearing experiment has gone no further than to express concern that it may be a problem to expose children to two such different environments, home and Headstart, particularly when one is being devalued.[247] Both home based programmes[248] and Parent-Child Centres[249] involve the parent and seem less likely to have this as a problem, but the system of shared childrearing which evolves has not been explored. Evaluating these experiences from the point of view of shared childrearing could be helpful.

Resources Insufficient for Demand

When a person's resources are not sufficient to meet the demands made on him/her, it seems reasonable to assume that childrearing will be affected adversely. While there is no research to date which examines this assumption, there are data which are consistent with it.

For example, data suggest that, as the number of children a person cares for increases, the cognitive development of the children is progressively less,[250] presumably reflecting less adequate care, quite possibly because of excessive demands. As the number of children parents have increases, the time spent caring for or interacting with their children does not increase proportionately.[251] Not only are parents likely to interact less with children as the number of children increases, the interactions they do have are less likely to be suited to the child's development. As the number of children increases, children are more likely to report that parents are autocratic, explaining their behaviour less and resorting to physical punishment more.[252] Other data confirm that it is the demands of having the children which produce these attitudes and behaviours. In a follow-up of college students six years after their attitudes towards children had been assessed, it was found that among women there was an increase in the tendency to reject children over the years directly related to the number of children they had.[253] Increasing rejection in this study was reflected by a tendency to endorse minimizing contacts with children, inhibiting children's demands for attention, and using harsh discipline.

In summary, it does seem that as the demands made on a parent increase, for example, in the form of increasing numbers of children or uninterrupted responsibility, the parent's ability to give individualized attention decreases, as does the likelihood that they will provide responsive care which supports a child's self-initiated exploration of the environment.

Childrearing is not the only demand on a parent's time. It is important to consider the effect of other demands as well, but the research has not been done. Even for the important issue of employment, not much is known about how it affects childrearing.[254] Most research to date has been primarily an attempt to note differences in the children of working and non-working mothers. Studies have not found that the consequences of the mother's working is less adequate development of competence, although there is some ambiguity with respect to sons.[255] In terms of the demands of work, time-use data do indicate that working mothers spend less time in child care than non-working mothers. However, it has also been found that working mothers spend equal amounts of time in one-to-one interaction with their children[256] and equal amounts of time interacting with the children in non-routine care activities.[257] But no one has asked if the time available for childrearing seems adequate to mothers or analysed the consequences of when it does not, of when demands exceed resources. One study does suggest that it is not working per se, but rather that it reflects a mother's satisfaction with her role either as mother or as working mother, which is a more significant predictor of the adequacy of care she provides, dissatisfied women providing less adequate care in both cases.[258] Perhaps dissatisfaction is in part a reflection of perceiving demands to exceed resources.

At this point it seems important to look at the way working fits into the balance between the demands and resources a woman manages to maintain. It would be an important addition to research into the effects of working per se on childrearing. Specifically, research clarifying how the time demands of working influence the quality of childrearing interactions by affecting a mother's or father's ability to be prompt, consistent, and effective in her/his responses to the children is important. It may be that working, as a demand, affects childrearing adversely only when demands exceed resources, for example, when satisfactory childcare is not available or when the demands of work drain available resources. It will be important to complement this research with studies assessing the adequacy in various situations of different forms of shared childrearing as a resource in support of working parents. It is also important to identify other demands on a person's time, to examine how these demands affect childrearing and to determine when shared childrearing can be an ameliorative response.

The original assumption was that childrearing is adversely affected when demands exceed resources. Having looked at situations which represent increasing demands, it is important to look at situations which represent diminished resources. It is in these situations particularly where demands are likely to exceed resources and where sharing childrearing may be a useful alternative.

What do we know about resources and how they are perceived that would help us to explore this issue? Not much, and it is an important concern. Time and money are both important resources in childrearing and presumably there is stress associated with an insufficient supply of either. There is yet another level of resource which needs more work as well. It has to do with emotional resources. What influences a person's capacity to deal with both exceptional and day-to-day demands? Some preliminary research suggests that the extent to which a person has other people to whom s/he can turn influences the likelihood that stress will affect childrearing adversely.[259] For example, a parent's effectiveness in interacting with his/her pre-school child during divorce is related to the support available to parents through their social networks (friends, family, and kin). 'By providing a loving and relatively consistent social environment which allays the doubts and frustrations of the parents, the social network may enable the parent to be more sensitive to the needs of the child.'[260] On a day-to-day basis a husband's support of his wife as mother is important. For example, data suggest that this support is related to the sensitivity and competence of a mother's feeding behaviour.[261] Also, as one would expect, based on the earlier discussion of the effect of the number of children, a father's absence is more detrimental to children's development the greater the number of children.[262]

These data suggest that having interpersonal supports can be helpful. Just how important can be seen in other data which link lack of support in a context of high demand to child abuse. As the demands increase because of single parent status and the stress of poverty and at the same time the interpersonal, economic, and informational resources decrease (less contact with kin, higher geographic mobility making social isolation more likely, poverty, and fewer educational resources) the incidence of child neglect and abuse is greater.[263]

In summary, the assumption that the quality of childrearing interactions depends on the extent to which a person perceives and has the resources sufficient to deal with the demands in his or her life receives some preliminary support. However, little is known in this area. Sharing childrearing might be helpful when there are a number of children or when mothers have uninterrupted responsibility for children. Also, when mothers perceive the demands for childrearing to exceed their capacities, whether or not they in fact do, sharing childrearing with someone else, however briefly, may relieve the stress of sole responsibility.

All of this is very sketchy. More information is needed about the demands people experience, both related and unrelated to childrearing, and how they respond to these demands in terms of analysing and marshalling needed resources. Answers to other questions, such as how important a priority childrearing is, would also be useful as an indicator of how vulnerable the quality of childrearing is as demands approach and exceed resources. Pursuing these and other issues is important to an adequate assessment of the value of shared childrearing.

Shared childrearing seems to be an important support to offer those parenting, specifically when the excessive demands derive from childrearing itself. What forms best suit the parents' needs in terms of supporting effective childrearing would need to be looked into, e.g. father compared with daycare. Shared childrearing may also be helpful when excessive demands derive from sources other than childrearing, but here other alternative supports seem equally important to explore, depending on the source of the problem, such as providing isolated people with interpersonal supports or providing housing which includes adequate play areas to allow a respite from childcare.[264]

To sum up, those caring for children are not always able to provide that which is important to their children's development. When this is the case, perhaps because of lack of knowledge, dysfunctional beliefs, excessive demands on their resources, or other reasons not elaborated on here, sharing childrearing can be a way of improving the situation. However, little is known about how shared childrearing can be most effectively implemented to meet needs. Nor has shared childrearing been examined in the context of other available responses to determine which is most appropriate. More work is needed in this area.

CONCLUSION

Perhaps the most important thing to say at this point is to reiterate what was said at the beginning of this chapter. Most children's rearing is shared. Therefore, to further our understanding of how children are developing under current circumstances, it is important to determine who shares and under what conditions and to explore both the nature of shared childrearing which results and its implications for various aspects of a child's development.

To date, the phenomenon of shared childrearing has been neglected as a guide in focusing research efforts and as a concept useful in explaining research findings. Introducing the concept into research efforts will be useful in several ways. First, focusing on the concept of shared childrearing brings several dimensions of a child's experience, which are otherwise in the background, into relief. It is not that these issues have not been raised before, but rather that they have seemed less important than they are. For example, when the prevailing assumption is that the mother has primary responsibility for raising the children, inconsistencies between her childrearing and the father's are not as developmentally significant as they are when the prevailing assumption is that childrearing is shared. When the prevailing assumption is that the mother has primary responsibility, a secure mother-infant attachment is of central importance. However, when the prevailing assumption is that child-rearing is shared, the mother-infant attachment is seen to be one of a possible cluster of infant attachments. It becomes important to understand the nature and consequences of various patterns of attachment for a child's security and development, thereby moving emphasis, though not interest, away from the mother-infant relationship.

Second, issues which have not been raised before are brought into focus in the process of examining the nature and implications of shared childrearing. One such issue suggested here is the impact of sharing responsibility for a child's rearing on those rearing the child. It is important to determine when sharing responsibility is an important support in a demanding task and when it inadvertently results in less attention to a child's needs.

Third, using the concept of shared childrearing puts research findings in a larger context, a context which more adequately represents the child's reality. For example, the greater belligerence observed in daycare girls[265] could be due to greater exposure to peer interactions, a different norm for behaviour in daycare settings, or it could be a response to the frustration of experiencing conflicting expectations in daycare and home environments. The last explanation is derived from the fact that childrearing is shared and is a plausible and important alternative to explore.

In closing, it does seem that if our efforts to understand children's development in contemporary society are to be successful, shared childrearing is an area in which more knowledge is needed.

NOTES

1 Being a social psychologist by training, I am deeply indebted to Richard Volpe and Fredric Weizmann for the perspective they provided as developmental psychologists and for their provocative and helpful reactions to earlier drafts of this chapter. I am also especially grateful to my colleagues at Child in the City, especially Katherine Catton and Bill Michelson, for their thoughtful and thorough readings and suggestions all along the way, to Brenda Billingsley and Valerie Farrer for their assistance in tracking down some of the detail, and to Catherine Gwin, Douglas Hodgson, and Penny Lawler for their very useful comments and important encouragement.

2 Fraiberg, S. *Every child's birthright: In defense of mothering*, New York: Basic Books, 1977.

3 It is important to note that the forms of shared childrearing considered in this paper do not by any means exhaust the possibilities. For example, communal childrearing is a form of shared childrearing. There is not much research on the effects of these alternatives on the child's development. One important exception is a project examining the effects of various family lifestyles, including nuclear families, non-married couples, single parents, and communal arrangements, on children's development. Weisner, T. Do nonconventional family styles adversely affect infants' gross developmental screening measures. Paper prepared for a symposium on The role of alternative life styles in the prevention of emotional disorders in children, London, Ontario, 1976; Weisner, T. and Martin, J. Learning environments for infants in communes and conventionally married families in California, Family Life Styles Project, Department of Psychiatry and Anthropology, University of California at Los Angeles, 1977. It is also important to note that while the focus of this paper is on the implications of shared childrearing for a child's development, shared childrearing also has implications for those who parent. It will be important to explore questions as to how the experience of parenting is altered by sharing it and what the consequences are for the person parenting. These questions are, for the most part, beyond the scope of this paper but do require consideration.

4 The term childrearing is used throughout this paper instead of child care. There is a euphemistic quality to the phrase child care. For example, the word daycare belies the fact that another person is sharing childrearing. It is more than substitute care. It is rearing. To call it 'care' can constrict the range of questions asked about the effects of shared childrearing. The word care does have emotional connotations as well which may provide reassurance on some levels, but the fact remains that the shared rearing aspect of daycare, and the like, has not been explored. It is hoped that using a more accurate label will focus attention on the dynamics of shared childrearing.

5 Cook, G. *Opportunity for choice*, Ottawa: Statistics Canada, in association with the C.D. Howe Research Institute, 1976.

6 Keniston, K. *All our children: The Carnegie Council on Children*, New York: Harcourt Brace & Jovanovich, 1977.

7 For these arguments and others along with statistical documentation see: Reid, J. Changes in family lifestyles and their implications for the care and well-being of children, unpublished staff working paper. Policy Research and Long Range Planning, Health and Welfare Canada, October 1977.

8 Ibid.

9 Calculated from *Vital statistics II: marriages and divorces*, Statistics Canada, 1973 and 1975.

10 *Vital statistics I: births*, Statistics Canada, 1973.

11 Reid, J. Changes in family lifestyles, viii. *Note*: Though specific statistics for pre-school children are not available, the increase is likely to involve them as much as any other age group.

12 Ibid.

13 Empey, LaMar T. The social construction of childhood, delinquency and social reform, in M.W. Klein, ed., *The juvenile justice system*, Beverly Hills: Sage Publications, 1976, pp. 27–54.

14 Robinson, J. *How Americans use their time: a social psychological analysis of everyday behavior*, New York: Praeger Publishers, 1977; Stone, P. Child care in twelve countries, in A. Szalai, P. Converse, P. Feldheim, E. Schenck, and P. Stone, eds., *The use of time*, The Hague, Netherlands: Mouton, 1972, pp. 249–65; Walker, K.E. and Woods, M.E. *Time use: a measure of household production of family goods and services*, Washington, D.C.: Center of the Family of the American Home Economics Association, 1976.

15 Berger, P., Berger, B., and Keller, H. *The homeless mind*, New York: Random House, 1973, p. 77.

16 Roberts, J.M. The self-management of cultures, in Ward Goodenough ed., *Explorations in cultural anthropology*, New York: McGraw-Hill, 1964; Sutton-Smith, B., Roberts J.M., and Rosenberg, B.G. Sibling associations and role involvement, *Merrill-Palmer Quarterly 10:* 25–38, 1964.

17 Berger et al. *The homeless mind*.

18 Rosenberg, B.G. and Sutton-Smith, B. *Sex and identity*, New York: Holt, Rinehart and Winston, 1972. They make a similar argument regarding sex-role socialization.

19 Slater, P. *Footholds: understanding the shifting family and sexual tensions in our culture*, New York: Dutton, 1977, p. 49.

20 These changes in childrearing are assumed to result in *relative* uncertainty or ambiguity. Parents are not charged with socializing their children in a total vacuum of values and prescriptions. Qualities such as autonomy are encouraged by the social values. However, compared to earlier communities, the behavioural specifications are less comprehensive.

21 Newson, J. and Newson, E. Cultural aspects of childrearing in the English-speaking world, in M.P. Richards, ed., *The integration of a child into a social world*, Cambridge: Cambridge University Press, 1974, pp. 53–82.

22 Bronfenbrenner, U. Socialization and social class through time and space, in E. Maccoby, T. Newcomb, and B. Hartley, eds., *Readings in social psychology*, 3rd ed., New York: Holt, Rinehart and Winston, 1958, pp. 400–25.

23 Wolfenstein, M. Introduction, in M. Mead and M. Wolfenstein, eds., *Childhood in contemporary cultures*, Chicago: University of Chicago Press, 1955, pp. 145–49.
24 Cook, G. *Opportunity for choice*.
25 Glick, P. A demographer looks at American families, *Journal of Marriage and the Family 37:* 15–25, 1975.
26 Glick, P. A demographer looks at families.
27 Ontario Provincial Secretariat for Social Development. Think about the family: a seminar on the family in today's society, May 1977, p. 37.
28 Reid, J. Changes in family lifestyles.
29 White, R.W. Motivation reconsidered: the concept of competence, *Psychological Review 66:* 297–333, 1959.
30 Others have made a similar assumption: Ainsworth, M.S. Mother-infant interaction and the development of competence, in K.J. Connolly and J.S. Bruner, eds., *The growth of competence*, New York: Academic Press, 1973, pp. 97–118; Lee, L.C. Toward a cognitive explanation of peer interaction, in M. Lewis and L. Rosenblum, eds., *Friendship and peer relations: the origins of behaviour IV*, New York: Wiley, 1975, pp. 207–21; Youniss, J. Another perspective on social cognition, in A.D. Pick, ed., *Minnesota symposium on child psychology 9:* Minnesota: University of Minnesota Press, 1975, pp. 173–93.
31 For a critique of developing competence in the interest of 'fitting in,' see Chombart de Lauwe, P.H. Interaction of person and society, *American Sociological Review 31:* 237–48, 1966; Richards, M.P. Introduction in M.P. Richards, ed., *The integration of a child into a social world*, pp. 1–10.
32 This concept fits in well with the perspectives like that offered by Riegal who argues that it would be beneficial to view people less as seeking stability and more as actively dealing with the frequent challenges brought about by change. Riegal, K.F. The dialectics of human development, *American Psychologist 31:* 689–701, 1976. See also White, R.W. Strategies of adaptation: An attempt at systematic description, in G.V. Coelho, D.A. Hamburg, and J.E. Adams, eds., *Coping and adaptation*, New York: Basic Books, 1974, pp. 47–69, for a discussion of the tendency individuals have towards growth as a drive underlying coping and adaptation.
33 Bowlby, J. *Attachment and loss, I: attachment*, London: Hogarth Press and the Institute of Psycho-Analysis, 1969.
34 Berlyne, D. *Conflict, arousal and curiosity*, New York: McGraw Hill, 1960; Hunt, J. McV. *Intelligence and experience*, New York: Ronald Press, 1961; White, R.W. Motivation reconsidered.
35 Piaget, J. *The origins of intelligence in children*, trans. Margaret Cook, New York: International Universities Press, 1952.

36 Freud, S. *Beyond the pleasure principle*, trans. James Strachey, New York:
    Bantam Books, 1928.
37 Piaget, J. *The origins of intelligence*, p. 269.
38 Watson, J.S. Smiling, cooing and 'The Game,' *Merrill-Palmer Quarterly 18:*
    38, 1972.
39 Zelazo, P. Smiling and vocalizing: a cognitive emphasis, *Merrill-Palmer
    Quarterly 18:* 349–65, 1972.
40 Brackbill, Y. Extinction of the smiling response in infants as a function of
    reinforcement schedule, *Child Development 29:* 115–24, 1958.
41 Provence, S. and Lipton, R. *Infants in institutions: a comparison of their
    development with family-reared infants during the first year of life*, New
    York: International Universities Press, 1962; Yarrow, L. Maternal depriva-
    tion: toward an empirical and conceptual re-evaluation, *Psychological
    Bulletin 58:* 459–90, 1961.
42 Skeels, H.M. and Dye, H.B. A study of the effects of differential stimulation
    on mentally retarded children, *Proceedings and Addresses of the American
    Association on Mental Deficiency 44:* 114–36, 1939.
43 Skeels, H.M. Adult status of children with contrasting early life experiences,
    Monographs of the Society for Research in Child Development 31: Serial
    No. 105; No. 3, 1966.
44 Riesen, A.H. Stimulation as a requirement for growth and function in be-
    havioural development, in D.W. Fiske and S.R. Maddi, eds., *Functions of
    varied experience*, Homewood, Ill.: Dorsey Press, 1961, pp. 57–80.
45 Bell, S.M. and Ainsworth, M.S. Infant crying and maternal responsiveness,
    Child Development 43: 1171–90, 1972; Haugan, G.M. and McIntire, R.W.
    Comparisons of vocal imitation, tactile stimulation, and food as reinforcers
    for infant vocalizations, *Developmental Psychology 6:* 201–29, 1972; Rhein-
    gold, H.L. The modification of social responsiveness in institutionalized
    babies, *Monographs of the Society for Research in Child Development 21:*
    Serial No. 63; No. 2, 1956.
46 Bradley, R. and Caldwell, B. Early home environment and changes in mental
    test performance in children from 6 to 36 months, *Developmental Psychology
    12:* 93–7, 1976; Wachs, T., Uzgiris, I., and Hunt, J.McV. Cognitive develop-
    ment in infants of different age levels and from different environmental back-
    grounds: an exploratory investigation, *Merrill-Palmer Quarterly 17:* 283–317,
    1971.
47 Watson, J.S. Smiling, cooing.
48 For extensive reviews of research to date see: Maier, S.F. and Seligman, M.E.
    Learned helplessness: theory and evidence, *Journal of Experimental Psycho-
    logy: General 105:* 3–46, 1976; Lefcourt, H.M. *Locus of control: current*

trends in theory and research, Toronto: John Wiley and Sons, 1976. For an alternative interpretation of the data see also: Wortman, C.B. and Brehm, J.W. Responses to uncontrollable outcomes: an integration of reactance theory and the learned helplessness model, in L. Berkowitz, ed., *Advances in experimental social psychology VIII*, New York: Academic Press, 1975, 277–336.

49 Kohn, M. and Rossman, B.L. Cognitive functioning in five-year-old boys as related to socio-emotional and background demographic variables, *Developmental Psychology 8:* 277–94, 1972.

50 Kohn, M. and Rossman, B.L. Relationship of pre-school socio-emotional functioning to later intellectual achievement, *Developmental Psychology 6:* 445–52, 1972.

51 Murphy, L. *The widening world of childhood*, New York: Basic Books, 1962; Murphy, L. Coping, vulnerability and resilience in childhood, in G.V. Coelho, D.A. Hamburg, and J.E. Adams, eds., *Coping and adaptation*, pp. 69–100; White, R.W. Strategies of adaptation. In a recent article, Harter identifies some of the pressing questions research efforts looking into the ongoing development of competence need to address and her article is highly recommended for anyone interested in this area. Harter, S. Effectance motivation reconsidered: toward a developmental model, *Human Development 21:* 34–64, 1978.

52 Horowitz, F.D. Learning, developmental research and individual differences, in L.P. Lipsett and W.H. Reese, eds., *Advances in child development and behaviour*, IV, New York: Academic Press, 1969, pp. 85–126; Uzgiris, I. Infant development from a Piagetian approach: introduction to a symposium, *Merrill-Palmer Quarterly 22:* 3–10, 1976.

53 Piaget, J. *The origins of intelligence.*

54 Yarrow, L., Rubenstein, J., and Pederson, F. *Infant and environment*, Washington, D.C.: Hemisphere Publishing Corp., 1975.

55 Elardo, K., Bradley, R., and Caldwell, B. The relation of infants' home environments to mental test performance from six to thirty-six months: a longitudinal analysis, *Child Development 46:* 71–6, 1975.

56 Bradley, R. and Caldwell, B. The relationship of infants home environments to mental test performance at 54 months: a follow-up study, *Child Development 47:* 1172–4, 1976.

57 Wulbert, M., Inglis, S., Kriegsmann, E., and Mills, B. Language delay and associated mother-child interactions, *Developmental Psychology 11:* 61–70, 1975.

58 Rubenstein, J. Maternal attentiveness and subsequent exploratory behaviour, *Child Development 38:* 1089–1100, 1969; Yarrow et al. *Infant and environment.*

59 In the Rubenstein study just cited, number of toys and variety of play opportunities were related to preference for novel objects (exploratory behaviour),

but so was maternal attentiveness. Since the number of toys and the variety of play opportunities were also related to maternal attentiveness (they occur together), it is not possible to state with confidence that the relationship between variety and exploratory behaviour is not what is called spurious, there only because variety occurred with maternal attentiveness. The Yarrow et al. study did pursue this and established that it is, in fact, variety that is the significant factor. However, this kind of follow-up is rare, and therefore, most of the assertions made in this chapter are best assumed to be tentative, pending further corroboration.

60 Yarrow et al. *Infant and environment.*
61 Haugan, G.M. and McIntire, R.W. Comparisons of reinforcers for infant vocalization.
62 Wachs, T. Utilization of a Piagetian approach in the investigation of early experience effects: a research strategy and some illustrative data, *Merrill-Palmer Quarterly 22:* 11–30, 1976.
63 Davis, E.A. The development of linguistic skill in twins, singletons, and sibs, and only children from five to ten, *University of Minnesota Institute of Child Welfare Monograph*, 1937, No. 14.
64 Mittler, P. Biological and social aspects of language development in twins, *Developmental Medicine and Child Neurology 12:* 741–57, 1970.
65 Lytton, H., Conway, D., and Sauvé, R. The impact of twinship on parent-child interaction, *Journal of Personality and Social Psychology 35:* 97–107, 1977.
66 Jones, P. Home environment and the development of verbal ability, *Child Development 43:* 1081–6, 1972. For a thorough review of this kind of finding during infancy see: Appleton, T., Clifton, R., and Goldberg, S. The development of behavioral competence in infancy, in F.D. Horowitz, ed., *Review of child development research IV*, Chicago: University of Chicago Press, 1975, pp. 100–86.
67 Wachs, T. Utilization of a Piagetian approach.
68 Wachs, et al. Cognitive development in infants.
69 See for example: Bruner, J.S. On perceptual readiness, *Psychological Review 4:* 123–52, 1957; Festinger, L. *A theory of cognitive dissonance*, Stanford: Stanford University Press, 1957; Kahneman, D. *Attention and effort*, Englewood Cliffs, N.J.: Prentice-Hall, 1973.
70 Piaget, J. *The origins of intelligence*; Hunt, J.McV. *Intelligence and experience*; Hunt, J.McV. Intrinsic motivation and its role in psychological development, in D. Levine, ed., *Nebraska Symposium on Motivation* XIII, Lincoln: University of Nebraska Press, 1965, pp. 189–282; Kagan, J. *Change and continuity in infancy*, New York: Wiley, 1971.

71 Appleton et al. The development of competence in infancy; Wachs, T. The optimal stimulation hypothesis and early development: anybody got a match?, in I. Uzgiris and F. Weizmann, eds., *The structuring of experience*, New York: Plenum Press, 1977, pp. 153–77.

72 Berlyne, D. *Conflict, arousal and curiosity.*

73 Eysenck, M.W. Arousal, learning and memory, *Psychological Bulletin 83:* 389–404, 1976.

74 Easterbrook, J.A. The effect of emotion on cue utilization and the organization of behavior, *Psychological Review 66:* 183–201, 1959.

75 Yerkes, R.M. and Dodson, J.D. The relation of strength of stimulus to rapidity of habit formation, *Journal of Comparative Neurology and Psychology 18:* 459–82, 1908.

76 McLaughlin, R.J. and Eysenck, H.J. Extraversion, neuroticism and paired-associate learning, *Journal of Experimental Research 2:* 128–32, 1967. For a discussion of a recent failure to replicate, see Eysenck, M. Arousal, learning and memory.

77 Callaway, E. and Band, R.I. Some psychopharmacological effects of atrophine: preliminary investigation. *Archives of Neurology and Psychiatry 79:* 1958, 91–102; Callaway, E. The influence of amobarbital (amylobarbitone) and methamphetamine on the focus of attention, *Journal of Mental Science 105:* 382–92, 1959. These data are just a hint of the work done involving the concept and influence of arousal. For the interested reader the following reviews are recommended: Berlyne, D. Arousal and reinforcement, in D. Levine, ed., *Nebraska Symposium on Motivation*, 1–110, 1967; Eysenck, M. Arousal, learning and memory; Kahneman, D. *Attention and effort*; Kiesler, C. and Pallak, M. Arousal properties of dissonance manipulations, *Psychological Bulletin 83:* 1014–25, 1976.

78 Wachs et al. Cognitive development in infants.

79 Clark, A. and Richards, C. Auditory discrimination among economically disadvantaged and non-disadvantaged pre-school children, *Exceptional Children 33:* 259–62, 1966.

80 Wepman, J.M. Auditory discrimination, speech and reading, *Elementary School Journal 60:* 325–33, 1960.

81 Wachs et al. Cognitive development in infants; White, B. and Held, R. Plasticity of sensorimotor development in the human infant, in J. Rosenblith and W. Allinsmith, eds., *The causes of behavior*, 2nd ed., Boston: Allyn and Bacon, 1966, pp. 60–71.

82 Yarrow et al. *Infant and environment.*

83 Bell, S. and Ainsworth, M.S. Infant crying and maternal responsiveness.

84 Watson, J. Memory and 'contingency analysis' in infant learning, *Merrill-Palmer Quarterly 13:* 55–76, 1967.

85 Stern has suggested that the inconsistent and the unexpected are part of what elicits attention and pleasure during play. This seems quite reasonable and, since play is likely to be important to learning, it is important to distinguish the inconsistency in play situations from the inconsistency being discussed here and assumed to have a negative impact on learning. In the present context, learning to be effective in eliciting desired outcomes is the concern. The responses being discussed are those to acts which infants intend to have certain effects. Inconsistency in this situation may well be disruptive of learning in the same way that response delay is disruptive. Each is likely to interfere with the perception of having an intended effect. The inconsistency in play, when it does not disrupt the experience of contingency, is likely to facilitate competence by expanding the infant's schema of human behaviour. Stern, D.N. Mother and infant play: the dyadic interaction involving facial, vocal and gaze behaviours, in M. Lewis and L. Rosenblum, eds., *The effect of the infant on its caregiver*, New York: Wiley, 1974, 187–214.

86 Becker, W.C. Consequences of different kinds of parental disciplines, in M.L. Hoffman and L.W. Hoffman, eds., *Review of child development research I*, New York: Russell Sage Foundation, 1964, pp. 169–208; Fein, G. and Clarke-Stewart, A. *Day care in context*, Toronto: Wiley, 1973; Kagan, J. Issues and evidence in day care, in W. Michelson, S.V. Levine, and E. Michelson, eds., *The child in the city: today and tomorrow*, ch. 10, Toronto: University of Toronto Press.

87 Watson, J. Smiling, cooing.

88 Coopersmith, S. *The antecedents of self-esteem*, San Francisco: W.H. Freeman, 1967.

89 Beckwith, L. Relationships between attitudes of mothers and their infants' IQ scores, *Child Development 42:* 1083–97, 1971; Stayton, D.J., Hogan, R., and Ainsworth M.S. Infant obedience and maternal behaviour: the origin of socialization reconsidered, *Child Development 42:* 1057–69, 1971.

90 Yarrow et al. *Infant and environment*.

91 Radin, N. The role of the father in cognitive, academic and intellectual development, in M. Lamb, ed., *The role of the father in child development*, New York: Wiley, 1976, pp. 237–76.

92 The role of behavioural self-initiation is particularly important in early childhood. However, not all learning is based on this trial and error method. Often, skills are learned by imitating others. And cognitive processes facilitate vicarious learning about what to expect from the world, by observing the outcomes for those perceived to be similar to us. However, these methods are not as important in infancy and early childhood as later on. Dollard, J. and Miller, N.E. *Social learning and imitation*, New Haven: Yale University Press, 1941; Bandura, A. Vicarious processes: a case of no-trial learning, in L. Berkowitz, ed., *Advances in Experimental Social Psychology*, vol. 2, 1965, pp. 1–55.

93 Condry, J. Enemies of exploration: self-initiated vs. other-initiated learning, *Journal of Personality and Social Psychology 35:* 459–77, 1977; Hunt, J.McV. *The challenge of incompetence and poverty*, Urbana, Ill.: University of Illinois Press, 1969.

94 Lepper, M.R., Greene, D., and Nisbett, R.E. Undermining children's intrinsic interest with extrinsic rewards: a test of the overjustification hypothesis, *Journal of Personality and Social Psychology 28:* 129–37, 1973.

95 Kelly, H.H. The process of causal attribution, *American Psychologist 28:* 113, 1973.

96 There may be a problem with attributing this sophisticated process to such young children. Condry reviews research which suggests that the discounting principle is not prevalent among young children. However, it is still an open question. There is another explanation of the data which is plausible. It has been found that, when given a number of tasks to perform people are more likely to recall the incompleted tasks than the completed tasks and are more likely to resume incompleted than completed tasks. Assuming that there is tension associated with incompleteness, completing the task alleviates the tension. How does this relate to the children in the Lepper et al. study? It is possible that those who worked for an award experienced closure when they received it, while those who were not working for award experienced less closure when the time was up, even if they received a reward unexpectedly. When given an opportunity to continue drawing in a freeplay session, those with less closure drew more. Whether it is one of these explanations or another that is involved, the observation that individuals are less likely to pursue an activity if it is performed for task extrinsic rewards is important. Developing competence requires sustained activity. Zeigarnik, B. Über das behalten von erledigten und unerledigten Handlungen, *Psychologische Forschung 9:* 1–85, 1927; Ovsiankina, M. Die Wiederaufnahmen von unterbrochenen Handlungen, *Psychologische Forschung 11:* 302–389, 1928; Lewin, K. *Field theory in social science*, New York: Harper and Row, 1951.

97 Discussing only one study gives an incomplete picture of the work done to date. The interested reader is referred to Condry's review (Enemies of exploration). In addition to elaborating on these findings, he discusses the possibility that verbal approval may not have the same effect as other rewards on motivation.

98 Stephen, M.W. and Delys, P.A. External control expectancies among disadvantaged children at preschool age, *Child Development 44:* 670–4, 1973.

99 Strickland, B. Delay of gratification as a function of race of the experimenter, *Journal of Personality and Social Psychology 22:* 108–12, 1972.

100 Ainsworth, M.S. The development of infant-mother attachment, in B. Caldwell and H.N. Ricciutti, eds., *Review of child development research III*,

Chicago: University of Chicago Press, 1973, pp. 1-94. See also: Dweck, C. and Repucci, N. Learned helplessness and reinforcement: responsibility in children, *Journal of Personality and Social Psychology 25:* 109-16, 1973.

101 Hiroto, D.S. and Seligman, M.E. Generality of learned helplessness in man, *Journal of Personality and Social Psychology 31:* 311-27, 1975.

102 Lefcourt, H.M. *Locus of control.*

103 Davis, W.L. and Phares, J. Internal-external control as a determinant of information-seeking in a social influence situation, *Journal of Personality 35:* 547-61, 1967; Seeman, M. and Evans, J.W. Alienation and learning in a hospital setting, *American Sociological Review 27:* 772-83, 1962.

104 Wolk, S. and DuCette, J. Monetary incentives upon incidental learning during an instrumental task, *Journal of Educational Psychology 66:* 90-5, 1974.

105 Lefcourt, H.M., Lewis, L. and Silverman, I.W. Internal vs. external control of reinforcement and attention in a decision-making task, *Journal of Personality 36:* 663-82, 1968.

106 Brecher, M. and Denmark, F.L. Internal-external locus of control and verbal fluency, *Psychological Reports 25:* 707-10, 1969.

107 Dweck, C. and Repucci, N. Learned helplessness and reinforcement; Hiroto, D.S. Locus of control and learned helplessness, *Journal of Experimental Psychology 102:* 187-93, 1974; Mischel, W., Zeiss, R., and Zeiss, A. Internal-external control and persistence: validation and implications of the Stanford Preschool Internal-External Scale, *Journal of Personality and Social Psychology 29:* 265-78, 1974.

108 Bell, S. and Ainsworth, M.S. Infant crying and maternal responsiveness.

109 Korner, A.F. and Thomas, E.D. The relative efficacy of contact and vestibular-proprioceptive stimulation in soothing neonates, *Child Development 43:* 443-53, 1972.

110 Yarrow et al. *Infant and environment.*

111 Yarrow, L. and Pederson F. Attachment: its origins and course, in W.W. Hartup, ed., *The young child, II,* Washington, D.C.: National Association for the Education of Young Children, 1972, p. 54. For a summary of difficulties in defining 'attachment,' see: Weinraub, M., Brooks, J. and Lewis, M. The social network: a reconsideration of the concept of attachment, *Human Development 20:* 31-47, 1977.

112 Yarrow, L. and Pederson, F. Attachment, 63-4, italics not in the original.

113 Ainsworth and her colleagues have done important work in this area, attempting to identify and understand the development and implications of different types of attachment. The mother-infant relationship described here is likely to result in what Ainsworth has called 'secure' attachment,

and in Ainsworth's work, as here, it is a secure attachment which is associated with an accelerated development of competence. In the discussion to follow, the benefits of attachment relate to a secure attachment.

Ainsworth's work suggests that there are relationships which result in attachment which is not secure (e.g. an ambivalent attachment). The distinctive developmental consequences of other types of attachment are being explored. This work of Ainsworth and her colleagues is highly recommended to the reader interested in this area. For reviews of the work see: Ainsworth, M.S. Mother-infant interaction and the development of competence.

114 Kessen and Mandler propose this as an aspect of learning and call it acquiring secondary inhibitory properties. Kessen, W. and Mandler, G. Anxiety, pain and inhibition of distress, *Psychological Review 68:* 396–404, 1961.

115 Cox, F.N. and Campbell, D. Young children in a new situation with and without their mothers, *Child Development 39:* 123–31, 1968. For similar findings see: Ainsworth, M. and Wittig, B. Attachment and exploratory behaviour of one-year-olds in a strange situation, in B.M. Foss, ed., *Determinants of infant behaviour IV*, London: Methuen, 1969, pp. 111–36; Rheingold, H.L. and Eckerman, C.O. The infant separates himself from his mother, *Science 168:* 78–83, 1970.

116 Anderson, J.W. Attachment behaviour out of doors, in N.G. Blurton Jones, ed., *Ethological studies of child behaviour*, Cambridge: Cambridge University Press, 1972, pp. 199–215.

117 Rheingold, H. and Eckerman, C.O. The infant separates himself.

118 Blurton Jones, N.G. and Leach, G.M. Behavior of children and their mothers at separation and greeting, in N.G. Blurton Jones, ed., *Ethological studies of child behavior*, 1972, pp. 217–248; Lamb, M. The role of the father: an overview, in M. Lamb, ed., *The role of the father in child development*, pp. 1–61.

119 Bowlby, J. *Attachment and loss.*

120 Ainsworth, M.S. The development of infant-mother attachment.

121 Harter, S. Mental age, IQ and motivational factors in the discrimination learning set performance of normal and retarded children, *Journal of Experimental Child Psychology 5:* 123–41, 1967. See also: White, B. and Watts, J.C. *Experience and environment I*, Englewood Cliffs, N.J.: Prentice-Hall Inc., 1973; Lytton et al. The impact of twinship on parenting. These studies report that infants who seek more attention have less responsive mothers.

122 Schaffer, H. and Emerson, P. The effects of experimentally administered stimulation on the developmental quotients of infants, *British Journal of Social and Clinical Psychology 7:* 61–7, 1968.

123 Zigler, E. and Butterfield, E.C. Motivational aspects of changes in IQ test performance of culturally deprived nursery school children, *Child Development 39:* 1–14, 1968.
124 Wachs et al. Cognitive development in infants.
125 Yarrow et al. *Infant and environment.*
126 Cole and Bruner in discussing the tendency to equate performance and capacity stated, in 1971, that 'although such misgivings abound, they have not yet crystallized into a coherent program of research and theory nor have the implications of accepting the need to incorporate an analysis of situations in addition to traditional experimental manipulations been fully appreciated.' This is still the case. Cole, M. and Bruner, J.S. Cultural differences and inferences about psychological processes, *American Psychologist 26:* 870, 1971. It is important to note that in reality programme intervention probably affects the competence of some children in terms of their capacity and others in terms of their performance capability. The alternative interpretation of the data has been stated in its most extreme form to make the contrast clearly.
127 Ainsworth, M.S. The development of infant-mother attachment.
128 Bell, R.Q. A reinterpretation of the direction of the effects of studies in socialization, *Psychological Review 75:* 81–95, 1968; Bell, R.Q. and Harper, *Child effects on adults*, Hillsdale, N.J.: Lawrence Erlbaum Associates, 1977.
129 Murphy, L. *Widening world of childhood.*
130 Stern, D.N. Mother and infant play.
131 Robson, K.S. The role of eye-to-eye contact in mother-infant attachment, *Journal of Child Psychology and Psychiatry 8:* 13–25, 1967; Fraiberg, S. Blind infants and their mothers: an examination of the sign system, in Lewis, M. and Rosenblum, L., eds., *The effect of the infant on its caregiver*, 1974, pp. 215–32.
132 Clarke-Stewart, A. Interaction between mothers and their young children: characteristics and consequences, *Monographs of the Society for Research in Child Development 38:* Serial No. 153; No. 6–7, 1973; Wolff, P.H. The natural history of crying and other vocalizations in early infancy, in B.M. Foss, ed., *Determinants of infant behaviour: IV*, 1969, pp. 81–110.
133 Birns, B. Individual differences in human neonates' response to stimulation, *Child Development 36:* 249–56, 1965.
134 Bell and Harper's book *Child effects on adults* is highly recommended to any reader interested in pursuing this topic. They suggest, for example, that the infant's influence on the mother's behaviour may begin during pregnancy and that some difficulties during pregnancy and during birth may originate with the infant and not with the mother as is usually assumed.

135 Sameroff, A.J. and Chandler, M.J. Reproductive risk and the continuum of caretaking casualty, in F.D. Horowitz, ed., *Review of child development research: IV*, 1975, pp. 187–245.

136 Bruner, J.S. Organization of early skilled action, *Child development 44:* 1–11, 1973; Fowler, W. A developmental approach to infant care in a group setting, *Merrill-Palmer Quarterly 18:* 145–77, 1971; White, B.L. *The first three years of life*, Englewood Cliffs, N.J.: Prentice-Hall, Inc., 1975.

137 Ainsworth, M.S. The development of infant-mother attachment; Bowlby, J. *Attachment and loss*; Fowler, W. A developmental approach to infant care.

138 Clarke, A.M. and Clarke, A.D. *Early experience: myth and evidence*, New York: Free Press, 1976; Kagan, J. The baby's elastic mind, *Human Nature 1:* 66–73, 1978.

139 See, for example, Kagan, J. and Klein, R.E. Cross-cultural perspective on early development, *American Psychologist 28:* 947–61, 1973; Kagan, J. and Moss, H. *Birth to maturity*, New York: John Wiley and Sons, 1962.

140 Yarrow et al. *Infant and environment*, p. 4.

141 Yarrow, L. Personal consistency and change: an overview of some conceptual and methodological issues, *Vita Humana 7:* 67–72, 1964.

142 Clarke, A.M. and Clarke, A.D. *Early experience*.

143 Goldberg, S. Social competence in infancy: a model of parent-infant interaction, *Merrill-Palmer Quarterly 23:* 163–78, 1977; Sroufe, L.A. Early experience: evidence and myth, *Contemporary Psychology 22:* 878–80, 1977.

144 Kagan, J. Baby's elastic mind.

145 Sroufe, A.L. Early experience, 879.

146 In a recent paper on the ecology of human development, Bronfenbrenner sets the stage for a more thorough examination of the issues involved in how children develop than has previously been undertaken. His paper is highly recommended and its influence is readily seen in the organization and range of issues considered in the remainder of this chapter. Bronfenbrenner, U. Toward an experimental ecology of human development, *American Psychologist 32:* 513–531, 1977.

147 Robinson, J. *How Americans use time*; Stone, P. Child care. This is not to ignore the growing efforts of fathers or overemphasize mothers. In societal forms which preceded industrial society (on which there are data), specifically hunter-gatherer societies, mothers have primary responsibility for childrearing in the first year in only 50 per cent and in none do mothers have primary responsibility after the first year. Weisner, T. and Gallimore, R. My brothers' keeper: child and sibling caretaking, *Current Anthropology 18:* 169–90, 1977.

148 Kotelchuck, M. The infants' relationship to the father: experimental evidence, in M. Lamb, ed., *The role of the father in child development*, 1976 pp. 329–44; Lamb, M. The role of the father.

149 Bowlby, J. *Attachment and loss.*

150 Parke, R.D. and Sawin, D.B. The father's role in infancy: a re-evaluation, *Family Coordinator 25:* 366, 1976.

151 Parke, R.D., O'Leary, S., and West, S. Mother-father-newborn interaction: effects of maternal medication, labour, and sex of infant. Reported in R.D. Parke, and D.B. Sawin. The fathers' role in infancy.

152 Parke, R.D. and O'Leary, S. Father-mother-infant interactions in the newborn period: some findings, some observations and some unresolved issues, in K.F. Riegal, and J. Meacham, eds., *The developing individual in a changing world*, The Hague: Mouton, 1975, pp. 653–63.

153 Greenberg, M. and Morris, N. Engrossment: the newborn's impact upon the father, *American Journal of Orthopsychiatry 44:* 520–31, 1974.

154 Whiting, B. and Whiting, J. *Children of six cultures*, Cambridge, Mass.: Harvard University Press, 1975.

155 Blanchard, R.W. and Biller, H.B. Father availability and academic performance among third-grade boys, *Developmental Psychology 4:* 301–5, 1971.

156 Some attempts to explain separation anxiety focus on it as a child's anxiety that the mother is abandoning him/her. As such it is attributed central importance in the developing child's emotional life. However, a more recent approach by Kagan explains the phenomenon in cognitive-motivational terms. Not all understanding emerges at once. Separation protest is assumed to reflect that point at which the child has a concept for his/her mother and her significance, and is just developing the capacity to imagine alternative consequences of her departure. Without being able to answer the question of where she is going, there is anxiety associated with her departure. This approach differs from the earlier one in that it assumes separation protest to be a likely consequence of cognitive development and not a noteworthy signal of an unusual anxiety about being abandoned. Kagan, J. Emergent themes in human development, *American Scientist 64:* 186–96, 1976; Spitz, R.A. *The first year of life*, New York: International Universities Press, 1965.

157 Kotelchuck, M. The infants' relationship to the father; Spelke, E., Zelazo, P., Kagan, J., and Kotelchuck, M. Father interaction and separation protest, *Developmental Psychology 9:* 83–90, 1973.

158 Kotelchuck, M. The infant's relationship to the father; Leibowitz, A. Education and home production, *American Economic Review 64:* 243–50, 1974; Robinson, J. *How Americans use time*; Stone, P. Child care.

159 Lamb, M. Interaction between eight-month old children and their fathers and mothers, in M. Lamb, ed., *The role of the father in child development*,

1976, pp. 307–28. Lamb's book is an excellent review and update of recent work done with fathers.

160 Rebelsky, F. and Hanks, C. Father's verbal interaction with infants in the first three months of life, *Child Development 42:* 63–8, 1971.

161 Ban, P. and Lewis, M. Mothers and fathers, girls and boys: attachment behaviour in the one-year-old, *Merrill-Palmer Quarterly 20:* 195–204, 1974; Pederson, F.A. and Robson, K.S. Father participation in infancy *American Journal of Orthopsychiatry 39:* 466–72, 1969.

162 Lewis, M. and Weinraub, M. The father's role in the child's social network, in M. Lamb, ed., *The role of the father in child development*, p. 172.

163 Brooks, J. and Lewis, M. Person perception and verbal labeling: the development of social labels, reported in M. Lewis and M. Weinraub. The father's role in the social network.

164 Ainsworth, M. *Infancy in Uganda: infant care and the growth of love*, Baltimore: Johns Hopkins Press, 1967: Schaffer, H. and Emerson, P. The development of social attachments in infancy, *Monographs of the Society for Research in Child Development 29:* Serial No. 94; No. 3, 1964.

165 Kotelchuck, M. The infant's relationship to the father; Lamb, M. Father-infant and mother-infant interaction in the first year of life, *Child Development 48:* 167–82, 1977.

166 Radin, N. The role of the father.

167 Lamb, M. and Lamb, J.E. The nature and importance of the father-infant interaction, *Family Coordinator 25:* 379–85, 1976.

168 Lamb, M. Twelve month olds and their parents: interaction in a laboratory playroom, *Developmental Psychology 12:* 237–44, 1976.

169 Spelke et al. Father interaction.

170 Weinraub et al. The social network.

171 Ibid.

172 Hartup, W.W. Peer relations and the growth of social competence, in M. Kent, and J. Rolf, eds., *The primary prevention of psychopathology, Vol. 3: promoting social competence and coping in children*, Hanover, N.H.: University Press of New England, in press; Konner, M.J. Relations among infants and juveniles in comparative perspective, *Social Science Information 5:* 371–402, 1976; Lewis, M., Young, G., Brooks, J., and Michelson, L. The beginning of friendship, in M. Lewis and L. Rosenblum, eds., *Friendship and peer relations*, 1975, pp. 27–66; Weisner, T.S. and Gallimore, R. Child and sibling caretaking.

173 Hartup, W.W. Peer relations.

174 Goode, W.J. *Revolution and family patterns*; Shorter, E. *The making of the modern family*, New York: Basic Books, 1975.

175 Sutton-Smith, B. and Rosenberg, B.G. *The sibling*, New York: Holt Rinehart and Winston, 1970. The book is a notable exception.

176 Sells, S.B. and Roff, M. Peer acceptance – rejection and birth order, *Psychology in the Schools 1:* 156–62, 1964. *Note:* Liking is assumed to be a response to a child's skill in interacting. However, Sells and Roff did not measure these social skills. It is possible that it is not social skills, but other processes altogether which mediate less acceptance of older and middle children. For example, first-born children achieve more and middle children may be more reliant on others for help. Even if all children had comparable social skills, these differences could mediate preferences for the younger children. Deutsch, A. Birth order effects on measures of social activities for lower-class preschoolers, *Journal of Genetic Psychology 127:* 325, 1975; McGurk, H. and Lewis, M. Birth order: a phenomenon in search of an explanation, *Developmental Psychology 1:* 366, 1972; Schacter, S. Birth order, eminence and higher education, *American Sociological Review 28:* 757–68, 1963.

177 Lieberman, A. Preschoolers' competence with a peer: relations with attachment and peer experience, *Child Development 48:* 1277–87, 1977.

178 The discussion to follow is based on Hartup, W.W. Peer relations.

179 Whiting, B. and Whiting, J. *Children of six cultures.*

180 Ibid.

181 Eckerman, C.O., Whatley, J., and Kertz, S.L. The growth of social play with peers during the second year of life, *Developmental Psychology 1:* 42–9, 1975.

182 Belmont, L. and Marolla, F.A. Birth order, family size and intelligence, *Science 182:* 1096–1101, 1973; Breland, H.M. Birth order, family configuration and verbal achievement, *Child Development 45:* 1011–19, 1974; Zajonc, R.B. and Markus, G.B. Birth order and intellectual development, *Psychological Review 82:* 74–88, 1975.

183 Gartner, A., Kohler, M., and Reissman, F. *Children teach children,* New York Harper and Row, 1971.

184 Olds, D. Cross-age tutoring and parent involvement, *Dissertation Abstracts 38:* 1305A, 1977.

185 Hartup, W.W. Peer relations.

186 Harlow, H.F. and Harlow, M.K. Effects of various mother-infant relationships on rhesus monkey behaviours, in B.M. Foss, ed., *Determinants of infant behaviour IV,* 1969, pp. 15–36.

187 Novak, M.A. and Harlow, H.F. Social recovery of monkeys isolated for the first year of life: 1. Rehabilitation and therapy, *Developmental Psychology 11:* 453–65, 1975; Suomi, S.J. and Harlow, H.F. Social rehabilitation of isolate-reared monkeys. *Developmental Psychology 6:* 487–96, 1972.

188 Furmen, W., Rahe, D., and Hartup, W.W. Social rehabilitation of low-interactive preschool children by peer intervention, University of Minnesota, in preparation.

189 Hartup, W.W. Social development and peer relations. Leighton McCarthy Memorial Lecture. Given at the Institute for Child Study at University of Toronto, April 1978.

190 Weisner, T. and Gallimore, R. Child and sibling caretaking.

191 Cicirelli, V.G. Effects of mother and older sibling in the problem-solving behaviour of the younger child, *Developmental Psychology 11:* 749–56, 1975.

192 Sutton-Smith et al. Sibling associations.

193 Gartner et al. *Children teach children.*

194 Olds, D. Tutoring and parent involvement.

195 Cicirelli, V.G. Concept learning of young children as a function of sibling relationships to the teacher, *Child Development 43:* 282–7, 1972; Cicirelli, V.G. Effects of sibling structure and interaction on children's categorization style, *Developmental Psychology 9:* 132–9, 1973.

196 Cicirelli, V.H. Siblings teaching siblings, in V. Allen, ed., *Children as teachers*, New York: Academic Press, 1976, pp. 99–112.

197 Cicirelli, V.H. Effects of mother and older sibling. Cicirelli interprets this finding differently. He suggests that the younger child's ability to use help provided by his/her mother is a function of having used help from the older sister. While possible and intriguing, because, if so, it is an example of how child-child interactions might alter parent-child interactions, it does not seem as plausible, as the interpretation offered here.

198 Mueller, E. and Lucas, I. A developmental analysis of peer interaction among toddlers, in M. Lewis, and L. Rosenblum, eds., *Friendship and peer relations*, 1975, pp. 223–58.

199 Bronson, W. Competence and the growth of personality, in K. Connolly, and J. Bruner, eds., *The growth of competence*, p. 225.

200 Ibid.

201 Lewis et al. The beginning of friendship.

202 Ibid.

203 Bates, E. Peer relations and the acquisition of language, in M. Lewis, and L. Rosenblum, eds., *Friendship and peer relations*, pp. 259–92.

204 Zajonc, R.B. and Markus, G.B. Birth order and intellectual development.

205 Data from one study suggest that older siblings may function as a secure base from which to explore. Children with older siblings at the same school cried less than children without older siblings when confronted with the

novelty of a daycare experience. More research along these lines is needed. Blurton Jones, N.G. and Leach, G.M. Children and mothers at separation and greeting.

206 Cochran, M.M. Comparison of group day care and family childrearing patterns in Sweden, *Child Development 48:* 702-7, 1977.

207 Wandersman, L.P. An ecological study of the interaction of caregivers and daycare children in family day care homes, *Cornell Journal of Social Relations*, in press.

208 Bronfenbrenner, U. Research on the effects of day care on child development, in *Toward a national policy for children and families*, National Research Council, Advisory Committee on Child Development, 1976, pp. 117-33; Hutchison, R. and Siegal, L. Developmental consequences of infant day care centre attendance. Manuscript submitted for publication, McMaster University Medical Centre; Kagan, J., Kearsley, R.B., and Zelazo, P.R. The effects of infant day care on psychological development, *Evaluation Quarterly 1:* 109-42, 1977.

209 Kagan, J., Kearsley, R., and Zelazo, P. The emergence of initial apprehension to unfamiliar peers, in M. Lewis and L. Rosenblum, eds., *Friendship and peer relations*, pp. 187-206; Kagan et al. Effects of infant day care. In another frequently cited study, daycare children were more wary of strange adults at two-and-a-half and at three-and-a-half years than home-reared children. The concerns about the affects of daycare on attachment and social relationships sparked by this study do not at present seem justified. Other related studies and specific attempts to replicate it have not resulted in similar findings. Blehar, M.C. Anxious attachment and defensive reactions associated with day care, *Child Development 45:* 683-92, 1974; Roopnarine, J.L. and Lamb, M. The effects of daycare on attachment and exploratory behaviour in a strange situation, *Merrill-Palmer Quarterly 24:* 85-96, 1978.

210 Ricciuti, H.N. Fear and the development of social attachments in the first year of life, in M. Lewis and L. Rosenblum, eds., *The origins of fear*, New York: Wiley, 1974, pp. 73-106.

211 It would be particularly interesting to see if and how such differences enter into the development of attitudes toward ethnic diversity. See Chapter 6 of this volume.

212 Bronfenbrenner, U. Is early intervention effective? in H.J. Leichter, ed., *The family as educator*, New York: Teachers College Press, 1974, pp. 105-29; Raph, J.B., Thomas, A., Chess, S., and Korn, S.J. The influence of nursery school on social interactions, *American Journal of Orthopsychiatry 58:* 144-52, 1968; Schwarz, J.C., Strickland, R.G., and Krollick, G.

Infant day care: behavioral effects of preschool age, *Developmental Psychology 10:* 502–6, 1974.

213 A look at other variables used indicates that careful scrutiny of how such variables as aggression are interpreted is required. For example, daycare children are more 'intolerant of frustration.' This conclusion is based on the fact that they are less able to tolerate interruptions or to accept failure. However, looked at in another way, this may mean the daycare children are better able to persist in self-initiated behaviours than home-reared children, not a matter for concern according to earlier discussion.

Since the value of daycare is at present an issue of considerable debate, it is important to identify the specific behavioural differences underlying conceptual labels, such as 'aggressive.' Conceptual labels can convey a value judgment which you as a reader may not share once the behaviours are identified.

214 One study suggests that family daycare providers do take more responsibility for socializing their own children than the other children they are caring for. Not only are more studies of this kind needed to confirm and elaborate on the finding, but research is also needed which adds observation of the socializing in the child-child interaction which coincides. Wandersman, L.P. An ecological study of the interaction of caregivers' own and day care children.

215 Lytton et al. The impact of twinship on parenting.

216 Biemiller, A., Avis, C., and Lindsay, A. Competence supporting aspects of day care environments: a preliminary study. Paper presented at Canadian Psychological Association meeting, Toronto, June 1976; Fowler, W. How adult/child ratios influence infant development, *Interchange 6:* 17–31, 1975.

217 The finding that home-reared and daycare children perform equally well on IQ tests does not control for the adult/child ratio in each setting. It may be that daycare and control children both come from large families and therefore daycare is not a disadvantage in terms of individualized attention. And the result is equal IQ test performance. It may also be that adult/child ratio is not as influential a factor in such complex settings as one might at first expect. Perhaps daycare providers, when trained, can facilitate learning quite effectively despite a higher adult/child ratio.

218 Cochran has begun to look at this. Cochran, M. Daycare and family childrearing.

219 Getzels, J.W. Preschool education, *Teachers College Record 68:* 219–28, 1966; Getzels, J.W. Socialization and education: A note on discontinuities, in H.J. Leichter, ed., *The family as educator*, pp. 44–51.

220 Getzels, J.W. Socialization and education.

221 Horowitz, F.D. and Paden, L.Y. The effectiveness of environmental intervention programs, in B. Caldwell and H.N. Riccuiti, eds., *Review of child development research* III, pp. 331–402.

222 Berlyne, D. *Conflict, arousal and curiosity.*

223 Elardo, R. and Caldwell, B.M. Value imposition in early education: fact or fancy? *Child Care Quarterly 2:* 6–13, 1973; Horner, W.C. Value imposition in day care: fact, fancy and irrelevant? *Child Care Quarterly 6:* 18–30, 1977.

224 Horner, W.C. Value imposition in day care.

225 Fowler, W. A developmental approach to infant care.

226 Blehar, M.C. Anxious attachment and day care; Caldwell, B., Wright, C., Honig, A., and Tannenbaum, J. Infant day care and attachment, *American Journal of orthopsychiatry 40:* 379–412, 1970; Cochran, M. Day care and family child-rearing; Doyle, A. Infant development in day care, *Developmental Psychology 11:* 655–6, 1975; Kagan et al. Effects of infant day care; Leiderman, P.H. and Leiderman, G.F. Affective and cognitive consequences of polymatric infant care in the East African highlands, in A.D. Pick, ed., *Minnesota Symposia on Child Psychology 8*, Minneapolis: University of Minnesota Press, 1974, pp. 81–110.

227 Caldwell et al. Infant day care.

228 Cochran, M. Day care and family childrearing. To test children in an environment which differs in familiarity complicates interpretation of the results. In the Caldwell et al. study children were observed at the daycare centre, a setting familiar to the daycare children, but not to the home-reared. The novelty of the environment may have elicited more exploratory behaviour from the home-reared children, reducing the extent of affiliative interaction with their mothers. If so, the equal amount of affiliative behaviour reported in the two groups of children would not be likely in environments equated for novelty. Daycare children will be comparatively less affiliative in their behaviour. However, the two other studies with settings equated for novelty eliminate this as an alternative interpretation of the Caldwell et al. data.

229 Doyle, A. Infant development in daycare; Ainsworth, M. and Bell, S. Attachment, exploration and separation: illustrated by the behaviour of one-year-olds in a strange situation, *Child Development 41:* 49–67, 1970.

230 Blehar, M.C. Anxious attachment and daycare. Leiderman and Leiderman's report that African children raised by more than one caretaker express more negative affect at their mother's departure than children raised primarily by their mothers may support Blehar's data. However, whether the negative affects reflect an insecure attachment for their mothers arising from sepa-

ration, or simply a situational recognition that their mother is less likely to come back needs further inquiry before a conclusion can be reached. Leiderman, P.H. and Leiderman, G.F. Polymatric infant care.

231 Roopnarine, J.L. and Lewis, M. The effects of day care.

232 Farran, D.C. and Ramey, C.T. Infant day care and attachment behaviour toward mothers and teachers, *Child Development 48:* 1112–16, 1977.

233 Kagan et al. Effects of infant day care.

234 Ricciuti, H.N. Fear and the development of social attachments; Vinay, M. Attachment behaviours in young children experiencing two primary caregivers, MA thesis, University of British Columbia, Vancouver, B.C., 1973. Reported in T.M. Williams, Childrearing practices of young mothers: what we know, how it matters, why it's so little, *American Journal of Orthopsychiatry 44:* 70–5, 1974.

235 Latané, B. and Darley, J. *The unresponsive bystander*, New York: Appleton-Century-Crofts, 1970.

236 Honig, A.S. and Lally, J.R. How good is your infant program? Use an observational method to find out, *Child Care Quarterly 4:* 194–207, 1975.

237 Weigand and Gross, study done at Michigan State University. Reported in P. Stone, Child Care.

238 Minturn, L. and Lambert, W. *Mothers of six cultures: antecedents of childrearing*, New York: Wiley, 1964.

239 A study being done at the University of Toronto School of Social Work by E. McIntyre and P. Lawler looking into the quality of relationships in childcare networks is an important exception.

240 Personality differences in mothers and fathers which influence their tendency to provide desired conditions are beyond the scope of this paper. So also, are issues of development for parents. In the latter case, there is actually very little work. Much of developmental psychology has focused on the first two decades of life. Recent work has intensified interest in infants and the elderly. However, as we turn to the capacity of parents it becomes important to ask how the developmental phases of adults influence their responses to the demands of childrearing. Erik Erickson's work, popular works like Sheehy's *Passages*, researchers who have recently begun to explore development in terms of the 'life span,' and work which explores the stresses of adult life all have something to contribute here. But it is just a beginning and it seems important that theoretical and experimental work move into this area for its own sake and to aid in our understanding of the conditions which influence the quality of childrearing. Bronfenbrenner, U. The experimental ecology of education, *Educational Researcher 5:* 5–14, 1976; Dohenwrend, B. and Dohenwrend, B.S. *Stressful life events: their nature and*

effects, New York: Wiley, 1974; Erikson, E. Identity and the life cycle, *Psychological Issues 1:* 1–173, 1959; Joulet, L.R. and Baltes, P.B. *Lifespan developmental psychology: research and theory*, New York: Academic Press, 1970; Sheehy, G. *Passages: predictable crises of adult life*, New York: Dutton, 1976.

241 Tulkin, S.R. and Cohler, B.J. Childrearing attitudes and mother-child interaction in the first year of life, *Merrill-Palmer Quarterly 19:* 95–106, 1973; Sameroff, A. Transactional models in early social relations, *Human Development 18:* 65–79, 1975.

242 Bernstein, B. Elaborated and restricted codes: their social origins and some consequences, in K. Danzinger, ed., *Readings in child socialization.* Toronto: Pergamon Press, 1970, pp. 165–86.

243 Coser, R.L. Complexity of roles as a seedbed of individual autonomy, in L.A. Coser, ed., *The idea of social structure: papers in honor of Robert R. Merton.* New York: Harcourt, Brace & Jovanovich, 1975, pp. 237–63.

244 Battle, E. and Rotter, J.B. Children's feelings of personal control as related to social class and ethnic groups, *Journal of Personality 31:* 482–90, 1963; Ramey, C.T. and Campbell, F.A. Parental attitudes and poverty, *Journal of Genetic Psychology, 128:* 3–6, 1976.

245 Falender, C. and Helser, R. Attitudes and behaviours of mothers participating in the Milwaukee Project. Unpublished manuscript, 1974, reported in S. Tulkin. Dimensions of multicultural research in infancy and childhood, in R.H. Leiderman, S.R. Tulkin, and A. Rosenfeld, eds., *Culture and infancy*, New York: Academic Press, 1977, pp. 567–86.

246 Fischer, C. *Networks and places: social relations in the urban setting*, New York: Free Press, 1977; Mechanic, D. Social structure and personal adaptation: some neglected dimensions, in G. Coelho, D. Hamburg, and J. Adams, eds., *Coping and adaptation*, pp. 32–44.

247 Cole, M. and Bruner, J.S. Cultural differences and inferences about psychological processes; Horowitz, F.D. and Paden, L.Y. Effectiveness of intervention programs.

248 Brofenbrenner, U. Is early intervention effective?; Dudzinski, D. and Peters, D.L. Home-based programs: a growing alternative, *Child care Quarterly 6:* 61–7, 1977.

249 Hunt, J.McV. Parent and child centers: their basis in the behavioral and educational sciences, *American Journal of Orthopsychiatry 41:* 13–38, 1971.

250 Belmont, L. and Marolla, F.A. Birth order, family size and intelligence; Breland, H.M. Birth order, family configurations and achievement.

251 Jacobs, B. and Moss, H. Birth order and sex of sibling as determinants of mother-infant interaction, *Child Development 47:* 315–22, 1976; Robinson, J

How Americans use time; Lytton et al. The impact of twinship in parenting.
252 Clausen, J.A. Family structure, socialization and peers, in M.L. Hoffman and L.W. Hoffman, eds., *Review of child development research* II, New York: Russell Sage Foundation, 1966, pp. 1–54. *Note:* The same pattern appears across classes. Therefore, it is not explained by the tendency of the lower and working classes, who have more children than the middle class, to use more physical punishment in disciplining their children.
253 Hurley, J.R. and Hohn, R.L. Shifts in child-rearing attitudes linked with parenthood and occupation, *Developmental Psychology 4:* 324–8, 1971.
254 For reviews of research on working mothers, see Etaugh, C. Effects of maternal employment on children: a review of recent research, *Merrill-Palmer Quarterly 20:* 71–98, 1974; Hoffman, L.W. Effects of maternal employment on the child: a review of the research, *Developmental Psychology 10:* 204–28, 1974.
255 Hoffman, L.W. Effects of maternal employment.
256 Goldberg, R. Maternal time-use and preschool performance, Graduate Faculty of Education, University of Pennsylvania, in preparation.
257 Robinson, J. *How Americans use time.*
258 Yarrow, M.R., Scott, P., de Leeuw, L., and Heinig, C. Child-rearing in families of working and nonworking mothers, *Sociometry 25:* 122–40, 1962.
259 Cochran, M. and Brassard, J. Child development and personal social networks, draft of a paper presented at the symposium on the Ecology of Human Development: Theory, Method and Preliminary Results. New Orleans, March 1977. *Note:* This paper presents an interesting discussion of the functions of personal social networks.
260 Hetherington, E.M., Cox, M., and Cox, R. Divorced fathers. *Family Coordinator 25:* 417–28, 1976.
261 Pederson, F.A. Mother, father and infant as an interactive system, Paper read at a meeting of the American Psychological Association, Chicago, September 1975. Reported in F.A. Pederson, Does research on children reared in father-absent families yield information on father influences? *Family Coordinator 25:* 459–64, 1976.
262 Sutton-Smith, B., Rosenberg, B.G., and Landy, F. Father-absence effects in families of different sibling compositions. *Child Development 39:* 1213–21, 1968.
263 Garbarino, J. A preliminary study of some ecological correlates of child abuse: the impact of socioeconomic stress on mothers, *Child Development 47:* 178–85, 1976; Giovanni, J. and Billingsley, A. Child neglect among the poor: a study of parental adequacy in families of three ethnic groups,

Child Welfare 44: 196–204, 1970; Prescott, J.W. and McKay, C. Child abuse and child care: some cross-cultural and anthropological perspectives, reported in J. Bernard, *The future of motherhood*, London: Penguin, 1974.

264 The earlier discussion points to other ways in which shared childrearing can contribute to a child's developing competence. For example, an only child might benefit from exposure to peers and both only children and last children might benefit from an early opportunity to teach, each of which could be provided through a mixed-age daycare setting. Also, role differentiation is likely to vary from culture to culture, with the consequence that father's involvement in childrearing is more important in some cultures than in others to a child's acquiring necessary competence. See: Radin, N. The role of the father.

265 Fowler, W. A development approach to infant care.

4

Children and the Law:
An Empirical Review

KATHERINE CATTON

I EMPIRICAL RESEARCH ON LEGAL ISSUES AFFECTING CHILDREN

In Canada in 1975, over 50,000 marriages ended in divorce, an increase of 12.4 per cent over 1974.[1] While our legal system has rules regulating this process, we do not know how, or even how many, children under 18 are affected by these divorces. Similarly, many children live with parents who are separated from their spouses. Less is known about how the separation process itself and the long-term living arrangements which result alter the lives of these children.

In 1976 in Ontario, more than 20,000 cases of children 'in need of protection' came into our legal system.[2] In these instances, the judge must determine whether the child's family has failed to provide him with a minimum standard of care. If the court so decides, it can permit social agencies to intervene coercively to protect the child 'at risk.' Yet how effectively these agencies enhance the well-being of the children involved, if at all, remains unknown at this time, although suspicion exists that their potential for harm at least equals their potential for good.

An even greater number of children are brought into our legal system as delinquents. Approximately 140,000 children were dealt with by the police in 1976 in Canada and, in 43 per cent of these cases, charges were either recommended to be laid or actually laid.[3] In all of these instances the legal system seeks to promote the child's 'best interest.' Yet, underlying policy is set in a vacuum, for little information exists to inform the decisions which underlie our legislative and judicial guidelines governing judgments affecting the child's best interests.

One central focus of both law and social science is human behaviour. Legal policies are based upon predictions about human behaviour. Yet these decisions are usually made without adequate knowledge about the probable consequences of adopting one policy or another. While much of our present jurisprudence is amenable to empirical analysis, few relevant data exist to enlighten the choices made. The body of this chapter examines several key areas of law noting where social science research may clarify issues, focus questions, or point out probable solutions to the many difficult problems confronting legislators and policy-makers when they seek to further the child's 'best interests.' In the end, there emerges a clear picture of the need for and yet regrettable lack of scientifically based factual information to inform these decisions.

This chapter is divided into a number of discrete segments. Introductory remarks on the need for and utility of an empirical analysis of the traditional assumptions of our jurisprudence on children will be presented. Following this, the legal and developmental approaches to ascertaining who children are will be reviewed. Some consequences of these definitional processes will be examined in the section which addresses children's legal and developmental capacity to consent to medical treatment. The issue of legal capacity and responsibility is inextricably bound up with what children know about law and what they can know from a developmental perspective, and this is the focus of section IV of the chapter. In section V, a number of issues affecting the processing of children through the courts are surveyed, including the wide discretion in decision-making, the child's participation in the hearing, the issue of legal representation, the use of social reports, and alternative forms of courts for families and children. In the sixth section, some special concerns related to delinquency are canvassed. In conclusion, the children's rights movement is examined with an emphasis on the changing legal status of children in our society.

The chapter draws its content from a variety of disciplines and is directed towards a varied audience, including lawyers, policy-makers, service delivery personnel and clinicians, as well as social scientists. While this diversity of perspectives may create many problems of definition, jargon, bias, priorities, and theoretical and methodological orientations, casting a wide net, in Nonet's[4] view, broadens our perceptions, obliges us to cross narrow disciplinary boundaries, and follow multiple paths of inquiry, hence facilitating the integration of legal and social research.

Yet to cross disciplinary boundaries successfully, for the legal scholar to make intelligent use of scientific methodology, and for the social scientist to undertake meaningful empirical research on legal issues, an in-depth appreciation of the other discipline is required. To this end, the social scientist must understand the nature and scope of the law he wishes to investigate. To date, says Freeley, researchers have taken a narrow view of the concept of law. This has often led to generalizations about law and society that are of questionable use.[5] To pose relevant questions and draw proper boundaries of inquiry, the social scientist must broaden his concept of law and enlarge his understanding of its many forms and functions.[6] Those who seek to answer the questions posed by our legal system through empirical analysis require more than a passing understanding of the nature, purposes, and processes of our laws and legal structures. Otherwise, they risk undertaking superficial analysis and drawing trivial conclusions. Similarly, policy-makers and legislators need to understand what social science research can and cannot do for them. What it can do is provide the policy-maker with an increased confidence in the probability that his decision will effect a certain outcome, that it will influence behaviour in one way or another. What it cannot do is eliminate the value judgments inherent in most policy decisions.

To encourage a meaningful empirical approach to legal issues pertinent to children, a brief historical review of some of the key bodies and concepts of law will be presented. Their present day application will then be noted. Following this, a review of some key concepts and techniques of analysis from the behavioural sciences will accompany an outline of the various ways in which empirical research can assist the policy-maker in understanding the legal system as it now exists, in making choices for reform and in evaluating the effectiveness of reforms. After a brief description of the scientific method and some of the research techniques social science employs to collect meaningful data, a caveat on the uses and limitations of scientific research will be filed. In conclusion, the need for a multidisciplinary analysis of the multifaced problems of children and law will become apparent.

The Legal Perspective
At the most fundamental level the first question the reader might reasonably pose is – what is law? A common but misleading answer, in Karl Llewellyn's view, defines law as a set of rules to govern conduct, enforced by external constraint, laid down by the state and addressed to the man on the street.[7] A more accurate approach, he suggests, focuses on what officials do in dealing with disputes. From this perspective, rules assume importance only insofar as they help people predict what officials will do should a dispute arise.[8] In this way, rules guide behaviour. But no matter what the definition, it is clear that law is concerned with both value and conduct, be it individual, group, institutional, or that of society as a whole. Yet these same concerns arise in the realm of social science – only here the approach is 'the scientific study of society and of individual relationships in and to society'[9] with a view to describing, predicting, and explaining behaviour.

To understand the present legal status of children requires an appreciation of the basic elements of law. Our law, says Glanville Williams, is 'composed of three great elements: common law, equity and legislation,'[10] each with its own historical tradition.

Historically, our law was nothing more than a collection of unwritten local or tribal customs.[11] After the Norman conquest of England in 1066, judges travelling around the country administering the local laws began to select out and apply only the best of these laws. Through this selection process, there developed a uniform, national body of unwritten customary law common to all of England, with the judges serving as guardians or interpreters of this body of learning. This system of unwritten common law rules, originally developed and administered by the ancient common law courts, forms the backdrop of our present legal system.

Law, however, should not be confused with justice. Justice is an end. Law is only a means of achieving that end. And the common law in early times was a most imperfect way of achieving justice, so much so that when the common law courts failed to provide relief, disappointed litigants often petitioned the king as the 'fountain of all justice' to provide extraordinary relief. Eventually, a separate court, the Court of Chancery, evolved to administer this 'equitable' relief. It attempted to provide fair and morally just remedies not available at common law. Thus, a separate system of law – the law of equity – with its separate court, developed alongside the common law. When the rules of common law and equity came into conflict, equity prevailed so long as the person seeking the equitable relief was himself free from any taint of wrongdoing. Today, these two branches of unwritten law remain separate. Their administration, however, is now fused so that one court administers both systems.[12]

An examination of the legal status of children illustrates the interaction between these two elements of law. At common law, children were virtually legal non-entities. The father's common law position as natural guardian of both the property and person of his child was almost absolute, even against the mother. As recently as 1878 an English judge described the right of a father to the custody and control of his child as 'one of the most sacred rights.'[13] Only when the father's conduct was such as to gravely imperil the life, health, or morals of the child[14] would the Court of Chancery exercise its historic equitable wardship jurisdiction, acting on behalf of the Crown as *parens patriae*[15] and intervene in the father-child relationship to assume the duties and obligations of the natural parent.[16]

The third element of law is statute law – codified rules passed into law by legislatures. Gradually, legislators have enacted statutes revising large portions of both the common law and equity. Today, in theory, our legislators have sole law-making power. Hence, legislation, where enacted, supersedes the unwritten common law.[17] Conversely, where no statute law exists, recourse must be had to the prevailing common law or equitable rules. Thus, despite the father's almost absolute power over his child at common law, beginning in the nineteenth century, a series of statutes intervened on behalf of the mother, strengthening her rights to custody of the child,[18] culminating in the 1920s with equal guardianship legislation. For example, *The Infants Act*[19] in Ontario declares:

Unless otherwise ordered by the Court and subject to this Act, the father and mother of an infant are joint guardians and are equally entitled to the custody, control and education of the infant.

Like all law, however, the legal status of children is an evolving concept. Moreover, it appears to be changing rapidly today. Yet in those areas of law where children's legal status has not evolved, either through legislation, policy, or court decision, the controlling jurisprudence may be outmoded.

Because sole law-making power is now vested in our legislatures, the judiciary claims only to discover and apply the law. In reality, however, judges create law in several ways. There is a hierarchy of courts, and judicial authority and the doctrine of precedent hold that the rule found in the decision of a higher court binds lower courts;[20] that is, when their material facts are the same, cases must be decided in the same way.[21] But a later court can reexamine an earlier case and, in effect, redefine the rule of that earlier case by restricting the rule to the particular facts of that case. In this way, a similar case with comparable material facts can now be distinguished from the earlier case and, therefore, be decided differently. In effect, the previous decision is redefined and, by the slow erosion of further redefinition, is effectively overruled and hence no longer binding. Thus, the law is changed.[22]

Similarly, judges are often called upon to interpret statutes. Statutes are general statements. They must cover a wide range of situations, some of which the legislators did not foresee when drafting the enactment.[23] But statutes do not stand alone. They draw their life from their words and phrases, some of which have long-established common law meanings. 'Technical terms used in a statute, undefined, must draw their meaning from the law which brought them forth' says Llewellyn.[24] So, here again, the case law is examined for guidance in defining statutory terms and in determining legislative intention. While maintaining the fiction of merely trying to discover the aim of the legislation, judges, through this process of interpretation, create new law to achieve just and sensible results. Thus, judicial law-making colours all three strands of our legal system – common law, equity, and legislation.

Cross-cutting all three elements of our legal system are two bodies of law which must be distinguished – substantive and procedural law. Substantive law deals with the substance of law – what ought to be. It creates, defines, and regulates rights and duties. It both affects and reflects the values of our society. Procedural law, on the other hand, regulates the working of the courts.[25] It is that body of law which prescribes methods of enforcing substantive rights and duties or otherwise sets out the formal steps which must be taken in judicial proceedings.

For example, when legislation authorizes the state to remove a child from his parents if his living environment falls below a minimally acceptable standard, this rule involves an issue of substantive law. It mirrors our belief that children are entitled to a decent home life. The formal steps which child welfare authorities must follow to achieve this end, for example, the steps necessary for notifying the parents of a judicial hearing, the procedure for forcing parents to bring their child to court if they refuse to do so voluntarily, the rules which determine what evidence is admissible – all these illustrate what is meant by the term procedural law. Similarly, our laws on delinquency and custody contain both substantive and procedural components.

Procedure is of critical importance in our legal system. When there is a dispute, procedural rules enter into and condition the realization of any right or duty set out in substantive law. Substantive law has no meaning apart from procedure.[26] For this reason, discussions of substantive law easily become misleading.[27] Without the procedure to allow the individual to reach his substantive right or remedy, such rights or remedies are otiose. When procedures are simple, rights are easily enforced; when procedure is complex or abstruse, rights may be virtually illusory.

In settling the disputes brought before them, our courts usually operate on an adversary model of procedure. The trial is a 'battle of strategy and wits, a judicial duel between counsel ...'[28] In private law, two private individuals are in dispute; in public law, it is the state in dispute with the individual. The person asserting a claim before the courts, the plaintiff or prosecutor, has the burden of proving his claim. He must prove his allegations to a certain degree – 'beyond a reasonable doubt' in criminal proceedings and on 'the balance of probabilities' in all others. The opposing party, the defendant, may choose to do nothing, but if he does not rebut his opponent's evidence, he runs the risk that the uncontradicted evidence will be believed and his opponent will be successful in asserting his claim.

This overview is intended to alert the reader to the complexity of our laws and legal process. Any statement of law must be interpreted in the light of the relevant legislation and case law, its true nature and purpose, form and function, being the result of a convoluted evolutionary process, not necessarily apparent at first glance.

Legal Research and Scientific Research

The focus of this chapter is research. Yet what the lawyer means by research and what the social scientist means are very different things. Thus, it is important to define this key term. Traditional legal research comprises a variety of activities whether it be undertaken to prepare argument for court or background documents for legislative reform. Statutes, where relevant, must be analysed to see if they apply to the problem at hand. They must be read for their plain meaning.

Then, the case law must be examined to learn how the statute has been interpreted both as a whole and for the particular word or phrase in question. Where no statute applies, the case law is the sole source of the governing principles. Scholarly commentary in texts or law journals may also be cited for its persuasive value.

When this preparation is undertaken to determine the merits of an individual case and thus predict judicial opinion on the matter, the fact situation and relevant law are parsed and analysed with a view to presenting arguments to persuade a court of a particular explanation of the facts and application of the relevant law. And if one set of arguments does not persuade the court, an alternative explanation may be presented. Despite the theatrical demand of witnesses that they testify to 'the truth, the whole truth, and nothing but the truth' our courts do not exist to establish objective truth.[29] '[A] lawsuit is not a scientific investigation for the discovery of truth, but a proceeding to determine the basis for, and to arrive at a settlement of, a dispute between litigants.'[30] Hence, legal research in preparation for court is directed towards constructing arguments which will persuade the court of a particular view of the fact situations favourable to one party in the dispute. Earlier cases which do not support the particular position to be advocated must be distinguished on their facts from the case at hand. Otherwise the judge may consider himself bound to follow the rule they establish. Note that, in court, 'fact' is something to be argued and eventually determined on the weight of the evidence.

At the law reform or policy level, a similar research process is followed. Statutes are analysed, cases parsed, and scholarly opinion considered. At this level, special-interest-group opinion and public opinion are also sought. Moreover, the views of the legislators themselves play a key role for they reflect the political climate for the reform under consideration. In all legal research much argument centres around what the facts might be, but seldom is an attempt made to determine what they are in a scientific manner.

Empirical research, on the other hand, seeks to establish objective scientific fact. Many questions treated by jurists as purely legal questions are really empirical questions. At the law reform or policy level, scientific research can complement legal research. Both the need for undertaking reform and suggested routes of achieving reform can be predicated on a data-based analysis of the problem and its possible solutions.

The Scientific Method
'[T]aking law in its largest sense as encompassing all aspects of government, the predominant mode of securing legal data is the dialectic method,' says Loevinger. 'The scientific method [on the other hand] is clearly a different and distinguishable approach to data gathering ...'[31] Science, like law,

... is a mode of securing agreement among individuals with respect to certain kinds of questions and problems. The strength of science derives from its objective and demonstrative, and therefore highly persuasive, techniques. The limitation of science is that it is not applicable to all kinds of questions ... Essentially the scientific method is applicable only to questions ... involving issues of 'fact.'

The basic methods of science are experimental, statistical and clinical ... Science recognizes no meaning that is not empirically definable and accepts no significance that is not empirically demonstrable.[32]

Hence what social science has to offer law is research methodology which facilitates the gathering of reliable information to inform legal decision-making. And, because empirical research deals with probabilities, its chief predictive value lies at the broad policy level rather than at the individual level. The utility of social science research as a tool in the law reform process will now be examined in more detail.

'[U] p to the present time,' Loevinger asserts, 'law has made little use of science, ... and ... lawyers generally have little understanding of science or its concepts and methods.'[33] Selznick observes that a social science interest in law is outside the mainstream of scholarship in both law and science.[34] Social science research can, however, make valid contributions to both substantive and procedural law reform in at least three ways – in accurately describing the existing system, in devising innovative reforms, and finally, in evaluating the success of the reforms once implemented. While there is much overlap in these three conceptual categories, for purposes of clarity they will be examined separately.

At the Descriptive Level
At the purely descriptive level, scientific information-gathering techniques can be used to monitor the effects of existing law so that accurate information about the operation of the various components of, for example, the present juvenile justice system, is available.[35] 'The law as it appears on the statute books may be only a partial and sometimes misleading guide as to the administered situation which in fact exists.'[36]

Because the basic data have not been gathered, no one knows exactly what happens. While there is no lack of claims of deficiencies based on hunches and surmise, concrete documentation is virtually non-existent. For example, there is a growing concern that our juvenile courts are failing to stem the tide of delinquency. Yet no official year-by-year record is kept of the delinquency charges laid to document the rise in delinquency or of juvenile court dispositions to show that these courts are doing a less adequate job than in the past. Before decrying the inadequacies of the delinquency process, a complete statistical picture of what is now happening should be available. Collecting data to describe the system and to clarify the nature and extent of any problems that exist must be the first step in any effective law reform process. Only once the problem is understood, can solutions be sought.

At the Legislative or Policy Level

Social science research may also assist policy-makers in devising solutions to these problems. Once a clear data-based *description* of the problem exists, this body of background data can also help to narrow and crystallize the issues and to predict the possible consequences of the various reform alternatives available.[37]

Yet, as Ellsworth and Levy note, '... efforts to apply social science data directly to the solution of legal problems are impeded because the social scientists' theoretical categories seldom coincide with the issues presented by legal doctrinal development.'[38] The existing psychological and psychiatric research relevant to the problems of child custody adjudication, for example, is minimal because social scientists have been engaged in formulating and trying to answer their own theoretical and empirical questions, and their questions seldom correspond with the questions to which policy-makers seek answers.[39] For example, '[d]irect studies of the effects of different types of custody arrangements are non-existent '[40] Yet, despite the absence of data to inform such decisions, legislative choices must be made.[41] Ellsworth and Levy conclude,

Until such studies are undertaken, ... the only contributions from psychological research are the few tentative indicators ... extending some tentative hypotheses ... Since the legislative responsibility cannot be held in abeyance pending the collection of more useful and conclusive data, for the time being it will have to be dealt with as it has been in the past – on the basis of hunches, guesses, surmises, and biases.[42]

Sound policy analysis, however, requires not only that good rules be formulated, but also that their probable impact on the overall system be considered.[43]

[T]he problems of children exist in the context of the culture and organizational structure of the social agencies involved ... The introduction of significant change into elaborately organized complex institutions is extraordinarily difficult. There is not much reason to believe the proposals for change will succeed if they ignore the social forces which make for organizational stability and inertia.[44]

Hence, policy-makers need to know the characteristics of the system they seek to change and this knowledge can only be obtained through basic empirical research.

Wald supports Ellsworth and Levy's view that social science research could have a significant impact on policy choice.[45] But even beyond the almost total absence of data to inform such decisions, many of these questions, says Wald, 'cannot be answered solely through research ...'[46] Facts alone cannot resolve normative issues. Their ultimate resolution rests on value judgments about the kinds of policies we wish to further for children. '[L]aw does, and should, embody value judgments that are beyond the reach of factual impeachment.'[47]

In the end, law deals with preference, and not truth. Prescribing norms is an essential component of law-making and this is not and cannot be scientific in any sense which the contemporary scientific community would recognize as such.[48] Empirical fact alone cannot resolve the value-ridden controversies inherent in many legal questions.[49] The ultimate responsibility to choose is vested in the policy-makers and legislators and they must not delegate this duty to the scientific expert. They must retain their power of choice, while employing empirical data to help them make the most informed choice possible. Thus, the utility of scientific research in devising reforms is its ability to narrow and focus the controversy, crystallize the issues, perhaps point to unsuspected solutions, and give indications of the probable effectiveness of proposed remedies.

At the Implementation Level: Evaluating Reforms

Social science research techniques can also help policy-makers evaluate the effects and effectiveness of their reforms. 'Living law,' says Friedman, 'is different from the law on the books.'[50] Katkin and his co-authors stress that 'changes in the law do not automatically result in predictable changes of behavior of real people in the real world.'[51] There is, they note, 'considerable danger that changes in the law will result in unanticipated changes in the behavior of people ..., and that those unanticipated changes will undermine or negate the law's intentions.'[52] Thus, reforms must be monitored not only to determine whether the predicted or desired outcomes occur, but also to assess unanticipated consequences.

Moreover, Kalven notes, because law has a multiplicity of ends, law-makers may try to escape the threat of empirical impeachment by shifting ground. 'Legal rules and ... institutions [usually] do not have a single avowed end or purpose against which their performance can be tidily measured.'[53] Because of this, the social scientist attempting to pin down a legal premise for testing may be frustrated in his efforts.

But while this multiplicity of ends may be a profound point about the nature of practical action and about law in particular, it is a shallow point in the relation of law to science. At most, it is a warning against too simplistic a scientific approach. To say that the purposes of law are multiple is not to say that they are indeterminate.[54]

Meaningful evaluation which can measure the impact of reforms is, however, dependent upon having a clear picture of how the system functioned before the reform was implemented. Thus the interdependency of the three levels of empirical research in the law reform process becomes apparent. Basic data gathering is necessary not only to help define the problem and to point to possible solutions which legislators should consider, but also to provide a baseline of comparison from which to measure the impact of reform for, as Campbell and Stanley observe, the process of comparison, of recording differences or contrast, is basic to the scientific method.[55]

Evaluation is applied research which employs scientific rigour and methodology to measure the effectiveness of a programme or reform in achieving its goals.[56] There are four distinct steps in this kind of research.

1 The goals or objectives of the reform must be clearly identified. Meaningful evaluation cannot be conducted on a programme which has confusing or contradictory objectives.
2 Operational measures must be formulated and criteria established which can be used to assess whether the reform achieves the goals.
3 Then, using a methodologically sound research design, data must be collected and analysed to measure the success of the programme.
4 Finally, recommendations for future programme activity can be made based on the interpretation of the data. In this way the output of evaluation research may form the basis of future legislative or policy reform.[57]

According to Donald Campbell, a leading research psychologist, 'modern nations should be ready for an experimental approach to social reform, an approach in which we try out new programs designed to cure specific social problems, in which we learn whether or not these programs are effective, and in which we retain, imitate, modify or discard them on the basis of apparent effectiveness ...'[58] Usually, today, Campbell notes, 'specific reforms are advocated as though they were certain to be successful.'[59] Then to avoid possible failure, 'most administrators wisely prefer to limit the evaluations to those the outcomes of which they can control ... Ambiguity, lack of truly comparable comparison bases, and lack of concrete evidence all work to increase the administrator's control over what gets said ...'[60] This may result in a failure to evaluate the reform realistically for if 'the political and administrative system has committed itself in advance to the correctness and efficacy of its reforms, it cannot tolerate ... failure. To be truly scientific we must be able to experiment. We must be able to advocate without the excess of commitment that blinds us to reality testing.'[61]

Even where there is a commitment to hard-headed evaluation, research may be directed towards measuring the competence of the administrator rather than the deficiencies in the programme he runs. In this situation, again the administrator has a vested interest in having the programme appear successful. Because of this, the data are sure to be biased in innumerable ways favourable to the administrator. Hence, *ad hominem* research designed to evaluate specific administrators rather than alternative policies should be avoided.

To ameliorate the contaminating effects of these factors, Campbell suggests a shift in the political approach to reform. In this approach, policy A would be instituted on an experimental basis. If after a few years there were no significant improvements, policy A would be discarded and policy B tried.[62] By explicitly acknowledging that the proposed solution appeared to be the best of several that the administrator could have advocated and by having a plausible alternative, the administrator can afford honest evaluation of the outcome of his reform. He would not jeopardize his job if reform A did not work because his job would be to keep after the problem till something was found that did work. Alternatively, a variety of programmes could be instituted on an experimental basis and their effectiveness compared. Then the programme demonstrated most effective would be retained.[63] This approach to research, designed to evaluate reforms rather than specific administrators, would minimize attempts to sabotage the measurement system or suppress unwanted research results.

The Need for Independence in Empirical Research

Empirical research must be both impartial and objective. Only through impartial assessment can the diverse alternatives found, for example, in our juvenile justice system, be meaningfully compared.[64] To maintain objectivity, empirical research must be conducted by independent investigators. Yet, there exist serious problems in maintaining researcher independence. Once the researcher moves into the 'real world,' he must rely to some degree on organizations to fund him and give him access to information. Independence and impartiality are hampered in those cases where government-sponsored programmes are the subject of research, government must give its consent to the research, funds the research, or attempts to or has control over the dissemination of the results.[65] When government dominates research, there is a danger that only favourable evaluations will be released.[66] Moreover, the political vulnerability our usual system of government reform creates by advancing a priori one specific programme as the 'solution' frequently precludes objective, hard-headed evaluations.[67]

The Responsibility of the Social Scientist

When applied social science research is used in the law reform process, social researchers are under an obligation to speak responsibly. According to Katkin and his co-authors, those who would influence social policy with knowledge derived from the social sciences are obliged (1) to develop a thorough data base which draws on the total body of relevant knowledge, and which proceeds from a profound awareness of the limitations on such data; (2) to develop an optimal plan, that is, one which is not only workable, but which offers greater benefits or less costs than other possible solutions to the problem posed; and (3) to anticipate possible unintended consequences of the reform which may alter existing political and social arrangements.[68] Social science knowledge, like all cultural artifacts, exists in a social context that can limit the researcher's perspective.[69] Social scientists desirous of having a powerful impact on governmental policy may be tempted to overstate their case[70] or overlook the limitations in their data.[71] Furthermore, the process translating social science concepts into social action is highly complicated and the social scientist far from an unbiased translator. Hence, legislators and others responsible for the formulation and implementation of policy should not be dazzled by the promise of the social sciences.[72] Policy-makers must develop a taste for empirical research on legal problems so that they can know 'what scientific inquiry can and cannot do for law.'[73] Yet, Kalven cautions that a little methodology may be a dangerous thing, for it may lead to simplistic approaches to complex problems.[74] There is a need in law for a much wider and deeper understanding of the empirical method and its implications and applications.[75] While no panacea, such research can be an important aid to delineating problems and evaluating solutions.

The Interdisciplinary Approach
Wald believes that there are many 'lawyers who are anxious to work with behavioral scientists in framing the questions and doing the research' on legal problems relating to children.[76] But both the lawyers and social scientists must understand that: 'The successful resolution of complex social problems requires that they be appreciated and understood from a range of perspectives. There is no single discipline (and certainly no single approach within a discipline) that is able to perceive and explain all the intricacies of human interaction.'[27] Ellsworth and Levy have summarized the problem most succinctly in recommending: 'To prescribe remedies requires ... empirical studies designed and executed by interdisciplinary teams. The studies would then take account of the theoretical and practical orientations of the law and provide relevant data ... to test the law's hypotheses, while profiting from the methodological rigor possible with a scientific approach.'[78]

A basic understanding of law, legal process, and the constraints imposed by tradition are prerequisites to undertaking an empirical analysis of issues respecting children and the law. Equally important is an appreciation of the uses and limitations of social science research on issues of legal policy and law reform.

With these perspectives in mind, a selected review of a number of key issues will now be undertaken to determine what is known and what directions future research might most productively take.

II WHO ARE CHILDREN?

The Legal Approach

Contemporary Western society shares a particular view of childhood as a distinct era of life with its own myths, psychology, and special needs requiring special institutions. Our legal policies respecting children derive from this conception of childhood, even though it is founded on belief rather than hard data regarding children's changing needs and capacities. Incompetence, notes Skolnick, is the one distinguishing feature of our view of all childhood, and our legal system, through the status of minority, reflects and codifies this conception. The law thereby shapes the social reality in which children live[79] at least as much as it reflects this reality.

An arbitrary line is drawn between adults and infants.[80] At common law, an infant attained majority at age 21. While this age still applies for purposes of federal law in Canada, most provinces now have passed legislation adopting a lower age of majority. For example, with the passing of *The Age of Majority and Accountability Act*[81] in 1971, a person in Ontario loses his infancy status and becomes a legal adult at age 18. The status of minority, sometimes called infancy, in large part determines the rights and duties of the child before the law regardless of his or her age or actual capabilities. Hence, while their needs and interests may be greater than those of adults, children have far fewer legal rights and duties.[82] Yet this dividing line obscures the differences among children of different ages and the similarities between older children and adults. And in Rodham's view, it is not only arbitrary but also simplistic.[83]

The general rule of law holds that anyone below the age of majority is legally incompetent. For example, no minor is bound by a contract unless it is for 'necessaries' of life.[84] Common law and specific statutory authority, however, create many exceptions to this general rule. The common law concept of 'age of discretion' serves as an illustration. It defines the age at which *habeas corpus*[85] will not lie to regain custody of a child against his will. For boys, this age is 14; for girls, it is 16. Marriage is a further example. At common law, boys age 14 and girls age 12 could give valid consent to marriage, but this common law exception to the general rule has now been further modified by statute, with almost every province today setting higher ages than were established at common law.[86]

Finally, Ontario's present child welfare laws, *The Child Welfare Act*[87] provide an example of legislation which within itself contains a number of different, and not entirely consistent, age-related provisions. A summary of only a few of its provisions demonstrates the complexity of determining who falls within the definition of child for any given purpose. Any child under 16 may be taken, with judicial authorization, into care by the Children's Aid Society (hereafter referred to as the CAS).[88] Both CAS and Crown wardship may last until a child is 18.[89] In special circumstances, Crown wardship may be extended to age 21.[90] Any person supervising a child under age 10 who leaves him unattended for an unreasonable time is guilty of an offence,[91] as is any person who attempts to induce a child under 18 and lawfully in care to leave premises where he has been placed.[92] No child under 16 is allowed to loiter in a public place without parental supervision.[93] Further, no boy between the ages of 12 and 15 shall engage in any street occupation after 9.00 P.M. Finally, the Act sets out a variety of age-graded provisions for termination of CAS powers. Other areas of law, too, contain numerous age-related and some sex-related provisions.[94]

This myriad of statutory and common law exceptions, and exceptions to exceptions, creates, as Freeman observes, 'a lack of consistency in ages chosen for children to be allowed to do certain things or enter certain legal relationships.'[95] When attempting to define a child's legal position in any given situation, one faces a hodgepodge of arbitrary, confusing, and often contradictory laws. And while Skolnick argues that the concept of minority reflects our beliefs about the incapacities of children, Rodham finds these legal age gradations neither rational nor supported by developmental psychology theory or data.[96] That children's legal capacity should reflect more accurately children's actual capacities is an issue that will now be scrutinized further.

The Developmental Approach

According to Hafen,[97] the presumption of a minor's incapacity is a fundamental element of our Western democratic tradition. In his view, this presumption has encouraged discrimination on the basis of age. But he sees it as positive discrimination which protects children from the excesses of their immaturity and promotes the development of their abilities. Compulsory public education is cited as an example of positive discrimination.[98]

This presumption of limited capacity accounts for the limitations imposed on minors exercising rights to make affirmative choices[99] as well as the development of special protections to secure their special needs. The natural development of children from incapacity to capacity is consistent with the presumption that capacity does not exist for children as a class until they reach a certain stage of development and the weight of evidence shows that a given level of capacity does exist.[100] Hafen concludes that the ultimate control over children's conduct must rest either with parents or the state as long as they do not have the capacities to assume full responsibilities for their own lives.[101] What the requisite capacity should be before a particular right is granted and at what point children reach this desired level of development are basic issues which Hafen ignores in his analysis. Yet, these issues are open to empirical investigation. Developmental psychological research can potentially have a profound impact on basic legal presumptions such as these.

Thus the rationale put forth for depriving a person in a dependency relationship of rights is, as Rodham notes, that the individual is incapable of taking care of himself[102] and therefore needs special protections and safeguards instead of rights. Children are uniquely susceptible to this rationale.[103] The obvious dependency of younger children is seen in their physical, intellectual, and emotional incapabilities. For adolescents, however, the dependency necessitating a deprivation of general rights and, in its place, a bestowal of special protections, is less apparent.

To reverse the presumption of incapacity, Hafen insists, would require that children as a class or, for example, above a given age, not be characterized by inability to form judgments and be able to assume economic responsibility and otherwise act independently on their own behalf.[104] Presently, in Ontario, the presumption of incapacity is reversed when a child reaches majority at age 18. But, as noted, this presumption is partially reversed in many ways for those under 18 through a variety of common law and statutory provisions which grant children of various ages an assortment of rights and duties. Yet these reversals are not based on any empirical determination of children's general level of development at these ages. Rather, they are based on surmise, common sense, tradition, and political convenience. Such decisions could, however, be better predicated on scientifically gathered developmental data, were the necessary research undertaken.

Foster and Freed, in their early seminal work on children's rights, conclude that children should be granted individual freedom commensurate with their maturation and development. The authors believe the burden should be on those who would abridge children's freedom to show that such restrictions are necessary.[105] They suggest a system of age-grading whereby each year or few years children get increased responsibility and duties in the external world according to the empirically established capacity of that age group.[106]

Tribe advocates a similar approach. He believes that, when a right is at stake, the general fact of youth alone cannot automatically justify its abridgement. The deprivation of liberty or opportunity, justified by reference to immaturity and its supposed consequences, should be based on a *demonstrated incapacity* to use the opportunity or liberty.[107] Rodham, too, endorses this concept. She suggests that the legal status of minority be abolished. Hence there would be a presumption of capacity rather than the existing presumption of incapacity.[108] She supports the Foster and Freed proposal that children's substantive and procedural rights be limited and modified on the basis of empirically established needs and capacities at various ages rather than on the basis of arbitrary policy decisions as is done now. In this model, the presumption that a child is competent to exercise a right or assume a responsibility could be defeated only on demonstrated proof to the contrary. 'The [crucial] difference between a rebuttal presumption of incompetency and a presumption of competency is that the former places the burden of proof on children and their allies, while the latter shifts it ... onto those who assert that the child is incapable and would force them to prove this assertion.'[109] Abolition of minority status would not, in Rodham's view, mean that children would be treated the same as adults before the law. Rather their rights would require limiting and modifying on the basis of empirically documented evidence about their needs and capacities at various ages.

Yet, as Leon notes, there exist no easy, or 'scientific,' answers to the question of either *who* should determine capacity or *how* it should be done.[110] Additional behavioural science research and theory is imperative to inform this type of legal and policy decision-making.[111] The behavioural sciences have not, for example, provided observable and verifiable measures for determining a specific child's *capacity* to choose between two parents in a custody dispute. Presently such determinations of capacity are made on the basis of general legal presumptions or loose judicial assessments of the particular individual child's 'maturity.' Yet, rather than relying totally on such individual assessments, which are open to severe criticism,[112] or, at the other extreme, relying on arbitrary presumptions, we should undertake empirical research to determine what capacity is necessary for a child to be able to make a given decision and then determine at what age children generally possess this capacity. On the basis of this type of scientific data, the legal presumption could be established that children of age X are capable of making decision Y *unless* in the given individual case there exists compelling evidence to the contrary.

While recognizing that children of the same age vary markedly in their development, and given the extent to which the elements of capacity remain unknown, and finally, while acknowledging the paucity of research directed specifically at the question of capacity, still researchers have started to collect behavioural science data relevant to the determination of legal capacity at given ages.

A review of the mainstream developmental psychology literature has not been attempted here. While child development issues such as ego-centrism, moral development, time perspectives, cognitive and language development, decision-making ability and competence, especially at the stages of later childhood and adolescence, are central to questions of children's capacity to exercise a variety of legal rights and responsibilities at varying ages, such a review is beyond the scope of this paper. Yet before empirical research is actually undertaken on the requisite elements of legal capacity, a synthesis of the mainstream child development theory and data is imperative.

Leon has selectively canvassed the relevant clinical and empirical research on a variety of behavioural attributes which may prove useful in determining the elements of developmental capacity necessary for a child to exercise basic legal rights.[113] While the focus of his analysis is the child's right to counsel in custody proceedings, any other basic right is amenable to this type of examination. Grisso and Vierling have, for example, reviewed the existing developmental psychology literature, specifically relating it to minor's ability to consent to medical treatment.[114] The legal capacity necessary to exercise the right to counsel is the 'capacity to instruct counsel.' Leon has broken down the requisite developmental capacity into several more basic elements: (1) the child's ability to communicate; (2) intellectual capacity; (3) the ability to understand others; (4) the ability to make a choice; (5) the ability to plan; and (6) the reliability of the child's understanding and assessment of fact situations. A summary of his review follows.

The Ability to Communicate

To participate in decisions about his own life, a child must be able to communicate his decision verbally. An adult's appreciation of a child's communication ability, however, also varies, depending on the adult's skill and experience in dealing with children. As expected, empirical research indicates that a child's ability to communicate increases with age.

According to Kraus and Glucksberg,[115] in learning to tailor their use of language to the demands of the particular listener and circumstances, children still do not achieve an adult level of competence even by age 13-14. However, as the communication task is simplified, the performance of even very young children begins to approach the adult level of competence. Beginning at ages 5-6, children increasingly appreciate that their message to another may have been meaningless or ineffective in conveying what was intended. Further, these authors conclude that the effective social use of language depends as much on the child's overall social facility as it does on knowledge of language itself.

One important factor is the child's *willingness* to communicate. At the individual level, children may hesitate to express their views on sensitive topics or when dealing with authority figures. Research indicates that direct interviews can be used as effective research tools, even with 4 year-olds, although pre-school children may persistently 'test' adults by refusing to respond or deliberately distorting responses.[116] While the child's communication abilities continue to improve during the middle years of childhood, clinicians note an intensified resistance to revealing feelings, concerns, and attitudes to adults.[117] The adolescent's 'resistance to adult attempts to probe his private world has acquired the status of a stereotype.'[118]

Understanding Others

Since many decisions are of a social nature, the child's ability to understand his social world becomes relevant. Here again, the focus is on describing the ability of children at different stages in their development to comprehend the views of others. In a recent review of the relevant social-psychological research, Shantz[119] isolates three pertinent social cognitive competencies.

First, there is the ability to infer what another is feeling, that is, to empathize. Pre-school children can accurately recognize simple emotions in highly familiar situations or with persons substantially similar to themselves, but with unfamiliar situations or dissimilar persons, accurate empathetic ability does not appear until middle or late childhood.[120] Secondly, by age 6, a child realizes that others may have thoughts or knowledge different from his own. By middle childhood, the child generally knows that others can think about *his* thoughts, feelings, and intentions.[121] Thirdly, by age 6, children can usually discriminate between the intended and accidental actions of others. As the consequences of others' actions, particularly negative consequences, become more extreme, however, children of this age are less able to distinguish intended from accidental actions. In sum, the child's ability to understand the feelings, thoughts, and intentions of others improves with increasing age.

Intellectual Capacity

By about age 12, according to Kagan, the child acquires a new cognitive competence – a disposition to examine the logic and consistency of his own beliefs.[122] Prior to this the child usually views his parents as omnipotent and omniscient. When confronted with evidence to the contrary, such as a failure by parents to understand him or irrational behaviour on their part, the 12 year-old is usually able to deduce that his parents have their limitations.[123] Younger children generally deny the existence of parental failure and find alternative motives for their parents' behaviour. The older child, however, changes his assumptions to fit the world as he sees it, and generally no longer believes his parents are perfect.

If the 12 year-old has the capacity to evaluate parental behaviour objectively, at least in non-stress situations, then he has, in part, the capacity to decide which parent he wants to live with. Yet, this decision is a highly emotion-charged one. Thus, emotional capacity must also be considered and its ability to distort reality recognized. Further, the development of children in early adolescence is particularly variable.[124] In attempting to specify an age at which a child can be presumed to be capable of reaching a specific decision, one must take note of this variability.

Ability to Choose

There is no empirical research which examines the child's ability to choose between parents. But this choice must be made before the child can instruct the lawyer to advocate his decision. The psychoanalytic perspective suggests that 'children of all ages have a natural tendency to deceive themselves about their motivations, to rationalize their actions and to shy back from full awareness of their feelings, especially where conflicts of loyalty come into question,'[125] although there is no comparison to suggest that they are any different from adults in this respect.

Based on clinical judgments, Levy[126] divides children of latency age and early adolescence, ages 5-13, into three categories on the basis of their responses to being asked directly to choose between parents. The first group, the 'uncommitted' or 'peacekeepers,' are unwilling or unable to choose a custodial parent; their wish is for their parents to re-unite. The second group saw no hope for parental reunion and tended to blame one parent for the divorce. They often saw the preferred parent as faultless and the non-preferred parent as having numerous faults. While overly sure of themselves on occasion, these children showed signs of ambivalence and anxiety about their choice and were often reluctant to tell the non-preferred parent of their decision or to inform the judge directly.

The third group, the 'emphatically decided' children, was subdivided into two categories. The 'truly decided' child could meaningfully discuss the pros and cons of his choice of parent even though he often displayed sadness and ambivalence over the loss of a parent.[127] The brainwashed or pathologically identified child, on the other hand, used exaggerated, repetitive phraseology in reciting complaints about the non-preferred parent. Because these children were so unyielding in their selection, it was difficult to give credence to their choice. In Levy's view, concern with the emotional effects of asking the child to choose is misplaced, since these children have usually been exposed to the continuing trauma of parental discord. Moreover, being asked to express a choice may have a considerably different effect from being asked to act on the choice.

Wallerstein and Kelly's clinical studies of children's responses to divorce are also pertinent to the child's ability to choose between parents. By age 5-6, the children they studied had a reasonable understanding of the divorce-related events,[128] although they coped by using extensive 'denial through fantasy.' In contrast, the 7 and 8 year-olds responded to the divorce process with 'pervasive sadness.'[129] None of the 7 and 8 year-olds was pleased about their parents' divorce, regardless of the prior degree of marital conflict. Unlike older children, these children retained their loyalty to both parents, refusing to align themselves with one or the other.[130] By age 9-10, children 'perceived the realities of their families' disruption with a [startling] soberness and clarity ...'[131] These children felt conflicting loyalties when called upon to take sides in the dispute. Those who refrained from making a choice 'felt alone and desolate, with no place to turn for comfort or parenting.'[132] For adolescents 13 and older, divorce was an extremely painful event.[133] The divorce process may force the adolescent to 'de-idealize' his parents at an earlier stage than is developmentally desirable.[134] Parental demands that the child align himself with one parent or the other may result in feelings of despair, anger, guilt, and depression. Some adolescents detach themselves from both parents to avoid aligning themselves with one parent and hence rejecting the other. This research is, however, based on clinical observations. For this reason, it can provide only tentative indicators of directions which should be pursued in future developmental research on the child's ability to choose between parents and then instruct counsel to advocate this choice.

The Ability to Plan

To make decisions that have binding consequences requires foresight. Children generally have a restricted future time perspective although this varies markedly with age. Cottle and Klineberg write that, while the pre-school child has an extremely limited view of the future, 'as children grow during the early school years they are generally able to endow increasingly distant future events with a sufficient sense of reality to support a preference for delayed rewards.'[135] As the child enters adolescence he is confronted with a variety of choices that have potentially irreversible consequences. Transformations in cognitive capacities, role expectations, and self-conception which occur at this age indicate that an adolescent's orientation towards the distant future is substantially different from that of a child.[136] By age 14 or 15, these authors suggest, the adolescent's image of future adult existence takes on a new sense of reality. Nevertheless, no comparisons have been made between the time perspectives of those over and under 18, a crucial comparison in view of the presumption of legal capacity at this age.

Reliability

The reliability of children's reports of past and present circumstances is usually considered in law in terms of the weight to be assigned a child's testimony given in legal proceedings.[137] Wigmore suggests four difficulties with children's testimony: the child's capacity to observe; the child's capacity to recollect; the child's capacity to understand the questions posed and to frame intelligent answers; and the child's sense of moral responsibility.[138] Cohen's literature review and data indicate that by age 9-11, the reports of children are as reliable as those of adults.[139] Similarly, in the context of psychiatric interviews, Herjanic et al.[140] find a high degree of consistency between the reporting of parents and that of their children age 6-16. In terms of content, children agreed most often with their parents on factual matters, with agreement successively decreasing on matters related to psychiatric symptoms, behaviour, and mental status.

This annotated summary of Leon's review of the research on the child's developmental ability to instruct counsel illustrates the utility of an empirical approach to the issue of capacity. Policymakers formulate presumptions about legal incapacity based on *assumptions* about developmental capacity, plus value judgments. Developmental research addressing those issues which the law now answers through arbitrary age-related provisions should lead to a more rational set of legal presumptions about children's capacities to participate in various behaviours at selected ages. Objections either that there should not be such a system of age-graded presumptions or that developmental research is not sufficiently advanced to direct itself to such questions must be answered by pointing out that the law respecting children already operates on an age-grading system, only its gradations are presently based on surmise and supposition about children's capacities rather than on empirically based fact.

As stated, in Ontario, along with the general presumption of legal incapacity for all those under 18, there exists a myriad of narrower presumptions of capacity in special circumstances. Further, on an individual basis, courts frequently create exceptions to the presumption of incapacity. In judicial proceedings, a child's capacity for a specific purpose may be demonstrated on the weight of the evidence. The law of torts, for example, has always required individual judge or jury assessments of the child's capacity to act 'reasonably,' based on a comparison with what should be expected from the normal child of like age, intelligence, and ability. The duty to exercise care is not imposed on the particular child in question unless the 'reasonable' child of that age would be capable of understanding the nature and likely consequences of the particular act.[141] The *Canada Evidence Act*[142] provides another instance of the law requiring an assessment of the individual child's capacity. Even though too young to understand the nature of the oath, a child of 'tender years'[143] is allowed to testify as long as he is shown to understand his duty to speak the truth and to possess sufficient intelligence to justify the reception of his unsworn testimony.

Since every day our courts are called upon to make individual assessments of a child's capacity and since our laws make many arbitrary overall exceptions to the presumption of incapacity, perhaps the time has come to reverse this general presumption of a minor's incapacity, as Rodham and several other leading scholars of children's law suggest. Yet, if all children were presumed capable of exercising all rights and responsibilities, the situation would be equally untenable.

Rodham, however, stresses that 'The abolition of minority ... need not mean that children become full-fledged miniature adults before the law. Their substantive and procedural rights could still be limited or modified on the basis of supportable [empirical] findings about needs and capacities at various ages.'[144]

Reversing the presumption of incapacity would stimulate empirical research aimed at aligning children's legal rights and responsibilities with their actual capability to exercise such rights and assume such responsibilities. Research should be directed towards developing a rational, empirically based set of age-graded classifications whereby children as a class at various pre-established ages are automatically presumed capable of exercising certain rights and responsibilities, unless, on an individual basis, evidence is tendered which rebuts the presumption of capacity for the given child in question. Through the use of developmental research, a more logical and orderly framework for granting children rights should emerge. Legislation thus developed should minimize anomalies such as exist in law today.

III CAPACITY TO CONSENT TO MEDICAL TREATMENT

The question of whether or not minors have the capacity in law and in fact to consent to medical treatment illustrates the difficulties that arise out of concepts like minority status, legal capacity, and consent. A minor's legal capacity to consent to medical care is ambiguous. Opinion varies among jurisdictions. Foster and Freed assert that 'it follows from the status of minority that minors lack legal capacity to give valid consent to medical treatment ... Such is the common law or general rule ...'[145] While this may accurately represent American common law, English authority takes the opposite stance. '[T]here is no rigid rule of English law which renders a minor incapable of giving his consent to an operation but there seems to be no direct judicial authority establishing that the consent of such a person is valid.'[146]

In tort law, the intentional touching of another constitutes a trespass to that person, commonly known as an assault, no matter how trivial and regardless of whether any harm is done. The notion of implied consent relieves us from liability for the touchings of everyday life, such as tapping another to get his attention. The performance of any medical procedure on a person without his consent, or that of the person entitled to consent on his behalf, is an assault for which the doctor may be held liable.[147] One of the prerequisites for valid consent is that the patient have the requisite legal capacity to give consent to the medical treatment.[148]

In Canada, diverse opinions exist with regard to the capacity of minors to consent to medical treatment. One school of thought considers all minors unable to give such consent by virtue of their legal minority status. The Report of the British Columbia Royal Commission on Family and Children's Law supports this view,[149] as do Foster and Freed.[150] A second view suggests that all children under the 'age of consent' are unable to consent to medical care.[151] The majority view, however, derived from the law of torts, asserts that age does not, of itself, render a minor incapable of giving valid medical consent.[152]

Because tort law has never held that children were under any legal incapacity to give consent to touching or to be liable for the consequences of their conduct, 'their capacity to consent is not limited by age but rather by the ability to know and understand what they are consenting to.'[153] Hence, the most prevalent view, based on individual assessments of capacity, holds that a minor may give medical consent, that is consent to being touched, as long as he has sufficient capacity to appreciate the nature and consequences of the act. To determine this, the particular child in question is compared with the reasonable or average child of like age, intelligence, and ability. The leading Ontario case of *Johnson* v. *Wellesley Hospital*[154] illustrates this approach. Here the court held that a minor has the right to consent if he is capable of appreciating fully the nature and consequence of the particular treatment. Thus Ontario law gives the child right to consent once he possesses the requisite capacity.

Many American jurisdictions have now legislated consent requirements similar to those found in Ontario common law, thereby reversing their common law rule that minors do not have the capacity to consent to medical treatment. Through such legislation, once the minor has the requisite capacity, his consent alone is sufficient. Yet the American case law indicates that only where the child is close to majority, fully understands the nature and consequences of the proposed treatment, and where the treatment is not major and is clearly for the child's benefit is this legislative rule strictly followed.[155]

Because a child of 'tender years' lacks the capacity to understand the nature and consequences of the act, the parent or guardian has the right, and indeed the obligation, to give or withhold consent.[156] But in Ontario at least, once the child has the capacity to consent, there should be no need for parental consent too. The question, therefore, becomes: When does the child possess this capacity? To this, there is no clear answer. The ethical guidelines of the Ontario College of Physicians and Surgeons, for example, state that a doctor may treat minors 16 and over without informing their parents. This opinion has been misunderstood to mean that it is *lawful* to treat only those 16 and over without parental consent,[157] a view which does not appear to accurately reflect Ontario law.

A number of jurisdictions have suggested or recently taken action to clarify their position on minors' medical consent.[158] In Ontario, for example, a regulation enacted pursuant to *The Public Hospitals Act*,[159] and therefore applicable only in public hospitals, requires parental consent to surgical procedures on unmarried minors under 16. Although there is some question as to the legal validity of this regulation,[160] Krever notes that it too has given the medical profession the incorrect impression 'that a child under 16 may, in no circumstances other than an emergency, be treated without parental consent.'[161]

Although Ontario case law supports the view that once a child has the capacity to consent, then his consent is valid and sufficient, the preceding discussion illustrates the uncertainty surrounding the consent question. What effect does this confusion have on the practising physician? Certainly, he has no desire to expose himself to liability and yet every day he experiences the pressing need to treat minors who are either unable or unwilling to involve their parents in their medical decision-making. Moreover, if he must make individual assessments of the minor's capacity, how is he to do this? Can and should the law guide him in this decision?

In 1975, the British Columbia Royal Commission on Family and Children's Law surveyed doctors on the issue of minors' medical consent.[162] They interviewed doctors who had experience treating minors, including paediatricians, public health doctors, gynaecologists, and general practitioners. The British Columbia legislation applicable at the time of the survey made a 16 year-old's consent effective if the doctor first made a reasonable attempt to obtain parental consent and, if unsuccessful, he or she secured the written confirming opinion of one other medical practitioner. Some highlights of this survey are as follows.

Virtual unanimity was found in the doctors' belief that married minors and those single minors living independently of their parents as adults are capable of consenting to their own general treatment. However, '[O]nly one-third ... would give general treatment to a minor under 16 in the same way as to an adult. Many said they would attempt to get parental consent first. They may have been influenced by the existing statute law concerning minors 16 and over.'[163] Very few stated that they would obtain a written confirming opinion from a second practitioner, as their legislation then required. 'The major reluctance doctors have in accepting a minor's consent surrounds the recommendation of an abortion. When the minor is living at home or is under 16, a majority believe that the parents should be informed. However, if the minor was independent or married, most doctors did not feel bound to inform the parents.'[164] When dealing with independent and married minors, a majority of the doctors, between 67 and 83 per cent, were prepared to provide treatment over the known objections of the parents. Where the patient was aged 16–18 and living in his parents' home, a majority of the physicians were still willing to treat the minor in all instances except that of abortion. Reluctance to disregard the parents' wishes[165] was predictably most manifest where minors under 16 were involved. In fact, only when the treatment concerned venereal disease were most of the respondents prepared to overrule the parents' wishes.[165]

The researchers concluded that doctors on the whole believed minors to be ready 'for independence' at age 16, or younger if living independently. For those under 16, the investigators acknowledged the desirability of doctors encouraging parental participation, but agreed with the doctors on the need to recognize the reality of the minors' maturity, and the impossibility of legislating into existence the ideals of a freely communicating, supportive family unit.[166] On the question of law versus practice, it was found that fewer than 50 per cent of the doctors were not even aware of the statute law and among those who knew of it, 64 per cent said it did not influence their practice.[167] Yet a large percentage of those who dealt with adolescents on an occasional or regular basis felt a strong need for legal reform, not only to clarify their own legal liabilities but also to acknowledge that many children, especially those who are emancipated or married, 'are capable of informed consent to medical treatment and, having assumed the responsibility of adults they deserve the rights of an adult.'[168]

Similar assessments should be undertaken in other jurisdictions to determine what doctors perceive the law of medical consent to be, how, in practice, they handle the treatment of minors, and what areas of law they see as needing reform or clarification. Sound policy and legislative reform can only emanate from a clear delineation of the problem itself.

When considering the medical needs of minors, there are five areas of special concern – venereal disease, drug and alcohol abuse, psychiatric care, contraceptives, and pregnancy and abortion. Investigation of the needs and problems unique to each area is required.

Venereal Disease

In North America, venereal disease has reached epidemic proportions.[169] Minors make up a substantial number of those who carry the disease. Early detection and treatment are not only in the minor's best interests but also in the public interest. Yet this medical need is a sensitive and private one. If minors think they require parental consent before obtaining treatment, regardless of whether the law requires it or whether doctors believe they do, they may delay or even neglect seeking treatment. In Foster and Freed's opinion, 'any requirement of parental consent to the treatment of a venereal disease is medically and psychologically absurd and not in the public interest.'[170]

The Alberta report on the Consent of Minors to Health Care[171] takes the position that '[p]rompt treatment is essential, and a requirement of parental consent might result in delay or even in neglect of treatment. If a person is old enough to contract venereal disease he should have the capacity to attend to it ...'[172]

Recognizing the need to remove all barriers to such treatment, by 1974, 36 of the United States had enacted legislation enabling any minor, regardless of age, to consent to treatment for venereal disease. Another 13 states grant the minor this right only after he has reached a certain minimum age, ranging from 12 through 16 years.[173] Similarly, in Canada, the age requirements vary from province to province.

Drug and Alcohol Problems

Some consider the abuse of drugs by minors to be epidemic. The magnitude of the problem is such that in probably no other area of the law have the various jurisdictions in the United States been so quick to act. Seeing the potential deterrent to seeking treatment of the American common law rule which presumes minors incapable of giving medical consent, a number of states have enacted laws validating a minor's consent for the purposes of drug treatment. In this way, they seek to encourage youths with drug problems to seek help.[174]

The Alberta report also recognizes the deterrent effect of 'perceived' parental consent requirements, whether or not such requirements exist in law. It cites the example of a treatment centre which, upon changing its policy to one of complete confidentiality relying solely on the minor's consent, found that attendance of young people 'increased rapidly and considerably and stayed at an increased level for quite some time.'[175] This report continued on to recommend that any minor needing assistance with a drug problem should be capable of self-consent.

Psychiatric Care and Counselling

The British Columbia Royal Commission[176] observed that, since psychiatric care technically involves no touching, no consent to a touching is required for such treatment. Thus, the issue of parental consent need not arise. However, Brian Fraser has stated that legal action could perhaps be based on the tort of enticement or, possibly, alienation of affections.[177] A further consent issue arises where a minor attempts to contest a mental health committal authorized by his parents. So here, too, further clarification of the minor's legal capacity to consent is needed.

Contraception

There is a widespread belief that minors are engaging in sexual activity more often and at younger ages than ever before.[178] Also increasing is the rate of illegitimate births.[179] The age of menarche has dropped significantly over the last decade.[180] This combination of factors leads to a central issue: Why don't minors engaging in sexual activities use contraceptives? No doubt a complex of variables bear on the problem. A leading cause though, Fraser suggests, is the difficulty unmarried minors have in obtaining adequate information and effective means of birth control.[181] While a complete review of the issue of adolescent sexuality is presented in Chapter 5, the problem of consent to contraception is examined here.

When either the child or his physician believes parental consent is necessary, this may lead to a neglect in seeking or a delay in obtaining appropriate contraception. As noted, Ontario common law allows children of sufficient capacity the right to consent to medical care. In 1970, British Columbia law was virtually identical with that now existing in Ontario. Yet, in that year their Court upheld their medical profession disciplinary body's ruling that a doctor who inserted an IUD in a 15-year-old girl without first informing her parents was guilty of unprofessional conduct. Thus, doctors are justified in being somewhat reluctant to rely solely on a child's consent.[182] Moreover, a doctor who prescribes contraceptives could possibly be held guilty of contributing to delinquency[183] or of aiding and abetting sexual relations with a girl under 16, although the Alberta report concludes that any doctor acting in good faith would not be so found. Still these possibilities do little to ease the physician's hesitance to rely solely on the child's consent.

The argument that readily available contraception will lead to an increase in sexual activity finds no empirical support.[184] The Alberta report concludes 'that the withholding of contraceptives is not a deterrent; and granted that minors are engaging in sexual intercourse, it is better for the minor to be able to avoid unwanted pregnancies. We ... make our recommendation accordingly.'[185] It, therefore, urges that a minor's consent be sufficient to obtain any form of contraception.

Pregnancy and Abortion
Subject to the *Criminal Code* provisions regarding abortion,[186] the same issues arise here as in all other areas respecting the minor's capacity to give medical consent. But because this is viewed as a serious medical procedure with possible psychological and moral repercussions, doctors take a much more conservative approach to this problem. In Toronto, the Hospital for Sick Children will not perform an abortion on a girl under 18 without parental consent unless not doing so would seriously endanger her emotional health, despite the Ontario regulation making the consent of a 16-year-old valid for all surgical procedures.[187] The British Columbia doctors' survey reported that few doctors would perform an abortion on a minor without first obtaining parental consent; 71 per cent would require parental consent for a minor aged 16-18; 80 per cent if the girl were under 16.[188] The British Columbia Royal Commission Report suggests that

for major treatment such as elective surgery and abortions,[189] parental consent should be required because it is a traumatic event and family support is apt to be beneficial.[190] They ignore possibilities such as parents' refusing to consent or rejecting the child as a result of such consent being requested.

Thus, a number of interrelated variables affect the delivery of health care to minors. First, there is lack of clarity in the law itself. Ontario common law on a minor's consent to medical treatment may be different from that of British Columbia or Alberta. Therefore a court decision in one province does not bind courts in another province. Moreover, piecemeal legislation on a minor's consent for various specific purposes, such as *The Public Hospitals Act* regulation in Ontario, further confuses the issue. Each jurisdiction may have its own statutory rules respecting consent. Because of this, medical governing bodies and individual doctors are uncertain of their legal position in treating minors as patients in their own right. Ontario holds that a minor may consent to his own medical treatment once he has the capacity to know and understand what he is consenting to. So, in reality, the doctor is placed in the position of having to assess the minor's capacity on an individual basis and hope a court will uphold his decision should the matter ever be litigated. Thus, even assuming the practitioner clearly understands the relevant law, his position remains somewhat tenuous, for he is required to make individual assessments of capacity and yet receives no guidance in law on how to do this

Empirical research assessing what physicians know about the law respecting minors' consent to medical treatment would be a useful first step in investigating problems of delivery of health care to minors. Since doctors' understanding of the legal framework will influence their behaviour, a next step would be to analyse how they handle the problem of minors' consent in their daily practice. How do physicians make assessments of the minor's capacity? What variables do they consider? Does the level of capacity required vary with the seriousness of the proposed treatment? Do doctors feel the law needs clarification or reform? Does this perceived need vary with the accuracy of their understanding of the law? A breakdown by medical specialities would help define whether or not particular consent issues align with particular health care needs.

Conversely, the minors' perception of the relevant consent law will also play a significant role in their seeking out health care. Thus, young persons themselves should be canvassed. A number of related concerns deserve further investigation, including what young persons' health needs are; what problems they experience in attempting to secure medical treatment, especially consent problems; how the perceived and actual difficulty of obtaining treatment affects their attempts to secure treatment; and, finally, what networks for obtaining and transmitting information respecting their health needs and appropriate treatment have been developed by the clients themselves, by intermediate social services or other community organizations, and by the medical profession.

Many jurisdictions have recommended enactment of specific age guidelines to permit minors over that age to consent to various forms of medical treatment.[191] Others argue for no age limits for consent where special adolescent medical problems are involved, while retaining age lines for medical treatment in general.[192] And still others advocate a flexible standard based on the individual physician's assessment of the particular minor's capacity to make the medical decision in question. Empirical research can help clarify the problems of both need and delivery, including issues of consent and capacity. Once this is done, policy-makers will be in a better position to know if the law needs reforming and, if so, what directions reform might take to ameliorate the situation.

IV CHILDREN'S KNOWLEDGE AND UNDERSTANDING OF THE LAW

When attempting to define developmental stages at which children of various ages may assume different legal rights and responsibilities, one key factor must be kept in mind. Children today have few opportunities to absorb accurate information about law. Most adults command remarkably little precise knowledge or understanding of our laws. The problem is even more acute for children. While it is true that our legal system is complex, it is equally true that few efforts are made to apprise our citizenry, and especially our children, about how our laws work, what purposes they serve, how laws affect and direct their daily lives.

This lack of basic information may prove a potent confounding variable in research on questions relating developmental capacity to legal capacity, for dealing with legal concepts necessitates some understanding of the law. For example, a researcher may wish to investigate children's ability to understand the reciprocal concepts of rights and duties. The little research undertaken in this area indicates that children do not acquire facility with such concepts until adolescence. Yet this may be a function of their not being exposed to such concepts before this age as much as it depends upon an inherent developmental ability to comprehend this type of abstract concept. Until efforts are directed towards teaching children these specific concepts to ascertain the stage of development at which they can be grasped, we cannot know whether such lack of facility is due to inherent developmental ability, lack of exposure, or a combination of such factors.

Reported Research
In a cross-cultural study on adolescent perspectives on law and government, Adelson and Beall[193] reported that children aged 11–12 had only a diffuse and

incomplete notion of political ordering. Younger adolescents, these researchers claim, see the function of law as restrictive and coercive: the citizen's duty is to obey the law and failure to do so merits punishment in their view. They do not see the citizen as having any rights. Young adolescents assume laws are enacted only for good and proper reasons, rarely imagining that they might be absurd, mistaken, or unfair and therefore in need of revision. But between the ages of 13 and 15, Adelson and his co-workers observed that the adolescents' authoritarian conception of law declines markedly. Instead, a critical, pragmatic view becomes dominant. These researchers suggest that the younger child's authoritarianism stems from his inability to abstract. The marked cognitive shift from concrete to abstract modes of discourse which occurs in adolescence leads to an understanding of abstract concepts such as society, laws, and community. Adolescents thereby come to understand that laws should serve the needs of the total community rather than the single individual.

Hess and Torney examined the socialization of the child into the United States political system.[194] In contrast with Adelson and Beall, these researchers found that political socialization was well advanced by the end of the eighth grade. They had hypothesized that the major developments in political attitudes would occur during high school. But this hypothesis was not supported by the data. Instead, they found an unexpected degree of political experience and learning occurred at the pre-high school level. Indeed, even 7-year-olds in grade 2 had very specific, although highly concrete and individualized, conceptions of government. These conceptions were, however, often inaccurate. Responses from fourth and fifth graders showed that even at this early age, government was not always seen as just and responsive.[195] The young child's basic trust in government declined rapidly between grades 2 and 5, although they still believed laws *should* be fair.[196]

In attempting to document the agents of political socialization, Hess and Torney observed that previous research overestimates the influence of the family. They found that the family played only an indirect role in influencing attitudes towards authority, rules, and compliance. The schools, they concluded, played the largest part in teaching attitudes and beliefs about the operation of the political system. Yet, in their view, the present curriculum overemphasized compliance with rules and regulations. Conversely, it underemphasized both the rights and obligations of the citizen to participate in government and the role and importance of conflict and procedures in the operation of our legal system. These researchers noted that the elementary school child lacked adequate information at the time he was acquiring his basic orientation towards law and government, that is, starting in grade 2. Because of the important role the schools play, these researchers conclude that more attention must be paid to its methods, curriculum, and timing of political socialization.[197]

Greenstein's research indicates that, by age 10, children in the United States are settled into lifelong party identifications which account for most voting behaviour and, by age 14, they are as well informed as most adults about major political institutions.[198]

The National Assessment of Education Progress[199] in the United States recently released the preliminary results of their 1971-2 survey on the political knowledge and attitudes of children aged 9, 13, and 17. Their data disclose serious gaps in children's understanding of fundamental areas of law and government. When questioned about criminal rights, the 13- and 17-year olds performed well. They knew that an accused had the right to have a lawyer represent him, to know what he was accused of, to remain silent, and not to go free even if he returned stolen property. The researchers speculated that television had played a major role here. One of every eight 17-year olds, however, believed the president was not required to obey the law. Only 9 per cent of the 17-year olds demonstrated knowledge of the Supreme Court's decision-making process and, in another question on the Supreme Court, only 30 per cent of the 13-year olds answered correctly, while 56 per cent of those 17 and 66 per cent of the adults responded appropriately. Similarly, many of the questions on political understanding indicated major gaps in knowledge. Of even more significance is the 1975-6 folllw-up study which showed a marked decrease in children's knowledge of the structure and function of government over the four-year period. Moreover, there was a decline in their understanding of and willingness to participate in the political process and in recognizing and valuing constitutional rights.

A 1974 Hamilton Report[200] notes the results of a 1970 Ontario Department of Education Survey on youth's knowledge of law. This study found that, while there was a marked improvement between grade 8 and grade 11 in knowledge about the law, still there remained noticeable gaps of knowledge in all grades tested. Questions in two areas, those involving concepts of rights and duties and those requiring knowledge of court and legal procedures, received the lowest scores. The researchers also observed a notable weakness in knowledge about juvenile law. Overall, they concluded, juveniles have very little appreciation of the laws affecting their lives.

Taken as a whole, this research suggests that even very young children should be given the opportunity to learn about the legal structure of the society in which they live. Such teaching would need modification to parallel the child's stage of development and ability to learn, that is, his capacity at any given age. But because children are already acquiring this type of information and because the information they are exposed to is often factually incorrect, efforts should be made to provide them with a clear and simple picture of the nature, purpose, and content of the laws which frame our society. An overview of the diverse goals which may be furthered through instructing children in law will now be undertaken. Some areas for future research will then be outlined.

The Ends Sought Through Educating Children in Law
A number of writers have advanced a variety of reasons, both philosophical and practical, for instructing children in law. They fall into several categories. Firstly, law is an important social phenomenon. It influences every member of our society, pervades all aspects of our lives and describes and delimits our social order. Dolding asserts that if general education is defined as that essential education which is fundamental for good citizenship regardless of occupational status, the common preparation needed by all persons to live harmoniously in our society, then some knowledge and understanding of the law must be an indispensable part of a person's general education.[201] To be a responsible citizen in a democratic society requires a basic understanding of law, legal institutions, and the law-making process.[202]

Secondly, ours is a complex society with an equally complex legal system. Because of this, a barrier has resulted between law and its institutions on the one hand and those whom it was designed to serve. There exists a large and unnecessary void in the public's knowledge of the law. People do not understand and appreciate what law is, how or why it works the way it does, and what its capabilities and limitations are. Because of this, people have inaccurate expectations of what the law can do. Disappointments resulting from such misunderstanding may lead to suspicion and mistrust of the law.[203] In Dolding's view, students should be taught about the compromise and balance of interests which lie at the heart of the legal system, so that they will have realistic expectations.[204] While the crisis of confidence in our laws may not result entirely from ignorance of the law, such ignorance may enhance the general feeling that law is something apart from society.[205] Possessing knowledge of the law may mitigate people's sense of estrangement from the legal system under which they live. In so doing, it may enhance positive attitudes towards the law. For example, Elson and Elson found that as children's general knowledge of law increased, there was a concomitant improvement in their attitudes towards law.[206] Enhanced positive attitudes may, in turn, lead to a direct reduction in crime.[207]

The study of law provides a valuable means of approaching history and examining moral issues of timeless concern, such as values, justice, equality, freedom, and responsibility.[208] Students may thereby gain an awareness of the complex relationship between law and social change. They may come to understand that our laws interact with and both affect and reflect the moral, political and economic forces within our society.[209]

Fourthly, students may, through this process, learn of the strengths and weaknesses of our present legal institutions. They may come to appreciate the manifold difficulties that stand in the way of reform. To initiate and obtain public support for effective reforms requires public sophistication of a fairly high standard and education is one step towards such public wisdom.[210]

Our *Criminal Code* states that 'ignorance of the law by a person who commits an offence is not an excuse for committing that offence.'[211] Since laws pervade all aspects of our life and 'if ... knowledge is power and ignorance is no excuse, then knowing the legal facts of life can do no harm, only good' according to Lamb.[212] The many penal statutes enacted for their deterrent effect can have no deterrent value unless people know the behaviour proscribed and the penalties that follow. What better place to apprise the public of our laws than through our education system?

Sixthly, young persons need basic information about the legal issues that affect them directly. They should learn how to avoid or deal with their legal problems in order to minimize loss or damage and to discover how, where, and when to seek legal assistance. By these means, the child's ability to cope with the vicissitudes of daily life may be enhanced. He can learn that frustrations may be vented and solutions obtained through legitimate channels. Recourse to extra-legal or illegal solutions might thereby be reduced. As Baetz et al.[213] observe, the importance of recognizing the legal implications of one's day-to-day activities cannot be overestimated. People, they note, commonly do not recognize their problems as legal ones or are unaware of available legal resources that could lead to solutions.

Further, the analytic, logical, and sytematic reasoning skills and the ability to consider and evaluate all possible alternatives required in the legal process may contribute to the development of rational and independent thinking by students.[214]

Finally, Stenning maintains that the study of law in schools provides a good vehicle for a re-examination of the legal and normative structure of the school itself. A student may, through this undertaking, achieve a greater understanding of his role within the school, that of teachers and parents, and of the rights and obligations which accrue from being a member of this group.[215]

Any of these reasons provides sufficient justification for teaching law in the schools. Cahn and Cahn provide a good summation when they state that if education in law 'affects basic perceptions at an early age, increases one's ability to resist injustice and to compel fair dealing, if it enables one to distinguish between real and fancied injustices and if it instills a sense of mutual obligation and mutual responsibility'[216] then it has major investment potential.

Considering the many beneficial effects that may accrue from educating children in law and in view of Hess and Torney's findings which suggest that even very young children are acquiring (often inaccurate) concepts of law and government, why then has the State through its schools only recently moved to meet this need? One reason is readily apparent. Many of the laws which we apply to children in our society are patently unfair. They repeatedly violate fundamental precepts of justice. How can children be taught that our laws are fair and just when the subset of law designed especially for them, to secure their 'best interests,' is often neither fair nor just? The concept of the 'status' offence, examined in detail in section 6 of this chapter, is illustrative.[217] Through this vague and all-encompassing concept, virtually any normal childhood nuisance behaviour may be adjudged a delinquency, with all the negative consequences that may flow therefrom. To teach children that our legal system is founded on concepts such as fairness, justice, and freedom and then to explain why, in their own best interests, children as a class are often excepted from these principles of law may indeed prove a difficult task.

The Trends
In the past few years, increasing efforts have been made to incorporate law into the school curriculum. Several hundred such programmes now exist in the United States.[218] The American Bar Association has added its prestigious force to the pronounced and rapidly accelerating movement to bring law studies into the schools by establishing a Special Committee on Youth Education for Citizenship. In the 18-month period between publication of its first Directory of Law Related Educational Activities[219] and the second, the number of projects increased by 50 per cent and many of the existing projects grew in size and effectiveness.

In Canada, several provincial governments conduct law courses in the later grades of high school. Throughout the summer of 1977, the federal government conducted an assessment of the national picture on law education in the schools, although the results of this survey are not yet available.

British Columbia appears to have the most advanced programme in their secondary schools. In a 1974 evaluation of this programme, Orr et al.[220] reported major deficiencies in teacher knowledge of the subject matter and a shortage of good teaching materials. Despite these difficulties, both the students and teachers recommended that the courses be expanded. The researchers noted that student responses to the curriculum were very mature and recommended that their views on the curriculum be incorporated into any change. The students recognized and appreciated the need to learn about certain areas of the law even though these areas were not the most interesting in terms of content.

Ontario Ministry of Education figures, which may be inflated by double enrolment, estimate that in 1976, approximately 8.5 per cent of Ontario public secondary school students were enrolled in law courses. In 1977 the percentage had risen to 8.95. In view of the Hamilton Report's data indicating many gaps in students' understanding of law, increased efforts are needed to get more students into better courses at earlier ages.

Yet to optimize efforts to teach children law, many questions need to be answered. For example, what is the optimal age at which to commence such courses? If, as Hess and Torney maintain, children begin to acquire such concepts in grade 2 and are fairly set in their overall attitudes by grade 8, these programmes should be started in the earliest school grades. Further, does learning about rights and responsibilities in any way alter children's perceptions or behaviours? Will teaching children specifically about legally proscribed behaviour, and especially the behaviour proscribed for them, in any way alter juvenile misbehaviour? If we seek to use such courses as tools for delinquency prevention, then such studies must begin before grade 7 or 8, for official delinquency rates rise sharply for those aged 11 to 12. Then the content of such courses could be systematically varied to determine which approach, if any, had deterrent value.

Through evaluating the effects of such courses, more may be learned about how children's attitudes towards authority develop and how their moral belief systems change as they mature.[221] Those effects attributable solely to developmental capacity may be teased out from those attributable to lack of exposure to legal concepts. Teaching children about abstract concepts such as justice, values, rights, and duties may stimulate their intellectual growth as might learning methods of legal reasoning. Exposure to common values may enhance the child's appreciation of and tolerance for ethnic diversity. At the same time, learning about unique features of our laws may enhance his sense of Canadian identity. At this time of concern for our Canadian culture, it is important to know how much of children's knowledge of and attitudes towards law are based on the 'Americanized-TV' version of justice. All these questions, and many more, can be narrowed and focused, and perhaps answered, only through empirical research relating developmental capacity to the child's knowledge and understanding of our legal structure.

V CHILDREN IN THE COURTS

Children come in contact with our legal system in many ways but nowhere does the law impinge more directly on their lives than when they become involved with our courts. Three types of judicial proceedings - delinquency, child welfare, and custody - are the focus of this review.

An understanding of the nature and purposes of the relevant substantive law and an appreciation of the essential differences among these areas of law is central to grasping the permutations of any given issue as it applies to either delinquency, child welfare, or custody. For this reason, a synopsis of the relevant legal framework is sketched in an appendix to this chapter. If the social science researcher does not appreciate subtle yet crucial differences in law, he may wrongly attempt to transpose an issue in one area of law directly to another, ignoring pivotal distinctions which may significantly alter the issue itself. To avoid superficial analysis and trivial conclusions, those who seek to answer the questions confronting our legal system through empirical analysis require more than a passing understanding of the nature, purposes, and processes of our laws and legal structures.

In examining the processing of children through the judicial system, whether in custody, child welfare, or delinquency hearings, several key questions emerge. Yet, the almost total absence of descriptive data available makes it difficult to define problems with precision.[222] For example, Statistics Canada keeps a record of the number and sex of children whose parents are involved in divorce proceedings. Their age, however, is not included. The custody disposition is recorded, but the reasons for the decision are not noted. No attempt is made to separate out those divorces where custody is in issue from those where it is not, or to keep any statistical picture of what happens in custody matters unrelated to divorce. On the basis of such sketchy data, it is difficult to elucidate with precision the problem areas in this process.

The statistical picture of the nature and extent of child welfare processing in Ontario is also underdeveloped, although efforts are now underway to improve the official data base. Finally, basic delinquency data, too, are gathered only sporadically.[223] Thus, there is no comprehensive, systematic, or continuous data collection in any of these areas. In consequence, we only have the vaguest notions, based on surmise and supposition, of what happens to children involved in court proceedings. Yet, as noted earlier, an accurate picture of what is presently going on is an essential first step in the reform process.

In this section, five key issues affecting children in the courts will be examined. These were culled from a large number of potential concerns as those ripe for empirical inquiry. The issues canvassed are first, discretion in the legal process; second, the child as participant in the hearing; then, legal representation; next, the use of social evaluation reports; and finally, alternative forms of court processing. These topics will be examined from the perspective of what is known and what needs to be known.

Discretion in Decision-Making in the Court System

The first issue to be explored is the wide discretion in decision-making which occurs at all levels of processing in the juvenile justice system, that is, prior to, at, and following the court hearing. This discretion cannot be considered legal discretion, for legal discretion requires effective guidelines,[224] and vaguely drawn substantive laws creating indefinite standards provide little guidance for decision-makers. Law is meant to provide the principal framework to inform and constrain official action.[225] But the 'best interests' standard prevalent in children's law is not really a standard at all. Rather, it serves as the decision-maker's rationalization to justify his judgments about a child's future. By offering no guidelines on how power should be exercised, this standard leaves the perceptions and prejudices of the decision-maker uncontrolled,[226] and unfettered discretion leads to individualized judgments. Yet individualized decisions offend the basic precept of our common law system which requires that similar cases be treated similarly. Thus, the best interests test serves little purpose for two reasons: it furnishes the decision-maker with little meaningful guidance in making his decisions and it requires him to make impossible predictions about the contingencies of life.

Discretion in the Delinquency System

The present Canadian approach to delinquency grew out of the wider nineteenth-century child saving movement.[227] In Lerman's view, this approach is characterized by broad, intolerant, morality-based legislation, tempered by administrative discretion on the part of police, court-intake workers, judges and ordinary citizens. This results in virtually unlimited scope and 'benevolent' discretion in this area of law.[228] Tappen has observed that the vast majority, if not all, normal children indulge in forms of behaviour which come within the purview of the delinquency laws.[229] Whether a child ends up being officially processed, however, depends upon the discretion of the officials he comes in contact with, upon their subjective interpretation of his behaviour.

The Canadian juvenile justice system, like its American counterpart, has confusing, even contradictory, objectives. Along with the rhetoric of treatment and rehabilitation,[230] which ostensibly justifies the broad discretionary intervention powers, there exists considerable sentiment for punishment and social protection.[231] Principles of punishment, however, must be governed by the rule of law, not individual discretion. Laws based on coercive sanction should be defined with specificity, certainty, and uniformity, so that the individual may thereby know exactly what conduct is proscribed.[232] An increased emphasis on these punishment and social control elements in our delinquency process should lead to a shift away from the rehabilitative rhetoric towards greater incorporation of criminal law jurisprudence and, as such, should lead to a decrease in discretion and a greater emphasis on due process.[233] The proposed new Canadian delinquency legislation, which encompasses only federal offences, represents precisely this type of philosophical shift. But whether this proposed reform, if enacted, will actually decrease the discretion exercised can only be determined empirically.

(a) *Discretion prior to the delinquency hearing – the problems with diversion.* The concept of diversion[234] encompasses a variety of activities, including police, social agency, and pre-trial screening to channel offending juveniles back to the family or social agency, or into a pre-trial settlement procedure, rather than on to court.[235] Most juvenile infractions are minor offences which do not reliably indicate future delinquency or adult maladjustment. Hence, diversion is considered by many to be desirable in terms of both time and cost. Indeed, the smooth operation of our juvenile justice system may require diversion. Otherwise, these courts could grind to a halt as virtually all children were brought before them.

Presently in Canada, however, there is no formal diversion policy or structure. Since no formal guidelines define the diversion process, officials must rely on their own discretion. Hence, irrelevant factors and personal bias frequently may come into play. In studying the extent to which factors *not* related to the alleged offence affected the probability of a juvenile being referred for a formal court hearing in the United States, Thomas and Sieverdes' research indicated that extra-legal as well as legal factors played major roles, including age (older referred to court more often), family instability (referred more often), co-defendants (referred more often), and race (blacks referred more often).[236] Moreover, other studies have shown that, overall, diversion tends to *increase* the number of children in official or semi-official hands.[237] That is, there is little diversion *from* the system. Rather it occurs mainly within the system. Thus as the number of diversion programmes has grown, so has the total number of juveniles brought within the juvenile justice system.[238] Hence, diversion, in practice, appears to accomplish exactly the opposite to what diversion theory seeks to accomplish.

To develop systematic and effective diversion programmes, effective guidelines are needed to help structure and control the diversion process. Then, those agencies performing diversion activities must be monitored and held accountable for their performance. In Canada, diversity in local attitudes and resources, which variably affects opportunities for diversion, provides a unique opportunity for experimentation and comparison.[239] To understand how such discretionary decision-making works and to know its role and function in the delinquency system requires basic empirical research. Only then can we seek to manage this discretion more effectively.[240]

(b) *Discretion at the delinquency hearing.* Again at the hearing itself, few guidelines exist to structure the judge's broad threefold discretion. First, judges decide *what* behaviour to process further, for in the omnibus clauses in delinquency legislation, judicial authorities find the discretion to impose upon youth whatever standards of behaviour they deem appropriate.[241] The judge, as statutory *parens patriae*, acts for the state in the role of a benevolent parent to 'aid, encourage, help and assist' a 'misdirected and misguided' child.[242] Yet the behaviour one judge considers 'misguided and misdirected' at one time, he may another time choose to ignore. Even if the individual judge is consistent in his approach, the behaviour he proscribes may differ radically from the behaviour proscribed by another judge. For example, one judge may go to great lengths to declare a child delinquent if it appears that the child needs help. Another will rely only on the behaviour which brought the child to court in determining delinquency. Hence, the process of defining delinquent behaviour is based on wide judicial discretion.

Secondly, the judge, to a large extent, is able to decide *how* the proceedings are conducted. Hearings are informal. Research has shown that, in practice, due process protections are often set aside despite the fact that the case law now enumerates a range of due process protections. Mr. Justice McRuer has argued that 'strict adherence to the procedure of the ordinary courts might well work to the detriment of the child. The function of the judge is not so much to determine guilt as to find out the underlying causes which have brought the child before the court, and when these have been determined to prescribe treatment.' In his view, while 'some basic' legal protections require recognition, the function of the judge, as 'a social physician charged with diagnosing the case and issuing the prescription ... cannot be properly performed if he is surrounded by too many legalistic trappings.'[243] Further, because our legislation limits appeals to cases where there exists a gross abuse of process and because the proceedings are not open to public scrutiny, there is limited review to check procedural abuse. In consequence, one juvenile court may be conducted in a highly legalistic manner while another totally disregards due process procedures.

Thirdly, judges decide *what penalty* to set. Since there is no specific fine, penalty or treatment for any given offence, the judge may invoke any one or combination of the dispositions set out in section 20 of our *Juvenile Delinquents Act*, ranging from adjournment with no finding to indefinite training school committal. In sum, it is apparent that all major decisions at the delinquency hearing are, to some extent, discretionary. And while both consistency and predictability are central to any system of law, there can be no consistency in a system which relies on discretion at every level.

The proposed new federal delinquency legislation, which limits the court's jurisdiction to encompass only those who commit federal offences and which circumscribes procedural discretion, reflects the prevailing dissatisfaction with this system of discretionary justice for juvenile offenders, even though little reliable data exist about the actual effects or effectiveness of the complex network of inter-related components making up our delinquency system. While the confusing and even contradictory goals in our present system make meaningful evaluation of its effectiveness difficult, presently, even the most basic descriptive research remains to be undertaken. Attempts should be made to develop a solid data-based description of the effectiveness of the present delinquency laws. Otherwise, there will exist no basis for comparing the new federal proposals when they are implemented and without such comparisons, it will be impossible to measure the effectiveness of these statutory reforms.

Discretion in the Child Protection System
The fundamental fault with our child protection laws, Mnookin claims, is the wide discretion they permit.[244]

(a) *Discretion prior to the protection hearing.* Prior to bringing on a child protection application, the child protection agency usually works with the family in an attempt to resolve their problems. Rodham suggests that this should be a prerequisite to intervention.[245] In her view, only after the state has been unsuccessful in ameliorating neglect by providing services to the child and family should other forms of intrusion be permitted.

As an alternative to protection proceedings, Ontario's legislation permits parents to place children into CAS care voluntarily when the parent is temporarily unable to care for the child or the child has special needs.[246] Yet little is known about how, when, why, or how often these 'non-ward care agreements' are employed. Their use appears to be entirely at the individual social worker's discretion. Because these agreements are private contracts requiring no judicial scrutiny, the agency may use them in place of care proceedings. Moreover, no external checks exist to prevent the threat of formal proceedings from being used to coerce families into entering non-ward agreements. Nor is there any monitoring or evaluation to see how successful such agreements are in comparison with other forms of intervention.

In a narrow range of circumstances, Ontario's legislation gives the CAS the power to place a homemaker temporarily in premises where a child has been left without proper care.[247] This option is limited to providing temporary care only and is not available as a broader family problem-solving technique. In theory, though, homemaker services have the potential for ameliorating a wide range of family problems which might otherwise lead to protection applications. Homemakers could be used to alleviate crisis situations, teach parenting, help families get to other needed services, protect children and perform a wide variety of other roles. Yet no study of their present or potential utility has been undertaken. The espoused goal of child welfare agencies is to rehabilitate families rather than remove children. Innovative experimentation with and evaluation of homemaker services and other forms of child care may help transform this policy into reality.

Finally, little is known about the process leading up to a protection hearing or about the exercise of worker discretion prior to a case reaching court. Is there a series of predictable stages through which each case must pass? Are there formal guidelines to delimit and standardize decision-making? If so, do they work? Especially important are the variables which enter into the decision to commence the hearing itself. For example, Greenland's Ontario study indicated that both within individual agencies and between different agencies, no common definition of what constituted child abuse obtained.[248] Thus, the need for understanding and controlling discretion prior to the hearing is apparent. Research which monitors standardization and effectiveness is one possible technique which may facilitate the achievement of this end.

(b) *Discretion at the child protection hearing.* Current criteria for declaring children in need of protection are couched in broad, vague statutory language. Yet because aiding children through coercive intervention has not been proven successful, Wald believes that overintervention into family life is a greater problem than underintervention. Neglect is often defined in terms of parental conduct or home conditions, rarely requiring a showing of actual harm to the child.[249] In Wald's view, vague concepts such as parental fault or moral neglect should be abandoned in favour of statutory standards based on specific types of damage which justify intervention.

In theory, there are two stages with two different standards in child protection hearings. The court should first find whether the child is in need of protection and, if this is so, the judge must then consider which disposition would serve the child's best interests. But, in practice, the two separate stages and separate standards overlap and individualized adjudications result. Yet, as noted, because the individual judges are forced to rely on their own personal biases, such discretionary determinations are frequently not consistent and often not fair. In a simulation study of judicial decision-making in child welfare hearings, Phillips[250] found that every judge operated on his own unique personal value system, different factors being important to different judges.

Like Wald, Mnookin, too, insists that the judge's discretion to remove a child from his home should be circumscribed. He suggests that objective measures be defined and that written judicial decisions, containing both the reasons for removal and an explanation of why proposed less drastic measures were found unsatisfactory, be required.[251] Whether some form of written decision could, in fact, check judicial discretion, and perhaps agency discretion too, is an empirical question. This and other possible techniques for controlling discretion merit further exploration.

In protection hearings in Ontario, a judge is faced with four alternatives: he can dismiss the case, leave the child in the home under agency supervision, remove the child from the home temporarily, or take steps to remove him permanently by declaring him a Crown ward.[252] If the child is found in need of protection, the present legislative standard for disposition – the best interest test – does not equip a judge to compare the probable consequences of the child's remaining in the home with the probable consequences of his removal.[253] The judge may not readily see the risks of foster care placement since only the risks of the child remaining in the home are placed before him.[254] This results in a substantial bias in favour of removal. More basic still, Wald points out, little is known about the consequences of placing the child under home supervision as compared with removal, for example.[255] But even if removal were to prove the better alternative, the benefits may not be sufficient to justify the substantial financial cost. The possible harmful effects of compelling unwilling clients to accept services must be investigated too, for this may have significant repercussions for the child.[256] Thus, the full range of innovative prevention measures should be evaluated and compared. One especially promising alternative, the 'no-questions-asked-drop-off centre,' where parents may deposit their children for a specified period of time, is now being implemented in a number of locations.[257] Approaches such as this merit serious assessment.

In conclusion, indeterminate, discretionary standards fail to force social welfare bureaucracies to plan adequately for children. In the plans they do make, the convenience of the social welfare system rather than the best interests of the child is often suspected to be the overriding factor.[258] Monitoring and evaluation, forcing accountability, could help overcome abuses. Systematic empirical research on the effects of removal and foster care can define and document problem areas. Such research can not only provide an effective tool in lobbying for legislative standards limiting discretion, it may also indicate innovative avenues of reform.

Discretion in Processing Custody Issues
Custody and access questions are essentially matters of private law. The state will perform a dispute-settling function only if the question is brought to court.

(a) *Discretion prior to the custody hearing.* The majority of custody disputes are resolved before reaching court. Eekelaar's recent study of divorce-related custody dispositions in England indicates that custody was still in dispute by the time the divorce reached the judicial hearing in only 2.1 per cent of the cases in his sample. Most custody dispositions were found to be *pro forma* judicial confirmations of private arrangements made between the spouses prior to court.[259] And when the parties settle the custody matter out-of-court, this decision-making process is virtually free from judicial review.

Indeed, formal procedures are being created to encourage private settlement. In Ontario, for example, the Unified Family Court[260] and the Family Law Division of the Supreme Court have established informal 'pre-trials' between the judge and the disputing spouses. These pre-trials seek to encourage spouses to reach accord privately on as many issues as possible, including custody, prior to their formal divorce hearings.[261] Yet without empirical research, we cannot know if these procedures actually effect satisfactory and lasting custody settlements.

(b) *Discretion at the custody hearing.* While most custody matters are settled out of court, litigated cases often make important contributions to the law of custody. Our custody legislation directs the court to make that order which is consistent with the 'best interests' of the child[262] but fails to elucidate the criteria on which this 'best interests' decision is to be made.[263] Hence, the judge must resort to the case law for guidelines. Yet the precedents often provide little assistance either because their rules are either too vague or too flexible to be unequivocal or because they involve different facts with different people while the 'best interests' test requires individualized decision-making.[264] Thus, the trial judge is left with substantial discretion in making his decision.

As a principle of law, Mnookin argues, the 'best interests' test is so wide that one cannot know when a judge has used it improperly.[265] Hence, except for appeals, there are no effective limits on judicial discretion in these proceedings.[266] Because no clear societal consensus exists on the best mode of childrearing[267] and because the test itself is indeterminate, the judge is forced to rely on his own value choices, or, alternatively, to depend on the reports of social workers or psychiatrists who make questionable claim to special knowledge and predictive ability.[268] In consequence, the decisions of one court may appear inconsistent with those of another and the fundamental principle that like cases should be decided alike may be violated or appear to be violated in the eyes of the parties.[269] Bradbrook concluded from his research on judicial discretion in contested custody matters that no universal principles exist in the law of custody. And on an individual basis, because the vagueness of this standard makes the outcome of litigation hard to predict, an increased number of cases are taken to court.[270]

To counter this broad judicial discretion, many have proposed that substantive guidelines or presumptions supplement the best interests rule.[271] Such presumptions may, by directing the court to consider a number of matters relevant to the issue, limit discretion. While guidelines such as these should be predicated on rigorous scientific study, the necessary research has yet to be undertaken. The need for increased knowledge of the long-term consequences of alternative custody arrangements, the central question in any custody matter, is apparent. Yet little relevant data presently exist.[272] Before guidelines can be formulated, we need to know how and under what circumstances custody arrangements cause emotional injuries to children and how various familial factors exacerbate or mitigate these effects.[273] Questions related to changes in mother-figures,[274] the effects of psychological ties, the need for continuity of relationships, the benefits of access, and the like are all empirical questions which require research to provide the much needed information on which to base guidelines aimed at structuring and defining discretion in the custody decision-making process. Then the effects and effectiveness of the guidelines themselves must be assessed.

The Child as Participant in the Hearing
Regardless of the type of hearing, serious questions exist about the child's participation, based on a variety of considerations. These include the child's status in the hearing, his ability to understand both the nature and purpose of the hearing and the manner in which it is conducted, his perceptions of the fairness of the procedure and the justness of the outcome, and his capacity to know and express his own views, either through a lawyer or directly to the court.

The Child's Status in the Hearing
The word 'party' has a precise meaning in legal parlance. It is that person by or against whom legal action is brought or who otherwise has a legally recognized interest in the proceeding, and who, therefore, has a right to participate fully in the proceedings.

In delinquency proceedings, the child clearly has party status.[275] In child protection and custody matters, however, his status is unclear. Moreover, opinion varies on whether the child should be considered a full legal participant. A recent Ontario case is of the view that the child is not a party in child protection proceedings.[276] Thus, the child has no right to participate. Section 25(3) of *The Child Welfare Act* in Ontario is permissive, though, and the judge may, if he chooses, hear any person on behalf of the child. Presumably 'any person' includes the child himself, but unless the judge permits the child to make representations to the court in the protection hearing, he will be unable to do so.[277]

In custody matters, a recent Ontario decision directed the Official Guardian to protect the interests of the children involved in the hearing and act for them *as if they were parties.*[278] Thus, there appears to be a shift in judicial opinion in Ontario towards granting the child party status in custody matters.

To possess party status in legal proceedings where one's rights are being affected is a fundamental tenet of our legal system. Without such status a person cannot compel the court to hear his views on the matters being adjudicated, even though his rights may thereby be affected. That children still lack party status in some proceedings where their lives are affected is an historical anachronism, a holdover from times when children were virtually legal non-entities. The trend today, however, is towards recognizing children as full citizens in our society. Yet as long as such anomalies in our legal system survive, they must be acknowledged and children's status determined accordingly.

The Child's Capacity to Understand the Proceedings

Delinquency charges cannot be brought against a child under 7 years of age. Custody and protection matters, on the other hand, often involve very young children incapable of directly participating in the hearing even if accorded party status. Stone has noted that 'the medical profession seems generally convinced that children aged 6 or 7 years, even if below normal intelligence may have decided ideas ... and should be heard.'[279] Yet no research has been undertaken to establish in a scientific manner the age below which most children are unable to understand the nature and consequences of legal proceedings and are thus incapable of meaningful participation. Therefore, no meaningful age line can presently be drawn below which children should be presumed incapable of participating.

The small body of empirical data which exists notes that, prior to a delinquency hearing, most children have no clear understanding of what to expect at the hearing.[280] Moreover, once the proceeding is over, the research indicates that they have little understanding of what actually happened in court.[281] This lack of comprehension obtained equally for those with a long history of court appearances as for those appearing for the first time. The research also suggests that most parents did not understand what had occurred in the hearing.[282]

These misunderstandings can be attributed to a variety of factors. Most legislation dealing with children is vague, broad in scope, and based on individualized 'best interests' determinations. And what actually occurs in these hearings often belies this espoused legislative goal. Parents and children have little factual knowledge of what should happen in court. The procedure may be unnecessarily confusing or complex. The informal nature of the proceedings may well contribute to the confusion, for there are few clear and predictable steps in the process. Moreover, recent American research suggests that children learn much of what they know about law from television.[283] If this finding holds true in Canada, children would, on this basis, expect strict American criminal law due process in court. If the child's parents equally do not grasp what is happening in court and the lawyer, if present, may not have or take the time to explain the process, confusion on the child's part is an understandable consequence of a delinquency hearing. Bewilderment and perhaps dismay may be normal reactions connoting real insight into the nature of children's legal proceedings and, as such, are indicative of a child's capacity rather than incapacity in this context.

The comprehensibility of the informal procedures in delinquency and child protection hearings should be subject to further research. The child's lack of understanding may stem mainly from poorly defined procedures or from insufficient knowledge of what to expect rather than from inherent deficiencies in his capacity to appreciate the legal process. The work Grisso and his colleagues are now undertaking on juveniles' comprehension of Miranda warnings and perceptions of the juvenile legal process should help to clarify these issues.[284] Because custody hearings are more formal, a comparison between children's comprehension in these proceedings and in the more informal delinquency and child protection hearings would be useful. Because no efforts are made to apprise the child of the functions of the various participants in the proceeding - the judge, the lawyer, social worker, 'prosecutor' - he may understand little about their respective roles in the hearing. But it is important to realize that children, like the rest of us, act and react on the basis of their expectations. Disappointed expectations, even though inaccurate, may lead to negative attitudes towards the law. On the basis of ignorance and misinformation, the child may react to his exposure to the legal system with a 'profound sense of injustice.'[285]

The Child's Capacity to Present His View to the Court
There is little point in giving the child the right to participate in proceedings affecting him if he is unable to ascertain or express his own views. Research on children's perceptions of delinquency hearings indicates that they frequently feel that they do not 'get their say' in court. They feel that they are treated in a routine and superficial manner.[286] These same feelings may also occur where the judge, in a custody matter, interviews the child in chambers, although no research has been undertaken on this point. To improve this situation, children are more frequently being provided with their own legal counsel. The ramifications of this will now be explored more fully.

Legal Representation
In examining the lawyer-child relationship, three central concepts must be reviewed: access - how and when do children retain counsel? capacity - when are

children able to instruct counsel? and finally, quality – how effective is the representation provided?[287]

Kleinfeld maintains that, for adults, the right to counsel is premised upon the incompetence of the ordinary layman to cope with the technicalities of legal proceedings. In his view, this logic compels an even broader right to counsel for infants because of their presumably even greater incompetence.[288] In delinquency proceedings, children, as parties, have the right to retain and instruct counsel.[289] In a recent custody matter, the Ontario Divisional Court appointed the Official Guardian to act as the legal representative for the children 'with full powers to act for these infants as if they were parties to the proceedings.'[290] Even more recently, in Ontario, children have appeared with their own independent counsel in a custody hearing.[291] In child protection matters, it was recently decided that the Ontario Provincial Courts (Family Division) have *no* authority to *appoint* the Official Guardian to make representations on behalf of a child. They may, however, *ask* the Official Guardian whether he wishes to do so.[292] Yet, as a matter of practice, children are sometimes represented by independent counsel in child protection hearings.[293] Elsewhere, too, the trend is towards providing children with some form of legal representation.[294]

The potential benefits of representation are numerous. Children, like adults, need assistance in understanding court proceedings. They need representation to ensure that their rights are upheld, to ensure procedural regularity, to protect them from potential abuse endemic in a system based on broad discretionary justice, to present impartially and articulately their views to the court, and to help make new law by appealing cases. Child advocates may also form an effective lobby for statutory changes.[295]

Judicial and legislative activity in this area has reflected the general upsurge in concern over legal representation for children. Hence, the issue today is not so much whether to provide children with legal representation as how to ensure that children obtain representation which is both timely and effective. Central to this issue is the child's capacity to instruct counsel and, in the obverse, the role the lawyer should assume. Should he act in his traditional adversary role as an advocate for the child's view, assuming he can determine what the child's views are? Should he modify his role to that of an *amicus curiae*,[296] assisting the court by bringing to its attention matters that might otherwise be overlooked? Or should he act as the child's guardian, advocating the decision he sees as being in the child's best interests?

Both the child's ability to instruct counsel and the philosophy and procedural structure of the court in which the lawyer acts may affect his final role definition. Based on their research in the Ontario Provincial Courts, Dootjes et al.[297] reported that lawyers representing children in delinquency hearings were under pressure to perform diametrically opposing roles in court. These researchers found that the lawyer's training as an advocate conflicted with the informal, social service orientation of the juvenile court. This conflict created pressure on counsel to assume a less adversarial stance. The judges and social workers were also found to have contradictory expectations about the function the lawyer should fulfil.[298] Some judges and social workers indicated that he should act in a highly legalistic manner; others insisted that he should do whatever is 'best' for the child. Stapleton and Teitelbaum[299] obtained similar results in their American study. They observed that lawyers themselves varied in their preferred orientation towards representing juveniles. Further, the role counsel was able to assume depended, to a large degree, on whether the court itself was legalistic or informal in its orientation. Finally, these data indicated that while the adversarial approach was highly successful in obtaining discharges in a 'legalistic' court, in an informal 'family model' court, the adversarial approach led to an increase in conviction rates.[300]

In custody hearings, which are formal adversarial proceedings based on due process procedures, the lawyer is expected to, and therefore does, perform a much different role than in informal, family model, delinquency or protection hearings. Thus a number of variables influence the exact role the lawyer finally adopts in any given proceedings, including the philosophy of the court, the model underlying the procedure, the lawyer's own preferred orientation towards the proceeding, the role that other participants in the hearing expect the lawyer to perform, and the lawyer's assessment of the child's capacity to instruct him. Each of these variables merits further research to determine what effects it has on the lawyer's role, the child and the hearing itself.

Whether the lawyer looks to the child for direction depends on his opinion of the child's capacity to instruct him. While a child as young as 7 years may have decided views and be a proper source of information, most children involved in protection proceedings and many in custody disputes are even younger than this. The lawyer may, therefore, be required to make an independent assessment of the child's best interests in this situation.

The psychological literature generally endorses the notion that children over 6 years have, to a degree at least, the capacity to make choices and convey information to direct a lawyer, and by about age 13 should be able to give counsel specific instructions.[301] Yet no empirical research has been directed specifically to this question. Since children are being represented with increasing frequency, the effects and effectiveness of legal representation should be explored more fully. In fact, the whole area of representation abounds with questions which can only be answered through empirical research. For example, at what point in the process must a lawyer be provided to be effective? What role should the lawyer perform? Should his role differ, depending on the nature of the hearing? What training does the lawyer need to help him communicate with and understand children? Conversely, what training do children need to help them deal with, speak to, and understand lawyers? Can procedures be modified to make lawyers more effective in representing children? If so, how? Does having legal representation really make any difference in the nature and outcome of the proceeding? If so, is it for the better? Should there be a full-time representative providing legal services to all children? Or should the judge have the discretion to appoint counsel as he sees fit? These and many other questions are ripe for empirical investigation.

In Ontario, the Official Guardian[302] provides a limited range of legal services for minors. He is required by statute to provide the court with a social report for all children involved in divorce proceedings, covering matters related to their care, maintenance, custody, and access, a total of 14,900 cases in Ontario in 1976.[303] The court may also request that he provide a report in a non-divorce custody proceeding. And in a growing number of cases the Official Guardian is being asked to act as counsel for children in contested custody and child protection matters. An analysis of the Official Guardian's role could be a useful first step in examining issues relating to legal representation for children.

Ontario also has duty counsel, provided through Legal Aid, to represent juveniles involved in uncontested delinquency proceedings.[304] This system, too, should be evaluated. Preliminary research[305] indicated duty counsel-child communication was so poor that some children did not even realize duty counsel was a lawyer present to represent them. Moreover, duty counsel was observed to make few attempts to advocate actively on the child's behalf in court.

When a child contests a delinquency charge, he may be able to retain a private lawyer through Legal Aid to represent him. Despite the unique opportunity for comparative research these two modes of delivering legal services to children provide, no evaluation has yet been undertaken. In 1977, however, the Ontario Attorney General's Committee on the Representation of Children[306] recommended that a series of pilot projects be established to assess the quality of present modes of delivering legal representation to children and to determine ways of improving this service. Preliminary work is now underway.[307]

The Use of Social Evaluation Reports in Court

Social evaluation reports usually come before the court in two ways. Either the court itself orders a social investigation[308] or one of the parties retains the assistance of an expert, such as a psychiatrist or psychologist, to prepare a report or present evidence in support of that party's claims.

Social investigation reports are designed to assist the court in deciding the case before it by expeditiously bringing to the judge's attention matters which he would not learn of otherwise. The scope of the report may depend on the judge's directions. Usually, though, it encompasses the complete personal and economic backgrounds of all parties before the court, the rationale being that almost any variable could be relevant in determining the 'best interests' of the child in question. 'Experienced and disinterested workers make an unbiased examination of the qualifications of each party and of the circumstances surrounding the child' according to Gozansky.[309]

The predictive inadequacy of present judicial guidelines accounts for the interest in behavioural science opinion as a source of decision-making assistance.[310] Traditional adversary procedures in custody matters seldom produce the kind of information a judge needs to determine the child's best interests. In protection and delinquency hearings, the justification for using such reports stems from the court's ostensible need to have a complete picture before it can act in the child's best interests.

Yet it is important to note that these reports are based on opinion rather than on scientifically based fact, for the research necessary to produce such knowledge remains undone. Thus, current use of such reports is, in Okpaku's view, based on the mistaken belief that the behavioural sciences are sufficiently advanced to supply answers to individual questions such as 'which long-term custody placement is best for this child?' Okpaku argues that, in its present unverified state, psychological theory can, at best, only suggest such questions as areas where research is needed. It provides no panacea to the decision-making dilemmas faced by our judiciary because the data on which to base such knowledge remain to be gathered.

The use of clinical psychiatric and psychological insight to inform judicial decision-making has been subject to much criticism. Virtually any conduct, Okpaku asserts, can be taken as symptomatic of a psychiatric disorder. Even without regard to bias, psychiatric judgments involve a high risk of error. That psychiatric and psychological judgments are highly unreliable is well documented.[311] Okpaku concludes that clinical judgments of doubtful validity presently serve as the basis for predictions about the long-range effects of a particular placement or treatment on the child; well-intentioned clinicians, convinced of the accuracy of their unsystematic observations, can find in their over-broad descriptions of childhood needs and harms support for virtually any opinion.

In Ontario, social investigations are mandatory in all custody matters and divorce actions involving children.[312] Freelance social workers investigate and prepare these reports in Toronto; in smaller centres, the child welfare agency is used.[313] In protection matters, court affiliated assessment clinics, where they exist, prepare such reports; otherwise, the local agency is used despite the conflict of interest between their role as the party commencing the protection application and their role as impartial investigator preparing an unbiased evaluation of the family situation. In delinquency proceedings, court clinics or court-appointed personnel prepare these evaluations at the judge's request.

Although many participants in court hearings rely heavily on the reliability and validity of these social reports, little is known about when judges request them, how they are used, or how accurately they portray the family situation. Kraus[314] reported in 1975 that, despite its importance, he could find no empirical research on how pre-sentence reports were used in juvenile court decision-making. His research into judicial use of these reports in the Australian Juvenile Court indicated that the most significant factor in judicial decision-making was not the report *per se* but rather its actual recommendations. These recommendations carried more weight in judicial decision-making than any other factor he analysed. In the deliberations of Scottish Children's Panels, Fox observed that discussion focused mainly on the contents of the social report.[315] Thus, courts appear to rely on such reports to a considerable extent. Moreover, while Smith and Lodrup[316] note that judges express a strong desire for this type of expert assistance, little empirical research on the accuracy and utility of expert social reports in children's hearings has been conducted.

The need for further data-based research is readily apparent, especially in view of the steady increase in the number of requests for these reports which occurs each year and the heavy judicial reliance on their recommendations.[317] Empirical research can further our understanding of the present use of the social reports and help establish directions for future policy.

Alternative Forms of Court

Spencer has stated that systems of justice, above all in relation to children, cannot be divorced from the structure of social services responsible for the assessment and care of the child and of his family.[318] But concern has been expressed about the effects and effectiveness of transferring decision-making away from either the legal process or the family where it formerly resided and into the hands of social service agencies. Some would contend that the social service system, while lacking the formal checks and restraints found in the legal process, has come to function as a quasi-legal system. This section of the paper therefore explores the need for data on the use and utility of some of the wide variety of social services relevant to delinquency, child protection, and custody matters.

Howlett,[319] in commenting on the establishment of the National Youth Services Bureau in the United States, concluded that this agency would only broaden the umbrella of ineffective services for children while further transferring the problems and responsibilities of the family away from the home, school, and community where they belonged and into the public domain. This agency, in his view, would divert from the legal system only those who should not be there anyway. Streib suggests that as the formal delinquency system in the United States found its discretionary powers circumscribed by the due process requirements of their Supreme Court, an informal system developed, composed of a collage of service agencies, which now parallels and competes with the formal system.[320] Thus, discretion and procedural abuse have not disappeared. They have simply re-emerged in another form. This informal service system performs exactly the same functions as the legal process but without the judge, without strict legal procedures, and without formal hearings. Its sanctioning mechanism is the threat of court. Yet rather than simply abolishing this informal system, which may provide a viable and less costly alternative to judicial processing, Streib says we need to learn more about how it operates and evaluate its effectiveness.

Courts exert little effective control or supervision over the decision-making of service agencies. In consequence, these agencies exercise virtually unbridled discretion. Because the variety of services surrounding the legal processing of children often have unclear or inconsistent goals and operating procedures, meaningful comparisons are difficult to undertake. But unless both supervision and evaluation are undertaken, Seymour notes, service agencies may tend to serve their clients according to the agency's function rather than the client's needs.[321] Yet if these service agencies prove no less effective than courts in controlling antisocial behaviour and achieve their results more simply, efficiently, humanely, or cheaply, then this option deserves further consideration. If, however, as Howlett predicts, research demonstrates that more children are netted by ineffective services, other alternatives must be sought.

The movement away from legal processing towards service processing as the preferred way of dealing with children's legal problems mirrors our dissatisfaction with the present system. In custody and protection proceedings, and to a lesser degree in delinquency matters, dissatisfaction focuses on the adversary system. Because it tends to entrench acrimony and further polarize those involved, the adversary system is often ineffective in achieving amicable and lasting dispute settlement. Those who advocate alternative approaches to solving family problems hope that informal procedures, fostering conciliatory attitudes and encouraging the parties themselves to participate in the dispute resolution, will lead to permanent, effective solutions. Dissatisfaction with the present system also centres in the trauma of court hearings, on overloaded court schedules leading to repeated delays, and on the time and dollars involved in litigating issues which might be settled more efficaciously by other means.

The alternatives, either proposed or operative, fall into three broad conceptual categories. First, there are procedures established prior to court which seek to settle as many issues as possible or to channel the case out of the legal system entirely. Examples of this are formal and informal delinquency diversion programmes and the conciliations, arbitrations, or pre-trials often used in matrimonial matters. Secondly, some systems eliminate judicial processing entirely. In its place, service hearings are substituted. The Scottish lay panel system is an example which has been empirically evaluated to some extent. Thirdly, some jurisdictions have attempted to unify the existing judicial and service elements of the family law process. The movement in Canada towards a system of unified family courts illustrates this approach. As stated, these three categories are conceptual only. Any of these service approaches, in combination or permutation, may be employed in seeking solutions to the deficiencies in the present system. The small amount of empirical research relevant to these three categories will now be examined.

Pre-Court Services

Diversion within the delinquency system has already been discussed in the section entitled 'Discretion Prior to the Delinquency Hearing.'

Mediation[322] is a method of conflict resolution whereby the parties to the dispute are made to realize that they themselves must find a way to solve the matter in dispute. The mediator cannot impose a solution. Rather he guides the parties into a willingness to accept their responsibility to seek a solution and points out alternatives that might have been overlooked.

In a crisis urban ghetto in the Bronx, a Neighborhood Youth Diversion Program[323] was established, geared towards intensive community participation in dispute resolution through informal mediation, using community residents trained as mediators. The mediation process sought to convince the disputants that they themselves had the responsibility to come to a mutually satisfactory solution. The powerlessness of the forum was seen as its greatest asset, for its success was totally dependent on the genuine consent of everyone involved. In this voluntary environment, mediation effected resolutions where coercive court processing had previously failed. Hence, the project demonstrated to the community that it had the capacity to deal with its own youth problems.

Mediation-based child care conferences have also been proposed as a method of dealing with child protection cases.[324]

Conciliation is the label applied to mediation of domestic disputes. As in mediation, the conciliator has no power to impose a settlement. Rather he attempts to bring the parties to an awareness of their own responsibility to achieve a mutually satisfactory solution. A number of conciliation projects are underway across Canada.[325] In Toronto, for example, the Family Court Conciliation Project provides specialists trained in the socio-legal aspects of short-term crisis-oriented matrimonial counselling. The service is voluntary but the court's authority is used to encourage people to take advantage of it. A team approach, utilizing professionals of varying backgrounds, is employed to enhance the possibility of resolving the dispute outside the formal court structure. Of special interest is the project evaluation which examplifies the type of empirical research seldom conducted but essential if meaningful conclusions are to be drawn from data collection. The investigators state that '[t]he plans for evaluation ... include the use of experimental and control groups. Clients will be randomly assigned to the control group (the existing court intake service) and the experimental group (the conciliation project) for the purpose of statistical comparisons.'[326] Methodologically strong empirical research like that being undertaken at the Toronto Family Court will enable policy-makers to base their decisions on solid, empirical data rather than mere surmise.

In this type of multidisciplinary approach to family problems, however, there is often no clear demarcation between the social and legal services provided. In consequence, the professionals affiliated with such services may experience serious role conflict or confusion. Such conflicts can jeopardize the success of the programme. Elkin has argued that lawyers should handle the strictly legal matters and leave the large social and personal matters of conciliation to the social workers.[327] Theuman observed that considerable friction among the various professionals working on a number of Canadian conciliation projects arose from their divergent views as to who should perform what duties along the social service-legal counselling continuum.[328] This problem merits consideration in the further assessment of such projects.

Service Hearings as a Substitute for Courts
In this second category, judicial hearings are eliminated and service hearings are held in their place. The most well-known example, which has been subject to some systematic research, is the Scottish lay panel system.

Children's panels were established in Scotland in 1971[329] to replace court proceedings in delinquency and protection matters with hearings before a panel of three lay persons. If the parents or child refuse to appear, deny the act in question, or do not accept the panel's determination, then the matter may still be referred on to court. The nature of the offence is irrelevant at a panel hearing, its sole function being to apply training measures appropriate to the child's needs.[330] The process promotes a highly individualized approach to each case and relies heavily on persuasion in attempting to obtain the co-operation of the delinquent and his family.[331]

According to Morris, one cannot talk accurately about the 'Scottish lay panel system.' Her research indicates that there are a number of systems operating within the same statutory framework.[332] The children referred to panel hearings generally were found to be petty delinquents, more social nuisances than social problems.[333] Yet, under this system, the number of children in residential treatment has increased even though the total number of cases being processed has not.[334] And while the panel system was designed to enhance community involvement, Bruce maintains that it has had little impact in the general community.[335] Spencer, on the other hand, feels it has sharpened community awareness of the real problems faced by children living in deprived circumstances.[336]

Sweden also had long held service hearings before their Child Welfare Boards. The Board has full authority to adjudicate both family and delinquency matters involving children under sixteen. The Board may, in delinquency matters, refer the child on to the courts.[337] Similarly, in 1974 British Columbia established a panel system, composed of two lay persons and a judge which, upon the application of a variety of persons including the child, may make a variety of dispositional decisions once the child is found in need of protection.[338] The effectiveness of these two systems has not, as yet, been subject to empirical assessment.

Unified Family Courts

The move towards unified family courts has developed in response to the inadequacies in the present system. The Ontario Law Reform Commission has summarized the deficiencies in the existing system as follows:

Four different branches in the judicial hierarchy ... administer family law in Ontario and this results in overlapping and competing jurisdiction ... and conflicts in philosophy and approach to the same problems among the different courts. The end result is inefficiency, ineffective treatment of family problems, and unnecessary confusion ... [Moreover] the provision of such ancillary services as exist (and these are by no means sufficient) has been haphazard, marked by lack of uniformity of policy and of standards ...[339]

Despite the absence of empirical data to support their views, the Commissioners concluded that '[o]nly if a Family Court is given comprehensive jurisdiction in all family law matters, will it be capable of meeting the needs of the community ...'[340] There was no question, in the Commissioners' view, that a strong, well-structured, well-equipped Family Court system, supported by adequate ancillary services, could be of inestimable value to the community.[341]

In response to such perceived deficiencies, the British Columbia Royal Commission on Family and Children's Law established a Unified Family Court pilot project in that province in 1974. Their final assessment of the project is soon to be released. While the interim reports appear to be highly subjective, they indicate that the project was considered a success. Ontario, too, has established a Unified Family Court pilot project. The problem of fragmented jurisdiction has been overcome by giving this court power to administer all legislation relating to families and children.[342] Thus, the one court can handle any family law matter. Further, attempts are underway to streamline the ancillary services considered essential for the ultimate resolution of family problems. And before further government commitment is made to this reform programme, a full-time researcher is evaluating the project's effectiveness.

Others, however, are not so optimistic about this trend. Theuman believes that the unified family court movement is based on the same rehabilitative philosophy that underlies the juvenile courts and the consensus of opinion, in his view, is that this philosophy has failed in that forum.[343] Judge Allard succinctly voiced this concern when he stated that '[a]ppraisals of American Family Courts are all too often marked by self-initiated statements of their own effectiveness and worthiness. Recent questionings of Juvenile Court practices will no doubt soon be extended to questioning of the handling of domestic disputes heard in the various courts.'[344] The Dysons, in their exhaustive review of Family Courts in the United States, remark that

[f]amily courts though little studied in depth, have garnered almost universal praise ... This uncritical consensus reflects a practice common in America, of looking to legal institutions for the correction of social ills. This tendency is dangerous; our experience is that courts seldom contain the answers to problems arising *outside* the legal system. We delude ourselves if we think that delinquency and family disorganization can be cured simply by reforms in legal institutions ...[345]

Thus, in any of the above-described ways, children who come in contact with the legal system find themselves, and often their entire families, inextricably bound up in a social service network of, as yet, unproven worth. This service dimension cannot be ignored. Many view services as alternatives to legal processing rather than as mere adjuncts. Yet few data exist to endorse this approach. Even the utility of the present service component of the Family Court system remains undemonstrated. Service approaches which appear to enhance individual involvement and responsibility in decision-making, which save time and dollars, or which increase the likelihood of lasting and satisfactory resolutions of family problems should be systematically evaluated to establish their efficacy. Then those programmes of proven value should be retained. In considering the service alternatives within the present legal system and services as alternatives to court, many questions remain unanswered. Scott warns us that '[i]t is the nature of services to develop like living organisms: to grow, to specialise, to seek more recognition and power'[346] and perhaps this alone accounts for their rapid proliferation. In terms of time, cost, and the needs of children, the merit of these recent service innovations requires empirical validation based on hard data to provide answers about their effects and effectiveness.

VI SPECIAL CONCERNS RELATED TO DELINQUENCY

There exists a misconceived tendency to focus on delinquency as the core problem when surveying issues regarding children and the law. Yet special concerns relating to delinquency do exist and some of these will now be examined.

Problems in Defining the Problem
In our *Juvenile Delinquents Act*[347] '"juvenile delinquent" means any child who violates any provision of the *Criminal Code* or any federal or provincial statute, or of any municipality, or who is guilty of sexual immorality or any similar form of vice, or who is liable by reason of any other act to be committed to an industrial school or juvenile reformatory under any federal or provincial statute.' According to Sellin and Wolfgang,[348] at least 34 types of behaviour fit within this definition, including offences such as disobedience, lack of respect, smoking, incorrigibility, running away, sexual activity, and 'other similar forms of vice.' Unfortunately, nuisance behaviour such as this is lumped in with serious criminal behaviour. Cohen and Porterfield found that 100 per cent of the college students they sampled had been involved in offences serious enough to warrant court action had this route been chosen.[349] The President's Commission on Law Enforcement[350] reported that nine out of ten children in the United States have committed an offence for which they could have been arrested. In view of the all-embracing definition of delinquency, however, it is surprising that the other one of the ten avoided such activities. The vague, imprecise nature of this definition fails to give the child notice of what behaviour is proscribed, and hence fails to establish clear boundaries for unacceptable conduct. In this way, our delinquency legislation violates a fundamental precept of law.

Williams and Gold[351] distinguish between 'delinquent behaviour' and 'official delinquency.' 'Delinquent behaviour' encompasses activities by a juvenile which, if detected by an appropriate authority, could result in legal sanction. 'Official delinquency,' on the other hand, is defined as the identification of and response to such behaviour by the police and the courts. Lerman[352] suggests that official delinquency rates probably provide a more accurate record of police and court behaviour than of youthful misbehaviour.

While between 1967 and 1972 officially reported delinquency rates in the United States rose sharply[353] and public concern increased even more rapidly than the demonstrated statistical increase,[354] Gold and Reimer[355] found an overall *decrease* in self-reported delinquency rates in that same time period. While no Canadian comparison data are available, there is little reason to suspect that the picture is any different here. The probability of youth engaged in 'delinquent' behaviour being netted into the juvenile justice system has been estimated at about 3 per cent.[356] Wolfgang and his co-workers'[357] suggest that since roughly 46 per cent of first offenders never get processed a second time, intervention to provide treatment at this point is wasteful. Moreover, an additional 35 per cent of second offenders do not come in contact with the system again. On the basis of these statistics, Wolfgang et al. conclude that only the three-time offender should be subject to intensive processing.[358]

These data should, however, be interpreted in light of the selective channelling which occurs at all stages in the delinquency system. Thomas and Sieverdes[359] found that many non-legal factors influenced decisions to proceed or divert. In their United States study, blacks, older children, those from unstable family backgrounds, and those with co-accused were all more likely than their counterparts to be processed further. In predicting whether further official action would be taken, the importance attached to the seriousness of the offence varied considerably when other factors were held constant. So while here justice is not blind, it is highly selective. This research indicates that becoming a first-time official delinquent is a highly random process, often only minimally related to the delinquent behaviour in question.

Several writers have called for standardized intervention criteria with a number of specific variables being taken into account. The frequency, duration, and seriousness of the behaviour have been suggested as possible factors to be considered.[360] A test based on these considerations could be applied at all stages of processing as a mechanism for controlling what is now almost absolute discretion.

Status Offences

Status offences are those offences which can only be committed by a child because the behaviour in question is proscribed only for those below a certain age. Children who fall within the status offender category are generally of three types: those who do not get along at home, those who do not get along at school, and those who get along too well with children of the opposite sex.[361] Hence status offences are non-criminal, uniquely juvenile offences encompassing activities such as unmanageability, truancy, running away, sexual activity, drinking liquor, and smoking.

Our present *Juvenile Delinquents Act* encompasses both status offences and *Criminal Code* offences. But the long-standing controversy over whether status offences are properly within the jurisdiction of the juvenile court appears to have been decided in Canada against those who prefer this approach and in favour of those who seek to restrict the concept of delinquency to criminal offences. Recent federal proposals to reform our delinquency laws proscribed for juveniles only that behaviour which is proscribed for adults.

Reform of this kind brings into question the proper role of the juvenile court. To what extent should it be asked to bear the burden of non-criminal youthful nuisance or antisocial behaviour? To what extent should it accept this role? Pink and White[362] suggest that the court restrict its role to setting limits or maintaining bounds. Courts should administer justice; they should not engage in social rehabilitation.[363] The argument of those who oppose the juvenile court's status offence jurisdiction may be summarized as follows: this broad jurisdiction is exercised capriciously, subjecting thousands of children to a system which interferes with their lives, stigmatizes them, and deprives them of their freedom in order to 'treat' them, despite the dearth of evidence showing that current modes of coercive treatment work and the growing body of evidence indicating that such treatment may actually be harmful.[364] What the concept of the status offence really represents, in Schur's[365] view, is our society's unwillingness to tolerate youthful misbehaviour.

A general survey of the court's actions in ungovernability cases revealed that it was easier to obtain jurisdiction over a child through this mechanism than via a delinquency charge.[366] This study further observed that the court's assessments were frequently inaccurate and that its dispositions failed to provide effective treatment, all at considerable cost to the taxpayer. Status offenders tend to be incarcerated longer than delinquents guilty of serious criminal acts and the younger the status offender, the longer the period of incarceration.[367] McCarthy warns that the patent unfairness of this legal concept may do incalculable damage to the institution of law.[368]

All this leads to a basic question. Should solutions to this type of social problem be sought through the legal system when all the evidence indicates that such problems are not amenable to legal solution? Yet, if the delinquency jurisdiction in Canada is narrowed to cover only criminal offences, thereby excluding our incorrigible, ungovernable, or sexually active teenage population from this court's control, what will happen to them? A caveat is sounded by Gilman.[369] He notes that when Florida's delinquency code was revised so as to remove status offenders from its ambit, their child welfare legislation was, at the same time, expanded to include these same youths. Hence the 'problem' behaviour was not excluded from legal processing; it was simply rerouted. In his view, this so-called 'reform' resulted neither in improved procedures nor in an amelioration of the standardless, discretionary power over the child.

A similar situation obtains in Ontario. Indeed, the definition of 'child in need of protection' in our child welfare legislation is so broad that it does not need expansion to encompass status offenders. Hence narrowing the definition of delinquency may simply result in these children being processed under our child welfare laws or, alternatively, under some other legislation enacted for the specific purpose of gaining control over misbehaving children. And, as in Florida, if status offenders are going to be processed in any event, they are better off going the delinquency route, for in this system children have a clear right to counsel and other procedural protections which do not exist in child welfare proceedings.[370]

In the final analysis, Thomson remarks, the route chosen to process the child matters little if he is adjudged delinquent or in need of protection because the child is then plugged into exactly the same service system,[371] a resource network not yet demonstrated in any way effective.

If the proposed delinquency reforms are enacted, there exists a unique opportunity to study how our society will respond to the problem of the 'unmanageable' child. Will he merely be shunted into the child welfare system with the same end result as in the delinquency system? Or will this legislative reform lead to unique responses to the problems of youthful misbehaviour? Steps should be taken to collect data on the present methods of processing of the status offender[372] so that the data base necessary to make this comparison will be available.

Female Delinquency
Most studies of female delinquency, according to Datesman,[373] suggest that such behaviour can be attributed to deficient family relationships which compel these girls to seek compensatory affection outside the home. 'It seems to be generally agreed that the female offender, whether for biological, psychological or social reasons, is emotionally disturbed, has not adjusted successfully to her sex role and ... is sexually promiscuous.'[374] These studies do not, however, consider the nature of the delinquent acts for which females are commonly apprehended; that is, because females are more often charged with sexual offences, theorists assume that this stems from an underlying sexual pathology rather than a defect in the juvenile justice system. Yet some researchers claim that the delinquency system enforces a female sex-role stereotype. To date, however, few studies have concerned themselves with the process by which adolescent females are referred to the courts or how the courts respond to this group.[375]

The official statistics support the view that the delinquent girl is emotionally troubled and promiscuous. Overall, official delinquency rates for girls are much lower than for boys.[376] Landau[377] found that, in the United States, England, and in Toronto in 1971, the arrest ratio of boys and girls was about five to one. Hence the male adolescent is several times more likely than the female to become officially recorded as delinquent. But is this because females commit fewer delinquent acts or because of different societal reactions to female delinquency? The studies based on self-reported delinquency show that, in terms of types of offences committed, male and female delinquency patterns are very similar, but overall girls do commit fewer offences.[378] Wise concludes from her self-report data that although middle-class girls are underrepresented in official statistics, both 'middle-class boys and girls engage in essentially non-coercive, non-violent forms of delinquent behaviour and participate about equally in sex and alcohol delinquencies.'[379] The self-report data indicates that sex offences and ungovernability are not primarily female offences, despite the official delinquency picture.[380] '[F]emale delinquency differs only quantitatively and not qualitatively from male delinquency.'[381]

What, then, accounts for the inaccurate picture of the female delinquent portrayed in official delinquency statistics? Although the *Juvenile Delinquents Act* and *The Training Schools Act* do not, on their face, discriminate on the basis of sex, Barnhorst asserts that 'it can be shown that boys and girls receive differential treatment at all levels of the legal system. The system itself tends to create a certain type of female delinquency which enforces sex-role stereotypes.'[382]

Canadian data support this hypothesis. '[W]ithin the onset of puberty,' Landau remarks, 'a large percentage of girls begin appearing in court on charges of sexual immorality, truancy' or incorrigibility.[383] Boys, on the other hand, are much more likely to appear in court for *Criminal Code* offences. Barnhorst notes that 1971 Statistics Canada figures support this view, observing that 'despite the almost five to one boy-girl [arrest] ratio, almost twice as many girls ... were charged with incorrigibility.'[384] Weiler[385] examined the records of 60 males and 60 females sent to training school under the now repealed s.8 of *The Training Schools Act* in 1972. She found that while 16 girls were committed specifically for promiscuity, no boys were; 23 girls as opposed to 12 boys were sent to training school for staying out late; and finally, 23 girls but only 13 boys were committed for running away.[386]

In 1975, Lambert and Birkenmayer observed that although the use of *The Training Schools Act* 'incorrigibility' provisions had declined as grounds for sending sexually active female adolescents to training school, the use of the sexual immorality provisions of the *Juvenile Delinquents Act* has resulted in an overall increase in the number of girls committed to training school for sexual activity.[387] Moreover, Landau suggests that while some judges are becoming increasingly reluctant to send the 'beyond control' child to training school, there is an increasing trend to refer these children to closed 'treatment' settings which differ in name only from training schools.[388]

The American research also supports the notion that the legal system creates a certain type of female delinquency by focusing on sex-role violations. In New York State, several thousand more boys than girls are brought to court for involvement in serious crime, but several thousand more females than males are eventually placed in rehabilitative settings. Fully one-half the minors incarcerated each year have committed no criminal activity whatsoever, most of them being sexually active girls.[389] Rogers reports that 80 per cent of the girls as opposed to 18 per cent of the boys in Connecticut institutions are there for status offences.[390] Both Terry[391] and Cohn[392] report that the legal system is more likely to deal with female delinquents more severely than their male counterparts. United States national statistics for 1960-71 show that, regardless of the offence, the average confinement for the female adolescent is two months longer than for males. Although there are no Canadian studies on severity of disposition to compare with these American data, there is no reason to suspect our situation is any different, in view of the similar official delinquency pictures in the two countries.

Chesney-Lind[393] concludes that because official statistics consistently underestimate the number of female offenders while overestimating the sexual nature of their offences, both the legal system's handling of the female offender and the assumptions underlying it need to be investigated. She feels that the broad definition of delinquency combines with the wide discretion in the system to enable the court to enforce society's double standard. Her analysis of court records in Honolulu from 1929 to 1955, indicate that 70 to 80 per cent of all adolescent females processed in their delinquency system were subject to sexual physical examinations as opposed to 12 to 18 per cent of the males, even though these examinations were often irrelevant to the offence.[394] She concludes that the legal system tends to 'sexualize' adolescent female offences by focusing attention on sex-role violations rather than on infringements of legal norms.

Weiler's findings[395] support this view. In examining hearing transcripts, she found that circumstantial evidence of a girl's staying out late or associating with undesirable companions appeared sufficient reason for a determination of promiscuity. Similarly, she states 'it is also evident that a girl will be considered sexually immoral and therefore beyond control if she has normal heterosexual relations.' An on-going stable relationship does not prevent a girl from being labelled promiscuous.[396] Young females, she concludes, are charged with promiscuity on the basis of 'surmise, suspicion or fear as to what they are like rather than proof.'[397]

There is a pressing need to focus on the adverse effects of sex-role stereotyping in the legal system. Little research has been done in Canada to compare self-reported delinquency rates with official rates, but the different nature of the official male and female delinquency picture should alert us to the need to examine legal processing with a view to preventing this type of abuse. Eliminating the status offence from our delinquency laws will not cause the problem to vanish but only to be redirected through other, possibly more coercive, legal channels, with perhaps more detrimental consequences.

Delinquency and the School System

Schooling, says Skolnick,[398] must have profound effects on a child's psychological development. Yet the psychologist typically does not study the effects of this enduring environment in which the child of today lives much of his life.[399] While Chapter 5 reviews the employment problem and its relationship to schooling, this section specifically addresses the connections among schooling, employment, and delinquency. Schur[400] believes that schools are now the major agency of social control of children and youth. Moreover, today, educational attainment rather than family status is the fundamental determinant of an individual's economic and social position in life.[401] Wenk[402] maintains that if schools fail to protect children from criminal involvement, practically nothing else stands between them and criminal careers. Balch[403] has suggested that the schools may, in fact, be creating and sustaining the very behaviour they are supposed to suppress. Because of its central role in children's lives, both the structure and goals of the school system must be scrutinized to see if they are meeting the needs of young persons.

Research supports the view that, regardless of social class or attitudes towards school, school status alone is the single most significant variable in predicting delinquent behaviour.[404] Polk and his co-workers,[405] in examining court records, found that, notwithstanding socio-economic status (hereafter referred to as SES), delinquency was related to low academic performance. Further the quality or type of delinquency did not vary with socio-economic class.[406] Jensen's[407] reanalysis of Wolfgang's work also supports this view, in that, while both race and achievement in school were related to delinquency, the relationship between achievement and delinquency was independent of race.

Vinter and Sarri[408] found almost all children place a high value on passing courses. Indeed, according to Reiss,[409] black and low SES children place a *higher* value on education than white or high SES children, even though the former were more often unsuccessful in the United States school system. Three individual factors have been identified which may lead to unacceptable behaviour or performance in school.[410] These are low commitment to school goals, low innate ability, and low acquired skills, that is, poor work habits or social skills required for interaction with peers and school personnel. Unacceptable school behaviour or performance frequently results in coercive, degrading sanctions[411] which debase and exclude the child rather than re-involve and re-commit him.[412] Yet research suggests that deviants frequently possess less innate ability or fewer acquired skills rather than less commitment to school.[413] Working on the false assumption that poor performance stems from low commitment and hence increasing the child's motivation without, at the same time, increasing his skills, may serve only to exacerbate the problem, for a highly motivated child will experience his failure more acutely than an unmotivated one. Other adverse consequences may then ensue.

The poor performer is easily locked into the deviant role. Poor achievement affects a child's self-image, as well as his peers' and parents' reactions to him. Poor achievers not only lose out on the primary rewards of school, good grades, but may also be excluded from the secondary rewards, such as classroom responsibilities or other school related tasks.[414] Such children are thereby denied legitimate alternative opportunities for recognition and success in school. Not only does a child's academic achievement affect his status in school; his status in school, in turn, affects his status in the larger community as well.[415]

Schafer[416] believes that underachievement and misbehaviour in school are not merely individual problems. Rather, they result from adverse school-child interactions. But, as Schafer and Olexa[417] point out, it is easy to see why a medical model of delinquency appeals to schools, for if problems like truancy and underachievement are attributed to the pathologies of individual students, the school is thereby absolved from responsibility. Elliott and Voss's[418] research supports the view that schools may, in fact, aggravate the delinquency problem. They found that dropping out of school led to a *decrease* in involvement in delinquent activities. We should not be surprised, they say, if youthful rebellion and delinquency result from our forcing youth to remain in frustrating situations where they are repeatedly subject to and stigmatized by failures. These authors recommend that our policy of trying to keep children in school be reviewed in light of their data.

Schafer[419] maintains that more research is needed to understand the complex nature of school-child interactions, focusing on how the variable effects of school structural arrangements, belief systems, and coping practices affect the orientations and achievement chances of students. Elliott and Voss[420] found that schools tend to push deviants out. Although the immediate effect of departure from school was positive in that their rate of delinquent activity decreased, the long-term life prospects of these children thereby decline. Polk and Schafer[421] believe that schools abdicate their responsibility for youth in trouble. What is needed, they say, are programmes which increase the educational success chances of the high delinquency risk population.[422] In their view, new ways of channelling children back into the educational process must be found. At present, no one has this responsibility.[423] We must then find ways to help them achieve once they do return. The reader is again referred to Chapter 5 for an analysis of these issues.

Breed[424] suggests that the school system needs to develop programmes specifically directed towards alleviating delinquency. He recommends a number of possibilities, including developing schools that are models of justice and democracy in terms of organization, opportunity, and relevant curricula. Alternate educational opportunities must be provided for those who can not fit within the traditional structure. The use of school facilities for community programmes involving the entire community in education should be encouraged.[425]

Bazelon[426] argues that schools have shunned their responsibility for keeping children's interest or, for that matter, keeping them at all. While speaking to a conference of juvenile court judges, he submitted that

[T]he argument for [the Court's] retaining beyond control and truancy jurisdiction is that the juvenile courts have to act in such cases because 'if we don't act, no one else will.' I submit that precisely the opposite is the case: because you act, no one else does. Schools and public agencies refer their problems to you because you have jurisdiction, because you exercise it and because you hold out promises that you can provide solutions.[427]

He believes that the schools, and not the courts, are the obvious place to turn when a community has problems with its children. Ideally a society dedicated to the elimination of crime and illness among its children would go back still further and ensure adequate prenatal care, child rearing, housing, nutrition, and health care. But since we have not made that commitment, Bazelon maintains that the school, because it is the only institution that comes into contact with almost every child,[428] provides us with our last clear chance for preventive measures.[429]

Delinquency and the Community

Lerman[430] reports that most persons do not believe that they as individuals can do anything about crime in their own neighbourhood. They see crime as a matter for police action rather than citizen action.[431] Yet because delinquency is so clearly related to other social problems such as poverty and employment, it cannot be isolated as merely a police problem. The basic thrust of the Report of the President's Committee on Juvenile Delinquency and Youth Crime was that delinquency stemmed from the community's failure to provide the conditions, services, and opportunities that enable young persons to participate competently in life.[432] Wheeler and his co-workers[433] assert that these two themes of opportunity and community competence still provide the most useful and promising orientation towards the delinquency problem.

While Chapter 7 presents an in-depth examination of the physical environment as it relates to children, this section concerns itself with the relationship between delinquency and the community. But what is meant by the term 'community' or 'neighbourhood'? The idea of community is hard to conceptualize. It is composed of a number of elements and forces all of which interact differently, depending on the perspective from which one chooses to view it. From the child's perspective, the meaning of community must change radically with increasing age. One also needs to understand what the idea of community means from the perspective of its typical adult resident, and from the viewpoint of its primary socializing institutions, its social service agencies and its institutions of social control. A city's administrative subdivisions seldom coincide with its functional community units. Spergel[434] maintains that an interorganizational approach to the study of community is essential. The community should be studied in terms of the interaction of specific organizational variables and the components of community integration described in terms of the horizontal and vertical relations which exist. Spergel thus defines community as a set of relations of people to each other and to the organizations they have created and respond to, usually within a particular territory, based on common interests, traditions, or concerns.[435]

Youth are most likely to acquire a legitimate identity when they have a stake in conformity, Pink and White suggest.[436] Children, like the rest of us, need a sense of competence, belonging, usefulness, and personal power.[437] But in our society, children are physically separated from the total community. By defining school as their proper sphere of activity, their participation in the larger community is effectively precluded. Moreover, the student role itself is essentially passive, with adults being dominant. Yet even children's out-of-school activities and friendship patterns are school related. And, as noted, the child's status in school invariably defines his status in the larger community.

School, however, is the only one of a variety of community variables which may mirror underlying conditions conducive to delinquency. All the formal organizations in a community are responsible in some manner for and responsive to community problems, including delinquency. Little theoretical or empirical work relating community structure to delinquency patterns has been done in recent years.[438] By focusing on how these institutions function, how they relate to each other and how they relate to the larger community, much can be learned about community problems.[439] The concept of community may provide a useful intervening notion to explain the process by which larger social, cultural, and economic pressures or constraints lead to different patterns of delinquency among various sectors of the population.[440] Contradictory delinquency findings, says Spergel, may not be contradictory at all when placed in a community structure context.[441]

Thus there exists a critical need, according to Wheeler et al., for empirical studies which provide data on the quantity and quality of delinquency in various types of communities and neighbourhoods. There is a lack of knowledge on the extent to which homogeneous patterns exist. Typologies need to be developed and patterns sought, based not only on the personal and social background characteristics of the delinquent, but also on the structure and organization of the community, both in terms of the social and physical environment in which delinquency occurs.

The community structure perspective should also provide a useful basis for analysing current strategies of delinquency control, such as diversion and other social service approaches, to see how these programmes interact with and are mediated by the community.[442] The youth and his particular social situation are often treated by service agencies as an atomized entity unrelated to the community. There has been little emphasis on service programmes which maximize the juvenile's identification with the agency and the community, and enhance the responsibility that all three must share in implementing such programmes.[443] Services may have a positive value in helping the individual adjust to his environment. Their effectiveness is maximized, however, only to the degree that they operate with an understanding of the larger community constraints. A strict service approach, Spergel believes, inherently alienates the individual and his family from their community and society. This, in turn, may lead to increased, rather than decreased, deviance.

Community institutions, especially schools and social service agencies, play a major role in validating the existence of serious youth problems which require court intervention. Walker[444] suggests that, as the number of agencies and youth workers handling delinquency increases, so does the official delinquency rate, even though self-reported delinquency remains a fairly stable phenomenon.[445] In essence, these community institutions define youthful misbehaviour as a problem that can only be handled within the legal system.

The question therefore becomes 'How do we get families, school, neighbourhoods, churches, and other community institutions to meet their fundamental responsibility to youth?' rather than turning such problems over to the legal system which can only respond by recycling misbehaving children through the service system or removing them from the community.[446] How can these institutions help set limits? How can they help youth establish legitimate identities? These institutions, rather than isolating youth, must help them re-enter the mainstream of community life. They must help children establish legitimate identities within the context of the entire community rather than limiting their frame of reference to peer groups. Pink and White propose that activities meaningful to the entire community in which all youth can participate, programmes covering the full range of community life, directed, funded, and supported by the legitimating institutions of the community, and not by persons affiliated with the juvenile justice system, must be developed[447] to integrate youth into the community. Such programmes can involve youth of all backgrounds in planning, organizing, and executing useful and necessary community services. In this way, youth may be re-integrated into the community and deviant behaviour thereby reduced.

Thus, these special concerns related to delinquency need to be viewed from a broader perspective. To see the problem as the child's alone or even as that of his family absolves the larger community of its responsibility to act. The individual 'treatment' approach has led nowhere. By avoiding a more fundamental, yet much more complex analysis of the problem, including a rethinking of the nature of the problem itself, time, energy, and dollars are wasted with few results. The time is ripe for a more comprehensive perspective and a broader and more innovative approach to solutions.

VII THE CHILDREN'S RIGHTS MOVEMENT

This chapter has canvassed a number of areas of law which affect children, pointing out the need for, and utility of, empirical research on many issues traditionally regarded by jurists as purely legal issues. One theme which has emerged repeatedly in this review is that of the changing definition and status of the child in today's family and today's society. There exists much conflict of opinion about what this definition and status should be, emanating from such diverse sources as the 'child savers' and the children's rights movement, on the one hand, and those who support the traditional family structure or who would increase parents' authority and control, on the other.

At the heart of this conflict, in Kleinfeld's[448] view, is the distribution of decision-making power and responsibility among children, their parents, and the state. Historically, a fundamental purpose of family law has been to support the family.[449] Hence, most of the authority for making decisions respecting children has been lodged with parents, although the degree of parental control has declined markedly over the past century so that today the state has wide power to interfere in the parent-child relationship when there is compelling justification to do so. Almost none of the legal decision-making power rests with those who are its focus – children. Recently, however, another important force has emerged as a strong contender for a portion of this decision-making power. That force is the child saving movement which seeks to replace, in part, both the parent and the state as decision-maker *on behalf of* children.

The critical question, in Coons and Mnookin's[450] view, is who should have what portion of the decision-making responsibility. Yet, the key to distributing such power and responsibility is the ability to exercise it and 'any broad assertion that age is ... irrelevant to legal autonomy inescapably collides with biological and economic reality.'[451] Hence the issue of capacity becomes critical, for below a certain age 'the question is not whether the child should decide, but which adult should decide on behalf of the child.'[452]

The child savers find their voice in the child advocacy movement. It is a broad movement of social reform, lodged mainly in the social service sector, concerning itself with social and moral rights, as well as legal ones. It seeks as its goals '(a) to know every child, (b) to know what each child needs, and (c) to make sure that needed services are available for him.'[453] It is a paternalistic movement envisaging a wide variety of persons fulfilling the advocate role, including teachers, social workers, community workers, and health professionals as well as lawyers.[454] Child advocates do not seek to give the child more decision-making responsibility. Rather, the child advocate, recognizing that children not only need protection from others but protection from themselves as well, accepts the responsibility of decision-making for children.[455] Hence while power is wrested from the family and possibly the state, it is shifted to the child advocate rather than to the child.

Proponents of the children's rights movement, on the other hand, couch their goals in strictly legal terms rather than in broader social ones, seeking new legislation as a framework for redefining and redistributing decision-making power among children, parents, the state, and those who can represent the child's views. The goal of this movement is to turn the power of decision over to the child. The most extreme exponents of children's rights hold that 'the rights, privileges, duties [and] responsibilities of adult citizens be made available to any young person, of whatever age, who wants to make use of them.'[456] More realistic opinion, however, maintains that all children have a right to 'know, comprehend, challenge and participate meaningfully in all decisions that vitally affect their lives.'[457] This right emanates from the general presumption that children should be allowed the same rights as adults unless there is significant risk of consequential damage or children do not possess the capacity to exercise such rights.[458] Hence, while both the child savers and the children's rights movement seek 'a basic shift in attitude toward' youth,[459] for the child savers it is a shift in attitude only, while for the supporters for children's rights there is a shift in power and responsibility too.

Those who seek to uphold or enhance the position of the family find these trends an anathema. Levy, for example, maintains that

the current 'children's rights' campaign, by increasing government intrusion into family decisionmaking, has at least the potential to upset the traditional compact that undergirds ... family-centered values.[460]

[W]e must take account of the terrible risks to private family decisionmaking that ... the current fascination with 'children's rights' pose(s); ... and we must create ... doctrines which ... adequately protect the interests of families.[461]

Hafen,[462] too, is concerned about the effects of policies which undermine traditional parental rights. Ile is of the opinion that 'those same policies will inevitably undermine the assumption of parental responsibility,' an unwise course of action in his view, since our society has no realistic alternative to offer.[463] Yet whether child advocacy and the children's rights movement reflect an erosion of confidence in the nuclear family as the sole childrearers in our society or are precipitating an erosion of confidence which, in turn, may lead to a decline in parental responsibility, are questions that remain unanswered at this time.

Certainly the traditional concept and role of the family are undergoing change. The women's movement, the redefinition of parental roles, the increase in marital breakdown, and the rise in the number of single-parent families all point towards critical transformations in our social organization. The increasing concern for children's rights, whether in the narrow legal sense or the broader social and moral sense, is a part of this major social change. While the interactions are complex and the causal relationships tangled and unclear, it seems reasonable to assume that mutual associations exist.

Our laws and legal institutions play a crucial role in this change. As noted, a fundamental purpose of family law has been to support our traditional family structure. 'As a general proposition, one would expect that law, particularly in an area so intimately related to family, would largely reflect the dominant cultural norms ...'[464] Yet because there is little consensus about variables such as, for example, the most desirable mode of childrearing, the optimum level of parent-child attachment, and the proper role of the family in today's changing society, our cultural norms, and in consequence our legal structure, are in a state of flux. 'Moreover, it is ... a well-established ... tradition to view law as a means of producing cultural change ...'[465] Hence, the delineation of the scope of children's rights and protections and, with it, the parcelling out of the authority and responsibility for children may have profound effects on the relationships of children to their families, children to the state, and the family to the state.

'[T]he proper distribution of power can profoundly affect policy conclusions, particularly in the face of factual uncertainties and value clashes.'

Coons and Mnookin maintain that the advocates for children's rights have failed to pay attention to the utility of theory in their arguments.[467] What a theory of children's rights could provide, in the view of these authors, is a conceptual structure which might help to explain or relate an observed set of facts.[468] Yet, to date, the requisite 'observed set of facts,' collected in a methodologically reliable fashion, is lacking. Solid, data-based information will enhance our understanding of present changes, help us better define the priority issues and better inform our future policy choices. For these reasons, empirical inquiry focusing on the nature and evolution of legal relationships of children to their families and to other institutions and structures is an essential first step in understanding social change and enhancing the well-being of our children.

APPENDIX

The Areas of Substantive Law

Delinquency[469]
The federal *Juvenile Delinquents Act*[470] confers jurisdiction on our Provincial Courts (Family Division) to deal with offenders below age 16. Technically the Act creates only one offence – a delinquency. Yet a virtually unlimited range of conduct falls within the purview of this concept. As the Act states, a

'juvenile delinquent' means any child who violates any provision of the *Criminal Code* or any federal or provincial statute, or of any municipality, or who is guilty of sexual immorality or any similar form of vice, or who is liable by reason of any other act to be committed to an industrial school or juvenile reformatory under any federal or provincial statute.[471]

Our juvenile court was created at the turn of the century to protect offending youngsters from the harsh treatment they received in adult courts. Indeed, at common law the criminal laws did not distinguish between adult and child once the child reached age 7 – the age at which he was presumed capable of forming criminal intent.[472] But, through the equitable doctrine of *parens patriae*, 'the idea of a sheltering juvenile court for all young people who need help was developed at the turn of the century ... The court ... was designed to be helpful and rehabilitative to the offender, not ... punitive or aimed at retribution.'[473]

The treatment philosophy which underlies the substance of our delinquency legislation gives the court broad discretion in pursuing its rehabilitative goals.

This, as well as the 'family' model, as opposed to the 'due process' model, of procedure upon which the legislation is based, is exemplified in s.3 of the Act which states that 'the care and custody and discipline of a juvenile delinquent shall approximate as nearly as may be that which should be given by his parents and as far as practicable every juvenile delinquent shall be treated, not as a criminal, but as a misdirected and misguided child, and one needing aid, encouragement, help and assistance.'

Because the judge, acting as a just parent would, seeks to further the child's best interest, the early reformers felt no need for legalistic due process or adversary procedures. In theory, the state and the child are not in opposition as they are in adult criminal proceedings.[474] Yet, despite this rhetoric, the proceedings have been held to be criminal in nature[475] and because the state brings charges against the child, they are in essence adversarial. Nonetheless, s.17(1) of the Act provides that the proceedings may be as 'informal as the circumstances will permit consistent with a due regard for the administration of justice' and s.17(2) specifies that no decision of the juvenile court shall be set aside because of any irregularity in the procedures, if it appears that the decision in the case was in the best interest of the child. Further, juvenile court proceedings are not open to the public and newspaper publicity is prohibited.[476]

The broad discretion and the procedural informality in juvenile court are justified as a proper exercise of the court's *parens patriae* function. 'As *parens patriae* the state invests the juvenile court with the power to act as the parent of the child. The judge is thus expected to assume a fatherly and protective stance in relation to those who appear before him. And if the juvenile court withholds from the child procedural safeguards granted to adults, it is only because it views him as having the rights to custody and care rather than the right to liberty.'[477]

A substantial body of case law has developed[478] under the *Juvenile Delinquents Act* which, despite the wording of the legislation, gives the child many due process protections. In summary, these judicial decisions hold that the nature of the offence

must be made clear to the child, who then has the right to make full answer and defence, including the right to cross-examine witnesses, to call witnesses and to testify in his own behalf (and be sworn if the meaning of the oath is understood). A juvenile also has the right not to give self-incriminating evidence, the right to require that an alleged statement or confession be excluded in the absence of proof of voluntarinesses, and the qualified right not to be questioned in the absence of a parent or counsel, or without being warned. Finally, a juvenile may be convicted only on legally sworn evidence, and is entitled to an open and fair trial.[479]

Yet, despite these fairly broad due process rights and protections, the procedural informality in actual juvenile court proceedings may often border on procedural abuse.[480]

In Ontario, Legal Aid[481] provides children in juvenile court with legal representation by 'duty counsel.' Alternatively, the child may retain a private lawyer through legal aid to represent him. This right to counsel is based on the child's status as a party[482] in the proceedings. Both the quality of legal representation children are receiving and the modes of delivery are examined in section V of this chapter.

Upon finding the child delinquent, the range of dispositions open to the judge is very broad.[483] These include any one or combination of the following: suspending final disposition, indefinite adjournment, a fine not exceeding $25, probation, foster home placement, Children's Aid Society placement, training school (but only as a last resort for children under 12),[484] and 'the imposition of such further and other dispositions as may be deemed advisable.'[485]

The term status offence applies to all those activities which are neither wrong nor illegal for adults but which are proscribed for children. Hence status offences are non-criminal, uniquely juvenile offences. Children who fall within the status offender category are generally of three types: those who do not get along at home, those who do not get along at school, and those who get along too well with children of the opposite sex.[486] Status offences include activities such as unmanageability, truancy, running away, sexual activity, drinking liquor, and smoking. Because of the broad definition of delinquent, status offenders are often processed under the *Juvenile Delinquents Act.* Alternatively, our child welfare laws can be used to obtain jurisdiction over the so-called 'beyond control' child.[487]

In early 1977, Ontario repealed its legislation allowing unmanageable children to be committed to training school.[488] This repeal, however, did not eliminate the concept of the status offence from our laws. As noted in section V, control over such children may still be obtained through our delinquency or child welfare legislation. Proposed federal reform of the delinquency laws, if enacted, will eliminate the concept of the status offence in federal law. Then only provincial statutes, such as *The Child Welfare Act*, will remain on which to base status offence charges, unless new provincial laws are passed specifically to fill any 'perceived' gap.

Child Welfare
Child protection proceedings, sometimes called neglect or care proceedings, under Part II of Ontario's child welfare legislation, are essentially civil rather than criminal proceedings. These proceedings provide the legal mechanisms

whereby the state may intervene in the parent-child relationship to protect children at risk. The protection proceeding is usually informal, based on a modified version of the adversary system.[489] It is a dispute between the state, through the Children's Aid Society (hereafter referred to as the CAS), and the parents over the well-being of the child. The informal nature of the hearing, says Dickens, often results in 'a failure to provide adequate protection of the rights of individuals, particularly children.'[490] Here again, as in delinquency hearings, the court operates on a welfare philosophy. Its function is essentially rehabilitative, ideally rehabilitating the child's family, but more often, in reality, removing the child from the home. Our family court exercises a statutory *parens patriae* jurisdiction here to further the 'best interests' of the child.

The scope of our child welfare laws is not limited to protecting children from physical abuse.[491] *The Child Welfare Act, 1978* sets out numerous grounds on which a child may be declared in need of protection. As the reader can see, virtually any child may be brought within the purview of this legislation. Section 19(1)(b) states that a 'child in need of protection' means: (i) a child who is brought, with the consent of the person in whose charge he is, before a court to be dealt with under this Part; (ii) a child who is deserted by the person in whose charge he is; (iii) a child where the person in whose charge he is cannot for any reason care properly for him, or where that person has died and there is no suitable person to care for the child; (iv) a child who is living in an unfit or improper place; (v) a child found associating with an unfit or improper person; (vi) a child found begging or receiving charity in a public place; (vii) a child whose parent is unable to control him; (viii) a child who, without sufficient cause, habitually absents himself from his home or school; (ix) a child where the person in whose charge he is neglects or refuses to provide or obtain proper medical, surgical or other recognized remedial care or treatment necessary for his health or well-being, or refuses to permit such care or treatment to be supplied to the child when it is recommended by a legally qualified medical practitioner, or otherwise fails to protect the child adequately; (x) a child whose emotional or mental development is endangered because of emotional rejection or deprivation of affection by the person in whose charge he is; (xi) a child whose life, health or morals may be endangered by the conduct of the person in whose charge he is.

Any police officer or person authorized by the CAS who reasonably believes that a child is in need of protection may take the child to a 'place of safety' and detain him there for up to five days. The matter is then brought before the court to determine if the child is, in fact, in need of protection.[492] Alternatively, the CAS may place a homemaker in the home to look after the child for up to 30 days, with possible extensions.[493]

Once the child is found in need of protection, the 1978 amendments to the Act allow the court to do one of three things: place the child with his parents or some suitable person under CAS supervision for not less than 6 months up to a maximum of 12 months, make the child a ward of the CAS for up to 12 months, or make the child a Crown ward which terminates when the child reaches age 18, marries, is adopted, or upon court order after a review of the child's status. For a Crown ward, the Crown assumes all the rights and responsibilities of the legal guardian, whereas the CAS is the legal guardian of a CAS ward.[495] The CAS is under a statutory duty to endeavour to secure adoption of Crown wards[496] and, while there is no statutory duty for the CAS to work towards reuniting the CAS ward with his family, in theory, this is their goal.

The CAS may avoid a judicial hearing and obtain control of the child by entering into a 'voluntary non-ward agreement' with the parents.[497] By this means, a child may be placed under supervision for up to 12 months if the parent is temporarily unable to provide for his child or the child has special needs. Note, however, that the written consent of any child age 12 or over who has sufficient capacity to give consent is also required.

At present, the child does not have party status under this legislation and, therefore, has no right to independent legal representation.[498] The Act does, however, place the judge under a duty to determine if representation is desirable to protect the interests of the child and, if it is desirable, the court shall direct that legal representation be provided for the child.[499]

These 1978 amendments, just described, are the result of a major re-examination of all child welfare laws. Yet whether these legislative revisions will result in actual reform in practice is an empirical question and one which merits further consideration.

Custody

As noted earlier, at common law the right to custody of a child originally lay with the father absolutely unless his conduct gravely imperiled the child's life, health, or morals. But today, by statute, the mother and father are joint guardians, equally entitled to custody, control, and education of the child. When living apart, parents may enter into private agreement as to which parent should have custody of the child.[500]

Thus, custody is essentially a private matter. The court seldom intervenes unless the parties are unable to reach accord between themselves. However, our High Court has inherent equitable *parens patriae* jurisdiction to review, upon request, any private agreement to ensure that the best interests of the child are protected. Contested custody proceedings, unlike delinquency and child welfare, are clearly adversarial in nature with strict due process procedures. Yet, as in delinquency and child welfare hearings, the court must act in the child's best interests when resolving custody issues.

The federal *Divorce Act*[501] provides that, upon granting a decree *nisi*[502] of divorce, the court may make 'an order providing for the care and upbringing of the children of the marriage.' Thus, custody issues may be determined as matters corollary to divorce. Provincial legislation, too, enables a number of different courts to determine custody issues upon separation. For example, custody applications under *The Family Law Reform Act, 1978*[503] may presently be heard in either the Provincial Court, County or District Court, Unified Family Court, or Supreme Court.

Because a variety of statutes with diverse purposes give different courts the powers to settle contested custody questions, problems of divided jurisdiction arise. This fragmented jurisdiction results in 'disparate and discriminatory'[504] powers lodged in different courts. Contradictory custody orders may emanate from different courts, the quality of justice may vary, and confusion and inequities arise.[505] Further, depending on the Act under which the custody question is initiated, and upon which the court has jurisdiction to hear the matter, questions such as who may commence custody applications, who may have notice of such proceedings, who may be joined as a 'party' to the proceeding and, most importantly, who may be awarded custody, may be answered differently.

When deciding custody issues, the welfare of the child is the 'first and paramount consideration,' no matter how the question came before the court, regardless of whether the child is legitimate, and even in custody disputes between a parent and an unrelated third party.[506] But what does this 'welfare' or 'best interests' test really mean? Several guidelines have been developed in the case law.

When assessing the fitness of the proposed custodian, courts may consider the following factors:

1 conduct, the rule being that only conduct having a direct bearing on the child's welfare should be considered;[507]
2 morality, such as adultery[508] or homosexuality,[509] is a factor considered along with all the other evidence to determine what is in the child's best interests;
3 mental fitness, mental instability being viewed as an undesirable trait in a potential custodian;[510]
4 physical fitness, in that an incapacitated parent will generally, but not always, be denied custody;[511]
5 age, courts being reluctant to award custody to either very young applicants or very old ones, although maturity and ability to care for the child are the prime considerations;[512] and,
6 finally, the future wishes and plans which the potential custodian has for the child are important in helping the court assess whether this person would be the best custodian for the child.

Several judicial rules of thumb relating to characteristics of the child have also developed although, considering the changing roles of parents today, they are not rigidly followed. In summary, in the absence of evidence to the contrary, very young children are considered better off with their mothers and older boys with their fathers.[513] Close siblings will usually not be separated.[514] As a general rule, the child's wishes, especially where the child is aged 10 or over, are considered and the older the child, the more important his views.[515] Our courts are of the view that the child's psychological ties are more important than his blood tie.[516] Indeed, today, preserving the child's stable, on-going relationships is the key factor in determining his 'best interests.' Recently in Ontario, a series of judicial decisions have held that the child's status in custody disputes is equal to that of a party, therefore, the child has the right to independent legal representation in such hearings.[517]

NOTES

Social science footnoting format, in accordance with University of Toronto Press guidelines, has been adopted.

The author would especially like to thank Bernard Dickens, Anthony N. Doob, Susan Hodgson, Roman Komar, and Suzanne Ziegler for their helpful comments and criticisms of various sections of this manuscript.

1 Vital Statistics, Vol. II Marriages and Divorces, 1974 (see update of Wednesday, 17 November 1976, at 4).
2 Ministry of Community and Social Services, Children's Services Division, Statistical Data Sheet, 1976.
3 These figures are estimates based on the statistics for December 1976 found in Law Enforcement, Judicial and Correctional Statistics, Vol. 5(2), Judicial Division, Statistics Canada, 7 May 1977.
4 Nonet, Phillippe For jurisprudential sociology, L. & Soc. Rev. 10: 526, 1976.
5 Feeley, Malcolm The concept of law in social science: a critique and notes on an expanded view, L. & Soc. Rev. 10: 509, 1976.
6 Ibid., 513.
7 Llewellyn, Karl The bramblebush: some lectures on law and its study, New York: Columbia University, 1930, p. 3.
8 Ibid., 3–5.
9 American Heritage Dictionary, 1969.
10 Williams, Glanville Learning the law, Eighth Edition, London: Stevens & Sons, 1969, p. 24.
11 The author would like to thank Roman Komar, law clerk to the Chief Judge of the Provincial Courts (Family Division) of Ontario for his helpful comments on legal history.

12 Williams, Glanville *Learning the law*, 26-7; see for example *The Judicature Act*, R.S.O. 1970, c.228.
13 *Re: Agar-Ellis* (1878), 10 CH. 49, pp. 71-2, per L.J. James.
14 Ontario Law Reform Commission, *Report on family law:Part V: Family Courts*, Toronto: Queen's Printer, 1974, p. 89.
15 The King is father of his country and through his courts will intervene on behalf of those under disability (for example, children) and, if necessary, assume guardianship over them.
16 Ketcham, O.M. Unfulfilled promise of the American juvenile court, in Margaret Rosenheim, ed., *Justice for the child: the juvenile court in transition*, New York: Free Press, 1962, p. 22; *Parental rights and duties and custody suits*, A Report by Justice, London: Stevens & Sons, 1975, p. 5.
17 Edgar, S.G. *Craies on statute law*, 7th edition, London: Sweet and Maxwell, 1971, p. 10.
18 Justice Report, *Parental rights*, 5-6; Freeman, M.D.A. Child law at the crossroads, *Curr. Legal Prob.*, 167, 1947.
19 *The Infants Act*, R.S.O. 1970, c.222, s.2(1).
20 Williams, Glanville *Learning the law*, 89.
21 Ibid., 72.
22 Llewellyn, Karl *The bramblebush*, 63.
23 Ibid., 76-77.
24 Ibid., 78.
25 Ibid., 7.
26 Ibid., 8.
27 Ibid., 9.
28 Ibid., 22.
29 Dickens, Bernard *Legal issues in child abuse*, A working paper of the Centre of Criminology, University of Toronto, 1976, p. 55.
30 Ibid.
31 Loevinger, Lee Law and science as rival systems, *U. Florida L. Rev. 19:* 534, 1976.
32 Ibid., 534-5.
33 Ibid., 535.
34 Selznick, P. The sociology of law, in Lawrence Friedman and S. MacCauley, eds., *Law and the Behavioral Sciences*, Indianapolis: Bobbs-Merrill, 1969.
35 Nejelski, Paul and LaPook, Judith Monitoring the juvenile justice system: how can you tell where you're going, if you don't know where you are?, *Am. Crim. L. Rev. 12:* 10, 1974.
36 Lempert, Richard Strategies of research design in the legal impact study, *L. & Soc. Rev. 1:* 118, 1966.

37 Wald, Michael S. Legal policies affecting children: a lawyer's request for aid, *Child Development 47:* 2, 1976.
38 Ellsworth, Phoebe C. and Levy, Robert J. Legislative reform of child custody adjudication, *L. & Soc. Rev. 4:* 182, 1969–70.
39 Ibid., 215.
40 Ibid., 198.
41 Ibid., 202.
42 Ibid., 215.
43 Katkin, David, Bullington B., and Levine, M. Above and beyond the best interests of the child: an inquiry into the relationship between social science and social action, *L & Soc. Rev. 8:* 669, 1974.
44 Ibid., 676.
45 Wald, Michael S. Legal policies affecting children, 2.
46 Ibid., 2.
47 Kalven, Harry, Jr. The quest for the middle range: empirical inquiry and legal policy, in G.C. Hazard, ed., The American Assembly, *Law in a changing America*, Englewood Cliffs, N.J.: Prentice-Hall, 1969, p. 66.
48 Loevinger, Lee Law and science as rival systems, 535.
49 Kalven, Harry, Jr The quest for the middle range, 67.
50 Friedman, Lawrence M. *The legal system*, New York: Russell Sage Foundation, 1975, p. 160.
51 Katkin, David et al. Above and beyond the best interests of the child, 676.
52 Ibid., 685.
53 Kalven, Harry, Jr. The quest for the middle range, 66.
54 Loevinger, Lee Law and science as rival systems, 538. A further difficulty noted by Loevinger arises because lawyers often see the problems of law as different from the problems of science and therefore not subject to empirical study. He states at p. 540: 'lawyers and law professors are generally so ignorant of science and its methods that they are neither able to distinguish problems which can properly be studied empirically from those which cannot, nor to formulate questions and designs for empiric investigation of appropriate problems.'
55 Campbell, Donald T. and Stanley, J.C. *Experimental and quasi-experimental designs for research*, Chicago: Rand McNally, 1963, p. 6.
56 Nejelski, Paul and LaPook, Judith Monitoring the juvenile justice system, 24.
57 Ibid., 24.
58 Campbell, Donald T. Reforms as experiments, *Am. Psychologist 12:* 409, 1969.
59 Ibid., 409.
60 Ibid.

61 Ibid., 410.
62 Ibid.
63 Nejelski, Paul and LaPook, Judith Monitoring the juvenile justice system, 25.
64 Ibid.
65 Llewellyn, Karl *The bramblebush*, 77.
66 Nejelski, Paul and LaPook, Judith Monitoring the juvenile justice system, 23.
67 Campbell, Donald T. Reforms as experiments, 409.
68 Katkin, David et al. Above and beyond the best interests of the child 672–81.
69 Ibid., 681. 'Thus, they promote the interests of their disciplines and professional ideologies and of their institutional and financial sponsors.'
70 Ibid., 683.
71 Ibid., 672–6.
72 Ellsworth, Phoebe C. and Levy, Robert J. Legislative reform, 215.
73 Kalven, Harry, Jr. The quest for the middle range, 56.
74 Ibid., 65.
75 Loevinger, Lee Law and science as rival systems, 550.
76 Wald, Michael S. Legal policies affecting children, 5.
77 Katkin, David et al. Above and beyond the best interests of the child, 672.
78 Ellsworth, Phoebe C. and Levy, Robert J. Legislative reform, 215.
79 Skolnick, Arlene The limits of childhood: conceptions of child development and social context, *L. & Contemp. Prob. 39;* 38, 1975.
80 Freeman, M.D.A. Child law at the crossroads, *Curr. Legal Prob,* 174, 1974.
81 S.O. 1971, c.98, as amended by S.O. 1972, c.95; 1974, c.63. and c.109.
82 Rodham, Hillary Children under the law, in *The rights of children,* Cambridge, Mass.: Harvard Educational Review, 1974, p. 2.
83 Ibid., 3.
84 Infants (and persons of unsound mind), normally incapable of making a binding contract, can contract to buy necessaries, i.e., goods suitable to the condition in life of such infant and to his actual requirements at the time of the sale and delivery. Osborn's Concise Law Dictionary, Fifth Edition, London: Sweet & Maxwell, 1964.
85 A writ directed to a person who detains another in custody commanding him to produce that person before the court and show legal cause why that person is detained.
86 See for example *The Marriage Act,* R.S.O. 1970, c.261, s.5, 7 and s.8.
87 *The Child Welfare Act,* R.S.O. 1970, c.64, as amended by S.O. 1971, c.98; S.O. 1972, c.109; S.O. 1973, c.75 and 1975, c.1.
88 Ibid., s.20.
89 Ibid., s.35.
90 Ibid.

91 Ibid., s.40(2).
92 Ibid., s.39(1).
93 Ibid., s.43(3).
94 The criminal law too contains a myriad of age-related provisions. For example, it is a criminal offence for a parent to fail to provide the necessaries of life for a child under age 16, thereby placing the child in necessitous or destitute circumstances or at risk of his life or permanent health (s.197, CRIMINAL CODE). Anyone who abandons or exposes a child under 10 so that his life or permanent health is endangered is liable to two years' imprisonment (s.200, CRIMINAL CODE). Females under 14 are given special protections from sexual abuse (s.146(1), s.166), those age 14–16 other protection (s.146(2) & (3)), and a girl over 14 in a dependent position of step- or foster-daughter is given added protection from intercourse with her surrogate father (s.153(1)). With regard to criminal offences committed by children, the *Criminal Code* specifies that a child under 7 cannot be convicted for a criminal offence (s.12), and further that a child shall not be convicted for a criminal offence committed while he was between the ages of 7 and 14 unless it is shown that 'he was competent to know the nature and consequences of his conduct and to appreciate that it was wrong' (s.13). The *Juvenile Delinquents Act* R.S.C. 1970, c. J-3 is federal legislation designed to deal with all offences, not just *Criminal Code* ones, committed by children under age 16.
95 Freeman, M.P.A. Child law at the crossroads, 174.
96 Rodham, Hillary Children under the law, 26.
97 Hafen, Bruce C. Children's liberation and the new egalitarianism: some reservations about abandoning youth to their 'rights,' *Brigham Young U.L. Rev*, 605, 1976.
98 Ibid., 613.
99 Ibid., 646–7.
100 Ibid., 648.
101 Ibid., 654–5.
102 Rodham, Hillary Children under the law, 7.
103 Ibid., 7.
104 Hafen, Bruce C. Children's liberation and the new egalitarianism, 649.
105 Foster, Henry, Jr. and Freed, Doris A bill of rights for children, *Family L.Q. 6:* 343, 1972.
106 Ibid., 375
107 Tribe, Laurence Childhood, suspect classifications, and conclusive presumptions: the linked riddles, *L. & Contemp. Prob. 39:* 11, 1975.
108 Rodham, Hillary Children under the law, 20–1.

109 Ibid., 22.
110 Leon, Jeffrey S. *Legal representation of children in selected court proceedings: the capacity of children to receive legal counsel*, Working paper of the Child in the City Programme, University of Toronto, 1978; the background work for this section can be found in this working paper.
111 Wald, Michael S. Legal policies affecting children.
112 Okpaku, Sheila Psychology: impediment of aid in child custody cases, *Rutgers, L. Rev. 29:* 1117, 1976.
113 Leon, Jeffrey S. Legal representation of children.
114 For a review of the developmental literature relevant to minors' consent to treatment see Thomas Grisso and Linda Vierling Minors' consent to treatment: a developmental perspective, *Professional Psychology 9:* 412, 1978.
115 Kraus, R.M. and Glucksberg, S. Social and nonsocial speech, *Scientific Am. 236(2):* 100, 1977.
116 Yarrow, L.J. Interviewing children, in P.H. Mussen, ed., *Handbook of research methods in child development*, New York: John Wiley, 1970, p. 565.
117 Ibid., 566.
118 Ibid., 567.
119 Shantz, C.U. *The development of social cognition*, Chicago: University of Chicago Press, 1975.
120 Ibid., 23–24.
121 Ibid., 32.
122 Kagan, Jerome A conception of early adolescence, *Daedalus 100:* 999, 1971.
123 Ibid., 1001.
124 Stewart, V. Lorne and Chamberlain, Clive *Age and criminal responsibility*, Research Report of the Centre of Criminology, University of Toronto, 1975, p. 29.
125 Freud, Anna On the difficulties of communicating with children – the lesser children in chambers, in J. Goldstein and J. Katz, *The family and the law: problems for decision in the family law process*, New York: Free Press, 1965, p. 262.
126 Levy, A.M. *Many facets of child custody consultation*, Paper presented at the Annual Meetings of the American Academy of Child Psychiatry, Toronto, 1976.
127 A related area of study in this regard is the response of children to the death of a parent: Kelly, J.B. and Wallerstein, J.S. The effects of parental divorce: experiences of the child in early latency, *Am. J. Orthopsychiatry 46:* 22,

1976, see generally, for example Gartley, W. and Beransioni, M. The concept of death in children, *J. Genetic Psychology 110:* 71, 1967.

128 Wallerstein, J.S. and Kelly, J.B. The effects of parental divorce: experiences of the pre-school child, *J. Am. Academy of Child Psychiatry 14:* 608, 1976. These results are based on a study of 34 children, 14 of whom were five to six years of age. McDermott reports that pre-school children are sensitive to their parents' feelings toward each other. McDermott, J.F. Parental divorce in early childhood, *Am. J. Psychiatry 124:* 1429, 1968.

129 Kelly, J.B. and Wallerstein, J.S. The effects of parental divorce, 23.

130 Ibid., 29.

131 Wallerstein, J.S. and Kelly, J.B. The effects of parental divorce: experiences of the child in later latency, *Am. J. Orthopsychiatry 46:* 257, 1976.

132 Ibid., 265.

133 Wallerstein, J.S. and Kelly, J.B. The effects of parental divorce: the adolescent experience, in E.J. Anthony and C. Koupernik, eds., *The child in his family: children at psychiatric risk*, New York: John Wiley, 1974, p. 485.

134 Ibid., 491.

135 Cottle, T. and Klineberg, Stephen *The present of things future: explorations of time in human experience*, New York: Free Press, 1976, p. 74.

136 Ibid., 91.

137 See generally: Bigelow, S.Y. Witnesses of tender years, *Crim. L.Q. 9:* 298, 1966; Cartwright, I. The prospective child witness, *Crim. L.Q. 6:* 196, 1963; Ontario Law Reform Commission *Report on the law of evidence*, Toronto: Queen's Printer, 1976, pp. 123–7; Law Reform Commission of Canada *Evidence: competence and compellability*, Study Paper No. 1 Ottawa: Information Canada, 1972, pp. 1–2.

138 *Wigmore on Evidence*, 3rd ed., para. 506. The latter two factors are sub-elements of 'communication.'

139 Cohen, Ronald *Children's testimony and mediated (hearsay) evidence*, Study prepared for the Law Reform Commission of Canada, n.d.

140 Herjanic, B., Herjanic, M., Brown, F., and Wheatt, T. Are children reliable reporters? *J. Abnormal Child Psychology 3:* 41, 1975.

141 *McEllistrum* v. *Etches* [1956] S.C.R. 787.

142 *Canada Evidence Act*, R.S.C. 1970, C.E-10, s.16(1); Dickens, Bernard *Legal issues in child abuse*, pp. 34–5.

143 The case law has defined 'tender years' to mean under 14 years of age. See *R.* v. *Antrobus* (1947) 2 D.L.R. 55, 87 C.C.C. 118 (B.C.C.A.).

144 Rodham, Hillary Children under the law, 22.

145 Foster, Henry, Jr. and Freed, Doris A bill of rights for children, 358.

146 *Report of the Committee on the Age of Majority, United Kingdom*, The Latey Report, London: Her Majesty's Stationery Office, 1967, Cmnd. No. 3342.
147 One exception to the consent requirement occurs in emergency situations where the person authorized to consent is unable to do so. To preserve the patient's life or health, the physician is justified in taking all necessary steps despite the fact that no consent has been obtained, provided that the express instructions of the patient are not thereby contravened.
148 Tomkins, Barbara Health care for minors: the right to consent, *Sask. L. Rev. 40:* 45, 1975.
149 Twelfth Report of the Royal Commission on Family and Children's Law, British Columbia, *The medical consent of minors*, Vancouver: Queen's Printer, 1975.
150 Foster, Henry, Jr. and Freed, Doris A bill of rights for children; this view holds that no minor can contract except for necessaries. At common law, however, health care was considered a necessary. Hence a child could contract for its supply; Tomkins, B. Health care for minors, this author argues that this viewpoint stems from an unwanted extension of the law of contract.
151 Tomkins, Barbara Health care for minors, 48; this opinion, in Tomkins's view, results from a mistaken extension of the criminal law. For example s.146 of the *Criminal Code* states that a female under 16 is unable to give valid legal consent to certain sexual acts.
152 The Canadian case law supports this view, see, for example, *Johnston v. Wellesley Hospital et al.* (1971) 2 O.R. 103, as does the recent Report of the Alberta Institute of Law Research and Reform, *Consent of minors to health care*, Edmonton: University of Alberta, Dec. 1975 and the British Age of Majority Report, 1967.
153 Tomkins, Barbara Health care for minors, 48.
154 *Johnston v. Wellesley Hospital et al.* (1971) 2 O.R. 103.
155 Tomkins, Barbara Health care for minors, 50-1.
156 Ibid., 53.
157 Krever, Horace Minors and consent for medical treatment, Lecture delivered to University of Toronto, reprinted in Bernard Dickens *Materials in medical jurisprudence*, University of Toronto: Faculty of Law, 1976, p. 4.85.
158 See, for example, ibid., 4.80-4.85
159 *The Public Hospitals Act*, R.S.O. 170, c.378, see Regs. 729 and 100.74 (March 9, 1974).
160 Krever, Horace Minors and consent for medical treatment.

161 Ibid.; Recent proposed amendments to Ontario's child welfare legislation would require parental consent for all medical treatment for those under 16 living in provincially funded residential care facilities, see Consultation Paper on Standards and Guidelines for Children's Services, *Children's Residential Care Facilities: Proposed Standards and Guidelines*, Ontario Ministry of Community and Social Services, Sept., 1978, p. 31.

162 Royal Commission on Family and Children's Law *The medical consent of minors*.

163 Ibid., 10.

164 Ibid., 7.

165 Ibid., Appendix I, 10.

166 Ibid., Appendix I, 15.

167 Ibid., Appendix I, 11.

168 Ibid., Appendix I, 14–15.

169 Paul, E.W., Pilpel, H., and Wechsler, N. Pregnancy, teenagers & the law, 1974, *Family Planning Perspectives 6(3):* 142, 1974.

170 Foster, Henry, Jr. and Freed, Doris A bill of rights for children, 361.

171 Alberta Institute Report *Consent of minors to health care*.

172 Ibid., 12.

173 Fraser, Brian The pediatric bill of rights, *South Texas L.J. 16:* 250–1, 1975.

174 Ibid., 267–8.

175 Alberta Institute Report *Consent of minors to health care*, 12.

176 Royal Commission on Family and Children's Law *The medical consent of minors*, 7.

177 Fraser, Brian The pediatric bill of rights, 266.

178 Alberta Institute Report *Consent of minors to health care*, 13; Fraser, Brian The pediatric bill of rights, 251; Krever, Horace Minors and consent to medical treatment, 4.74.

179 Krever, Horace Minors and consent to medical treatment, 4.74.

180 Ibid.

181 Fraser, Brian The pediatric bill of rights, 252.

182 Alberta Institute Report *Consent of minors to health care*, 18.

183 Ibid., 14.

184 Fraser, Brian The pediatric bill of rights, 252, see footnote 44 citing Cutright Illegitimacy, myths, causes and cures, *Fam. Planning Perspectives 3:* 25, 1973.

185 Alberta Institute Report *Consent of minors to health care*, 14.

186 *Criminal Code*, s.251.

187 The Public Hospitals Act, R.S.O. 1970, c.378, see Regs. 729 and 100/74 (March 9, 1974).

188 Royal Commission on Family and Children's Law *The medical consent of minors*, Appendix I, p. 6.
189 Ibid., Appendix I, p. 16.
190 Ibid.
191 See, for example, Fraser, Brian The pediatric bill of rights.
192 Alberta Institute Report *Consent of minors to health care*, 22.
193 Adelson, Joseph and Beall, L. Adolescent perspectives on law and government, *L. & Soc. Rev. 4:* 495, 1970.
194 Hess, Robert and Torney, Judith *The development of political attitudes in children*, New York: Doubleday, 1967.
195 Ibid., Chapter 1.
196 Ibid., 47.
197 Ibid., 247–53.
198 Greenstein, F. *Children and politics*, New Haven: University Press, 1965, pp. 71–2.
199 *Political knowledge and attitudes*, 1971–2, Report from the National Assessment of Educational Progress, 1973; National Assessment of Education Progress, Changes in political knowledge and attitudes, 1969–76, Report #07-CS-02; Education for citizenship: a bicentennial survey, Report #07-CS-01.
200 Social Planning and Research Council of Hamilton and District *Youth and the law: a report on knowledge about the law*, Final Report of the Committee on Youth and the Law, Hamilton, 1974.
201 Dolding, Leslie *Law focused education in elementary and secondary schools*, unpublished paper, Osgoode Hall Law School, 1975, p. 27.
202 Stenning, Philip Legal education beyond the law school walls: teaching law in Ontario's high schools, *L.S.U.C. Gazette 7:* 136, 1973.
203 Whittler, J. Public legal education *J. Family L. 12:* 278–9, 1972–73.
204 Dolding, Leslie *Law focused education*, 23.
205 Elson, A. General education in law for non lawyers, in G.C. Hazard, ed., The American Assembly, *Law in a changing America*, Englewood Cliffs, N.J.: Prentice-Hall, 1968, p. 184.
206 Elson, A. and Elson, M. Educating teachers and children in law: an approach to reduced alienation in inner city schools, *Am. J. Orthopsychiatry 40:* 877, 1970.
207 Whittler, J. Public legal education, 279–82.
208 Maxwell, R., Henning, J., and White, C. Law studies in the schools, *J. Legal Ed. 27:* 158, 1974–5.
209 Dolding, Leslie *Law focused education*, 2.
210 Elson, A. General education in law for non lawyers, 185–6.

211 *Criminal Code*, s.19.
212 Lamb, E.B. The story of 'You and the Law,' *Crime & Del. 7:* 241, 1961.
213 Baetz, R., Brooke, R., Chadwick, J., and O'Brien, A. *Law education in secondary schools: a preliminary survey*, Canada Council on Social Development, 1975.
214 Stenning, P. Legal education beyond the school walls, 18; Maxwell R. et al. Law studies in the schools, 159.
215 Stenning, P. Legal education beyond the school walls, 21.
216 Cahn, E.S., and Cahn, J.C. Power to the people or the profession?: the public interest in public interest law, *Yale L.J. 79:* 1022, 1970.
217 This concept is dealt with further in sections five and six of the text.
218 Maxwell, R. et al. Law studies in the schools; Directory of law-related educational activities (Parts I and II), American Bar Association; see also Law-related education in America: guidelines for the future Report of the American Bar Association, Special Committee on Youth Education for Citizenship, 1975.
219 Ibid.
220 Orr, J., Peters, R., and Swift, R. *Legal education in B.C. secondary schools: an in-depth look at Law II*, Report to the Justice Development Commission, 1974.
221 Tapp, June L., and Kohlberg, Lawrence Developing senses of law and legal justice *J. Soc. Issues 27:* 65, 1971; Kohlberg, Lawrence *Collected papers on moral development and moral education*, Cambridge, Mass.: Moral Education and Research Foundation; see also June L. Tapp and Felice Levine *Law, justice, and the individual in society*, New York: Holt, Rinehart and Winston, 1977.
222 In the United States the National Assessment of Juvenile Corrections, University of Michigan, has commenced data collection on the effectiveness of the juvenile courts with reference to the policies, standards, and goals for which there is some societal consensus. See Sarri, Rosemary and Hasenfeld, Y., eds., *Brought to justice? juveniles, the courts and the law*, University of Michigan, Ann Arbor: National Assessment of Juvenile Corrections, 1976.
223 The last full report was *Juvenile Delinquency – 1973*, Statistics Canada; see also Law Enforcement, Judicial and Correctional Statistics, vol. 5(2) Judicial Division, Statistics Canada, 7 May 1977.
224 *R. v. H.* (1931) 2 W.W.R. 917.
225 Mnookin, Robert Foster-care – in whose best interests?, *Harv. Educational Rev. 43:* 599, 1973; as reprinted in *The rights of children*, Cambridge, Mass.: Harvard Educational Review, 1974, p. 161.
226 Ibid., 177; Rodham, Hillary Children under the law, in *The rights of children*, Cambridge, Mass.: Harvard Educational Review, 1974, p. 27.

227 Parker, Graham Some historical observations on the juvenile court, *Criminal Law Quart. 9:* 476, 1966.
228 Lerman, Paul, ed., *Delinquency and social policy*, New York: Praeger Publishers, 1970, p. 4.
229 Tappan, Paul *Juvenile delinquency*, New York: McGraw-Hill, 1949, p. 32.
230 *R. v. Gerald X.* (1958), 121 C.C.C. át 120 (Man. C.A.); Royal Commission Inquiry into Civil Rights, Report 1, vol. 2, Toronto: Queen's Printer, 1968, pp. 554–5.
231 Nejelski, Paul and LaPook, Judith Monitoring the juvenile justice system, 24; Parker, Graham The century of the child, *Can. Bar Rev.*, 749, 1967.
232 Fox, Sanford Juvenile justice in America: philosophical reforms, *Human Rights 5:* 66, 1975.
233 *R. v. Gerald X.* (1958), 121 C.C.C. at 125 (Man. C.A.).
234 Diversion refers to the process whereby certain types of delinquent behaviour are handled by some means other than the juvenile court. It is characterized by the halting or deferring of juvenile justice processing for youth who are in immediate jeopardy of a court appearance.
235 Canada Law Reform Commission, *Studies on diversion*, Working Paper on Diversion, Ottawa: Information Canada, 1975.
236 Thomas, C. and Sieverdes, C. Juvenile court intake: an analysis of discretionary decision-making, *Criminology 12:* 413, 1975.
237 Pink, William and White, Mervin Delinquency prevention: the state of the art, in M.W. Klein, ed., *The juvenile justice system*, Beverley Hills: Sage Publications, 1976, p. 10.
238 Sarri, Rosemary and Vinter, Robert Justice for whom? varieties of juvenile correctional approaches, in M.W. Klein, ed., *The juvenile justice system*, Beverley Hills: Sage Publications, 1976, p. 164.
239 Wilson, L.C. Diversion: the impact on juvenile justice, *Can. J. Crim. Corr. 18:* 161, 1976.
240 Pink, William and White, Mervin Delinquency prevention, 10.
241 Note, *Parens patriae* and statutory vagueness in the juvenile court, *Yale Law J. 82:* 747, 1973.
242 *R. v. Gerald X.* (1958), 121 C.C.C. 103–120 (Man. C.A.) p. 120–5; Parker, Graham The century of the child, 749.
243 Royal Commission Inquiry into civil rights.
244 Mnookin, Robert Foster-care, 188–9.
245 Rodham, Hillary Children under the law, 28.
246 *The Child Welfare Act*, R.S.O. 1970, c.64, s.23a(2).
247 Ibid., s.222, see also Manitoba: Section 12d, *The Child Welfare Act*, 1974, c.30.

248 Dickens, Bernard *Legal issues in child abuse*, 11.

249 Wald, Michael State intervention on behalf of 'neglected' children: a search for realistic standards *Stanford L. Rev. 27:* 1000, 1974-5.

250 Phillips, M., Shyne, A., Sherman, E., and Haring, B. Factors associated with placement decisions in child welfare, 1971, referred to in R.H. Mnookin, Child custody adjudication: judicial functions in the face of indeterminacy, *L. & Contemp. Prob. 39:* 263, 1975.

251 Mnookin, Robert Foster-care, 190.

252 *The Child Welfare Act*, R.S.O., 1970, c.64, s.26; see fn. 55 of Dickens, Bernard Legal responses to child abuse, *Can. J. Fam. L. 1:* 100, 1978, for how things are done elsewhere in Canada.

253 Mnookin, Robert Foster-care, 174.

254 Ibid., 181.

255 Wald, Michael State intervention on behalf of 'neglected children,' 996.

256 Ibid., 998.

257 Dickens, Bernard Legal issues in child abuse, 24-5.

258 Mnookin, Robert American custody law: a framework for analysis, in J.C. Westman, ed., *Proceedings of the University of Wisconsin Conference on child advocacy*, Madison: University of Wisconsin, 1976, p. 142.

259 Eekelaar, John An enquiry into custody disposition in divorce cases, in Ian Baxter and Mary Eberts, eds., *The child and the courts*, Toronto: Carswells, 1978, p. 1; Ellsworth, Phoebe C. and Levy, Robert J. Legislative reform of child custody adjudication, *L. & Soc. Rev. 4:* 202, 1969-70.

260 See rules 33, 34, and 36 of Ont. Reg. 450, 1977 under *The Unified Family Court Act*, S.O. 1976.

261 Lieff, A.H. Pre-trial of family law in the Supreme Court of Ontario: simplify and expedite, *L.S.U.C. Gazette 10:* 300, 1976.

262 For example, s.1(1) of *The Infants Act*; *The Family Law Reform Act, 1978* R.S.O. 1978, c.2, s.35(1).

263 Manchester, A.H. Custody, the child and the legal process, *Family Law 6:* 67, 1976.

264 Mnookin, Robert Child custody adjudication.

265 Ibid., 253.

266 Ibid., 231.

267 Ibid., 260.

268 Okpaku, Sheila Psychology: impediment or aid in child custody cases, *Rutgers Law Review 29:* 1153, 1976.

269 Mnookin, Robert American custody law, 146.

270 Manchester, A.H. Custody, the child and the legal process, 67; Mnookin, Robert American custody law, 146; Bradbrook, Adrien An empirical study

of the attitudes of the judges of the Supreme Court of Ontario regarding the workings of the present child custody laws, *Can. Bar Review 49:* 557, 1971.

271 Weiler, Karen Re Moores and Feldstein: a case comment and discussion of custody principles, *Osgoode Hall L.J. 12:* 219, 1974; *Parental rights and duties and custody suits,* A Report by Justice, London: Stevens & Sons, 1975, p. 35.

272 Okpaku, Sheila Psychology, 1141.

273 Ibid., 1139; but see Doris S. Jacobson The impact of marital separation/divorce on children: 1. parent-child separation and child adjustment, *Journal of Divorce 1(4):* 341, 1978 for preliminary research on the effects of separation on children; Mel Roman and William Haddad *The disposable child: the case for joint custody.* New York: Holt, Rinehart and Winston, 1978; see also pp. 195–200 of text.

274 Ibid., 1141.

275 Report of the committee on the representation of children in the Provincial Court (Family Division), Ontario Ministry of the Attorney-General, June 1977, p. 21.

276 *Re Helmes* (1976), 13 O.R. (2d) 4 (Ont. Div. Ct.); ibid., 18.

277 In two other provinces, Manitoba and Quebec, the child has a specific statutory right to independent legal representation. Section 33 of the 1978 amendments to Ontario's legislation enables a child 10 years or over to be present at the judge's discretion. Section 20 gives the judge power to appoint a lawyer if the child is not already represented by counsel.

278 *Reid v. Reid* (1976), 11 O.R. 622 (Ont. Div. Ct.); In Alberta, paragraph 10(2)(b) of *The Family Court Act,* R.S.A. 1970, c.133, specifically allows the *child* to make application in respect of his or her own custody or access.

279 Stone, Olive M. The welfare of the child: its assessment, representation and promotion in judicial proceedings, in I. Baxter and M. Eberts, eds., *The child and the courts,* Toronto: Carswells, 1978, p. 242.

280 Langley, Michael, Thomas, Brenda, and Parkison, Ronald Youth's expectations of their initial juvenile court appearances, *Can. J. Crim.* 49, 1978.

281 Lipsitt, Paul D. The juvenile offender's perceptions, *Crime and delinquency 14:* 49, 1968; Catton, Katherine and Erickson, Patricia *The juvenile's perception of the role of defence counsel in juvenile court: a pilot study,* A Working Paper of the Centre of Criminology, University of Toronto, May 1975.

282 Ibid., Catton and Erickson.

283 Political Knowledge and Attitudes 1971–2, Report from the National Assessment of Educational Progress, 1973; National Assessment of Education Progress, Changes in political knowledge and attitudes, 1969–76, Report #07-CS-02; Education for citizenship: bicentennial survey, Report #08-CS-01.

284 Grisso, J.T. and Manoogian Juveniles' comprehension of Miranda warnings in P. Lipsitt and B. Sales, eds., *New directions in psychological research*, New York: Van Nostrand Reinhold, 1979, in press.

285 Maher, B. and Stein, E. The delinquent's perception of the law and the community, in W. Wheeler, ed., *Controlling delinquents*, New York: John Wiley, 1968, p. 187.

286 Matza, David *Delinquency and drift*, New York: John Wiley, 1964; Catton, Katherine and Erickson, Patricia *The juvenile's perception of defence counsel.*

287 For a more complete review of issues regarding child representation, see Leon, Jeffrey S. *Legal representation of children in selected court proceedings*, Working Paper #1 of the Child in the City Programme, University of Toronto, 1978; see pp. 195–200 of text for a review of his work.

288 Kleinfeld, Andrew The balance of power among infants, their parents, and the state, *Family Law Quart. 4:* 323, 1970.

289 Report of the committee on the representation of children, 21.

290 *Reid* v. *Reid* (1976), 11 O.R. 622 (Ont. Div. Ct.).

291 *Rowe* v. *Rowe* (1976), 26 R.F.L. 91 (Ont. H.C.).

292 *Re Helmes* (1976), 13 O.R. (2d) 4 (Ont. Div. Ct.); proposed amendments to *The Child Welfare Act* will give the judge the power to appoint counsel.

293 Report of the committee on the representation of children, 19; s.25(3) of *The Child Welfare Act* authorizes the judge to hear any person on behalf of the child.

294 Catton, Katherine and Leon, Jeffrey Legal representation and the proposed *Young Persons in Conflict With the Law Act, Osgoode Hall L.J. 15:* 107, 1977; Report of the committee on the representation of children, 7-11.

295 Rodham, Hillary Children under the law, 23.

296 Friend of the court: one who calls to the court's attention some point of law or fact which otherwise might be overlooked.

297 Dootjes, Inez, Erickson, Patricia, and Fox, Richard Defence counsel in juvenile court: a variety of roles, *J. Crim. Corr. 14:* 132, 1972.

298 Erickson, Patricia The defence lawyer's role in juvenile court: an empirical investigation into judges' and social workers' points of view, *U.T.L.J. 24:* 126, 1974; Erickson, Patricia Legalistic and traditional role expectations for defence council in juvenile court, *Can. J. Crim. Corr. 17:* 78, 1975.

299 Stapleton, W. Vaughn and Teitelbaum, Lee *In defense of youth: a study of counsel in American juvenile courts*, New York: Russell Sage, 1972.

300 Ibid., 67-8, and 78-9; Catton, Katherine Models of procedure in juvenile court, *Crim. L.Q. 18:* 181, 1976.

301 See pp. 195–200 of text; Mnookin, Robert Foster-care, 189.

302 Essentially the Official Guardian is a public solicitor appointed by the legislature with complete authority to represent the civil rights and interests of children under the age of 18 years residing in Ontario. He may bring an action on behalf of a minor if there is no other person ready or willing to do so or he may defend an action on his behalf in similar circumstances. *The Judicature Act,* R.S.O. 1970, c.228, s.107.

303 *Globe and Mail,* 4 July 1977; Annual Report of the Ministry of the Attorney-General of Ontario, 1975–76.

304 *The Legal Aid Act,* R.S.O. 1970, c.239; R.R.O. 1970, Reg. 557, s.69.

305 Catton, Katherine and Erickson, Patricia *The juvenile's perception of defence counsel,* 20.

306 Report of the committee on the representation of children.

307 The Child in the City Programme, University of Toronto, is assisting the Attorney-General's Committee on the Representation of Children in designing the research component of these pilot projects; see Katherine Catton *Legal representation for children in family court: a research proposal,* Appendix to the 2nd Report of the Ontario Attorney-General's Committee on the Representation of Children, September 1978.

308 In Supreme Court custody proceedings, the judge's inherent *parens patriae* jurisdiction gives him power to order such reports. Some question whether family court judges have the power to order such investigations, especially at adjudication.

309 Gozansky, N. Court ordered investigations in child-custody cases, *Williamette L.J. 12:* 552, 1976.

310 Okpaku, Sheila Psychology, 1132.

311 Ennis, B.J. and Litwack, T.R. Psychiatry and the presumption of expertise: flipping coins in the courtroom, *Cal. L. Rev. 62:* 693, 1974.

312 Annual Report of the Ministry of the Attorney-General, 1976–7, p. 31.

313 Ibid.

314 Kraus, J. Decision process in the children's court and the social background report, *J. Research Crime and Del. 12(1):* 17, 1975.

315 Fox, Sanford Juvenile justice reform: innovations in Scotland, *Am. Crim. L. Rev. 12:* 61, 1974.

316 Smith, Lucy and Lodrop, P. The child in the divorce situation – factors determining the custody question and the use of experts in custody cases in Norway, in I. Baxter and M. Eberts, eds., *The Child and the courts,* Toronto: Carswells, 1978, p. 25.

317 Bradbrook, Adrien J. An empirical study on the attitudes of the judges of the Supreme Court of Ontario regarding the workings of the present child custody adjudication laws, *Can. Bar Rev. 49:* 561, 1971.

318 Spencer, John Alternatives to the judicial process: the Scottish system of children's hearings, in I. Baxter and M. Eberts, eds., *The child and the courts*, Toronto: Carswells, 1978, p. 253.

319 Howlett, Frederick Is the youth services bureau all it's cracked up to be? *Crime and Delinquency 19:* 485, 1976.

320 Streib, Victor L. The informal juvenile justice system: a need for procedural fairness and reduced discretion, *John Marshall J. of Practice and Procedure 10:* 52, 1976.

321 Seymour, J.A. Youth Services Bureau, *L. and Soc. Rev. 7:* 251, 1972.

322 Most arbitrators and mediators in family law problems possess training in marital and family counselling.

323 Statsky, W. The training of community judges: rehabilitative adjudication, *Colum. Human Rights L. Rev. 4:* 401, 1972; Statsky, W. Community courts: decentralizing juvenile justice, *Capital U. L. Rev. 3:* 1, 1974.

324 Cruickshank, David Alternatives to the judicial process: court avoidance in neglect cases, in I. Baxter and M. Eberts, eds., *The child and the courts*, Toronto: Carswells, 1978, p. 203.

325 Theuman, Richard *An assessment of four Family Court Conciliation Projects funded by the Department of National Health and Welfare*, submitted in partial fulfillment of a Master's Degree in Social Work, Wilfred Laurier Univ., 1977.

326 Irving, Howard and Gandy, John Family Court Conciliation Project: An experiment in support services (1977), 27 R.F.L. 47 at 52.

327 Elkin, Meyer Conciliation courts – the re-integration of disintegrating families, *Fam. Coord. 22:* 63, 1973.

328 Theuman, Richard *An assessment of four Family Court Conciliation Projects.*

329 *Social Work (Scotland) Act 1968*, Part III.

330 Morris, Allison, Scottish juvenile justice: a critique, in R. Hood, ed., *Crime, criminology and public policy*, New York: Free Press, 1974, p. 368.

331 Fox, Stanford Juvenile justice reform.

332 Morris, Allison Scottish juvenile justice.

333 Ibid., 368.

334 Ibid., 371.

335 Bruce, N. Children's hearings: a retrospect, *Brit. J. Crim. 15:* 343, 1975.

336 Spencer, John Alternatives to the judicial process.

337 Dahl, Tove Stang The Scandinavian system of juvenile justice: a comparative approach, in Margaret K. Rosenheim, ed., *Pursuing justice for the child*, Chicago and London: University of Chicago Press, 1976, p. 327.

338 *Protection of Children Amendment Act*, R.S.B.C. 1974, c.2.

339 Ontario Law Reform Commission, *Report on Family Law, Part V: Family Courts*, Toronto: Queen's Printer, pp. 3–4, 1974.
340 Ibid., 3.
341 Ibid., 6.
342 *The Unified Family Court Act*, S.O. 1976, c.85.
343 Theuman, Richard *An assessment of four Family Court Conciliation Projects.*
344 Allard, H. Family Courts in Canada, in D. Mendes da Costa, ed., *Studies in Canadian family law*, Toronto: Butterworths, 1972, p. 3.
345 Dyson, E. and Dyson, R. Family Courts in the U.S., *J. Family Law IX:* 89–90, 1969; also *J. Family Law VIII:* 507, 1968.
346 Scott, P. Children's hearings: a commentary, *Brit. J. Crim. 15:* 346, 1975.
347 *Juvenile Delinquents Act*, R.S.C. 1970, c.J-3 s.2(1).
348 Sellin, T. and Wolfgang, M.E. The legal basis of delinquency, in P. Lerman, ed., *Delinquency and social policy*, New York: Praeger Publishers, 1970, p. 20.
349 Cohen, A.K. *Delinquent boys*, New York: Free Press, 1955; Porterfield, A.L. Delinquency and its outcome in court and college, *Am. J. Sociology*, 199, 1943.
350 President's Commission on Law Enforcement and Administration of Justice, *The challenge of crime in a free society*, Washington D.C.: Government Printing Office, 1967, p. 55.
351 Williams, Jay and Gold, Martin From delinquent behavior to official delinquency, *Soc. Prob. 20(2):* 209, 1972.
352 Lerman, Paul *Delinquency and social policy*, 6.
353 Gold, Martin and Reimer, D. Changing patterns of delinquent behavior among Americans thirteen to sixteen years old: 1967–72, *Crime and Del. Lit. 7:* 483, 1975.
354 Miller, W.B. Inter-institutional conflict and delinquency prevention, in Lerman, Paul *Delinquency and social policy*, 407.
355 Gold, Martin and Reimer, D. Changing patterns of delinquent behavior.
356 Williams, Jay and Gold, Martin From delinquent behavior to official delinquency.
357 Wolfgang, Marvin, Figlio, Robert, and Sellin, Thorsten *Delinquency in a birth cohort*, Chicago: University of Chicago Press, 1972, p. 254.
358 Ibid.
359 Thomas, C. and Sieverdes, C. Juvenile court intake, *Criminology 12:* 413, 1975.
360 Wolfgang, Marvin et al. *Delinquency in a birth cohort*, 253; Pink, William and White, Mervin Delinquency prevention: the state of the art, in M. Klein, ed., *The Juvenile Justice System*, Beverley Hills: Sage Publications, 1976, p. 10.

361 Note: Nondelinquent children in New York: the need for alternatives to institutional treatment, *Columbia J.L. and Soc. Prob. 8:* 254–5, 1971–72.

362 Pink, William and White, Mervin *Delinquency prevention*, p. 10.

363 Ibid., 13.

364 Abadinsky, H. The status offender dilemma: coercion and treatment, *Crime and Del. 22(4):* 456, 1976; Frisell, D. The status offender and the juvenile court, *Williamette L.J. 12:* 557, 1976; Thomas, C.W. Are status offenders really so different? *Crime and Del. 22(4):* 438, 1976; Policy Statement: Board of Directors, National Council on Crime and Delinquency, Jurisdiction over status offences should be removed from the juvenile court, *Crime and Del. 21(2):* 97, 1975; Teitelbaum, Lee and Gough, Aidan, eds., *Beyond control: status offenders in the juvenile courts*, Cambridge, Mass.: Ballinger Co., 1977.

365 Schur, Edwin *Radical non-intervention: rethinking the delinquency problem*, Englewood Cliffs, N.J.: Prentice-Hall, 1973, p. 167.

366 Note: Ungovernability: The unjustifiable jurisdiction, *Yale L.J. 83:* 1383, 1974.

367 Policy Statement: Jurisdiction over status offences, note 364.

368 McCarthy, F. Should delinquency be abolished? *Crime and Del. 23(2):* 196, 1977.

369 Gilman, D. How to retain jurisdiction over status offences: change without reform in Florida, *Crime and Del. 22(1):* 48, 1976.

370 Report of the committee on the representation of children, 17–21.

371 Thomson, George Comments, in W. Michelson, S.V. Levine, and E. Michelson, eds., *The child in the city: today and tomorrow*, Toronto: University of Toronto Press, 1979, pp. 155–158.

372 Note that the most recent federal government statistics (December 1976) ignore this as a category. It is impossible to determine from their table where the status offender is classified although the most likely slots are provincial statutes and *Criminal Code* sexual offences.

373 Datesman, Susan and Scarpitti, F. Female delinquents and broken homes, *Am. J. Crim. 13:* 33, 1975; see also Sherrie Barnhorst, Female delinquency and the role of women, *Can. J. Family Law 1:* 254, 1978.

374 Ibid., 260

375 Chesney-Lind, Meda Judicial enforcement of the female sex role: the Family Court and the female delinquent, *Issues in Criminology 8(2):* 51, 1973.

376 Barnhorst, S. Female delinquency, 260.

377 Landau, Barbara The adolescent female offender, *Can. J. Corr. 17:* 146, 1975.

378 Jensen, Gary and Eve, R. Sex differences in delinquency, *Criminology 13:* 429, 1976; Gold, M. *Delinquent behavior in an American city*, California: Wadsworth Publishing Company, 1970.
379 Wise, Nancy Juvenile delinquency among middle-class girls, in Edmund Vaz, ed., *Middle class juvenile delinquency*, New York: Harper and Row, 1967, p. 187.
380 Barnhorst, S. Female delinquency, 267.
381 Ibid., 268.
382 Ibid.
383 Landau, Barbara The adolescent female offender, 463.
384 Barnhorst, S. Female delinquency, 261–4.
385 Weiler, Karen *Section 8 of the Training Schools Act*, unpublished Masters thesis for LL.M. degree, York University, 1974.
386 Ibid., 62.
387 Lambert, Leah and Birkenmayer, Andrew *An assessment of the classification system for placement of wards in training schools*, Planning and Research Branch, Ontario Ministry of Correctional Services, 1972, Table 4.
388 Landau, Barbara The adolescent female offender.
389 Conway, A. and Bogdan, C. Sexual delinquency: the persistence of a double standard, *Crime and Del. 23(2).* 133, 1977.
390 Rogers, K. For her own protection ...: conditions of incarceration for female juvenile offenders in the state of Connecticut, *L. and Soc. Rev. 7:* 223, 1972.
391 Terry, Robert Discrimination in the handling of juvenile offenders by social control agencies, in Peter G. Garabedian and Don C. Gibbons, eds. *Becoming delinquent*, Chicago: Aldine Press, 1970, p. 78.
392 Cohn, Yona Criteria for the probation officer's recommendation to the juvenile court, in Peter G. Garabedian and Don C. Gibbons, *Becoming delinquent*, Chicago: Aldine Press, 1970, p. 190.
393 Chesney-Lind, Meda Judicial enforcement of the female sex role.
394 Ibid., 54.
395 Weiler, Karen *Section 8 of the Training Schools Act*.
396 Ibid., 66.
397 Ibid., 69.
398 Skolnick, Arlene The limits of childhood.
399 Ibid., 69–70.
400 Schur, Edwin *Radical non-intervention*, 162.
401 Polk, Kenneth and Schafer, Walter The changing context of education, in Kenneth Polk and Walter Schafer, eds., *Schools and delinquency*, Englewood Cliffs, N.J.: Prentice-Hall, 1972, pp. 10–11.

402 Wenk, E. Schools and delinquency prevention, *Crime and Del. Lit. 6:* 236, 1974.

403 Balch, Robert The medical model of delinquency, *Crime and Delinquency 21:* 124-5, 1975.

404 Phillips, J. *The creation of deviant behavior in high schools: an examination of Cohen's general theory of subculture*, Dissertation, Ann Arbor, Michigan University microfilms, 1974.

405 Polk, Kenneth, Frease, D., and Richmond, F. Social class, school experience and delinquency, *Criminology 12(1):* 84, 1974.

406 Ibid.; see also Power, R. Benn, R., and Morris, J. Neighborhood, school and juveniles before the courts, *Brit. J. Crim. 12(2):* 111, 1972.

407 Jensen, Gary Race, achievement and delinquency: a further look at *Delinquency in a birth cohort, Am. J. Sociology 82:* 379, 1976.

408 Vinter, Robert and Sarri, Rosemary Malperformance in the public school: a group work approach, *Social Work 10:* 3-13, 1965.

409 Reiss, Albert Jr., and Rhodes, Albert A sociopsychological study of adolescent conformity and deviation, United States Office of Education, Cooperative Research Project, Number 507, 1959, in Kenneth Polk and Walter Schafer, eds., *Schools and delinquency*; Polk, Kenneth and Schafer, Walter The changing context of education, 167.

410 Schafer, Walter Deviance in the public school: an interactional view, in Kenneth Polk and Walter Schafer, eds., *Schools and delinquency*, p. 156.

411 Schafer, Walter and Polk, Kenneth School career and delinquency, in Kenneth Polk and Walter Schafer, eds., *Schools and delinquency*, p. 168.

412 Ibid., 170.

413 Schafer, Walter Deviance with the public school, 158.

414 Ibid., 161-2.

415 Pink, William and White, Mervin Delinquency prevention, 23.

416 Schafer, William Deviance in the public school, 147-8.

417 Schafer, Walter and Olexa, Carol *Tracking and opportunity: the locking-out process and beyond*, Scranton: Chandler Publishing Company, 1971.

418 Elliot, D. and Voss, H. *Delinquency and drop-out*, Lexington, Mass.: D.C. Heath and Co., 1974.

419 Schafer, Walter Deviance in the public school, 163.

420 Elliot, D. and Voss, H. *Delinquency and drop-out*.

421 Schafer, Walter and Polk, Kenneth School conditions contributing to delinquency, in Kenneth Polk and Walter Schafer, eds., *Schools and delinquency*, p. 235.

422 Ibid., 240.

423 Ibid., 256.

424 Breed, Allen *Educational reform and delinquent youth*, California Youth
Authority, 1974.
425 Ibid., 6.
426 Bazelon, David Beyond control of the juvenile court, *Juv. Court Judges
J. 21:* 42, 1970.
427 Ibid., 44.
428 Ibid., 50.
429 Ibid., 44.
430 Lerman, Paul *Delinquency and social policy*.
431 Ibid., 354.
432 Wheeler, S., Cottrell, L.S. Jr., and Romasco, A. Juvenile delinquency –
its prevention and control, in Paul Lerman *Delinquency and social policy*,
429.
433 Ibid., 430.
434 Spergel, Irving Interactions between community structure, delinquency and
social policy in the inner city, in Malcolm Klein, *The juvenile justice system*,
Beverley Hills: Sage Publications, 1976.
435 Ibid., 59.
436 Pink, William and White, Marvin Delinquency prevention.
437 Ibid., 23.
438 Spergel, Irving Interactions between community structure, 86.
439 Pink, William and White, Marvin Delinquency prevention, 15.
440 Spergel, Irving Interactions between community structure, 86.
441 Ibid., 87.
442 Ibid., 88.
443 Ibid., 91.
444 Walker, Pamela The law and the young: some necessary extra-legal
considerations, *U.T. Fac. L. Rev. 29:* 58–9, 1971.
445 Gold, Martin and Reimer, D. Changing patterns of delinquent behavior
among Americans.
446 Pink, William and White, Mervin Delinquency prevention, 5.
447 Ibid., 17.
448 Kleinfeld, Andrew Jay The balance of power among infants, their parents
and the state (1970), *Fam. L.Q. 4:* 319, 1970; 410, 1970; *Fam. L.Q. 5:*
64, 1971 (3-part article).
449 Ibid., 438.
450 Coons, John E. and Mnookin, Robert H. Toward a theory of children's
rights, in I. Baxter and M. Eberts, eds., *The child and the courts*, Toronto:
Carswells, 1978.
451 Ibid.

452 Ibid.
453 Westman, Jack C. Child advocacy: a program report in Jack C. West-man, ed., *Proceedings of the University of Wisconsin Conference on child advocacy*, Madison, Wisconsin: University of Wisconsin, 1976, p. 5.
454 Ibid., 8.
455 Ibid., 185; Westman, Jack C. and Stiles, Christine A field trial of child advocacy in Wisconsin, in Jack C. Westman, ed., *Proceedings of the University of Wisconsin Conference on child advocacy*, Madison, Wisconsin: University of Wisconsin, 1976, p. 185.
456 Holt, John *Escape from childhood*, New York: Ballentine Books, 1974, p. 1.
457 Wald, Patricia Making sense out of the rights of youth, *Center Quarterly Focus*, 5–6, 1975.
458 Ibid., 5.
459 Westman, Jack C. and Stiles, Christine A field trial of child advocacy in Wisconsin, 193.
460 Levy, Robert J. The rights of parents, *Brigham Young U.L. Rev.*, 693, 1976.
461 Ibid., 697.
462 Hafen, Bruce C. Children's liberation and the new egalitarianism: some reserv tions about abandoning youth to their rights, *Brigham Young U.L. Rev.*, 605, 1976.
463 Ibid., 656.
464 Coons, John E. and Mnookin, Robert H. Towards a theory of children's rights.
465 Ibid.
466 Ibid.
467 Ibid.
468 Ibid.
469 For general review, see E. Dianne Caldwell, Children's right to legal representation in juvenile court proceedings, unpublished paper, University of Toronto Law School, 1976.
470 *Juvenile Delinquents Act*, R.S.C. 1970, c.J-3, s.2(1).
471 Ibid.
472 Leon, Jeffrey The development of Canadian juvenile justice: a background for reform, *Osgoode Hall L.J. 15:* 71, 1977.
473 Wang, Ketchem The continuing turbulence surrounding the *parens patriae* concept in American juvenile courts, *McGill L.J. 18:* 222–3, 1972.
474 This is the theory, despite s.5 which states that the proceedings 'shall, *mutatis mutandis* be governed by the provisions of the *Criminal Code* relating to summary convictions insofar as such provisions are applicable.'

For a discussion of the 'family model' of procedure, see Katherine Catton Models of Procedure and the Juvenile Court, *Crim. L.Q. 18:* 181, 1976.

475 *A.G.B.C.* v. *Smith* (1968), 65 D.L.R. (2d) 82.

476 *Juvenile Delinquents Act* R.S.C. 1970, c.J-3, s.12(2) and (3).

477 Fox, Richard and Spencer, Maureen The Young Offenders Bill: destigmatizing juvenile delinquency?; *Crim. L.Q. 14:* 193, 1972.

478 Catton, Katherine and Leon, Jeffrey Legal representation and the proposed act, 108.

479 Ibid., 109–110.

480 Catton, Katherine and Erickson, Patricia *The juvenile's perceptions of defence council.*

481 Report of the Committee on the Representation of Children; *The Legal Aid Act*, R.S.O. 1970, c.239.

482 Party is a technical word and has a precise meaning in legal parlance. It is the person(s) by or against whom legal action is brought and who therefore has a right to fully participate in the proceedings.

483 *Juvenile Delinquents Act* R.S.C. 1970, c.J-3, s.20(1).

484 Ibid., s.25.

485 Ibid., s.20(1).

486 Note, Nondelinquent children in New York.

487 *The Child Welfare Act* R.S.O. 1970, c.64, s.20(1).

488 *The Training Schools Act* R.S.O. 1970, ch.467, c.8; Weiler, Karen Unmanageable children and Section 8, *Interchange 8:* 176, 1977–8.

489 Dickens, Bernard *Legal issues on child abuse*, 57.

490 Ibid., 58.

491 At common law, parents have the right to physically punish their children provided that the amount and form of force applied is reasonable considering the nature of the child's offence, the child's age, sex, and strength.

492 *The Child Welfare Act, 1978* S.O. 1978, s.21, s.27 and s.28.

493 Ibid., s.23.

494 Ibid., s.30, s.38 and s.42.

495 Ibid., s.40 and s.41.

496 Ibid., s.68.

497 Ibid., s.25.

498 Report of the Committee on the representation of children, 18.

499 Ibid., 18–19; *The Child Welfare Act, 1978* s.20.

500 *The Family Law Reform Act, 1978* R.S.O. 1978, c.2, s.53(d).

501 *Divorce Act* R.S.C. 1970, c.D08, s.11(1)(c).

502 Every decree of dissolution of marriage, whether for divorce or nullity, is in the first instance a decree *nisi* not to be made absolute until three months have elapsed, unless the court orders a shorter time; ibid., s.13.

503 *The Family Law Reform Act, 1978* R.S.O. 1978, c.2, s.35 and s.1(c).

504 Justice Report *Parental rights*, 36.

505 Ontario Law Reform Commission, *Report on family law. Part V*, 3.

506 *Re Moores and Feldstein* (1974), 12 R.F.L. 273 (Ont. C.A.); leave to
appeal to the Supreme Court of Canada refused on 22 November 1973.

507 *Talsky* v. *Talsky* (1976), 21 R.F.L. 26 (Supreme Court of Canada); Robinson,
L.R. Custody and access, in D. Mendes da Costa, *Studies in Canadian
family law*, Toronto: Butterworths, 1972, vol. 2, p. 545.

508 *Berger* v. *Berger* (1975), 17 R.F.L. 216 (Ont. H.C.).

509 *Case* v. *Case* (1975), 18 R.F.L.132 (Sask. Q.B.).

510 *Berger* v. *Berger* (1975), 17 R.F.L. 216 (Ont. H.C.).

511 Robinson, L.R. Custody and access, 589.

512 *Re Protection of Children Act, Re Jepson and Maw (an infant)* (1960), 32
W.W.R. 93 (B.C.S.C.); *Voghell* v. *Voghell* and Pratt (No. 2) (1962), 35 O.L.R.
(2d) 592 (Man. Q.B.); see also Robinson, L.R. Custody and access, in D.
Mendes da Costa, ed., *Studies in Canadian family law*, p. 591.

513 *Dunn* v. *Dunn and Holcombe* (1954), O.W.N. 561 (H.C.); *Hind* v. *Hind and
Wilson* (1962), 31 D.L.R. (2d) 622 (B.C.S.C.); see also Robinson, L.R.
Custody and access, in D. Mendes da Costa, ed., *Studies in Canadian
family law*, p. 543.

514 *Currie* v. *Currie* (1975), 18 R.F.L. 47 (Alta.).

515 *M.* v. *M.* (1975), 20 R.F.L. 346 (Man. Q.B.).

516 *Re Moores and Feldstein* (1974), 12 R.F.L. 273 (Ont. C.A.).

517 *Reid* v. *Reid* (1976), 11 O.R. 622 (Ont. Div. Ct.).

5

Issues for Adolescents in a Modern Urban Context

MARTHA FRIENDLY, SAUL V. LEVINE AND LINDA HAGARTY

One of the major roles which all human societies share in common is that of socializing their young for eventually assuming the responsibilities of the tribe, culture, or nation. The passing of the torch or assuming some measure of adulthood almost always occurs sometime in the teen years, depending upon the needs of the particular society. Most children's worlds are relatively circumscribed; in societies where significant choices during childhood are possible, most of the decisions are made for the child by the family.

Although a significant part of what happens to a teenager during his adolescent years is determined by a combination of the circumstances and characteristics with which he enters adolescence, and while significant socialization continues to take place within the family, adolescence is primarily a time of beginning to strike out on one's own, of establishing patterns which may persist into adulthood, and of making choices which may be, if not irrevocable, significant turning points for the future. It may be a time for the beginning of the assertion of a favourable identity which will lead to a successful adult life, or it may be filled with frustrations which are difficult to resolve, leading to an unfulfilling future.

This chapter considers the adolescent within the context of the changes occurring in our society in the latter part of the twentieth century. Rapid technological advances, multiple options, and an altered family structure have presented adolescents, who are themselves undergoing rapid changes in mind and body, with new and important uncertainties.

The first part of the chapter presents an historical view of adolescence, followed by a brief discussion of the physical, cognitive, and relational changes which occur, and a consideration of the concept of a development of identity as one of the adolescent's major tasks. The latter part of the chapter develops an in-depth view of two key issues which the twentieth-century adolescent must confront and which have become problematic. The key issues of the transition to adult sexuality and the transition from school to work, are, today, areas which provide many questions and few answers. The dilemmas of developing a satisfactory belief system and an adequate base of information and experience on which to base sexual, familial, job, and career choices are particularly grave in a time of unstable social and economic conditions. Following a presentation of empirical evidence from a variety of disciplines, some research directions are explored.

I THE NATURE OF ADOLESCENCE

Adolescents today are viewed in various ways, depending upon the biases of the viewer. Some of the older generations in North America see their own young people as overly critical, emotionally troubled, shiftless, or promiscuous. Others see adolescents today as carrying their hopes for a better world; young people are viewed by some adults as honest, idealistic, or loving. Positive traits which the previous generation lacked are frequently attributed to them.[1]

These observations are generalizations and probably neither is completely true: they are based upon non-systematic observation of a small visible number of adolescents. There is evidence that generation gaps have existed throughout history and that the twentieth century is not unique in this regard. Writers from the Greeks on have commented, generally unfavourably, upon the differences between themselves and the adolescent generation of their time. Thus, Shakespeare, in the words of Polonius in *Hamlet*, commented,

By Heaven, it is as proper to our age
To cast beyond ourselves in our opinions
As it is common for the younger sort
To lack discretion.[2]

An Historical Perspective

'... to every period of history, there corresponded a privileged age and a particular division of human life: "youth" is the privileged age of the seventeenth century, childhood of the nineteenth, adolescence of the twentieth.'[3]

In calling adolescence the privileged age of the twentieth century, Aries, in 1962, described the popular and scientific preoccupation with adolescence which developed in this century. This is not to say that modern attention to and concern with the age approximating puberty has solely been the domain of philosophers and scientists, parents and social critics in the twentieth-century. The notion of adolescence as a time of change and of testing oneself, of excesses and idealism is one that has pervaded ideas about this period of life from the time of the Greeks who viewed adolescence or youth as a separate and distinct period.

Although by the Middle Ages distinctions between post-infancy children and adults had become quite blurred, the distinction was revived with the eighteenth-century emphasis on the development of reason and on the socialization of children.

To Rousseau, the capacity for self-consciousness developed in middle childhood, between 6 and 12, and at about 12 years the capacity for rational thought began to waken. During the seventeenth, eighteenth, and into the nineteenth century, the adolescent years (which were then typically viewed as extending into the middle or late 20s) were seen as a time needing guidance because of the uncertain, self-centred, and, especially, sinful proclivities of youth. In order to promote a safe arrival at a moral Christian adulthood, clergymen emphasized the need for a heavy measure of guidance, as youth is 'carried with more headlong force into vice, lust and vain pleasures of the flesh.'[4] Contiguous with the view that adolescence was a time during which extreme caution needed to be exercised, there was a feeling that 'youth were possessed of strength and vigour, or purer conscience, and a softer heart than an old man.'[5]

Although conceptions of the adolescent or youth period of life are not new, and, in the past seem to have included much of the ambivalence with which teenagers are viewed today, it has been during the twentieth century that serious attention has been paid to the special problems and tasks of adolescence. The publication of Hall's *Adolescence* in 1904 is regarded as the beginning of a scientific study of this stage of development.[6] Indeed, in a consideration of the study of human development, Hall's synthesis of concepts from the fields of philosophy and natural science is regarded as a first step toward a scientific notion of human development.

Hall is often understood as having emphasized only the biological or maturational aspects of adolescent development and ignoring the effects of culture. However, although it was upon genetic theory that his ideas were based, he suggested that it was at adolescence when 'primitiveness' and 'savagery' gave way to 'more civilized ways of life' and in this, cultural influences play an important role. Indeed, Hall says, 'Young children grow despite great hardships but later adolescence is more dependent upon favoring conditions of the environment, disturbance of which more readily cause arrest and prevent maturity' and 'no age is so responsive to all the best and wisest adult endeavor.'[7] Hall concluded that the response to children during the reduced growth period which precedes puberty should be repression, but that once adolescence is reached, the control should be loosened to encourage development.

'The only duty of young children is implicit obedience,' says Hall, but 'with the teens this all begins to be changed and many of these precepts must be gradually reversed. Individuality must have a longer tether. Plasticity is at its maximum. The mind at times grows in leaps and bounds ...'[8]

Hall's work is important because his application of the principles of natural science to the study of human development paved the way for consideration of important questions which, although empirical evidence has been collected, have not yet been answered. First, the relative importance of biological givens and cultural influences and how they interact is not yet fully understood, although bits and pieces have been added to our understanding of this issue. Although it is clearly known that an interaction between the biological and the cultural or social exists, it is not known what conditions are best for promoting optimal growth for societies or individuals. Part of what is unknown has to do with the intrinsic nature of development in adolescence; that is, it is not known whether it is necessarily characterized by the upheaval and stress frequently reported by clinicians and popularly assumed to be part of the age, or conversely, whether adolescence, given the proper conditions, may in fact be a smooth, placid transition to adulthood.

Storm and Stress

Although Hall's recapitulation theory of human development has become antiquated with new knowledge based on empirical research, his related notion that adolescence is a period of upheaval, storm, and stress has persisted with many theorists and practitioners and in popular mythology.

Hall and his contemporary, Sigmund Freud, both gave strong support to this notion, Hall's based on his view of the changes in adolescence as rapid, abrupt, and discontinuous, and Freud's upon his vision of the individual as a battleground where the Id and the Ego warred for supremacy. The battle, which was for Freud quiescent during pre-puberty (latency), was re-encountered with the onset of the hormonal and psychological changes brought on by puberty; it became an important part of the adolescent's search for independence and identity. The psychoanalytic view of the storm and stress of adolescence, although modified and in some ways expanded by Freud's successors, still has a major influence today.

Blos wrote, in 1962, '... it is the typical expression of the adolescent's struggle to regain or retain a psychic equilibrium which has been jolted by the crisis of puberty';[9] and Gustin, in 1961 '... Picture an adolescent now poised at the brink of adulthood, racked by sexual desire, frustrated by outer prohibitions and inner inhibitions; desperately longing for independence yet fearful of isolation; eager for responsibilities yet fraught with anxieties about inferiority; flooded by irrational impulses yet committed to rules of propriety, he is hopelessly and helplessly confused and an enigma to everyone and himself.'[10]

Although there is some evidence that indicates that normal adolescence may not be as Gustin has described, it is interesting to consider Friedenberg's point that 'adolescence *is* conflict; protracted conflict – between the individual and society' and his comment about Mead's anthropological study of adolescent girls that 'there are cultures in which this conflict seems hardly to occur; but where it does not, the characteristic development of personality which we associate with adolescence does not occur either ... their people do not seem to us like adults.'[11] This view that some conflict during adolescence may provide an opportunity for development of a rich identity is one to which others subscribe, as did Mead herself.

Mead's description in *Coming of Age in Samoa* indicates that Samoan adolescent girls make an easy passage through adolescence; Mead concluded that the ease of relationships in the Samoan culture demanded little and that turmoil and conflict were not an inevitable, universal part of the age but a 'cultural invention.' However, she felt that a puberty without conflict affected Samoan identity, and that adult interpersonal relationships were, as a result, rather superficial.[12] Anna Freud, who felt that rebellion was a normal part of adolescence, and would be outgrown, expressed concern with adolescents who built up excessive defences against so-called 'normal' conflict.[13] Douvan and Adelson, in discussing their finding based on a large representative sample of American adolescents, also attached negative value to their population's relative lack of turmoil.[14]

Bandura, in rejecting the storm and stress hypothesis, used notions from learning theory, evidence from physiological psychology, anthropological data and common sense to present a persuasive argument that much adolescent stress is culturally engendered.[15] Similarly, the Offers, who conducted a series of studies over a ten-year period of a sample of 3000 middle-class American boys, concluded that, contrary to the writings of Freud and others in the psychoanalytic tradition, turmoil was relatively low in adolescents. The Offers found, first, that although anxiety, guilt, depression, and 'bickering' with parents were rather common, these tended to be mild and, second, that the boys in the sample appeared to fall into three relatively homogeneous groups, only one of which seemed to show the degree of turmoil presumed to be normative.[16] Daniel Offer, in presenting his conclusions with regard to the effects of the seeming low conflict of his sample, said, 'Implicitly ... investigators have adopted the position that lack of turmoil is a bad prognostic sign and must necessarily prevent the adolescent from developing into a mature adult. All our data, including the psychological testing, point in the opposite direction. The adolescents not only adjusted well; they were in touch with their feelings and developed meaningful relationships with significant others.'[17]

Masterson has published findings from his research indicating that adolescents who underwent extreme conflict in adolescence were, in fact, at risk, and continued to manifest pathological symptoms beyond the adolescent period.[18] This finding does not contradict those of the Offers; the Offers' is a widely drawn, presumably more normative sample, while Masterson's research deals with adolescents who were already known to be in difficulty.

A Time of Change

Although it is not clear that, for most of the population, adolescence is filled with turmoil, it is undeniably a time of rapid change - physical, psychological, and social change. Perhaps most important, all of these rapid changes occur simultaneously. As was suggested earlier in this chapter, although it is known that interaction between biology and culture is a continual process throughout an individual's development, the precise nature of the effects of one upon the other is not yet known. What is known is that these changes occur and that they, together with the effects of earlier experiences, influence the development of the adolescent to an adult.

Physical Change

Some of the most obvious signs of adolescence are the physical changes that occur. Changing bodily dimensions, accelerated physical growth, development of sexual characteristics, and increased sexual drive all occur rapidly and obviously. Physical growth and change are affected by heredity, influenced by social class and other factors including nutrition and climate.

The culture of which the adolescent is a member may mark his or her physical maturation with ceremony, or may make the subject taboo, and may, in general, influence whether the physical changes occurring are a source of confusion, pride, anxiety, or shame. The individual's feelings about his own body which develop during adolescence may remain a part of his identity for a long time after adolescence, as indicated, for example, by the findings from Jones's research that late-maturing boys were likely, in their 30s, to still be relatively less responsible, less self-controlled, and more dependent than early developers.[19]

It should be emphasized that physical change in adolescence tends to be uneven, to occur by stops and starts in each individual; this discontinuity may make an adolescent even more uncertain about his or her physical status. In addition, the range of normality for the beginning, the rate and the schedule of physical puberty is extremely wide; a class of eighth-graders may include little boys and girls and more mature men and women.[20] The combined effects of these uneven individual and group developmental rates, together with extreme mood variability created in part by an adjusting hormonal system, may be profound. The adolescent may not only not know who he is, or how he appears relative to his peers, but he may also be unable to handle his new feelings.

The interaction of personality development and one's body image has aroused much interest in recent years. Previously, the theory of somatotypes held that some aspects of temperament and character were determined biologically, as, for example, the old stereotype about the good-natured overweight person. Stereotypes still exist and the reactions to adolescents by others who hold those stereotypes will undoutedly influence a developing self-image.[21] This is one aspect of development in which the role of popular culture may be seen. As we are continually confronted with the society's notions of ideal body configuration, it may be difficult for an adolescent who deviates from the ideal to develop a positive image of his own body.

It is not the purpose of this paper to report comprehensively on the theoretical positions and the results of empirical research with regard to physical changes during adolescence but to emphasize that physical change is one important aspect of the developing adolescent identity which is universal, and with which the social and cultural context interacts.

Cognitive and Intellectual Change

Another area in which important changes occur during adolescence is in cognitive and intellectual capacity. The gains in these abilities allow the adolescent to approach the demands of the teenage years in ways of which the younger child would be incapable. The development of academic and vocational skills, of social, moral, and personal values, and the developing sense of identity, are all facilitated by the intellectual and cognitive gains of adolescence.

It has been suggested that adolescence is a time when the capacity to acquire and assimilate knowledge is at 'peak efficiency.' This notion is supported by a body of longitudinal data collected by Bayley which indicates that the rate of increase of overall mental ability is rapid throughout childhood, and slows in young adulthood, with the level of ability remaining relatively stable into the later adult years.[22]

The quantitative approach to intellectual development, exemplified by the work of Binet on intelligence testing in the very beginning of the twentieth century, preceded the more recent emphasis on the qualitative, or cognitive aspects of development, which considers the process of intellectual performance. Piaget has suggested a stage theory of cognitive development, emphasizing the necessity for mastery of each successive stage before the next can be attained. The highest stage of development from what Piaget has termed childish, or *concrete* thinking, to *abstract*, or adult reasoning ability, generally emerges in early adolescence and is an important qualitative change necessary for making the kinds of decisions the adolescent will have to make to establish himself eventually as an individual with a distinct and separate identity. Piaget's emphasis upon a fixed sequence of stages does not deny that differences in intelligence and different rates of progress through the sequence of stages exist.[23,24]

The adolescent who has reached what Piaget has called the stage of logical reasoning is characterized by an ability to think hypothetically and to be introspective in a way in which the younger child cannot be. This cognitive ability may mean that the adolescent, rather than accepting a decision from his parents, will be able to consider a number of alternatives before reaching a decision on his own. This ability may play an important role in the striving for relative independence which becomes so important in the relationship between the adolescent and his family.

A concept related to the Piagetian notions of cognitive development which plays a large role in the emotional state of adolescents is that of adolescent egocentricity. Adolescents (unlike younger children) are able ... 'to conceptualize the thought of other people. It is this capacity to take account of other people's thought which is the crux of adolescent egocentrism ... he (the adolescent) fails to differentiate between the objects toward which the thoughts of others are directed and those which are the focus of his own concern ... this belief that others are preoccupied with his appearance and behaviour constitutes the egocentricity of adolescence.'[25]

The adolescent, therefore, may project his feelings about himself to others and is, as a result, frequently performing before an 'imaginary audience' to whom he attributes his own attitudes and views about himself. These views may be approving but are likely to be critical, and may contribute to his extreme self-consciousness. Continually performing before an audience which he believes is acutely aware of his feelings may enhance the feeling of uniqueness to which adolescents are so susceptible. This may, for example, lead a teenage girl to believe that pregnancy can 'happen' to her friends but not to her, may characterize the peculiarly romantic nature of adolescent love; or may increase a boy's feeling that 'no one understands.'

As with the discussion of physical development in adolescence, the purpose of this chapter is only to provide a brief description of adolescent cognitive development; the reader may refer to other sources for more in-depth discussion of this important issue.

Development of an Identity

From Dependence to Independence
During childhood, although children make important friendships and develop peer groups which are important to them, it is the family circle that dominates

their lives. The pre-school and school-age child has friends on 'the block' and at school, but his family determines where his block is, where he goes to school, what he wears, what he eats, and so on. Although the family plays perhaps the most critical role in determining what the child will be like when he enters adolescence, and through adolescence will continue to help him make a smooth adjustment to the demands of the age, one of the most important transitions which adolescents make is from a childish dependence upon the family to relative independence as an adult.

As Douvan and Adelson have pointed out, 'The problem the parent faces is loosening the control to the child's capacity to regulate himself, letting the reins slacken at the right time and in the right way, neither holding them so tightly that the child resists nor releasing them so lightly as to endanger him.'[26] The achievement of this balance is important to children of all ages but it is during adolescence that the problems of managing it successfully are likely to become acute. If one of the major tasks of adolescence is the establishment of an identity which includes independence from one's parents, it is necessary for an adolescent to have the opportunity to reach out for that independence. Particularly in times of significant and rapid social change such as we are experiencing today, it is difficult for parents to be able to be sensitive to the difference between what are to the adolescent reasonable demands for autonomy and acceptance by his peers, and what are to them dangerous behaviours against which their child should be protected. Isolation of age groups from one another, altering of community bonds (particularly in cities), and perhaps, most important, the rapidity of social change have created a significant impact upon the ability of one generation to understand the accepted practices of the other. It may be in Conger's words, 'a world they never knew' from the parents' perspective, or 'a world they never made' from the perspective of the adolescent.[27]

Some writers today suggest that, because of changes in the structure and nature of the family, and in the nature of our society itself, the family has lost the ability to assist its young people into maturity. Although the ways in which families help or hinder adolescents are not entirely clear, the movement from dependence to independence and the accomplishment of a number of other important developmental tasks are clearly the domain of the adolescent. The family influences its children and continues through adolescence to play an active role in helping or hindering its young in their move to independence. Abundant literature exists dealing with the nature of these relationships. The effects of social class, ethnicity, and education are only a few of the ways in which families are known to influence their children; some of these effects are dealt with elsewhere in this chapter, and in other chapters in this book.

It is perhaps the lack of blueprints against which parents of today's adolescents are reacting; it is true that not only are adolescents confronted with situations that are unknown, that lack boundaries and rites of passage, but their parents, too, are dealing with situations and issues in which it is unclear what they should do in order to be 'good parents.' It is here where (according to Mead) the substance of the contemporary 'generation gap' may develop.[28]

A clear example of the kinds of conflict which may arise between adolescents and their families is generational difference with regard to attitudes towards use of marijuana. In the 1960s, along with other symbols of the youth culture, marijuana use among adolescents increased tremendously; although statistical studies reporting numbers and percentages of marijuana smokers showed wide variations, it is undeniable that use became reasonably widespread among young people.[29] Initial adult response to the phenomenon was one of concern, and alarm, and frequently punishment. Parents from a generation which had viewed all illicit drug use as irrevocably addicting and destructive to physical and intellectual capacities were often panic-stricken when they learned of their own adolescent's use of marijuana. Such use was seen by many adults as symbolic of an entire way of life with which they had little experience, and which they feared.

It is interesting to note that although peer drug use is a more powerful correlate, a number of studies have reported a positive correlation between parental use of licit drugs like alcohol, tobacco, tranquillizers, amphetamines, and barbiturates with their offspring's use of marijuana and other illicit drugs.[30] Kandel has called the inter- and intra-generational influences 'synergistic';[31] the correlational evidence for the influence of the family on the adolescent in the area of drug use is suggestive.

It is undeniably true that the modern family is being transformed in a variety of ways, and that, as a result, the ways in which adolescents become independent of their families are being affected both by the changes in the institutions of the family itself and by its social context. Nevertheless, almost all children are still raised in families which are ultimately responsible for their rearing and almost all young adults eventually become independent of their families. The modern adolescent must, like his predecessors, move towards independence, and modern parents, like their predecessors, must try to achieve the appropriate balance between protecting and granting autonomy to the maturing individual in their midst. While physical and intellectual maturity will come to normal adolescents without any special effort of their own, the struggle for independence is in large part an attempt to incorporate their new capabilities into a comprehensive and satisfactory adult self-image. This consolidation is the struggle for identity, one of the major tasks of adolescence.

The Role of Beliefs in Adolescence*

Evolving a personal value system and set of ideals and beliefs is a fundamental and important part of the task of identity resolution. It is known that moral values and attitudes begin to evolve at an early age[32] even before the child makes the transition from concrete to abstract reasoning.[33] Younger children are taught and most often espouse the values of their parents and, in fact, many adolescents adhere to the same attitudes, aspirations, and even prejudices of their parents.[34,35] Adolescent values which are engendered by peer group relations often turn out to be more superficial and transient than those fostered by their parents. Nonetheless, adolescents do often adopt ideologies which are at variance with their parents' point of view, and for the first time in their lives, these beliefs and values are largely autonomously derived and sustained.

An ideology or set of values is as vital to adolescents as to adults. It is, in part, a measure by which an individual can assess himself and it becomes more important as the adolescent grows older. Adelson, in some pioneering work makes a clear distinction between younger and older adolescents.[36] The former are much more absolutist, concrete, rigid, and inflexible than the latter. Both groups are wrestling with identity related issues and both are looking for causes in which they can believe, and which will even inspire them.[37] In the younger group, firmly held ideas and, more often, action-oriented behaviour are utilized to question the omniscience of the once idealized parents. These more fixed ideas and behaviours also help to overcome confusion in adapting to rapidly changing biological impulses (e.g. sexual, aggressive) and accelerated cognitive and sensory stimulation. In older adolescents, however, existential questions come more into focus, and experiences of alienation are much more common.[38,39]

Over the past few years adolescents have either been maligned or have themselves been idealized by our youth oriented society. We have learned much about the mythology of contemporary youth,[40] that they are neither paragons of virtue nor purveyors of iniquity. As in the general population, there are obviously those who are antisocial, even dangerous. Similarly, there are among our youth creative and dedicated idealists. But we are speaking here of the majority of adolescents, neither violent, nor saintly, nor disturbed. Numerous studies have shown that, while most adolescents appear to be resilient, adaptive, and enthusiastic about life,[41] many others of our youth manifest feelings of confusion, instability, and uncertainty.[42,43,44]

Adolescents have always noted and criticized the foibles and faults of their elders. This has been done on a personal level within families, in groups opposed

---

* This section, *The Role of Beliefs in Adolescence*, was written by Saul V. Levine.

to institutional procedures (e.g. school rules), or even within the context of mass movements. At times the criticism and campaigning have had beneficial effects on the social system involved – the family, the institution, or the society. At other times the criticisms have evolved into attacks which have been destructive to all concerned. But aside from effects on the social system involved, the adolescents' ability to believe in the rightness of their position serves an important personal protective device. For without an object to criticize, believing in oneself is more difficult to accomplish; it helps to define and crystallize one's own views. With a belief system there is a raison d'etre, and often a support group of like-minded peers. Further, without a set of values and beliefs, alienation and demoralization may result.[45,46,47]

For these reasons, adolescents are (and always have been) highly susceptible to ideologies, belief systems, and mass movements.[48,49,50] These movements have often been seen by their parents' generation as misguided, unsavory, or even dangerous or destructive. Movements or groups as diverse as political organizations, revolutionary groups, drug users, counterculture exponents, antisocial gangs, religious cultists, and others have all been labelled at one time or another along these lines. Again, we are not here speaking about clinically disturbed adolescents. But those who are feeling confused and unhappy are particularly vulnerable or receptive to easy answers. Voluntary membership in socially dissonant cults or group belief systems and subsequent behaviour patterns are most often a result of feelings of alienation and loneliness.[51] Feelings of loneliness or, conversely, feelings as an integral part of a group are important determinants of low or high self-esteem, respectively. Rosenberg has shown that susceptibility to beliefs and indoctrination is increased in adolescents with low self-esteem. Conversely, self-esteem rises in those who believe in their cause, and who feel that they belong to a cohesive group with shared activities and values.[52]

The conceptual framework of theorists who emphasize the intense social bonding needs of adolescents is primarily psychosocial, while the orientation of those who emphasize developmental issues is primarily intrapsychic.[53,54,55] However, the prevailing view of identity resolution as the primary task of adolescence certainly encompasses both perspectives.

We adopt Rokeach's view that a belief system represents an all-embracing set of attitudes, values, and beliefs which essentially define an individual's perception of and relationship with his or her external world.[56] Social bonding has been shown by anthropologists, ethologists, and psychiatrists to be as inherent a need of individuals as biological drive reduction. Yet, in contemporary society these two phenomena, beliefs and relationships, have been at least as decimated as any other. The detrimental effects of excessively rapid change have been well documented.[57,58] Leighton's components of psychosocial disintegration are in evidence.[59] All age groups have been affected, yet adolescents may have particular difficulty with instability. A sine qua non of this age group is change but in addition to responding to external flux, adolescents must cope with the internal physiological and cognitive changes. They are in double jeopardy, as it were. Families, which in the context of stability maintain a strong belief system and traditional family structure, seem best able to shield their youth from alienation, anomie, and destructive antisocial behaviour, like drug use.[60,61] Yet both elements seem to be waning in contemporary society: the family seems no longer sacrosanct, and common belief systems are less in evidence than ever before.[62]

We find that there are literally thousands of adolescents and youth across North America who have for a variety of reasons become immersed in social systems different from traditional family structure, or in conflict with dominant social values. They may adopt 'alternate' living arrangements on a voluntary basis, for example, religious ashrams, communes, therapeutic communities, drug houses, drop-in or runaway centres – crash pads, political groups, free clinics, alternative schools, or they may have such living arrangements imposed upon them as in the case of group homes, halfway houses, training schools, hospitals, therapeutic or corrective work farms, detention centres, pioneer programmes. Adolescents in the latter group may have been in conflict with the law, or societal values, or labelled as disturbed by professionals or lay individuals. Even in the voluntary group, however, the members are often in overt conflict with mainstream middle-class social values and lifestyles. Whatever the basis for their departure or extrusion from the family, these young people feel outside the system, and see themselves, and are seen by others, as not belonging. They fit Seaman's definition of alienation: feelings of normlessness, powerlessness, isolation, self-estrangement, and meaninglessness prevail.[63] In Frank's terms, because of their obvious demoralization, many clinicians would feel that these adolescents were prime candidates for various types of psychotherapy.[64]

Studies on contemporary youth over the past few years in urban communes, fringe religious movements, and work with normal adolescents, or those in therapeutic communities, group homes (corrective and therapeutic), and in psychotherapy, have shown that adolescents need a set of values and ideas to inspire them, and a group of peers to support them.[65] It may well be that the extent to which an external belief system, and a sense of belonging to a participating community exist in any of the above-mentioned social systems, will by and large determine the success or failure of the programme, the future direction of the young person, and even acceptance by the dominant society.

There are ongoing attempts to make use of the susceptibility of antisocial or alienated young people and the strengths inherent in belief systems and belonging in therapeutic, correctional, and rehabilitative programmes.[66,67,68,69] In these circumstances, the adolescents involved are already alienated, have started on the path of society's 'losers,' have been labelled by professionals as 'sick' or 'bad,' and will have significant emotional problems in a few years.[70]

But institutionalized adolescents are not the major focus of this discussion. *All* individuals in this age group benefit from a set of values and a sense of participating in and belonging to some form of social system. In the majority of instances, this is accomplished smoothly and informally. The beliefs and the *group* strengthen the individual's faith in himself and his society.

As was stated earlier, adolescents have to deal not only with a rapidly changing body and mind, but in moving towards a comprehensive sense of identity for the first time they are grappling with multiple external stimuli from an ever-changing reality. Added to this Zeitgeist – this era of unpredictability, of rapid technological advances, changing values, and multiple options, there is the spectre of double digit unemployment for urban youth. In a period of rapid social change and high unemployment for urban youth the possibility exists that we are creating conditions ripe for the utilization and possible exploitation of the energy, idealism, and commitment of young people on the one hand, and their alienation, demoralization, and anger on the other. Movements or behaviours mentioned above that are seen as deleterious to youth or to society can capture the imagination of young people. A belief system or a raison d'etre is provided there and a strong supportive group is engendered.

In North America the period of adolescence, at least as socially defined, has been prolonged artificially, largely because of higher education and economic dependence on parents. And their peculiar hiatus status – between childhood and adulthood – is partly enhanced by the unwillingness of adults to integrate them into the dominant society. The frustration in being told that they are capable and responsible, and yet not being given the corresponding rights, plays into their needs for a social system that *will* accept them.

Most adolescents are functioning well. They are part of cohesive families, have a shared value system, and feel accepted by their peers and others. It is the significant and potentially growing number who, for a variety of possible reasons feel alienated from society's potential, are of concern to us. Adolescents who have time and energy at their disposal, without constructive and meaningful social outlets, can get into trouble in a variety of ways. For example, the diverse areas of work and sexuality (see next section) are just two of the many possible sources of problems. To the extent that society cannot or will not fill the needs of believing and belonging in adolescents, we can expect to see the behavioural manifestations of frustration and unhappiness in many young people. This might take the form of membership in less than salutory groups for some, or apathy, restlessness, and demoralization in others. And this will be reflected in the unemployment, school dropout, crime and welfare statistics, which are dominated by 'normal' youth who are outside the mainstream of society.[71, 72] These young people are still disproportionately from lower socio-economic classes, but this is by no means universal. Recently more middle-class youth are increasingly represented in these statistics.[73, 74] Certainly in the drug scene and in religious cults, middle-class adolescents have comprised the majority of the members.[75] Hence socio-economic status is not the useful marker that it once may have been, at least in this context, because the problems of society are permeating *all* social classes.

If youth cannot believe in their society, it is a tremendous loss to them personally and to society as a whole. In order to minimize the social and psychological effects of societal dysfunction on adolescents, it is vital for this society first to realize that it *has* a problem, and second that it can only be mitigated or prevented if youth perceive that they have, and indeed *do* have, an important and respected role to play in a social system with a purpose.

Who Am I?

A man's character is discernible in the mental or moral attitude in which, when it came upon him, he felt himself most deeply and intensely active and alive. At moments there is a voice inside which speaks and says, '*This* is the real me.'[76]

Eric Erikson has used the words of William James to illustrate what he calls a sense of identity. The formation of identity, says Erikson, is a process 'by which the individual judges himself in the light of what he perceives to be the way in which others judge him in comparison to themselves ...; while he judges their way of judging him in the light of how he perceives himself in comparison to them.'[77]

A critical task of adolescence is finding, or beginning to find, an answer to the question 'who am I?' For many social scientists, adolescent socialization is synonymous with the formation of identity, the differentiation of oneself as a distinct personality, related to, but not bounded by one's family and society.

Identity formation begins early in childhood, and continues throughout one's lifetime. However, adolescence, to Erikson, is the time when identity formation 'meets its crisis.' It is in adolescence that decisions are made which are, if not irrevocable, frequently difficult to undo, and are, more often than in childhood, made by the adolescent himself. Choices that are bad from the point of view of the individual are those which lead to a lack of coherence of the personality and may mean identity confusion. This does not imply that 'good' choices are necessarily those which are normative and approved. As was mentioned earlier in this chapter, some experts believe that conflict between the adolescent and his society is necessary to successful personality integration and that a character formed in the easiest of conditions will be a weak one.

It is important to note two critical aspects of notions about the development of identity in adolescence. First, one's own identity develops throughout childhood out of the variety of identifications with individuals such as parents, teachers, relatives, friends, heroes, and with cultural, religious, national, ethnic, or other groups; it is the sum, and yet greater than the sum of these identifications, which eventually may tell the individual who he is. Second, the individual and the culture cannot be separated in a discussion of the formation of identity, because, as Erikson says, 'the two help to define each other, and are truly relative to each other.'[78]

As Conger has pointed out, young children may not need to have an integrated sense of themselves because their cognitive abilities are limited, their world is protected, and the choices they must make are few and simple.[79] The adolescent, while undergoing a variety of complex simultaneous changes physically, emotionally and cognitively, is faced with the need to make decisions which, if not in the long term, certainly in the short term, have profound implications for him.

Particularly in a time of rapid social change, presented with contradictory information about what are the correct and possible choices for him to make, and with plural and ambiguous adult role models, it is easy for the adolescent to fall victim to confusion about who he is and where he is going.

Conclusions from empirical research on how modern adolescents may best be prepared for and assisted through the task of developing an identity in a broad sense are notably lacking. The term identity, as Erikson used it, is an intentionally broad one and for our purposes here has been used in that way. At the same time, it is important to consider some substantive areas where adolescents of today may encounter problems in developing a full sense of who they are.

II THE TRANSITION FROM SCHOOL TO WORK

In his discussion of the demands of adolescence in the formation of identity, Erikson has said, 'In general, it is the inability to settle on an occupational identity which most disturbs young people,'[80] and, as Bronfenbrenner has pointed out, 'if a child is to become a responsible person, he not only must be exposed to adults engaged in demanding tasks, but he himself must participate in such tasks.'[81] However, there is evidence that today at least some of this inability may be quite external to the adolescent and may have to do more with changing technology, the economy, and the lack of opportunities for testing possible occupational identities than with adolescents themselves.

The time of entry into the labour force is a time of transition which is experienced by most members of our society. The adolescent moves from school to work, from economic dependence to independence and from youth to adulthood in the same space of time. One of the important decisions that an adolescent must make is the kind of work at which he will spend, usually, the next four or five decades of his life. From his or her work an individual derives income, self-esteem, satisfaction (or dissatisfaction), interests, and friends.

The boundaries of this transitional phase are not clearly defined; for many people, the first steps towards career choice are made early in childhood, long before the actual move into adulthood occurs; even when career choices are made, the possibility exists that changing technology and demography may necessitate shifts in careers. Currently, education 'finishes' at graduation; it is not yet considered an open-ended or lifelong process. Adolescents may begin moving into the labour force while still in school by holding a part-time job, by involvement in a work experience programme, or as a student in a vocational programme. Sometimes a choice is never made, and a worker may spend his life switching jobs or careers.

At one time in North America, and still, in more traditional societies, decisions about what kind of work to do were circumscribed by gender, position in the community, and what kind of work one's parents did. Today, however, although the boundaries of mobility are still defined for much of the population by social class, educational opportunities, gender roles, and geography, the limits are much less clearly drawn.

In traditional agrarian societies, the occupational choices available to youth were limited; vocations were defined for children by the roles of their parents and filled the needs of a simpler culture. The transition to adult work was gradual, moving from observation and apprenticeship into fully adult work roles. Education was both informal and work centred, so that education and occupation were simultaneous and interrelated. In effect, there was no transition from school to work; schooling was 'on the job.'

However, with advances in technology, in much of the world jobs have become highly specialized and the number of possibilities has proliferated. At the same time, with increased urbanization, adolescents have been isolated in their own institutions: the school system, youth recreational places or facilities, and, in the latter part of the twentieth century, in the 'youth culture.' Our relatively affluent society has played a major role in lengthening the time adolescents stay in school, remain economically dependent, and avoid the world of work.

Unlike agrarian societies, where socialization occurred through contact with parents and other adults in the community, in industrial societies the effect of the combination of increased specialization and isolation has in effect been to remove adolescents from contact with the world of adult work. Although even today adolescents in small towns or in a few well-integrated urban neighbourhoods may have the opportunity to become familiar with a small number of occupations, in general, the work-world contains thousands of jobs with which most adolescents have no contact and about which they have no information.

School as Preparation for Work: Functions and Purposes

The goal of education in pre-twentieth century America was to transmit academic knowledge; as Herman et al. have pointed out, 'old fashioned American high schools, with their classical curricula, used to graduate an elite; educationally, they were terminal points (college was for a much smaller elite); occupationally, they were way-stations for the solid citizens of tomorrow.'[82]

The high schools of today educate a much larger proportion of students; yet data on how well they are being educated in traditional academic subjects indicate that, as Silberman believes, longer and more expensive schooling does not necessarily mean better schooling.[83] Although educators still consider training in basic skills to be one of the goals of an educational system, some express concern about the decline in these abilities.[84] Studies indicate that, in recent years, Canadian and American students have had declining scores on a variety of traditional measures of academic achievement.[86] Although over the past 25 years studies indicate that on standardized tests of basic skills students have made some gains in the long term,[87] in recent years Canadian and American students have had declining scores on a variety of traditional measures of academic achievement.[88,89]

The family and the community were at one time the primary institution proving most of the socialization for adult work for children; now it is the school that dominates this function. During the critical years between six and sixteen, most children are enrolled in public schools, spending about 30 hours a week there, and an additional number of hours engaged in homework and other school-related activities. Although the family with its own sociocultural values and dynamics is the predominant influence on the child's future as an adult, and determines the nature of the school experience, the family's effect is mediated through the school system, and vice versa.

As the influence of other social institutions (the family, the community, the work place, and the church) has been reduced in western culture, the role of the school has expanded. Not only are contemporary schools responsible for the development of academic skills required by a labour market demanding increasing specialization and credentials; they are now regarded as the obvious institution to train non-academically inclined youth for work and to develop a variety of non-cognitive abilities and values. Historically, we are at a point where, as Herman et al. have pointed out, 'interest (in youth) leads us almost reflexively to talk about education which they often take to be a universal nostrum. It is so regarded at this moment by a whole host of observers, laymen and experts alike.' Discussion of delinquency prevention includes a nod to the accumulated evidence that delinquency is frequently associated with poor school performance and adjustment, low self-esteem, and dropping out without marketable job skills. In recent years, a great deal of emphasis has been placed on the importance of the school's role in encouraging personal growth by development of creativity, curiosity, and social skills in special courses[90] or, at least, by providing environments which would not stifle these characteristics held by many to be innate features of childhood. Other activities for youth which were once outside the scope of the school system's sphere are a range of extra-curricular programmes, community projects, and work-related activities.

Perhaps the most important social responsibility which has been thrust upon the school system in the past ten or twenty years has been that of serving as a panacea for society's inequalities. This has taken shape in Canada as special attention paid to the rights of New and Native Canadian children to learn English in special programmes, and, at the same time, to develop self-esteem by maintenance of their cultural integrity in special multi-ethnic programmes. In the United States, too, the civil rights movement demanded compensatory education and open admissions for those who had been inadequately compensated for oppression in the social order. Many have argued that schools have perpetuated society's inequities· early streaming and stigmatization have been linked to lower motivation and interest, lower educational expectations, and lower levels of education for poor, immigrant, and minority group children.[91]

The responsibility of being the agent of providing social mobility by offering an opportunity for every student to get an equal education, together with the recognition that difference in academic interest and aptitude exist, has created what is known as streaming, or tracking. Rather than rewarding students differentially for a variety of talents, it rewards some by encouraging them to pursue further education, and assumes that those who are unable to go on will, by default, need to be trained to work at a trade. As Evans has pointed out '(American) education is designed for one basic purpose – to prepare the student for subsequent schooling ... Intelligence tests are designed to predict success in only one undertaking – schooling. Guidance counselling is limited almost entirely to helping the student to choose and prepare for a higher level of schooling. Teachers and curricula alike are judged on the proportion of students who succeed at the next higher level of schooling.'[92]

School Programmes: Influences and Choice
One of the 'choices' with which adolescents are confronted early in this period is which programme to enter in high school or, in some localities, which high

school to enter. The range of possibilities may be as small as a choice between an academic or non-academic diploma or, in a large city like Toronto, for example, entrance into any one of six levels of programme, including academically competitive high schools in which the student body is university bound, vocational or technical schools offering vocational programmes and a general diploma. Of course, the student's choice has essentially been made for him by his prior record in school, which is, in turn, determined by his innate intellectual ability, his socio-economic status, and the influence of his family.

Belonging to a particular social class influences one's vocational future in a number of ways, beginning with experiences in school. It has long been recognized that students from economically advantaged backgrounds have significant advantages over their working-class or disadvantaged peers in terms of their perception of their own ability[93] and standard school achievement.[94] Although the interaction among economic status, parental levels of education and aspirations, self-esteem, and student's attitudes towards school are subtle, it may be said with certainty that as a group, middle-class youth are better students than their poorer schoolmates, for whatever reason.

However, it also seems to be true that peer and parental influences may serve to override the general effects of social class on academic success and that, indeed, the term 'middle class' is being used as a surrogate for other factors. Students from poor families who go to 'high-status' schools are more likely to go on to university than their poor peers who go to 'low-status' schools.[95,96] This principle, which was behind the emphasis on busing in the United States, fails to operate if the character of the school is changed by moving too many poor students into the area. Additionally, influences within the family itself, based on ethnic or individual attitudes serve to create an orientation towards education.[97] In a study of adolescent boys by Bachman et al., it was found that socio-economic status was not as accurate a predictor of attitudes towards school as relations within the family.[98] Similarly, Simpson found that although middle-class status was one factor in predicting high educational and vocational aspirations, adolescents from working-class families which held high educational and occupational hopes for their offspring had higher educational aspirations than youth from middle-class families who had lower aspirations.[99]

Vocational Programmes
A goal which has been more and more widely accepted as one of the roles which the school system should play is that of preparing youth for work. Although commentators on education have argued that the primary function of the school system has become, de facto, that of educating youth for more and more education,[100,101] it has become obvious that higher education is neither reasonable nor

desirable for everybody and that a disservice is being done youth who are encouraged to believe this is so. Venn emphasizes the importance of vocational and technical education as the occupational preparation for most youth[102] and, as youth unemployment rates have risen higher and higher in the 60s and 70s, the need for career and vocational programmes, vocational counselling, work experience, and co-operative education programmes has been increasingly emphasized.

The purpose of vocational or occupational programmes is to train youth to make a direct transition to work at the conclusion of the programme. Although all instruction may be said to have value for occupational purposes, a typical vocational curriculum includes a combination of laboratory work, classroom instruction related to the occupation being studied, general education in reading and spoken English, elementary social studies, and in some cases, more advanced academic subjects. One of the emphases of vocational education is upon helping students see practical applications of theory, a value which educators have stressed in recent years for all students.[103]

The dichotomy between general, academic and vocational education is controversial; although some vocational courses have tried to enhance the prestige of their programmes by selecting the best of the students available to them, the highest status has been reserved for academic, post-secondary bound students. Even with the development of a range of vocational programmes, including highly specialized training for those with the most ability, and special programmes for those with more limited capabilities, they are, as Mihalka has observed, frequently seen as a holding area for young people from low income families.[104]

The history of vocational education in North America reaches back into the nineteenth century, with the introduction of commercial training, agriculture, household science, and manual training into the secondary school curriculum, and separate day and night schools specializing in the same subjects. The trend in the early part of the twentieth century was for the development of separate vocational and technical schools; later, in the period after World War II, the trend reversed and composite schools were established, with one aim being the social mixing of students from various programmes. Today, in large cities there are often a variety of alternatives, with some specialized vocational and technical schools offering a wide range of subjects, and composite schools with both academic and vocational students. Although there is a trend in some rural areas to establish area vocational schools, outside large cities the composite school is most common.[105]

With the rise in youth unemployment through the 60s and 70s, increased emphasis has been placed on training young people for specific jobs, and although for a period a university degree has been seen as the most necessary credential for success, there have been many individuals who stress the utility of vocational training and have called for a rethinking of some of its problems.[106,107]

In an era of rapidly changing technology and job categories, one of the flaws of which vocational programmes have often been accused is that of too narrow specialization. Yet Evans has observed that, to the contrary, vocational education is often broad enough to prepare a student for a fairly diverse range of jobs within a specialty; for example, as Evans has noted, skills learned in a metals trades programme actually prepare a graduate to enter about 200 different jobs defined in the *Dictionary of Occupational Titles*.[108]

Another problem of vocational programmes is the stigma, or labelling which may result. Students are streamed into occupational or vocational programmes for a variety of reasons. Some are identified as slow learners as early as elementary school and may enter directly into a vocational programme. Others, with the direction and encouragement of teachers and guidance personnel, have the 'option' of transferring into a vocational programme at the beginning of high school. In some places – Ontario, for example – it is possible for vocational students of higher academic ability in a composite school to take advantage of courses in the general academic stream. Others entering vocational programmes may be young adults returning to school to learn a trade, students with a variety of learning disabilities, students from training schools, and those with language and behavioural problems. In almost every case, emphasis is placed not on the reward of different abilities and the real acceptance of individual difference, but on an implicit acceptance of a status hierarchy which rewards those who do well academically and stigmatizes and lumps together those adolescents who 'cannot cope' with academic work.[109]

Evidence exists to support the fact of stigmatization. A Toronto Board of Education study indicated that students in the vocational programmes studied often refuse to admit outside the school that they attend a vocational school, and Harvey and Masemann also commented that in their study there was evidence of stigmatizing by other students and by the local school board.[110,111] This is not surprising when one considers that the streaming system in most school systems, although developed as a way of practically helping each student develop to the maximum of his potential, has, because of the overlay of the culture's emphasis upon status defined by education, helped to perpetuate the very status hierarchy which the demands for equality of opportunity of the 60s and 70s sought to abolish. Because the school operates within a social context with its set of values firmly entrenched in the culture, the system of streams, tracks, or levels of a school system places students who succeed academically in the 'top' post-secondary bound stream, and those who are unsuccessful in the vocational, lower or work-force bound stream.

The problem is further compounded by the fact that in a tight economy, jobs go to higher-achieving students.[112,113] Although some vocational students move on to further education or training after completion of the vocational programme, graduates often do not qualify academically for apprenticeship programmes; Harvey and Masemann report that the vocational programme completion certificate is often not accepted by employers as the proper credential. Thus graduates are frequently prevented from working in the areas for which they were trained.[114] One reason for this may have to do, again, with the prestige assigned to education in our culture; frequently in a buyer's job market, when jobs for youth are in short supply, employers establish educational requirements which may not actually be necessary to do the job. In a sense, the stigmatizing process that has poorly served vocational students throughout their school careers follows them through the transition from school to work and into the labour market.

School Dropouts: Who They Are and What Happens to Them

Dropping out of school, that is, leaving school without a high school diploma or certificate, has been considered a waste of the talents of our young people; many people feel that the young dropout is likely to be seriously disadvantaged in later life. Efforts in the form of media campaigns are made to encourage adolescents to stay in school and programmes are designed to help them re-enter the high school system if they have dropped out.

In addition, the costs to a society, in monetary and human terms, have been considered. Dropouts, because their employment opportunities are limited, are seen as potential welfare recipients, as payers of low or no tax revenues to support government services, unproductive members of society from an economic point of view, as potentially delinquent or criminal and requiring expenditures for related support services, as unlikely to be fully involved as voters or politically informed, and as likely to be the parents of the poor of the next generation.[115]

How valid are these arguments which have been marshalled against adolescents dropping out of school? Copious research has investigated the reasons for leaving school before graduation and somewhat fewer studies have looked at the consequences of dropping out. There is agreement among researchers on a number of the antecedents of dropping out but less concurrence on the interpretation of data on the consequences.

Bachman has presented a 'stereotyped dropout picture - a "loser," delinquent, with low self-esteem, lacking in ambition and unable to control his own destiny.'[116] Peebles, in summarizing research on dropping out, expands this stereotype, citing studies investigating ability and school-related factors (average or below average intelligence, poor reading skills, one or more grades repeated, little or no participation in extracurricular activities, discipline problems, dislike of school courses, failure to see relationship between courses and future employment, and insecurity in school status, family related factors (low socio-economic level, large family, low academic aspirations, frequently a member of a 'drop-out-prone family,' lack of encouragement [at home], low occupational aspirations, broken home, and individual personality and behaviour factors [low self-esteem, feeling of isolation and alienation and anxiety]). There is general agreement among a large number of studies, with, of course, some individual variation on this stereotype.[117] Bachman makes the case that dropping out is 'symptomatic of certain background and ability characteristics, school experiences and traits of personality and behavior'[118] which are mismatched with a typical high school environment.

In Bachman's view, with which others concur,[119] it is not the act of dropping out per se that is important. Rather, he argues that the dropout was a 'loser' even prior to dropping out of school; in Bachman's before-and-after sample, the characteristics listed above were present when the sample was first encountered at grade 10. Although the background, school, and ability factors are related to dropping out, the consequences may be as related to these factors as to the actual act of dropping out. That is, dropping out is another symptom, rather than a problem in and of itself.

The most common public conception is that high school dropouts will have a difficult time finding work in a slow labour market, are likely to be delinquent, and will be less satisfied with their jobs and income than high school graduates. Although relationships have been established between dropout status and some of these variables, it is questionable whether the relationship is causal. And, secondly, data on some of these questions are contradictory.

There is no clear evidence that dropouts are likely to be unemployed. Although data on unemployment rates by age group and educational attainment have been interpreted as meaning that '14 - 19 year olds not completing high school have unemployment rates verging on a disastrous 20 percent,'[120] figures for a comparable age group who were completing high school were unavailable because most of them were still in high school. Even though it is true, as mentioned earlier in this paper, that employers may tend to require credentials out of proportion to the job, the high unemployment rate for this group may also have to do with their age and lack of training, rather than with their having dropped out. In Bachman's study, which collected data on a cohort of young men as they moved through and out of school, about 71 per cent of dropouts were employed full time, compared with 87 per cent of high school graduates of the same age. Several Canadian studies found that unemployment rates for dropouts were lower than those in the United States discussed by Levin;[121,122] some of the contradictions between these data may be attributable either to local labour markets or to differences in survey techniques. However, when trying to clarify the relationship between dropping out of school and unemployment, a number of factors must be considered.

First, the official statistics available are confounded by the number of very young workers who, by necessity, fall into the dropout category. Second, it is obvious that lack of education and training are serious obstacles to job placement, and, according to Canadian census data, those who are at the greatest disadvantage educationally, the earliest dropouts, are less likely to receive vocational training of a variety of kinds after entering the labour force.[123] Third, as Bachman has suggested based on data from his four-year study, it is necessary to consider the antecedents of dropping out when looking at the consequences. If one looks at what is known about today's slow job market, which has few jobs for young people in any case, higher unemployment rates for dropouts may be associated as much with family, school, and ability characteristics, the reasons for which they dropped out of school, as with the fact that they are dropouts.[124] It should be noted that research considering the relationship between dropping out of school and unemployment is most typically done shortly after leaving school; in this regard, Super's comment that dropouts tend to move down the occupational ladder after acquiring several years experience is relevant.[125]

Similarly, the view that the relationship between high delinquency rates and dropping out is causal has been questioned by Bachman and by Wenk. Perhaps, as Wenk has suggested, dropping out is part of a progressive phenomenon in a series of delinquency-associated unproductive school experiences.[126] The Bachman study reports that, although on the dimension of delinquent and rebellious behaviour, dropouts distinctly stood out from stayins, and that these behaviours may be seen as a precursor of dropping out, there was no indication that delinquency increased as a result of dropping out.[127]

Investigation of dropouts' satisfaction with jobs and income has produced contradictory results. Bachman found that in his sample, employed dropouts' incomes were almost equal to those of graduates; more of the dropouts (3/4) than of the graduates (2/3) rated themselves as 'quite' or 'very' satisfied with their jobs.[128] However, American census data indicate that the income differential between high school graduates and non-graduates has increased and Levin's interpretation of the data indicates that the differential is unlikely to decrease.[129] Job satisfaction was one issue considered in a Canadian study, and although dropouts were not considered separately within the sample of young workers surveyed, some inferences may be drawn from the finding that the vast majority of the youngest workers, under 19, felt that they were not in 'career' jobs, and indicated a desire to be so.[130] Together with information about the fewer opportunities for those at the lowest end of the educational spectrum, the dropouts entering career ladders, it may be seen that long-range job satisfaction may be questionable for dropouts.

One of the most important things to understand about the issue of dropping out of high school is that distinctions in income, mobility, and satisfaction are more evident when contrasting individuals who attend university with all those who do not, than between high school dropouts and high school graduates. Viewing this together with statistics relating family background, and ability characteristics to motivation to succeed in school and the likelihood of university entrance, it may be seen that educational achievement lies along a continuum with variables associated with high socio-economic status generally defining the university-bound contingent at one end of the continuum, and factors related to low socio-economic status defining the other end, the dropouts. Although some writers on the problems of dropping out are still using the landmark of a high school diploma as a cut-off point below which one is inadequately educated,[131] Bachman's data which show very small differences on a number of dimensions between dropouts and high school graduates, and larger ones between the university bound and all others, would support the view that a high school diploma may no longer be the key to success, economic or otherwise.[132]

The Limits of Schooling
It is true that because of its universality, as Coleman has pointed out, 'school is the sector of society that can be explicitly designed to meet the needs of the young. However, one problem which derives from the nature of the school-learning situation itself is that, because he is in the role of a learner, an absorber rather than a doer, a student's opportunity to take other roles which would prepare him for adulthood is limited by the school environment. A variety of needs can only be served by a variety of institutions. Up to a point, the variety may be provided within a single comprehensive structure. But there are limits on how far any organization can be asked to stretch and still function effectively, especially when it is vulnerable to a turbulent environment of contradictory and shifting group demands. There are also limits on how comprehensive any educational organization can be without blandness eroding all sense of purpose and enterprise.'[133] As the schools have become the primary institutions which serve youth, they have been overwhelmed with the burden of trying to be all things to all people. As their goals have become diffuse and blurred, it has become obvious that they have been unable to fulfil well any of their multiple goals.

Perhaps it is in trying to meet a variety of goals which are essentially in conflict, for all members it serves, that the schools have run into the morass of problems with which they are now confronted. A goal of helping each student develop to a maximum of his potential as an individual, together with the reliance on education as the great social leveller, encourages teachers to help students to get as much schooling as they can, and to raise their expectations as high as possible. On the other hand, economic forces beyond the control of educators have created a job situation which means that many of the heightened expectations of youth for careers, interesting work, and some autonomy may not be met in the workplace.

Adolescents in the Labour Market
Traditionally, economists have studied the relationship of youth and the labour market only in the context of more general studies of the supply and demand for labour in different occupational categories. However, in the 1970s, youth unemployment has assumed proportions large enough to indicate the makings of a massive social problem and has created the impetus for an aroused interest in the place of youth in the labour market. In a transition from school to work, even with the best possible counselling and preparation, and a work ethic equal to that of the early Calvinists, there must be places available to which adolescents may make a transition. In the latter part of the 1970s, the hard reality with which youth are confronted, whether they leave school early, leave after high school graduation, or complete any one of a number of possible post-secondary courses, up to and including the PHD, is that there are too few appropriate places in the work force into which they may move.

Youth unemployment is not a new problem; in Canada, it was the vision of large numbers of unemployed young people idling in the cities of the late 1800s which provided the initiative for the first compulsory education law in 1870. At that time, as now, a major factor creating unemployment was new technology – in that case, the move to industrialization in factories and on farms. Some years later, at the time of the Great Depression of 1929, young people were once again idling, with no jobs and no prospects. The entry into World War II pulled the economy out of the doldrums to the prosperity of the 40s and early 1950s.

However, even before World War II had drawn to a close, Canadians were looking forward to a future when once again we would be faced with young people with nothing to do. The *Canadian Youth Commission*, established in 1943, considered the post-war situation: 'it would appear that as many as three-quarters of a million young people under the age of 25, possibly closer to a million, will be in need of new jobs or other constructive peacetime occupation in the period of post-war adjustment. What is the prospect of such opportunities being available to them?,' the Commission asked.[134]

Even at the time that the Commission published its report in 1945, it was recognized that when work is scarce, youth, especially the youngest group under 21, have a more difficult time finding work than older, more experienced workers.

Teenagers have always been more susceptible to unemployment than other age groups, and have been the group most affected by cyclical economic variations. However, in Canada in the last 20 years, a steady trend has caused an already high youth unemployment rate to reach, in 1978, in some regions of Canada, over 30% for 15-19 year-olds. Although young workers constitute less than 30% of the labour force in Canada, they make up nearly 50% of the unemployed. Actual unemployment rates among young people vary considerably from province to province, but the seasonally adjusted unemployment rate for young people is close to 15% or about 400,000 young Canadians in 1977.[135] In Ontario, statistics on unemployment rates by age and sex groups from 1973 to 1976 indicate that youth unemployment is a high and increasing percentage of total unemployment, and a more serious problem statistically for young males. Canada is not anomalous in this; the United States and much of the West show similar trends.[136]

These official unemployment rates are seen as underestimates by many experts. For example, a recent report comments that, according to the 1971 census, there were 187,000 15-19 year-olds who were neither in school nor working.[137] Even if some of these teenagers were women with young children who had chosen not to seek work, it may be reasonable to assume that some of the others were 'discouraged workers,' that is, those who have left the official labour force by ceasing to seek jobs. In addition, there is the phenomenon of involuntary part-time employment. Interpretation of Statistics Canada reports indicate that there are many youthful workers, especially young women, who are working part-time only because full-time work was unavailable.[138] It has also been suggested that the seasonal presence of students in the labour force is buried in the aggregate youth unemployment rate figures and hides a relatively higher rate for the group which has the most problems finding jobs, the non-students or those who have left school.[139]

Finally, the problem of underemployment should be considered. Although there has been no official calculation of this problem, one indication of the problem of underemployment, from the point of view of the youthful worker himself, is the finding in *Canadian Work Values* that almost 3/4 of workers aged 16-24 wanted to be in jobs leading to 'careers' but, in their own view, were not.[140] Whether or not underemployment is a phenomenon related merely to increased formal credentials and to high expectations, but not to skill, is unknown. However, high aspirations and expectations related to having a specialized skill or a degree do not ensure finding a job in one's field or any job, for that matter.[141] Finally, it is known that some youths who would prefer to work stay in the school system because it is difficult to find work.[142]

Whatever the precise percentages of the youth unemployment rate, it is generally agreed that it is a problem of sizeable magnitude.[143] The youth unemployment situation is potentially explosive politically and economically and a recently released report by Statistics Canada indicates that the idea that the situation will be eased as the 'baby boom' population ages is a myth.[144] It has been suggested that young workers who suffer long periods of unemployment, or who work at low level, dead-end jobs, will be affected permanently by their experiences; unemployed young people today may carry poor work patterns into the future.[145] The labour force entry point has profound consequences for the individual's work history; although there certainly are exceptions, generally, a low-paying dead-end first job means a different kind of work history than a first job which is prestigious, and carries the possibility of upgrading and training.

When the population and participation rate changes are put together, it is indicated that the young labour force will continue to grow until 1981. Therefore, the unemployment situation is serious for youth not only today but has significant implications for the future. How has this situation developed?

First, high youth unemployment rates have become a consistent feature of the economic environment; in Canada, in only 3 of the past 18 years has the unemployment rate for young men aged 14–19, the group with the highest rate, been below 10 per cent.[146] This condition of high consistent youth unemployment has also been true for American populations. It has been suggested that one of the primary causes of this has been technological advances which have abetted the disappearance of entry level jobs for unskilled or semi-skilled youth for whom one historical route into work began with these jobs. Now the bottom of the occupational ladder frequently demands qualifications that the youngest group of workers lacks.

Secondly, the cyclical variation of the youth unemployment rate is greater than that of all other groups in the labour force. That is, at times of economic decline when jobs are in short supply, youth, especially teenagers, are the most severely affected. The adage 'last hired, first fired' seems to apply here; adolescent workers lack seniority, are rarely union members and, in an employment market where there are adults competing with teenagers for jobs, employers will tend to hire older, more experienced workers.[147]

Thirdly, today's young people are present in the labour force today in unprecedented numbers. During the 1965-70 period, the growth in the youth labour force was due almost solely to population increases – the so-called 'baby boom' population reaching maturity. Since 1970, however, in addition to a continued increase in the size of the youth population, there has been an increase in the labour force participation rate for teenagers. That is, the long-term downward trend in the participation rate for teenagers, due to an increase in industrialization and a demand for better trained manpower, increased access to higher education, and increased familial pressures to more education stemming from parents' higher educational attainment resolved by teenagers' staying in school longer, has been interrupted by a short-term trend in the 1970s which has resulted in more young people (relative to the previous 10 years) leaving school to enter the labour force.[148]

Other factors have been suggested which would exacerbate the high rate of unemployment: low levels of motivation to work; insistence on unrealistically high wages and conditions; rise in the minimum wage together with low productivity of adolescent workers which does not warrant payment of a minimum wage by employers, and a mismatch in supply and demand of skills and work.

In economic terms, the major factors which statistically swell the youth unemployment figures are both frictional and structural. Analysis of frictional unemployment uncovers non-economic bases which contribute. Frictional unemployment refers to the amount of job changing which occurs, resulting in periods of unemployment while the worker is seeking a new job. Young workers exhibit a greater propensity to leave jobs, to shop around in the labour market, and even to completely change fields than older workers.[149,150,151] Indeed, Piker has suggested that this 'shopping around' period following school-leaving should be considered as part of the occupational choice process, and seen as pre-entry into the labour force.[152] Certainly, young workers, still in the process of personal development may need forays into a variety of kinds of jobs before embarking on a career choice, particularly in view of the lack of information and experience they get while still in the school system. Nevertheless, high frictional unemployment for young workers means that there are large numbers of them periodically swelling the ranks of job seekers competing for the small number of entry level jobs available.

Structural unemployment has to do with a mismatch in the supply and demand for labour. Some of this is, in Canada, geographical or regional. Although there has recently been considerable geographical mismatch between supply and demand in all occupations, the mismatch is even more pronounced in what are considered to be youth intensive occupations. The Atlantic, Pacific, and Quebec regions have had a disproportionate share of unemployment in general, and youth unemployment in particular.[153] Further than geographical mismatch, however, is the problem of a mismatch in the qualifications of young people and those which the whole labour market requires. This is certainly related to the school system, whether it is due to the particular training adolescents are receiving for work in occupations where no jobs exist, while other occupations lack trained workers, or to lack of training at all. If a considerable amount of the preparation for the work world takes place in the school, the kind of links forged between the educational system and the labour market are salient.

*Youth Employment Programmes**

In response to the growing problem of youth unemployment, a number of initiatives have been taken during the past decade, primarily by government. While some new programmes are geared exclusively to in-school students as part of their curriculum, and others exclusively to unemployed, out-of-school young 'workers,' increasingly programmes are designed to address the school-to-work transition. The desire to 'bridge the gap' between school and work, the theme of a major conference in Ontario in 1975, is expressed in the title of a coordinating group in metro Toronto which brings together representatives from a variety of youth employment projects and concerns.[154]

Major sponsors of programmes directed to the problem of youth unemployment in both Canada and the United States are senior levels of government, although there are marked differences between the two in overall philosophy and approach.

Canadian Programmes[155]

In contrast to the centrally planned and evaluated American programmes described subsequently in this section, those operating in Canada represent a patchwork of seemingly uncoordinated efforts with very uneven evaluation components. Under a wide variety of federal and provincial auspices, and directed towards different goals and different groups within the youth population, they generally defy succinct description. A recent government report,[156] for example, lists over thirty distinct programmes typically identified by acronyms or initials (JET, LEAP, OCAP, OYEP, CSYEP, YAT, YES, etc.).

In general, most of the existing programmes in Canada can be classified into three types on the basis of their intent and population served: those which provide a work experience as part of a school programme, those addressing the search for or selection of a job or career, and those which provide a job or work experience to young people who have permanently or temporarily (summer students) left school.

Work experience programmes offered in conjunction with formal secondary schooling are variously titled 'cooperative education,' 'work experience,' 'work study,' 'community involvement,' etc. Most such programmes have emerged in response to the growing concern, articulated by critics such as Coleman[157] and Illich,[158] that adolescents have become isolated from direct experience and that schools are out of touch with the 'real' world. As a result, cooperative education programmes, to use the term most commonly in use in Ontario, place students in

---

* The following section, *Youth Employment Programmes*, was written by Linda Hagarty, with the assistance of Lyn Uzans.

job settings for periods ranging from one or two weeks per year to half-time in alternating school-work blocks. In return for their contribution, students are rewarded either with academic credits or payment at the minimum wage at least.

Guidelines for cooperative education issued by the Ontario Ministry of Education[159] prescribe that 'a certificated teacher on the school staff ... must be involved in the out-of-school portion to the extent of identifying objectives ... working cooperatively with outside supervisors ... visiting and monitoring the out-of-school activities ... and evaluating the student's performance.' Interpretations of the guidelines by different boards of education can result in either expanded or restricted work opportunities for students.

Although cooperative education programmes have received considerable attention in educational literature and the popular press, systematic evaluations are rare. As Weaver has concluded, 'most recent publications in the field have been more descriptive than definitive, more promotional than analytical, and more practical than theoretical.'[160] In reviewing the literature for one of the few published evaluations, in this case of a community involvement programme in Etobicoke, Ontario, which placed students in community service agencies, Usher cites a handful of American studies and one previous Canadian evaluation of a similar programme by the Ontario Institute for Studies in Education.[161] Usher's study found the positive benefits for the participating students included gains in knowledge of community and social agencies, personal and social maturity, self-concept and attitude towards education, and clarification of vocational goals towards social services. Critiques focused on the lack of sufficient orientation to agency programmes, lack of student progression from simple to more demanding responsibilities, and lack of communication between the school and the participating agencies.

Because cooperative education programmes are seen as a means of facilitating the entrance of young people into the labour force, the federal government is committed to providing funds at 50 per cent of the cost of new projects. In Ontario, both the Ministries of Education, and Colleges and Universities, have received federal funds for this type of programme.

Career guidance and selection programmes exist in a variety of forms aimed at both students in secondary schools and unemployed young people who have left school. Given the large and increasing number of occupations to which a young person could be attracted, the informational aspect of career guidance is critical. In addition to their traditional printed materials for the use of school guidance counsellors, the federal government has developed a computer based occupational information system. CHOICES (Computerized Heuristic Occupational Information and Career Exploration System) stores information on approximately

700 primary occupations, representing 90 per cent of Canada's labour force, and 3000 related occupations. At ten terminals throughout Ontario (five on a demonstration basis in secondary schools and five in Canada Employment Centres), young people can access career information directly from the computer, using such question routes as interests, aptitudes, educational preparation, earnings, hours of work, physical demands, and future occupational outlook. Outcomes expected include more informed use of career counsellors, more awareness of the narrowing effects of limited education, and more analysis of values with respect to career choices. At the same time, a programme like this presumes considerable motivation and self-direction on the part of the user.

For unemployed young people requiring more personal guidance in career selection, a programme entitled Creating a Career, consisting of forty to sixty hours of instruction, was designed to equip unemployed youth with increased skills in career selection and job search. Originally pre-tested in western Canada, the programme is administered in Ontario by the Ontario Careers Action Program, using the staff of community colleges as instructors. To be eligible, applicants must be registered with Canada Employment. They receive no pay while on the course. Open-ended comments of participants to date have generally been favourable, e.g. 'where was this when I was in school.' The package is available to secondary schools but is still relatively costly.

With respect to the more specific search for a job, several pamphlets on job search techniques have been widely distributed but again presume a relatively well-motivated reader. Some outreach services have been developed to meet the needs of unemployed young people who do not make use of regular Canada Employment centres. For example, in Metropolitan Toronto, Trigger is a centre for unemployed youth, located in a large public housing project which employs innovative methods and various community resources to assist young people to obtain work. Special employment centres for students have also been set up in various areas of high unemployment, but the seasonal nature of these (May to October) is a disadvantage.

The third type of youth employment programme which provides a work experience to young people permanently or temporarily out of school, is intended in part to counteract lack of experience as a factor in unemployability of young people. Several of the largest scale Canadian youth employment programmes feature government subsidies to employers who are willing to hire a young person. In Job Experience Training (JET), the federal government will subsidize up to 50 per cent to a current maximum of $1,560 per participant. At the end of the subsidized period, employers are expected to keep the young person on permanent staff. Aimed at 16 to 24 year-olds who have been out of school a minimum of three months, the programme is viewed with considerable optimism by local representatives. Although no formal evaluation has been made available, employer response has been favourable, particularly to the pre-employment orientation which includes information on getting and keeping a job.

A summer version of this programme provides potential school-leavers in the 16 to 19 age group with a subsidized experience to help them decide whether to remain in the labour force or return to school. Students who would benefit from the programme are referred by their schools. It is one project within the overall Canada Summer Youth Employment Program (CSYEP), a $96.2 million interdepartmental programme for students, with the goal of creating 60,000 summer jobs and placing students in 250,000 positions across Canada through Canada Employment centres for students. Among the ten federal departments involved, the Young Canada Works Program, under the Department of Immigration, is the largest.

Provincially, the Ontario Youth Employment Program (OYEP) is a subsidy programme which provides grants to employers hiring young people during the summer period. To qualify, positions must be newly created, but an employer may hire up to six persons with the subsidy. The young person obtains employment privately and the employer applies for the subsidy.

Also operated by the provincial government, with the assistance of federal funds, is the Ontario Career Action Program (OCAP) which subsidizes employers to hire unemployed young people (16 to 24 years) who are encountering difficulty in obtaining permanent employment. They are hired for periods of up to six months, paid an allowance, and given the opportunity for additional help such as access to the Creating a Career package mentioned previously, assistance with job search techniques, and time off to search for work. Initially all jobs were within government but the province has allocated $2.5 million for the expansion of this programme to industry.

An evaluation of this programme[162] which was planned from the outset and carried out by project staff including an evaluation team of external consultants, compared a random sample of graduates of the programme with a sample of those who were unselected. Since the selection process was designed to be nondiscriminatory, it was expected that the characteristics of the two groups would be similar. Primary outcome measures were the number finding permanent employment in a job of their choice, supervisors' assessment of trainees, and trainee's satisfaction with his or her work experience.

Selected applicants were more likely to be female because of the larger number of clerical openings. Similarly, the small percentage with post-secondary education were over-represented among the selected applicants. While supervisors' perceptions of trainees' work and gains in job skills were generally positive, the differences in employment outcomes between the two groups were less marked than one would hope. A telephone survey two months after trainees had left the programme revealed that 54 per cent of OCAP graduates had gained full-time employment compared with 49 per cent of unselected applicants. However, since 44 per cent of graduates had re-entered the educational system compared with 30 per cent of the unselected group, and those actively seeking employment represented 25 per cent of the OCAP group and 35 per cent of the unselected, 'the unemployment rate of unselected applicants is substantially greater than that of graduates.'[163] Moreover, the employment of graduates was more challenging, more closely related to career goals, and generally better paid, a finding expected to lead to less 'job-hopping.' Recommended changes in the programme included more supervisor involvement in selection, clearer training plans, a more intensive monitoring of the programme, and reduction of the stay from a year to a maximum of six months to make the 'job search a more immediate concern.'[164]

One of the only examples of a work experience programme sponsored by the private sector (with the assistance of federal funds) is the Bank of Montreal's Youth Project.[165] Socially and economically disadvantaged youth are hired as bank employees, paid the minimum wage and given seven months of on-the-job training supplemented by a human relations component which includes life skills and interpersonal sharing. An evaluation follow-up of the project found that 75 per cent of those enrolled complete the programme and are placed in permanent jobs. Interestingly, the major effect of the programme is seen as increased self-confidence leading to greater employability.

In summary, in Canada there is currently in existence a large number of programmes dealing with the problem of youth unemployment. Cooperative education programmes offered in schools, programmes geared to career selection or job search, and work experience programmes for students are all addressing the transition of young people from school to the labour force. On the other hand, job experience programmes for unemployed out-of-school youth are remedial in nature, attempting to enhance employability in a variety of ways.

From the perspective of either a young person seeking employment or an employer willing to hire a young person, the existing programmes present a bewildering and frequently competitive array. The obvious problems of coordination being addressed locally in Toronto, for example, by organizations such as the Youth Services Network and Bridging the Gap, an incorporated group of representatives from government, business, and youth agencies are as yet only scratching the surface. Interviews and data gathering for this review of programs reveals considerable rivalry, lack of knowledge of the current scope of youth employment programmes, and competition for the same resources, despite the contribution of a number of obviously dedicated people.

American Programmes[166]

In the United States, federal spending on employment related programmes totals almost $10 billion annually. In August 1977, the Youth Employment and Demonstration Projects Act was signed into law to employ and increase the future employability of several hundred thousand young persons. As its name suggests, it is a 'demonstrations projects' Act, and as such is providing funds to various projects on this basis.

YEDPA funding is divided into four areas: Young Adult Conservation Corps; Youth Incentive Entitlement Pilot Projects; Youth Community Conservation and Improvement Projects; and Youth Employment and Training. Each of the four areas has a federal and regional administrative staff, but individual projects are initiated and operated by local groups, which may be public, private, or voluntary agencies. Detailed guidelines have been set down for qualifying projects, as have detailed evaluation methods. The projects are geared to the spectrum of unemployed youth, and include programmes for in-school and summer students, out-of-school youth, the economically disadvantaged, as well as the non-disadvantaged. The goal of the Act is to provide the knowledge base for more comprehensive youth employment policies. The evaluation component has been heavily emphasized, and will utilize the following: (1) documentation of process, (2) client profiles, (3) tracking, (4) outside monitoring and assessment, (5) inside assessment reviews, and (6) impact assessment.

The Young Adult Conservation Corps, administered by the (federal) departments of Labor, Agriculture, and Interior, is geared to providing jobs for unemployed youth and accomplishing needed conservation works, and has as its target group youth from areas of substantial unemployment.

Youth Incentive Entitlement Projects is addressed to the 16 to 19 year old youth who are economically disadvantaged and either in school or prepared to return. It is a two-tier programme, with the first tier guaranteeing jobs (part-time, summer) in an effort to test whether this will increase high school retention, return, and completion. Because of the high cost of this tier, it was to be tested in seven areas (individual schools) across the country. The second tier funding was alloted to various smaller projects with a more specific focus (e.g. attracting unwed mothers back to school).

Youth Community Conservation and Improvement Projects focuses primarily on out-of-school youth between 16 and 19 years, although some projects will include in-school youth. This project appears to resemble closely Canadian co-operative education programmes by utilizing the work itself as the source of training and giving academic credits for successful completion. In addition, this segment of YEDPA plans to test the idea of neighbourhood-based decision-making by funding a few such groups to implement youth projects. The work itself must be of tangible benefit to the community.

Youth Employment and Training division will fund various projects which enhance employment prospects, including work experience opportunities, training, services such as outreach, counselling and occupational information, education-to-work transition, job restructuring, and child care.

This package of youth project funding differs from the current Canadian approach in its total concept of purchase of project rather than having the government both sponsor and run individual projects, and in its concept of using a funded demonstration model as a basis for future policy-making.

The Job Corps is a comprehensive educational, training, support programme that includes physical, dental, and mental health services in addition to job training and placement.

It is intended to serve those youth who have the fewest chances of success on their own, the severely disadvantaged. More than half of their clients are black and one-tenth are Spanish speaking; 85 per cent are school dropouts and less than half have a grade six or lower education; half are from families of five or more persons, and three-quarters of the families have annual incomes of less than $5,000.

The Job Corps programme began in 1964, with a total residential component that had never been offered before on such a large scale. Today it remains primarily residential, although there are some non-residential programmes also being offered.

The Job Corps is federally funded and coordinated with centres across the country. The linkage between centres is provided through common goals and shared information, but each centre operates autonomously, and the centres are administered by a variety of public and private agencies, including large corporations in some areas.

The components of the Job Corps[167] include: (1) Civilian Conservation centres operated by departments of Interior and Agriculture, designed exclusively for males, and more likely to offer earth moving or construction trades; (2) Residential Manpower centres located in urban areas and utilizing community training and educational resources; (3) Men's Urban centres with an enrolment capacity of 1000 to 2000, located on former army bases in rural areas (usually more than fifteen miles from a town); and (4) Women's centres, operated mostly by private business.

The theory behind the large size of Men's Centres was to make it practical to offer a greater variety of trade training. However, the quality of service was found to differ greatly from centre to centre and there were problems with discipline and homesickness.

The Women's Centres appear to attract an older and relatively better educated clientele, and three-quarters of the participants are from minority groups. Most of the training offered is in four clusters: business and clerical, child care, food service, and health.

The Job Corps has been repeatedly used as a political football with multiple shifts with each presidential change. Several evaluations have been done over the years, but because of the type of clients served, follow-up has been difficult. Soft data indicate that the Job Corps does serve a real need, but hard data indicate that the dropout rate is high and cost-benefit analysis is inconclusive.

In contrast to the American programmes, those in Canada lack an overall conceptual framework and long-term planned approach. Although as noted in the previous sections, the causes of youth unemployment are frequently structural and system-related, by definition most youth employment programmes address individual-related causes such as lack of job search skills, lack of motivation, lack of training, and lack of experience.

Despite frequent reference to the fact that programmes are being carefully evaluated, published evaluations of Canadian programmes are rare, and criteria are not made explicit to local representatives. Most serious perhaps is the lack of expressed commitment to serving the needs of the most disadvantaged youth in Canada. At a time of economic constraint, when all social programmes are in some financial jeopardy, there is considerable danger that existing organizations and programmes will fail, by focusing on youth who can use them best, to serve those who need them most.

Attitudes of Adolescents Towards Work: The Work Ethic

One of the concerns about youth in the 60s and 70s has been the belief that the work ethic is dead, or has changed, or does not apply. This has been reflected in newspaper articles describing how, in a time of high youth unemployment, jobs listed at Manpower centres go unfilled, and has motivated some research on the attitudes of youth towards work.[168]

The definition of the work ethic with which most modern writers have concerned themselves is that developed by Max Weber in the context of seventeenth-century German Calvinism; that is, industriousness was a way to gain personal satisfaction, as well as a social obligation and, most important, it was a way of establishing spiritual virtue.[169] Certainly, industriousness has existed and does exist in societies other than those in which conditions have facilitated the development of capitalist civilization. As Burstein et al. have pointed out, 'almost identical work attitudes have been found among small cultural groups usually labelled primitive by modern industrial standards.'[170] And, certainly, personal industry is a keystone of the social and economic life of modern China and other socialist states. Fears about the decline of the work ethic are not limited to 1977. As Tilgher has pointed out, 'every country responds to the lament that the work-fever does not burn in the younger generation.'[171]

Why then is there such widespread concern that young people today don't, or won't, want to work? Or, more specifically, that they won't want to work for the same rewards, or in the same way, or at the same kinds of things that previous generations did?

There is some feeling that the work ethic as it has been known in North America has indeed been affected in some way not yet understood but with its roots in movements of the 1960s among the youth population. Whether or not the work ethic has evolved enough to be called, as Yankelovich has done, the 'New Values,' remains to be seen; nevertheless, there is evidence that the younger segment of the population is in the process of striking a balance between the Calvinist work ethic and some as yet unspecified new way of spending their work lives.[172]

A recent Canadian study suggested that some of the popular stereotypes regarding the preference of youth for collecting unemployment insurance and remaining idle rather than working were inaccurate, and secondly, that the old work ethic was changing in some way. Motivated by concern over an unemployment rate in Canada which refused to drop below 5 per cent (and has since risen much higher), coupled with labour shortages in some geographical and occupational areas, the Department of Manpower and Immigration suggested that perhaps young Canadians had either lost the traditional work ethic or were not gaining satisfaction in the work available in the current job market. The authors stated, 'In either case we are dealing with a change in *attitudes* which may have been sufficiently widespread to affect unemployment statistics ... there is little such attitudinal data in Canada ... but certain recent changes lend credence to the assumption that traditional work attitudes have been modified.'[173]

This survey found, first, that young workers (age 16-19 and 20-24) were no less likely to derive life satisfaction from work for the attainment of success than older workers. Indeed, the post-adolescent group were more likely to depend on work to achieve self-fulfilment than any other group.

Considering this, together with the greater willingness of young workers to change jobs compared with older workers, and with Yankelovich's American finding that young workers tend to feel that the greatest obstacle to job advancement lies in lack of education, and often would be anxious to advance their careers by obtaining further education or job training, even with a cut in pay to compensate for time off work, it may be inferred that youthful expectations are for careers, rather than jobs.[174,175]

Young Canadians were generally similar to older groups in preferring work to benefits (although feeling entitled to public assistance if unemployed). Thus it seems that Canadian youth value work and, indeed, want to work. However, the interesting differences which emerged between younger and older populations in Canada had to do with what they were working for. The importance of doing interesting work and using one's talents decreased with age, and an emphasis on more pay increased. These emphases were supported in a separate survey of youth working in OFY programmes who, although they were generally oriented towards work in the same ways as the general population (in terms of commitment and derivation of personal satisfaction), in an ideal job situation ranked 'a chance to be of service to other people,' and a 'sense of accomplishment' ahead of 'salary' in importance.[176]

These Canadian findings indicate that the popular stereotype of youth as idle layabouts who prefer to collect handouts from government may not be true. What does seem to be true, however, is that Canadian youth have high personal aspirations about the kind of work they will do.

In an attempt to determine whether the new orientation towards work expressed by a small minority of youth in the 60s had spread beyond the ranks of the counterculture, and indicated that societal transformation was in the making, Block and Langman suggested that rejection of the hard-work ethic of the dominant culture had been the province of a privileged group at elite universities in the late 1960s. Their results with college students at an American 'blue collar' university in 1971 showed that there had been 'a rapid diffusion of countercultural values by 1970,' including more emphasis on expressive interests like creativity, concern with one's special abilities and the desire to help others, and less emphasis on instrumental values like money, status, and prestige.[177]

This finding was extended by Yankelovich in 1974 in the latest of a series of reports on the changing values of American youth. Yankelovich found that diffusion of what he called New Values had occurred, extending New Values from a university elite to working and high school youth between 1969 and 1973. In the early 1970s, he reports, the traditional work ethic had been somewhat strengthened on college campuses but had weakened (from its previously strong position) among non-college youth. Indeed, what appears to be in the process of occurring is diffusion of New or counterculture values to segments of the population other than the original elite student group, and a synthesis of new and old values. That is, although youth are willing to work hard, they expect a reasonable payoff for hard work.[178]

The new North American dream emphasizes personal satisfaction and interest in one's work and while there is a desire in young people for monetary recognition for services rendered, goals related to materialism are balanced by other satisfactions. Whether or not these goals are realistic when considered together with evidence about youth's possibilities in the labour market, the role of schools in preparing them for a life's work, and the role of social class and gender in attaining satisfaction, remains to be seen.

III THE TRANSITION TO ADULT SEXUALITY

The transition made by the adolescent from childhood to adult sexuality is one of the most dramatic and readily observable events in adolescence. It is physiologically based, with some obvious and relatively abrupt physical occurrences and with more subtle changes that are both physical and psychological. The sexual transition challenges the adolescent's sense of identity, and the manner in which the sexual area is handled during and after puberty may determine the nature of the future adult's interpersonal and sexual relations for a very long time. The way an adolescent handles his or her emerging adult sexuality depends upon physical attributes, an individual hormone schedule, integration of parent-child relationships, peer group relations and pressure, the particular context in which he lives, and wide contemporary standards: 'hormonal puberty is a time when the motors of sexual drive ... are set in high gear. Gender-identity has already been effectively differentiated ... ahead of time; puberty is the time for it to declare itself.'[179]

Social Context
A significant shift in the understanding of sexuality has occurred since Freud pointed out in the late nineteenth century that infants and growing children are sexual beings. It is known, for example, that sexual behaviour and attitudes, in large part, are learned, and there are wide variations from culture to culture. Childhood sexuality may be acceptable in a culture, or forbidden but permitted during adolescence. Homosexuality may be permitted, ridiculed, encouraged, or strongly prohibited.[180] Even within Western society, there are national variations in attitudes towards sexuality.[181]

In societies less culturally diverse than ours, acceptable and unacceptable sexual behaviour is usually more clearly defined; an adolescent is not likely to have to make his way through a confusion of contradictory attitudes held by his peers and adults. In addition, there is frequently a formal period of training for adulthood and rites of passage marking the transition to adult sexuality. Most often, other adult roles accompany the new adult sexual role; new occupational status, or a new dwelling place might also come at the end of the official adulthood ritual.

Although official and obvious puberty ceremonies have usually not been the practice in Western culture, there was more general agreement in the past within the society on acceptable and unacceptable sexual behaviour and on the roles individuals were expected to take within sexual and interpersonal relationships. For example, in our culture in the past, sex was officially sanctioned only within marriage, and the relationship of marriage implied that the partners would take certain roles. Although sex outside of marriage, divorce, and separation existed, these were deviations from an accepted norm. Today, not only are divorce and separation, premarital sex, and common-law relationships widespread, but adult authorities with a wide variety of perspectives have sanctioned them. Aspects of male-female relationships, within and outside marriage, ranging from the purely sexual to the economic, are being questioned and tested, and large numbers of people are expressing new attitudes towards these issues.

Some writers see our society as extremely ambivalent about sexuality; Johnson has called it sexcentric but sexrejecting.[182] Although sex is presented with increasing openness in the media, there are recurrent efforts to censor, edit, and ban a wide variety of materials. These efforts range from restricting certain films to adult audiences, editing existing films for television, removing materials from school libraries, to occasional prosecution under existing obscenity laws. However, although pressures are still exercised against an open acceptance of sexuality, it is undeniable that the culture is a more visibly open one than it was some time ago. Media obscenity has been broadly interpreted, changes in behaviour like private and semi-public nudity, attitudes towards and behaviour of homosexuals, changes in abortion and contraception laws and practices, prolific sex research, and increasingly open programs of sex education in the schools have been documented anecdotally and in research. Attitude surveys have indicated that the trend is for more and more respondents to be permissive in their attitudes towards premarital sex, birth control services for teenagers, abortion, and homosexuality.[183,184] At the same time, Kirkendall and Libby have commented that the importance of sex itself has been de-emphasized and the quality of the interpersonal relationship has grown in importance for much of the population.[185]

The developing adolescent of today, then, must make an accomodation between his own changing and often fluctuating physiology and psychology and a social set of norms which are also in the process of evolving from an earlier, more monolithic standard to one that includes a number of options.

The importance of physiological change in adolescence is discussed earlier in this paper; however, it is important to understand that one of the major tasks of adolescence is the successful handling of a changing physical self, and a whole set of unpredictable feelings, impulses, and fantasies related to sexuality. The developing awareness of these important questions both affects and is affected by the practical choices that are made.

As has been pointed out earlier in this chapter, the world of the young child is relatively circumscribed and rules are generally established by the family. Although a sense of values is developing throughout childhood, it is not until adolescence that the necessity for important choices among alternatives demands that personal values be examined and developed.

A choice of a route to a job or career means that emphasis placed on conventional material success, or upon personal autonomy must be determined; patterns of sexual exploration require the weighing of societal, parental, and peer values. The ability to make these kinds of choices is determined by cognitive abilities which, as discussed earlier in this chapter, develop during adolescence.

The Attitudes of Adolescents Towards Sexuality

Reiss has proposed a way of integrating several levels of social influences and individual factors for a consideration of the development of attitudes towards sexuality. According to Reiss, sexual values are acquired in much the same way as are other values and are affected by a number of social factors in the same way as are other learned attitudes.[186]

Children learn their basic attitudes from an assortment of significant groups: first, from parents, a bit later from friends and from relevant social institutions such as schools. As the child approaches adolescence, he is influenced more and more by peer values which are often more permissive in the sexual area than are those of his family. Whether or not the adolescent strongly responds to these more permissive pressures depends on their strength, the basic attitudes he brings to puberty, and upon his own particular physical schedule. Reiss has pointed out that courtship (or dating) and the family are the two basic institutions which are of key importance in the development of sexual attitudes and behaviour. Generally, the peer group is relatively permissive in its attitudes and behaviour and the family institution is, in general, relatively more conservative. The adolescent's particular evolution of his own sexual attitudes and behaviours vary in accord with a variety of sociocultural factors: his social class, gender, regional values, religious attitudes, and level of general liberalism of the whole culture. These influences, together with the biological changes of adolescence, combine to promote a beginning of the formation of the sexual attitudes and behaviour that the adolescent will hold as an adult.

Among writers who have considered the issue of changing adolescent attitudes towards sexuality, there is agreement that there has been, in the late 1960s and 1970s, more emphasis on openness, honesty and intimacy, and less conformity with traditional social codes.[187,188] Rather than basing their standards upon traditional courtship and marriage roles, adolescents tend to stress the nature and quality of human relationships. As Conger has summarized recent findings on these emphases, 'What many adolescents appear to be saying is that the morality of sexual behaviour can often be judged not too much by the nature of the act itself but by its meaning to the persons involved.'[189] In addition, the importance of the right of individuals, in what are seen by adolescents as private matters, to make their own decisions concerning premarital sex, homosexual relationships, and abortion has become increasingly important.

Sorenson, in research on the attitudes of a large sample of American adolescents, found that gender and age differences existed; that is, girls tended to be somewhat more conservative than boys, and older adolescents, those 16–19, were less conservative than their younger counterparts. Perhaps most important was Sorenson's finding that there were differences between what adolescents said that they would consider acceptable behaviour for other people, and what they said they would do themselves. For example, abortion was an alternative to continuing pregnancy to term in general but fewer respondents in the sample said that they themselves would choose an abortion (or would choose one for their girl friends) as an alternative. This finding supports the notion that, as Yankelovich's poll suggests, sexuality is viewed as an area where the individual should be allowed to make his own decisions.[190,191]

Very little research on sexual attitudes has been done in Canada, and almost all of what has been done has used university students as its sample. However, a cross-national survey of university students' attitudes towards sex and sex roles included a Canadian as well as an American sample and a number of European ones. Luckey and Nass's findings in this research indicated that Canadian students were, in general, somewhat more conservative in their attitudes than their American counterparts.[192] Although it is not possible to draw direct inferences from the attitudes of these university populations in the 1960s to Canadian adolescents in the late 1970s, the paucity of Canadian studies in this area insists that American research on adolescent samples be, at least, considered.

The adolescents in one small Toronto sample were quite similar to their American counterparts in their attitudes towards sex; they emphasized the importance of the relationship within which sex occurred, and felt that decisions regarding their sexual behaviour should be made by themselves.[193]

Adolescent Sexual Behaviour

The comparison of most contemporary researchers on adolescent sexuality is generally with the landmark work done in the early 1950s by Kinsey. Although a number of research studies have dealt widely with a range of sexual behaviours from kissing and petting to masturbation, the greatest public concern (perhaps because of the possible consequence of pregnancy) and, as well, the largest well-documented body of data, deals with the incidence of sexual intercourse among adolescents. It was documented by Kinsey that changes in the incidence of premarital sexual intercourse increased, in females, in each successive generation since 1900. Kinsey's data indicate that, of females born before 1900, only 2 per cent had intercourse prior to age 16; the figures jumped only to 4 per cent for the mothers of today's adolescents.[194]

Although a 1965 study done in Great Britain shows that only 6 per cent of the 15-year-old boys and 2 per cent of the 15-year-old girls had experienced intercourse,[195] it has been suggested by a comprehensive study of the literature on premarital sexual behaviour, most of which has focused on college student populations, that it was in the late 1960s that the first evidence of a significant increase in premarital sex since the 1930s had occurred.[196]

Sorenson's survey of adolescent sexuality in the United States indicated that 30 per cent of 16-year-old girls (and 44 per cent of 16-year-old boys) have had intercourse. Indeed, Sorenson's 1974 study indicated that, for the first time, a majority of American adolescents, aged 13–19, report being fully sexually active.[197] Kantner and Zelnick reported on adolescent sexual behaviour in 1972 and again in 1977.[198,199] In their 1971 sample, 26.8 per cent of teenaged never-married women had engaged in sexual intercourse; in 1976 the figure had jumped to 34.9 per cent. The median age had dropped slightly from 1971 to 1976: from 16.5 to 16.2. In addition, Zelnick and Kantner found that while frequency of sex had declined in the time between their two surveys, the number of partners had increased.

Although there is some disagreement on the precise size of the trend towards adolescent involvement in full sexual activity, most researchers agree that it is clearly in the direction of earlier sexual intercourse for a larger number of adolescents. Further, it is clear that there have been two important changes in the pattern of sexual behaviour; these changes are, first, changes in gender differences, and, second, an acceptance of options or alternative sexual patterns.

Although according to Sorenson, gender differences in sexual activity do still exist, and girls in general still tend to be more conservative than boys, the gender differential seems to be decreasing. The double standard of acceptable male and female behaviour no longer adequately describes adolescent sexual experience. The system of options which a number of researchers have commented upon includes 'serial monogamy' and 'sexual adventuring,' or sex with multiple partners for both boys and girls as options of active sexual behaviour.[200, 201]

Findings that, although the gender differential is decreasing but still exists, should be considered in the context of what was assumed in the past to be true about the differences in male and female sex drives. In the past, it was assumed that women had a biologically weaker sex drive. However, as Gagnon has pointed out, assumption of 'gender variation in the strength of biological impulse is not supported by any body of data on human beings '[202]

A number of theories have been advanced to account for the gender differential in overt sexuality. However, although the interaction of the biological and the cultural is not clearly understood, it appears to be at the very least partially attributable to traditional attitudes towards female sexuality. It is significant, when considering the decrease in the gender differential in sexual activity cited above, to note Hunt's finding in a recent American survey of adolescent girls: only one in ten said that they believe that 'women have innately less capacity for sexual pleasure than men' and more than 66 per cent believed that 'women enjoy sex as much as men.'[203]

Overall trends in sexual attitudes and behaviour, then, indicate that some changes have occurred in adolescents in the last ten years. Although there is diversity within the adolescent population by such factors as age, gender, socio-economic and educational level, religion, race, geographical area, and national group, the general trend is towards earlier and more sexual activity, and towards more permissive and private attitudes. Whether or not this constitutes a teenage sexual revolution depends upon one's perspective. Further, the effects of this trend upon adolescents and upon the society are, to a large extent, unknown.

Sex Education

Where do adolescents get their information about sex? Guyatt's study of adolescent girls at a family planning clinic found that their sources for information about sex and birth control were school and girl friends; although mothers were frequently mentioned as a source, it was usually only as a source of information about menstruation.[204] Sorenson found that 70 per cent of all boys and girls in his survey replied that they did not talk 'pretty freely' with their parents about sex.[205] A PSYCHOLOGY TODAY survey questioned a non-random sample of young adults with a clip-out-and-mail questionnaire. Two-thirds of the male respondents and one-half of the females said that friends had been the primary source of their information about sex, while less than one-tenth of the men and one-sixth of the women responded that they had received most of their sex education from their parents.[206] It is possible that adolescents often have difficulty in getting information from their parents about sex, sometimes because they are uneasy about approaching their parents and sometimes because parents are unwilling or uncomfortable.

One issue which has been raised, particularly by opponents of sex education and available birth control information for adolescents, is whether or not this would encourage an increase in premarital sexual relations. Although many schools have initiated sex education and birth control programmes, these programmes are frequently attacked on this basis. Conger has stated, 'In the light of statistics on current adolescent premarital intercourse, pregnancy, and abortion, as well as the general social climate, it is difficult to see how sex education for adolescents could be viewed as 'premature.'[207] Reiss states that while 'the presence of contraceptive information is not a major cause of coitus, the absence of it is a major cause of premarital pregnancy.'[208]

The whole issue of sex education is one that needs to be evaluated much more systematically. The effects of programmes of sex education in the schools have been difficult to evaluate because, while there is some evidence that providing information on fertility and contraception has not been effective, the particular content and approach of programmes needs to be considered carefully. In Hunt's sample, 98 per cent of the female adolescent respondents wanted schools to provide sex education programmes and about half the sample reported that they had had instruction in school. However, when asked what they thought should be included in the courses, many of the adolescent girls in his sample wanted a wide-ranging discussion of human sexuality, including consideration of ethical and philosophical issues.[209] It is possible that the mechanics of sexuality, which are frequently discussed in school sex education programmes, need to be placed within a context of a wide consideration of the psychological and emotional aspects of human sexuality. When considering the issue of contraception for adolescents, which follows, it may be seen that these issues are extremely important and may play as large a role as an understanding of the mechanics.

Contraception

Why are adolescents not more conscientious about using birth control? It has been suggested that it is difficult for adolescents, particularly those below local ages of medical consent, to obtain reliable contraceptives. Several surveys of physicians in the United States indicate that some of them, at least, will prescribe birth control to teenagers. One study indicated a relationship to the age of the patient, with physicians becoming more willing to prescribe without parental consent as the patient's age increased.[210] Although some physicians for ethical or legal reasons do refuse contraceptives to adolescents,[211] many feel that it is their ethical and medical duty to help adolescents prepare for sex by providing a range of contraceptive services. So it would seem that contraceptives are available to adolescents if they know where to go – to sympathetic physicians, clinics, or counselling services.

Many researchers in this area believe that one important reason for adolescent failure to use contraceptives is related to the psychology of the developing adolescent. As Cvetkovich et al. have pointed out, 'the adolescent is as yet uncertain of his ability to live up to demands of adult sexuality. Indeed, there are some who are probably uncertain that they want anything to do with the whole business of sex ... The adolescent may not be ready, cognitively or emotionally, to accept his sexuality to the degree that allows premeditated sex. To prepare for sex by using contraception is to admit to one's self ... a willingness to accept adult sexuality.'[212] Other studies support this point of view.[213,214] For contemporary teenagers, guilt may be associated more with planning for sexual intercourse by using contraceptives than with the actual act itself. It has been suggested that the unpredictability, sporadic nature, and infrequency of sexual activity and a belief in the naturalness and spontaneity of sex influence adolescents and increase the chances that they will not use adequate contraceptives.[215] This is supported by evidence in the Sorenson study, that the adolescents who are most likely to use birth control are those who have a regular sexual partner.[216]

It has been suggested that a 'personal fable,' as Elkind has described, may encourage adolescent girls to believe that although others may, they, themselves, will not get pregnant;[217] the fantasy may be reinforced if an adolescent has intercourse and does not become pregnant.[218] This is supported by evidence that even adolescents who do use contraceptives frequently use them irregularly and inconsistently.[219]

Another factor which may contribute to the failure of adolescents to use adequate contraception is their apparent misunderstanding of important facts about sex and contraception. For example, fertility periods during the menstrual cycle and the relative methods of birth control[220,221] are misunderstood. Kantner and Zelnick found that, although more young women in their sample who had taken sex education courses were slightly better informed, still only 41 per cent knew the time in the menstrual cycle when risk of pregnancy was high.[222]

Adolescent Pregnancies, Abortion and Young Parenthood

One of the major reasons that there has been so much concern on the part of parents, educators and others about the sexual activity of adolescents is that it may culminate in an unwanted pregnancy. Adolescent pregnancy has future implications for the prospective young mother, the father, and their offspring.

The trend in numbers of illegitimate births from about 1945 to 1970 nationally in Canada, in the U.S., and in some other industrialized nations has paralleled the demographic trends for Ontario during that period of time. The figures across Canada, the U.S., and in Ontario showed a considerable rise, doubling in Ontario for most age groups. From the 1950s into the 1970s, in Canada, an increasing proportion of unmarried mothers were under 20; in Ontario, the figure rose from about 28 per cent in 1945 to about 56 per cent in 1973. Although 1970 was the peak year for births-out-of-wedlock for all age groups in Ontario, the statistics dropped abruptly for all age groups but the under 20s; those are still rising.[223]

The trends clearly indicate that more adolescent girls than ever before are becoming pregnant. The traditional literature on adolescent pregnancy has asked why adolescent girls become pregnant. Osafsky has reviewed the literature on adolescent pregnancy and concluded that there has been a history of theories naming such causes as immorality and bad companions (in the 1920s), cultural-anthropological theories citing cultural variation in attitudes towards illegitimacy (in the 1930s and 40s), Freudian-based theories developing notions of symptomatic attempts by the girl to solve family or emotional conflicts (in the 1930s and 1940s), and, most recently, what Osafsky has called theories of 'society as patient,' naming contemporary morality, and unavailability of counselling, contraception, and education about sexuality as causal.[224]

Guyatt has suggested that, rather than asking why adolescent girls get pregnant, a more relevant question to ask would be why they do not.[225] If the number of adolescent girls who are sexually active is as large as it is, and if they are as unprotected by contraceptives as they appear to be, it is certainly not surprising that some of them become pregnant. Indeed, it has been reported by Sorenson and supported by Kantner and Zelnick that nearly 10 per cent of all American female adolescents and about 29 per cent of all non-virgin female adolescents have, by their own report, been pregnant at least once.[226,227]

In the past, most adolescents who became pregnant either married (the shotgun wedding) or gave their babies up for adoption. Abortion, adoption figures, married statistics, and research findings indicate that a large number of teenage marriages, 25 per cent, according to some research are still preceded by conception.[228] Two new trends are apparent, however. First, of those who remain single, more are choosing abortion and, of those who choose not to abort, most are retaining custody of their children.[229] These trends may be explained by some changes in social attitudes and legal changes. Together with liberalization of other attitudes about sex, there is more public acceptance of unmarried mothers and their children. Indeed, many adolescents believe that one should bear and raise the child of a premarital pregnancy.[230] Further, more permissive attitudes towards abortion and liberalized abortion laws have created a climate of easier access to abortion.

In 1969 abortion laws in Canada were liberalized. The new provision was for therapeutic abortion, with the consent of an approved hospital committee if continuation of the pregnancy would endanger the life and health of the mother. The effect has been to allow widespread therapeutic abortions in some localities for women who know which physician and hospital committee will grant approval. After 1970, the proportion in Canada of abortions to live births rose from 3 per cent in 1970 to 14 per cent in 1974; in Ontario, the trend was steeper (3.9 per cent in 1970 and 20 per cent in 1974). Canadian age specific figures for all provinces, except Ontario and B.C., and the Yukon indicate that 33 per cent of total therapeutic abortions were performed on girls under 20 and that 97 per cent of these were single.[231] In other localities, too, liberalization of abortion laws have allowed large numbers of pregnant adolescents easier access to abortions. For example, in New York state, in the first year and a half following the passage of the N.Y. state liberalized abortion law, of the 250,000 abortions performed on women in the state, 10 per cent involved women 17 or younger.[232]

The attitudes of adolescents towards abortions seem to be somewhat less permissive than their other attitudes in the area of sexuality, and these attitudes indicate some differences between what they accept for others and what they say they themselves would do if faced with the problem of pregnancy. In Sorenson's study, 51 per cent of all adolescents, 59 per cent of non-virgins, 55 per cent of all boys, and 45 per cent of all girls agreed that, in the abstract, it is alright to abort an unwanted child. Indeed, almost half of the adolescents interviewed agreed with the statement 'It's immoral to bring an unwanted child into this overpopulated world, especially now that abortions are so easy to get.'[233] However, fewer adolescents in the sample said that they would have (or want their girl friends to have) an abortion. In a study at a family planning clinic, Goldsmith found, as had Sorenson and Gabrielson et al., that younger adolescents (13-15) had more conflict over the idea of abortion than did the older group (16-17).[234,235,236]

Besides the increased use of abortion as a way of resolving premarital pregnancies, the other trend noted in the late 1960s and 1970s has been the increase in the number of pregnant adolescents who rear their children themselves. This trend is evident from the decrease in the number of infants available for adoption and from the experience of those involved in direct service to pregnant adolescents. In Ontario, in 1970, more than 50 per cent of single mothers retained custody of their children; in 1975, the figure had increased to about 75 per cent. Guyatt's research on pregnant teenagers in a family planning clinic noted that of the young women who chose not to abort their pregnancies most retained custody of their children.[237]

IV RESEARCH DIRECTIONS

Adolescents and Work

In the area of the transition of adolescents to adult work, a number of potentially fruitful research directions need to be followed. Because the current state of the Canadian economy and the status of adolescents within the labour market does not inspire optimism, the topic of adolescents and work most often becomes one of adolescents and unemployment. Government policy in providing job opportunities for young people needs to be analysed more systematically, including opportunities for vocational and personal growth and mobility. A component of this analysis is a consideration of the opportunity for training and skill development which now is most often provided only in the school system.

The effects on adolescents of the lack of opportunities for developing a sense of responsibility and for testing themselves vocationally throughout adolescence need to be assessed, both psychologically and in terms of social costs.

Finally, there has been no broad, systematic examination of the effects on youth of a school system which fails to prepare them for the 'real world'; one that in turn fails to provide sufficient numbers and quality of work. Does this social system produce a significant number of alienated youth? How are we to harness their energy and potential commitment to socially constructive goals? What is the price of failing to do just that?

Although some information about the attitudes of adolescents towards work has been collected, more work in this area needs to be done. In particular, the effects of lack of information about the labour market, together with high expectations, need to be assessed.

Adolescent Sexuality

Research in the area of adolescent sexuality has most often taken the form of asking what adolescents do. Studies which consider the effects of earlier sexual activity on the developing adolescent's sense of identity, and what it means for their lives as adults have been notably lacking. This is one area where fruitful and informative research needs to be done.

Another, more directly practical area has to do with the use, or the non-use, of contraceptives by adolescents. The effects of advertising, and of particular kinds of sex education programmes, and the effects of greater availability of the right kinds of birth control techniques through clinics, physicians, and other sources need to be explored.

A third direction for research is in the area of the effects of young parenthood, and on appropriate support systems for adolescent parents and their children. Even if more effective ways to adequately prepare adolescents with contraceptive information and techniques are found, it has been observed that there are occasionally adolescent girls who want to have babies. Ways of supporting them and their children need to be investigated too.

CONCLUSION

Two issues in adolescence - sexuality and the school-work transition - seem to embrace two of the dilemmas adolescents face: attempting to develop a set of beliefs, values, and behaviours about relationships that are discontinuous with past experience and attempting to make practical choices with limited information, no experience, and no preparation for the responsibility. Sexual beliefs and values may develop without an adequate informational or experiential base and unbridgeable gulfs may develop between valued and actual employment also for lack of good information and experience. Through it all, the young adult encounters a wide variety of perspectives and many alternatives, especially at a time when many older adults are expressing new attitudes towards these issues.

In the past 10 years, values and attitudes of adolescents with respect to sexuality have increased in openness and honesty, have emphasized permissiveness and the quality of interpersonal relationships, and the importance of individual discretion with respect to intimacy. According to available research, parents have participated little in dialogue with their children about this attitude evolution and about the increase in adolescents' reported sexual activity. Many schools have attempted to initiate sex education and birth control programmes which have been difficult to evaluate. Do these programmes give adolescents information about and preparation for social choices? Response to the programmes indicates that the mechanics of sexuality need to be placed in the context of the psychological aspects of human sexuality. Perhaps this approach will help uncover some of the reasons why adolescents who are sexually active fail consistently to use contraceptives, even though they have knowledge about them and access to them. Future studies should consider the effects of early sexual activity on the adolescent's developing sense of identity and what it may mean for their lives as adults.

Recent trends among teenage girls indicate an increase in both pregnancies and abortions, as well as an increase in the number of girls retaining custody of their children. What effect do sex education classes, peer counselling, and other approaches have on these choice patterns? Future research should attempt to learn about the effects of young parenthood and to help establish appropriate support systems for adolescent parents and their children.

Adolescents have to choose a career path at an early age when most time is spent in an educational system isolated from 'real' life and a system in which graduation means completion. Requirements of technology and the economic system in our society change often, demanding additional, different, and specialized job training and retraining. There is little possibility, given the present system, that adolescents, when they leave school, will be sufficiently well-informed or experienced to make optimal career choices. Through the 1900s as schooling reached more and more youths for longer periods, it also came to mean an education for all, despite their capabilities. Schools have sponsored academic and non-academic training programmes designed to foster expression and creativity, extracurricular activities, and social equality but may have fostered the status hierarchy they sought to abolish. Paradoxically, although education should be preparation for the world of work, schools give most prestige to students who are preparing for further schooling.

In the 1970s renewed discussions of the place of youth in the labour market have been prompted by the lack of appropriate 'beginning' jobs for them, resulting in substantial youth unemployment for school dropouts, and high school and university graduates as well. Employers prefer experienced workers when work is scarce. As the employment opportunities decrease for all youth, even those with adequate education, more youth are entering the labour market as a result of the 'baby boom' and earlier school leaving. If preparation for the work world takes place in the school, the kind of links forged between the education system and the labour market are salient.

Recent research indicates that in the 1960s the work ethic was modified among young people. While young workers are no less likely to derive life fulfilment from occupational success than other workers, their expectations are for careers, not jobs. Young people do value work, they want to work at something that is interesting to them, and has a reasonable pay-off.

Government policy in providing job opportunities for young people needs to be assessed in light of the current educational system, labour market conditions, and expectations of youth for the present and future. Whom have recent job creation programmes served and how successful have they been in providing jobs and training in the long as well as the short run? Are such jobs and training perceived as desirable by the recipients? What are the links between the job creation programmes and 'real' jobs? What opportunities could exist for training and skill development within the school system and outside in the real world? What are the psychological and social costs of lack of opportunity for young people?

To once again quote Erik Erikson,

... to enter history, each generation of youth must find an identity consonant with its own childhood and consonant with an ideological promise in the perceptible historical process ... no longer is it merely for the old to teach the young the meaning of life. It is the young who, by their responses and actions, tell the old whether life as it is represented to them has some vital promise, and it is the young who carry in them the power to confirm those who confirm them, to renew and regenerate, to disavow what is rotten, to reform and rebel.[238]

Each generation of young must be considered within the social context of the time, as part of a historical process. Opportunities must be available for them to develop their own ways of dealing with issues which have been historically, and continue to be, part of the adolescent transition from childhood to maturity.

The nature of the experiences and opportunities needed in adolescence for the transition to adulthood remains unclear. Adolescence is a time of striking out on one's own while significant socialization continues to take place in the family. In the context of family relationships and circumstances, the adolescent begins to develop a set of values and beliefs modified by the personal characteristics with which he enters adolescence, and the circumstances of his own physiological changes.

NOTES

1 Conger, J.J. A world they never knew: the family and social change, *Daedalus 100:* 1105–34, Fall 1971.
2 Shakespeare, W. The tragedy of Hamlet, Prince of Denmark, in *Shakespeare, The Complete Works*, G.B. Harrison, ed., New York: Harcourt, Brace and World, Inc., 1962, p. 152.

3 Aries, P. *Centuries of childhood: a social history of family life*, New York: Vintage Books, 1962, p. 32.

4 Kiell, Norman *The universal experience of adolescence*, Boston: Beacon Press, 1967, pp. 18–19.

5 Smith, S.R. Religion and the conception of youth in seventeenth century England, *History of Childhood Quarterly 2:* 513, 1975.

6 Hall, G.S. *Adolescence: its psychology and its relations to physiology, anthropology, sociology, sex, crime, religion and education*, Vol. I, Vol. II, London: Sidney Appleton, 1904.

7 Hall *Adolescence* Vol. I., 1904, p. 47.

8 Hall *Adolescence* Vol. II., 1904, p. 454.

9 Blos, P. *On adolescence: a psychoanalytic interpretation*, New York: Free Press, 1962, p. 11.

10 Gustin, J.C. The revolt of youth, *Psychoanalysis and the psychoanalytic Review 98:* 83, 1961.

11 Freidenberg, E.Z. *The vanishing adolescent*, Boston: Beacon Press, 1959, p. 12.

12 Mead, M. *Coming of age in Samoa*, New York: William Morrow & Company Inc., 1961.

13 Freud, A. Adolescence as a development disturbance, in G. Caplan, and S. Lebovici, eds., *Adolescence: psychological perspectives*, New York: Basic Books, Inc., 1969, pp. 5–10.

14 Douvan, E. and Adelson, J. *The adolescent experience*, New York: John Wiley & Sons, Inc., 1966.

15 Bandura, A. The stormy decade: fact or fiction? *Psychology in the Schools 1:* 224–31, 1964.

16 Offer, D., Marcus, D. and Offer, J.L. A longitudinal study of normal adolescent boys, *Am. J. Psychiatry 126:* 917–24, 1970.

17 Offer, D. and Offer, J.B. *From teenage to young manhood: a psychological study*, New York: Basic Books, Inc., Publishers, 1975.

18 Masterson, J. The symptomatic adolescent five years later – he didn't grow out of it. *Am. J. Psychiatry 123:* 1240–42, 1966.

19 Jones, M.C. The later careers of boys who were early or late in maturing, *Child Develop. 28:* 113–28, 1957.

20 Tanner, J.M. *Growth at adolescence*, Oxford: Blackwell Scientific Publications Ltd., 1962 (2nd ed.).

21 Lerner, R.M. The development of stereotyped expectancies of body build-behaviour relations, *Child Develop. 40:* 137–41, 1969.

22 Bayley, N. Development of mental abilities, in P. Mussen, ed., *Carmichael's manual of child psychology*, Vol. I, New York: John Wiley & Sons, Inc., 1970 (3rd ed.) pp. 1163–1209.

23 Piaget, J. The intellectual development of the adolescent, in G. Caplan, and S. Lebovici, eds., *Adolescence: psychosocial perspectives*, New York: Basic Books, Inc., Publishers, 1969, pp. 22–26.

24 Inhelder, B. and Piaget, J. *The growth of logical thinking from childhood to adolescence*, New York: Basic Books, Inc., Publishers, 1961.

25 Elkind, D. Egocentricism in adolescence, *Child Develop. 38:* 1025–34, 1967.

26 Douvan and Adelson *The adolescent experience*, p. 163.

27 Conger, J.J. A world they never made: parents and children in the 1970's, Invited address, American Academy of Pediatrics Meetings, Denver, 16 April 1975.

28 Mead, M. *Culture and commitment: a study of the generation gap*, Garden City, N.Y.: Natural History Press/Doubleday & Company, Inc., 1970.

29 Smart, R.G., Ferjer, D., and White, J. The extent of drug use among Metropolitan Toronto Schools: a study of changes from 1968 to 1970, Subsidy #523, Toronto: Addiction Research Foundation, 1970.

30 Smart, R.G. and Fejer, D. Drug use among adolescents and their parents: closing the generation gap in mood modification, *J. Abnorm. Psychol. 79:* 153–60, 1972.

31 Kandel, D. Inter and intragenerational influences on adolescent marijuana use, *J. Soc. Issues 30:* 107–35, 1974.

32 Kohlberg, H. Moral development and the education of adolescents, in *Adolescent readings in behavior development*, ed. by Evans & Hinsdale, Illinois: The Dryden Press Inc., 1970.

33 Piaget, J. *Six psychological studies*, New York: Random House, 1967.

34 Offer, D. *The psychological world of the teenager*, New York: Basic Books, 1967.

35 Mead, M. *Culture and commitment*, 1970.

36 Adelson, J. The development of ideology in adolescents, *Adolescents in the life cycle*, S. Dragastin, G. Elder, eds., New York: John Wiley & Sons, 1975, pp. 63–78.

37 Erikson, E. *Identity: youth and crisis*, New York: W.W. Norton & Company, 1968.

38 Keniston, K. *The uncommitted: alienated youth in American society*, New York: Brace & World, Inc., 1965.

39 Adelson The development of ideology.

40 Levine, S. The mythology of contemporary youth. *Canad. Med. Assoc. J. 113:* 501–04, Sept. 1975.

41 Offer, D. *The psychological world of the teenager: a study of normal adolescent boys*, New York: Basic Books, Inc., Publishers, 1969.

42 Pasmanick, B., Roberts, D.W., Iemkau, P.W., and Krueger, D.B. A survey of mental disease in an urban population, in *Epidemiology of mental disorder*, American Psychiatric Association, 1959, pp. 183–201.

43 Masterson, J.F. *The psychiatric dilemma of adolescence*, New York: Little Brown and Company, 1967.
44 Rutter, M., Graham, P., and Chadwich, O. Adolescent turmoil – fact or fiction, *J. Child Psychol. Psychiat.* (in press).
45 Keniston, K. *The uncommitted.*
46 Levine, S. Adolescents, believing and belonging, *Ann. adolescent Psychiat. 7*, Spring 1979 (in press).
47 Conger, J.J. *Adolescence and youth: psychological development in a changing world*, New York: Harper & Row, 1977.
48 Adelson The development of ideology.
49 Braungart, R. Youth and social movements, in *Adolescence in the life cycle*, S. Dragastin, and G. Elder, eds., New York: John Wiley & Co., 1976, pp. 255–89.
50 Toch, Hans *The social psychology of social movements*, New York: Bobbs-Merrill Co., Inc., 1965.
51 Levine, S. and Salter, N. Youth and contemporary religious movements: psychological findings, *Canad. Psychiat. Assoc. J. 21:* 411–20, 1976.
52 Rosenberg, M. The dissonant context and adolescent self-concept, in *Adolescence in the life cycle*, S. Dragastin and G. Elder, eds., New York: John Wiley and Co., 1978, pp. 97–116.
53 Kohlberg, L. Moral development, 1970.
54 Piaget, J. *Six psychological studies*, 1967.
55 Erikson *Identity*, 1968.
56 Rokeach, M. *The open and closed mind: investigations into the nature of belief systems and personality systems*, New York: Basic Books, Inc., 1960.
57 Slater, P. *The pursuit of loneliness: American culture at the breaking point*, Boston: Beacon Press, 1970.
58 Toffler, A. *Future shock*, New York: Basic Books, Inc., Publishers, 1971.
59 Leighton, D. The empirical status of the integration-disintegration hypothesis, in *Psychiatric disorder and the urban environment*, B. Kaplan, ed., New York: Behavioral Publications, 1971.
60 Keniston, K. *The uncommitted*, 1965.
61 Blum, R. & Associates *Society and drugs: social and cultural observation*, San Francisco: Jossey-Bass Inc., Publishers, 1969.
62 Braungart, R. Youth and social movements, in Dragastin and Elder, eds., *Adolescence in the life cycle*, New York: J. Wiley & Co., pp. 255–89.
63 Seeman, M. On the meaning of alienation, *Am. sociolog. Rev. 24:* 783–91, 1959.
64 Frank, Jerome Stimulus/Response: the demoralized mind, *Psychol. Today*, April 1973, p. 22.

65 Levine, S., Carr, R., and Horenblas, W. The urban commune: fact or fancy, promise or pipe dream, *Am. J. Orthopsychiat. 43:* 149–63, 1973.
66 Randal, D. and McClure, G. The effectiveness of residential treatment, Proposed study, Ontario Ministry of Health, 1977.
67 Doherty, G. Teaching acting-out youth acceptable ways of exerting control over their environment, *Canada's Mental Health 22*, June 1974.
68 Delryer, P. Evaluation of elan, Chicago, 1975.
69 Angell, M. Positive peer culture, *Texas Quart. XIV:* 165–72, Summer 1977.
70 Robins, L.N. Follow-up studies of behavior disorders in children, in H.C. Quay, and J.S. Werry, eds., *Psychopathological disorders of childhood*, New York: John Wiley & Sons, 1972, pp. 414–450.
71 Moynihan, D. Some thoughts on the 1960's and 1970's, *The public interest 32:* 3–12, Summer 1973.
72 International Labour Organization, Geneva, March 1977.
73 Coleman, J. Chairman. *Youth: transition to adulthood, a report of the panel on youth of the President's Science Advisory Committee*, Chicago: University of Chicago Press, 1974.
74 Conger, J.J. *Adolescence*, 1977.
75 Levine, S., Lloyd, D., and Longdon, W. The speed user: social and psychological factors in amphetamine abuse, *Canad. psychiat. Assoc. J. 17:* 229–41, 1972.
76 Erikson, E. *Identity*, 1968, p. 19.
77 Ibid., p. 22.
78 Ibid., p. 23.
79 Conger, J.J. *Adolescence*. 1977.
80 Erikson, E. *Identity*, 1968, p. 132.
81 Brofenbrenner, U. The origins of alienation, *Scientific American 231:* 60, 1974.
82 Herman, M., Sadofsky, S., and Rosenberg, B. *Work youth and unemployment*, New York: Thomas Y. Crowell Co., 1968, p. vii.
83 Silberman, C.E. *Crisis in the classroom: the remaking of American education*, New York: Random House, 1970, p. 18.
84 Pitman, W. in *The Toronto Star*, 15 July 1977.
85 U.S. Department of Health, Education and Welfare. *Toward a social report*, Washington, D.C.: U.S. Government Printing Office, 1969, 66–90.
86 Godway, C. and Wilson, H.A. *Functional literacy – basic reading performance: technical summary*. Denver: The Education Commission of the States, 1975.
87 *Secondary/post secondary interface study*. Summary report. Ontario Ministry of Education/Ontario Ministry of Colleges and Universities, 1976.
88 Herman et al. *Work, youth*, 1968, p. 8.

89 Pink, W.T. and White, M.F. Delinquency prevention: the state of the art, in M.V. Klein, ed., *The juvenile justice system*, Beverly Hills, Calif.: Sage Criminal Justice System Annual, Vol. V., 1976.

90 Deisach, D. *Family life education in Canadian schools*, Toronto: The Canadian Education Association, 1977.

91 Coleman, J.S., Mood, A.M., Campbell, E.Q., et al. *Equal educational opportunity*, Washington, D.C.: Government Printing Office, 1966.

92 Evans, R.N. School for schooling's sake: the current role of the secondary school in occupational preparation, in *The transition from school to work*, Princeton, N.J.: Industrial Relations Section, 1968.

93 Bachman, J.G., Green, J., and Wirtanen, I.D. *Youth in transition*, Vol. III, *Dropping out - problem or symptom*, Ann Arbor, Michigan: Institute for Social Research, Univ. of Michigan, 1971.

94 Johnson, J.S. *Update on education: a digest of the national assessment of educational progress*, Denver: The Education Commission of the States, 1975.

95 Buttrick, J.A. *Who goes to university from Toronto?* Toronto: Ontario Economic Council, February 1977.

96 Boyle, R.P. The effect of the high school on students' aspirations, *Am. J. Sociol. 71:* 628–39, No. 131, 1966.

97 Bordua, D.J. Educational aspirations and parental stress on college, *Soc. Forces 38:* 262–69, 1970.

98 Bachman, J.G. et al. *Youth in transition*, 1971.

99 Simpson, R.L. Parental influence, anticipatory socialization, and social mobility, *Am. Sociol. Rev. 27:* 517–22, August 1962.

100 Mihalka, J.A. *Youth and work*, Columbus, Ohio: Charles E. Merrill, 1974.

101 Evans, R.N. School for schooling's sake, 1968.

102 Venn, G. *Man, education and manpower.* Washington, D.C.: American Association of School Administrators, 1970.

103 Coleman, J. *Youth: transition to adulthood*, 1974.

104 Mihalka, J.A. *Youth and work*, 1974.

105 Princeton Manpower Symposium, *The transition from school to work*, 1968, Princeton, N.J.: Industrial Relations Section.

106 Mihalka, J.A. *Youth and work*, 1974.

107 Coleman, J. *Youth: transition to adulthood*, 1974.

108 Evans, R.N. School for schooling's sake, 1968.

109 Harvey, E.B. and Masemann, V.L. *Occupational graduates and the labour force*, Toronto: Ontario Ministry of Education, 1975.

110 Work Group on Vocational Schools, *Vocational schools in Toronto: an interim report*, 1973, Toronto Board of Education.

111 Harvey, E.B. and Masemann, V.L. *Occupational graduates*, 1975.
112 Mihalka, J.A. *Youth and work*, 1974.
113 *Vocational schools in Toronto*, 1973.
114 Harvey, E.B. and Masemann, V.L. *Occupational graduates*, 1975.
115 Levin, H.M. *The costs to the nation of inadequate education*, report prepared for the Select Committee on Equal Educational Opportunity of the U.S. Senate, January 1972.
116 Bachman, S.G. et al. *Youth in transition*, 1971.
117 Peebles, D. *Dropping out: a review of the research and literature*, Toronto: Department of Educational Research Services, Board of Education, Borough of North York, January 1973.
118 Bachman, J.G. ct al. *Youth in transition*, 1971.
119 Peebles, D. *Dropping out*, 1973.
120 Sangster, D.L. *Youth unemployment in Canada: a detailed analysis*, Ottawa: Department of Manpower & Immigration, Research Projects Group, 1976.
121 Stobo, H. and Ziegler, S. A survey of high school dropouts in two schools in the Borough of York, Toronto: The Board of Education for the Borough of York, May 1973.
122 Reich, C. and Young, V. Patterns of dropping out, Toronto: Research Department, Board ot Education for the City of Toronto, December 1974.
123 Sangster, D. et al. *Youth unemployment*, 1978.
124 Bachman, J.G. et al. *Youth in transition*, 1971.
125 Super, D.E. Vocational development of high school dropouts, in D. Schreiber, *Guidance and the high school dropout*, Washington, D.C.: American Personnel and Guidance Association, 1961.
126 Wenk, E. Schools and delinquency prevention, *Crime and delinquency Literature 6:* 236, 1974.
127 Bachman, J.G. et al. *Youth in transition*, 1971.
128 Ibid.
129 Levin, H.M. *The costs to the nation*, 1972.
130 Burstein, M., Tienhaara, N., Hewson, P., and Marrander, B. *Canadian work values: findings of a work ethic survey and a job satisfaction survey*, Ottawa: strategic planning and research, Dept. of Manpower and Immigration, 1975.
131 Levin, H.M. *The costs to the nation*, 1972.
132 Bachman, J.G. et al. *Youth in transition*, 1971.
133 Coleman, J. *Youth: transition to adulthood*, p. 15.
134 Tuttle, G. *A reference manual for the Canadian Youth Commission: youth and jobs in Canada*, Toronto: Ryerson Press, 1946, p. v.
135 Statistics Canada, *The labour force*, April 1978, Catalogue F1001, Table 32.

136 U.S. Dept. of Labor, Manpower Administration, *Manpower report of the President*, Washington, D.C.: U.S. Government Printing Office, 1974.
137 Collins, K. *Youth and employment: a source book*, Canadian Council on Social Development, December 1976.
138 Ibid.
139 Ibid.
140 Burstein, M. et al. *Canadian work values*, 1975.
141 Harvey, E.G. and Masemann, V.L. *Occupational graduates*, 1975.
142 Collins, K. *Youth and employment*, 1976.
143 Canada's time bomb: unemployed youth 'a powder keg' politicians, professors warn. The *Toronto Star*, 3 September 1977.
144 *Future trends in enrollment and manpower in Ontario*, Ottawa: Statistics Canada, 1976.
145 Piker, J. *Entry into the labor force*, Ann Arbor, Mich: Institute of Labor and Industrial Relations, 1968.
146 Lazar, H. and Donner A. The dimension of Canadian youth unemployment: a theoretical explanation, *Indust. Rel./Industrielles, 21:* 295–321, 1967.
147 Kolachak, ed. *The youth labor market*, Ann Arbor, Mich.: Institute of Labor and Industrial Relations, 1969.
148 Sangster et al. *Youth unemployment*, 1976.
149 Burstein, M. et al. *Canadian work values*, 1975.
150 Lazar, H. and Donner A. The dimension of Canadian youth unemployment, 1967.
151 Kolachak, E. *The youth labor market*, 1969.
152 Piker, J. *Entry into the labor force*, 1968.
153 Statistics Canada *The labor force*, April 1978.
154 *Bridging the gap: a mandate for action to important transitions between education and employment.* A progress report from the Bridging the Gap Conference held in Metropolitan Toronto, Ontario, in May and November 1975. Prepared by Michael Sinclair with Brian Oxley. Toronto: Bridging the Gap Policy and Planning Committee. December 1976.
155 Unless otherwise specified, the material on Canadian programmes is based on the press releases of speeches by the Honourable Bud Cullen, Minister of Employment and Immigration, and pamphlets and brochures issued by the federal and provincial governments.
156 Bedville, Gwen A report on youth activities in the Ontario region, paper presented at the National Conference of Youth Consultants at National Headquarters (Employment and Immigration, Canada), Ottawa, 18–21 October 1977.
157 Coleman, James *Youth: transition to adulthood*, 1974.

158 Illich, Ivan *De-schooling society*, New York: Harper & Row, Harrow Books, 1970.
159 Ontario Ministry of Education Guidelines for Cooperative Utilization of Community Facilities.
160 Weaver, Donald C. A case for theory development in community education, *Phi Delta Kappan*, November 1972, p. 157.
161 Usher, Brian R. *Etobicoke community involvement program evaluation.* Evaluation of a secondary school programme involving students in community and social service activities. Ministry of Education, Ontario, Queen's Park, 1977.
162 Ontario Ministry of Colleges and Universities *Ontario career action program, phase II*, evaluation report, Ministry of Colleges and Universities, Queen's Park, Toronto, Ontario, January 1977.
163 Ibid.
164 Ibid.
165 Eaton, Ivan The bank of Montreal youth project ... a way in training, Fall 1975, pp. 24-27.
166 Unless otherwise specified, material on the American programmes is drawn from the Youth Act Kit, U.S. Department of Labor, Employment and Training Administration. Office of Youth Programs, 1977 – a compilation of information on the goals, objectives, intent, and plans of the Employment and Training Administration (ETA) for implementation of new youth programmes, funded under the Youth Employment and Demonstration Projects Act (YEDPA) of 1977 and the Job Corps.
167 The following information on the Job Corps, including evaluation commentary are based on Sar A. Levitan and Benjamin H. Johnston *The jobs corps: a social experiment that works*, Baltimore, Maryland: Johns Hopkins University Press, 1975.
168 Burstein, M. et al. *Canadian work values*, 1975.
169 Weber, M. *The Protestant ethic and the spirit of capitalism*, New York: Charles Scribner's Sons, 1958.
170 Burstein, M. et al. *Canadian work values*, 1975.
171 Tilgher, A. *Homo faber: work through the ages*, Chicago: Regners, Henry & Co., 1964, p. 143.
172 Yankelovich, D. *The new morality: a profile of American youth in the 1970's*, New York: McGraw-Hill, 1974.
173 Burstein, M. et al. p. 7.
174 Ibid.
175 Yankelovich, D. *The new morality*, 1974.
176 Burstein, M. et al. p. 7.

177 Block, R. and Langman, L. Youth and work: the diffusion of 'counter-cultural values,' *Youth and society 52:* 411–32, No. 4, 1974.
178 Yankelovich, D. *The new morality*, 1974.
179 Money, J. and Erhardt, A. *Man and woman, boy and girl: the differentiation and dimorphism of gender identity from conception to maturity*, Baltimore: Johns Hopkins Univ. Press, 1972, p. 186.
180 Conger, J.J. *Adolescence*, 1977.
181 Luckey, E.B. and Nass, G.D. A comparison of sexual attitudes and behaviour in an international sample, *J. Mar. & Fam. 31:* 364–79, No. 2, May 1969.
182 Johnson, Clara L. Attitudes toward premarital sex and family planning for single-never-pregnant-teenage girls, *Adolescence*, 9: 255–62, No. 34.
183 Greenglass, E. Attitudes toward abortion, *Family planning in Canada*, Schlesinger, B., ed., Toronto: U of T Press, 1974, pp. 207–13.
184 Pomeroy, R. and Landman, L.C. Public opinion trends: elective abortion and birth control services to teenagers, *Family planning perspectives 4:* 44–45, No. 4, 1972.
185 Kirkendall, L.A. and Libby, R.W. Interpersonal relationships – crux of the sexual renaissance, *J. Soc. Issues 22:* 45–58, April 1966.
186 Reiss, I.L. *The social context of premarital sexual permissiveness*, New York: Holt, Rinehart & Winston, 1967.
187 Sorenson, R.C. *Adolescent sexuality in contemporary America*, New York: World Publishers, 1973.
188 Kirkendall, L.A. and Libby, R.W. *Interpersonal relationships*, 1968.
189 Conger, J.J. 1977, *Adolescence*, p. 283.
190 Sorenson, R.C. *Adolescent sexuality*, 1973.
191 Yankelovich, D. *The new morality*, 1974.
192 Luckey, E.B. and Nass, G.D. Comparison of sexual attitudes, 1976.
193 Shymko, D.L. Current sex research in Canada, in *Sexual behaviour in Canada*, Schlesinger, B., ed., Toronto: U of T Press, 1977.
194 Kinsey, A.C., Pomeroy, W.B., Martin, C.E., and Gebhard, P.H. *Sexual behavior in the human female*, Philadelphia: Saunders, 1953.
195 Schofield, M. *The sexual behaviour of young people*, London: Longmans Press, 1965.
196 Cannon, K.L. and Long, R. Premarital sexual behaviour in the sixties, *J. Mar. & Fam. 23:* 36–49, No. 1, February 1971.
197 Sorenson, R.C. *Adolescent sexuality*, 1973.
198 Zelnik, M. and Kantner, J.F. The probability of premarital intercourse, *Soc. Sci. Res. 1:* 335–41, No. 3, 1972.

199 Zelnik, M. and Kantner, J. Sexual and contraceptive experience of young unmarried women in the United States 1976–71, *Family Planning Perspectives 9:* 55–71, No. 2, 1977.
200 Sorenson, R.C. *Adolescent sexuality*, 1973.
201 Orthopharmaceutical Corporation *Teenage and premarital sexual counselling*, Ortho Panel 3, Raritan, N.J.: Orthopharmaceutical Corp., 1968, pp. 4–7.
202 Gagnon, J. The creation of the sexual in early adolescence. In J. Kagan and R. Coles, eds., *Twelve to Sixteen: early adolescence*, New York: W.W. Norton & Co., 1971.
203 Hunt, M. *Sexual behavior in the 1970's*
204 Guyatt, D. *Adolescent pregnancy*, Faculty of Social Work, University of Toronto, unpublished dissertation, 1976.
205 Sorenson, R.C. *Adolescent sexuality*, 1973.
206 Hunt, M. *Sexual behaviour in the 1970's.*
207 Conger, J.J. *Adolescence*, 1977, p. 281.
208 Reiss, I.L., ed. The sexual renaissance in America, *J. Soc. Issues 22:* No. 2, 1966.
209 Hunt, M. *Sexual behavior in the 1970's.*
210 Burks, J.L. Contraception for minors: report of a physician survey, *J. pediat. Med. 5:* 152–53, No. 4, 1970.
211 Guyatt, D. Family planning and the adolescent girl, in *Family Planning in Canada*, B. Schlesinger, ed., U of T Press, 1974, pp. 176–82.
212 Cvetkovich, G., Grote, B., Sjorseth, A., and Sarkissian, J. On the psychology of adolescents, use of contraceptives, *J. Sex. Res. 11:* 256–70, No. 3, 1975.
213 Sorenson, R.C. *Adolescent sexuality*, 1973.
214 Guyatt, D. *Adolescent pregnancy*, 1976.
215 Orthopharmaceutical Corporation *Teenage and premarital counselling*, 1968.
216 Sorenson, R.C. *Adolescent sexuality*, 1973.
217 Elkind, D. Egocentricism, 1967.
218 Guyatt, D. *Adolescent pregnancy*, 1976.
219 Sorenson, R.C. *Adolescent sexuality*, 1973.
220 Orthopharmaceutical Corporation *Teenage and premarital counselling*, 1968.
221 Guyatt, D. *Counselling*, 1968.
222 Zelnik, M. and Kantner, J.F. Sexual and contraceptive experience, 1977.
223 Guyatt, D. *Adolescent pregnancy*, 1976.

224 Osofsky, H.J. Teenage out-of-wedlock pregnancy: some preventive considerations, *Adolescence 5:* 151–86, No. 18, 1970.
225 Guyatt, D. Family planning, 1974.
226 Sorenson, R.C. *Adolescent sexuality*, 1973.
227 Zelnik, M. and Kantner, J.F. Premarital intercourse, 1972.
228 Guyatt, D. Family planning, 1974.
229 Guyatt, D. *Adolescent pregnancy*, 1976.
230 Sorenson, R.C. *Adolescent sexuality*, 1973.
231 Guyatt, D. *Adolescent pregnancy*, 1976.
232 Hausknecht, R. The termination of pregnancy in adolescent women, *Pediat. Clin. N. America, 19:* 803–10, No. 3, 1972.
233 Sorenson, R.C. *Adolescent sexuality*, 1973.
234 Ibid.
235 Goldsmith, N.S. Teenagers and abortion: some special considerations, Abortion techniques and services, proceedings of a symposium, New York: June 1971. Amsterdam: *Excerpts Medice*, p. 147–50.
236 Gabrielson, I.W., Goldsmith, J., Potts, C., Mathews, V., and Gabrielson, M.O. Adolescent attitudes toward abortion: effects on contraceptive practice, *Am. J. Pub. Health 61:* 730–38, No. 4, April 1971.
237 Guyatt, D. *Adolescent pregnancy*, 1976.
238 Erikson, E. *Identity*, 1968.

6

Ethnic Diversity and Children

SUZANNE ZIEGLER

There is a very old tradition in the English-speaking world that associates cities with moral corruption, and with the degeneration of children. English novelists of the eighteenth and nineteenth centuries, like Fielding and Dickens, vividly described the physical and spiritual indignities likely to be visited upon children who live in cities. The theme of the purity of the country, the benevolence of its air, its open spaces, and its honest society, in contrast to the toxins of the city is as alive today as it was then. From *Tom Jones* to *Huckleberry Finn* to the latest edition of *The Whole Earth Catalogue*, we have continually renewed our subscription to the idea that the country is the best place to raise children, that God's country is outside cities, that the simple and basic skills of subsistence are more ennobling than the skills which insure survival and success in the city.

A current version of this old idea is that small towns, rather than cities, because they provide a more ideal environment for child rearing, breed the most competent and the best-adjusted adults. Popular magazines have featured articles pointing out that all American presidents but one were small-town boys.[1] Scientists have described the benefits of small-town life for developing children's ability to cope with their environment, and feel comfortable in it.[2]

Suburbia can be seen as an attempt by a very large segment of the population to move their children as far as possible from the centre of the city while the parents remain within commuting distance of their city jobs. And the recent revitalization of urban cores depends heavily on the lowered birth rate, as increasing numbers of single people and couples without children renovate city houses and occupy new downtown apartment towers. There is an increasing acceptance of the idea that cities may be good places for people to live – but maybe not for children.[3]

Why should the countryside, or small towns, or suburbs be thought better places for children? Some reasons are obvious: cities have more automobile traffic, which is dangerous for small children. Cities have more industry, thus creating air and soil pollution, which in some forms (notably lead pollution) is much more dangerous to children than to adults. But cities are increasingly striving to limit automobile use, and to control industrial pollution. Cities have fewer open spaces where children can explore nature and use their imagination; but increasing numbers of imaginative playgrounds are being created by architects and planners skilled at designing open spaces which maximize the natural landscape and optimize opportunities for creative play. It is certainly not beyond the scope of our imagination, in 1979, to picture a city with reasonably clean air and water, carefully controlled traffic patterns, good and varied housing, and sufficient and well-planned open spaces.

Such a city would still differ from small towns and suburbs in a significant way, assuming that the population of our city remained relatively stable. Cities differ from smaller centres socially, as well as physically. The simplest and most basic statement of this difference can be stated in a word: diversity. Small towns and suburbs are, relative to cities, characterized by social homogeneity. Class and ethnic[4] variation is far more restricted. Children are far less likely to be exposed to variation in class, race, national origin, language, and the value differences which arise therefrom. One of the early, sociological definitions of the city was offered by Louis Wirth, in 1935. Wirth distinguished three criteria for urban settlements: size, density, and diversity. The human heterogeneity of cities, he asserted, is not simply the predictable product of greater numbers, and therefore greater variance:

... the city shows a kind and degree of heterogeneity of population which cannot be wholly accounted for by the law of large numbers or adequately represented by means of a normal distribution curve ... The city has historically been the melting-pot of races, peoples and cultures ... It has brought together people from the ends of the earth *because* they are different and thus useful to one another rather than because they are homogeneous and like-minded.[5]

The heterogeneous character of urban life has also been described across cultures by anthropologists. Robert Redfield listed heterogeneity as an urban trait, in contrast to the cultural homogeneity of the folk tradition of peasants. In fact, according to one commentator, the cultural heterogeneity of cities is 'the only "urban" characteristic of Redfield's "folk-urban" model that has held up to all attacks on the model.'[6] In spite of its powers of endurance, heterogeneity has been largely ignored as a focus of urban studies in anthropology and sociology in favour of studies of particular neighbourhoods, ethnic groups, or deviate subcultures. The heterogeneous, urban context in which the slum, the ghetto, and the gang exist and operate has been neglected, as have the interactions which occur within and between class and ethnic groups.[7]

Traffic and pollution are urban evils; they are bad for everyone's health, most especially children. Is social heterogeneity, which is at least equally likely in cities, equally undesirable? While relatively few people are committed to such a strong negative position on diversity, people do differ on how much of what kind of heterogeneity they find desirable. Many people who would have no objection to working in a mixed setting with respect to race, national origin, or class, would shun such a mixture in a neighbourhood setting. Indeed, familiar tools of social science, such as the scales to measure social distance, are based on just such premises. Urban planners are familiar with the idea of the tipping point: the degree of integration which is seen as too much by majority group members. Urban neighbourhoods are often far more homogeneous than the city of which they are a part, as people voluntarily or involuntarily create and perpetuate ethnic, racial, or class enclaves.

Why do so many people prefer neighbours who are similar to them in some basic respect to neighbours who are different? Is it ethnocentrism, preference for one's own kind, an attribute of human groups which many suggest is universal? Are fear and dislike of different others an inevitable fact of the human condition? Are children born with it, or do they learn it in the cradle? Can anything be done to alter such attitudes? Can governmental and school policies and programmes which officially sanction cultural alternatives and the maintenance of ethnic traditions and identity have an effect on majority attitudes to diversity? Can they strengthen ethnic boundaries in a positive way at the same time that they encourage tolerance for diversity?

In the following pages, some of these questions are answered. We know, for example, that children do not have negative associations with visible or non-visible human differences until well past infancy and we know that some kinds of experiences in childhood are more likely to enhance intolerance of diversity than others. We know that some techniques for changing children's (and adults') negative feelings to different others are relatively effective, and others are not.

But there is a great deal we do not know. As children become aware of human diversity in their environment, do they inevitably feel less secure about their own identification and self-value than children who lack this experience? Do they feel their world is less predictable and that their control of it is more limited than children without such awareness? If awareness of diversity does result in increased security, is this a passing or a permanent effect? Is it possible that such an experience is transitional and is followed by greater self-confidence, as children learn to operate successfully in a more complex world? Emotional, moral, and cognitive development in children are said to proceed in a step-wise fashion, with new development followed by stabilization, and even by occasional regression. Perhaps children's growing awareness of human differences is a stage in their development during early childhood which, if properly understood and dealt with in a nurturant environment, would lead naturally to a heightened appreciation of the richness of human diversity, and to a sense of increased competence. Obviously, we do not live in an ideal world. Some children will be exposed to narrow-minded parents, teachers, neighbours or relatives. But programmes, centred in schools and the community, which facilitate meaningful contact and create positive intergroup experiences may offer some hope of effecting increased understanding and appreciation of ethnic diversity.

For minority-group children, the effect of successful programmes and policies would be to dissociate felt inferiority from minority-group status; to reduce parent-child conflict which is intercultural in nature; and to make participation in both ethnic and non-ethnic networks and activities more attractive and available.

For majority group children, successful programmes and policies in this area would lead to a positive approach to ethnic differences, and to the development of a sense of being one among many groups, with majority status carrying no special privilege or innate superiority. Individual characteristics would be clearly distinguishable from group differences, and an awareness of cultural uniqueness would not obscure the reality of universally held values and principles.

Population diversity is a common characteristic of cities, and interethnic contact a fact of urban life for most of us, and especially for children. It cannot be avoided; how can it be exploited?

Can the social heterogeneity of cities promote security and competency in children? The children of immigrants live, to an overwhelming degree, in large cities, not small towns. If they are to learn to cope successfully with their environment, they must be able to perceive their ethnic identity positively. At the same time, they must learn to be comfortable in the world of school and of their ethnically diverse peers. They must be able to maintain filial relationships with their parents, in spite of the pressure for linguistic and cultural change, pressure which is much greater for them than for their parents.

For majority group children, can the human heterogeneity of an urban environment be horizon-expanding? Can children who are different be perceived as a positive stimulus instead of a target for discrimination? For all children, can the experience of human diversity not place them at a disadvantage, through confusion about their own identity and crippling prejudice turned against themselves or others; but at an advantage, because they, more than small town or suburban children, know how to live well in a world of multiple possibilities and alternatives? A girl who left Molise in rural Italy for Toronto when she was twelve years old says of her experiences of school in Canada: 'School prepared me to mix with anyone of any nationality. It prepared me so that I'm not too shy to go and talk to another person because here in Canada there's an awful lot of ethnic groups and making friends with all of them prepares you to go out into the world and not be scared to mix with any other group.' And a girl who was ten when she came to Toronto from Rome says of the same experience of exchanging majority for one-among-many minority-group status: 'It has enabled me to look at many things in many different ways, because there are so many different ethnic groups here in Canada ... I was looking at prejudice more freely than I would have been in Italy, and I was acquiring friends that were not in the same ethnic group ... I think it really helped me to *see*, in a broader sense.'[8] Planners, teachers, parents, and all city dwellers face the challenge of making the comfortable independence of the girl from Molise, the understanding and vision of the Roman girl the common share of more and more urban children, immigrants and natives alike.

In this chapter, though it is a review of the literature on interethnic and intraethnic relationships among children, the reader will find little mention of issues like competence, tolerance, or appreciation of diversity. Instead, there are descriptions of a multiplicity of studies of prejudice, and several of intergenerational conflict in immigrant families. As in many areas of social research, the problem orientation of the majority of investigators has left a conspicuous gap in our understanding of what is involved in successful adjustment – in this case to urban ethnic heterogeneity. We shall return to this focus in the last section of the paper, which deals with topics for future research.

I THE CANADIAN CONTEXT

Recency of Immigration
Two kinds of heterogeneity characterize modern human groupings: socio-economic differences (class) and cultural differences (ethnicity). Of these, the latter, as Louis Wirth noted, is essentially an urban phenomenon. In twentieth century Europe and North America, immigrants, whether internal or external, have moved from the country to the city. In Canada, recent growth in large cities is due primarily to immigration. The immigrant population has been more urbanized than the native population according to every Canadian census since 1921. In 1961, when 67.5 per cent of the native population was in cities, the figure for foreign-born was 81.4 per cent.[9] Immigration following World War II has increased the ethnic heterogeneity of Canadian metropolitan areas enormously. In Toronto, where this change has been the greatest, the proportion of British-origin (in the city of Toronto, the central core of the metropolitan area) declined from

80 per cent in 1931 to 46 per cent in 1971. (For the metropolitan area as a whole, in 1971 57 per cent of the population was of British descent.) Recent immigrants include Asians, West Indians, Europeans, and Latin Americans.

The situation of immigrants and ethnic groups in Canada differs in important ways from that extant in the United States and Australia, the source of most of the literature we survey. In the United States, 'ethnic' most often means indigenous and black. Thus, the field of interethnic relations among American children is one dominated by a very clear status hierarchy in which the racial minority group, in spite of centuries of life in the United States, occupies a very low socio-economic position. Children's relationships do not occur in a vacuum, and American children are early aware of the congruence between race and status. In Canada, on the other hand, racial minorities are recent arrivals in most parts of the country. (Notable exceptions are blacks in Halifax, Chinese in Vancouver, and native peoples throughout Canada.) An ethnic status hierarchy is by no means obvious. 'By and large, ethnic groups in Canada are not in massive opposition to one another in their perception of the distribution of economic and political advantages.'[10]

Canadians of non-British and non-French origin may not be conspicuous on the boards of large corporations,[11,12] but non-majority group members do prosper and are increasingly recruited to positions of power and prestige. Statistics released in Canada in 1975 showed immigrants out-earning non-immigrants on average. Minorities in Canada, possibly excepting the native people, are not frozen into an inferior position vis-à-vis the majority, such that a negative self-image is the inevitable social inheritance of their children.

Australia resembles Canada far more than does the United States with respect to demography. Both commonwealth countries have experienced heavy postwar immigration which has radically altered the ethnic composition of many, if not most, of their major cities. But Australia, unlike Canada, has been heavily committed to an assimilationist policy (although this commitment may be diminishing in recent years).[13] Their immigration policy has deliberately excluded non-Europeans, on the basis that they would be too difficult to absorb culturally. The obvious goal of the policy is to minimize the differences between natives and immigrants until, with time, these differences disappear entirely.

Policy of Multiculturalism

In Canada, on the contrary, at the same time that Canadian cities have been growing increasingly diverse with respect to ethnicity, there has emerged an official policy, at the federal, provincial, and municipal levels, which endorses and supports multiculturalism, and makes a variety of resources available to persons and groups interested in maintaining ethnic diversity in such forms as ethnic histories, folklore associations, performing groups, and anti-discrimination bodies. In Toronto and elsewhere, Boards of Education have begun to institutionalize policies of multiculturalism and ethnic pluralism, by offering in the high school and in adult classes, courses in the languages of the communities they serve. For example, 18 modern languages, besides English and French, are offered by the city of Toronto Board of Education. While it is doubtful that the various governments' commitments are to extensive and thorough-going pluralism – for example, no language but English or French can be used as a permanent language of instruction in schools, in spite of repeated petitions – there is, however, a positive emphasis on cultural variation, one goal of which is to legitimate diversity and to heighten the awareness of cultural differences on the part of the host population.

The government's endorsed policy of multiculturalism – the encouragement and maintenance of cultural diversity – is imposed on the basic dualistic (French/ English) institutional structure which exists at the national level. The guarantees made to both founding nations of the right to preserve their languages and cultures gave Canadian society a pattern which, from its beginnings, could not be mono-cultural. While many French-Canadians question their ability to maintain their language and culture within Canada, largely because of pressures from the world of commerce and finance to use English and think English, the legal guarantees of institutional dualism remain. While other ethnic communities do not have the same status as the French – their languages do not have official standing – neither has there been the expectation that they would disappear. Recently, the prime minister of Canada, in a speech to the United States Congress at the time of a separatist victory in a Quebec provincial election, reaffirmed the Canadian commitment to cultural pluralism, and anchored the maintenance of ethnic diversity solidly within the context of French-English relations in Canada. Referring to 'the many cultural minorities who dwell throughout Canada,' he said,

These communities have been encouraged for decades to retain their own identities and to preserve their own cultures. They have done so and flourished ... The sudden departure of Quebec would signify the tragic failure of our pluralist dream, the fracturing of our cultural mosaic, and would likely remove much of the determination of Canadians to protect their cultural minorities.[13a]

This distinction in attitude and policy between Australia and Canada applies, at least until very recently, to the United States as well. Thus Lipset sees a major difference between the United States and Canada in their emphases on universalism (a single set of values and behaviour patterns for all groups) and particularism (where groups maintain distinctive values and behaviour patterns) respectively, and describes the 'melting pot' concept in the United States as 'achievement orientation applied to entire ethnic groups.'[14] The degree of universalism or particularism which obtains has consequences for the frequency, and perhaps the quality, of inter- and intra-group relations. In all three countries, interethnic boundaries exist because of pressures from within the minority groups as well as from outside them. But in Canada official policy[15] acts to strengthen such boundaries from without. Whether stronger external boundaries cause stronger internal boundaries is an empirical question; certainly that is the intention of a multicultural policy. (A more extended discussion of boundaries is presented in section III.)

Some provinces and municipalities, following the federal lead, have adopted a multicultural policy for children. Generally this has occurred within the framework of the educational system, at the pre-university level. Provincial ministries of education have, in some cases, devised courses of study which emphasize the multiethnic nature of Canadian history. In Ontario, a 'Heritage Languages Program' has recently been created to provide extracurricular instruction at the elementary school level in the language of a child's heritage, paid for and provided within the public school system.

At the local level, multiculturalism has been advanced by some boards of education as a policy to encourage ethnic parental participation through the use of community workers and other out-reach strategies; and to use the schools to maintain and strengthen ethnic ties. Such maintenance efforts focus on third language and culture programmes, such as the Heritage Languages Programs; the inclusion of staff members who reflect the ethnic makeup of the neighbourhood; and a general attempt to bridge the gap between ethnic group members, especially immigrants, and the majority culture, with the goal of altering the system so that cultural diversity becomes an advantage rather than a handicap for individual students and student bodies. Where such attempts are being made, considerable controversy exists within local communities as to their advisability, their constraints, and their probable success.

Opponents of multicultural policies and programmes usually argue that such efforts will cause a heightened awareness of racial and cultural difference which will result in greater interethnic prejudice, and that such programmes also will unnecessarily retard the assimilation of immigrants, which is seen as a desirable goal.

Proponents, on the other hand, insist that multicultural programmes enhance mutual respect across ethnic lines and hence lessen prejudice, and that social and cultural assimilation are of dubious desirability; rather, cultural diversity is a valued end state. This is the view that is commonly stated by government representatives at all levels, and which receives considerable endorsement in the press. How widely accepted it is by various segments of the public, however, is difficult to estimate.

Ethnicity as an Intervening Factor in Urban Settings

Thus, in many Canadian cities, simultaneously with dramatic, recent increases in ethnic heterogeneity has come an important change in the officially sanctioned view of how people ought to treat diversity. The idea that a peculiarly urban characteristic, human heterogeneity, might enhance the quality of life seems aberrant historically. The city, as we said earlier, has not traditionally been viewed as a good place in which to grow up. Urban sociology, the science of cities, has reflected this view. Indeed, any historical review of urban studies would send the reader away with a strong sense of the negative aspects of urban life. Urban studies emphasize disorganization, delinquency, anomie, social distance, non-cooperation, impersonality, crowding, and so forth. This has been true, almost without exception, until quite recently. Even the study of immigrant groups in urban settings has been shadowed by a generally bleak view of what cities do to immigrants, most often rural Europeans. American cities are seen as corrosive for immigrants, who suffer from the loss of a coherent culture, of close extended family relationships, and of their native language as an effective means of communication. Gans[16] dates a change in this tradition as emerging about 1954, with writers beginning to reject the Wirthian thesis that urban life is necessarily anomic, and instead to describe such phenomena as the persistence of primary groups.

The recent trend to look for evidence of primary group relationships and non-isolation in cities, which Gans dates to the mid-50s, was tied to the discovery of the persistence of ethnicity in urban enclaves. Gans's own work, *The urban villagers*,[17] documents class and ethnic cultural identity in a second and third generation population in an urban setting. Suzanne Keller in *The urban neighborhood*, cites 'ethnic or immigrant enclaves in urban areas' as similar to small towns and rural areas in 'placing greater reliance on neighbors than the larger, more heterogeneous, more urbanized settlements.'[18] Urban villages and urban neighbourhoods were discovered to be home to hundreds of thousands of first, second, and third generation 'ethnics.'

Toronto: An Urban Instance

Metropolitan Toronto, an urban area of over two and a half million residents according to the 1971 census, has a population that is two-thirds Canadian-born, one-third foreign-born. If children are ignored, the proportion of immigrants increases: half of the family heads in Toronto in 1971 were foreign-born. Slightly more than half of the respondents (all household heads) identified their ethnicity as British Isles. The other groups were Italian, German, French, Asian, Polish, and Ukrainian, all in numbers exceeding 50,000, with the Italians, the largest minority group, numbering 275,000. A substantial Greek community also existed by 1970. Since 1970, the city has been further diversified by large migrations from Portugal, and the West Indies, and increasing numbers from India, Pakistan, Hong Kong, and South America.

People continue to maintain their ethnic identity: although half the household heads in a 1970 survey were Canadian-born and slightly more than half of these were third generation or more, only slightly more than a quarter of the total identified themselves as 'Canadian' without other qualification. This latter group included about 14 per cent of the foreign-born and 39 per cent of the native-born.[19] Thus, more than one-third of native-born Canadians identified as much or more with an ancestral culture as with Canada.

In Toronto, ethnic boundaries are strengthened by a high degree of residential segregation, institutional completeness,[20] and extensive kinship networks. Many immigrant groups here have followed a pattern of chain migration, which has permitted former neighbours to regroup themselves in residential enclaves which are scaled-down models of former villages in Italy, Portugal, or Greece. Even within an ethnic group which has a more individual, less kin-extended pattern of migration, like the West Indians, West Indian food shops, hairdressers, newspapers, radio programmes, etc. permit strong dependence on own-group culture and identification.

Residential segregation and institutional completeness affect children in specific ways. One effect of residential segregation for pre-school children is a lack of contact with members of other ethnic groups. For a smaller, but still very sizable number of children, residential segregation extends to the school: in the city of Toronto, 48 per cent of the elementary schools have at least 10 per cent of the student body falling into one ethnic group. For 11 per cent of the schools, a single group makes up 25–39 per cent of the school, and in 8 per cent (or 18 schools), a single ethnic group comprises 40 per cent or more of the student body. These most homogeneous schools have heavy concentrations within four groups: Italian, Portuguese, Greek, and Chinese. Thus, the possibility of ethnic segregation within the school community exists for a great many children.

Many pre-school children attend nursery schools which are sponsored and used by a particular religious or ethnic group. In Toronto, one can find Ukrainian, Greek, Italian, Jewish, Armenian, and West Indian nurseries and daycare centres. Some religious groups run alternative school systems, kindergarten to university. And many ethnic and religious groups – Chinese, Germans, Greeks,

Jews, Ukrainians, and probably others as well - operate after-school language and cultural programmes. Such programmes are receiving increased financial support from the federal government as part of its multicultural thrust.

The local context, then, is one of recent immigration, institutionally well-developed communities and an official policy favouring the maintenance of a multiethnic society. While such a policy assumes that total assimilation is both unlikely and undesirable, it does not ignore the probability that the transition from one culture to another will be difficult, even in a multicultural context. Indeed, one goal of some multicultural programmes is to lessen intrafamilial strain between parents and children, whose understanding of and commitment to old and new cultures inevitably differ. Nowhere is this made more explicit than in some recently developed school-based multicultural programmes.

Schools, in Canada, have traditionally been assimilationist. They are perhaps the only institutional sector which has consistently been so: 'Nor has any vigorous effort been made to assimilate continental European peoples in Canada, except through the public schools.'[21] While a policy of multiculturalism in the schools would be consistent with the particularism that has been encouraged in adult society, the maintenance of ethnic identity and efforts to that end have generally been confined to the voluntary, private sector, with governmental support. State support of multiculturalism within a majority institution, as opposed to support channelled through ethnic schools or community groups, is a new and controversial idea. Only the French minority have long-standing and formally guaranteed public support for separate institutions - including schools.

The multicultural programmes which have been recommended in the city of Toronto and other municipalities in and around metropolitan Toronto include such non-controversial areas as the teaching of English as a second language, and the inclusion of more and better cross-cultural training in teacher education. The aspects of the programme which are controversial are those that recommend that the school take an active role in helping students to maintain or develop the ancestral language; that non-official languages be integrated into the elementary school curriculum either as subjects of instruction, or as media of instruction. In Toronto, in 1977, the Work Group on Multicultural Programs abandoned such recommendations, for lack of both public and governmental support. Since then, the policy has been altered to include non-official languages as subjects of instruction, but only as an adjunct to, and not a part of, the curriculum.

The premise which underlies the attempt to incorporate students' languages, and thereby their cultures, into the school curricula from the earliest grade levels, is that children from non-majority backgrounds will suffer from a sense of alienation from school or family or both if there is no linguistic and cultural link between home and school. 'In order for these children to develop a positive self-image and feel good about participating, both as members of a family unit and as members of a classroom unit, the schools should provide them with a means of recognizing their own cultural and linguistic heritage as a matter of routine school experience.'[22] In other words, the motivation is to close the culture gap between minority, and especially immigrant minority parents and their children by altering the school, so that its assumptions and demands are not incompatible with, or even unrelated to, those of the home. The difficulties and unhappiness and the degree of intrafamilial conflict which may result when schools do not make such effort are assumed, not extensively documented, although some eloquent, if unsystematic, descriptions do exist.[23] These attempts to ease the special generation gap imposed on immigrant families can perhaps soften what has been seen as an inevitable course: 'The attainment of full ego identity within the new country is, among immigrant children, definitely connected with a detachment from the setting of their family of orientation and a stronger identification with the universalistic patterns of the new country.'[24]

In a setting in which recent immigration from a multitude of English and non-English-speaking countries has diversified the society of cities which were more ethnically homogeneous, many questions of personal values and social policy centre on the desirability of assimilation and acculturation. Given a recent historical trend to stress the power of ethnicity as an enduring dimension of personal, social, and political behaviour over generations, and the dualistic character of Canadian history and culture, it is not surprising that a policy should have evolved at all levels of government which favours the maintenance of a multicultural society. The implications of such a combination of policy and historical trends, for the newcomers and for the receiving society, is, in a general way, the focus of interest of this paper. The research which we shall review below deals with such issues as they affect the attitudes and behaviour of minority and majority groups of children, both in families and as members of peer groups.

II INTRA-GROUP RELATIONS OF CHILDREN

Canadian Studies

Research in the area of intrafamilial relations in immigrant families is informed by a similar concern for intergenerational strain. In Toronto, several researchers have focused on first and second generation minority group children. There are studies of Italian, Greek, Korean, and Chinese adolescents, and of West Indian school children. A common focus, in several of these studies, is on the differential degree of acculturation of parents and their children, and the intrafamilial conflict which may result.

All the studies cited here look for parent-child differences between the first and second generation in such areas as ability in English or adherence to traditional values. Most look also for evidence of conflict, with mixed results. Of the six studies cited, three find that conflict between parents and children over children's demands for greater autonomy is greater for daughters than sons, and two find that language is also a factor in parent-child conflicts – both parents' lack of English and children's indifference to their parents' language.

Intrafamilial conflict has been a focus of several studies of immigrant children in Toronto. Danziger[25,26] found conflict in Italian families over boys' and girls' desires for increased autonomy. Girls, especially, feel the gap between their Canadian peers' freedom and their own lack of it. Such problems are characteristic of Italian families in the immigrant generation only, according to Danziger's data. Even in the immigrant generation, increasing length of residence in Canada is associated with substantial increases in autonomy especially for boys, and an increased role in family decision-making for children and their mothers.[27] By the second generation, Italian girls gain freedom similar to that of other Canadian girls, and Canadian-born Italian mothers' use of reason and authority in child-rearing conforms to North American, not to first generation Italian-American norms.[28]

Colallio's sample of Italian adolescent girls was entirely first generational.[29] Within an immigrant cohort, she found significant differences in conflict over ethnicity and extended-family relationships among girls, according to the degree of linguistic acculturation of their mothers. Those whose mothers had some competence in English were more positive about intraethnic and intrafamilial ties. Colallio's finding suggests that, even in the absence of real change in parental behaviour regarding daughters' independence, the mothers' ability in the new language may have symbolic value: mothers may be seen as more modern, and hence their directions become more acceptable.

Linguistic acculturation was the major bone of contention between Greek adolescents and their parents according to Economopolou's study.[30] Her sample of adolescents attending after-school Greek language and culture programmes reported more conflict at home over language use than over out-group friendships. This is less surprising when considered in light of the fact that the children, though their linguistic acculturation and self-identification as Canadians was far greater than that of their parents, showed much weaker value acculturation. Their values towards dating, arranged marriage, family solidarity, and female independence, among others, were closer to their parents' values than to those of their Canadian peers. This was particularly true for the boys. The girls were somewhat less traditional, and they are more immediately affected in areas like chaperoned dating and female independence.

Kim, similarly, found immigrant Korean girls to be less traditional in their values, and to come into increased conflict with their parents as their length of residence in Canada increases.[31] In fact, contrary to prediction, the boys showed little sign of non-traditionalism, or of parental conflict. Like Italian and Greek girls, Korean girls are traditionally given considerably less freedom than boys, and the possibility for conflict in Canada is accordingly greater for them.

One of Kim's measures, for which he hypothesized an association with parental conflict, was locus of control, which indicates a person's faith in his own ability or inability to control events in his life. His hypothesis was that immigrants would have less sense of control, less confidence in their ability to predict from cause to effect, because of the conflict between traditional and Western values and attitudes (the same conflict that would be interpersonalized within the family). This was the finding of a study of Italian immigrant students in Toronto, which compared them with a sample of Italian students in Italy and with Canadian-born Italian students.[32] Kim was able to replicate this finding for Korean girls, but not for boys.

Beserve[33] also uses the locus of control measure in his study of West Indian children, mostly first generation, in Toronto. He documents ways in which many West Indian-born parents in Toronto fail to provide home environments which are ideally suited to maximizing children's school-readiness and school progress. The result for the children of inconsistency between home and school values may be conflict in both environments.[34] Beserve found positive relationships between children's degree of internal control – that is, sense of being in control – and a positive learning environment (i.e., press for achievement, provisions for general learning) in the home. If one accepts the idea that internalized feelings of control over oneself indicate good emotional health, and an absence of parent-child conflict, as suggested by Kim, then Beserve's findings imply not only poor school performance, but also parent-child conflict for children whose homes provide relatively poor learning environments.

Beserve's study is unusual in examining the possible relationship between parents' 'strength of ethnicity' and facets of their own and their children's behaviour. In fact, he found no relationship between parents' intragroup solidarity, as measured by number and intimacy of within-group friendships, membership in ethnic organizations, and any of the home environment variables he measured. These included, in addition to learning-related factors, the variable of 'family security.' Furthermore, parents' intragroup solidarity was not related to children's verbal or perceptual abilities, self-concept, or degree of internal control.

Whereas Economopolou found considerable difference between Greek and Canadian children judged by traditional Greek values, when Wolfgang and Shell[35] compared recently arrived Chinese (with an average residence in Canada of 2¾ years) to Canadian-born high school students on a scale of items, some of which reflected traditional Chinese values and some Canadian values, they found that most of their items, although designed to get at intragroup differences, failed to differentiate between the two groups. Questions tapped family relationships, attitudes to sex and marriage, non-verbal behaviour, interpersonal relations, education, and self. Thus, Canadian students were as likely to agree that 'respect for elders is important' and 'embarrassing others is most inappropriate' as were Chinese. And Chinese were as likely as Canadians to reject the statement that 'a teacher's decisions should not be questioned' and to agree that 'to be independent is very important.' A possible explanation of this similarity in values is that the majority of Chinese immigrants to Toronto are from urban Hong Kong, and thus share with Canadians certain norms which are characteristic of urban, industrialized societies.[36]

Since most studies of immigrants discussed above are dealing with people from rural areas, there is the possibility of taking as Canadian/European differences in values and behaviour what are more basically urban/rural differences. Like the male/female dimension, the urban/rural origin difference may be central in explaining value conflict, or its absence.

These recent Canadian studies of the relationships between immigrants and their children are clearly grounded in a conceptual framework in which change in children's behaviour and values and intergenerational conflict resulting from this change are central. When either is found missing, as in Kim's study, the prediction of the author is not confirmed.

There is no evidence that parents attempt to limit their children's cross-ethnic friendships, at least prior to dating and marriage. Economopolou looked for it but did not find it. There is evidence of conflict over language between parents and children, with each generation concerned that its preferred language be acquired and maintained. If there is a struggle on the part of each generation to pull the other into its own orbit, the struggle appears to be at the symbolic level of language more than at the level of everyday social relations.

Other Research

Australian Studies
Australian studies of intragroup relationships mirror the more assimilationist policy which that country has adopted. Unlike Canadian studies, they tend to look at absorption more than adjustment, and to find rapid change, little intergenerational conflict, and relatively little ethnic loyalty. Whether such findings corroborate the effectiveness of government policy, we cannot judge. But in light of the fact that the receiving society resembles Canada (outside Quebec) linguistically and culturally, and that most of the immigrant groups which are represented in Australia have also come to Canada, the Australian studies become important here, not only for their intrinsic value, but also as the reflection, both

in their design and in their results, of a policy very different from that prevailing in Canada. While a two-continent comparison is far removed from a laboratory situation, there is a sense in which, given a certain basic similarity between the host countries and their recent immigrants, the policy becomes the significant independent variable, in comparing the Canadian and Australian literature on immigrants and ethnicity.

Australian studies, like Canadian studies, date from the mid-twentieth century, and focus on immigrant and second-generation children and their parents. Taft and Johnson studied the children of Polish immigrants[37] and found that, as in several of the Toronto studies, language was the prime area of intergenerational conflict. Like Colallio, they found that parent-child conflict was related negatively to parental assimilation. But unlike Colallio, the authors conclude that the influence of immigrant parents on the adolescent children in their sample seems to be indirect and limited, especially on the boys, whose rate of assimilation was negatively related to that of their parents. (By contrast, Reiger,[38] working with Yemenite adolescents in Israel, found that the children followed their immigrant parents' lead in identifying or not identifying with the dominant Israeli culture; and Dawson, Ng, and Wing-Cheung[39] also found very high correlations between parents' and children's traditional attitudes, in Hong Kong.)

Taft and Johnson's is the only study which addresses the issue of parent-child differences as a potential source of intrafamilial conflict. Most of the Australian work focuses not on conflict in the immigrant family, but on assimilation in the second generation; indeed, there is an apparent assumption that assimilation will occur in one generation. Johnson, in her book-length study of Polish, German, and 'Australian' Australians, never defines the last group, except to say that they are Australian-born.[40] They could have been no more than second generation; but the assumption about assimilation in Australia is such that there is no need to define ethnically anyone beyond the immigrant generation. Doczy's work is an exception, in looking for and at ethnic differences in a second-generation sample.[41]

Taft studied intergenerational change over three generations among Australian Jews.[42] He found that, within each generation – first, second, and third – children (aged 16–25) self-identified less strongly as Jews, both socially and religiously, than their parents, though they identified more strongly with Israel. They also found that assimilation was proceeding across all generations (of adults and youth). By the third generation, young people expressed no preference for intraethnic social relationships.

Feather and Wasyluk's study of second-generation Ukrainian-descended university students and their parents[43] is typically Australian in its approach: it documents the acculturation of the children, and the measure is one that is not really culture-specific. Rather than examining adherence to traditional Ukrainian values, the authors looked at terminal values like a comfortable life, freedom, a world at peace, and instrumental values like honesty and courtesy, which presumably have meaning in all cultures. In fact, the Ukrainian students' terminal values (which are defined as more basic to attitude formation than instrumental values) are closer to those of the Australian parents than to those of their own parents. The children, lacking their parents' experience of the economic and social hardships which both motivated and directly followed their migration, are interested in excitement as much as comfort, in love more than security. And where their parents are much more concerned with salvation (whose institutionalization, for Ukrainians, is found in an ethnic church), the children emphasize the universalistic 'true friendship.' These findings are quite different from those reported by Economopoulou or Kim in Canada. A possible explanation is that value change is slower in Canada than in Australia, because of the greater encouragement of ethnic diversity here.

American Studies
Contemporary Canadian investigators have only a very sparse earlier literature from which to draw. Australian studies are contemporaneous; and among American studies of immigrants and ethnic groups there is little description of any sort of the assimilation of the children of earlier waves of immigrants, 'other than general observations that the children are usually more assimilated than their parents (e.g. Warner and Srole) or that second generation children are correspondingly more assimilated.'[44] Rather than attempting to capture the process, sociologists traditionally have documented end-states: degrees of acculturation or assimilation, by ethnic groups, at a point in time. Their subjects are almost always adults. And American anthropologists, until the 1970s, really did not interest themselves in immigrants at all.

The lack of data, of even a simple descriptive nature, about the children of immigrants is surprising. After all, no one really thought the immigrants themselves would melt; rather it was their children, born and/or raised on American soil, educated in that great democratic, upwardly mobilizing institution, the American public school, who would all smoothly and unconsciously give up mother tongues and old country ways. To the extent that ethnic neighbourhoods, an ethnic press, ethnic endogamy, and ethnic voting patterns survive, they do so in spite of the overwhelmingly common prediction that the children, by mingling freely with their peers of other backgrounds, would be culturally homogenized in the process, an assumption which few earlier writers saw any need to test.

There do not appear to be any studies of ethnically identified American children in the process of sociocultural change. The classic American studies do not focus on children, although Warner and Srole briefly discuss intergenerational problems within the family,[45] Francis Ianni, who has published several studies of Italian-Americans, has written a brief overview of the Italo-American teenager over three generations.[46] He traces a pattern of increasing assimilation resulting from weakening family ties. In the first generation, membership in street-corner gangs, common among Italian male adolescents, can be seen both as compensation for the decreased saliency of the family, and as symptomatic of the conflict the boys felt between their parents' values and those of their American peers. Ianni sees this adolescent generation as conflicted and confused about their ethnic identity.[47] The second and third generations of Italian adolescents, however, are increasingly integrated into lower-class American society, and accept its morés. Like Gans, Ianni sees class replacing ethnicity as a determinant of behavioural patterns for Italian-Americans but he is also aware that it is ethnic identification from outside or inside – from peers or parents – 'which preserves some element of ethnicity in the Italo-American teenager.'[48] Ianni predicts that even this boundary will eventually disappear, and assimilation will soon be complete.

Because the Americans expected, as the Australians appear still to do, that acculturation and assimilation would be complete within, at most, two generations, contemporary students of ethnic relations find themselves with a surprisingly sparse body of research on which to base hypotheses. But a major theoretical development in recent years has made an important contribution to the field of intragroup and intergroup relationships. This is the concept of the boundary as a shifting but constant delineator of intergroup differences and intragroup solidarity. Simultaneously, a research tradition has evolved which examines interpersonal relationships by describing social networks; that is, a group is defined on the basis of the ties which are found to exist among its members. Boundaries and networks are both ways of defining groups *de facto* instead of *a priori*, and as such offer new and exciting possibilities for empirical studies of intragroup and intergroup relationships.

III ETHNIC BOUNDARIES AND SOCIAL NETWORKS

Ianni's article, appearing in 1961, preceded the work of Gordon, Greeley, and the others who were responsible for altering the tendency to see assimilation as ultimately inevitable for American ethnic groups. One hazards a guess that Ianni's perspective now might be different, that he might not be willing to assert that '... the third generation (Italo-American) teenager is quite similar to other lower class teenagers ... As the process of assimilation continues, even these (remaining status-related) differences will disappear, and he will soon be indistinguishable from other teenagers.'[49] Evan Alba, who has recently strongly criticized the contention of Gordon, Greeley, and others that social assimilation is a relatively weak force, does not take as strong a point of view as Ianni.[50]

But if his certainty about assimilation seems a dated concept, Ianni's description of the pressures that maintain ethnic identification – '... the fact that he is still identified as being an Italian-American by his peers and his parents' – seems a forerunner of the immensely useful concept enunciated by Barth[51] almost twenty years later: the notion that the boundary between groups, rather than the cultural content on either side of the boundary, is the important and enduring determinant of ethnic identification.

Barth's contribution makes sense of the pattern of ethnic continuity maintained in spite of cultural change which anthropologists and sociologists have described all over the world, particularly in pluralist societies, where, as a result of colonialization or immigration, distinct cultural groups have met, mingled, changed, and yet remained separate. Barth says that

... the nature of the continuity of ethnic groups is clear: it depends on the maintenance of a boundary. The cultural features that signify the boundary may change, and the cultural characteristics of the members may likewise be transformed, indeed, even the organizational form of the group may change – yet the fact of continuing dichotomization between members and outsiders allows us to specify the nature of continuity ...[52]

Seen in these terms, the secularization and Anglicization of American ethnic groups is, from the point of view of ethnic identity, non-disruptive. Italian-American newspapers are no less Italian, even though they are now published in English, just as Greek social organizations are no less Greek, even if they have lost their religious character. People may have lost distinguishing cultural differences – but their social divisions are still as strong and as ethnic as before.

Ethnic boundaries, according to Barth, are based on both 'criteria and signals for identification,' whereby members recognize like and unlike others, and also 'a structuring of interaction which allows for the persistence of cultural differences.'

Stable interethnic relations presuppose ... a set of prescriptions governing situations of contact, and allowing for articulation in some sectors or domains of activity, and a set of proscriptions on social situations preventing inter-ethnic interaction in other sectors, and thus insulating parts of the cultures from confrontation and modification.[53]

These prescriptions and proscriptions which regulate interethnic relations are boundary-maintainers, which operate to reduce the frequency or the intensity or the meaningfulness of interethnic contact.

With the discovery of the persistence of ethnic identity has come a close examination of those aspects of social and cultural life which contribute to the maintenance of that identity. There is extensive research on residential segregation, on institutional completeness of ethnic groups, on the maintenancy of mother tongue, on endogamy – in short on all kinds of boundary-maintaining devices.

There is abundant evidence that ethnic residential segregation exists in American and Canadian cities. Darroch and Marston,[54,55] and Schwirian and Matre[56] document high rates of residential segregation in Toronto, no matter whether birthplace or mother tongue is used as the criterion of ethnicity. This segregation, measured by an index of dissimilarity from the British-origin population, is definitely ethnic in character. 'Socioeconomic differences by themselves account for only relatively small proportions of the ethnic segregation in all cases.[57] The ethnic neighbourhood is often multiclass.

Similarly, in a recent study of four American cities, Kantrowitz[58] and Guest and Weed[59] found that ethnic residential segregation does not disappear over time; and that although it is highly related to socio-economic status, it 'would continue to exist even if social status differences among ethnic groups disappeared.'[60] Thus, another aspect of ethnicity which was supposed to disappear according to the traditional 'Chicago school' view[61] is with us still, and shows no sign of disappearing.

The effects of residential integration on boundary maintenance are not wholly unambiguous. While proximity does promote contact[62] and while distance may help to inhibit it and so preserve boundaries, such contact may be ineffective in forming positive interpersonal relations. Thus Molotch[63] asserts that propinquity can inhibit, as well as promote, positive relationships. Suttles[64] discusses some of the inhibiting factors in the neighbourhood he studied. Cultural differences, he found, were effective barriers to communication.

Conversely, many researchers have found that the maintenance of social networks, often kin-based, does not depend heavily on propinquity, since good transportation and the telephone make distance less salient. For most children, furthermore, the immediate neighbourhood ceases to be an effectively bounded unit as soon as they go to school, since school catchment areas typically encompass more than one ethnic group, even in cities with reasonably high rates of ethnic residential segregation, like Toronto.

One of the significant correlates of residential segregation is institutional completeness, which may be far more important to the maintenance of an ethnic community, over time, than physical propinquity. Breton[65] shows that 'The degree of institutional completeness and the magnitude of the ethnic interpersonal network are interdependent phenomena ... once a formal structure has developed, it has the effect of reinforcing the cohesiveness of already existing networks and of expanding these networks.'[66] Breton, working in Montreal, finds a correlation between institutional completeness for ethnic minorities, and the proportion of the group which cannot speak a majority group language (English or French).

The one ethnic institution which exists solely to serve children is the ethnic school, which may be an all-day parochial school or an after-school language and culture programme. It is common for ethnic groups to support such alternate or additional educational programmes for the purpose of maintaining their religion, language, and ethnic identity in their children's generation. Interestingly, such schools seem to be generally ineffective as boundary-maintaining mechanisms.[67,68,69,70]

Language maintenance has been studied in the United States by Fishman[71] and in Canada by O'Bryan et al.[72] Both studies document clearly the erosion of ethnic languages over time, and the necessity of new immigrants (or perhaps new and different deliberate efforts on the part of government) to maintain minority languages. Fishman sees one causal factor as the lack of any ideological commitment to or value placed on ethnicity by the twentieth-century immigrants to the United States, whose orientation was to becoming American. Thus, the desire of American society to melt the ethnics (or at least their cultural distinctiveness) met with little conscious resistance from the ethnics themselves. Similarly, O'Bryan et al. found that a majority of ethnic group members in urban Canada, while they favoured their children's maintenance of their mother tongue, said they did so not because they cared for it as a way of maintaining customs and traditions (only 35% did) but because of its usefulness as a second language (according to 89%). (The fact that its utility might be in the maintenance of tradition was apparently not uppermost in the respondents' minds.) Whether it is this lack of ideological commitment to mother tongue as a mark of ethnicity, or other factors, it is true that the use of ethnic languages in Canada, as in the United States, disappears in the second or third generation.[73] It is intriguing and instructive that, while heritage language schools, sponsored by ethnic origin groups are manifestly unsuccessful in their professed goal of perpetuating a language - and by implication a culture - they continue to exist. Perhaps they function to strengthen social boundaries, and perhaps this latent function always has been more important to the schools' sponsors than the manifest one.

If ethnic boundaries are maintained in the absence of continuing immigration, as we know they are, such boundary maintenance cannot be wholly dependent on linguistic barriers. What in fact has happened, in many instances, is that ethnic organizations whose meetings were originally held in the mother tongue now conduct business in English; but ethnic identity remains the basis for membership in these groups.[74]

Primary group relationships appear to be far more fundamental to ethnic self-identification than cultural variables.[75] The well-known work of Gans[76] and Gordon,[77] among others, supports the notion that, long after cultural differences disappear, ethnic friendship networks and ethnic endogamy persist. The process of ethnic cleavage (that is, voluntary social segregation by ethnicity), begins early in childhood and is maintained in marriage and maturity. In Gordon's terms, structural (social) assimilation proceeds much more slowly than cultural assimilation. Social boundaries may be maintained mostly from outside - as a result of prejudice against minorities, especially visible ones - or they may receive strong support from within the minority, as an expression of self-preference. The degree to which each force is operating will differ, depending on the nature of the minority and the majority group. Thus we find, for example, that in settings as diverse as Australia and Canada, Dutch immigrants place relatively little value on ethnic solidarity or endogamy compared to Eastern European and Mediterranean groups.[78,79,80,81,82]

The importance to this chapter of the idea of the ethnic boundary, as the threshold across which interethnic communication flows, but at a lesser frequency than intraethnic communication on either side of the boundary, is twofold: first, we are made aware of the reciprocal and complementary nature and development of interethnic and intraethnic behaviour and attitudes; and second, the concept of ethnic boundaries provides an explanatory device that helps to account for the persistence of ethnicity as a factor in interpersonal relations, a factor which is relatively unaffected by the erosion of cultural distinctiveness.

The companion concept to the boundary is the social network. Social networks are the patterns of social relationships in which individuals are embedded. Everyone has a network, but individual networks vary in size and quality. Peoples' networks are sources of support and of information. They both form links to a larger society, and at the same time form and are formed by social boundaries, which inhibit outside communication.

The pioneering work in exploring and describing personal networks has been done in the last twenty years by writers like Bott,[83] Boissevain,[84] and Mitchell,[85] who have shown that who one knows has a great deal to do with what one knows, with the decisions one makes, and with effective need-satisfaction.

Access to health and social services is one kind of need whose satisfaction is clearly related to personal networks. Several writers have built on the work of

Bott and others by looking specifically at the relationship between personal networks and attitudes to, information about, and utilization of health services. Much of the recent literature in this area is reviewed in Chapter 2 of this volume. While several characteristics have been defined to describe the quality of personal networks, such as size, density and multiplexity, most studies of the relationship between networks and health behaviour have focused mainly on the relationship of each member of a network to the individual in question.

The degree to which a person's network is composed of relatives, either nuclear or extended, or of friends may have different significance to his likelihood of being linked to health services and institutions. (See Chapter 2.)

What is perhaps more important than either the degree of kinship or the size of a personal network in determining access to good information, is the diversity of the network. When a network is dense – that is, composed of many people who know each other, and are in frequent interaction,

the members ... tend to reach consensus on norms, and they exert considerable informal pressure on each other to conform to norms ... but when most of the people a person knows do not interact with one another, that is, when his network is loose-knit, more variation in norms is likely to develop in the network, and social control and mutual assistance will be more fragmented and less consistent.[86]

Kinship, class, and ethnicity are all boundary-creating mechanisms, and tend to impose a restricting homogeneity on social networks. Suchman's study of health care attitudes of members of five ethnic groups in New York City[87] found that the looseness of the individual's network, that is, the degree to which it included people who were not long-time acquaintances of the respondent and his family or of one another, was the most important predictor of a modern (or scientific) rather than a 'popular' (or non-scientific) attitude towards health care. Suchman's scale of social organization of network included, besides the 'friendship solidarity' dimension just described, a measure of 'ethnic exclusivity,' which asked if most friends were of the same ethnic background, and if shopkeepers of the same ethnic background were preferred. Suchman found ethnic exclusivity, like friendship solidarity, to be negatively related to knowledge about disease, and positively related to scepticism of modern medical care. He also considered ethnic group membership, independent of the social organizational dimensions of ethnic exclusivity and friendship solidarity, and found that only for one group, the Puerto Ricans, did ethnic group membership, independent of network characteristics, relate to health care attitudes. However, only Puerto Ricans, of the five groups included (Black, white Protestant, native white Catholic, and

Irish-born Catholic) were recent immigrants from a traditional folk culture. Thus in a setting such as Toronto, where many ethnic groups represent a majority of recently immigrated rural folk, ethnicity, even as a residual, cultural variable, which remains after removing the network variables of ethnic exclusivity and friendship solidarity (which, themselves, vary by ethnic group), may be significant in predicting health care patterns.

That a large and institutionally complete ethnic community may serve as a deterrent in finding one's way to health and other social services, as Suchman's work suggests, is supported by the findings of Breton and others that such communities are tightly bounded and inhibit communication across their boundaries. Thus, as an example, Gans's study of Italians in Boston's west end[88] found that they depended heavily on one another for support and friendship[89] (and particularly on same generation relatives), and were very sceptical of local physicians (who were not Italian). In Suchman's study, it was the Puerto Ricans and the Blacks who were least knowledgeable about medicine and most sceptical of physicians.[90] Whether or not their ethnic communities were larger or more institutionally complete than those of the white Protestants, Catholics, or Jews of the area we are not told. Suchman implies that it is network homogeneity, not size or institutional completeness of the ethnic enclave, which is the most salient factor predicting health care attitudes and utilization. Katz's work on American immigrants in Israel[91] also supports the idea that, within the same ethnic group, bounded and unbounded networks exist, and are participated in by different individuals. Size of the ethnic enclave alone, then, does not determine the nature of the network. However, one can reasonably assume that the opportunities for network homogeneity, which includes ethnic exclusivity, are considerably greater when people of a given ethnicity are numerous and densely settled, as is true for many ethnic communities in Toronto.

Perhaps the important missing link to the larger society for many people who are part of homogeneous ethnic networks of extended kin and friends is the broker, or intercultural middle-man. A few studies offer evidence of this kind of linkage. Salloway[92] studied a small and non-random sample of Gypsies living in an eastern United States city, and found them to be surprisingly well-informed about the availability and quality of local health services. He suggests that certain of them, whom we could call brokers, take advantage of their contacts with outsiders to gather information which is rapidly and effectively transmitted throughout an all-Gypsy network.

Wong,[93] studying New York's Chinatown, finds that the new 'elites,' who are American-born Chinese social service workers and professionals, are consciously attempting to link their prospective clients, who have traditionally looked only within the Chinese community for support and service, to health and social service agencies of the larger society.

Snyder describes the person we have called a broker as a gatekeeper. 'Gatekeepers are individuals who, because of their experience, knowledge or socioeconomic position, provide linkages between the dominant urban society and the ethnic urban enclaves. The gatekeeper serves to facilitate adaptation and problem-solving.'[94] He was able to find some use of gatekeepers among all five of the ethnic groups he studied in Los Angeles. In fact, knowledge of gatekeepers and knowledge of public services, which included employment programmes, public health programmes, public health clinics, food stamps, and welfare programmes for dependent children and for the disabled, consistently co-varied. The more people in a group were aware of the one, the more they were aware of the other.

The relationship between knowledge and *use* of gatekeepers was less clear, however. American Indians, who had knowledge of many gatekeepers, made little use of them, while Arabs and Chicanos came much closer to making maximal use of the gatekeepers they knew. When one looks at use of public services, it appears that utilization patterns are more closely related to knowledge of gatekeepers than to direct use of them – suggesting that gatekeepers are functioning within networks, where their indirect influence (at second or third hand) is much wider than their direct influence. (Snyder found that most migrants do have fairly extensive personal networks at the time of arrival.) Interestingly, the Arabs, who were the only international immigrant group in the sample, rely more on gatekeepers than on services, suggesting that in such a recently formed immigrant community, a gatekeeper, besides being a link to services, may also be a supplier of needed information or help, such that no further referral is made or sought.

While brokers may exist in any neighbourhood or network, including a white English-speaking majority one, they are particularly critical where language and/ or cultural differences make direct access to services difficult. In at least one study, broker-like persons were formally hired and trained by a Public Health Department. They functioned as health guides, to inform and steer clients to appropriate health services, and contact with these brokers resulted in improved use of services.[95]

In a study of inter- and intra-ethnic relationships of individuals, a delineation of personal networks and boundaries is basic. Such links and barriers in parents' social worlds serve as models for children in developing their self-identity and attitudes towards others; and the breadth and diversity of the maturing child's own contacts will significantly affect his view of himself and the world he lives in.

IV INTER-GROUP RELATIONS OF CHILDREN

We have reviewed some evidence that children's intraethnic relationships are altered by interethnic contact. We shall now look at the contact experience itself, as it affects childrens' attitudes and behaviour towards their peers. But it is worth pointing out, at this juncture, that of the various studies which explore intrafamilial or peer relations of minority or majority children, none look at both kinds of relationship – the ethnically continuous and the ethnically discontinuous – as they are mutually interdependent, through networks and across shifting boundaries.

Canadian Studies of Prejudice and
Discrimination by and towards Children

There are no studies of interethnic contact, ethnic cleavage, or its converse, interethnic friendship, among children in Canadian cities.[96] Four recent urban studies focus on prejudice: they examine children's attitudes towards minority group members. Three other studies record minority group members' self-reported experiences of discrimination against them by peers and adults.

Rosenstock and Adair[97] used a slide presentation with written responses as well as group discussions to explore prejudice and stereotypes held by 255 ten-to-fifteen year old schoolchildren in Toronto and Ottawa. (Twenty-nine of the 255 subjects were members of visible minorities.) The experimenters showed a series of 46 slides, featuring persons of various racial backgrounds – white, black, East Indian, Amerindian. Subjects were given a choice of several alternative descriptions of what was happening and asked to choose one, or they were asked to indicate like or dislike for the person pictured. Slides and responses were designated to look for stereotypes regarding wealth, social status, and professional status of the various racial/ethnic groups. The investigators found abundant evidence of what they interpreted as stereotyping;[98] for example, Amerindians were only identified as such when they were portrayed as poor. The problem with such an interpretation is twofold: first, the slides had not been subjected to any reliability tests, and may not have been recognizable representations of the intended racial and ethnic groups; secondly, is a stereotype a stereotype when it accords with the reality of a person's experience? Native people, as a group, are the poorest in Canada and physically they are not as obviously different from the majority group as are Blacks or Chinese, for example. Consequently, the fact that 85 per cent of the students failed to identify a group of well-dressed native children as such, while 87 per cent did identify correctly a picture of a poor native woman and child is not as convincing to the reviewer as it was to the investigators.

On the slides that showed a person against little or no background and to which subjects were to respond along a like/dislike continuum (with, unfortunately, no neutral alternative), the evidence of stereotyping is also mixed. Nonwhites had the highest rejection rates – but not if they were young. The highest rejection rate (20% said 'I don't like this person') was expressed towards two pictures, one of a man in his twenties, on a park bench, who had 'a moustache, a swarthy complexion, and is what might be described as a "Mediterranean type."' The other most disliked man was a Sikh, in a turban. A young Canadian Indian, however, and a black student leader type (shown on a university campus), were no more rejected than the white models. And again, while background was intended to be minimal and of no significance to a value judgment, it is hardly surprising that school children respond more positively to a young man, of whatever colour, on a university campus than to an unshaven man, of whatever colour, on a park bench. Thus the Rosenstock and Adair study is inconclusive. Their technique for eliciting response, while highly flawed, is interesting in that even when no neutral response was allowed, almost all students were willing to choose an answer; and while it is not possible to make any strong generalizations on the basis of the study, it is not unreasonable to view it as suggestive of children's willingness to make judgments of individuals on the basis of non-individual characteristics.

A far less problematic method for studying interethnic hostility is the one used by Labowitz[99] in studies using Anglophone university students as subjects. In his study, the same written summary of a sociological study was attributed to eight different authors, differing in sex and ethnicity (English-Canadian, French-Canadian, and Canadian Indian). Respondents were randomly assigned to groups; each group read the passage with one author's name attached. The English names were rated most favourably (male was preferred to female); and the French male was ranked last. Another very similar method was used by Larimer;[100] subjects heard a recorded message in one of two conditions: each time read by the same bilingual speaker, but once attributed to a French speaker and once to an English speaker. Respondents described the speaker's personality, based on his voice. Again, the French-named speaker was described less positively than the English-speaker.

Labowitz warns that the results of his study 'should be interpreted with caution as indicators of intergroup antagonism. Responses to names may be far removed from the way people interact with those from other groups.'[101] While this is a necessary caveat, at least Labowitz's and Larimer's procedures are far less fraught with ambiguity than Rosenstock's and Adair's, and consequently a better measure of attitude, even though one cannot, in either case, assume generalizability to behaviour.

Another measure of prejudice was developed by Kehoe[102] who had secondary school students in Vancouver and other cities in British Columbia respond to a pretested series of items, each of which represented one of seventeen human rights principles. An example is freedom of religion. The same principle was embodied in items which referred to the majority and some minority groups. He found very substantial rejection of some human rights principles when applied to minority groups, with differences depending on the group. Like Rosenstock and Adair and Labowitz, he found high rejection of native people. For example, while 35 per cent of the respondents defended the right of an apartment house manager to refuse to rent to a mixed black/white couple, 80 per cent defended that decision when applied to a mixed white/native couple.

Rosenstock and Adair, Labowitz, Larimer and Kehoe were investigating prejudice, hostile attitudes towards out-groups, from the point of view of the majority group. Ramcharan[103] and Head[104] investigated the experience of discrimination from the viewpoint of a minority group in Toronto, using a survey method. Ramcharan interviewed 290 West Indian parents in Toronto. He found 20 per cent who said their children had experienced discrimination in school, mostly from white classmates. A total of 31 per cent said their children had reported racially derogatory statements made about them. These parents were over-representative of blue-collar workers, of darker-skinned West Indians, and of inner-city dwellers from high density West Indian neighbourhoods.

Head's (non-random) sample of Blacks in Toronto, most of whom are West Indian immigrants, included an adolescent group (n = 53). Each subject was interviewed on a number of topics including experience of discrimination, school experiences, feelings about interracial mixing, and self-concept and ethnic identity. Thirty-one of the fifty-three adolescent respondents (59%) reported having experienced discrimination. The most common setting, involving 28 per cent of the sample, was the school, and the most common discriminatory experience there was 'unfair treatment by teacher or administration.' Seventy per cent thought that textbooks contain derogatory references to Blacks and other minority persons.

While 41 per cent of the sample had not personally experienced discrimination, they agreed with the others that discrimination, mostly of a subtle rather than an overt nature, does exist in Toronto. The area most mentioned was housing. Most of the sample think there is 'a little' or 'some' discrimination in schools. Sixty-one per cent think that teachers discourage blacks from aiming for high educational goals, either by streaming them into non-academic programmes (30%) or by an explicitly unencouraging attitude (57%). Many thought that the effect of such teachers' attitudes is to create a negative attitude towards school among black students. (45% think black students do hold such attitudes.) But the majority did not believe that their colour, by itself, would negatively affect the achievement of their educational goals, if they persevered.

Eighty-two per cent of Head's subjects thought that other visible minorities also encounter discrimination in Toronto; in fact, Canadian Indians are seen as more discriminated-against than Blacks.

Ninety-six per cent believed that interracial friendships are desirable; but inter-racial dating is accepted by only 57 per cent, and interracial marriage by 50 per cent. Few had experienced disapproval from friends or strangers of their interracial acquaintances. Interracial and interethnic mixture in the neighbourhood of residence is seen by some as an advantage, by others as a drawback.

Eighty-seven per cent of the sample thought it very important for West Indians to maintain their culture in Toronto, especially as a way of strengthening black identity, an interesting reflection of the dominance of paticularism in the Canadian social environment. Just over one quarter saw their minority status here as a threat to their identity; almost half, however, thought their minority status did not interfere with their lifestyle. And some thought that 'a mixed community encourages growth and development.'

Discrimination in the schools was a topic included in a recent survey of 119 randomly selected families of grade eight children in a municipality within Metropolitan Toronto.[103] Forty-two (or 36%) of the family heads were born in Canada, four in England and one in the United States. Thirty-six, or 31 per cent, were born in Italy, 19 (16%) elsewhere in Europe, predominantly in Eastern Europe, and 16 (14%) in the West Indies.

On the subject of ethnic stereotyping as a form of discrimination, 15 per cent of the parents agreed that it exists in some form in the school, particularly on the part of other pupils. The most common form of stereotyping attributed to teachers was that they think of Canadian-born children as being more capable than immigrants. (Sixteen per cent of the Canadian parents agreed that teachers expect more of Canadian children.) Fifteen per cent of West Indian parents believe that teachers have negative expectations of their children, based on ethnocultural stereotyping. This is a considerably lower proportion than Head found: 42 per cent of his adult sample, 61 per cent of whom are parents, and some but not all of whom have experienced Canadian schools through their children, feel that teachers discourage Blacks from striving for high academic goals. Eleven per cent of the Italian parents, and none of the other Europeans, felt that their children were negatively stereotyped. Some parents mentioned negative stereotyping in textbooks, and other instructional materials.

Few parents – a total of six, representing all three non-Canadian-born groups – assert that their child has experienced discrimination personally at school.

Only two of these six accused teachers of discrimination; the other four incidents involved other pupils.

While actual discrimination was rarely perceived, and stereotyping generally disavowed, a substantial minority (33%) believe that schools suffer from racial tensions. Italian-born parents are less likely to perceive it than Canadian-born parents (22% compared to 26%); but other European parents, and especially West Indian parents, are far more likely to see their children's schools as having racial tension (39% and 56%, respectively). This racial tension is perceived as basically caused by prejudice and hostility passed on to children by their parents. In most cases, teachers are not seen as responsible. (It is possible that the parents, although assured of anonymity, were reluctant to direct accusations against teachers, who are supported by the school system which sponsored the survey.)

These several studies of prejudice and discrimination support the idea that both exist in Canada,[106] the former more than the latter. While some of the measures of prejudice developed are good ones (Labowitz's and Larimer's particularly), information is lacking on their relationship to actual behaviour; this is a very important gap in our knowledge of the connection between attitudes and behaviour.

Research in the Development of
Inter-Group Attitudes and Behaviour among Children
There are few points of contact between the studies of intergroup relationships among children reviewed above, and the theoretical literature on the subject. Thus local studies have used survey techniques to sample opinion rather than investigating experimentally the development of interethnic attitudes and behaviour; whereas the main topics which have absorbed the energy of social and developmental psychologists, who have been the principal students of intergroup relations, include the development of out-group attitudes and behaviour, their correlates, and the development of effective strategies to alter undesirable attitudes and behaviour. Aboud and her colleagues, working in Montreal, have made a contribution to our understanding of the complex area of children's ethnic identity in a multi-ethnic context. Her work also has implications for the understanding of attitudes towards different others. These studies and the one described below by Kalin et al.,[107] are almost the only ones carried out in Canada to date which contribute to the literature on the development of out-group attitudes in young children. But there is no dearth of studies from the United States, and some from Australia, England, and Israel, most of which have been extensively reviewed.[108-113] Bhatnagar, in an article for a Canadian journal,[114] is forced, for lack of Canadian studies, to review mainly English and American data on children's interethnic interaction.

It is important to look briefly at this body of literature in order to point out possible gaps in it, and missing links between it and Canadian studies.

The major subdivisions within the literature appear to be: (1) the early development of racial and ethnic awareness; (2) the development of own-group and/or other group preference; (3) determinants of intergroup attitudes including intelligence, class, child-rearing techniques, and intergroup contact; and (4) the effectiveness of various attempts to change attitudes and behaviour in the direction of (a) increasing regard for ethnically different others; and (b) increasing self-regard on the part of members of low-status minority groups. We shall summarize briefly the findings and the unknowns in each of these areas.

The Development of Racial and Ethnic Awareness

The studies in this area are reviewed by Proshansky, and summarized below. More recent work has been done by Aboud and her colleagues. Besides the two studies by Aboud referred to below,[115,116] which find minority group children (Black, Chinese, and Native) delaying self-identification by one year or more (to age 6 or 7) beyond white children, another of Aboud's studies[117] found that Native children showed superior ability at role-taking from the perspectives of members of other cultural groups, when compared with majority (white) children in the United States, Switzerland,[118] or Britain.[119] Aboud and Mitchell interpret this finding as an indication that conflict about self-identification (which emerged relatively later in this same Amerindian group) may result in greater cognitive flexibility.

Summary

What is known about the development of racial and ethnic awareness.

1 The sequence involved in the development of children's awareness of and attitudes towards ethnic and racial difference is reasonably well established, with age correlates. The stages can be described as ethnic awareness (ages 3–4); ethnic orientation (4–7), and ethnic attitudes; or a finer breakdown can be established after Katz's categorization.[120] Racial and ethnic differences become increasingly salient with age. Before age 7 or thereabout, awareness does not predict ethnic exclusiveness.

2 Self-identification by race, ethnicity, or nationality is far less common in young children than is self-identification by gender.

3 Awareness and understanding of racially or ethnically different others probably emerges later than self-identification. (Age 4 for the latter and age 6 for the former, according to one researcher.[121])

4 Awareness and understanding of racially or ethnically different others may emerge at a different age for minority and majority group children.

What is not known.

1 Do minority children become racially or ethnically self-conscious before majority children[122] or after them?[123,124]

2 Does age at emergence of self-identification or age at emergence of identification of others have anything to do with the direction or intensity of later-appearing attitudes and behaviour towards other groups?

The Development of Own-Group and Other-Group Preferences
(a) *Their evolution.* The complement to awareness of differences is awareness of similarity. Children's ethnic awareness, placing themselves in relationship to others who are different or similar, develops as early as the third year of life and, over the next four to five years, acquires evaluative connotations. Ethnic cleavage, in terms of intergroup relationships, is ethnic solidarity from the point of view of intragroup relationships.

All groups of children learn to prefer their own racial or ethnic group. But for minority children, the preference may develop somewhat later. By age 6-7, children show high awareness of racial and ethnic differences, a growing tendency to use race as a term of identity for themselves and others, and a persistent tendency to accept or reject others on racial and ethnic grounds.

Ethnic self-preference, or ethnocentrism, appears to be a virtually universal characteristic of human groups.[125] Piaget and Weil[126] demonstrate the relationship of ethnocentrism to egocentrism in young children. While own-group identification emerges much earlier, not until children are about 10-11 years old do they understand and appreciate ethnic or national loyalties which differ from their own.

But minority status may intervene to invalidate the general law of own-group preference for young children, especially if they are of lower rather than higher socio-economic status. Several studies of black and white pre-school children in the United States and in England show relatively low own-group preference for the black children on both doll-choice and semantic-differential measures.[127,128] Further, '... data from England, South Africa, New Zealand and Hong Kong, ... support the generalization that young children of ... subordinate racial groupings tend to prefer and perceive themselves similar to those in the dominant racial grouping.'[129] A Canadian study of black and white nursery school children shows the same pattern.[130] A few recent studies, however, do not support this trend.[131] A more detailed review of the literature in this area is available.[132]

Among black children in the United States, own-group preference begins to develop after entrance into school, and, congruent with the development of other ethnic attitudes, becomes stronger and more consistent with increasing age. The general finding is that prejudice increases with age[131] and attitudes towards particular groups are stable and consistent by later adolescence, if not before.[132] Kalin et al.'s recent Canadian study found children showing somewhat lower rates of egocentrism and higher acceptance of multiculturalism as an ideal than adults; but unlike other studies, it also found that interethnic tolerance increased with age within the juvenile sample (age 10–18).[135] Lambert and Klineberg's cross-national study of children's views of foreigners indicates that they tend to rate foreign people as similar or dissimilar to themselves in a non-evaluative way;[136] but, contradicting Kalin et al., the tendency towards evaluation such that 'dissimilar' becomes correlated with 'disliked' increased with age from early childhood to adolescence. The patterns of preference repeat adult patterns and are the same for majority and minority group members, except that each group tends to rank itself as the most preferable.

Adolescents' ethnic solidarity has been shown to be directly related to that of their parents.[137] Several studies find higher own-group preference among minority than majority group members in high school populations.[138,139,140] Beserve reviews studies which find high self-preference among West Indian children in England and high rejection of them by non-black children, and suggests that, for minority children, own-group preference may be the result of rejection by others.[141] Several studies find higher own-group preference for majority and minority members of racial and religious groups in integrated versus segregated school settings, but contradicting findings exist.

(b) *Relation of attitudes to behaviour.* In spite of ample evidence that intergroup attitudes do not reliably predict behaviour, for adults or children, the majority of studies continue to examine attitudes, not behaviour. The general finding is that attitudes show more exclusiveness than does behaviour.[142] Most recently, Gerrard and Miller report discouraging results from a longitudinal study of children in an integrated school; ethnic cleavage, as measured by sociometric tests, increased over time. But they observed an increase in interethnic interaction on the playground. Such a discrepancy is consistent with the general finding on direct measures (observed behaviour) versus the indirect (self-report, sociometric) measures of intergroup contact used in the classroom.[143] Furthermore, in the Gerrard and Miller studies, as well as in the dozens of others dealing with black and white children in integrated schools,[144,145] situational factors may be highly relevant, since most measurements, even in the rare instances when they extend to include some direct observation, are confined to the classroom, where black children are typically operating at an academic disadvantage compared with their white classmates, and may thus make less desirable partners than they would in a non-academic setting.

British studies also measure attitudes and self-reported (that is, non-observed) interaction. Interethnic interaction is the exception, in these integrated elementary and secondary schools. Jellinek and Brittan[146] found, in a survey of 8-14 year old British, Asian, West Indian, and European children, that 90 per cent of all reported friendship patterns were ethnically homogeneous, and that this relationship increased with age, especially between 10 to 12 year olds. But they also found that homogeneity of *desired* friendship patterns, while high, decreased with age. Their study is particularly interesting because it is unique in distinguishing between actual and desired friendship patterns.

(c) *Relationships of own-group to other-group attitudes.* An Australian study of first- and second-generation Greek children found that interethnic friendships decreased as age increased and noted that this was 'not surprising, as 93.5% of parents ... expressed personal preference for Greek peer relationships for their sons and daughters.'[147]

It is reasonable to assume that, as prejudice increases with age throughout childhood and into early adolescence, so does ethnic self-preference. Studies of American black children support that assumption. We do have one finding to the contrary: Jellinek and Brittan's previously cited observation that, while homogeneity of friendship patterns did not decrease with age (from 8 to 14 year olds), the felt desirability of such homogeneous relationships did decrease. This was true for majority as well as minority group members. The more usual finding, however, is that minority children (racial and religious) increasingly identify with their own group socially and with the majority group culturally as they move into adolescence.[148, 149]

If one sees in-group solidarity and out-group hostility as reciprocal and correlated, then high own-group preference for minority group members (who are so identified by themselves and/or by others) must be associated with high outgroup (other-group) prejudice. While this is a common assumption, it is not extensively documented. Some supportive evidence is found in a study of a sample of second-generation Italian, Polish, and Dutch adolescents in Australia, which found that those who showed the highest degrees of ethnic solidarity were the offspring of parents who held unfavourable attitudes towards Australia and Australians.[150]

Self-esteem, at the individual level, may be seen as the corollary of esteem for the group of which one is a member. Studies of self-esteem within a racial or ethnic context include those reviewed by Rosenberg and Simmons[151] and St John,[152] which focus on the effect of school desegregation on black and white children's self-esteem. A weak, general trend of the numerous studies reviewed is a negative relationship between black children's self-esteem and their presence as a minority group in the integrated school. The hypothetical explanation is that black children attending previously all-white schools tend to be of lower socioeconomic class and to have lower levels of academic achievement than the majority (white) pupils to whom they, therefore, compare themselves unfavourably.

Paralleling the study of black children in mainly white schools are a few studies of ethnic and racial minorities in integrated neighbourhoods. Rosenberg found that Catholic, Protestant, and Jewish children have lower self-esteem when they comprise a minority, rather than a majority, in their neighbourhood.[153] St John, however, cites evidence of black adults having higher self-esteem in integrated than in segregated neighbourhoods, if they were products of integrated schools.[154]

While it is reasonable to suppose that self-esteem has a relationship to positive feelings towards one's own group, especially for minority group members, it is not reasonable to see self-esteem at the intra-individual level, as a mirror image of own-group preference.

Summary

What is known about the development of own-group and other group preference,

1 In the majority of studies of pre-school black and white American children, white children show own-group preference by age 4, while black children may not show own-group preference until age 6 or 7. More recent studies[155] are less supportive of this finding than earlier[156] ones, but the weight of evidence is still in that direction.

2 Even after own-group preference emerges clearly for minority as well as majority children, minority children are more likely to make unreciprocated sociometric friendship choices from the majority group than vice versa. This finding has been reported in the United States and in Great Britain, and includes religious as well as racial minority groups.

3 Prejudice increases with age. Ethnic group preferences and stereotypes begin to be stable and consistent after age 11, and change little after late adolescence.

What is not known.

1 The race of the examiner may affect children's response, especially on measures such as doll-choice, picture-sort, and other measures involving a high degree of subject-examiner interaction; but the exact nature of examiner-effects is not well known.

2 Ethnic cleavage may or may not be associated with out-group hostility, with weak or strong self-concept, and with strong ethnic self-identification. Each of these factors may differ between majority and minority group children, and between visible and non-visible minorities. While we know that ethnic cleavage exists, and increases with age throughout childhood, we know little about what it means to the involved parties.

3 American studies are primarily concerned with severely disadvantaged, visible minority children. Contemporary Canadian cities, on the other hand, offer a laboratory in which to examine the strength of ethnic cleavage among minori-

ties whose place in the social order is far less discrepant, and where children are less likely to be influenced by well-developed adult prejudgments.

4 The relationship between self-esteem and tolerance for others in minority and majority group children is largely unexplored.

Determinants of Intergroup Attitudes and Behaviour

Intergroup attitudes are learned. There is substantial agreement that they have multiple causation, and are rooted both in a social environment and in psychological processes that determine individual behaviour.

(a) *Direct transmission.* Prejudice may be learned from the society if norms legitimate it. It may also be learned directly from teachers, camp counsellors, and parents, although the evidence here is 'scanty and inconsistent.'[157] Such learning could be through direct verbal transmission of attitudes, or through modelling on adult behaviour. A recent study supports modelling as the transmission mechanism by finding a correlation between amount of interethnic contact of fathers and sons; but daughters are unaffected.[158]

Some studies find that parents are unaware of the prejudices they are teaching their children, and that such teaching is unintentional. Proshansky states that, 'considering the many other environmental sources for acquiring ethnic prejudice, the development of positive ethnic attitudes in the child requires not only the absence of such prejudice in the home, but also the directed attempts of the parents to inculcate positive ethnic orientations in their children.'[159]

The significant role played by teachers and other adults in transmitting positive and negative attitudes towards others is explored in the work of Meltzer,[160] Brittan,[161] James,[162] and Clark,[163] in addition to studies cited by P. Katz.[164] Fishman finds that parochial schools, however, are relatively ineffective, compared to earlier home influences, in affecting attitudes towards same and other ethnic or racial groups.[165,166]

(b) *Personality factors.* Many studies, beginning with *The authoritarian personality*[167] argue for a link between parental authoritarianism and childhood ethnocentrism (own-group preference, out-group rejection). The basic theory of Adorno et al. that parental authoritarianism, expressed in rigid modes of child-rearing, creates authoritarian personalities in children, has continued to interest psychologists. Many studies, throughout the 50s and 60s, corroborate the basic premise (for a review, see Katz).[168] While the basic conclusions of Adorno et al. are upheld again and again, the studies suffer from a lack of sufficient controls, especially for intelligence and education; and from an inability to distinguish between indirect transmission of prejudice (where authoritarian child-rearing patterns create childhood ethnocentrism without direct expression of prejudice present) and direct transmission (prejudiced parent → prejudiced child), since the authoritarian parents are themselves ethnocentric. Nonetheless, while causal links between child-rearing, authoritarianism, and the development of ethnocentrism in children are not proven, there is sufficient evidence to indicate that fundamental personality dispositions, however acquired, may be translated into negative intergroup attitudes.

Another kind of personality variable which may figure in interethnic attitudes is frustration, which some theorists see as the antecedent of interpersonal aggression. Thus researchers find anti-Semitism higher among people who are dissatisfied with their jobs than among those who are contented (but not among English Canadians).[168a] Similarly, positive relationships are found between economic deprivation and hostility to Blacks. Some researchers have demonstrated the relationship experimentally among older adolescents and adults. But there is some evidence that frustration-aggression theory is most applicable to people who are already prejudiced; that is, it is prejudiced persons who tend to display hostility, when frustrated. If so, the theory is not useful in explaining the origins of prejudice.

The relationship between frustration and prejudice has been demonstrated among pre-adolescent children, as well as university students and adults. Most of these studies focus on anti-Semitism, but Mussen's study of anti-black prejudice among white boys in summer camp is related.[169] Katz, in reviewing the area, concludes that 'personality factors seem to be only tangentially related to racial attitudes ...'[170]

(c) *Cognitive processes.* A series of studies exists 'based on the hypothesis that the development of ethnic prejudice ... is facilitated by general tendencies toward premature categorization, overgeneralization, and rigidity of thought.'[171] The classic study is that of Frenkel-Brunswick, who looked at children from 11 to 16 years of age, and found that prejudiced children were intolerant of ambiguity, showed a high degree of sex-role stereotyping, and saw family position in hierarchical terms.

Rokeach's research is based largely on the notion that bigots are more concrete in their thinking than others, and that dogmatism is associated with a greater rigidity in thinking. He confirmed this hypothesis among strongly prejudiced and strongly *un*prejudiced subjects, and concluded that dogmatism transcends the content of ethnic attitudes.

Other researchers have found a relationship in young children and in adolescents between intolerance of ambiguity, a lower level of abstract reasoning, and poor ability in concept formation and deductive logic (with controls for intelligence). Most recently, Glock et al. concluded, in their study of anti-Semitism and anti-black attitudes among adolescents, that '... prejudice is nurtured especially among youths who have not developed the cognitive skills and sophistication to combat it.'[172] Under 'cognitive skills and sophistication' they include interest in intellectual pursuits, tolerance for ambiguity, and a 'non-cynical' interpretation of human nature.

Whether or not formal education is associated with a decrease in prejudice is debated. Stember reviews the literature, and states that most earlier studies were inconclusive, and based on ungeneralizable measures and situations. He concludes that '... the impact of education is limited. Its chief effect is to reduce traditional provincialism ... and to diminish fear of casual personal contact. But the limits of equality are sharply drawn; while legal equality is supported, full social participation is not.'[173] Curtis and Lambert, whose measure of out-group rejection was a simple self-report, which did not allow for the subtleties mentioned by Stember, found that education was associated with a decrease in hostility towards ethnic and racial minorities and a decrease in 'preference for cultural uniformity.'[174]

Another cognitive factor associated with prejudice is assumed dissimilarity in belief. Studies such as that by Bryne and Wong[175] demonstrate that assumptions that attitudinal differences exist between members of different ethnic groups are common, and such assumptions are correlated with prejudice. At least one study confirms that this phenomenon operates among adolescents, as well as among adults.[176]

The work of Piaget describing childhood egocentrism is relevant; only Aboud and her colleagues seem to consider it, however.

(d) *Perceptual factors.* P. Katz[177] summarizes her own work and that of others in exploring the relationship to interethnic and interracial attitudes of such perceptual factors as visible cues and the labels which may affect perception. Katz's work with young children found that labels significantly affected white children's perception of colour cues. Black children, however, appear to respond to colour cues, without interference from verbal labels.

The symbolic significance of black and white as darkness and light, good and evil is extensively studied by Williams and Moreland[178] who argue that the burden of meaning attached to black and white by Judaeo-Christian tradition affects children's perception of the two races.

(e) *Personal contact.* Prejudice exists where there is no contact between groups, and where there is. Degree of interethnic contact in childhood is highly related to degree of contact later in life.[179] Casual and superficial contact appears to maintain or even increase pre-existing prejudice.[180] Allport has asserted that there are four variables which are of basic importance in determining the quality of the contact situation. These are the presence or absence of status equality, shared goals, intimacy, and institutional support.[181]

(1) Equal-status in the contact situation. Allport's assertion that status equality in the contact situation is essential to the reduction of prejudice is supported by numerous studies. An effective alternative to equal status contact for reducing prejudice in majority group members is contact between majority group members and higher status minority group members. Studies which show either of these alternative status-in-contact situations to be effective in reducing prejudice among juvenile majority group members include these by Williams[182] and Bjerstedt.[183] The converse, that negative attitudes result from interethnic contact in unequal status situations, is illustrated by Sapir using Israeli children as subjects.[184] The extensive body of literature on ethnic cleavage, cited earlier, can be understood as evidence of the ineffectiveness of contact where social status is unequal, because the children involved are members of racial or ethnic groups who occupy unequal status positions in American or British society and who are well aware of the existing status hierarchy.

A recent re-examination of the effectiveness of equal status contact in reducing prejudice was made by Robinson and Preston,[185] who investigated the attitudes of white and black teachers participating in a training programme on the problems of school desegregation. The participants, all voluntary, and all pursuing common goals, were of equal status (college graduates, school teachers). The training institute incorporated a great deal of interpersonal contact and cooperative action into its programme. After the twelve day-long sessions were concluded, white participants showed statistically significant, positive attitude change on all measures (including stereotyping, distastefulness, general prejudice, etc.). But black participants did not significantly change their attitudes. In a follow-up study of a larger sample of institute participants, with a control group of non-participating teachers, the findings were similar. The training sessions altered the attitudes of white teachers more than of black ones. There was a trend towards more positive attitudes to Whites on the part of black participants in the training programme, but the differences between them and black non-participants, while in the expected direction, did not reach statistical significance, as it did between the participating and non-participating white teachers. Ford's study of white and black housewives in an integrated housing project shows a similar result.[186] Greater reduction in prejudice for the majority than the minority groups resulting from personal contact has also been shown by Wen and Yu[187] among American and Chinese students.

Robinson and Preston's work confirms the effectiveness of Allport's conditions for reducing prejudice: institute participants became less prejudiced than non-participants, as a result of a favourable contact situation; and this lowered rate of prejudice was still measurable 16 months later. But contact, according to the authors, has a different meaning for Blacks and Whites, and hence different results. Several hypotheses are advanced to explain this difference. The authors posit that more intimate contact might have been more effective. They also cite Cohen and Roper's finding, in their study of black and white junior high school boys, that it is necessary to treat peoples' prior expectations first, if interracial interaction is to be genuinely equal-status.[188] It is interesting that few studies have looked at minority group members as holders of out-group prejudices, no doubt because such prejudice is not perceived as socially meaningful or effective in barring majority access to goods and services. Nonetheless, it could be an important barrier to positive intergroup relations.

Recently Amir[189,190] suggested that positive intergroup contact may be possible without equal status, but does not dispute that an equal-status condition, albeit not essential in all cases, is far more ideal than status inequality, in the contact situation.

(2) Superordinate goals in the contact situation. Allport specifies the importance of a common goal, shared by interacting members of different ethnic groups, to harmonious relationships. Researchers generally find that competition hinders, and co-operation furthers the formation of positive intergroup relationships. One study which showed both effects with 4–6 year old children was done recently in Australia.[191] The classic study of the importance of a superordinate goal in reducing intergroup conflict among children is Sherif's Robber Cave study,[192] where intergroup conflict was artificially induced among 12-year olds, and then eliminated. Race and ethnicity were not variables. Other than Sherif, investigators of competition and co-operation in intergroup situations have studied adults, not children, and have focused on economic competition. An exception is a study of 16-year old Dutch boys artificially assigned to competing groups. The investigators failed to support their hypothesis that intergroup competition would increase in-group solidarity.[193] This hypothesis, though it can be derived from Allport's thesis, is not identical with it.

Weigel, Wiser, and Cook did find that co-operative, interdependent learning in small groups of grade 7 and 10 white, black, and Chicano children lessened cross-ethnic conflict and increased cross-ethnic helping, and was more effective in achieving both than was intergroup contact in classes led by the same teachers but not using the small group technique.[194] Slavin's results, in a similar team learning approach involving white and black children in Grades 7 and 8, confirm the positive findings of Weigel et al.,[195] as do Aronson's, using his 'jigsaw' techniques of cooperative learning.[195a] Finally, Amir[196] points out that it may not be necessary for two groups in contact to share the same goal. They may have different goals which can be achieved through co-operation.

(3) Frequency and intimacy of contact. While there is some evidence that proximity produces more frequent intergroup contact, frequency of contact can have negative as well as positive results on intergroup relations. Positive effects are usually found to be linked to intimate rather than casual or superficial contact, however frequent it may be. Close personal relations are required before people generalize approval of someone ethnically different from a specific situation to other situations. Thus the ethnic cleavage observed among children in school settings may be seen as the result of a lack of intimate, meaningful contact, despite great proximity and frequent casual contact; so might the persistence of prejudice in spite of contact among the adolescents in Glock's study.[197] One study of black and white children in close personal contact at summer camp did find a significant reduction in racial cleavage after two weeks.[198] A study with mixed results is that of Reich and Purbhoo (1975) who rated immigrant and native students in high schools having a high or low proportion of immigrants, on tolerance for diversity,[199] using several pencil-and-paper tests. Their hypothesis that increased opportunity for interethnic contact increases tolerance for diversity was upheld for the immigrants, but not for the indigenous students. Studies which indicate the importance of intimate contact for prejudice reduction among adults include interracial housing studies in the United States, interethnic residential settings in Israel, and a study of attitudes towards Italians in England,[200] as a function of residential proximity and closeness of contact. Amir has suggested that the effect of intimate contact may be that the individual begins to see an out-group member as an individual, and not as a member of a stereotyped group.[201]

(4) Institutional support, or approval of an authority, in the contact situation. 'The effectiveness of interracial contact is greatly increased if the contact is sanctioned by institutional support.'[202] Allport's principle of the importance of institutional support has an interesting application in the school situation. If pupils do not perceive teachers to be unprejudiced, an important positive factor is missing in the contact situation. In the only set of studies which examined teachers' and students' intergroup attitudes and relationships in the same (English) schools, Brittan[203] found that a majority of teachers were assimilationist in thinking, unwilling to adapt the curriculum to the needs of the ethnic population, and had strongly stereotyped opinions about West Indian children. Thus, Jellinek and Brittan's finding, cited earlier, of strong ethnic and racial cleavage among students in the same schools can be seen as an instance of contact which lacks both intimacy and real institutional support. Institutional support for positive interethnic attitudes, in the contact situation, may be seen as an instance of direct transmission of attitudes, by teachers, bosses, and others.

Summary

What is known about the determinants of inter-group relationships.

1 While direct instruction, personality (including child-rearing) variables, cognitive and perceptual factors, and intergroup contact have all been shown to be relevant to the formation of intergroup attitudes, cognitive, perceptual, and contact variables appear to have more promise for future research and application.

2 Determinants of intergroup attitudes differ between minority and majority group members, at least in the area of intergroup contact and its effects.

What is not known.

1 What is true of the work on the developmental sequences in intergroup relationships is also true of the work on the determinants of intergroup relationships: far more is known about attitudes than behaviour, and the links between the two are not self-evident.

2 While common sense dictates a strong relationship between parents' and children's attitudes and behaviour in the area of intergroup relationships, there is little in the way of strong, unambiguous support for either direct or indirect transmission.

3 As is true of the work in attitude development, the studies of determinants of attitudes typically distinguish between white and black children, seldom between majority and minority white children. Exceptions are some studies of the effects of contact done in Israel; but most of these involve adults, not children.

4 Little is known of the demography of contact situations. While there is evidence that minority and majority status in the larger society differentially affect the outcome of contact for the participants, there is an absence of studies which look at the effect of different ethnic mixes within a setting like a school.

V EFFECTS OF DELIBERATE ATTEMPTS TO CHANGE CHILDREN'S INTER-ETHNIC AND/OR INTRA-ETHNIC RELATIONSHIPS

Measures of change used in the various studies reviewed in this section include direct questionnaire techniques, picture preference tests, projective techniques, social distance scales, disguised or unobtrusive measures, sociometric measures, and rarely, behavioural measures. There are relatively few of the last. Few studies use multiple measures, although there is wide agreement that attitudes have multiple components. One study that does so[204] fails to find high intercorrelations on the various measures used. And few studies attempt to relate changed attitudes to changed behaviour.

Contact and Change

Most studies of children's ethnic relationships are non-experimental and simply describe the behaviour of children in ethnically or racially mixed settings, such as integrated nurseries and schools. School desegregation studies, for example, are almost all of this type.

The results of these studies are, as we have seen, mixed. The presence or absence and the direction of attitudinal and/or behavioural change may differ for minority and majority groups depending on age, status, setting, intimacy of contact, attitude of authority figures, and other factors or combinations of factors. A few studies exist of deliberate attempts to affect children's attitudes and behaviour towards different others. Here too the results are mixed. The work of Sherif, in successfully creating and destroying intergroup enmity among artificially created, non-ethnic groups of boys has already been mentioned. I. Katz's study[205] of black and white adolescents in an interracial, voluntary group parallels Sherif's. When competition arose within the group over leadership and became a source of intergroup conflict, it was possible for a well-liked leader to reduce the tension and to change negative attitudes to a degree, although with more success among white than among black group members. However, existing stereotypes were maintained.

Rabbie and Wilken's study, also previously mentioned, was unsuccessful in attempting to create in-group solidarity through intergroup competition, again with artificially created, non-ethnic groups.

Trubowitz paired black and white children in grades 4 and 5 from segregated schools, in a series of three field trips and follow-up discussions. By creating interracial pairs, which were maintained over the six contact experiences, he hoped to create a degree of frequency and intimacy of contact which would aid in improving interethnic contact. In fact, however, none of the white children, and only one out of four groups of black children (grade 5 girls) showed any significant improvement over the controls in interracial attitude.[206] Even if Trubowitz's results had been more positive, one would have to wonder how much such changed attitudes would generalize to other persons in other situations, or, from attitudes to behaviour. Certainly many studies support the contextual specificity of attitude change, particularly where contact is confined to work (or school) settings. For example, a long-term effort was undertaken in the schools of Springfield, Mass. in the 1940s to alter prejudice in school children which included contact, interdependence, and strong institutional support. However, the programme failed to lessen out-group hostility towards the minorities present in the community.[207]

Two recent studies which created small interethnic, interracial work groups in a classroom situation, instead of the traditional classroom as a single unit, found positive effects on inter-group attitudes as a result of this increased dependence. DeVries and Edwards[208] divided a grade-seven class into four-member study teams, and found increased interracial (black/white) choices on a sociometric measure. Weigel et al.[209] created small study groups which included white, black, and Chicano junior high and secondary school students in newly integrated schools. They found that this interdependent grouping produced more cross-ethnic helping behaviour, and increased the respect, liking, and sociometric friendship choice of Chicanos by whites. But ethnic attitudes did not change, for any of the three ethnic groups.

Weigel et al. examine their results, and suggest that increased positive change in intergroup attitudes may result from lengthening the daily small-group experience (to beyond the one-half of one school period out of seven, obtaining in their experiment), and from building in some problem-oriented content which might generalize from an improved attitude towards an individual to include his ethnic group (following Cook[210]).

Information and Change

While most investigations have reported that possessing more information about a group is associated with holding more favourable attitudes towards that group, the direction of this effect cannot be determined: information may change attitudes, or favourable attitudes may predispose people to gain more information. Deliberate attempts to change inter-group attitudes through the provision of information have obtained mixed results. Proshansky summarizes the effects of specific school courses, saying that 'significant favourable changes in attitudes are reported about twice as often as no changes.'[211] Kehoe[212] reports that emphasis on similarities between cultures, not differences, is most effective in building tolerance. He advocates a discussion method, based on Kohlberg's moral dilemma format, in which students take a position in a human rights-related case, and attempt to generalize their position to other minorities and also to take the reverse to their original point of view, in order to grow in understanding and empathy of their own and others' viewpoints, and to become decreasingly ego- and ethno-centric.

As with the contact situation, the effect of information changing attitudes is greatest if certain conditions are met: (1) the information presented is favourable; (2) the instructor communicates a more favourable attitude than the students hold; (3) the relationship between teacher and students is positive; and (4) the course is of some length and includes some intimacy, as in workshop or seminar situations. P. Katz,[213] in her review, cites emotional involvement of participants (through role-playing, or through direct discussion of prejudice) as the essential ingredient of successful educational (informational) attempts to alter intergroup attitudes. She does, however, report on one study of a multi-ethnic reader, used without other modification to the curriculum, which resulted in improved interracial attitudes on the part of the grade two, white pupils.[214]

Almost all attempts to change attitudes are directed at improving interethnic and interracial relationships. The only exceptions are a few studies of the effect of a particular curricular experiment on the self-concept or intergroup attitudes of minority members. Such studies include, for example, attempts to evaluate the effects of black studies programmes on black students. One interesting study of this genre was reported by Lefley.[215] Native children were exposed to a ten-week course on Indian culture. Afterward they were compared to a matched group of native children who did not take the course. Measures of results tapped self-concept, self-esteem, and Indian self-esteem, a measure of pride in Indian identification. The experimental group showed no change in self-concept, but significant gains in self-esteem and Indian self-esteem. The inclusion of the three different outcome measures makes the results more differentiated and meaningful than is often the case, in similar evaluative studies, and suggests a possibly fruitful direction for further research in the neglected area of improving intragroup attitudes of minority members, which is generally a principal intention of multicultural programmes.

A different kind of manipulation is reported by Kehoe,[216] who describes a study in which minority children were instructed in a skill to level of competence equal or superior to majority children. Only in the condition of superior competence did the minority children's self-confidence improve such that their participation increased in a decision-making game, played subsequently to the skill demonstration.

Propaganda, as distinguished from information, has also been studied as a means for interethnic attitude change. Peterson and Thurstone used films to produce both favourable and unfavourable attitude shifts towards specific national racial and ethnic groups, in high school students. Some of the attitude changes showed persistence over reasonably long periods of time.[217]

The television programme, *Vegetable Soup*, evaluated by Mays, was found to have a very positive effect in improving intergroup attitudes, particularly with younger children.[218] Bogatz and Ball also found positive effects on preschool children's interethnic attitudes from long-term viewing of the programme *Sesame Street*.[219] P. Katz points out the surprising lack of studies of the effect of mass media on children's intergroup attitudes.[220] One could add that there is a total absence of studies of the effect of such programmes on intragroup attitudes.

The only study which attempts to compare the relative efficacy of contact versus information on interethnic attitude change was done by Berg and Wolleat.[221] They found information to be more effective than contact, among third and fourth grade children. The implications of their study, however, are difficult to evaluate, because there is no description of the intimacy of contact, or of the nature of the groups in the contact setting. A more recent study, however, reports that intraracial contact in a school setting is more effective than more indirect measures (such as race relations workshops for teachers, or class discussions of racial issues) in increasing cross-race friendship choices, and in positively affecting interracial attitudes, especially for the majority group.[222]

A study of a large sample of grade 3 and grade 5 children in Sweden indicated that teaching about human rights and prejudice, using gypsies as an example, was more successful in classes which included immigrant children, although none of the immigrants were gypsies.[223] It seems reasonable to suppose that a combination of contact and information, both under optimal conditions, would be more successful in altering attitudes and behaviour than either technique by itself.

An interesting contrast between contact and information as agents of change can be made by comparing the study which created interdependent groups, by Weigel and his colleagues, to a more recent one by Van der Keilen, in which she evaluated the effectiveness of a curriculum in Ojibway language and culture in changing white Canadian pupils' attitudes towards their Native schoolmates, and towards Native peoples in general.[224] She found that there was significant change in the latter, as measured by an attitude scale, but not in the former, as measured by friendship-choice (on a sociometric, paper-and-pencil measure). She suggests that choice of friends is less amenable to change because friendship choices depend on previously established individual interaction patterns. By contrast, the essence of Weigel's strategy was to change established interaction patterns, so that new alliances would be formed. However, generalized attitudes did not change, perhaps because in his study, unlike the Ontario study, the content of the programme had no implications for social relations. Ideally, one would like to combine the two strategies, so that curriculum control and working conditions would operate to affect attitudes and behaviour, respectively.

Reinforcement and Change

Several studies have used reinforcement principles to alter young children's attitudes toward Blacks. For example, children are rewarded for choosing black-coloured stimuli, or punished for not choosing them. In some cases, the result is an increase in children's expressed preference for black people as on picture-sort tests.

Perceptual Manipulations and Change

Various attempts at perceptual training or re-training have resulted in attitude modification among children. Such manipulations include: the teaching of Piagetian-type logical operations; the taking of a physically different perspective, in a drawing-exercise; role-taking; exposure to facial pictures, to increase familiarity; and learning labels for and making same-different judgments about pairs of other-race faces. P. Katz[225] reviews these studies.

Although these studies, like so many others discussed here, have some methodological problems, they tend to support the potential effectiveness of perceptual manipulation in altering children's intergroup attitudes.

Summary
What is known about changing children's intergroup and intragroup attitudes and behaviour.
1 It can be done. In fact, some suggest that children's attitudes can be changed more easily than adults'.
2 Reinforcement and perceptual strategies have reasonable success with young children.
3 Intergroup interdependence, within a school setting, can be effective even in the absence of curricular change.
4 Curricular change, especially if some emotional involvement is built in, is effective.
What is not known.
1 As has been stated in earlier sections of this paper, much more is known about intergroup attitudes than about behaviour. Similarly, in the area of change more is known about how to alter attitudes than behaviour.
2 The multiple components of intergroup attitudes need more and better multiple measurement.
3 While a developmental sequence is well-established for the formation of intergroup attitudes, little attention has been paid to the best combination of age and type of change manipulation.
4 If parental attitudes are transmitted to children, changes in such attitudes should also be transmitted. No studies exist of attempts to change children's attitudes by changing those of their parents – or, vice versa.
5 Efforts to improve the ethnic self-identification of minority group members are widespread, but evaluation of such efforts is very sparse. This is true both in the area of school curricula and of the media.

VI THRUSTS FOR FUTURE RESEARCH

Inter-Ethnic Relations

Methodological Contributions
The study of children's interethnic relations is deficient in studies of behaviour as opposed to attitudes, and in studies of the relationship between behaviour and

attitudes. A series of observations should be made in classrooms, on the school grounds, and, ideally, in the children's neighbourhoods, to examine children's friendship patterns, and the amount and quality of interethnic and interracial contact which exists. (A recent and rare attempt to look at frequency of inter-ethnic friendship in school and its relationship to ethnic density of neighbour-hood is described by Sullivan et al.[226]) Such observations could be made in schools and neighbourhoods which are ethnically and racially more and less hete-rogeneous and which differ in socio-economic class. They should include both quantitative measures of frequency of contact, and a recording of the content of such contact in various settings. Toronto is an excellent setting for such research and has not been exploited in previous studies.

At the same time attitudinal measures should be taken and related to observed behaviour. The most commonly used techniques, like doll choice and socio-grams, could be used to examine their predictability to behaviour. Additionally, and perhaps more importantly, some measures which have promise of being more closely related to behaviour could be tried. One such measure, used by ex-perimenters in the area of study called proxemics, is that of desired interpersonal physical distance, which shows strong correlation to observed and reported lik-ing.[227,228] Another measure which could be applied is the slide show, described in a study of relationships between retarded and non-retarded children in the same school. Slides of the target children are shown, and the respondents write the child's name if they know it, and indicate how frequently and how recently they have had friendly interaction with the pictured child.[229] Observation is costly, and should be used not as an end in itself, but as a means of validating more economical, less direct methods.

Measures of own-group attitudes tend to reduce themselves to measures of ethnocentrism, an extreme form of in-group identification which includes out-group hostility. More practical and sensitive measures are needed, if we are to be able to examine the assumption underlying multicultural policies: that pride in one's own group may be positively related to tolerance for ethnic diversity.

Intensive observation and related attitude measurements on populations vary-ing in class, heterogeneity, and age would provide a valuable contribution to the literature on interethnic and intraethnic relations where, according to one re-viewer, the dozens of studies that exist are, in the main, unsatisfactory. The sug-gestion is made that 'far more illuminating would be small-scale studies involving anthropological observations of the process of interracial schooling, across sett-ings diverse' in racial and class ratios, and in educational philosophies and tech-niques.[230]

The use of participant observers who could establish a personal relationship to several children would permit the use of informal interviews which, combined with observation, might begin to suggest answers to questions such as what ethnic cleavage means to members of different groups, and the degree to which they perceive themselves as active or passive in creating the fabric of their peer relations. Such information, based on subjects' perceptions and not imposed by researchers, could serve as a basis for designing valid survey instruments to gather data from a larger and more representative population.

Experimental Manipulation

Schools and classrooms differ, as St John suggests, in educational philosophies and techniques. While observations of interethnic relationships in schools could and perhaps should include some attempt to describe such variables, as well as the general atmosphere of the school, for which validated measures are available, an important area for further research goes beyond observation to experimental manipulation of such teaching-learning variables such as curriculum, seating patterns, individual vs. group work, lecture vs. seminar method, and others. The important study cited earlier of Weigel et al., plus the observations of Allport, Amir, P. Katz, and others, on the importance of institutional support and shared goals to the quality of the contact situation, points out the direction that future studies should take in the area of experimental manipulation of the contact situation in the classroom setting. While there is still substantial interest in the question of the effects of contact on interethnic relationships, there seems little point to stopping at the evaluation of contact as a single variable. Rather, a variety of manipulations which increase the positive, affective quality of interpersonal contact needs to be perfected and to be evaluated. The work of Weigel, Slavin, and Aronson indicates that such manipulations are practicable with even small changes in classroom procedure. Ideally, one might try such experiments in classrooms of different age levels, within otherwise similar school settings, in an attempt to determine the age at which such manipulations are most effective and most economical.

The transmission of attitude change from parent to child also could be examined within the context of a school or pre-school setting to learn whether successful intergroup contact among parents measurably alters their own and their children's attitudes and behaviour.

The effectiveness of such procedures can be measured in a variety of ways, including observation of change in friendship patterns if any; and by any of the many attitudinal measures described earlier.

Intra-Ethnic Relations

Inter-Generational Relations

The dynamics of parent-child cultural transmission in immigrant families is largely unstudied. The studies which document interfamilial conflict have little generalizability beyond whatever empirical data they gather, both because they seldom have representative sampling procedures and because their approach is limited to a simple question and answer format, which leaves no opportunity to discover processes which might apply across content areas. Why, for example, do studies find more parent-child conflict centring on language maintenance than on social relationships? How are such conflicts precipitated, how are they alleviated, under what circumstances are they resolved? While studies of acculturation are not rare, they usually focus on ethnic communities as units in contact with a host or colonial society. Studies of the dynamics of intergenerational cultural change are almost non-existent. We are all aware of the magnitude of the change in the behaviour from immigrant to second generation, but we are largely ignorant of the process. Hence, it is difficult for concerned educators and policy-makers to know how to ease the transition.

A particular area of interest with respect to ethnic groups and socialization, and which is important for both inter- and intra-ethnic relationships, is in the study of social networks. In the context of the 'Child in the City,' the study of people's embeddedness in differing kinds of social networks, and the impact of such network membership on health care information and utilization can be seen as a potentially significant domain in which to examine socialization processes. To what extent is a parent's reliance on kin or non-kin, ethnically similar and ethnically different service deliverers, brokers, and gatekeepers learned by the child as a set of roles determining whom one can trust, how wide the horizons of one's social world should extend, and how much one should depend one oneself and others to be effective? Is the transmission of such patterns of behaviour disrupted, for first- and second-generation children, by their awareness of differences between the larger culture and the family culture? A study of network formation among parents and their children, of the attitudes towards oneself, other people, and decision-making which may underlie personal social organization, and of the process of transmission of such behaviour and attitudes in a different cultural mileu (what has been called socialization as cultural communication) could tell us much of great potential importance about children in a multi-ethnic city.

Peer Relations

Breton et al.[231] note that there has been little work which examines ethnic identity as a dependent variable which develops and diminishes under various circumstances. Two variables whose relationship to ethnic identity should be explored are (a) contact and (b) curriculum.

(a) Contact. Most studies of contact look at its effect on interethnic relations. The only exception, in studies of children, is the literature which examines American black children's self-concept in newly integrated schools and generally finds it to be lower than in segregated settings. But, aside from the question of whether this finding would apply to less socially handicapped groups, or in a less polarized society, two other, unexplored areas of great interest are the effect of meaningful contact on the self-concept and social competence of majority members; and the effect of contact on minority children's attitudes towards their own ethnic group. Does increased interethnic contact increase majority children's sense of social competence – their ability to cope well with different kinds of people? Does it change the degree to which they value diversity in their own lives? Does it heighten their own sense of ethnicity? And, for minority children, does meaningful contact with majority members increase their identification with the majority culture? Does it lead them to reject their parents' values and the friendship of children of their own ethnicity? Or does it strengthen their sense of ethnic difference and separateness? While schools have traditionally been seen as promoters of cultural, if not social assimilation, the question of whether meaningful as opposed to random and unexploited contact leads to such results, is not answered.

(b) Curriculum. The multiculturalism programmes which are being variously implemented in schools in Ontario and elsewhere in Canada seek, as a major aim, to alter the traditional educational system so that the minority-group child or his parent no longer gets a message 'that the cultural base which previously provided that personality with its identity and all the necessary assurances of its validity is, inexplicably no longer valid.'[232] Consequently, one measure of the success of such programmes would be an increase in self-esteem as an individual and as a member of an ethnic group. While multicultural programmes, mostly in the form of more pluralistically oriented social studies programmes, are of recent origin locally, it should be possible to find settings in which they are being implemented and to evaluate their impact on the self-esteem and ethnic identification of minority children.

CONCLUSION

Breton et al. comment that while

... the manifest intention of the policy of multiculturalism has been to encourage and assist the preservation of cultural differences, many members of various ethnic groups ... see the policy as a way in which they can gain public recognition of their diverse subcultures not as foreign, but as Canadian. On the psychological level this may serve to integrate ethnic identity with Canadian identity. Yet probably few members of the Anglo-Saxon group would perceive the policy in this way.[233]

While it may be premature to look for evidence of great changes in Canadian culture as a result of multicultural programmes, or even as a natural result of post-war immigration, it is possible to investigate children's self-identification to see whether second-, third-, and older-generation children maintain any sense of ethnic identity. It is also possible to look at how majority and minority children, in various degrees of contact with one another and experiencing deliberately multicultural school policies, define Canada and Canadians. One interesting question, for example, is whether the federal policy of bilingualism is seen more sympathetically by children whose school experience, both social and academic, is multicultural. The work of Aboud and her colleagues indicates a heightened ability in minority children to identify with others, perhaps as a result of some early confusion about their own ethnic identity coming out of their minority status. Can this same ability to see things from the point of view of someone ethnically, racially, or linguistically different be developed in majority group children, through meaningful contact with minority group children in a school setting where diversity is positively valued? Or is it too late by the time children are six years old; or is the school setting too ineffective compared to home?

Many of these are old questions, but they are a long way from having been definitely answered. Toronto offers an excellent setting in which to investigate the effects of deliberate attempts to alter both intergroup and intragroup behaviours and attitudes in children. But the importance of such basic questions as whether intragroup pride and intergroup co-operation can co-exist in children and adults, or whether an appreciation for human diversity can be developed by exploiting the social heterogeneity present in the school and the community goes far beyond local concerns.

NOTES

1 Sidney, H. Why small-town boys make good, *Time 107:* 16, 24 May 1976.
2 Murphy, Lois and Moriarty, Alice *Vulnerability, coping and growth*, New Haven: Yale University Press, 1976.
3 *New York Times* 28 March 1971, p. 31.
4 '"Ethnic" throughout this paper includes visible and non-visible groups with identity based in natural origin. Thus, West Indians are an ethnic group in Canada, and Blacks, or Afro-Americans are an ethnic group in the United States.

'Definitions of "ethnicity" vary. According to one writer, ... there is no commonly agreed upon definition. In general, the term refers to situations in which different groups are in continuing interaction while maintaining separate identities. A group is ethnic only if there are "out-siders" and if it exists within a wider political field.' (Silverman, Sydel Ethnicity as adaptation, *Reviews in Anthropology 3:* 626–36, 1976.

5 Reiss, Albert J., Jr. *Louis Wirth: on cities and social life*, Chicago: University of Chicago Press, 1964, pp. 61–9.

6 Gulick, John The city as microcosm of society, *Urban Anthropology 4:* 5–15, 1975.

7 Suttles, Gerald D. Urban ethnography, in A. Inkeles, ed., *Annual Review of Sociology 2:* 1–18, 1976.

8 Ziegler, Suzanne *Becoming Canadian*, Toronto, Ontario: Borough of York, Board of Education, 1977. Mimeo.

9 Forcese, Denis and Reicher, Stephen *Issues in Canadian society*, Scarborough, Ontario: Prentice-Hall of Canada Ltd., 1975, p. 408.

10 Roseborough, Howard and Breton, Raymond Perceptions of the relative economic and political advantages of ethnic groups in Canada, in B. Blishen, F. Jones, K. Naegele, and J. Porter, eds., *Canadian society*, Toronto: Macmillan of Canada, 1968, p. 608.

11 Porter, John The economic elite and the social structure in Canada, B. Blishen et al., eds., *Canadian society*, Toronto: Macmillan of Canada, 1968, pp. 754–69.

12 Kellner, Merrijoy Ethnic penetration into Toronto's elite structure, in W.E. Mann, ed., *Canada: a sociological profile*, Toronto: Copp-Clark Publishing Co., 1971.

13 Taft, Ronald and Johnston, Ruth The assimilation of adolescent Polish immigrants and parent-child interaction, *Merrill-Palmer Quarterly 13:* 111–20, 1967.

13a *Globe and Mail*, Toronto, Feb. 23, 1977, p. 7.

14 Lipset, Seymour M. Canada and the United States: a comparative view, *Canadian Review of Sociology & Anthropology 1:* 173–85, 1965.

15 Isajiw, Wsevolod W. Definitions of ethnicity, *Ethnicity 1:* 111–23, 1974.

16 Gans, Herbert J. Urbanism and suburbanism as ways of life. In Herbert G. Gans, *People and plans*, New York: Basic Books, 1968, pp. 34–52.

17 Gans, Herbert J. *The urban villagers*, New York: The Free Press, 1962.

18 Keller, Suzanne *The urban neighborhood*, New York: Random House, 1968.

19 Richmond, Anthony Language, ethnicity and the problem of identity in a Canadian metropolis, *Ethnicity 1:* 175–206, 1974.

20 'Institutional completeness,' a term coined by R. Breton, is a measure of the extent to which an ethnic community can offer its members goods and services in their native tongue, as alternatives to the commercial and service institutions of the majority group.

21 Clark, S.D. *The developing Canadian community*, Toronto: University of Toronto Press, 1962, p. 196.

22 Toronto Board of Education Final report of the work group on multicultural programs. Toronto: 12 Feb. 1978, p. 22.

23 See Covello, Leonard Accommodation and the elementary school experience, in Joseph A. Ryan, ed., *White ethnics*, Englewood Cliffs, NJ: Prentice-Hall, Inc., 1973.
24 Eisenstadt, S.M. *From generation to generation*, New York: The Free Press, 1956, p. 175.
25 Danzinger, Kurt The acculturation of Italian immigrant girls, in K. Ishwaran, ed., *The Canadian family*, Toronto: Holt, Rinehart and Winston of Canada, Ltd., 1976.
26 Danzinger, Kurt *The socialization of immigrant children*, Toronto: York University, the Institute for Behavioural Research, 1971.
27 See also Ianni, Francis A. The acculturation of the Italo-Americans in Norristown, Pennsylvania, Pennsylvania State College, 1952.
28 See also Greenglass, Esther R. A comparison of maternal communication style between immigrant Italian and second generation Italian women living in Canada. *Journal of cross-cultural Psychology 3:* 185–92, 1972.
29 Colallio, Giuiana Culture conflict in the adolescent Italian girl, Toronto: Unpublished MA thesis, University of Toronto, 1974.
30 Economopoulou, Louisa Assimilation and sources of culture tension of second generation Greek pre-adolescents of Toronto, Toronto: Unpublished MA thesis, University of Toronto, 1976.
31 Kim, Bo-Kyung Attitudes, parental identification and locus of control of Korean, New Korean-Canadian and Canadian adolescents, Unpublished PHD dissertation, University of Toronto, 1976.
32 Wolfgang, Aaron A cross-cultural comparison of locus of control, optimism toward the future and time horizon among Italian, Italo-Canadian and the new Canadian youth, *Psychology Abstracts 8:* 299–300, 1973.
33 Beserve, Christopher Relationship between home environment and cognitive and personality characteristics of working-class West Indian pupils in Toronto, Toronto: Unpublished PHD dissertation, University of Toronto, 1976.
34 For a related discussion of Greek families in Australia, see: Noble, Toni and Ryan, Maureen What does school mean to the Greek immigrant parent and his child? *Australian Journal of Education 20:* 38–45, 1976.
35 Wolfgang, Aaron and Shell, Nina Development of a value scale that compares Chinese immigrant students with Canadian-born students, 1977, in press.
36 Lai, Vivien The new Chinese immigrants in Toronto, in Jean L. Elliot, ed., *Immigrant Groups in Canada*, Toronto: Prentice-Hall of Canada, 1971.
37 Taft, Ronald and Johnston, Ruth Assimilation of adolescent Polish immigrants.
38 Reiger, H. The problem of acculturation of Yemenite youth in Israel, *M'gamot 3:* 259–91, 52.

39 Dawson, John L.M., Ng, William, and Wing-Cheung Effects of parental attitudes and modern exposure on Chinese traditional-modern attitude formation, *Journal of cross-cultural Psychology 3:* 201-07, 1972.

40 Johnston, Ruth *Future Australians*, Canberra: Australian National University Press, 1972.

41 Doczy, A.G. The social assimilation of adolescent boys of European parentage in Western Australia, *British Journal of educational Psychology 39:* 193-94, 1969.

42 Taft, Ronald Intergenerational change in ethnic identity among Jews in Australia, in J.W. Berry and W.J. Lonner, eds., *Applied cross cultural psychology*, Amsterdam: Swets and Zeitlinger, B.V., 1975.

43 Feather, N.T. and Wasyluk, G. Subjective assimilation among Ukrainian migrants: value similarity and parent-child differences, *Australia and New Zealand Journal of Sociology 9:* 16-31, 1973.

44 See Spiro's excellent summary and analysis of acculturation studies in the United States: Spiro, Melford E. The acculturation of American ethnic groups, *American Anthropologist 57:* 1240-52, 1955.

45 Warner, W. Lloyd and Srole, Leo *The social systems of American ethnic groups*, New Haven: Yale University Press, 1945.

46 Ianni, Francis A.J. The Italo-American teenager, *Annals of the American Academy of Political and Social Sciences 338:* 70-8, 1961.

47 There is some evidence that juvenile delinquency rates are higher for the second than the first generation in Canada. See Elkin, Frederick *The family in Canada*, Ottawa: The Vanier Institute of the Family, 1971.

48 Ibid.

49 Ibid., 78.

50 Alba, Richard D. Social assimilation among American national-origin groups, *American sociological Review 41:* 1030-46, 1976.

51 Barth, Frederic *Ethnic groups and boundaries*, Boston, Mass.: Little, Brown & Co., 1969.

52 Ibid., 14.

53 Ibid., 16.

54 Darroch, A. Gordon, and Marston, Wilfred G. Ethnic differentiation: ecological aspects of a multidimensional concept, *International Migration Review 4:* 71-95, 1969.

55 Darroch, A. Gordon and Marston, Wilfred G. The social class basis of ethnic residential segregation: the Canadian case, *American Journal of Sociology 77:* 491-510, 1971.

56 Schwirian, Kent P. and Matre, Marc The ecological structure of Canadian cities, in Kent P. Schwirian, ed., *Comparative urban structure*, Lexington, Mass.: D.C. Heath and Company, 1974, pp. 309-23.

57 Darroch, A. Gordon and Marston, Wilfred G. Social class basis, *American Journal of Sociology 77:* 491, 1971.

58 Kantrowitz, Nathan *Ethnic and racial segregation in the New York Metropolis*, New York: Praeger, 1973.

59 Guest, Avery M. and Weed, James A. Ethnic residential segregation patterns of change, *American Journal of Sociology 81:* 1088–1111, 1976.

60 Ibid., 1088.

61 Park, Robert E., Burgess, Ernest, and McKenzie, R.D., eds., *The City*, Chicago, University of Chicago Press, 1925.

62 Williams, Robin M., Jr. *Strangers next door*, New Jersey: Prentice-Hall, 1964.

63 Molotch, Harvey *Managed integration*, California: University of California Press, 1972.

64 Suttles, Gerald *The social order of the slum*, Chicago: University of Chicago Press, 1968.

65 Breton, Raymond Institutional completeness of ethnic communities and the personal relations of immigrants, in B. Blishen, F.E. Jones, K.D. Naegele, and J. Porter, eds., *Canadian society*, Toronto: Macmillan of Canada, 1968, p. 91.

66 Ibid., 91.

67 Fishman, Joshua *Language loyalty in the United States*, The Hague: Mouton & Company, 1968.

68 Lampe, Philip E. The acculturation of Mexican Americans in public and parochial schools, *Sociological Analysis 36:* 57–66, 1975.

69 O'Bryan, R.G., Reitz, J.G., and Kuplowska, O.M. *Non-official languages*, Ottawa: Ministry of Supply and Services, 1976.

70 Woolfson, Peter Public or parish: a study of differences in the acculturation of Franco-American schoolchildren. Unpublished paper, presented at the annual meeting of the Northeastern Anthropological Association, Burlington, Vermont, 1973.

71 Fishman, Joshua *Language loyalty*.

72 O'Bryan, R.G. et al. Non-official languages.

73 This is not to say that linguistic distinctiveness, where it exists is not perceived as a powerful determinant of ethnic identity. Taylor (1975) indicates that it is more salient, as a self-identifier, than ethnic origin, among both English and French monolinguals and bilinguals in Quebec. By contrast, Aboud (1977) found that American Indian children, accustomed to bilingualism within their own families, 'had developed an understanding that language differences did not disrupt ethnic affiliations.' And in studies of children from age 6 to 11, in French language immersion programmes in Canada (Genesee, 1974), language was more related to social identification

for the younger children, while ethnic origin became more salient with increasing age. References:

Taylor, Donald M. Ethnic identity: some cross-cultural comparisons, in J.W. Berry and W.J. Lonner, eds., *Applied cross-cultural psychology*, Amsterdam: Swets and Zellinger, B.V., 1975.

Aboud, Frances E. Role-taking and self-identification, *International Journal of Psychology*, 1977, in press.

Genesee, F.H. Bilingual education: social psychological consequences, Montreal: Unpublished PH D dissertation, McGill University, 1974.

74 Fishman, Joshua *Language loyalty*.

75 Although this may be more true for some ethnic groups than others. See for example, Dreidger, Leo. In search of cultural identity factors: a comparison of ethnic students, *Canadian Review of Sociology and Anthropology 12:* 150–62, 1975.

76 Gans, Herbert J. *Urban villagers*.

77 Gordon, Milton *Assimilation in American life*, New York: Oxford University Press, 1964.

78 Wiseman, R. Integration and attainment of secondary school students in Adelaide, *Australian Journal of Education 15:* 253–68, 1971.

79 Feather, N.T. and Wasyluk, G. Subjective assimilation, *Australia and New Zealand Journal of Sociology 9:* 16–31, 1973.

80 Dreidger, Leo and Church, Glenn. Residential segregation and institutional completeness, *Canadian Review of Sociology and Anthropology 11:* 30–52, 1974.

81 Cimbos, Peter D. Immigrants' attitudes towards their children's inter-ethnic marriages in a Canadian community, *International Migration Review 5:* 5–17, 1971.

82 Cimbos, Peter D. A comparison of the social adaptation of Dutch, Greek, and Slovak immigrants in a Canadian community, *International Migration Review 6:* 230–44, 1972.

83 Bott, Elizabeth *Family and social network*, London: Tavistock Publications, 1957.

84 Boissevain, Jeremy. Friends of friends, Oxford: Basil Blackwell, 1974.

85 Mitchell, J. Clyde, ed., *Social networks in urban situations*, Manchester England: Manchester University Press, 1969.

86 Bott, Elizabeth *Family and social network*, p. 60.

87 Suchman, Edward A. Sociomedical variations among ethnic groups, *American Journal of Sociology 70:* 319–31, 1964.

88 Gans, Herbert *Urban villagers*.

89 More than other groups, in fact. While class and education alter this relation-

ship for others, for Italians it remains very strong. See, for example: Michael Gordon and C.E. Noll, Social class and interaction with kin and friends, *Journal of Comparative Family Studies 6:* 239–49, 1975.

90 It is interesting to note that, in a multi-ethnic study, Puerto Ricans and Blacks in New York city had the highest admission rates to mental hospitals, and Jews the lowest. Put side by side with Suchman's data, we see that the ethnic groups with the least knowledge about, and least positive attitude to medical care are the highest users of mental health facilities. The Jews, on the contrary, had quite 'modern' attitudes to medicine, but had the lowest admission rates to mental hospitals. While the data come from different populations (Rabkin & Streuning's covers a much larger area of New York city), it is interesting to speculate on the relationship between boundaries of social network and attitude to health care on the one hand, and susceptibility to mental breakdown on the other. Does isolation from the larger society create feelings of inadequacy, or depression? Or could routine physical health care have uncovered problems before an emotional crisis developed? Rabkin, Judith G., and Streuning, E.L. Ethnicity, social class and mental illness, Working Paper no. 17, Institute on Pluralism and Group Identity, New York, May 1976.

91 Katz, Pearl Acculturation and social networks of American immigrants in Israel. Buffalo: Unpublished PH D dissertation, State University of New York at Buffalo, 1974.

92 Salloway, J.C. Medical care utilization among urban gypsies, *Urban Anthropology 2:* 113–26, 1973.

93 Wong, Bernard. Elites and ethnic boundary maintenance, *Urban Anthropology 6:* 1–22, 1977.

94 Snyder, Peter Z. Neighborhood gatekeepers in the process of urban adaptation: cross-ethnic commonalities, *Urban Anthropology 5:* 35–51, 1976.

95 Warnecke, Richard B.; Graham, Saxon; Mosher, William; and Montgomery, Erwin B. Health guides as influentials in central Buffalo, *Journal of Health and Social Behavior 17:* 22–34, 1976.

96 The study by Van Der Keilen, discussed in a later section, is concerned with such variables, but because its major focus is on the evaluation of a strategy for attitude changes, it is included in section V. See Van Der Keilen, Marguerite. Some effects of a special Indian culture oriented program on attitudes of white and Indian elementary school pupils, *Canadian Journal of behavioural Science 9:* 161–8, 1977.

97 Rosenstock, Janet and Adair, Dennis *Multiracialism in the classroom.* Ottawa: Secretary of State's Office, 1976. Mimeo.

98 Stereotyping, the ascription of a set of characteristics to a group and to its individual members, is understood to be a manifestation of prejudice, and is often used as a measure thereof.

99 Labowitz, Sanford Some evidence of Canadian ethnic, racial and social antagonism, *Canadian Review of Sociology and Anthropology 11:* 247–54, 1974.
100 Larimer, George S. Indirect assessment of intercultural prejudices, *International Journal of Psychology 5:* 189–95, 1975.
101 Labowitz, Sanford Some evidence of social antagonism, p. 253.
102 Kehoe, John *A report to the Secretary of State on a series of teacher participation workshops*, Ottawa: Secretary of State's Office, 1976. Mimeo.
103 Ramcharan, Subhas Special problems of immigrant children in the Toronto school system, in A. Wolfgang, ed., *Education of immigrant students*, Toronto: The Ontario Institute for Studies in Education, 1975.
104 Head, Wilson *The Black presence in the Canadian mosaic*, Ontario: Ontario Human Rights Commission, 1975.
105 Borough of York Board of Education *Survey of parents of grade eight children on issues related to multiculturalism and the schools*. Toronto, 1976. Mimeo.
106 As does a very recent report for Metropolitan Toronto. See Pittman, Walter *Now is not too late*, a report submitted to the Council of Metropolitan Toronto by the Task Force on Human Relations, Municipality of Metropolitan Toronto, November 1977.
107 Kalin, Rudolph, Scott, P., and Powell, J. Ethnic and multicultural attitudes among children in a Canadian City, Unpublished report to the Secretary of State, Ottawa, July 1977.
108 Proshansky, Harold M. The development of intergroup attitudes, in L.W. Hoffman and M.L. Hoffman, eds., *Review of Child Development Research*, Vol. 2, New York: Russell Sage, 1936.
109 Amir, Yehuda Contact hypothesis in ethnic relations, *Psychological Bulletin 71:* 319–42, 1969.
110 Amir, Yehuda The role of inter-ethnic contact in change or prejudice and ethnic relations, in Phyllis A. Katz, ed., *Toward the elimination of racism*, New York: Pergamon Press, Inc., 1975, pp. 245–308.
111 Brand, E.S., Ruiz, N.A., and Padilla, A.M. Ethnic identification and preference, *Psychological Bulletin 81:* 860–90, 1974.
112 Katz, Phillis A. The acquisition of racial attitudes in children, in Phyllis A. Katz, ed., *Toward the elimination of racism*, New York: Pergamon Press Inc., 1976.
113 Katz, Phyllis A. Attitude change in children, in Phyllis A. Katz, ed., *Toward the elimination of racism*, New York: Pergamon Press Inc., 1976.
114 Bhatnagar, Joti Education of immigrant children. *Canadian Ethnic Studies 11:* 52–69, 1976.

115 Aboud, F.E., Cvetkovich, G.T., and Smiley, S.S. Interest in ethnic groups: information seeking in young children, in J.W. Berry and W.J. Lonner, eds., *Applied cross-cultural Psychology*, 1975, pp. 162–67.

116 Aboud, F.E. Interest in ethnic information: a cross-cultural developmental study, *Canadian Journal of behavioural Science 9:* 134–46, 1977.

117 Aboud, F.E. and Mitchell, F.G. Taking the role of different ethnic groups, *International Journal of Psychology*, 1977, in press.

118 Piaget, Jean and Weil, Anne-Marie The development in children of the idea of homeland and of relations with other countries, *International Social Science Bulletin 111:* 561–78, 1951.

119 Middleton, M.R., Tajfel, H., and Johnson, N.B. Cognitive and affective aspects of children's national attitudes, *British Journal of social and clinical Psychology 9:* 122–34, 1970.

120 Katz, Phyllis A. Attitude change in children.

121 Vaughn, G. Concept formation and the development of ethnic awareness, *Journal of genetic Psychology 103:* 93–103, 1963.

122 Horowitz, E.L. and Horowitz, R.G. Development of social attitudes in children, *Sociometry 1:* 301–38, 1938.

123 Aboud, F.E., Cvetkovich, G.T., and Smiley, S.S. Interest in ethnic groups, in J.W. Berry and J.W. Lonner, *Applied cross-cultural psychology*, 1975.

124 Aboud, 1977.

125 Levine, Robert A. and Campbell, Donald T. A proposal for cooperative cross-cultural research on ethnocentrism, *Journal of Conflict Resolution V:* 82–108, 1961. Recent work in Canada corroborates the reality of ethnocentrism among both adults and children. See John W. Berry, Rudolph Kalin, and Donald M. Taylor, *Multiculturalism and ethnic attitudes in Canada*, Ottawa: Secretary of State, 1978; and see also Kalin et al., *Ethnic and multicultural attitudes*, 1977.

126 Piaget, Jean and Weil, Anne-Marie Development of idea of homeland.

127 Williams, John E. and Morland, J.K. *Race, color and the young child*, Chapel Hill, NC: University of North Carolina Press, 1976.

128 Beserve, Christopher *West Indian children: some problems of adjustment*, Unpublished MA thesis, University of Toronto, 1973.

129 Brand E.S. et al. Ethnic identification.

130 Clark, Barbara S. Pre-school programs and black children, in Jean L. Elliott, ed., *Immigrant groups*, Scarborough, Ontario: Prentice-Hall of Canada Ltd., 1971.

131 Williams, John E. and Morland, J.K. *Race, color*, p. 247.

132 Milner, David *Children and race*, London: Penguin Books, 1975.

133 Brand, E.S. et al. Ethnic identification.

134 Wilson, W. Cody Development of ethnic attitudes in adolescence, *Child Development 34:* 247–56, 1963.
135 Kalin et al. Ethnic and multicultural attitudes.
136 Lambert, W.E. and Klineberg, Otto *Children's views of foreign peoples,* New York: Appleton-Century Crofts, 1967.
137 Wiseman, R. Integration and attainment of secondary school students in Adelaide, *Australian Journal of Education 15:* 253–68, 1971.
138 Loomis, C. Ethnic cleavage in the Southwest as reflected in two high schools, *Sociometry 6:* 7–26, 1943.
139 Gottlieb, David School integration and absorption of newcomers, *Integrated education 3:* 69–75, 1963.
140 Lundburg, G.A. and Dickson, L. Interethnic relations in a high school population, *American Journal of Sociology 58:* 1–10, 1972.
141 Beserve, Christopher *West Indian children.*
142 Brand, E.S. et al. *Ethnic identification.*
143 Gerrard, Harold B. and Miller, Norman *School desegregation,* New York: Pergamon Press, 1975.
144 Weinberg, M. *Desegregation research: an appraisal,* Bloomington, Ind: Phi Delta Kappa, 1970.
145 St John, Nancy H. *School desegregation outcomes for children,* New York: John Wiley and Sons, 1975.
146 Jellinek, Milina M. and Brittan, Elaine M. Multiracial education 1: Inter-ethnic friendship patterns, *Educational Research 18:* 44–53, 1975.
147 Isaacs, Eva Ethnic groups in urban education. *Australian Journal of Social Issues 4:* 303, 1974.
148 Williams, John E. and Moreland, J.K. *Race, color.*
149 Fishman, Joshua A. Negative stereotype concerning Americans among American-born children receiving various types of minority group education, *Genetic Psychology Monographs 51:* 107–82, 1955.
150 Wiseman, R. Integration and attainment.
151 Rosenberg, Morris and Simmons, R.G. *Black and white self-esteem,* Washington, D.C.: American Sociological Association, 1971.
152 St John, Nancy H. *School desegregation outcomes.*
153 Rosenberg, Morris and Simmons, R.G. *Black and white self-esteem.*
154 St John, Nancy H. *School desegregation outcomes.*
155 Katz, Phyllis A., Sohn, M., and Zalk, S.R. Perceptual concomitants of racial attitudes in urban grade-school children, *Developmental Psychology,* in press.
156 Clark, Kenneth B. and Mamie, P. Racial identification and preference in negro children, in T.M. Newcomb and E.L. Hartley, eds., *Readings in social psychology,* New York: Holt, 1947.

157 Katz, Phyllis A. Acquisition of racial attitudes.
158 Orive, Reuben and Gerrard, H.B. Social contact of minority parents and their children's acceptance by classmates, *Sociometry 38:* 518–24, 1975.
159 Proshansky, Harold M. Development of inter-group attitudes, p. 35.
160 Meltzer, H. Hostility and tolerance in children's nationality and race attitudes, *American Journal of Orthopsychiatry 11:* 662–75, 1941.
161 Brittan, Elaine Multiracial education: 2. Teacher opinion of aspects of school life, *Educational Research 19:* 96–107; 182–191, 1976.
162 James, H.E.O. Personal contact in school and change in intergroup attitudes, *International Social Science Bulletin 7:* 66–70, 1955.
163 Clark, Barbara S. Pre-school programs.
164 Katz, Phyllis A. Acquisition of racial attitudes.
165 Fishman, Joshua Negative stereotypes.
166 Fishman, Joshua A. Childhood indoctrination for minority group membership, *Daedalus 90:* 329–49, 1961.
167 Adorno, T.W., Frenkel-Brunswik, E., Levinson, D.J., and Sanford, R.N. *The authoritarian personality*, New York: Harpers, 1950.
168 Katz, Phyllis A. Acquisition of racial attitudes.
168a Curtis, James E. and Lambert, Ronald D. Educational states and reactions to social and political heterogeneity. *Canad. Rev. Sociolog. Anthropol. 13* (2): 189–203, 1976.
169 Mussen, R.H. Some personality and social factors related to children's attitudes toward negroes, *Journal of Abnormal and Social Psychology 45:* 423–41, 1950.
170 Katz, Phyllis A. Acquisition of racial attitudes, p. 136.
171 Proshansky, Harold M. Development of intergroup attitudes, pp. 339–40.
172 Glock, Charles Y., Winthrow, R., Piliavin, J.A., and Spencer, M. *Adolescent prejudice*, New York: Harper & Row, 1975, p. 164.
173 Stember, Charles H. Education and attitude change, New York: Institute of Human Relations Press, 1961, p. 171.
174 Curtis, James E. and Lambert, Ronald D. Educational status and reactions.
175 Byrne, Donn and Wong, Terry J. Racial prejudice, interpersonal attraction and assumed dissimilarity of attitudes, *Journal of Abnormal and Social Psychology 65:* 246–53, 1976.
176 Stein, O.D., Hardyck, J.A., and Smith, M.B. Race and belief: an open and shut case, *Journal of Personality and Social Psychology 1:* 281–90, 1965.
177 Katz, Phyllis A. Acquisition of racial attitudes.
178 Williams, John E. and Moreland, J.K. *Race, color.*

179 Williams, Robin *Strangers next door*, Englewood Cliffs, N.J.: Prentice-Hall, 1964, p. 184.
180 The only evidence we have to the contrary, that mere repeated exposure to a stimulus increases liking of it, comes from Zajonc whose experimental stimuli were letters of the alphabet, nonsense syllables, and photographs, but not people. Zajonc, Robert B. Attitudinal effects of mere exposure, *Journal of Personality and Social Psychology 9:* 1–27, 1968.
181 Allport, G. *The nature of prejudice.* Cambridge, Mass.: Addison-Wesley, 1954.
182 Williams, D.H. The effects of an interracial project upon the attitudes of negro and white girls within the Y.W.C.A., in Arnold Rose, ed., *Studies in reduction of prejudice*, Chicago: American Council of Race Relations, 1948.
183 Bjerstedt, A. Informational and non-informational determinants of nationality stereotypes, *Journal of Social Issues 48:* 24–9, 1962.
184 Sapir, R. A shelter, *M'gamot 3:* 8–36, 1951.
185 Robinson, John W., Jr. and Preston, James D. Equal-status contact and modification of racial prejudice: a re-examination of the contact hypothesis, *Social Forces 54:* 911–24, 1976.
186 Ford, W.S. Interracial public housing in a border city: another look at the contact hypothesis, *American Journal of Sociology 78:* 1426–47, 1973.
187 Wen, L. Li and Yu, Linda Interpersonal contact and racial prejudice, *Sociological Quarterly 15:* 559–66, 1974.
188 Cohen, E.G. and Roper, S.S. Modification of interracial interaction disability, *American Sociological Review 37:* 643–57, 1972.
189 Amir, Yehuda Factors in improving ethnic relations between hostile groups, in J.W. Berry and W.J. Lonner, eds., *Applied cross-cultural psychology*, Amsterdam: Swets and Zeilinger, B.V., 1975.
190 Amir, Yehuda Role of inter-ethnic contact.
191 Fulcher, Dianne and Perry, David G. Cooperation and competition in inter-ethnic evaluation in pre-school children, *Psych Reports 33:* 795–800, 1973.
192 Sherif, M. *Group conflict and cooperation*, London: Routledge and Kegan Paul, 1966.
193 Rabbie, J.M. and Wilkens, G. Intergroup competition and its effects on intra-and inter-group relations, *European Journal of Social Psychology 1:* 215–34, 1971.
194 Weigel, R.H., Wisner, P.L., and Cook, S.W. The impact of cooperative learning experiences on cross-ethnic relations and attitudes, *Journal of Social Issues 31:* 219–44, 1975.
195 Slavin, Robert E. Effects of biracial learning teams on cross-racial friendship and interaction. Baltimore, Maryland: Johns Hopkins University

center for social organization of schools, Report no. 240, November 1977.

195a Aronson, Elliot *The jigsaw* classroom. Beverly Hills: Sage, 1978.

196 Amir, Yehuda Role of inter-ethnic contact.

197 Glock, Charles Y. et al. *Adolescent prejudice.*

198 Yarrow, M.R., Campbell, J.P., and Yarrow, L.J. Acquisition of new norms, *Journal of Social Issues 14:* 8–28, 1958.

199 Reich, Carol and Purbhoo, Mary The effect of cross-cultural contact, *Canadian Journal of behavioural Science 7:* 313–27, 1975.

200 Chadwick-Jones, J.K. Intergroup attitudes: a stage in attitude formation, *British Journal of Sociology 13:* 57–63, 1962.

201 Amir, Yehuda Role of inter-ethnic contact.

202 Amir, Yehuda Contact hypothesis.

203 Brittan, Elaine Multiracial education.

204 Katz, Phyllis A. et al. Perceptual concomitants of racial attitudes.

205 Katz, I. *Conflict and harmony in an adolescent interracial group*, New York: New York University Press, 1955.

206 Trubowitz, Julius *Changing racial attitudes of children*, New York: Frederick A. Praeger, 1969.

207 Kehoe, John Report to Secretary of State.

208 DeVries, D.L. and Edwards, K.J. Student teams and learning games, *Journal of educational Psychology 66:* 741–44, 1974.

209 Weigel, R.H. et al. Impact of cooperative learning experiences.

210 Cook, S.W. Motives in a conceptual analysis of attitude-related behaviour, in W.J. Arnold and D. Levine, eds., *Nebraska symposium on motivation* (vol. 17), Lincoln, Nebraska: University of Nebraska Press, 1969.

211 Proshansky, Harold M. Development of intergroup attitudes, p. 350.

212 Kehoe, John *Report to Secretary of State.*

213 Katz, Phyllis A. Attitude change in children.

214 Litcher, J.H. and Johnson, D.W. Changes in attitudes toward Negroes of white elementary school students after use of multiethnic readers, *Journal of educational Psychology 52:* 339–43, 1968.

215 Lefley, Harriet P. Effects of a cultural heritage program on the self-concept of Miccosukie Indian children, *Journal of educational Research 69:* 462–66, 1974.

216 Kehoe, John *Report to Secretary of State*, p. 8.

217 Peterson, R.C. and Thurstone, L.L. *Motion pictures and the social attitudes of children*, New York: Macmillan, 1933.

218 Mays, L. et al. An evaluation report on *'Vegetable Soup,'* New York State Education Department, Bureau of Mass-Communication, 1975.

219 Bogatz, G.A. and Ball, S. *The second year of Sesame Street: a continuing evaluation*, Princeton, New Jersey Educational Testing Service, 1974.
220 Katz, Phyllis A. Attitude change in children.
221 Berg, M. and Wolleat, P. A comparison of the effects of information on children's attitudes toward other national groups, *California Journal of Research on Education 23:* 200–08, 1973.
222 Madden, Nancy and Slavin, Robert E. School practices that improve race relations. Paper delivered at annual meeting of the American Psychological Association, Toronto, August 1978.
223 Almgren, E. and Gustafsson, E. Training in world citizenship responsibility, *Pedagogisk-Psykologiska Problem*, 1973, no. 227.
224 Van Der Keilen, Marguerite Some effects of a special Indian culture oriented program.
225 Katz, Phyllis A. Attitude change in children.
226 Sullivan, Mercer L., Ianni, Francis A., and Orr, Margaret Desegregation, culture, contact and the social organization of the high schools, Paper delivered at annual meeting of the American Educational Research Association in Toronto, Ontario, April 1978.
227 Haase, R.F. and Markey, M.J. A methodological note on the study of personal space, *Journal of consulting and clinical Psychology 40:* 122–5, 1973.
228 Sommer, Robert *Tight spaces*, Englewood Cliffs, N.J.: Prentice-Hall Inc., 1974.
229 Hambleton, D. and Ziegler, S. The study of the integration of trainable retarded students into a regular elementary school setting, Toronto: Metropolitan School Board, Research Dept., 1974.
230 St John, Nancy H. *School desegregation outcomes.*
231 Breton, Raymond, Burnett, Jean, Hartman, Norbert, Isajiw, Wsevolod, and Lennards, Joseph Research issues in Canadian cultures and ethnic groups, *Canadian Review of Sociology and Anthropology 12:* 81–94, 1975.
232 Toronto Board of Education, The bias of culture, Toronto 1974. Mimeo.
233 Breton, Raymond et al. Research issues, p. 86.

7

Children and the
Urban Physical Environment

WILLIAM MICHELSON AND
ELLIS ROBERTS

This chapter is about the physical settings in which children live in large cities. Topics like housing, play facilities, neighbourhoods, and the means of transportation by which children get to know and use the city are covered, as well as others which are less well recognized but relevant to urban children.

Although there have been some excellent reviews in the realm of the general topic in recent years,[1] each has taken a partial view of the subject. Some, for example, focus on tangible architectural and landscaping improvements best suited to fit the needs of children; others exhaust known psychological theories linking children with spaces they use. Still others focus on special facilities, such as playgrounds, schools, or day nurseries. The major intention here is to explore the range of considerations in the urban environment which research and theory indicate as relevant to the health, welfare, and well-being of children. The chapter is meant to highlight significant contexts, indicating where much is known and where much more needs to be learned.

Such an exploration may be justified on a number of grounds.

First, although its roots go back at least to the so-called scientific management and design work around the turn of the century, best illustrated by time and motion studies in factories and kitchens alike, the systematic empirical study of people and the man-made environment they use every day is a very recent phenomenon.

The establishment of coordinated research and curricular efforts did not take up from the work of isolated (though far-sighted) individuals until about the 1950s in selected European nations[2] or the late 1960s in North America. The major treatises on so-called man-environment relations have only come out in the last 10 years.[3]

If an effort to learn about people of all ages in their environmental context is only just gathering momentum, we can certainly not now expect knowledge of children in this respect to be sizable. What is remarkable, however, is how *little* of the focus to date has concerned children. A major new sociological treatise about *The Urban Experience*[4] fails to suggest any special considerations about children on the subject. Another recent work, by a prominent environmental psychologist, makes clear that children's perception of urban places is different from that of adults, but it nonetheless fails to provide details of a more specific nature.

Trowbridge really argued that there are two systems, one used by 'civilized minds' and the other by 'birds, beasts, fish, insects, etc., but also, in all probability, by young children and by a large proportion of mankind living in an uncivilized state.'[5]

Even an exhaustive study on newly built American suburbs came no closer to an understanding of the spatial world of the child than an examination of whether communities, in the eyes of adults, were a good 'place to raise children' and if these communities did or did not have certain facilities and institutions commonly used by children. It ignored entirely the particular interface of children and environment.[6]

We cite these three examples not to single them out for particular condemnation but rather to illustrate treatment which is more the rule than the exception.

If the general treatises, starting from an emphasis on *environment*, have not gone deeply into the situation of children, neither have similarly recent, major policy statements on *children* dealt explicitly with specific aspects of the physical environment.[7]

Even a highly thoughtful and no doubt pathbreaking statement by Bronfenbrenner[8] entitled and clearly directed 'Toward an Experimental Ecology of Human Development' fails to relate such an interest to the specific kinds of spaces and places constituting the urban ecology.

Therefore, an explicit review, not consciously restricted to any single application or theoretical perspective, which points out those aspects of the urban physical environment which are of particular significance to children, may address a gap in the general literature. Such a gap, moreover, may be serious for several reasons.

Those kinds of factors in the urban environment which impinge on children may have far more lasting consequences for them than those which impinge on their elders. By and large, children are smaller and weaker than all but elderly and handicapped persons, who clearly share many of the problems children encounter in cities. Children's physical context serves as the setting for their formative years. By definition, children do not have prior experience in dealing with that which they encounter. And they seldom command the economic means of adaptation found in the adult world, except through the intervention of their parents. Children are not legally entitled to exercise political influence or control, and hence, except when adults take up their causes, they are more easily ignored.

Recent demographic trends show that the percentage of children in the total population is declining, while the percentage of elderly persons is rising. We are becoming a more adult population which is showing tendencies of becoming more adult *centred*. The general response to such a trend has been one of cutting back on provisions for children (e.g., the value per capita of school budgets) rather than on exploring the many ways in which children lack sufficient opportunities in large cities even before cut-backs.

Thus, there are many reasons to justify a concentration on children and their urban environment. Nonetheless, speaking of children and the urban physical environment is much like speaking of adults and their urban physical environment. Just as there are many kinds of people and many aspects of environment at the adult level, a great number of distinctions concerning children and forms of environment must be made.

Let us turn our attention to the lens or lenses we must use in order that these considerations come into realistically sharp focus.

I WAYS OF VIEWING CHILDREN AND THE ENVIRONMENT

What children experience in their urban environment is partly a function of their stage of development and of the nature of the surroundings with which they do or might come into contact. What these experiences leave them with is varied, a function of different forms of causation which link environment and people. Hence some factors requiring explication in this context are as follows: (1) stage of children's development, (2) scale and range of environment, (3) effects on children, and (4) types of causation.

Each consideration is instructive, because it indicates a way in which the subject must be differentiated and seen in closer detail. The existence of a variety of sources of differentiation tells us also that the overall subject is surely multidimensional and hence complex. To deal with all of the valid considerations surrounding the child-environment context, we must think in terms of a matrix reflecting the variety of differences found as a result of viewing all these factors simultaneously.

Thus, although these four kinds of factors are conjoint in the real world, we must start by examining them one by one, to understand their meaning and complexity. Unfortunately, multi-dimensional matrices do not lend clarity to the *exposition* of the content of a subject area. We must first recognize the nature and legitimacy of each factor with which we must cope.

Stage of Development

Children pass through several stages of development, and the public recognizes this by paying close attention to children's ages for many purposes. We age-grade children, for example, for purposes of school, competitive sports, and movie admissions. As Chapter 4 documents, the very definition of what children are and what they can and cannot do is set down to a great extent by age-graded law. Implied in all this is the notion of capacity – what children are able to do responsibly during their formative years.

The design of urban environment does not ignore differences in age. Facilities designed specially for the very young are common, and recreation rooms in new houses appeal to some needs of teenagers. Nonetheless, facilities directed to the special needs of age categories or which simultaneously serve all groups through a single vehicle (e.g., a multi-functional community centre) are not ubiquitous. More common is the designation of certain aspects of a plan as 'for the children,' such as a single kind of playground or a street pattern which excludes heavy traffic from the vicinity of homes. Studies of children and their use of urban space, however, make clear that children have greatly different abilities and needs at different ages, with definite implications for the physical environment.

Dahlén's careful study of new suburbs in Sweden, for example, indicates that children themselves maintain highly segregated groups according to age. Dahlén argues for a form of comprehensive community planning which systematically includes from the outset provision for the needs of *all* relevant age groups, lest children fail to optimize growth during any particular period of development as a result of lacking environmental supports.[9]

In a parallel vein, Bronfenbrenner urges that both children and adults can best be understood by viewing their behaviour as the outcome of a continuous mutual accommodation throughout the lifespan of the human organism and its environment.[10] To Bronfenbrenner, the environment includes dimensions of culture, social structure, and specific interpersonal situations, as well as relevant aspects of the physical setting, with dimensions of time and space. Although Bronfenbrenner does not specify which aspects of physical environment are important in relation to human development, other authors have been more explicit.

Most notable among these is Pollowy.[11] In her seminal work on children's environment needs, she stresses that age is associated with several dimensions of development: (1) intellectual and perceptual development, (2) physical growth and associated activities, and (3) personal and social development, including forms of relationships with other people. Although noting differences in these dimensions pertaining to even more specific age norms, she puts particular emphasis on three age groupings: infancy, the later pre-school years, and what she calls middle childhood (corresponding to the pre-teen school years). Each of these stages of age and development is then systematically related in her work to relevant design objectives and to the guidelines and criteria felt desirable for the achievement of the objectives.

Whether one takes these categories of development or prefers other divisions documented in the literature of child development, it is not difficult to understand that children at various ages have differential ability *to cope safely* with various features of the home and environment, *to traverse an increasingly larger territory* as part of the daily routine, and *to come into contact with other people* in increasingly more specific activities and autonomous groupings.

A recent study focused on the activities, contacts, competencies, and responsibilities of children from a wide range of backgrounds, living in a number of different locations, and taking stages of development into consideration. Age was the major factor explaining differences in all the foregoing behavioural atttributes of the children studied.[12]

There is no need to belabour this point. No one disputes the existence of age-related developmental stages; we quarrel only about the exact nature of the stages and about the importance and reversibility of what happens in a particular stage. For the present, however, it is enough to take as a starting point that there is a variety of stages which relate to the design of physical environment in ways which are relevant to the health, well-being, and opportunities available for children.

Yet, it is one thing to give general lip service to this point and quite another process, less customary and more demanding, to implement it fully when planning or providing services to any particular area. Indeed, a major Swedish government review of the situation of the contemporary child concluded a section on 'What are the implications of the design of physical environment' by emphasizing this very point: 'It is of the utmost importance for children that the environment provide activities for *all* ages ...'[13]

Scale and Range of Environments

What are the different kinds of environment towards which our concerns should be directed? A customary picture is of the child at home, in school or playing in a formal playground or, possibly, of unsupervised children on street corners or in shopping centres.

Perhaps because people normally (though likely mistakenly) credit the architectural and educational experts with having fully thought out the design parameters of home and school for children of all ages, empirical attention has for the most part been concentrated on the design of playgrounds. Such a fixation of attention has been noted recently by several authors:

Obviously we have considerable information from developmental studies, but what about the various settings in which they (children) live? Representative of their bias towards the validity of formalized play, most of the answers to this question come from works dealing with children's play: play activities, play environments, preferences in play equipment, problems with play. While some studies deal with the question in terms of the residential milieu, more are concerned with the specifics of various playgrounds.[14]

Physical planning for children has almost always come to mean the planning of playgrounds.[15]

Despite such a concentrated focus, both logic and evidence justify taking explicit notice of the range and scale of environments relevant to children's lives. In setting up such an expanded focus, one does not reject the importance of home and school environments. They occupy major portions of a child's daily life, so much so that students of children's daily time schedules customarily note a prevailing sameness about the daily activities of those old enough to go to school.[16] Nonetheless, there is a block of time not restricted to essential activities at home or school on school days, weekends, holidays, and school vacations; a substantial part of a child's life is played out during these periods, depending upon the age of the child, not to speak of the facilities available. Some of this time may be spent in the kind of formal playgrounds which provide the bulk of the research picture. But not all! What this third sector in the life of the child requires of the urban environment beyond formal play space is highly variable – from nothing at all to the whole world; it depends upon the situation of the child, the particular family, and the entire culture. Normally, however, as children get older, they are considered able to venture further from home and school; not coincidentally, they have more economic and recreational interests to pursue, and these are not uniformly satisfied in just one place. How far an older child will eventually go is circumscribed by what attractions are available relevant to his or her interests and by the ability to get there; access is partly determined by locational and siting decisions, forms and costs of available transportation, and parental support. We shall return to questions of land use, transportation, and play, but the present point is simply that *with increasing age, children are considered to have the capacity and motivation to cover larger and larger territories when they are not required to be at home or school.* Such a phenomenon is customarily referred to as the 'home range,'[17] or 'orbit.'[18] A daily or weekly orbit potentially involves a wide range of types of places. While some of them are intended for children of particular ages, like the playground to which we refer so frequently, other relevant aspects of environment include such different scales of place as locations outside a child's own unit but still within the same apartment house, areas immediately adjacent to residential buildings (gardens, doorways, walkways, etc.), stores, play spaces, streets, formal recreational or educational facilities, places of employment, and indeed, anywhere likely to be of interest – whether planned and provided for children or not.

The variety of places relevant to children's various purposes, going well beyond the traditional playground, and the importance of their availability and design, are suggested in a French study:

This third context for life activities, despite its importance in the daily life of the child and for his socialization, is the least studied. ... From the point of view of the child's social life, this context corresponds to the times and places where he gains access to the creative activities with his peer group. But it is often constraining, frustrating, and a source of multiple restrictions.[19]

Most authors distinguish among what is contained within the individual dwelling unit (also called the private domain[20]), the external interior (e.g., lobbies, hobby rooms, etc.), the immediate exterior (e.g. gardens), the block, the neighbourhood, and the urban fabric more generally (which would include both the kind of structure constituting the metropolitan area and where and how any local sub-area fits into it). The larger the scale of environment under consideration, the more likely it is that its implications for children are not fully recognized, or confused with expectations usually pertaining to adult users. The part such environments play in the lives of children, nonetheless, is not diminished by our non-observance of their significance to children.

Furthermore, the relevance of even very small scales of environments for children is not restricted by their original intent. It is a common observation that children appear to prefer spending time in places not made for them. Safe, protected areas go unused, for example, while children play on paved parking areas for which they have supposedly been given a better alternative. Kevin Lynch also notes the intense use by children of back alleys, garage roofs, building sites, and vacant lots.[21] The vivid memories of childhood involve the bricks and concrete of sidewalks and passageways not intended for use by children for their play. These spaces are commonly referred to as 'invisible environments'[22] or 'hidden structures.'[23] In many instances, the significance of a 'hidden' space goes beyond its unintended nature; being hidden from the eyes of other segments of the population can be attractive to children, even though this is not characteristic of all 'hidden spaces.'[24]

At *any* age or stage of development, some of the places where children spend time are intended for children's use, while others are hidden spaces. But as children get older, a greater percentage of the environment they effectively use will almost certainly be of the hidden variety, shared with grownups who often do

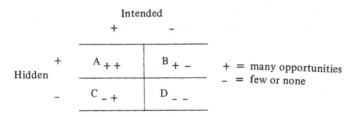

FIGURE 1 Configuration of environmental opportunities for children.

not expect multiple usage. This lack of acceptance by the adult world at the same time as the adolescent is reaching inevitably towards adult status and behaviour is surely another example of the ambiguities of transition from childhood to adulthood discussed in Chapter 5. There is no a priori logic which assigns virtue to children's environment as being either wholly intended or wholly invisible: what must be recognized is that children draw upon both types of spatial setting for the crucial third sector of their life activity. One may broadly evaluate residential areas in terms of the presence or absence of each kind of place, and there is no limit as to the number of both kinds of settings. This makes a fourfold table (Fig. 1).

Box A represents the kind of area which already has a great number of amenities for a given age group, whether from man-made enterprises or from nature, to which have been added others specifically earmarked for the given age group. An example of such a given place might be a well-organized, progressive residential area in a central city or suburb, where the commercial structure and recreational opportunities have grown organically over the years.

In contrast, B is the kind of area where, even though we say nothing has been provided for children, young people nonetheless keep occupied in the back lanes, the stores, and even the streets, with activities which they find engrossing, however mysterious or troublesome such behaviour may appear in the eyes of adults. Many think that B is more typical of older central city areas than A.

Box C represents the situation of many new suburbs or communities built quickly and with economies of scale. In this case, many natural amenities are not maintained, while low densities and strict zoning militate against the establishment of a rich commercial fabric in the vicinity of residential areas. Playgrounds and pools are often constructed; but in the absence of other hospitable places for children in the area, the overall outcome may still be relatively spartan.

Nonetheless, the most sterile situation is represented by box D in which 'richness,' whether physical, social, or commercial, is not already part of the environment but where little investment is put into specific new public attractions geared to children. Such is typical of newly constructed housing for marginal social classes around the world, whether in capitalist or socialist societies. Sadly, such housing has often been carefully 'planned.'

Figure 1 helps us to understand why, in retrospect, many newly planned communities or projects turn out to be no more attractive or effective for children than the slums they were meant to replace. Children's environment is surely more than home and school, its relevant aspects are of extremely variable degrees of scale, and indeed many critical aspects are neither intended to pertain to the everyday needs of children nor are recognized as doing so.

In the discussion of specific topics which constitutes the second half of this chapter, we shall return to the question of land use in newly developing areas, as we consider this a source of problems in metropolitan areas which is not fully recognized. Now, however, let us turn to several other major factors which have to be considered when dealing with children and the urban physical environment.

Effects on Children

To this point, we have examined children and urban environment in general terms to establish the need for taking a view which is more complex than conventional wisdom or practice in urban planning and management dictates. Now we must add to the formula the reason why we have to be concerned about the interface of the previous two factors. Although most of us profess to care about children, and therefore to do things which we generally feel to be to their advantage,[25] our actions can be more carefully directed and more highly focused if we are aware of the specific nature of the effects of such choices for children.

This is another source of complexity, for there are many potential effects of environmental conditions. This does not mean, however, that the kind of effect of any stimulus is indeterminant. One reason for focusing more closely on effects is to become more realistic about what can or cannot be a consequence of an existing condition, as well as what should or should not be expected to result from any particular ameliorative effort. Furthermore, consideration of effects provides some basis for choosing which situations to ameliorate first, assuming some valuative standpoint for assigning priority to one or another kind of effect.

Some effects are a matter of life and death. But even here, some subtlety might be entertained. There are *clear and immediate dangers* to life from airborne and domestic pollutants and poisons, from non-random accidents such as traffic, bodies of water, or falls, and from the actions of other people. On the other hand, environmental effects which are just as lethal may work slowly, building up dangerous levels of substances in the body or reducing degrees of resistance so that the point of recognition may be too late for ameliorative efforts.

Although health-related situations may be dramatic, as just suggested, they can operate at other levels, too. Housing studies to which we shall refer suggest, for example, a relationship between quality of housing and the incidence of disease. The observer may consider as well the relationship between environment and fitness in the larger sense.

Although health outcomes are relatively unambiguous, even though not necessarily universally recognized, they are but the tip of the iceberg. Another kind of effect has to do with personality. As Schorr points out in *The Child in the City: today and tomorrow*, Plant[26] made the first major assertion about environmental effects on the personality of children. He wrote that poor children growing up in high density settings, with little shielding from the realities of daily life among a variety of adults, could not maintain positive illusions about such matters as safety, sex, and marriage. They incorporate certain degrees of cynicism and fatalism into their personal outlooks, which may be realistic and useful but which differ from the outlooks of children in other circumstances.

There is a resurgence of interest among sociologists and psychologists (not to speak of social psychologists) concerning the outcome of urban living on the personality. Their concern now has to do with certain concepts like stimulus overload and alienation.[27] Whether the total urban context actually has effects on children is a matter of conjecture and a point to be considered subsequently. However, it takes no great stretch of the imagination to apply to specific situations affecting children the kind of reasoning exemplified by Plant and embodying concepts parallel to those of the macroscopic theorists to specific situations facing children.

Competence, for example, a concept central to other chapters in this book, is surely affected by the various kinds of environmental settings facing our children. Where, for example, children are able to complete particular tasks or to polish specific skills, we should expect the development of competence in their personalities.[28] Where such opportunities are lacking, the opposite should occur. A feeling of control may develop in response to children's ability to determine the use of particular areas of space. Occasionally, children have this power (although usually when abdicated by adults), sometimes their parents have it (more likely regarding their own home but sometimes regarding building complexes and neighbourhoods), but often neither have it. Sennett's work on urban anarchy, although surely a period piece of the late 1960s, gives graphic examples of potential forms of local control, together with purported supportive outcomes for the persons involved.[29]

Still others point to the capacity of the physical environment to support or enhance various forms of social contact. People are often concerned with whether neighbourhoods provide enough or too many children for appropriate play-groupings, whether there are suitable places where children of different ages can get together to do appropriate things, and whether these places are secure, costly, proximate, easily supervised, etc. In addition, however, many other forms of social contact are related to the urban context. The particular structure of urban housing and neighbourhood is associated with various forms of segregation. These involve ethnicity and race, socio-economic status, age, and whether or not a high proportion of children is present or absent in a neighbourhood (a modern form of segregation which is growing, with decided implications for the child in the otherwise childless neighbourhood). The kinds of groups which can form in any area are a function of the dimensions (physical and social) of the area.[30]

Another potential structural consideration has to do with how the segregation of residential areas from places of employment can effect children's knowledge of and attitudes towards gainful employment.

In other situations our concern is a directly behavioural one. We are concerned with what children do as the outcome of a complex of opportunities or the lack of them. Behavioural outcomes, however, are surely not cut-and-dried. They assume an endless variety, and our interest is at many levels. Even the most preliminary thinking about play, for example, illustrates our multiple concerns. At one level, we are concerned about whether or not children do, in fact, assume some kind of active, animated behaviour (physical or mental) in response to whatever opportunities are included in an area designated for play; the unwanted alternative is lethargic apathy. If the children are active, our concerns do not end. Is the activity safe or dangerous? Does it single out only the best competitors? Does it lead to intellectual enrichment or the learning of skills? Does it encourage aggressive or even destructive behaviour among some?

Behaviour outcomes are surely not unrelated to the other effects just noted, as well as to the earlier considerations of age and environment. It would seem too elementary to ask whether, at present, most neighbourhoods provide positive opportunities for social and recreational activities for all ages of children and youth, except that the answer is 'no' all too often. It is unusual, for example, to find places for teenagers to gather, particularly in newly built areas, hence leading to the use of hidden spaces like shopping centres in ways which are neither intended nor appreciated.

Behaviour does not occur in a vacuum, but in settings which accommodate some forms of behaviour better than others. How children and youth act is at least partially a function of suitable opportunities, as well as the 'paths of least resistance' regarding the settings utilized. Much delinquency is simply behaviour defined as such by adults, and some degree of delinquent behaviour is only activity deemed inappropriate on adult turf which occurs there only in the absence of more fully developed alternative turfs. The provision of behavioural opportunities for young people through appropriate physical settings is therefore more than a matter of amenity.

Thus, when we assess behavioural effects, we must consider not only those of particular intended environmental settings, but also those of the larger network of opportunities for any age group made possible by the *range* of settings available for their use.

Psychological effects are not unrelated to behavioural effects. It is not difficult to see how the development of personal feelings of competence and control, for example, relate respectively, to opportunities to carry to completion particular efforts and to the use of particular places without dominance by outside parties.

We have to this point focused on children as unique entities regarding their spatial needs, particularly with respect to discretionary activities. While such an emphasis is, in our opinion, generally underdeveloped in relation to its importance, it should not be taken to the point of exaggeration. As Chapter 2 indicates, most children still have their way into the world planned and facilitated by their parents and other members of their immediate family. And parental involvement applies not just to the home, but to coping even with dispersed, low density land-use patterns in the role of chauffeur.[31] Although children have their own needs and orientations, young people are clearly not autonomous.

But environmental conditions which affect the way adults can deal with children are surely meaningful as well for children, even if one step removed from the initial effect. Therefore, our interest in children and the urban physical environment must also include situations which aid or inhibit parents from participating in desired relationships or activities with their children. In some cases this may have to do with styles of child raising; in other cases, with ability to supervise, related in turn to what children are then allowed to do. In still others, with travel behaviour.

A parallel consideration takes the same ingredients, but puts them in a separate order. As Chapter 3 emphasizes, there is an increasing number of situations in urban society where the parent is unable to exercise direct supervision, particularly during the work day. While this applies to pre-school children, it is not restricted to them; many working parents, for example, begin or end their day at times which are at variance with the opening and closing times of schools. Social planners are rightly concerned with many dimensions of surrogate child care, including programmes, costs, and visibility to those desirous of such services.

The dimension we must emphasize here is location; child care services demanding high costs of travel and time obviate their intended benefits.

Thus, when studying children and their urban and physical environment, one must assume explicit awareness of the effects intended and observed. And for the child, such effects may be encountered firsthand or secondhand, in the short or long run, and in a host of ways.

Types of Causation

We are slowly building an equation. To this point we have kaleidoscopic combinations of children and environments (not excluding adults where relevant) leading to a variety of specific effects. Missing still is the notion of *how* the ingredients produce these effects. Dealing with any phenomenon surely requires knowledge of causation.

This is not the place for a complex theoretical discussion, which is readily available elsewhere.[32] Nonetheless, several basic premises must be elucidated in order that the dynamics of how environments come to bear on children and their lives are clear. Our major assumptions are as follows.

(1) It should be apparent to this point in the chapter that we do not regard environment as totally irrelevant to the lives of children. A few writers disagree; their point of view is that social policies and conditions are far more influential in peoples' lives than environment, which they regard as an epiphenomenon. Our assumption, though, does not suggest the *absolute* importance of any single kind of condition, which, even for an individual, is probably a metaphysical phenomenon.

(2) We do not regard physical environment, when of explanatory value, as necessarily deterministic. It is still a premise of some studies, though less than previously, that the physical environment produces results among people which are inescapable and of a certain, predictable nature. Public housing, for example, was once justified on the grounds of its supposed ability to improve the personal relationships of its occupants. But this rather simplistic hope has been dismissed by later evidence.[33] A deterministic theme which has worn somewhat better over the years suggests that, all else being equal, people form friendships according to the access of their homes to one another; one observer went so far as to suggest that neighbourhood planners are thereby enabled to create friendship patterns for the persons who will reside in the areas they have designed.[34] Today, considerable attention is focused on whether living in high densities determines one or another form of pathological response.

We do not see most child-environment relationships as inherently deterministic, but we do allow for situations in which the impact of environment affects the child directly. Causes of such a potentially direct impact are pollution, various forms of accidents (including traffic accidents), and aspects of physically bad housing.

(3) In the more common child-environment relationship, the effects occur in a non-deterministic, relatively volunteeristic manner. Something does not *happen to* the child. The child elects to do or not do something, at least partly on the basis of how well he or she assesses it could be done within the constraints of the physical setting(s) available. This view takes the assumption that environment is generally enabling or constraining, seldom vetoing or determining. One speaks of the degree of 'fit' between desired activity and physical setting; they are more and less 'congruent' with one another.[35]

Under this perspective, the nature and design of the environmental setting provides varying amounts of opportunity for different behaviours. Just because the opportunity is present, however, it does not necessarily follow that the desired or anticipated behaviours will ensue. The saying, 'You can lead a horse to water but you can't make him drink,' is not an untoward analogy when applied to most situations regarding people and physical environments.[36] Conversely, the crucial notion for planning is that 'the horse can't drink unless you provide water in a suitable container.'

One has to ask in a given situation whether the aspects of physical design contained there are really supportive of the behaviour assumed to follow. If the answer is 'no' (that is, an opportunity is not provided and the child-environment fit is incongruent), the ensuing effects will not be as desired – either in terms of non-participation or 'misuse.'

Nonetheless, as the above horsesense suggests, sheer opportunity in a congruent relationship does not by itself produce the desired behaviour. A host of other factors have to be examined regarding their bearing on the eventual performance or non-performance of what was expected. How well aspects of environment fit with the customs, traditions, and unwritten rules has a bearing on their use.[37] Whether design enables aspects of environment to be perceived in terms of their use is an additional factor pursued as important by social scientists at many different levels of scale.[38] In addition, the constraints of costs are hardly irrelevant.

Ease of access is surely a major factor regarding the use or non-use of facilities, as well as the mental image people have of them. Access should be considered as one of the basic dimensions of places built or maintained for children's use, as children have limited means of locomotion. If these facilities are located on sites which are largely inaccessible to the necessary mass of users, according to customary norms of access, then they are in effect incongruent in a significant way.

Thus, our search for how the particular combination of children and environment produces the effects that occur most frequently requires the examination of a non-deterministic situation involving varying degrees of opportunity, as well as the assessment of a number of more subjective dimensions explaining children's orientation to even functionally favourable environments.

(4) We must recall that not all environmental effects reaching children come to them first-hand. Some come, in consequence of a contextual phenomenon occurring first to someone else, usually a parent. In this situation, our explanation must include that which occurs at the adult level, as well as how this becomes meaningful for the child. In other cases, the environment-person relationship should be expected to follow either of the models in points (2) and (3) above, with an extension to children following the lines of a rather different form of understanding.

The effects on children of adult interfaces with the environment, moreover, go beyond overt behaviour or activity. The nature or consequences of adult social organization having to do with physical environment have consequences for children. For example, the structure of management of an apartment complex at the adult level may be highly central to children's feelings of environmental control; children tend to notice when their parents are at the mercy of an authoritarian building superintendent. Adult mobility decisions which create neighbourhood homogeneity, to take another example, have a bearing on the social relations of their children.

Furthermore, the place of adults regarding environmental effects on children takes on considerations of an even more macroscopic level. To understand how to change the child-environment formula so as to produce 'better' effects, we need to understand not only the dynamics of the interface between child and environment (however transmitted or managed by significant adults in the life of the given child) but also which adults were instrumental in creating the overall context in the first place (and for what reasons). Who was responsible for the whole first half of the equation we have been building? Merely knowing how to do something better in the future does not mean that it will be done that way. One must understand why it has been done as it has in the past in order to appreciate the constraints against better practice which are active in the real world.

For example, it might be easy to discover ways in which apartments might be designed more suitably for use by children. If, however, it could be shown that landlords have reasons for preferring to house families without children, then we might recognize their reluctance to implement designs which would attract families with children.[39] Such an explanation is hardly a solution. But the solution must be based on the knowledge of how significant persons are predisposed to act.

Thus, in the simplest of terms, adults are considered according to two different causal models.

(a) environment → adults → children,
(b) adults → environment → children.
Moreover, there is no reason why the two models can not be found together in certain situations, although one group of adults may have 'caused' the environment and another may serve to transmit the effects to children:
(c) adults → environment → adults → children.

In sum, an adequate explanation of how environmental effects are visited on children requires, at the least, a sensitive dissection and consideration of *all* the previous factors. There is no single a priori explanation of environmental effects on children. Explanatory paradigms may go in a variety of directions, although central to most (though not totally explanatory of the final outcome) are concepts involving environmental opportunity and adult social structure.

These theoretical premises therefore suggest a focus on at least three types of explanation, bringing in all relevant variables in the process: (a) environment as a determinant (as justified), (b) environment as spatial opportunity, and (c) environment as brought about and/or mediated by adult social organization.

The major purpose of this section of the chapter remains to elucidate some of the major factors contributing to necessary complexity regarding children and their urban and physical environment. We have made a breakdown of (1) children by age and developmental stage, (2) environment by scale and nature, (3) effects by type, and (4) explanatory reasoning by the logic joining environment and children. While there is considerable serious empirical content to be mastered, in order to pay due attention to the spatial needs of children in large cities, such content cannot be comprehensively represented in a simple, straightforward manner. The matrix to which we referred at the start of this section is at least four dimensional, with each dimension made up of no less than several possibilities, with the maximum number now unknown.

Figure 2 shows a simplified representation of the parts in our equation.

Inasmuch as we wish to go beyond the point of sensitizing the reader to necessary perspectives of children and environment and to come to grips with what is known and unknown regarding this complex of relationships, some choice must be made as to the framework of the more concrete discussion to follow. Even if the existing amount of information were to justify such detail, an encyclopaedic inventory touching upon each known combination of variables in the dimensions discussed would surely be formidable to the reader. And the superstructure would be greater than a single chapter could bear.

Therefore, in the second half, we shall discuss a selection of the major manifest and latent issues concerning children and their urban physical environment, as grouped according to the *type of causation* involved. We choose this last form of classification because it incorporates in its point of departure the various other

Age of children (developmental stage):	X	Scale and nature of environment:	=		Effects
a. infants		a. interior of home	a. directly		a. health
b. toddlers		b. other interior space inside multiple family dwelling	b. through provision of opportunity as motivated and directed by additional factors		b. personality
c. pre-school		c. immediate exterior	c. as mediated by adult social organization		c. social relationships
d. ca. 5–10 years		d. block or project			d. behaviour
e. 11–14 years		e. neighbourhood			e. care by adults
f. 15–16 years		f. city sector			
g. ca. 17 years+		g. city and its structure			

FIGURE 2 Selected factors requiring detailed attention when considering children and urban physical environment.

components of the equation we have built in this section. Assessing such issues under the primary perspective of the explanatory pattern helps to keep in the forefront the nature of remediation necessary if evidence shows that the issue is one that requires a change in policy.

Thus, we shall examine some of the major concerns about children and environment according to whether the effects of environment seem to occur determinatively to children, whether the matter is better viewed regarding the amount of opportunity provided by the environment in the light of children's voluntaristic and culture-based motivations, or whether adults and their social organization cause and/or transmit environments and consequences of relevance.

The City as a Holistic Phenomenon – Pro and Con
Although we are not disaggregating the subject matter entirely, such a focus of attention – on *selected* issues in *particular* age groups and *scales* of environment – poses one overarching question. Are there aspects of urban life *per se* which have a uniform effect on all children who live in cities? In other words, is there some way in which the constituent parts of the city are aggregated into a form of whole which transcends its parts, which has meaningful effects on children there that differ from what faces them in other forms of settlements?

The question is posed well by Mercer:

Bring your children up in the middle of a rural environment. Now start all over again but this time bring them up in the middle of a city. How different would they be? Do different types of physical environment have different effects on the developing child's view of the world, which might form the basis for later adult modes of thought or action?[40]

And it is intensified and given values by Coates:

In the heavily populated urban centres automobile traffic and the decreasing availability of open space conspire to limit the child's free exploration of his neighborhood environment. Combined with overcrowding in the home and related social problems such as working mothers[!], fatherless households, and intolerance by neighbors of the presence of children and the noise they create, it is clear that the urban child's freedom is severely restricted. The child in the suburb who is dependent on adults and the automobile for access to playgrounds, stores, movies, and other meaningful settings, is not very much better off.[41]

One body of thought, expounded early this century and then rediscovered in recent years, rules that the answer is yes. Simmel, basing his observations on German cities during the earlier period, noted that those who live in cities are surrounded by more people than they can hope to know or place personally. Furthermore, they are surrounded by sounds and signals of considerable detail and complexity. People respond, according to Simmel, by the use of impersonal forms of legitimation and communication. Traffic lights replace personal judgments. A fixed-price system replaces bartering with the monetary nexus, the central consideration of trade and commerce. Uniforms and identification cards replace knowledge of personal character. The individual brought up and living in the city learns to place head before heart. Furthermore, Simmel points out the blasé personality as an outcome of this process.[42]

Wirth continued in the tradition of Simmel but proceeded to specify three global characteristics of cities hypothesized to affect the lives of residents. These were large size, high density, and population heterogeneity. The range of effect of these 'stimuli' was observed to be more diverse than Simmel suggested, including aspects of interpersonal relationships, social mobility, and overall social structure. Nonetheless, the overall effects suggested by Wirth parallel those of Simmel rather closely. Urban life was felt to contribute to impersonality, anonymity, and the like.[43]

During the period between the 1930s, when Wirth wrote, and the present time, there have been many attempts to characterize the purported effects of urban life *per se*. This literature was for many years inconclusive, as writers largely failed to agree about the effects, as well as whether or not certain effects noted were not more easily attributable to social characteristics like occupational status. Nonetheless, social scientists are increasingly viewing the city from the perspective of social psychology, resulting in a new round of literature on the subject.

Milgram, for example, has explicitly updated Simmel's suggestions in terms of the concept of sensory overload. People in cities are exposed to more people and more phenomena than they can handle. Milgram feels that two adaptive responses by urbanites are to pay no attention to matters considered of lesser importance and to give less time to any single matter. Furthermore, special forms of behaviour are adopted to screen or ward off unwanted contacts.[44] Other forms of response noted in this literature are stricter spatial segregation, alienation, and, more positively, tolerance.[45]

Such a view of the macroscopic determinative effects of living in cities is tantalizing. We must view it, though, with some suspicion. First, it is, with few exceptions, based on theories about and studies of adults. But even if one were to make the leap in applying these considerations to children, a leap which may well be justified in this case were the conclusions firmly supportable, there are other reasons which may intervene to drain the credibility of such a perspective.

First, a number of recent writers have noted that all urbanites do not share a common world of experience. As Chapter 6 surely suggests, the city is a mosaic of smaller areas differing from one another in terms of social factors such as status, ethnic or racial background, demographic and family structure, and, increasingly, lifestyle. Areas of the city differ with respect to physical structure, including such aspects as the nature and condition of the housing stock, the availability and condition of public facilities and services, aesthetics, and access to other parts of the city.

One school of thought, which placed itself in explicit contradistinction to the earlier deterministic schools of thought, said that the characteristic ways of life in particular parts of cities are attributable almost entirely to the kind of local group with which one lives.[46]

A more recent view, by Fischer, synthesizes the previous disputes in a logical and straightforward manner. As we noted in Chapter 1, Fischer suggests that one crucial attribute of cities is their size, which enables large enough groups of people to assemble to allow the simultaneous existence of diverse subgroups able to carry out specialized interests and activities. His 'subcultural theory' of urban life holds that the groups that are attracted to any city and where they live within it are partly functions of the economic and physical characteristics of the city. Thus, although the direct explanation of behaviour may be tied to membership in a particular subgroup, the ultimate explanation goes back farther to the basic characteristics of the city in allowing for specific groups.[47]

Fischer's line of theoretical development, however, warns us against the expectation of uniform traits among children simply on the basis of their residing in a large city. Different areas present highly different contexts in which to grow up.

This does not mean, though, that individual neighbourhoods are entirely self-contained. They vary greatly in their degree of territorial focus and insularity. People from different backgrounds and living in different areas spend very different amounts of time in and have varying amounts of emotional attachment to their local areas.[48] The most common way of viewing local neighbourhoods at this point is as areas of 'limited liability';[49] the local area is not usually the whole world to its residents, even though people with certain similarities who live in close proximity can enjoy religious, commercial, and other common lifestyle benefits. And their inward focus is enhanced under pressures from the existence of other nearby groups or from threats of change by city fathers.[50]

If our first point, then, is that people in cities grow up in at least partially different social worlds, in turn related to internal differences in physical environment, our second point follows rather automatically. People are surely not exposed to the exact same physical contexts, even though they share the same city.

Third, even if we accepted the global view of the city and its effects, it would be difficult to separate physical causes from social causes. To some extent, this entire book is devoted to the exploration of recent changes facing children in cities, and it would be difficult, if not impossible, to deal with all its considerations simultaneously, even if one were to suppose they had a singular holistic effect.

A series of studies of children in Poland illustrates the dilemma of having to select from among alternative causes of holistic urban-rural differences. Detailed measurement was made of developmental and health characteristics of children in a variety of settings. Although a number of differences were found, it is hard to relate them to the opposing forms of settlement. Differences in poverty, diet, and daily regimen were all more logical forms of explanation which more closely fit the data.[51]

In a work of major policy importance, which culminated in the formation of Canada's Ministry of State for Urban Affairs, Lithwick attempted to make a distinction of phenomena which are 'in the city' as opposed to those which are 'of the city.'[52] The former refer to objects of policy interest which could theoretically occur anywhere but happen to be of interest to urban policymakers because they are of a particular scale or importance in the city. Phenomena 'of the city' are those that are intrinsic to cities. Although this distinction is highly useful for conceptual clarity, it is our opinion that most, if not all, phenomena of interest fall on the first list.

Finally, even if that were not the case, our interest lies with issues about which one can take pragmatic steps. There is little one can do, in a direct way, even if justified, to alter any Gestalt which would characterize the city as a whole. Action is taken at the level of trees, not the forest.

Certainly, particular kinds of issues and places do not stand in isolation. Ecologists say that individual entities, and changes in them, can be fully understood only through assessment of their interconnectedness. Nonetheless, that we must understand the larger context of a given entity does not alter the fact that most changes are addressed and implemented one by one. We sometimes go so far as to create more inclusive, apparently more rational systems of phenomena, but in the overall urban context these are inevitably subsystems of larger systems yet – and dependent, at the least, on the validity of their individual parts.

Let us therefore turn our attention away from the city as a whole, away as well from the formal matrix of necessary considerations, and towards an examination of a variety of specific issues, organized according to the form of explanations involved.

II SELECTED ISSUES ON CHILDREN AND THEIR URBAN PHYSICAL ENVIRONMENT

Direct Effects

Pollution
Evidence justifies reference to two kinds of pollution and their effect on children: air pollution and noise pollution.

(a) *Air pollution.* In a major review on airborne pollutants, Kane[53] indicates that definitive knowledge of the effects of air pollution on children is not at hand. Many pollutants are not commonly monitored. When they are monitored, it is rarely done with systematic geographic coverage. Levels of pollution in outdoor areas vary greatly according to location, topography, weather, and season. Indoor levels are not subject to public monitoring. Furthermore, such standards as have been established reflect adult criteria and, with exceptions, consequences of existing levels of pollution for children are not definitively known, since so many of the effects are chronic rather than acute. It takes a dramatic and widespread outbreak, like Minimata disease among ordinary citizens in Japan, for officials to link effects to environmental causes (in that case, mercury pollution, water-borne).[54] Nonetheless, Kane gives a number of reasons why we should be particularly sensitive to even low levels of pollution, whose effects might anticipate chronic conditions.

1 Children breathe in much more air per unit of body weight than do adults because they breathe more frequently. Hence, they inhale a more significant amount of any pollutant than do adults.

2 Children are normally more physically active than adults. In Los Angeles, for example, authorities consider it necessary to broadcast warnings against outdoor play by children when pollution levels get too high.

3 Many pollutants, such as lead, are heavy and settle on or near the ground. Because children are smaller, they are in closer proximity to such pollutants.

4 In the course of play, children are more exposed to dirt, in which pollutants lodge.

5 Children are more likely to breathe through their mouths, thus filtering out harmful substances less effectively.

6 Physiological conditions make exposure to pollutants more likely to result in harmful consequences among the unborn and among younger children.

The effects of air pollution are multiple. The most obvious, noted for years in Britain, is respiratory malfunctioning. This can be fatal within the first year of life, but also, when not acute, can lead to chronic bronchitis and the aggravation of asthma (estimated to occur among five to fifteen per cent of children).[55] Air pollution from sulphur dioxide, nitrogen oxide, dust, arsenic, ammonia, fluorides, and the like are felt responsible, in addition, for difficulties in growth and development.

Mental health consequences are also considered common. Carbon monoxide damages the brain, and airborne lead is harmful to intellectual, neurological, and motor development. Both of these latter two substances are products of gasoline powered vehicles, and they can reach children, depending upon the circumstances, whether they are passengers in motor vehicles, or outdoor consumers of exhaust fumes.

Other common sources of polluted air are industries, heating and cooking units, and indoor 'personal' substances like tobacco smoke and aerosol chemicals.

In addition to harmful effects from ingesting pollutants, problems occur when air pollution screens out some of the beneficial products of sunlight. As Wagner points out, necessary vitamin D is produced by ultraviolet rays transmitted by sunlight to the skin. He links the smoke and dirt of European cities in the nineteenth century with the incidence of rickets at that time.[56]

A Tokyo study indicates how air pollution acts as an indirect factor as well in children's health. Children in a variety of settings, including more and less polluted areas, were studied with regard to their environment, hours of play, and health. Children in the worse settings engaged less in active outdoor play and, in turn, were less healthy. The researcher concludes that reduced outdoor activity is the direct cause of poorer health with the atmosphere as the reason why children stay outside fewer hours.[57]

Although we are clearly aware of the need to avoid obvious excesses of air-borne pollutants, a number of unanswered questions remain. How is such pollution as we now have distributed? Are there concentrations in particular types of setting which go largely undetected, but to which children are exposed? To take a classic parallel case, hydroelectric rights of way are generally kept apart from enterprises which might harm them, and hence overt accidents are relatively few. But in Ontario, for example, children's outdoor play facilities are allowed under Hydro lines, and children are thereby exposed more directly than any other persons to the electromagnetic fields generated by the power lines.[58]

Furthermore, documentation of standards relevant to children regarding any substance requires much more empirical (largely longitudinal) study of persons with less than acute (and sometimes not even obvious) symptoms, lest long-range build-ups of toxic substances escape detection until too late.

(b) *Noise.* Noises surround children from many angles and from many sources. As Stevenson notes, they reach children from surface vehicles, airplanes, amplification equipment, trash collections, air conditioners, sirens, tests, and other people nearby.[59]

The adult literature shows a clear connection between noise and stress related diseases.[60] Noises considered harmful are those which are loud, intermittent, and outside the control of the individual. People do not have to be consciously aware of these noises for a negative effect to occur, and it is common for people to feel they have acclimatized themselves to some noises; nonetheless, the interruption, even at a subconscious level, of ongoing thoughts, dreams, and similar processes gives rise to various forms of psychiatrically diagnosable syndromes, not to speak of disorders like ulcers and colitis. In the occupational context, sustained loud noises are associated with loss of hearing, and preventive gear is more commonly required at present.

Among children, a parallel to occupational and emotional disorders may be found. Prolonged exposure to the discotheque atmosphere, with loud music between 90 and 100 decibels, is a common source of hearing loss.[61] Stevenson also notes documentation of interruptions to children's speech, and school activities coming from common sources of noise. He reports mental illness among children near Heathrow Airport in London.

Cohen, Glass, and Singer studied a thirty-two storey apartment building in Manhattan, indicating that the amount of street noise was inversely related to the height of residence in the building. Among children who had lived in the building at least four years, the higher the floor in which they lived, the greater was their auditory discrimination. Inasmuch as auditory discrimination is related to reading ability, they found that the children living on the lower floors read less well than those living higher up.[62] We can observe that noise has also indirect affects on children, but will reserve our discussion on this to later.

We see at this point that we must be concerned with at least three sources of noise: (1) intermittent noises of a largely non-residential character, (2) self-imposed, continuously loud noises, and (3) disruptions from adjoining dwelling units and residential spaces. These have several typical effects. The continuous, loud noises affect hearing; the intermittent, disruptive noises affect personal make-up. Some forms of adaptation to the latter clearly occur; teachers for example, have noted that children from chaotic home situations generally 'tune out' all but what they really want to hear, which often involves tuning out the teacher. Such an adaptation is a negative consequence in settings other than where developed. Indeed, a relatively new problem surrounds children in those *open plan* classroom settings where the circumstances or organization generate unaccustomed noise; many children cannot function as well with intermittent auditory disturbances.

In the school situation, it is easy to see what can be done. Where we stand on other questions is rather mixed. There is general agreement on the need to tone down discotheque music, and the standards to be applied to both live and recorded music are known. It simply remains for action to be taken where large numbers of young people *willingly* subject themselves to a form of pollution bearing potentially negative consequences.

Similarly, governments are aware of the need for standards concerning transportation noise, construction noise, and the like. It is unlikely that any government in North America or Western Europe would now build the old-style New York elevated trains that virtually entered living-rooms, tracks for bullet trains going well over 100 miles an hour every six minutes through the heart of congested residential areas (as in Japan), or new housing seen in Taiwan immediately adjacent to the end of jet runways. We still have relics of such situations from other decades, but elaborate hearings normally accompany new developments and projects with implications for noise. What we do not know, however, are the exact boundaries of noise tolerance, because the syndromes exhibited at less than clearly intolerable levels are not explicit and exact. Increasing epidemiological research on the fringes of noise pollution areas are clearly justified.

Furthermore, although it may be difficult to say how extensive safeguards against great public nuisances must be, it is surprising that there is no concerted effort to soundproof individual dwellings more fully. Surely the materials and technology are known, and the act of soundproofing does not in itself stifle any competing public or private interest of a non-economic nature. But it adds to the costs of construction of multiple dwellings and hence of residence in them. At a time, however, when so many other priorities having to do with the basic aspects of daily life are being re-examined (for example, energy, insulation, transportation, and health care), why is soundproofing - a factor which affects families directly every day - not treated more adequately? Why do builders provide so many amenities on occasion, but neglect this one so often?

As far as children specifically are concerned, more research on the broader consequences of the several effects of noise pollution early in development and education are justified. We suspect that the consequences are not the same as those occurring to older persons exposed to the same noises.

Traffic Accidents

A colleague of ours is fond of remarking, 'If a child hits a car, it's vandalism; but if a car hits a child, it's an accident.'[63]

By definition, the word accident implies a chance occurrence which could have been prevented. Yet, occurrence is much more than chance, even though the probability that such an event will occur to any particular victim is much less than certain. To understand accidents, we must recognize there is always an inflicting body or property and a victim. There would be many fewer accidents if we could exercise better control over the separation of the two parties to accidents. We must not attach a priori blame either to perpetrator or victim, but rather must understand the nature of each and how they come in contact in the city.

Accident prevention, particularly having to do with automobiles, is an area where considerable progress concerning the health of children, can be made rapidly through environmental design and management, well above that from post-accident treatment. As the National Academy of Sciences in the United States noted, 'Prevention of accidents ... may depend more on the design and function of cities than on bio-medical research.'[64] Indeed, accidents are the leading cause of death in children over one year of age. What we refuse to tolerate from wars and natural disasters, we accept from accidents because we label them as such; much more of a preventive nature, however, can and should be done.

Accident statistics tell us some of the specific things about children's fatalities or injuries in automobile accidents and point towards remedies. As Table I indicates, recent statistics from the Province of Ontario for persons aged 19 and under show that the lion's share of both injuries and fatalities occurs to children who are passengers in automobiles, in contrast to our customary view of young children at play as the most frequent victims. Fifty-seven per cent of such children and youths who were killed were passengers, while 64 per cent of those injured were travelling in an automobile at the time of the accident.

TABLE I
Juvenile victims of motor vehicle accidents by role and age (1976)*

Role	Age							
	Fatalities				Injuries			
	0–4	5–14	15–19	Total	0–4	5–14	15–19	Total
Passenger in vehicle	18	31	121	170	1379	3467	6907	11753
Pedestrian	18	42	29	89	503	2554	884	3941
Cyclist	1	26	13	40	30	1803	842	2765
Total	37	99	163	229	1912	7914	8633	18459

* Adapted from Ontario Ministry of Transportation and Communications, *Motor Vehicle Accident Facts*, 1976, p. 34.

Such a heavy emphasis on presence in a vehicle among victims partly reflects the 15 to 19 year old age group. Among the fatalities, for example, 71 per cent of those in the role of passenger occurred among those in the late teens. None-theless, even in the other groups, passengers account for a significant share of the fatalities and injuries. Young children (those under five) also find most of their problems coming from travel inside automobiles. Only 26 per cent of their injuries, for example, happen when they are on foot; 72 per cent happen as passengers of a motor vehicle. Only the five to fourteen year age group follows to some extent the popular image of problems with pedestrian and bicycle safety, but even with this group, a third of the fatalities and 44 per cent of the injuries come from riding as a passenger.

In every city I know, elaborate precautions are taken for pedestrian safety when children go to and from schools. Traffic safety is a traditional urban worry of parents with small children; training for traffic safety is considered an essential part of child-raising. Streets and highway departments have an arsenal of devices and techniques which, *if employed*, can reduce 'accidents.'

Although any preventable accident deserves the taking of appropriate steps, suggesting that we should certainly support the fullest implementation of safety devices and training for pedestrians and cyclists, we note the necessity of greater efforts to protect passengers. To some extent, this involves the minimization of accidents *per se*, as intended by recent experiments in lowering speed limits, cracking down on drunk drivers, and the like. For children, though, we suggest that a parallel avenue of effort focus on the provision of sufficient numbers of effective restraining devices (appropriate for different ages) and on the enforcement of their use. People customarily wink at the number of children placed in motor vehicles, in light of the provision of restraining devices for *adult* sized passengers.

Statistics on passenger seat belt usage, for example, are enlightening. In 1976, in Ontario, for example, for all traffic accidents involving passengers and automobiles in which seatbelts were installed, fatalities were more than ten times greater when seatbelts were not used than when they were. Regarding just injuries, 57 per cent more occurred among those not using the seatbelts supplied.[65] Underlying both the difficulty documented and the challenge to overcoming it is the kind of attitude both of victims and (in this case only) parents suggested by the discussion of teenage pregnancy in Chapter 5. Few if any will reject the *possibility* of difficulty from not taking precautions, but most have to overcome the attitude, 'it won't happen to me.'

Studies by the Insurance Institute for Highway Safety report that 'nearly half of all infants traveling in autos are held on the lap of an adult, while about 26 percent of children from 1 to 2 are held on laps.'[66] Yet, these studies show that the lap is the most dangerous place for auto travel, because children are crushed between their protectors and fixed objects in the car (e.g., front seat, dashboard).

This contrasts with the situation concerning pedestrian safety, where much is known and implemented already. The question here may rather be one of whether authorities are compulsive about implementing what they already know *everywhere* in the city.

There is rather common agreement that the most effective way to minimize traffic accidents when children are pedestrians is to separate traffic and children. Developmental studies, for example, indicate that up to about the age of eleven, children are not physiologically capable of taking enough precautions to avoid accidents.[67] If children, particularly when allowed out to go to school and to engage in the expanded range of play of school age children, cannot entirely avoid cars, then the cars must be channelled to avoid children in a way that goes beyond the immediate skills and reflexes of the individual driver.

Toronto has been particularly active in recent years in experimenting with a variety of designs intended to keep through traffic off residential streets. These include speed bumps, street closings, and traffic mazes. These are all reactions to known statistics which indicate that accident rates are highest in straightforward, unrestricted gridded street patterns.

When neighbourhoods are constructed from scratch, designs are also available and frequently utilized which involve differentiating thoroughfares by size and straightness so that the rational motorist would never choose to enter a residential neighbourhood unless that were his or her destination. Such was the major feature of the neighbourhood unit plan introduced in North America in the

1930s and which has become a basic feature of most new town planning and planned unit developments in recent years.[68] What must be emphasized, however, is that traffic avoidance plans may be implemented on *both* existing and newly designed neighbourhoods.

Sandels also notes specific site characteristics which cause difficulty to children. Hedges and fences conceal children from oncoming traffic. Parking areas near housing are meeting points for children, not least because the comings and goings of people and automobiles are of interest to children even when quiet, alternative spaces are provided elsewhere; one need only consider what settings attract which people to realize the necessity for the most sensitive planning of parking areas. Children are also injured frequently in those locations where they are picked up outside schools, daycare centres, and other children's institutions. Supervision must complement design in this latter case.[69]

As with previous factors, traffic affects children indirectly. Appleyard and Lintell, for example, suggest that heavy traffic reduces the use of streets for play and interaction with other children.[70]

No separate mention has been made to this point about bicycle safety in traffic. Table I does not show this to be a particularly high risk situation, regarding *total numbers* of injuries and deaths. Nonetheless, bicycle accidents have increased in recent years along with bicycle usage. The statistics do not show the number of accidents per unit of exposure. If one were to envisage an entire city at about 4:30 on a warm weekday afternoon in the spring, many more children would be playing on foot in one or another location than would be seated on bicycles. That bicycle injuries are so high under the circumstances suggests room for amelioration.

Bicycles are regarded with ambiguity by the public. They are toys, and they are also transportation. Legally, bicycles are classified as vehicles subject to traffic laws, and cyclists are expected to use the streets. Nonetheless, they leave riders in a fragile position regarding faster traffic, and riders often have no other qualifications or experience with vehicles in traffic. A logical alternative is another degree of separation – of bicycles from both cars and pedestrians. This is commonly found in Scandinavia, where separately marked lanes are often provided for bicycles between the traffic lanes and the sidewalks. Completely separate bicycle paths through the middle of superblocks, parks, and other open spaces surely serve the same purpose well, but it is difficult to add these to built-up central cities to fulfil the bicycle's role in everyday transportation. Most totally separated bicycle paths extend where people go only for recreational purposes. Even less serving, however, of any positive purpose are the kinds of designated bicycle routes found in central Toronto; a sign on a post specifying a normal city street as a bicycle route does nothing to secure the safety of the rider on that street.

Where bicycles must share common rights of way with other vehicles, the training of the cyclist and the safety features of the bicycle are important. Children must learn that they are not privileged users of roads and that mistakes can be fatal. Such training is essential inasmuch as juvenile use of bicycles can be a legitimated form of play rather than transportation from place to place; such usage does not take children as far as bicycle paths or special lanes on the streets. Safety organizations stressing suitable habits are expanding their reach to children in schools. What is lacking, though, is enforcement. If a driver breaks established rules, there is a reasonable probability of a penalty; this is seldom the case with respect to cyclists, who commonly break even the most widely observed rules of traffic (for example, running red lights).

Furthermore, the vulnerability of cyclists suggests the necessity that they be at least seen in traffic. Most municipalities maintain legal standards for reflective equipment and night-time lighting. Once again, however, observance is minimal. Furthermore, more safety equipment is available on the market than the law requires and people acquire. As of the date of writing, there is no universal set of standards regarding the required effectiveness of front lighting and reflective devices, let alone additional equipment (used in Europe) to encourage traffic to keep safely distant to the left. Considering the relatively low cost of safety equipment, and in view of the obvious dangers, stricter requirements and enforcement procedures are not unjustified.

Housing Conditions
We can speak of effects of housing in different ways. In this section, our discussion will focus upon such effects as might be relevant to the child in a *direct* way from the physical conditions and circumstances of his or her housing. Consideration of housing *type* will be reserved to our later discussion of opportunities found in different environmental settings.

A report by Canada's Central Mortgage and Housing Corporation on housing conditions in twenty-three Canadian metropolitan areas, released in 1977, established three types of problematic conditions in housing: physical quality, crowding, and cost. The last factor, cost, is most frequently the problematic factor. Nonetheless, CMHC estimated that 7 per cent of all dwellings in Canada are deficient with respect to two of the three types of conditions.[71]

It is hardly a foregone conclusion, however, that deficient housing is primarily urban. Indeed, crowding has traditionally been higher within Canadian rural dwellings, and standards of sanitation and safety are higher and more strictly enforced in urban areas. Nonetheless, we must assess whether or not there is a basis for concern for children with respect to urban residences of low quality and high crowding. Inasmuch as the effect of housing costs on children is indirect (however vital a factor it might be in the family and/or housing policy), we shall not consider it in this section.

The rationale for building publicly supported housing and for distributing individual units has up to now been highly solicitous of families with young children. Adults with unsatisfactory housing, particularly single persons, have seldom been considered as deserving of support, because we view children as still open to salvation. We assume that putting a decent roof over the head of a child may enhance the life chances and productivity of the child, an assumption we rarely make about grown people. Such traditional assumptions, however, must be strongly qualified by available evidence.

Data do support the provision of assistance to families in low quality housing. Nonetheless, as Schorr notes,[72] the effects of moving from poor quality to standard quality housing appear limited to those whose initial housing was 'desperately inadequate.' Features such as poor roofing, inadequate heating, and vermin infestation account for consequences which will change when replaced with sounder conditions. Cold and damp conditions, for example, bring about respiratory illnesses and tuberculosis. What has been shown is that improvements from such low starting points can improve children's health, and, in the process improve such other situations in their lives as are a function of health, like school attendance and participation.[73] Many of the other characteristics noted among 'slum' populations, and cited as rationale for slum eradication, reflect poverty, discrimination, and a deficiency of intended neighbourhood opportunities for children. Unless these factors are also changed when families are rehoused, changes in the family lifestyle beyond basic health-related aspects are unlikely to change. Rehousing, thus, must not be ignored when conditions are terrible, but is hardly a miracle cure for problems whose roots do not lie in housing per se. It is perhaps for this reason that municipalities once accepting of needy families are now more resistant, in view of the more clearly recognized need for accompanying social infrastructure, with high costs to municipalities either for providing them or for the consequences of not providing them.

Nonetheless, even in housing which is not desperately inadequate, there are common sources of domestic accidents and other difficulties. Most of these are well known.

Modern standards cover most contingencies concerning fire and electrocution; the major weak link in this regard is usually the enforcement of accepted municipal standards in poorer neighbourhoods, often reflecting the inability of families or the unwillingness of landlords to bring dwellings up to standard. One-time grant programmes to owner-occupants is generally considered the most effective way to keep residential buildings up to standard.

Redesigned drug bottles and an awareness of the need for precautions by parents are established ways of avoiding accidental poisoning from prescription drug supplies. A greater problem is poisoning from lead paint. Although most housing standards now prohibit the use of interior lead paint, the remains of earlier coats of paint are still present in many homes. Children between the ages of one and five typically injest chips of paint which they dislodge in the course of other actions. Although acute lead poisoning is visible (128 juvenile deaths between 1964 and 1974 in the United States), chronic poisoning leading to brain damage is asymptomatic, and it is thought that one in fifteen children in ghetto areas suffers from lead poisoning.[74] This would, however, not be such a problem if housing standards were enforced.

Falls, whether from obstacles inside housing units or from windows and balconies, can be controlled by known design products.[75]

In contrast to the above relatively finite problems, there is considerable ambiguity concerning the assumed and feared consequences of overcrowding. As cited earlier, much of the theoretical work on cities started with the premise that crowding had detrimental effects, particularly on children. Such a strongly held belief appears widely shared by social scientists, who continue to seek the ultimate proof of this assumption, despite a legacy of results which individually provide only scattered pieces of proof or disproof, but which collectively add up to a picture of no support for the negative findings.

Such an overall picture is clouded by a number of specific problems in the conduct of such studies:

1 There is considerable disagreement about what is meant by crowding, and different researchers support different conceptions.

2 Specification of how any particular kind of crowding (or density) is supposed to effect people is insufficiently developed and often missing entirely from analyses.

3 There is little understanding as to whether or not there are absolute standards of crowding. In any case, despite popular images, cities are becoming progressively less crowded rather than more so, and it is unclear whether studies which label areas as crowded and uncrowded refer to variations of crowding of any significance.

4 Investigators usually seek negative effects of crowding in their studies, and they typically ignore the possibility of finding positive effects. Furthermore, they look only in one direction along the crowding continuum, ignoring the consequences of very low densities or isolation.

5 Researchers of crowding have been restricted by the use of data based on aggregate levels. They are limited by the kind of information available for such areas and by an inability to see whether relationships based on areas actually

apply to individuals. But even the occasional studies dealing with individuals in a real setting have been restricted by the other four drawbacks.

Now let us look at the arguments one by one. The problem of definitions makes the entire issue more diffuse. Generally people think of crowding with respect to the residential setting, though some focus on phenomena like work places, subway stations, and the like; the former is generally considered the most relevant because it is more closely tied to essential activities and family life. Housing density or crowding may still be viewed in a number of ways, however. 'Crowding,' for example, is usually attached to a measure of persons per room within dwelling units. Sometimes, however, the measure is adjusted to refer to ratios of persons per bedroom, because it is standard practice to allocate housing on the basis of how many persons of which sex and age correspond to a given number of bedrooms.[76] 'Density' is generally applied to the measure of the number of people who live on a given square measure of land. This can be a gross measure corresponding to all of the surface measurements or a net ratio relating to just that amount of land devoted to residential purposes. Still another kind of measure is housing unit density, which focuses on the number of dwelling units situated upon a given unit of land. In this regard, people speak of housing density. Zoning regulations refer to so-called site density or coverage, which refers to the ratio of the floor area of a residential building to the area of its lot. Finally, regardless of the type of measure chosen, there is disagreement as to whether the major concern should be with the objective facts of crowding or density or with people's subjective impressions of being crowded.

Over time, each of the perspectives has been shown *more and less* fruitful than the others by analyses. Proponents of the crowding definition claim that the density outlook is too remote from the experience of the individual,[77] while others claim that the individual family can do more to control conditions within their own dwelling unit than they can about people in the neighbourhood with whom they have less intimate ties, hence making density the more potentially distressing concept.[78]

The explanatory paradigms employed to relate crowding to one or another kind of effect are generally not sophisticated. The single most popular of these is derived from animal experiments in which crowding was shown to relate to disastrous changes in social behaviour and health, through intermediate changes in glandular function.[79] The results, anti-social behaviour and pathology, have been applied uncritically to the situation of disadvantaged human populations, with little subsequent empirical support for theoretical elaborations. Derived from the first theory is one of 'interpersonal press,' whereby people in close proximity literally 'get on each other's nerves.'[80] A major alternative theory purports that persons living in high densities will be at odds with one another if paucity of facilities or services per capita leads to competition or congestion in the procurement of scarce resources.[81] Some of the more common findings of controlled experiments are that women respond more favourably to crowded situations than do men, findings that are aided little by these or other existent theories.[82]

Densities in North America, even at their height, are small compared with densities found, for example, in Southeast Asia. Yet, studies in Hong Kong have shown fewer of the effects purported to come from high density than are shown in many North American cities.[83] Where cultures have evolved so as to adapt to changed residential conditions, people have coped with the purported consequences of density and crowding.[84] This leads us in any case to wonder what, if anything, is being measured when North American researchers draw conclusions from study areas which may differ in density, but only marginally so on the total scale of possible residential density.[85]

As we suggested before, most researchers appear to undertake research on crowding because they themselves believe that negative effects are there to be found if only optimal research procedures are followed. Hence, they select measures which attempt to indicate most sensitively these negative effects. Hence, it comes as a surprise when an occasional positive effect of density is found. As one writer remarks of his study on grades four and five children:

The main weakness of this model, apart from the great shortage of empirical support, is that it leaves unexplained the lower neuroticism scores of the crowded girls; detailed examination of the most crowded girls found that their scores were even lower ... It is possible that within the crowded home there is a higher degree of cooperation required, and experience, between mother and daughter in the running of the house ...[86]

Only the occasional writers like Jacobs[87] and Freedman[88] have looked at such positive outcomes as security and co-operation as consequences of high-density situations.

Finally, even the most analytically sophisticated investigators have been bound by the sources of their data. Since surveys of individuals are difficult to carry out, because of the expense of surveying, researchers have turned to information already available. This latter kind of information is generally aggregated according to geographical units like census tracts or public health planning areas. Although increasing varieties of multivariate analysis can be applied to this information, it is seldom the exact same information one would ask for given a choice; and there is no analytic technique which will allow the researcher to see if what seems generally true for large numbers of people who share an area actually applies to the individuals there. For example, even if high levels of internal crowding seem related to juvenile delinquency, when one looks at a number of areas around town and the variations of these figures among them, this does not tell us whether it is really the families in crowded circumstances who produce the delinquent children. Furthermore, even when researchers are able to poll individuals or individual families, findings are bound by the absolute density levels found there and by theoretical preconceptions. It is also extremely difficult to gather as many individual cases as one should in order to document sufficiently variations in pathological phenomena which by and large do not occur frequently in a human population.[89]

Some relatively interesting results have come from experimental studies in laboratories of the subjective side of crowding. But inasmuch as several studies show rather unambiguously that people are resistant to situations of temporary crowding, generalizing from controlled experiments in the laboratory to regularly experienced long-term residential situations is fraught with difficulty.[90]

We therefore have little belief in answers as yet provided with respect to the effects of crowding or density on children. Furthermore, the very difficulties which we feel have sapped results to date are not likely to be easily overcome. We do not recommend only more studies of a marginally improved character. For light to be shed on the subject, a number of existing obstacles must be dealt with simultaneously.

Moreover, the effects of *low* densities should also be included in any future calculus. Alexander, for example, makes the proximity of a certain *minimum* number of other children a *sine qua non* of his design for optimal new family housing.[91] Numbers of persons in proximity also create opportunities, not just problems, as Fischer's critical mass concept suggested for the whole metropolis.

One adaptation of the density literature *has* proven fruitful, however. And its derivation has come from studies of children. It comes from the theories of Roger Barker,[92] and it deals with the concepts of 'overmanning' and 'undermanning.'[93] Barker propounded a perspective on the physical environment which, greatly simplified, says that to understand the incidence of the typical behaviours we see in our communities, we have to understand the mutual confluence of people, places, rules, and customs. Not all behaviours are expected to or can physically fit in all places; but, over time, we have grown accustomed to certain kinds of activity occurring in particular kinds of places, following regular formats and rules. Barker illustrates this with reference to places like soda fountains, school gymnasiums, and picnics.

Applying this orientation to schools, Barker and his colleagues observed that a certain range of activities of a curricular and extracurricular nature have become normal expectations within schools. Furthermore, they are expected to occur whether the school has many or few students. What they subsequently observed, however, is that the result is very different for the students involved, according to whether there are many of them or few of them available to fill the roles involved with the fixed number of activities. If there are few students in a school, the individual student ends up highly active in attempting to spread himself or herself over all the demands placed by the school context; this is the context of undermanning. On the other hand, if more students are available than conceivably needed for the number of roles traditionally available, overmanning is in effect. The latter situation is considered the source of much potential alienation, and observers of modern urban society are anxiously questioning the extent that this way of thinking might be applied to urban institutions.

In the case of overmanning, we are not thinking in strictly physical terms, but in terms of the number of persons per valued role in society. Where in fact many persons are present but few are needed, a situation not inapplicable to youth unemployment, we should be concerned about the outcome for the unneeded individuals and what this means for the health of the entire society.

Much more work on the concepts of undermanning and overmanning is recommended, in contrast to work with a more traditional focus on crowding and density.

Although overmanning is typically found in urban settings and undermanning in rural settings, this is not inevitable. Recent trends in rural consolidation of schools sets the potential for parallels to the urban situation. The fact of urban overmanning may be the path of least resistance, but it is surely not the only alternative to how schools can be organized and financed. Indeed, although the effect reaching children in this case reflects the density of children per 'standard school role,' the path of explanation goes back to the organizational world of adults and 'school politics.' In this regard, we could easily have considered this topic also under the heading 'Causation and Mediation by Adult Social Organization' in this half of the chapter.

Now let us turn to the consideration of some issues concerning children and their urban physical environment, where the explanatory dynamics appear to fall along the lines of environmental fit and opportunity.

Effects through Opportunities

Most conscious design efforts fall within this explanatory perspective. Although some design professionals sincerely believe that their actions are determinative, most activities of most architects and planners go into the creation of buildings and spatial arrangements intended to give people the *chance* to carry out what are seen to be common desires. If these fields had a long tradition of empiricism, testing whether or not the designs produced actually solve the problems posed, we could be confident in the sensitivity of design products in their applications to children. As we suggested at the outset, however, systematic empirical follow-up is a relatively recent phenomenon – and one which is not as yet fully integrated into most design efforts. Hence, the normal range of considerations required in providing housing for families is one about which uncertainty prevails. Such uncertainty is compounded even further by the kinds of recent changes in urban structure which the *Child in the City* seeks to address, as cited in Chapter 1 of this volume.

The material we provide in this chapter must of necessity be selective, concerning itself with some of the major issues highlighted by recent changes. Even though some of the perennial questions facing those who design family housing are only in the process of being faced, we must leave comprehensive design suggestions about housing per se to others.[94]

Even with this selective emphasis on our part, certain trends which affect 'regular' housing design should be noted.

First, urban design has typically focused on assumptions about the average person or family. Yet, one of the major characteristics of recent societal and urban development has been the increasing presence of diversity within the population, with urban scale permitting a sufficient population base for the parallel existence of many ways of life.[95] Besides differences in demands such as might reflect ethnic diversity, the evidence of this volume also supports a focus on family structure diversity. All families are not traditional ones with husband, wife, and children all present. Nor do all families have either two or three children. The modal range of two and three bedroom apartments with self-sufficient facilities and/or three or four bedroom houses (whether attached or detached) takes little regard for the spatial needs of single-parent families, communal living groups, or large families. Thus, even though design based on actual usage of space is in its relative infancy, its range of application must apply to a wide enough range of needs.

Second, a special kind of consideration reflects the needs of exceptional children – those with one or another form of physical or mental handicap. Recent work and experience indicates that many such persons live more harmoniously, and at tremendously less cost to society, in their own families' residential settings, provided that special devices and spatial allowances are designed into their homes. There is surely no need for young people to grow up learning the role of a dependent patient if prior design (and relatively lower capital investment) can make them non-patients.[96]

Third, although it is both useful and helpful to establish certain design standards to facilitate known everyday needs and activities, we must realize also that all potential design objectives are not equally important, while some, in fact, are mutually exclusive. We typically fail to differentiate among possible goals in a way that reflects how people regard these alternatives. Thus, while people may normally appreciate certain standards of commerce and recreation associated with living in high densities (and, indeed, may choose to benefit from it for a period of time), they may prefer certain benefits even more which are attainable only in lower density settings (e.g., private open space, quiet).[97] Above all, we must recognize that criteria for housing design are no more static in the lives of individuals and families than across different groups of users at any one time. Therefore, beyond basic functional requirements in housing, we have to consider the absolute level of support for various design goals and their distribution within populations.

Finally, when analysing the suitability of any given design with respect to children, we must consider not just what is there, but the extent to which children have actual access to it. Consideration of the total amount of space within a dwelling unit, for example, is not sufficient if parents typically restrict the use their children make of certain areas. Measurements of amounts of open space surrounding residential buildings are irrelevant if the greatest percentage of this space is fenced off against children.

The issues on which we shall expand below are few, but, we trust, central. As noted in Chapter 1, the issues at the fore at any time are highly transitory. They largely reflect changes from past experience and products which are new to great numbers of people. Thus, without claiming an eternal logic for our choice, we turn to selected aspects of housing, security, and land-use (including transportation, and, at a greater level of specificity, the design of playgrounds).

Housing
We generally do not study that with which we are familiar and which we think is functioning well. Hence, the objects of investigation over the years have switched among various aspects of housing, as introduced and experienced. A preoccupation in the first four decades of this century with so-called slums and (usually public) replacement housing gave way in the 1950s to a fixation on the suburbs, which, although surely not a novel concept, became mass phenomena after the end of World War II. Much concern was expressed about changing styles of life exhibited, growing political conservatism, isolation and frustration among housewives, and unsuitable behaviour on the part of youth. It is interesting to note in retrospect that few if any of the concerns arising from the suburban development were attributable to the type of *housing* so characteristic in the two decades from the end of the war: single family, detached housing. Although political conservatism was thought related to newly acquired ownership status (a belief *not* supported by subsequent research),[98] ownership is not tied to any one kind of dwelling. And even though detached houses are generally built in lower den-

sity patterns than are other forms of housing, housing type is surely not the crucial problematic aspect of the *land-use patterns* typical of the new suburbs which became the butt of the suburban criticisms. Turning to housing itself, it is the high-rise apartment, increasingly the home for many families with children since the mid-1960s, which has invited a good deal of recent public concern.[99]

This section, therefore, will focus heavily on the opportunities of children living in high-rise apartments. Although we are more accustomed now to the suburbs of the 1950s and 60s, we shall nonetheless return later to the question of residential land-use in new communities, as this issue is hardly dead. The problematics of suburban land-use are increasingly exacerbated when high-rise buildings for families are built in suburban areas, intertwining and multiplying difficulties coming from two types of source. Indeed, the respective implications of housing type and land-use require clarification, because public action based on inaccurate perception of the cause of problems is unlikely to prove effective.

There is a litany of worries about the effects on children of their living in high-rise apartments. Let us look at some of the features and why they are considered problematic:

(1) In most conventional apartment buildings, kitchens and all but the master bedroom have traditionally been small, and they are getting smaller. Yet, studies indicate that children are nearly always allocated the smallest bedrooms, spend a significant amount of time there, and are mostly in the kitchen when not in their own rooms.[100] This is, in itself, confining, but the generally low square-footage and shortage of storage space within most family apartments is thought to restrict children to pastimes at home requiring little space. Thus, activity in craft work and collecting, for example, are thought to give way to such hobbies as television watching.[101]

(2) The problem of minimal space, when coupled with sound transmission, is felt to inhibit pastimes which involve physical activity and production of noise.[102] In this regard, gymnastics and the playing of musical instruments become anti-social activities.

(3) The height of high-rise buildings is felt significant in several ways. First, access to and from the individual unit is mostly by elevator. Young children typically can not use elevators, and adults feel that older children misuse them. Elevators are essential for mothers with very young children in carriages or strollers above the ground floor, and they are increasingly important for people and their possessions with increased height of residence. Several studies indirectly note the value of elevators compared to the walk-up apartment situation; there is an increasing reluctance to go out with the greater the number of floors one has to 'climb,' and low-rise stairways serve as a funnel for noise.[103] Nonetheless, elevators and children are not felt to mix well, whether because of the mechani-

cal aspects or of the possibility that children will either disturb or be disturbed by others while en route up or down. This is one reason why many people advocate the restriction of families to dwelling units with direct ground access. While family occupancy could still occur in a high-rise building, most units are off limits, by definition, when this guideline is followed.[104]

(4) Most apartment buildings contain few if any spaces suitable for play as part of interior, non-private space. The economics of most buildings depend upon renting the greatest amount of space, and hence reserving for children's play otherwise rentable areas near the 'home' dwelling unit is extremely unusual. Apartment buildings which have a single row of units on a floor, accessed by wide exterior entrance walkways, provide some such space for very young children, but the value of such space depends partially on a number of factors like climate and an absence of families without children who would be disturbed by the noise.

The net result is a general separation between dwelling units and play spaces. This kind of separation is felt to hinder opportunities for play for younger children, as parents are neither free to go out and supervise at all times, nor able to do so from their own apartments. A corollary to this occurs for older children. Without a place to meet with friends inside the dwelling unit, they are left to venture farther from the home to be with friends, to situations less supervised than would otherwise be the case.[105]

Another aspect common to high-rise buildings which affects young children and their play is the separation of play facilities not just from the home base, but specifically from the toilet facilities found there. Ground floor, open bathrooms for children create difficulties in the absence of close supervision by grownups; yet, in their absence, children often fail to last the amount of time it takes to get home, in the process fouling themselves and/or elevators and lobbies.[106]

Small children also tend to play close to entrances to buildings.[107] This is generally a cause of some concern to adults who dislike the congestion, noise, and bother, and who typically feel that children's congregating behaviour is negative. Nonetheless, such a restricted home range appears typical of children in the early stages of development and should be recognized through the provision of appropriate play facilities close to entrances, rather than being made by design of space to appear out of place.[108] We might consider separate children's entrances to buildings, located so that parents can get to their children directly, without the children clustering around areas where they bother others.

(5) The scale of high-rise buildings presents the opportunity for children to have contact with very many more children than normally populate the face-to-face city block which serves as the initial basis for children's contact and play.

Parents worry in this respect about a lack of control over whom their children might fall in with, given the larger range of background and behaviour patterns possible, as well whether such larger numbers make more possible the existence of disruptive subgroups of children. The net result is also to inhibit opportunities for play.[109]

One consequence which people hypothesize from a combination of these aspects of the high-rise building is a lower level of fitness among apartment children. People feel that fewer opportunities for active behaviour have the effect of producing children whose formative years do not include sufficient opportunity to get and stay in top physical shape. Some limited support for this point of view was provided in a study from one of the boroughs in Toronto, where virtually the only difference among school children from high-rise as opposed to single family homes was the level of gross motor development; those from apartments were less well developed.[110] Clinical reports suggest that, not surprisingly, children brought up in apartments are less skilled at stair climbing.

The above considerations all relate to opportunities provided or denied by specific aspects of high-rise buildings. They are not trivial, but they are not global or impossible to deal with, either. Much concern about high-rise living for families, though, is a consequence of widely spread assertions of even greater consequences of high-rise living for children.

Farley investigated a variety of these popular claims. Do children in high-rises have less interaction with friends and neighbours than children living elsewhere? Do older children spend less time at home and hence have less contact with other members of their families? Do they end up with nothing positive to do? And is their attachment to community organizations like churches and organizations less close than that of other children?[111]

In his review of data comparing children in high-rise apartments with those in single family houses in the same suburban locations, Farley found that none of these assertions could be supported. Suburban high-rise children indeed had more friends, and participated actively in the range of pastimes as were convenient to their homes, some of which were the kind approved by adults (e.g. sports). The classic passive recreation, television watching, was no more pronounced among those living in suburban apartments than among those in suburban houses, although downtown-suburban differences are found to differentiate those living in houses in this regard.[112] In fact, the higher density of apartment families makes possible the provision of common sports facilities unavailable in the residential setting to children living in houses at lower densities. Another analysis of the same body of data, by Hagarty, came to a finding of 'no difference' with respect to children's contact and activities with parents at home.[113]

The specific, rather than general, nature of any effects that might come from high-rise living is illustrated in a Swedish report:

In some studies people have claimed to have found differences in children's behaviour, but they have been uncertain when dealing with causes. For example, there was an early study which showed that children from high-rise areas showed more aggressiveness and recklessness in their outside play than children from low-rise areas. When the study was extended to cover children's general behaviour ... no clear differences between children from high and low-rise areas were found.[114]

The report went on to question whether such differences as researchers do find reflect the physical nature of high-rise living or rather various differential background characteristics of the children and families under observation, though allowing for the possibility that some aspects of high-rise situations can 'stimulate or constrain'[115] social activities.

Whether such constraints as are present in a given high-rise building are crucial varies according to the absolute value placed on these phenomena by residents (no doubt reflecting as well the degree of difficulty presented in any given situation). The study of families in greater Toronto drawn upon by Farley and Hagarty indicates that both the adults and children living in high-rise who were interviewed were likely to take advantage of the opportunities and not dwell heavily on the constraints because they saw themselves as in a state of transition leading to a different and preferred kind of residential environment, the detached house. Only when they viewed themselves as unable to progress through their desired 'family mobility cycle' did they find the constraints of high-rise living untenable.[116]

Hence, we underline the various physical constraints facing children in high-rise for which experimental remediation may well be in order. There does not, however, appear to be a solid empirical basis for such blanket condemnation of high-rise buildings for children as has come from some quarters.

Security

A second consideration is derived from studies of high-rise housing but extends as well to other forms of housing. It is security. Apart from the proverbial worry about 'dark alleys,' most considerations of personal safety and vandalism in residential areas centred, until the late 1960s and 1970s, around police protection, tenant screening, parent control over children, and the like, rather than on spatial design. Then, several developments brought design considerations to the fore, indicating as they did that some spatial arrangements give more opportunity for criminal behaviour than others.

First, a high-rise public housing development in St Louis called Pruitt-Igoe became such a dangerous place in which to live that it was dynamited by public authorities within 10 years of a much heralded opening (which included design awards for its architects). When attempting to understand the level of criminal behaviour in many of the buildings, investigators turned partly towards their design. Elevators, for example, which stopped only on every fourth floor for efficiency, forced adults and children alike from the other floors to take stairways which were hidden from public view to reach their units; these stairways were the scene of frequent robberies and assaults. Dwelling units there were located off closed-in skywalks; children, however, could not play there nor would adults stay because they were not protected from others by public view. Although sheer opportunity for criminal behaviour was surely not the sole explanation for what happened, the Pruitt-Igoe situation put a spotlight on vulnerable areas more commonly found in multiple dwellings of all types.[117]

A seminal work, entitled *Defensible Space*, by Oscar Newman[118] brought together a number of major insights concerning the conditions under which opportunity for criminal behaviour could be enhanced or displaced by design considerations. These notions obviously do not occur in a vacuum, and other considerations such as management practices, the degree of social cohesion of residents, and criminal intent combine to determine what happens in any given place. Nonetheless, despite what many regard as a suspicious statistical basis of support for his reasoning, Newman's insights have won considerable respect.

Newman points out that criminal activity typically occurs where a perpetrator is least likely to be recognized and apprehended. This refers to places in and around buildings where a criminal or potential criminal is not likely to be seen by the victim or others *and* where he, even if seen, is not judged in advance to be an intruder. Displacing such activity involves creating buildings and complexes which (a) open as many spaces as possible to view by other people and (b) contain spaces which residents will collectively personalize, so that outsiders become easily recognized. The first goal is served, for example, by more extensive use of glass in lobbies, elevators, and stairways, as well as by electronic devices and careful siting of walkways by resident windows. Social contact among neighbours is fostered, according to Newman, by such designs as shorter hallways.

Newman's insights were greatly aided by the earlier observations of Jane Jacobs.[119] She noted that where she lived, in Greenwich Village, there was safety for children on the streets because they were constantly in view of neighbours peeking out of apartment windows and storekeepers lining the first floor along the streets of the area.

With respect to security, children of different ages are victims and aggressors in the same context. Research on defensible space concepts[120] is not highly developed. Nonetheless, it would be useful to learn whether the implementation of such ideas would not only lessen the amount of crime involving children, but also in so doing widen the opportunities for young children to play unmolested.

Land-Use and Opportunity

A review of a new book called *The Child in the City*[121] makes the following observation about places designated for children: 'If you examine any English city, you will find a ghetto cordoned off for certain of its citizens. They don't wear a yellow star or cook curries. They're marked out by their diminutive stature and low status and may be charmingly referred to as "the little blighters". They are children.'[122]

We noted in the first half of this chapter that places intended for children are usually not equally appropriate and available for all age groups (though intended places are hardly the only places visited). This would represent an appropriate maldistribution (i.e., that those who require the smallest range of specially designed spaces in fact get them, while older children with a larger home range and more specialized tastes fit with the diversity that the larger community has to offer) except that current land-use patterns do not typically make satisfactory provisions for any age group.

What are some of these environmental requirements and considerations for the distinct needs of children in different stages of development?

Stearns, a biologist, put his finger on a number of our concerns: 'For a balanced urban habitat, we must provide brood cover for small children, safe territory for useful exploration, flocking, trysting, and roosting habitats for young adults and, finally, stable and well defined territories for older cohorts.'[123] As Stearns appears to suggest, there is common agreement that preschool children require protected areas where they can play under supervision. The amount of space required is not generally considered great, but its location *vis-à-vis* the dwelling unit is critical. The neighbourhood unit plan,[124] which became such a popular part of post-war suburban development, strongly emphasized houses with private, fenceable yards, on quiet winding streets, removed as much as possible from the strange people and mechanical dangers of stores, factories, and other land-uses attracting people. While this plan had attractions for school age children as well, including the focus of the neighbourhood around a safely reached school building, its most tangible social attraction was for the very young child who could be left to play freely in the immediate vicinity of his or her own residence. Such a view was evidently attractive to the men who planned new areas and to the men who had to choose a setting in which to leave their wives and children in good conscience as they set off to work every day.

The low density, traditional suburban land-use pattern which segregates homes from other land-uses has been shown to have a number of drawbacks, however. Few will quibble about the self-contained house satisfying many basic adult goals (for autonomy, privacy, security of tenure, adaptability, etc.). However, the land-use pattern accompanying this dream is one which is envisaged as if it were perennially May and blossom time. Nonetheless, in most continental and northern climates, toddlers are in fact not left out for long periods of time, year round. While the house itself provides additional opportunities for children's activities, these typically include only a small range of potential behaviours and seldom include other children except by prearrangement.

Neighbouring toddlers can be put together in one or another yard or home. But this must usually be engineered, and the number of toddlers who are available on any block is unlikely to support any kind of major facility for them within the block; furthermore, the typical suburban land-use pattern divides all the land among the residents, seldom allocating common, safe, interior parcels for the joint use of younger children – a practice more familiar in Europe. Although much play by young children is self-centred, a general question concerning land-use is whether space and facilities exist for a gradual transition away from individual play and towards co-operative effort.

The segregation of land-uses means that parents with young children are seldom able to walk with them to stores and institutions during the normal week day. Although not a form of play, in the usual sense of the word, non-residential land-uses offer the chance for variety and learning to children, where they see different people carrying on different activities. Such trips are a vital relief from a child-centred home existence if the mother is not employed outside the home. Although shopping trips are possible by automobile or by public transit, ability to walk is a crucial consideration. Families must usually have two cars before the wife has one for her daily use,[125] but, even then, taking the child out shopping by car requires overcoming a certain amount of inertia. People generally hesitate to take children on shopping trips by public transit because of the physical difficulties of coming and going with strollers, packages, and the like.

If the mother is employed, another aspect of land-use segregation becomes accentuated. Where does she find institutions such as daycare centres? Their existence, even in great numbers, in the urban area at large, may satisfy the need for a *place* for her child. But a difficult logistical problem is found when they are located away from places of residence and work.[126] The time and trouble of taking a child, usually by public transportation, from home to daycare and then proceeding from there to work, with the process repeated in the evening, is difficult and expensive for mother and child alike, and it creates a very long day for the child. The logistics become particularly difficult when the mother works any but the most typical hours, unless the daycare centre is able to keep its doors open many hours of the day and night.[127]

But there is no necessity for both spouses to be employed for the non-integration of institutions and services into local communities to be problematic. Other institutions like medical centres, libraries, and welfare offices, not to speak of the kinds of outdoor space enjoyed by young children, must be realistically accessible to the potential users according to the actual conditions of their everyday lives. Otherwise, they will not be utilized.

Still another aspect of these areas supposedly planned for toddlers is that, by their design, they tend not to include the elderly, for whom these spatial and housing attributes have even less appeal. A consequence for children is that they lack opportunity to see older people during their daily routines and subsequently develop an aversion to the normal attributes of old age as somehow unnatural.[128]

Other considerations arise for children of grade school age. They usually go to school by themselves, and, when otherwise allowed out, are generally given somewhat more latitude to play within the block or neighbourhood. One consequence of this greater degree of freedom is their ability to select or reject places intended for children. The grade school age range is a time when children like to explore, to engage in physically active recreation, and to relate continuously with other children. This is also the age range when the various kinds of full-scale playgrounds come into the forefront. There is little argument that children need play. Bruner, for example, argues that play is much more than recreation; it is learning, experience, and growth – necessities before adulthood.[129] Primates are just not born intact and perfect like reptiles; primates have a childhood, with play, as a vital preparatory period.

There is controversy, however, about the most desirable forms of play space. The traditional playground with slides, swings, and other familiar fixed apparatus is being challenged by programmed playgrounds and by adventure playgrounds. The programmed playground is carefully designed by professionals to place known and novel pieces of equipment which draw upon different physical skills and which incorporate different textures and colours into such a system of spatial relationships on a site that children will be encouraged to proceed from piece to piece in a way which they will find interesting and entertaining, as well as supportive of desires for challenge and the achievement of physical skills. This approach is one which is pre-determined by experts (though it is hoped with some consultation and empirical basis) and which relies on a finite number of formal pieces of equipment. In many respects, it resembles the traditional playground; but it goes beyond it in terms of the emphasis on a wide range of skills and through the integration of all the pieces on the site.

Adventure playgrounds, in contrast, do not rely upon fixed pieces of equipment. The raw materials are made available for children 'to build their own play environments under adult supervision.'[130] The makings of adventure playgrounds are typically junk, building supplies, and the tools and conditions to grow flowers, vegetables, plants, etc. Because adventure playgrounds are currently advocated by so many students of play, yet do not fall within customary North American terms of reference for playgrounds, owing to the need for supervisory personnel as well as the more customary capital expenditures, special mention should be made of this alternative.

The originator of the adventure playgrounds, Christian Sørensen of Denmark, made its object a comprehensive one quite different from that of other kinds of playgrounds: 'The object must be to give the children of the city the substitute for the rich possibilities for play which children in the country possess.'[131]

A number of objectives have been expressed over the years. Moore, for example, stated two major purposes for a playground he helped design:

1. To provide for children an environment to stimulate creative and imaginative play, motor action and manual skills, cognitive developments and the acquisition of knowledge; sensory stimulation and powers of perception; and social skills (self awareness, personality and emotional development, social adeptness, and a sense of humour);
2. To provide an identifiable locus for community activities meetings, celebrations, and interactions.[132]

Cooper lists a number of purported merits of the adventure playground. First is the variety of potential activities, which is not circumscribed by fixed equipment. The variation of what children can put together from junk, build with tools and lumber, or grow is neither limited nor closed to experimentation and change. Second, it can accommodate larger numbers of children, working and playing side by side on a relatively small surface area. She cites examples of up to 300 children absorbed at one time on a one-third acre site. Third, she supports with preliminary evidence a hypothesis that the interests activated by the self-conceived jobs in adventure playgrounds relieve the boredom that serves as the chief motivation for vandalism, with the effects of reducing school and community vandalism. Fourth, she sees adventure playgrounds as a community focus not only for children but for adult supporters who can parley this into additional forms of community organization and betterment. Finally, Cooper sees the adventure playground as a feasible type of recreation in low income, high-density neighbourhoods, because the land requirements are so small and functions served so much needed in such neighbourhoods.[133]

There is common agreement, however, that the absolute necessity for success with adventure playgrounds is a skilled, paid leader. The materials and organization of adventure playgrounds are too complex, portable, and otherwise useful to allow such an operation to go unsupervised. The leader, however, is a catalyst rather than an autocrat. According to one of the leading advocates of adventure playgrounds, Lady Allen of Hurtwood: 'The key to a successful adventure playground lies largely in the quality and the experience of the leader. He or she must be a mature person who provides the background for the children's own initiative and is willing to act rather as an older friend and counsellor than as a leader.'[134]

Adults, especially in North America, customarily find that adventure playgrounds look messy, and they think that they are dangerous. Cooper, however, counters the latter belief with evidence to the contrary, that children working step by step on a valued product are more cautious than they are with untutored play.[135] Moore counters the former assertion not with a denial but with a justification for the obvious untidiness: 'The only way to provide for a high degree of individual expression and choice is to ensure that environment is ambiguous, open-ended, and changeable, so that children can manipulate it physically and mentally to suit their own ends.'[136] Nicholson describes this situation in a 'theory of loose parts.'[137]

At present, there are relatively few adventure playgrounds. Many proponents have themselves designed adventure playgrounds with virtues they admire. Nonetheless, systematic empirical foundation for many of the important claims made as to its effects (e.g. lowering vandalism) is not as yet on hand. For such evaluation to occur, adventure playgrounds must be neither extremely novel nor based on an area other than the normal neighbourhood whose community life is involved.

Some observers feel that adventure playgrounds should be a last resort. They think that the residential neighbourhood itself should be made safe and absorbing, not just a corner of it. We do feel, however, that the stated objectives warrant further experimentation, provided it is accompanied by serious research.

Nonetheless, playgrounds are only part of the environment utilized by children, often only a small part. Even the best playgrounds do not necessarily remove the attraction of alternative land-uses for the imaginative play entered into by grade school children. Gray and Brower, for example, borrowed a technique which Hart and Barker had pioneered in the small town atmosphere;[138] they had children in Baltimore give them tours of the actual places in their neighbourhoods which the children found meaningful and important in their daily lives. Stores and institutions were mentioned as frequently as were facilities designed for recreation. Many of the activities cited were passive and social in nature.

Boys pointed out a number of informal settings where they could spend time with some of the men of their neighbourhood.[139] These 'hidden spaces' were interesting to the children, even though they did not have the form or contents recognized by experts in play.

Thus, what proves of interest determines use. As Cooper put it, 'children will be attracted to the safe interior landscaped areas ... only if they are more interesting as play spaces than the surrounding roads and parking areas.'[140] In proceeding to specify what creates interest, she notes that children prefer areas that are of moderate size but with boundaries which are varied and full of surprises. Grass is less useful for most purposes of this age group than is a hard surface.[141]

There is general agreement that, within a given circumscribed space, there are several ingredients of interest, whether the space is intended for children or not. One is an appropriate surface. Children are closer to the ground than adults, and for both functional and aesthetic reasons, children are sensitive to the nature of surfaces. Lynch, for example, notes memories among adults of interesting brick pavements on which they played as children.[142]

Second, areas with differences of level and/or shape in the environment provide more opportunity for imaginative play.

Third, the boundaries must somehow separate the area from surrounding areas. This kind of barrier should not only serve to differentiate children's own space from an amorphous miscellany of continuous expanse, but to protect against elements like wind. In his new review of children's perceptions in six cities around the world, Lynch points to a common inability to delineate this way in both unplanned 'bulldozed' suburbs and in highly planned, monotonously repeated suburbs.[143] Some kind of tangible boundaries help make a space a space, but these are very different from formal fences.

Fourth, such spaces must physically allow for a range of movement. Otherwise they are boring and do not leave room for the imagination.

Fifth, it is desirable that contact be made with elements of the natural world: animal, vegetable, and mineral.

Sixth, it is space where control over activity has been consciously or by default given over to the children. The adventure playground might represent the former, while a back alley may represent the latter.

Finally, it is free from the dangers of heavy traffic. Streets themselves become popular juvenile territories if traffic is light. When the traffic is only moderately higher, a Baltimore study suggests expanding the size of sidewalks as a relatively safe method of expanding space which children find suitable.[144]

There is clearly no cut-and-dried blueprint for interesting spaces, guaranteed to be used by children. Nonetheless, applying some of the insights of persons contributing to the literature on children's actual use of space helps us to understand why children find some spaces intended for their use so inappropriate, while they gravitate to places which no one expects them to use.

A Swedish study, for example, focused on why virtually identical playgrounds in a large new housing area were used to differing degrees of intensity. Those with practically no usage had little in the way of geographic relief shielding the area and differentiating them from the surrounding area, while those used intensively had been provided with their own perceptual integrity.[145]

Lynch suggests some procedures to make spaces more hospitable for children. These include steps to reduce or eliminate traffic, widening sidewalks, giving 'under-used or abandoned rights of way, wastelands, and other left-over spaces' to children, in addition to ordinary parks and playgrounds, and landscaping those spaces already there.[146] According to Lynch, Utopia for growing children has trees, friends, quiet, a lack of traffic, small size, and cleanliness.[147] Such steps are an inexpensive, personnel-free approach to expanding the *de facto* opportunities of children. It is much cheaper than planning and building formal playgrounds.

Dahlén carries this reasoning even further than we do: '... the planning of grounds, in the sense of childrens' reserves, must in the long run be opposed.'[148] We urge attention both to the appropriate development of intended and the opportunity to have hidden spaces for children, according to the situations at hand.

The preceding discussion has appeared to accept the assumption that most children of grade school age remain within their own residential areas and are subject to the opportunities found there. This assumption, though, has several flaws. Parents frequently chauffeur their children to external sources of activity. Normally, however, these reflect formal commitments and obligations, like music lessons, supplementary classes, or religious instruction. Chauffeured activity does not substitute for the informal, spontaneous play characterizing the more typical third sector of activity.

Nonetheless, as children reach the upper boundaries of this age group, it is clearly possible that they make trips themselves to sites of recreational interest. Whether or not they can do so on a meaningful basis is a function of their residential location and the public transportation available. Ironically, it is typical that those already closer to the centre of the city, who have a more varied and potentially rich hidden environment immediately around them, also have easier access to alternative opportunities. Even when children in far-flung areas are fortunate enough to have public transportation, the amount of travel time involved makes it difficult to incorporate external visits into the already tight daily timetable. Travel time also represents an obstacle to setting out on weekends.

Public transportation, of course, is not the only link or blockage to reaching suitable play spaces. The age of the child will help determine how far he or she is likely to be permitted or able to go. If suitable attractions are beyond the normal range of travel, or, if they are blocked by busy roads, railroad tracks, property lines, or the like, underutilization will occur. On the other hand, facilities which are intentionally provided for children's use and in decent proximity must be perceived as interesting by the children themselves. Normally, formal institutions like schools are more appropriately located *vis-à-vis* residential units than are relevant play facilities.[149]

In any case, if we return to the logic of Figure 1, on intended and hidden spaces, we understand some of the many sources of difficulty facing younger children in all but the most exemplary surburban areas. Lack of opportunity in some kinds of housing may be exacerbated when land-use patterns do not conveniently provide: (a) commercial and institutional opportunities; (b) opportunities for outdoor play, intended or hidden; and (c) public transportation.

It is not difficult to understand why problems appear when the internal opportunities lacking in high-rise apartments are added to those missing in the typical suburban milieu. The combined setting can be extremely desolate (despite the likelihood of an abundance of green grass!). Such a woeful picture, however, is not uniform. What strongly needs documentation is some picture of where the children now live, related to what opportunities (of the various kinds) are realistically available to them – and by what means of access.

The one institution commonly located within pedestrian reach is, of course, the grade school. Yet, jurisdictional and budgetary considerations have traditionally restricted school buildings and campuses to school use only except in cases of *ad hoc* rental. Although community use is now a recognized possibility, it is still the exception, even though the school's locational characteristics recommend it for parallel recreational, institutional, or even local commercial usage.

Perhaps because the spatial patterns of ordinary teenagers from many walks of life, as compared to gangs or teens in special inner-city 'turfs,' have been more diffuse, less focus has been placed on their study. Yet, it is evident that the ambiguity about teenage needs is not one which has meant an absence of resulting problems. Some central environmental needs of teenagers were articulated by Stearns, when, in his earlier cited passage he spoke of habitats for flocking, trysting, and roosting. To these, we might add exercising, observing, learning, and 'becoming.'

As noted in Chapter 5, teenagers start from the confines of the family and from the role of children. Eventually, most of them end up as adults. Yet relatively few people are seriously concerned with the *process* of metamorphosis from cocoon to butterfly or moth. It is assumed to occur anyway, and people worry more about the excesses demonstrated, hoping to keep them in line by luck or force. But people observe little of the *meaning* of what adolescents undergo, missing the fact that some of their needs are rooted in the physical environment.

One particular need from the earlier chapter is the need to *belong*. If no longer comfortable merely as part of a family, nor accepted as a regular part of adult society, teenagers typically turn to groups of all kinds, often with exaggerated demands for loyalty – religious groups, sports groups, rock supporters groups, gangs. Only a few of these groups (e.g. gangs) have any reference to neighbourhood or community. Although we know of no hard data on the subject, we surmise that most areas lack places to serve as a locus of teenage integration in the community. There are few places in North America consistently open and accepting of teenagers except by appointment and under adult control. As a consequence, whatever peer loyalties teens establish are accomplished on their own, often taking directions which diverge from the mainstream of community life. During the 60s, community drop-in centres attempted to approximate this ideal, but they were closely tied with the drug culture and lifestyle crises of that particular period, often offered on an *ad hoc* basis by adults as an attempt at a stop-gap cure of a perceived evil.

What do we provide for youth? We construct sports facilities, playing fields, tennis courts, hockey arenas, etc. This is surely not inappropriate for a period of life in which young people are at the peak of their energies, yet are not called upon for physically hard work. How these facilities are used, though, varies greatly from community to community. Running major sports complexes and organizing teen sports are not accomplished without careful planning. One danger of emergent organization is that it may fail to provide sufficient opportunities for the total *potential* demand for participation (some of which is always latent), creating a situation of overmanning and hence alienation among non-participants. Every encouragement and opportunity must exist for children to participate. They must be deterred neither by premature professionalization nor by fees for which they lack resources (and which their families may begrudge or be unable to provide). Cooper, for example, notes the extreme importance in the San Francisco Bay area of basketball courts, facilities for which activities can be spontaneously implemented.[150] Stevenson, furthermore, notes the desirability of ball-playing as a focus for *intergenerational* contact.[151]

The matter of cost is another problem related to land-use for teenagers. If they generally lack places constantly open for meetings of their own, then they must find alternatives. These are typically locations set up *for* adult congregation *by* other adults, for commercial purposes. Teenagers do not spend enough to justify to adults their long hours there, and they are thought to deter adult use of the same commercial facilities. A typical response to this dilemma in the Toronto suburban area was the institution of a requirement on the local premises of a well-known hamburger chain that every customer spend at least 75 cents every twenty minutes, even though (or because) the place serves as a magnet to teenagers.

Even *in*appropriate attractions for teenagers are commonly missing *inside* newly constructed, non-central areas. Hence, transportation has always been a major factor in the life of a teenager. The quality of public transportation is vital, and the use of an automobile at the earliest legal age is considered highly desirable by teenagers, if for no other reason than that they cannot fulfil their lifestyle expectations without getting away from home and, expeditiously, to somewhere that is 'someplace.'

At present, the most convenient place for 'flocking' is the shopping plaza. It is not impossibly far away. It is either protected or enclosed, and, while food is normally available, there is no requirement to pay for admission, or a minimum to remain. Nonetheless, because such plazas were not intended as community centres for teenage socializing, with owners usually feeling that teenage presence reduces business, strenuous efforts are often made to discourage teenage use of this solution to their flocking problems. It is unusual to see the opposite attitude,[152] where developers attempt to promote the use of their shopping centres as genuine community centres, giving space and time to groups within the local area; according to this attitude, the various sectors of the population will develop a loyalty to the community and its centre which is not likely to hurt business. Teenagers are also less likely to vandalize places which are felt to be their own.

Where do boys meet girls and girls meet boys? Where can they stay together? Where can this occur without the need for expense and artificial formality? Elaborate facilities are designed by commercial entrepreneurs for wealthy young adults. But we decline to face directly such needs as develop among youth. Granted, contact occurs in schools and on streets, but these are not the most fruitful places for anything but superficial meeting.

Our land-use patterns also tend to separate teenagers from first-hand observation and experience with the world of work, excepting certain kinds of commercial roles. This is, of course, a function of zoning for major functional, aesthetic, and health considerations, so that the intrusion of noxious enterprises will not affect the everyday lives of those not involved in them. Nonetheless, this form of segregation is one which serves as a partial obstacle to the realistic development of adult roles among teenagers.

Within families and through individually arranged, non-universal tutoring or coaching, we make it possible for young people to develop skills and to establish feelings of competence as they progress to adulthood. What we largely lack are opportunities in the *community* where these feelings *can be combined* with those of belonging, harnessed to a vehicle which is always there, universally welcoming, and not bearing undue economic burdens. Boy Scouts, Girl Guides, or music lessons, for example, go only so far in integrating the young person into the community as it really is.

The entire subject of adolescent *spatial* needs is virtually untouched and requires extensive attention. We currently recognize the existence of reactive problems among young people in those areas characterized, in Lynch's terms, by 'experiential starvation.'[153] But we seldom go beyond identification of the symptoms, let alone towards the systematic pursuit of causes.

Now let us turn to the third type of explanation of phenomena linking children with their environment.

Causation and Mediation by Adult Social Organization
In the previous two subsections dealing with two forms of explanation linking environment and children, we have touched indirectly upon many situations in which adult organization is an additional factor in the equation – either as ultimate cause of the situation or as a mediating force between environment and children. We shall make our focus more explicit at this point, despite the virtual lack of a literature, because the need to recognize the more complex paradigm which includes adult social organization is so important and underexplored.

The Parental Influence
Parents' reactions to environmental conditions are surely not irrelevant to children. As we noted earlier, styles of childraising are felt to vary considerably according to housing type. Raven, for example, noted that the worst aspect of bringing up children in multiple dwellings with poor soundproofing is not the sheer amount of noise children make while bothering others, but the degree that parents go to *inhibit* the actions of their children to prevent bothering neighbours.[154] Parents, furthermore, are known to restrict the comings and goings of younger children in high-rise apartments when they cannot visually supervise the scene and when they distrust the characteristics of potential playmates. Later on, parents face the dilemma of acting either over-restrictively or too liberally when their children must of necessity meet other children farther from the family home than would otherwise be the case.

Neither is the larger land-use pattern incidental to child raising. The land-use pattern is a partial determinant of the housewife's state-of-mind, as a function of restrictions or opportunities for her own movements and whether or not children are cooped up at home with 'nowhere else to go.' Whether parents are thrust into the role of chauffeur is a function of several factors, including land-use, public transportation, and the extent that the given household places a heavy emphasis on the development of skills in the individual child.

How children regard environment is strongly related to how parents feel about it. Parents, for example, with no basis for a proprietary interest in their surroundings should be less capable of communicating community responsibility to their children. One might expect the opposite impression to be cast by parents who themselves maintain some feeling of power and control over their residential environment. There is a need, for example, for much research on the effects of living in condominium and co-operative housing. Do these systems of common ownership and control over management give the individual families a greater feeling of control than they experience when everything is in the hands of a commercial landlord, present or absent? Do any such differences filter through to children?

There is also the earlier question as to the physical location of institutions like daycare centres, which themselves assume surrogate parenting dimensions in the lives of the individual families.

Production, Planning, and Design of Housing and Land-Uses

Sometimes it is difficult to know which consideration should be given highest priority. Our normal tendency in research is to ask what the implications are of given forms of housing and land-use. Nonetheless, those affected by such existing forms are seldom those with the responsibility for having brought them about or for changing them. Turner, for example, puts the matter very directly. Housing, he says, is a *noun* to most of us – something which comes to us in the form of a product, presented by somebody else. It would be more fruitful, he urges, to think of housing as a verb, something with a process which we ourselves join in to guide.[155]

If we look at many of the specific causes of concern touched upon in the preceding discussions, we find that some of the environmental considerations are the consequence of reasoning which relates to children and their activities in only a circuitous way. Housing, for example, is produced in North America for the most part by entrepreneurs for profit. Such a requirement, indeed, pre-establishes how spaces may be used, what equipment may be provided, and even the quality of materials affecting considerations like soundproofing. An economic system which allows and, in many respects, encourages speculation accounts largely for the existence of so many high-rise apartments for families – the result of the skyrocketing cost of land.[156] They are not a function of demand, qualitatively. Even the recent emergence of so many condominium units is a function in the Toronto area of three parallel events: (1) a new provincial landlord/tenant act which makes it far less desirable for developers to build rental accommodation; (2) the imposition of a form of rent controls, with the same consequences; (3) federal policy innovations specifying maximum National Housing Act mortgage amounts within given urban areas for the production of new, owned accommodation, without specifying the building type in which it might be found. In fact, the widespread legacy of suburban land-use patterns is a function of an earlier generation of construction financing based on a rigid set of guidelines hypothetically related to security of investment.

Hence, to make better environments for children, we must understand also how the adult society organizes to provide housing and to determine housing type and land-use. The question is greater than design and technology, extending also to who designs, for what purposes, and in whose interest.

Children's Control over Space

A number of our previous points came down to the question of the extent that children feel that a given space or place is really theirs. In legal terms, this is not as yet possible. When it occurs, it is through an act of commission or omission of adults. Yet a number of arguments can be mustered to support some degree of control by children.

First, it is generally felt that scarce resources will be used better when children can get involved in the administration of their own facilities. Second, more appropriate designs may emerge when children introduce their own operational perspectives. For example, the Urban Design Centre in Vancouver shows that nursery school children can design highly appropriate institutional plans for their use, which differ in marked ways from conventional adult designs for the same group.[157] Third, as noted before, advocates of adventure playgrounds hypothesize that youthful control of their facilities will reduce vandalism. Such control is also thought to reduce intergenerational and interage conflicts. Finally, some degree of control is seen as of educational value; how do children turn into adults who have the ability to adapt and cope without having started to learn this in some tangible way? Nicholson, among others, hypothesizes that children's control over space leads to their becoming more active adults.[158]

We do not advocate turning over complete power of selected community facilities to children if delegation of accompanying physical and legal responsibilities is inappropriate and/or impossible. Nonetheless, there are less total forms of involvement which approximate control and which might be highly salutory. The current divorce of control from children's efforts, as exercised arbitrarily by the adult world, is clearly illustrated in an account by Spivack, who worked with local youth in Boston to redesign an underused and vandalized playground. What the children did engaged their enthusiasm and loyalty, but its appearance so confounded the adults of the area that they succeeded in having the city of Boston pave over the area, regardless of its meaning to the children involved.[159]

How such a process of decentralized control should be handled requires considerable experimentation, with accompanying research.

Neighbourhood Composition

A final point about the effects of adult organization should be made in passing. The kinds of residential situations serving as the context for consideration in Chapter 6 on multiculturalism in large cities do not occur in a vacuum, but as consequences of adult decision-making processes. In some cases members of a group choose to live together for positive reasons having to do with their culture and its institutions. In other cases they are guided to particular areas by persons .dealing with the allocation of real estate and apartments, or they do not have the knowledge or wherewithal to live elsewhere. Some adults wish their children to grow up in a particular social and/or educational milieu.

In some cases, neighbourhood homogeneity or change is a function of the housing market. Desired new homes are typically available only to persons with high incomes, under current economic and housing subsidy systems. Furthermore, financial organizations can exert a decisive influence on the population of a local area (and changes to it) by their lending patterns; so-called 'red-lining' is an invidious system in some American cities in which banks and insurance companies single out specific areas as insecure, suggesting to current residents that they should leave.

The causes of neighbourhood composition are many and complex. It is easy to call families racist when they leave areas with a changing ethnic or racial composition and move to other areas which are homogeneous in their own image, particularly in the face of practices like red-lining or forced bussing. While it is unlikely that racial or ethnic change is not a partial factor precipitating the move away, such moves would, nonetheless, not serve as a successful defence against practices like bussing were these families not able to cross 'medieval' boundaries into 'safe' municipalities. Nor would the general pattern of flight be so influential in establishing the characteristics of both origin and destination neighbourhoods, were access to new housing units based on processes other than sheer economic power.

Thus, even the overall framework of the changing city is itself dependent on larger forms of social organization in operation. The tragedy – but also the challenge – is that such macroscopic happenings inevitably have a bearing for children.

Indeed, this is the general message of the present chapter. Our consciousness of what affects our children goes well beyond that which we recognize and that with which we deal. Our practices, our experiments, and our supporting information must all be expanded to every direction if the situation of our children in cities is to improve.

III CONCLUDING REMARKS

This entire chapter is a summary, so another summing up would be redundant. We also pointed out, as we reached them in the body of the text, a number of areas in which additional research is needed. Therefore, at this point, we shall make some concluding observations of a more synthesizing nature.

The logic of the first half of the paper urged a perspective on children and environment taking into consideration (a) the various stages of children's development, (b) specific details of environment concerning a wide range of scale and latitudes, (c) particular effects hypothesized to occur from (a) and (b), and (d) the causal mechanisms by which (a) and (b) would produce (c), including adult social organization. This logic was shown fruitful in 'demythologizing' several public concerns.

Such problems as children face in the city cannot be reduced to anything as simplistic as 'high-rise living,' for example. There are pragmatic ways, mostly known, in which we can improve high-rise apartments (e.g., soundproofing, making defensible spaces, design and allocation of play space), but the evidence does not support condemnation. Indeed, many of the dysfunctions are exacerbated by factors outside the immediate realm of housing which have to do with the land-use patterns of the surrounding areas, as they narrow opportunities for children of certain ages and their parents.

One major unresearched question deserving attention is whether the quality of children's lives is significantly improved by defensible space measures, since children rely most on having the opportunity for unstructured play in the vicinity of their homes.

Our review of the crowding and density literature also concluded that both public and scientific fears do not adequately reflect the detailed nature of residential density. What we urge attention to, in consequence, is not more study or new policy having to do with physical crowding or density, but explicit recognition of overmanning in urban institutions. The literature suggests that overmanning can be a cause of considerable malaise in cities.

If we do not join the nay-sayers on phenomena as undifferentiated as high-rise living and crowding, we surely reject a view of the city as a global entity bearing inherent problems for children. We note instead a number of relatively specific practices which the adult world simply needs to face squarely. People know now about traffic planning, seat belt use, and bicycle safety practices, but they must make evident the benefits to be gained for children from compulsive implementation and enforcement of what's known. People know how to provide adequate soundproofing, but they do not provide it. People recognize ways in general that pollutants are harmful, but they have to measure more closely how and where children encounter them – and with what effect.

Social scientists are generally concerned with the importance of concepts like competence and control, particularly with regard to growing children, and the literature suggests that this extends to the spatial world. It is difficult to attempt to instil such attributes in young people during occasional structured sessions if such opportunities are clearly denied in the planning and spatial nature of the communities where they spend the greatest portion of their time. More attention in land-use planning and management to the behavioural and psychological needs of young people is essential if adults want them to be more than 'little blighters.'

There are *fads* in the area of children's environment, as in many others. Neighbourhood design is a traditional fad, but the design of recreation facilities, particularly playgrounds is another. There is everything to be gained by the implementation of new ideas, provided that there is sound research follow-up to see if they work (and why). Much of this kind of research is needed to establish the merits and/or drawbacks, for example, of programmed and adventure playgrounds.

The evidence of the entire chapter makes clear that almost all aspects of the lives of urban children and their parents have a locational dimension. It is not enough to say that there are play spaces, stores, daycare centres, and other facilities and amenities *somewhere*. Where they are, what spatial characteristics they have, and how they are reached are crucial.

We speak not just of facilities and amenities planned for children, but of the wider range of places which they can and do use. When improvements are considered, thought must, therefore, be given not only to satisfying a spectrum of ages, but to taking advantage of the most immediate and appropriate opportunities, many of which may require marginal changes to places not formally built for children, rather than funding and planning unique formal facilities.

In any case, the general public lack of attention given to children's needs in cities, apart from the context of a few situations (e.g. schools, safety around schools, formal sports facilities), is indicated by common ignorance of the overall system of the de facto spatial and locational opportunities for children in specific cities and how they relate to the residential distribution of families throughout these cities. We therefore urge an *accounting* for the needs of children as they arise in their everyday lives. If we can produce maps of crimes or of poverty, can we not document also the location of opportunities for children, so we can assess whether most of them have access to enough of these opportunities?

Finally, this chapter offers evidence that the environment itself does not cause aggression, vandalism, and other behaviours which adults decry. But failure to account for and to provide for basic opportunities for young people in spatial terms causes a vacuum which they are left on their own to overcome. If some resultant actions are destructive, it is not the fault of cities but of the adult world's failure to deal with them adequately, let alone optimally.

Not with anguish, but with challenge, we urge the most explicit attention to meeting the needs of children in cities. The result is a higher quality of life for all ages.

NOTES

1 See, for example, Gump, Paul V. *Ecological psychology and children*, Chicago: University of Chicago Press, 1975; and Pollowy, Anne-Marie *The urban nest*, Stroudsburg, Pa.; Dowden, Hutchinson and Ross, Inc. 1977. In this review of our own we are extremely grateful for guidance and advice to the following colleagues: Howard Andrews, Katherine Catton, John Gandy, Polly Hill, John Hitchcock, Susan Hodgson, James Lemon, William Rock, Myra Schiff, Joel Shack, Norman Shulman, Anna-Rose Spina, James Stopps, Willem van Vliet, Anne Whyte, and Suzanne Ziegler.

2 Most notably Great Britain and Sweden.

3 See, for example, Summer, Robert *Personal space*, Englewood Cliffs, N.J.: Prentice Hall, 1969; Robert Gutman, ed., *People and buildings*, New York: Basic Books, 1973; and W.M. Ittelson et al. *An introduction to environmental psychology*, New York: Holt, Rinehart and Winston, 1974. These are among the first of a now-growing number.

4 Fischer, Claude *The urban experience*, New York: Harcourt, Brace and Jovanovich, 1977.

5 Cantor, David *The psychology of place*, London: Architectural Press Limited, 1977, p. 141.

6 Zehner, Robert *Indicators of the quality of life in new communities*, Chapel Hill: University of North Carolina Press, 1977.

7 For example, National Academy of Sciences, *Toward a national policy for children and families*, Washington: The Academy, 1976; and Kenneth Keniston, and the Carnegie Council on Children, *All our children*, Harcourt, Brace and Jovanovich, 1977.

8 Bronfenbrenner, Uri Toward an experimental ecology of human development, *American Psychologist 32:* 513–31, July 1977.

9 Dahlén, Uno *Småhusbarnen*, Stockholm: Liber Förlag, 1977.

10 Bronfenbrenner, Uri Toward an experimental ecology.

11 Pollowy *Urban nest*. This is an excellent source of great numbers of specific environmental needs of children, together with ways of meeting these needs. We are unable to treat these phenomena as specifically as Pollowy and refer the interested reader to her work.

12 Boocock, Sarane Unpublished report to the Russell Sage Foundation, 1978.

13 Socialdepartementet *Barnens Livsmiljö*, Stockholm: Statens Offentliga Utredningar, 1975, p. 74. Translation by the senior author: emphasis in original text.

14 Pollowy, Anne-Marie *Urban nest*, p. 34.

15 Dahlén *Småhusbarnen*, p. 266.

16 Mårtensson, Solveig Childhood interaction and temporal organization, *Economic Geography 53:* 99–125, April 1977; Farley, John Effects of residential settings, parental lifestyles and demographic characteristics on children's activity patterns, Doctoral dissertation, Department of Sociology, University of Michigan, 1977; Medrich, Elliot A. The serious business of growing up, A study of children's lives outside of school, University of California, Berkeley School of Law, Children's Time Study, Winter 1977.

17 See, for example, Andrews, Howard F, Home range and urban knowledge of school-age children, *Environment and Behaviour 5:* 73–86, no. 1, 1973.

18 Parr, A.E. In Search of Theory VI, reprint from Arts and Architecture Sept. 1965, pp. 2–3.

19 Chombart de Lauwe, Marie-Jose et al. *Enfant en-jeu*, Paris: Editions du Centre Nationale de la Recherche Scientifique 1976, p. 39 (translation by the senior author).

20 Pollowy, Anne-Marie *Urban nest*.

21 In Volume I of the current series (*The child in the city: today and tomorrow*), Ch. 5, The Spatial World of the Child. Some childhood memories of the city, *Journal of the American Institute of Planners 22:* 142–52, 1956.

22 Parr, A.E. In search of theory.

23 Grabow, Stephen and Salkind, Neil J. The hidden structure of children's play in an urban environment, in Peter Suedfeld and James A. Russell, eds., *The behavioral basis of design*, Book I, Stroudsburg, Pa.: Dowden, Hutchinson and Ross, 1976, pp. 164–71.

24 This is an example of Erving Goffman's notion of 'backstage.' See his *The presentation of self in everyday life*, New York: Free Press, 1959; and *Behavior in public places*, Garden City, N.Y.: Doubleday Anchor Books, 1963.

25 For an illustration of the widespread phenomenon of husbands and fathers justifying suburban living because of its purported benefits for their families,

even at the same time that other members of the families protest a number of specific conditions of their suburban existence, see William Michelson, *Environmental choice, human behavior, and residential satisfaction*, New York: Oxford University Press, 1977, Chapter 8.

26 Plant, James S. The personality and an urban area, in Paul K. Hatt and Albert Reiss Jr. *Cities and society*, New York: The Free Press, 1957, pp. 647–65.

27 See, for example, such works as Helmer, John and Eddington, Neil A. *Urbanman*, New York: Free Press, 1973; Lofland, Lynn *A world of strangers*, New York: Basic Books, 1973; and Karp, David et al. *Being urban*, Lexington, Mass.: D.C. Health, 1977. We must note that such works deal with only some of the widespread conceptions of the concept alienation.

28 See Dattner, R. *Design for play*, New York: Van Nostrand Reinhold Co., 1969.

29 Sennett, Richard *The uses of disorder*, New York: Knopf, 1970. See also Freire, P. *The pedagogy of the oppressed*, translated by Myra Bergman Ramos, New York: Seabury Press, 1970.

30 See Beshers, James *Urban social structure*, New York: The Free Press of Glencoe, 1962, for a statement that parents wish to segregate their children from intergroup contact, with regard to an outcome concerning marriage partner selection.

31 Vanek, Joanne Time spent in housework, *Scientific American 231:* 116–20, no. 5, November 1974.

32 See, for example, Michelson *Environmental choice*; Michelson *Man and his urban environment: A sociological approach*, Reading, Mass.: Addison-Wesley, rev. ed. 1976; Perin, Constance *With man in mind*, Cambridge, Mass.: M.I.T. Press, 1970: Stokols, Daniel, ed., *Perspectives on environment: theory, research and application*, New York: Plenum Press, 1977; Moos, Rudolph *The human context*, New York: Wiley Interscience, 1976.

33 Wilner, D.M., et al. *The housing environment and family life: A longitudinal study of the effects of housing on morbidity and mental health*, Baltimore: The John Hopkins Press, 1962.

34 Whyte, William H., Jr. *The organization man*, Garden City, N.Y.: Anchor Books, 1956. See also Festinger, Leon, Schachter, Stanley, and Back, Kurt *Social pressures in informal groups*, New York: Harper and Brothers, 1950; and Michelson *Man and his urban environment*, Chap. 8.

35 See, for example, Michelson *Man and his urban environment*, Chap. 2; and Moos, *The human context*.

36 Michelson The case of the equine fountains: local neighborhood as design opportunity, *Design and Environment*, Winter 1971, pp. 129–31, 159.

37 Hall, Edward *The hidden dimension*, Garden City, N.Y.: Doubleday, 1966.
38 Goodey, Bryan *Perception of the environment*, Centre for Urban and Regional Studies, the University of Birmingham, 1973, Occasional Paper #17; Goodey *Images of place*, Centre for Urban and Regional Studies, University of Birmingham, 1974, Occasional paper #30, and Downs, Roger, and Stea, David, eds., *Image and environment*, Chicago, Aldine, 1973.
39 See, for example, Rose, Albert Housing and family policy, paper presented to Conference on Family Policy, Canadian Council on Social Development, Ottawa, April 1977.
40 Mercer, Charles *Living in cities*, Baltimore: Penguin Books, 1975, p. 98.
41 Coates, Gary *Alternative learning environments*, Stroudsburg, Pa.: Dowden, Hutchinson and Ross Inc., 1974, p. 192 (emphasis added).
42 Simmel, Georg The metropolis and mental life, in Hatt and Reiss, Jr., eds., *Cities and society*, pp. 635–46.
43 Wirth, Louis Urbanism as a way of life, *American Journal of Sociology 44:* 1–24, 1938.
44 Milgram, Stanley The experience of living in cities: a psychological analysis, in Helmer and Eddington, *Urbanman*, Chap. 1.
45 Karp, Stone, and Yoels, *Being urban*. Lofland *World of strangers*.
46 Gans, Herbert J. Urbanism and suburbanism as ways of life: a re evaluation of definitions, in Arnold M. Rose, ed., *Human behavior and social process*, Boston: Houghton Mifflin, 1962, pp. 625–48; Bell, Wendell et al., eds., *The new urbanization*, New York: St. Martin's Press, 1968, pp. 132–68.
47 Fischer, *Urban experience*.
48 For a comprehensive discussion of this matter, see Wellman, Barry The community question, University of Toronto, Centre for Urban and Community Studies, Research Report No. 90, 1977.
49 Janovitz, Morris *The community press in an urban setting*, New York: Free Press, 1972.
50 Suttles, Gerald *The social construction of communities*, Chicago: University of Chicago Press, 1972.
51 Wolanski, Napoleon Environmental modification of human form and function, *Annals of the New York Academy of Science 134:* 826–40, 1966.
52 Lithwick, N. Harvey *Urban Canada: problems and prospects*, Ottawa: Central Mortgage and Housing Corporation, 1970.
53 Kane, Dorthea Noyse Bad air for children, *Environment 18:* 26–34, no. 9, 1976.
54 Indeed, it took the spotlight directed by Japanese investigators to make clear that there is an outbreak of the same disease among remote Indian groups in Northern Ontario, inasmuch as it is so easy to blame other aspects of the

lives of victims for their chronic illnesses. See Science Council of Japan, *Science for better living*, Tokyo: Asahi Evening News, 1977.

55 American Lung Association *Introduction to lung disease*, Fairfax, Va.: The Association, 5th ed., 1973.

56 Wagner, Richard H. *Environment and man*, New York: Norton, 2nd ed., 1974, p. 18.

57 Hirosima, K. Natural condition for infants – their outdoor play environment and healthiness in urban ecosystem, in M. Numata, ed., *Tokyo project interdisciplinary studies of urban ecosystems in the metropolis of Tokyo*, Chiba: Chiba University, 1977, pp. 235–50.

58 These concerns are articulated in a presentation by Roberto Vigotti, DS-ENEL, Rome, at a meeting on Urban Ecosystems, UNESCO Man and the Biosphere Programme, Poznan, Poland, 27 September 1977.

59 Stevenson, Gordon N. Noise and the urban environment, in Detwyler, Thomas R. et al. *Urbanization and environment*, Belmont, Cal.: Duxbury Press, 1972, pp. 195–228.

60 Michelson *Man and his urban environment*, Chap. 7.

61 Stevenson Noise and the urban environment, pp. 221ff.

62 Cohen, S., Glass, D.C., and Singer, J.E. Apartment noise, auditory discrimination and reading ability, *Journal of Experimental Social Psychology 9:* 407–22, 1973.

63 See the remarks of Patricia MacKay in Volume I of this series, Chap. 1.

64 National Academy of Sciences *Toward a national policy*, p. 64.

65 Ontario Ministry of Transportation and Communications *Motor vehicle accident facts*, 1976, Toronto, p. 17.

66 Riding on adult's lap is found dangerous, *New York Times*, 30 April 1978, section 1, p. 29.

67 Sandels, Stina *The Skandia Report II: Why are children injured in traffic: can we prevent child accidents in traffic?* Stockholm: Skandia Insurance Co. Ltd., 1974, p. 68; Bunge, W.W. et al. *The Canadian alternative: survival expeditions and urban change*, Toronto: York University, Geographical Monograph, 1975, no. 2, p. 44.

68 Perry, Clarence The neighborhood unit formula, in William L.C. Wheaton et al. *Urban housing*, New York: Free Press, 1966, pp. 94–109; Stein, Clarence *Towards new towns for America*, New York: Reinhold, 1951; Buchanon, Colin *Traffic in towns*, London: H.M.S.O., 1963.

69 Sandels *The Skandia Report II*.

70 Appleyard, Donald and Lintell, M. The environmental quality of city streets: the residents' viewpoint, *Journal of the American Institute of Planners 38:* 84–101, 1972.

71 Cited by Canadian Press, Report zeros in on housing ills of city dwellers, *The Globe and Mail* (Toronto), 30 March 1977.

72 Schorr, Alvin *Slums and social insecurity*, Washington: Social Security Administration Research Report No. 1, 1963. See also, Glazer, Nathan The effects of poor housing, in Jon Pynoos and Chester Hartman, eds., *Housing urban America*, Chicago: Aldine, 1973, pp. 158–65.

73 Wilner et al. *The housing environment.*

74 Wagner *Environment and man*, pp. 250–51.

75 See, for example, the design conditions for apartment balconies set by Pollowy *Urban nest*, p. 59.

76 See Pollowy *Urban nest.*

77 Galle, Omer et al. Population density and pathology: what are the relationships for man, in Kent P. Schwirian, ed., *Comparative urban structure*, Lexington, Mass.: D.C. Health, 1974, pp. 198–213.

78 See Michelson, William and Garland, Kevin The differential role of crowded homes and dense residential areas in the incidence of selected symptoms of human pathology, University of Toronto Centre for Urban and Community Studies, 1974, Research Paper No. 67.

79 See, for example, Hall, Edward Hidden dimension, Calhoun, John Population density and social pathology, in L.J. Duhl, ed., *The urban condition*, New York: Basic Books, 1963.

80 Galle et al. Population density and pathology.

81 Zlutnick, Steven and Altman, Irwin Crowding and human behavior, in J.F. Wohlwill and D.H. Carson, eds., *Environment and the social sciences*, Washington: American Psychological Association, 1972, pp. 48–58.

82 See Freedman, Jonathan *Crowding and behavior*, San Francisco: Freeman, 1975.

83 Schmitt, Robert C. Implications of density in Hong Kong, *Journal of the American Institute of Planners 24:* 210–17, 1971.

84 Mitchell, Robert E. Some social implications of high density housing, *American Sociological Review 36:* 18–29, 1971.

85 This is one criticism attached to what was otherwise an exhaustive effort by Alan Booth, with this consideration putting considerable doubt on the validity of the claim to the definitive study, showing no results of significance from residential density differences observed in Toronto. Booth, Alan *Urban crowding and its consequences*, New York: Praeger, 1976.

86 Murray, Russell The influence of crowding on children's behavior, in David Canter and Terence Lee, eds., *Psychology and the built environment*, London: The Architectural Press, Ltd., 1974, p. 116.

87 Jacobs, Jane *The death and life of great American cities*, New York: Random House, 1961.

88 Freedman *Crowding and behavior.*
89 This type of criticism is very hard to overcome without funds for a truly epidemiological sample. It is another drawback limiting the results of the study by Booth *Urban crowding.*
90 See, for example, Biderman, Albert et al. *Historical incidents of extreme overcrowding,* Washington, D.C.: Bureau of Social Science Research, Inc., 1963.
91 Alexander, Christopher The city as a mechanism for sustaining human contact, in William R. Ewald, Jr., ed., *Environment for man: the next fifty years,* Bloomington: Indiana University Press, 1967, pp. 60–109.
92 Barker, Roger *Ecological psychology,* Stanford, Cal.: Stanford University Press, 1964.
93 See Barker and Gump *Big school, small school,* Stanford, Cal.: Stanford University Press, 1964.
94 For some good examples, see Pollowy *Urban nest* and Cooper, Clare *Easter Hill Village,* New York: The Free Press, 1976; and Central Mortgage and Housing Corporation *The use and design of space in the home,* Ottawa: CHMC, 1973.
95 Michelson Urbanism as ways of living, *Ekistics 40:* 20–26, July 1975.
96 Scott, Robert A. *The making of blind men,* New York: Russell Sage Foundation, 1969.
97 See Michelson *Environmental choice* for an elaboration of this theme.
98 Berger, Bennett *Working class suburb,* Berkeley and Los Angeles: University of California Press, 1960; and Gans, Herbert J. *The Levittowners,* New York: Pantheon Books, 1967.
99 It is interesting to note that in Sweden, where mass high-rise construction preceded mass suburbanization, those scholarly concerns were raised in inverse order.
100 Socialdepartementet, *Barnens Livsmiljö,* and Keller, Suzanne discussion on panel, Meeting of American Sociological Association, September 1977.
101 For supportive data, see Michelson *Environmental choice.*
102 Raven, John Sociological evidence on housing: 2. The home environment, *Architectural Review 142:* 236–40, 1967; and Rosenberg, G. High population densities in relation to social behavior, *Ekistics 25:* 425–27, 1968.
103 Fanning, D.M. Families in flats, *British Medical Journal 18:* 302–86, 1967.
104 See, for example, Jephcott, Pearl *Homes in high flats,* Edinburgh: Oliver and Boyd, 1971; Stevenson, A. et al. *High living,* Melbourne University Press, 1967; Stewart, W.F.R. *Children in flats,* Melbourne: National Society for the Prevention of Cruelty to Children, 1970; and Homenuck, H. Peter *A study of high rise: effects, preferences, and perceptions,* Toronto: Institute of Environmental Research, Inc., 1973.

105 Kumove, Leon A preliminary study of the social implications of high density living conditions, Toronto: Social Planning Council of Metropolitan Toronto, 1966, mimeo.
106 Moore, William *The vertical ghetto*, New York: Random House, 1969.
107 Socialdepartementet, *Barnens Livsmiljö*, p. 137; and Akermans, Eddy *The vicinity of the home used as a play area*, The Hague, Netherlands Institute for Preventative Medicine, 1970.
108 Pollowy *Urban nest.* See also Marcus, Clare Cooper Children in residential areas: guidelines for designers, *Landscape Architecture Quarterly 64:* 376, October 1974.
109 Wallace, A.F.C. Housing and social structure, Philadelphia Housing Authority, 1972: and Littlewood, J. and Sale, R. *Children at play* London: Department of the Environment (England), 1972.
110 Crawford, P. and Virgin, A. *The effects of high rise living on school behavior*, Toronto: Board of Education of the Borough of North York, 1971.
111 Farley Effects of residential settings.
112 Michelson *Environmental choice.*
113 Hagarty, Linda The family at home: a comparison of the time-budgets of families in highrise apartments and detached houses in suburban Metropolitan Toronto, University of Toronto, Doctor of Social Work thesis, 1975.
114 Socialdepartementet, *Barnens Livsmiljö*, p. 74 (translation by senior author).
115 Ibid.
116 Michelson *Environmental choice.*
117 Yancey, William L. Architecture, interaction and social control, *Environment and Behavior 3:* 3–21, 1971.
118 Newman, Oscar *Defensible space*, New York: Macmillan, 1972.
119 Jacobs *Death and life.*
120 Also known as crime prevention through environmental design (CPTED). See, for example, Jeffrey, C. Ray *Crime prevention through environmental design*, Beverly Hills, Cal.: Sage Publications, 1971.
121 Ward, Colin *The child in the city*, London: The Architectural Press, 1978.
122 Karpf, Anne Children at bay, *The Guardian*, 26 March 1978, p. 21.
123 Stearns, Forest The city as habitat for wildlife and man, in Detwyler et al. *Urbanization and environment*, p. 275.
124 Perry Neighborhood unit formula.
125 Michelson *Environmental choice.*
126 Johnson, Laura *Who cares?* Toronto: Social Planning Council of Metropolitan Toronto, 1977.
127 For a comprehensive analysis of the time and space dimensions of daycare and children of working spouses, see Mårtensson Childhood interaction.

128 The Canadian Housing Design Council, in a short film, *Family House*, strongly urges the segregation of generations as understandable and right. The CDHC may have their interests, but they are not necessarily the interests of children.

129 Bruner, Jerome S. The nature and uses of immaturity, in Bruner et al. *Play – its role in development and evolution*, Baltimore: Penguin, 1976, pp. 28–64.

130 Cooper Adventure playgrounds, *Landscape Architecture Quarterly 10:* 18, 1970.

131 Sørensen, Christian Theodore, as quoted in Lady Allan of Hurtwood *Planning for play*, Norwich (England): Jarrold and Sons, 1968, p. 55.

132 Moore, Robin The diary of a volunteer playground – with heavy neighborhood input and a high funkiness quotient, *Landscape Architecture Quarterly 63:* 217, 1973.

133 Cooper Adventure playgrounds, in Gary Coates, ed., *Alternative learning environments*, pp. 195–215.

134 Lady Allen of Hurtwood *Planning for play*, p. 56.

135 Cooper Adventure playgrounds.

136 Moore, Robin S. Anarchy zone: encounters in a schoolyard, *Landscape Architecture Quarterly 64:* 366, 1974.

137 Nicholson, Simon How not to cheat children – the theory of loose parts, University of Wisconsin at Milwaukee Conference on Children and the Urban Environment, October 1976.

138 Hart, Roger The genesis of landscaping: two years of discovery in a Vermont town, *Landscape Architecture Quarterly 64:* 356–62, 1974; and Barker and Wright, H.F. *One boy's day*, New York: Harper and Row, 1951.

139 Gray, La Verne and Brower, Sidney Activities of children in an urban neighborhood, unpublished paper, Baltimore City Department of Planning, April 1977.

140 Cooper Children in residential areas, p. 375.

141 Ibid.

142 Lynch Spatial world of child.

143 Lynch *Growing up in cities*, M.I.T. Press and UNESCO, 1977.

144 Robinson and Associates *Street games children play*, Baltimore Department of Planning, 1977.

145 Socialdepartementet, *Barnens Livsmiljö*, p. 174.

146 Lynch *Growing up in cities*, pp. 56–7.

147 Lynch *Growing up in cities*.

148 Dahlén, *Småhusbarnen*, p. 267 (grammatical error in original text).

149 Grabow and Salkind Hidden structure of children's play.
150 Cooper Children in residential areas, p. 377.
151 Stevenson, A. et al. *High living*, p. 88.
152 Demonstrated, for example, by the Rouse Corporation, a major developer of shopping centres, centred on the east coast of the U.S.A.
153 Lynch *Growing up in cities*, p. 24.
154 Raven Sociological evidence on housing.
155 Turner, John, F.C. *Housing by people*, London: Marion Boyars, 1976. See also Andrews, Howard and Breslauer, Helen Reflections on the housing process: implications for a case study of cooperative housing, University of Toronto, Centre for Urban and Community Studies, Report No. 74.
156 For a full discussion of this point, see Michelson *Environmental choice.*
157 Pfluger, Luther W. and Zota, Jessie M. A room planned for children, in reprint, *Design for childcare*, Urban Design Centre, Vancouver, 1974, p. 45.
158 Nicholson How not to cheat children.
159 Spivack, Mayer The political collapse of a playground, *Landscape Architecture Quarterly 59:* 288-91, 1969.

8

Emergent Themes and Priorities

SAUL V. LEVINE WITH
WILLIAM MICHELSON,
ANNA-ROSE SPINA AND
SUSAN HODGSON

The last one hundred years have witnessed a remarkable migration to and growth of cities of the western hemisphere. With this burgeoning change has come energy, excitement, and the promise of enlightenment on the one hand, and confinement, confrontation, and the potential for constriction on the other. Nowhere is this dichotomy seen more clearly than in the world of urban children. They represent to their parents and other adults all the fears and anxieties, yet all the hopes and aspirations that the city represents. If the city is the cutting edge of social change, then we are obviously dealing with a double-edged sword. But we shall remain in a state of relative ignorance if we are satisfied to rely upon past assumptions and knowledge.

What we have learned over the past year's search of the literature in our various fields and our mutual edification confronts us with the enormity of the task ahead. We are faced with voluminous bodies of knowledge paradoxically pointing to just how little is known about the effects of the urban context on its youngest citizens.

Some suggest that the sine qua non of this era is rapid change. While rampant changes in structures and values affect us all, they are even more influential in the lives of children and adolescents. Nowhere are the rapid changes that technology and unbridled growth have wrought more manifest than in the city. New neighbourhoods appear, old familiar haunts vanish, almost overnight. The predictability and constancy of the city's structures are as transient and ephemeral as social attitudes and values. Whether a child is affected positively by the phenomenal diversity offered by the city, or succumbs to the pressures inherent in this cauldron, is dependent on many factors, both personal and social.

While the vast majority of our children and youth now live in cities, we are still in the Dark Ages when it comes to knowing the consequences and implications of urban life. We *do* know that the city represents the forefront of change in society, change which has wrought pain and pleasure, promise and pessimism. Indiscriminate, rapid social change might disproportionately affect the lives of children, who themselves are undergoing intrinsic developmental changes, while society swirls about them.

Recent urban social trends focus on the child and the family as an institution and the relationship between institutions. While the vast majority of Western urban children still grow up in families, the family is faced with changes and potential stresses. Family changes have pointed to the necessity for changes in provisions for child care arrangements, community and neighbourhood services of all types, as families seek to share the job of childrearing. Families with a shifting membership through divorce and separation, remarriage and children with parents both working have requirements that cannot always be met by the family, relatives, and friends; and the requirements change with the ages of family members. It has become clear that families need to obtain resources from outside, and to coordinate these resources in order to sustain the family group. It is also clear that all families may need social support in addition to other resources, sometimes offered by family members, relatives, and friends and neighbours, but sometimes not.

Informal community networks of communication and support may be inadequate or may not exist at all for some families. Formal community or agency services, often specialized and administered by professionals who are specialists, make it necessary for the family least able to coordinate and utilize such resources to do just that. And, lacking this ability, the resulting family problems when they surface, are dramatic.

A prime instance of the need for social support (*not* just for problem families) is in the area of child care. As an increasing majority of mothers of young children take work outside the home, urban child care is being turned over increasingly to surrogates in formal and informal facilities, often unsupervised, unstandardized, and unsatisfactory. The role of childrearer is becoming dispersed and fragmented. This in itself need not be detrimental, if the commitment and affective investment is present. But too often it is not.

Children have become increasingly isolated from adults and the rest of society. Parents, relatives, neighbours, and other caring adults have been replaced by hours of television, increasing influence of peer groups, and growing loneliness. So-called 'latch-key' children, who return from school to an empty house, are an omnipresent and growing phenomenon. Other factors conspiring to isolate children are the separation of business and residential areas, the disappearance of neighbourhoods, zoning regulations, occupational mobility, the absence of the apprenticeship system, separate patterns of social life for separate age groups, rigid age segregation, working parents, and the delegation of child care and education to 'specialists.'

Other indices of severe social and psychological disintegration[1] in the city are also found in current urban statistics. Child abuse and other forms of domestic violence, and child and adolescent suicide have increased markedly in the past two decades. Two-thirds of the deaths between the ages of 5 and 18 years of age are caused by violence. Youthful abuse of alcohol has become a major problem. Venereal disease, therapeutic abortions for girls under the age of 16, and premarital teenage pregnancy have all increased within the past few years. Almost one-fifth of children have a severe educational, physical, or psychological handicap, yet the facilities for identifying and treating them early are sadly lacking. Official juvenile delinquency statistics indicate a considerable rise in rates among all social classes in the United States, especially as manifested by urban vandalism, even though self-reported statistics show little change. Youth unemployment looms as a major factor in their increasing alienation and attraction to dissonant paths. The divorce and separation rates among families with children have risen exponentially even within the last decade. All the data cited point to a disproportionate representation of these phenomena and behaviour in urban, as opposed to rural, settings.

Why does the city, with all its potential for stimulation, edification, and inspiration, also serve as the focus for some of the worst that organized society has to offer? The evidence seems to point to intrinsic detrimental pressures in the city disproportionately influencing those who are most vulnerable. Even controlling for the migration of disturbed individuals and families into urban areas, there are still disproportionate manifestations of children's problems. The cities just have more of these psychiatric, educational, or antisocial problems than do rural areas. Some of the specific deleterious factors or stressors include overcrowding (number of persons per room, as opposed to neighbourhood), isolation (lack of a sense of community), rapid change or mobility (in neighbourhood, family, values), certain schools, unemployment, poverty (and low social status), handicapping conditions (educational, physical, psychiatric), and severe familial discord.[2] The various stressors are interactive, potentiating, and cumulative.

It is not our intention here to review the findings and conclusions of all our work in our disciplines from the literature cited in earlier chapters. They are clearly stated in each chapter and in fact culminate in our research and demonstration projects, which speak for themselves. There are, however, recurrent underlying themes in each of the areas we have covered which merit some attention as foci for further consideration and investigation. While they are mentioned independently, it will soon be obvious to the reader that these themes are overlapping and related.

I THEMES

Competence

One theme which is touched on directly or tangentially in all our areas relates to urban *competence*. It indicates the child's ability to cope with, adapt to, and, to the extent that it is possible, to master and even control the complex and changing environment in which he lives. Urban competence is an extension of 'locus of control,' a recurrent concept in all our work. It concerns the degree to which an individual has a sense that he has *some* control over his environment; that rather than being overwhelmed by his city, the child sees it as a source of opportunities to be used, exploited, and enjoyed.

If a child is overwhelmed by the complexity of his social context, it will be more difficult for him to achieve a necessary degree of autonomy and independence; his sense of worth and self-esteem will inevitably suffer. While much of a child's degree of competence is related to his personality, his natural resources, and his immediate family's influence, much also depends on the attitudes of his society to children, the laws and services which pertain to children, the nature of his educational experience, and the quality of his physical and human environment, both inside and outside the home. If all these factors contribute to giving the child a sense of comfort with a mastery of his environment, and a belief in himself and in his society, we can expect that he will go on from competence and self-confidence to become a constructive member of that society.

We do not know how far short we are falling of this potential, either on an individual basis or across a wide representation of young people. If the central task of adolescence is defining one's self-concept or identity,[3] it behooves us to learn how best to structure society and its services so that our youth may realize that goal.

Rights and Responsibilities

Directly related to the issue of children's competence is the combined theme of *rights* and *responsibilities*. Urban society is in a quandary when it comes to granting rights to children. Too often our so-called child-centred society has denied youngsters their rights, has chosen the route of expediency or cost-saving to the detriment of the legitimate rights and best interests of children (as in contested custody cases, or in the provision of needed services like daycare). But the other side of the coin is just as confusing. To grant rights to youngsters is also to imply that they have attained a given level of competence, that certain standards of behaviour may be expected, and that they can assume concomitant responsibilities to duties. This pertains most directly to the legal and correctional systems, but, in fact, permeates our entire society. A void which comes up repeatedly in our work is the lack of standards of behaviour which one might appropriately expect from children at a certain age. Paradoxically, in families with problems, legal decisions are often made to 'clarify' the individual capabilities, rights, and responsibilities of various family members that remain unclear for most people otherwise.

We know that expectations are powerful shapers of children's behaviour,[4] but we do not know what we should reasonably expect, especially during the period of early adolescence. We have no definite behavioural correlates of growth, health, and maturity. This has implications for issues as mundane but important as driving and voting, but also for sensitive areas like sexuality, alcohol use, judicial representation, and financial responsibility. Social and developmental psychology have not provided satisfactory elucidation of what the components of competence are at various ages. As a result, legislators and others have been reluctant or too confused to impose absolute standards. We too often are forced to operate in at least partial ignorance when we impose responsibilities on a child, as well as when we bestow a right. Both are as often as not the product of current social values and predominant opinions, rather than a result of scientific findings.

Accountability

Another kind of responsibility, one owed by social institutions to the individuals they serve, is what is often called *accountability*. In the case of children, the accountable parties are adults and/or their institutions who provide, maintain, or introduce services that they perceive are needed by children. We have already discussed the discrepancy between the availability and the utilization of various services. There is no doubt that there are gross deficiencies and inequalities in the types of services provided. Furthermore, even if the felt need is validated, even if the institutionalized service is available, and lastly, even if the service is utilized by the children in need, too often the effectiveness of the service is either not monitored or is seen to be inadequate. Criteria for evaluating the efficacy of services are seldom spelled out, and those that are delineated are usually invalid. Too often a child-directed service is perpetuated to serve the needs of adults, rather than of those children who are supposed to benefit from the service.

Where does the buck stop? It is no accident that the child advocacy movement has burgeoned over the last few years, because too often the last individuals to be considered are children. There is still no effective lobby for children.

There *is* a tremendous superstructure of children's services and institutions employing thousands of adults and spending millions of dollars. But the answer to the question, 'Does the (any) service accomplish what we want?' is as yet unknown in the majority of instances. Until we get close to that point, the concept of accountability continues to be a myth, accepted in principle, but seldom executed.

Interconnectedness

Another pervasive theme is the *interconnectedness*, the interaction and mutual effect of different agents and agencies impinging on children. This finding reaffirms the wisdom of our original plan to take an interdisciplinary approach at the Child in the City. While this has added greatly to the complexity of our work, it acknowledges the multiplicity and complexity of factors affecting children living and growing in the city. A child is influenced by his physical surroundings, his family, the schools he attends, his peer group, and the various services which he utilizes. These in turn interdigitate with and influence each other. One child can make use of a variety of institutions and facilities that the city provides – transportation, education, recreation, etc. If a child is unique in any of a wide possibility of ways – from a broken home, delinquent, handicapped, learning disabled, emotionally disturbed, a recent immigrant, etc. – added services enter into his experience. For example, social, health, or correctional services, to name a few, might be involved as dictated by circumstances. Upwards of 20 per cent of children fall within this 'special' group. The city's structures and services are sufficiently complicated for children who have no particular deficits, but this complexity is exponentially increased when there are problems. The problems interact with and potentiate each other, and they affect and are influenced by the environmental context.

But for all the interconnectedness of the agencies, there is often a lack of organization and coordination. Children might be served by a number of agencies, and yet 'fall through the cracks' because no one takes the ultimate responsibility (accountability again). Redundancy, conflict, and competition abound between agencies serving the same child and family. There is an ongoing attempt in Ontario to overcome this confusing morass via a unified Children's Services Ministry serving all the needs of children (mental health, corrections, social). We wish it well.

Another aspect to the theme of interconnectedness is the relationship between the various environments among which children move. This experience might be a source of enrichment for them on the one hand, or might create confusion and conflict on the other (see Environmental Mosaic).

The Environmental Mosaic

The environmental mosaic is a repetitive theme. This refers, in part, to the social context in which children live in the city - their homes and neighbourhood, and the people who affect them, even indirectly. Just as we say in terms of services that the child cannot be looked upon in isolation, so too and even more so this message applies here. Whether the city is perceived as a hostile, alienating place or as a source of pleasure and stimulation to be enjoyed often depends in large part on the environmental mosaic. If the child lives in a dilapidated crowded dwelling, surrounded by or with access to luxurious homes and lifestyles, this will tell him much about prevalent inequities. It will also affect his self-concept and his self-confidence. Similarly, if his parents and his teachers convey discrepant messages about values and goals, the plurality of environments is a source of potential conflict. But where parents, educators, health workers, and others provide links in the form of effective formal or informal networks (home and school committees, neighbourhood centres), the same environment may benefit a child by giving him effective examples of how to function in a variety of situations.

Environmental mosaic also refers to the spatial and physical context in which children live. The access a child has to urban facilities and resources - via urban transit, sufficient income, acceptable population density, for example - will also affect his sense of control in his environment. The degree to which a child of a certain race, ethnic group, or sex is accepted or rejected by urban activities and groups will obviously shape his perception of both the urban context and, even more so, himself.

The complexity and diversity of the physical and social environment in cities - the relationship between population groups of different ethnic and racial backgrounds - and the relationship between people, their homes and communities, and the physical environment introduce a diversity and complexity that provide the backdrop and the content for urban life. How aspects of the family and the urban context affect the ability of a child to develop a positive self-image, intellectual and social competence, and social relationships, as he grows to maturity, offer complexities and dilemmas to those who attempt to sort them out and seek to understand them.

The environmental context also determines much of the behaviour of children and adolescents merely by providing certain facilities and denying others. But beyond the institutionalized or formal resources, the urban child has access to information and popular trends among peers from afar because of the instant transmission of information. Critical mass or sheer numbers ensure that many aberrant activities, even those seen as potentially destructive, like drug taking, early adolescent sexuality, vandalism, etc., will be pursued by a sizable number of youngsters, and even institutionalized by subgroups. Conversely, only the city can offer so much in the way of exchange of cultures, ideas, and intellectual and artistic stimulation, again due to the numbers and varieties of accessible experiences. However, we do not as yet know the critical point, where population density, for example, becomes destructive.

Poverty

A recurrent theme in all the subject areas has to do with the discrepancies between the haves and have-nots in lifestyles, service availability, utilization, and behaviour. This is, simply put, *poverty*. It undercuts any thrusts by agencies or institutions to provide more optimal environments for urban children. Socioeconomic class largely determines a family's physical space, neighbourhood, and mutual relationship with services (schools, police, hospitals, daycare, etc.). The stereotypes and expectations of the poor that others harbour are powerful, albeit simplistic, and usually negative. They, in turn, serve to further engender alienation from, hostility to, and fear and resentment of the dominant society.

There are obviously many other factors which serve to shape the urban child's destiny – quality of education, peer group, family dynamics, the parents' backgrounds, attitudes and values, the child's personal strengths, and the like. But inferior schools, delinquent peers, families in conflict, and non-thriving children are highly correlated with poverty. Being poor neutralizes much of the thrust of the research in our various fields; 'quality of life' becomes a fatuous or meaningless concept when one lives a deprived existence. Poverty colours a child's perception of his environment and his relationship to it; perhaps more importantly, it too often confers a negative self-perception on the child. A disproportionate manifestation of the indices of urban misery prevails among the poor. Unfortunately, we are witnessing a dynamic process, so that children born into poverty have less of a chance to 'make it' (however this is defined) during the course of their lives.

Research

Finally, a recurrent but complex theme which comes up in each of our areas is the general issue of *research*. From reviewing the contribution in each of the preceding chapters, the reader should by now be aware of the dearth of social planning which is based a priori on research findings or hard evidence. There is almost a tendency to impose services or structures in the face of countervailing data. Of course, beyond this bias, there are tremendous gaps in our knowledge which can only be filled by further research. We are not here discussing esoteric, pure academic studies, but rather policy research and social experimentation which would affect institutional practices, laws, and services. To quote Donald

Campbell,[5] our society 'should be ready for an experimental approach to social reform, an approach in which we try out new programs designed to cure specific social problems, in which we learn whether or not these programs are effective, and in which we retain, imitate, modify or discard them on the basis of apparent effectiveness on the multiple imperfect criteria available.'

Social scientists, politicians, and clinicians have for too long shied away from built in evaluation of any programme. There are recent moves afoot in the United States and Canada to look at 'family impact studies,' or the effects on families of legislation and/or proposed practices based on research findings. Similarly, there are proposals designed to explain or translate research language for legislators and the public, and more importantly, to evaluate the studies and their recommendations. These are significant moves, but until we incorporate monitoring, assessment, and accountability into our research and demonstration projects, and especially *our services*, we will not know if we are accomplishing our described goals.

II WHERE DO WE GO FROM HERE?

We have found it remarkable just how little is known about the effects of cities on their populations, despite the fact that the vast majority of the inhabitants of the Western world live in urban as opposed to rural environments. It is also remarkable that so little research in this vein has been done. After reviewing much of the literature in our respective fields, it is obvious that glaring deficiencies in our knowledge confront planners, clinicians, educators, politicians, and researchers. Yet many of these gaps can be filled, by a combined policy research and planning process. Let us look at some of the areas of relative ignorance, where potential for edification is greatest and which relate most closely to our interests and goals.

We do not really know where and how children in the city spend their time. Via census data we do know about population density and distribution of children. But there has not been an integrated analysis and graphic representation of children, their living conditions, land usage, health and social status, and needs, recreational facilities, etc., carried out in such a way as to examine issues like the locational relevance of services, facilities, and amenities for children of different ages, appropriateness of adult decisions regarding children's needs, and an ultimate assessment of the degree to which municipalities achieve the goals they set for their children.

There is a dearth of information regarding pathways to services in the city. How do children and adolescents get to services? On what basis are services for them set up? Issues such as utilization of services, access to them, and their availability are seldom studied or even discussed. When one goes beyond this to issues like appropriateness, monitoring and evaluation of the service offered, and accountability, we are in a veritable wasteland. These areas are in dire need of study in every type of service offered to children in the city, be it social, medical, legal, educational, correctional, or recreational.

The transition between school and work is an area that has barely been studied. We do not know if the myriad of governmental 'make-work' projects for youth, whether in school or out, have any degree of success in engendering a sense of competence and self-esteem in the individuals involved. Further, we do not know to what extent the youth who are not employed or otherwise occupied feel that they are an integral part of their society, or alienated from it.

The modern city is a diverse and complex environment, and children now live in a variety of milieus and social structures that were not as prevalent even a few years ago. Two parent, single-parent, communal, and extended families, various kinds of daycare, and hired caretakers take part to varying extents in the child-rearing of different children. We do not know how different family arrangements influence role behaviour, responsibilities, and time spent at different activities. We *can* learn about the kinds of domestic setups that are particularly vulnerable or resistant to typical (or atypical) stresses and pressures, and what kind of effective or innovative approaches can be taught or built in a priori.

Information is lacking regarding the advisability of doing early medical and developmental screening of young (2–3 years of age) children in various daycare facilities. There is evidence from some demonstration projects that screening of children aged 4–5 years can pick up correctible abnormalities in about 5–12 per cent of those tested. But the comparable data are not available for children younger than this. Further, we do not know whether the daycare population is particularly at risk in this regard, or whether those cases that are picked up belong to any particular demographic groups.

Many North American cities are made up of a mosaic of ethnic and racial minorities. For example, in Toronto, Chinese, Portuguese, West Indian, and Greek children often live in enclaves adjacent to and mixed with each other. We do not know the extent to which a child's attitudes towards other groups, his self-esteem, and his degree of comfort in the urban environment is directly correlated to the size of his minority in his immediate environment – school and neighbourhood, in particular. We also lack information regarding the patterns of utilization by ethnic groups of various services in the community, and the role that informal networks play in determining attitudes towards and usage of these services. There is very little written about 'degrees of ethnicity' and how it is affected by the relative representation of the particular group in the local population.

We do not know what constitutes 'optimal daycare,' or what particular elements are most important (e.g., playground, information, support, etc.) for children or parents. While there is a growing body of knowledge about alternative forms of caring facilities for young children, there is still a lack of good data on the long-term effects of various forms of daycare experiences on children. Here again, patterns of utilization of these services are not documented. There is little hard information available regarding parents who usually stay at home alone with their children, and the positive and/or negative effects of this experience on both. There is much written and paradoxically little *really* known about 'support for parenting,' or the extent to which the experience of having and raising children is implicitly or explicitly supported by contemporary urban society.

As was pointed out in Chapter 5, the efficacy of sex education in the schools is still doubtful. The goals of sex education are far from elucidated, and the few concrete objectives that have been delineated have not been attained. Optimal types of sex education geared to specific populations of children and adolescents have not been attempted. It has not as yet been shown that any kind of sex education is related predictably to sexual attitudes and behaviour, birth control usage, pregnancy, venereal disease statistics, and other measures of sexuality in our youth.

We do not know what attributes of the physical environment of the city – the neighbourhood organization, the nature of housing, the proximity to services, etc. – determine (and to what extent) a child's perception of his city, his degree of comfort and security in his environment, and his ability to make use of the city's services and facilities. Further, to what extent are a child's sense of control over his environment and himself, his self-esteem, and even his commitment to his society determined by his physical environment?

In the area of children and the law, the reader will have concluded from Chapter 4 that we still have much to learn. We do not know the effect of judicial discretion – that is, decisions left largely up to the opinion of the judge – on children and families in private dispute resolution (e.g., custody cases), or public dispute resolution (child welfare, state vs. parents, or delinquency, state vs. child). We do not know how children learn to perceive the laws of their society. To what extent are the pathways to police and legal services (as with other services) determined more by socio-economic status, race, ethnicity, age, sex, and fortuitous circumstances than by issues directly related to the law, like type of offence, threat to society, etc. We do not know the extent to which this can be affected by improving legal education in the elementary and high schools.

The whole area of medical consent and confidentiality, especially as it pertains to adolescents, is in a muddle. The status of the laws in these areas is vague, and there seems to be confusion among all three involved groups – adolescents, their parents, and doctors and others working with them.

We also do not really know the effect of child advocacy, the legal representation of children, on the prescreening of cases and on the children involved. Are the different types of advocates appointed by the courts acting on the child's, the court's, or their own best interests? As we discussed in our list of recurrent themes, there are few data on which to base an assessment of a child's competence in the eyes of the law. At what age, or by which attributes are we to adjudge one youngster as mature enough to assume complete responsibility in law for his own behaviour, and another as incompetent or not yet ready? We do not know if the removal of status offences (offences determined as such solely on the basis of age) from the criminal code makes any discernible difference in the disposition of youngsters in the judicial process.

What are the Tasks before Us?
How can we expose children to *meaningful* relationships with more adults, who can serve as friends, counsellors, models? Can we provide intergenerational exposure, access, and interdependence? How can we encourage the development of high quality daycare without further undermining the primary child-caring role of the family? Parents might all be involved in the planning and operation of the child-care facilities. How do we overcome the lack of support for parenting as a vital, meaningful, role in our urban society? Should we build informal and formal community networks, for communication, support, and a sense of neighbourhood participation? We need alternative community centres which can serve many social needs and service requirements. Part time employment for parents is certainly a worthwhile goal. Legislation and clinical practices which will make parenting easier are important. How can we provide meaningful, gainful employment for *all* ages? How do we reduce adolescent alienation and demoralization, and prevent their pursuit of potentially destructive paths? How do we provide ideals for them to believe in, and provide a social fabric in which they feel an integral part? How do we pick up handicapping conditions in our youngsters early enough so that they do not effectively and severely compromise children's lives? Can we institute large scale screening (developmental, medical, nutritional, dental) to pick up deficits early enough so that they can be corrected?

The Child in the City programme, having reviewed much of the literature in our respective fields, is now embarked on designing and implementing a number of research and demonstration projects. Our own aims are to add to knowledge, to suggest more fruitful practices, and to change policies. But even as the review presented here shows the enormity of the remaining task, it is clear that the efforts of any one group like ours will be minor if done in isolation. Urban children are many – and their health, welfare, and opportunities must be the concern of many. Should children develop under less than optimal conditions because too few cared to think hard and plan diligently on behalf of the next generations? Do we really care so little about our own society in the future that we pay less than adequate attention to those who will be at its centre?

NOTES

1 Leighton, D. The empirical status of the integration-disintegration hypotheses, in B. Kaplan, ed., *Psychiatric Disorder and the urban environment*, New York: Behavioral Publication, 1973.
2 Rutter, M. and Nodge N. *Cycles of disadvantage: A review of research*, London: Heinemann, 1976.
3 Erikson, E. *Identity: Youth and Crisis*, New York: Norton, 1968.
4 Rosenthal, R. and Jacobsen, L. Pygmalion in the classroom, New York: Holt, Rinehart and Winston, 1968.
5 Campbell, Donald T. Reforms as experiments, *American Psychologist 12*: 409–29, 1969.

APPENDIX

Criteria for Selecting Specific Projects
In determining our own research priorities, reflected in the concluding section of Chapter 8, we applied explicit criteria to the myriad suggestions and proposals which were generated or submitted for consideration. Certainly the themes discussed in Chapter 1 played a major role in our selections of subjects for research. Those which had little or no relevance to our goals or themes were soon excluded.

Following this, proposed subjects were subjected to a three-stage process which we shall outline briefly. The first stage consisted of four global criteria: The first was feasibility (time, money, results), the second was the lack of good (or any) previous work in the area, the third was relevance to Toronto, and the fourth, the relevance of the subject to other Western industrialized cities.

The second stage of project screening involved asking questions about subjects which had to do with (1) amount of public concern on the subject, (2) the number of children potentially concerned, (3) potential relevance in the future, and (4) orientation towards primary prevention.

The last stage rated the 'short list' of subjects according to (1) the amount of leverage which the pursuit of any topic would have regarding changes in policy and practices pertaining to children, and (2) the degree of interdisciplinarity inherent in the proposal.

The potential priorities were discussed successively by our own research staff (with external consultation via our resource groups), our Advisory Committee,[1] and the presidents of the University of Toronto and the Hospital for Sick Children Foundation, respectively.[2] More than sixty projects were examined, and the above criteria were applied in the designation of approximately ten as of highest priority, with about the same number again just behind. The last section of Chapter 8 reflects these priorities.

1 At the time, it consisted of Professor L.S. Bourne (chairman), Dr Thomas Egan, Professor Bernard Green, Professor Merrijoy Kelner, Dr Quentin Rae-Grant, and Professor Alan Waterhouse.
2 Dr John Evans and Mr Claus Wirsig, respectively.

Author Index

Subject Index